IA-64 Linux® Kernel

Design and Implementation

ISBN 0-13-061014-3

90000

9 790130 610149

Hewlett-Packard® Professional Books

OPERATING SYSTEMS

Diercks	MPE/iX System Administration Handbook
Fernandez	Configuring CDE: The Common Desktop Environment
Lund	Integrating UNIX and PC Network Operating Systems
Madell	Disk and File Management Tasks on HP-UX
Mosberger, Eranian	IA-64 Linux Kernel: Design and Implementation
Poniatowski	HP-UX 11i System Administration Handbook and Toolkit
Poniatowski	HP-UX 11.x System Administration Handbook and Toolkit
Poniatowski	HP-UX 11.x System Administration "How To" Book
Poniatowski	HP-UX System Administration Handbook and Toolkit
Poniatowski	Learning the HP-UX Operating System
Poniatowski	UNIX User's Handbook, Second Edition
Rehman	HP Certified, HP-UX System Administration
Roberts	UNIX and Windows 2000 Interoperability Guide
Sauers, Weygant	HP-UX Tuning and Performance
Stone, Symons	UNIX Fault Management
Weygant	Clusters for High Availability: A Primer of HP Solutions, Second Edition
Wong	HP-UX 11i Security

ONLINE/INTERNET

Amor	The E-business (R)evolution: Living and Working in an Interconnected World, Second Edition
Greenberg, Lakeland	A Methodology for Developing and Deploying Internet and Intranet Solutions
Greenberg, Lakeland	Building Professional Web Sites with the Right Tools
Klein	Building Enhanced HTML Help with DHTML and CSS
Werry, Mowbray	Online Communities: Commerce, Community Action, and the Virtual University

NETWORKING/COMMUNICATIONS

Blommers	OpenView Network Node Manager: Designing and Implementing an Enterprise Solution
Blommers	Practical Planning for Network Growth
Bruce, Dempsey	Security in Distributed Computing: Did You Lock the Door?
Lucke	Designing and Implementing Computer Workgroups

ENTERPRISE

Blommers	Architecting Enterprise Solutions with UNIX Networking
Cook	Building Enterprise Information Architectures
Missbach, Hoffmann	SAP Hardware Solutions: Servers, Storage, and Networks for mySAP.com
Pipkin	Halting the Hacker: A Practical Guide to Computer Security

IA-64 Linux® Kernel

Design and Implementation

David Mosberger

Stéphane Eranian

Hewlett-Packard Company

www.hp.com/hpbooks

Prentice Hall PTR
Upper Saddle River, New Jersey 07458
www.phptr.com

A CIP catalog record for this book can be obtained from the Library of Congress.

Editorial/production supervision: *Jane Bonnell*
Acquisitions editor: *Jill Harry*
Editorial assistant: *Sarah Hand*
Cover design director: *Jerry Votta*
Cover design: *Talar Boorujy*
Marketing manager: *Dan DePasquale*
Manufacturing buyer: *Maura Zaldivar*

Publisher, Hewlett-Packard Books: *Patricia Pekary*

 Published by Prentice Hall PTR
A division of Pearson Education, Inc.
Upper Saddle River, New Jersey 07458

Prentice Hall books are widely used by corporations and government agencies for training, marketing, and resale.
The publisher offers discounts on this book when ordered in bulk quantities. For more information, contact Corporate Sales Department, Phone: 800-382-3419; FAX: 201-236-7141;
E-mail: corpsales@prenhall.com
Or write: Prentice Hall PTR, Corporate Sales Dept., One Lake Street, Upper Saddle River, NJ 07458.

Printed in the United States of America
10   9   8   7   6   5   4   3   2   1

ISBN 0-13-061014-3

Pearson Education LTD.
Pearson Education Australia PTY, Limited
Pearson Education Singapore, Pte. Ltd.
Pearson Education North Asia Ltd.
Pearson Education Canada, Ltd.
Pearson Educación de Mexico, S.A. de C.V.
Pearson Education—Japan
Pearson Education Malaysia, Pte. Ltd.

To my parents, Marta and Erwin,
and my wife, Ning,
with deepest gratitude and love.
    — *David Mosberger*

To my parents,
my sons, Alexandre and Thomas,
and my wife, Florence.
    — *Stéphane Eranian*

CONTENTS

List of Figures

List of Tables

FOREWORD

by Bruce Perens
Senior strategist, Linux and Open Source
Hewlett-Packard Company

This book is a landmark in the development of operating systems software. It couples a powerful, fully open operating system with a unique look into the mind of the kernel architects who brought that kernel to an entirely new CPU architecture. It's accessible to the student in operating systems programming, but could teach seasoned kernel programmers a trick or two. It conveys a deep technical understanding of a modern CPU, its instruction set and architecture, and the Linux kernel. It shows how modern microprocessor designers build for efficiency and scalability. It goes over the kernel's design goals at the hardware-independent level, and then the specific implementation that stands between those hardware-independent portions and the IA-64 architecture. It covers all of the decisions that the kernel architects made in porting Linux to IA-64, showing how they fit hardware and software together into a working system.

One of the authors of this book is on the short-list of people who could succeed Linus Torvalds in leading the Linux kernel development. Both authors are employed in the research labs of HP, the company that created the IA-64's direct ancestors and their architecture and then went on to co-develop the IA-64 architecture with Intel. The two authors led the port of the Linux kernel to the IA-64 processor, and are thus the best possible teachers of this subject matter.

This book is for you if you'd like to understand the IA-64 architecture from a systems programmer's perspective, if you'd like to understand the Linux kernel on its deepest level, or if you are faced with the task of improving any software's use of any processor, porting an operating system to a new processor, or even designing a new CPU. For any student of operating systems, it provides an important bridge between theory and practice. This is where the rubber meets the road: where abstract goals of architectural cleanness and portability meet the challenge of having to execute efficiently and reliably on an actual CPU.

But one of the most revolutionary things about this book is the fact that it is available to you at all. Just a few years ago, the information in this book and the source code that comes with it would probably have been a *trade secret*, and the companies that own it would have assessed its value at tens of millions of dollars. You would have had to get a job in one of just a few departments at HP simply to be able to see our IA-64 kernel source code. A merely curious person or a student would not have been given the chance. Indeed, in the early 1990s, AT&T valued the intellectual property in its UNIX system at a quarter billion dollars. Well-funded colleges could sometimes buy the privilege to grant postgraduate researchers access to the UNIX source code, but only once those researchers had entered into an odious non-disclosure agreement. Times have changed: you are now granted access to the full source code of the operating system kernel. Want to give your friend a copy of the source? Go right ahead!

What made this change possible? The reason is that Linus Torvalds and hundreds of collaborators have made the Linux kernel available in source code form, and most importantly, under the revolutionary GNU General Public License (GNU GPL). The GPL's model of *Free Software* allows free use and distribution of the system and its source code, allows everyone to collaborate in developing the system, and makes partners of individual developers and the business world while at the same time making it difficult for any partner to take unfair advantage of another. You're invited to join that partnership.

To understand the importance of the GPL to Linux, one must consider how, all through the late 1980s and early 1990s, UNIX was perceived to be dying. Business people were convinced that the entire world would soon run Microsoft NT on their computers. During that period Steve Jobs, founder of Apple and NeXT, even capitulated and placed a Windows system, rather than one of his own products, on his desk at Pixar. But UNIX was saved by two factors: Microsoft had promised to deliver an enterprise-quality NT, but slipped its schedule by more than 5 years. And the GNU/Linux system resurrected the UNIX revolution.

GNU and Linux re-ignited the UNIX world only because of their open, shared nature, while also *uniting* it around a common operating system that ran on all vendors' hardware. UNIX had suffered from over-differentiation: every vendor made changes intended to lock in the customer, and vendors were so hungry to pay off their sizable R&D expenditures that they charged UNIX customers by the number of users and handicapped their systems so that they'd refuse to log in more people than the customer had paid for. But the GPL-ed Linux was less vulnerable to forcible differentiation and intellectual-property hoarding: the terms of the GPL require that improvements to the software must be shared with everyone, and they state that the software can be modified by anyone who has it. Once you are able to modify the software, you are able to remove any locks that restrict the system.

The share-and-share-alike provisions of the GPL tend to commoditize the operating system and the underlying hardware. This cuts into vendor margins, but is all to the customer's advantage. The net effect is that vendors have begun to treat operating systems as *enabling software*, rather than as the direct basis of their profits. This is possible because the collaborative nature of Free Software means that no individual or company is burdened with too much of the cost of developing or servicing it. Companies can, and do, share the development of this non-differentiating software with their direct competitors. For example, IBM and HP, while competing for Linux market share, are enthusiastic collaborators on a number of Free Software projects. The two companies can do together what their budgets would not allow them to pursue alone.

So, here's the logical outcome of the Free Software revolution: work that would have been proprietary only a few years ago is now available for you to examine and modify, and the people who did that work, rather than hoard their skills for the exclusive use of their employer, are about to tell you everything about how they did it. This book is a deep technical introduction to the IA-64 architecture and its version of the Linux kernel. Because the Linux system is yours to explore, this book hides nothing from you. With the lessons here, you can port the Linux kernel to another processor, add features, or even write an entirely new operating system for IA-64. Alternatively, you can simply become more knowledgeable about how your applications get service from an operating system, and why they run the way they do. The choice of how to use this information is yours. The secrets are out of the lab, the intellectual property police have gone elsewhere, the doors of the operating system are flung open. The revolution is here: come in and explore.

— Bruce Perens

PREFACE

This book grew out of the simple desire to describe exactly how Linux works on an IA-64 machine. By realizing that desire, we hope not only to shine a light on the inner workings of Linux, but also to share some of the excitement and the creative processes that are involved in solving the many technical challenges that arise when designing an operating system for a platform as radical and innovative as IA-64. Many of the innovations in IA-64 are targeted at increasing performance by giving a compiler more control over the CPU. However, as we see in this book, IA-64 also comes with a powerful system architecture which supports—indeed encourages—innovative solutions at the operating-system level.

Linux is a no-nonsense operating system, sticking to tried and true principles whenever possible. At the same time, Linux has always been able to adapt quickly to genuine advances in hardware and operating-system technology. Thus, while we believe that the design and implementation described in this book provide a solid foundation, we also believe that there is plenty of room for improvement. In this sense, we hope to encourage research and development around this platform. Of course, the fact that Linux is an Open Source operating system also helps make it an ideal test bed for exploring new ideas. Unlike more speculative operating systems, Linux offers the opportunity to turn truly inspired solutions into practice almost overnight.

Given that the Linux source code is freely available, some people may wonder whether it would not be possible to learn Linux and its IA-64 implementation directly from reading the source code. It is true that the source code contains the most *precise* description of how Linux works, but too much precision sometimes hurts: it can make us see all the trees but miss the forest. Source code also can explain only *how* things are done, not *why* they are done in a particular way. This book is designed to compensate for these shortcomings.

When introducing a new topic, we start at a high level, describing the ideas, principles, and motivations for the approaches taken by Linux. Then we describe the hardware abstraction interfaces used by Linux and, finally, their IA-64 implementations. Throughout these discussions, the focus is always on *what* needs to be accomplished. How they are accomplished is described also, but at a sufficiently high level that avoids drowning a reader in details. This implies that this book can be used in two primary ways: readers mainly interested in an overview of Linux/ia64 find a self-contained and authoritative description. Readers interested in gaining hands-on experience find a smooth introduction to the world of Linux/ia64 and the underlying source code. To assist with the latter, the descriptions in this book have embedded in them pointers to key pieces of the Linux source code. Those pointers tend to be most accurate for Linux kernel version v2.4.14, though they also apply to earlier and later versions.

INTENDED AUDIENCE

This book is primarily targeted at professionals interested in learning more about how the Linux kernel works on IA-64. In addition, hardware architects may find the book useful as a case study of how one particular operating system takes advantage of IA-64. Similarly, software architects interested in designing other operating systems for IA-64 will find many tips on how to handle some of the more advanced features of IA-64. For example, the book discusses the operating-system impact of speculative execution, the register stack, and the virtual hash page table walker. Finally, students in the area of Computer Science and Engineering may find the book interesting as a description of how a real, general-purpose operating system works on real hardware.

Among the Linux professionals, the book should be of most direct value to general kernel programmers, authors of device drivers, and application programmers interested in tuning performance for IA-64. Beyond that, the descriptions of the Linux hardware abstraction interfaces are valid independently of the target platform. We believe that the interface descriptions in this book are among the most accurate and most comprehensive descriptions in existence. But we should caution that these interfaces were developed by a large group of developers over a long period of time and, to some degree, they continue to evolve. For that reason, we cannot claim that the descriptions are authoritative beyond the IA-64 platform, though we did try to make them as inclusive as possible.

Knowledge of the C programming language is a prerequisite for this book. Familiarity with basic operating-system concepts, assembly programming, and the machine organization of computers are also helpful, though not strictly required. No prior knowledge of IA-64 is needed.

ORGANIZATION

The first two chapters of this book contain introductory material. Chapter 1, *Introduction*, provides background information on the evolution of both microprocessor architectures and Linux. The second half of the chapter is dedicated to an overview of the Linux kernel. As part of this overview, we also establish the terminology used throughout the remainder of the book.

Chapter 2, *IA-64 Architecture*, introduces the IA-64 architecture and software conventions. IA-64 is a rich architecture that cannot be learned overnight. Because of this, we recommend that this chapter first be read in a fluid fashion, without undue attention to details. Once a basic familiarity has been established, the reader may then want to revisit the chapter from time to time and study specific aspects in more detail.

The next three chapters describe the most fundamental components of Linux and how they work on IA-64: Chapter 3, *Processes, Tasks, and Threads*, describes aspects related to scheduling and execution. It starts with an overview of key data structures, then moves on to describe the Linux thread interface and the various synchronization primitives that Linux supports. Chapter 4, *Virtual Memory*, describes the virtual memory system of Linux. A brief introduction is followed by detailed descriptions of all hardware abstraction interfaces and their IA-64 implementations. Topics covered include the Linux page tables, linearly-mapped virtual page tables, TLB (translation lookaside buffer) management, page fault handling, and memory coherency. Chapter 5, *Kernel Entry and Exit*, describes all aspects related to entering and exiting the kernel. In particular, it explains how system calls and signals work, as well as how data is passed across the user/kernel boundary. Like the preceding two chapters, this one starts by describing the Linux aspects that apply to all platforms and completes the discussion with descriptions of the IA-64 implementations.

The next three chapters are fairly independent of each other. Chapter 6, *Stack Unwinding*, discusses the general topic of stack unwinding. While the topic is not really IA-64 specific, it does play a more important role on this platform. Indeed, anyone wishing to write IA-64 assembly code needs to be familiar with the material presented in the third section of this chapter. The other sections describe the IA-64 kernel unwinder and its implementation. Chapter 7, *Device I/O*, describes aspects related to device input/output (I/O). Specifically, it covers the hardware abstraction interfaces for programmed I/O (both memory-mapped and port-based), DMA (direct memory access), and device interrupts. The interface descriptions are followed by descriptions of their IA-64 realizations. Chapter 8, *Symmetric Multiprocessing*, discusses aspects specific to multiprocessor (MP) machines. Where appropriate, the other chapters cover MP aspects in the course of normal discussion, but this chapter covers all remaining issues. In particular, the first section provides an overview of the Linux locking principles and the MP support interface. The remaining two sections cover the handling of CPU-specific data areas and the issue of maintaining high-resolution timestamps on MP machines.

The final three chapters are mostly IA-64 specific. Chapter 9, *Understanding System Performance*, introduces the IA-64 performance monitoring support, its Itanium implementation, and the associated *perfmon* kernel subsystem. This chapter should be of great value to anyone interested in characterizing and tuning the performance of IA-64 programs, whether the programs are normal applications or part of the Linux kernel. Chapter 10, *Booting*, covers all aspects related to booting a machine. The first two sections contain an overview of the IA-64 firmware and the IA-64 bootloader. The third section covers the Linux bootstrap interface and its implementation on IA-64. Chapter 11, *IA-32 Compatibility*, describes how Linux/ia64 manages to provide backward compatibility with IA-32. By its very nature, this discussion is IA-64 specific. However, most 64-bit Linux platforms provide backward compatibility with some 32-bit platform. For this reason, many of the topics and solutions discussed here apply to other platforms as well.

A glossary of terms and abbreviations used in this book is provided in Appendix E. We would like to encourage the reader to refer to it whenever encountering an acronym that may seem unfamiliar.

ACKNOWLEDGMENTS

Many people contributed to this book, some directly, others indirectly.

First, we would like to thank Cary Coutant, Dale Morris, Dong Wei, Jerry Huck, Jim Callister, and Jim Hull, all of HP, as well as Asit K. Mallick and Rumi Zahir, both of Intel, for patiently answering our questions on some of the more esoteric aspects of IA-64 and the Itanium CPU.

The official reviewers for the book were Brian Lynn, Hans Boehm, and Khalid Aziz, all of HP. We greatly appreciate their feedback. Brian, especially, spent countless hours reviewing multiple revisions of each chapter, always providing insightful comments. We also were fortunate enough to have the help of several volunteer reviewers. In order of reviewed chapter, we would like to thank Sverre Jarp of CERN for reviewing the description of the modulo-scheduled loop hardware and Cary Coutant for helpful corrections and comments on the description of the IA-64 software conventions. David K. Raila of University of Urbana–Champaign and Christophe de Dinechin of HP reviewed the virtual memory chapter. Kevin Buettner of Cygnus Solutions (now Red Hat Solutions) reviewed the chapter on stack unwinding. Asit K. Mallick of Intel reviewed both the Device I/O and Multiprocessing chapters and contributed helpful clarifications and thoughts. Jes Sørensen of Wild Open Source also reviewed the Device I/O chapter and helped find an error in the draft version of the chapter. Jim Callister of HP was instrumental not just in reviewing the content of the System Performance chapter, but also in unlocking some of the secrets behind the Itanium performance monitoring unit. Dong Wei of HP reviewed the ACPI section in the Booting chapter, for which we are especially grateful. Don Dugger of Independent Storage reviewed the chapter on IA-32 compatibility, and we would like to thank him for that. Sunil Saxena of Intel solved the puzzle of why IA-32 ELF binaries use such an odd load address.

We are greatly indebted to all reviewers and thank them for their countless contributions. At the same time, we need to emphasize that the accuracy of the book is entirely our responsibility. Should a reader find any errors, we would appreciate hearing about them. See the next section on how to contact us.

As far as the production of the book is concerned, we would like to thank Susan Wright and Pat Pekary of HP Books Publishing. Susan was instrumental in getting this book on track. We would also like to thank our acquisition editor, Jill Pisoni Harry, and our production editor, Jane Bonnell, of Prentice Hall PTR. Together with their resourceful staff, they helped us get this book published with a minimal amount of distractions.

Last, but by no means least, we would like to thank Linus Torvalds for creating Linux and the Linux community for making it into such a terrific Open Source operating system. By the same token, we would like to thank HP Labs management for giving us the freedom and the substantial amount of required time to prepare this book.

The manuscript and layout of this book was prepared with LaTeX 2ϵ, xfig, GNU Emacs, and the X Window System running on top of Linux. Most of the book was written on an OmniBook 5700CTX laptop from HP, with the final layout being produced on an HP i2000 Itanium workstation. Special thanks go to Brian V. Smith, the maintainer of the xfig package. On short notice, he was able to accommodate changes to xfig that simplified the production of this book.

PROVIDING FEEDBACK

While we strived to make this book as interesting, useful, and accurate as possible, we encourage our readers to provide feedback on how to improve future editions. For this purpose, we set up a web site at the following address (URL):

```
http://www.lia64.org/book/
```

Please visit this site to report errors or to make suggestions for improvements. The web site also contains an up-to-date errata, links to related software and tools, and a summary of the evolution of Linux as it pertains to this book.

David Mosberger and Stéphane Eranian
Palo Alto, California
November, 2001

Chapter 1

Introduction

The fundamental task of an operating system such as Linux is to take the complex and varied hardware resources of a machine and abstract them into easy-to-use, abundant, and machine-independent software resources. For example, a limited amount of physical memory is abstracted into abundant virtual memory, a limited number of CPUs are abstracted into abundant "threads of execution," and complex input/output (I/O) device interfaces are abstracted into easy-to-use concepts such as files, graphical windows, or network sockets (connections).

Given this role, Linux is necessarily closely tied to the hardware that it is running on. In this chapter, we begin to explore how Linux turns the raw hardware resources of a machine into useful high-level software abstractions. We start by describing the context that gave rise to Linux. As is common for operating systems, there are a hardware component and a software component to this: the first section explores the hardware component and briefly examines the history of microprocessor evolution. As we will see in the second section, microprocessors played an instrumental role in the creation of Linux. Arguably, they influenced Linux in at least two ways. First, in 1991 they enabled Linus Torvalds, a student at the University of Helsinki, to have his own personal computer on which he began developing Linux. Second, microprocessors fueled the explosion of the Internet during the following years. This was important because it enabled nearly instantaneous communication among a worldwide community of Linux developers. Without this community, Linux simply would not exist in its current form. After describing this background, the chapter moves on to describe what Linux looks like today. Specifically, the third section provides a general overview of the Linux kernel: its key abstractions and the major components that are needed to realize them. For the curious and practical-minded reader, the fourth section gives a short overview of the Linux source code.

1.1 MICROPROCESSORS: FROM CISC TO EPIC

Let us start with a brief tour of the evolution of microprocessor architecture [10]. Since this book focuses on IA-64, we will also use this as an opportunity to provide the context and motivation for this architecture.

Microprocessors can be classified according to the *paradigm* that they follow. A paradigm is a loose set of rules that defines the basic flavor of an architecture. There are four

1

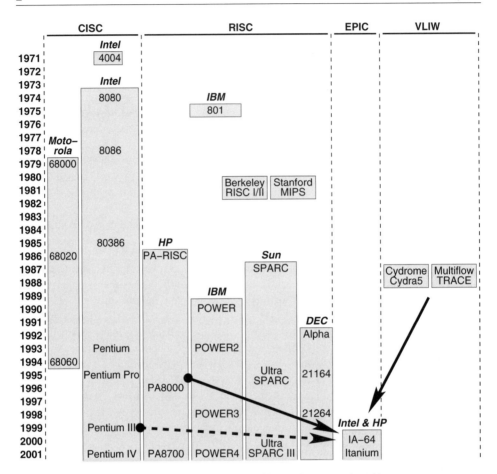

Figure 1.1. Microprocessor paradigms and history of some sample architectures.

common paradigms: *complex instruction set computing (CISC), reduced instruction set computing (RISC), very long instruction word (VLIW),* and *explicitly parallel instruction set computing (EPIC).* We will use the diagram in Figure 1.1 as a guide to explain these terms. The figure shows major microprocessor-related events, starting with the year 1971 at the top and ending in year 2001 at the bottom. We should warn that because of space limitations, the diagram is not meant to be complete. For example, the MIPS and PowerPC architectures have been omitted. Similarly, the figure focuses on microprocessors only: mini- and mainframe architectures such as the DEC VAX and the IBM 390 are not included.

At the top of the diagram, we see that Intel introduced the 4004 in 1971. This CPU is widely regarded as the first microprocessor. It is listed in the CISC column even though by today's standards it is all but complex: it had only a handful of instructions, could address only 640 bytes of memory, and was implemented with just 2600 transistors! The reason it is listed there is that it gave birth to the CISC paradigm: initial microprocessors had such limited numbers of transistors that their functionality was severely limited. The primary goal of subsequent microprocessors, therefore, was to overcome these limitations and to pack more and more functionality into each chip. As microprocessor technology became more sophisticated, these chips grew increasingly complex. By the time Intel introduced its first 16-bit microprocessor, the 8086, and Motorola started its 68000 series, the primary metric of a "good" microprocessor was how many fancy instructions and addressing modes it supported.

It did not take long before various architects started to notice that while these microprocessors provided powerful instruction sets, they did not necessarily run as effectively as possible. It turned out that, in some cases, complex instructions could be replaced with a sequence of simpler instructions and the resulting program ran *faster*! Moreover, compilers often were overwhelmed by the multitude of instructions available and ended up choosing suboptimal instruction sequences. To counter these situations, around 1981 various teams started to explore the possibility of building streamlined, highly efficient microprocessors that provide just the most basic instruction sets. Specifically, at the University of Berkeley, a team led by David Patterson started to work on the RISC I architecture. Almost simultaneously, a Stanford University team led by John Hennessy created MIPS. The resulting architectures were called RISC designs because, compared to their CISC brethren, they had a much simpler architecture and provided only a minimal (primitive) set of instructions that could readily be exploited by a compiler.

In retrospect, it is clear that in the year 1975, an IBM project called 801 created the first RISC design. However, this design was ahead of its time, well before the term "RISC" was even coined, and IBM did not successfully commercialize RISC technology until much later, in 1990, with the introduction of the POWER architecture. The academic projects later transformed into commercial RISC designs, with Sun SPARC being based on the Berkeley design and the Stanford design transforming into the commercial MIPS architecture. Hewlett-Packard (HP) introduced its own RISC design in 1986 with the PA-RISC architecture. However, PA-RISC was influenced more by the IBM 801 than by the Berkeley/Stanford projects. This is not surprising considering that some of the same people that worked on the 801 were behind PA-RISC. Consequently, PA-RISC was not as extreme as the academic projects in streamlining the instruction set, though clearly both approaches shared many of the same goals. In particular, all RISC architectures share the load/store model, where all operands need to be loaded from memory into registers before they can be operated on.

Just as the first commercial RISC designs started to become popular, there were also initial attempts to commercialize VLIW architectures. Specifically, around 1987 there were two projects, called the Cydrome Cydra5 and the Multiflow TRACE architecture. VLIW is similar to RISC in that it also uses streamlined instruction sets. However, unlike RISC, VLIW packs multiple instructions into bundles of "very long instruction words," which are then executed in parallel. As such, VLIW has the potential to perform better than a straight RISC design. Indeed, the VLIW architectures were moderately successful for scientific applications, but they failed to catch on as mainstream architectures because they lacked binary compatibility, which prevented a program compiled for one generation of VLIW machine to run on the next generation. Another issue was that they achieved less than stellar performance on irregular workloads such as those exhibited by many commercial applications. Despite these issues, the principal ideas behind VLIW are sound and there are popular VLIW architectures for embedded environments.

1.1.1 Summary of microprocessor taxonomy

Let us summarize the discussion so far. A *paradigm* defines a loose set of rules, which are then refined by specific *architectures*. Each *architecture* defines a specific instruction set that is used by applications to implement particular programs. Within an architecture, there are typically several chip implementations, or *CPU models*. Since they share the same instruction set, a given application can generally run on any implementation of the same architecture. However, in some cases, later CPU models implement architecture extensions that are not supported by earlier models. For example, the PA-8000 CPU model introduced a 64-bit extension to the original 32-bit PA-RISC architecture. This implies that older applications can run on PA-8000 but the reverse may not necessarily be true. Apart from paradigms, architectures, and CPU models, another important concept is the *microarchitecture*. This term refers to the implementation framework that is shared within a family of CPU models. While different members of a family share key implementation aspects, they may use different implementation parameters. For example, the Intel Pentium Pro and Pentium II models share the same basic microarchitecture, though they run at different clock speeds, may have different cache sizes, and so on.

1.1.2 The IA-64 architecture and Itanium

In the early 1990s, HP Labs started to explore designs for a future architecture that would significantly raise the performance levels above what could be achieved with pure RISC designs. This project was variously called *PA wide-word (PA-WW)* or *super-parallel PA (SP-PA)*. The basic idea was to take advantage of the lessons learned from past designs and build a wide-instruction word architecture that solved the traditional problems of VLIW. The ultimate goal was to build an architecture that could go beyond the performance levels of traditional RISC (or CISC, for that matter). Later on, the resulting paradigm was named EPIC: like VLIW, it expresses parallelism explicitly in the instruction stream but does so in a fashion that avoids the binary compatibility problem associated with VLIW.

HP invited Intel to participate in the effort to design and build the architecture. This led to the HP/Intel alliance that would proceed to define the IA-64 architecture [26]. While the architecture was co-designed by HP and Intel, the actual IA-64 chips are produced by Intel and are available to other computer manufacturers. In this sense, IA-64 is an open architecture. As Figure 1.1 illustrates, the architecture is influenced both by PA-RISC and the early VLIW projects. The dashed arrow from the original Intel line of microprocessors indicates that the IA-64 architecture is backward compatible with Pentium III, even though the IA-64 instruction set itself has no elements of a CISC design.

The first chip implementing the IA-64 architecture is called Itanium and was introduced in May of 2001. Appendix A contains a summary of the model-specific aspects of

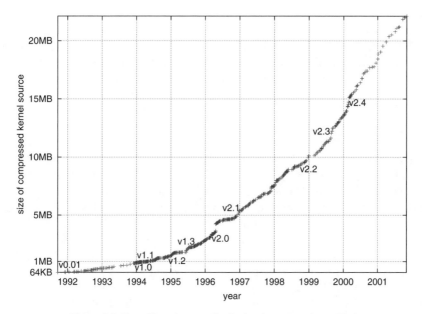

Figure 1.2. Size of kernel source distribution (compressed `tar` files).

Itanium and the follow-on model, code-named "McKinley." We should mention that the IA-64 architecture is often called the *Itanium processor family (IPF)*. However, throughout this book, we use the term IA-64 because it helps clarify the distinction between the *architecture* and its *implementations* (e.g., Itanium). This distinction is important because an operating system design is much more influenced by the architecture than by specific implementations. In other words, since Linux/ia64 is designed for the IA-64 *architecture*, it will continue to run without major changes even as Itanium is replaced by increasingly faster implementations. Similarly, this book uses the term *IA-32* to refer to Intel's traditional 32-bit line of microprocessors, which started with the 80386. To be more precise, we use this term to refer to the CISC instruction set implemented by the Pentium III model [25].

1.2   A BRIEF HISTORY OF LINUX

One way to start looking at the evolution of Linux is to plot the size of the kernel source distribution as a function of time. This is illustrated in Figure 1.2. As shown there, the Linux kernel started late in 1991 with version 0.01. It was just about 64 Kbytes in size. From then on, it grew exponentially, with v1.0 having a size of 1 Mbyte, v2.0 a size of 4.7 Mbytes, and v2.4 taking up more than 15 Mbytes! The figure also illustrates nicely how even-numbered releases (e.g., v1.0 and v1.2) are usually quickly followed by odd-numbered releases (e.g., v1.1 and v1.3). This reflects the fact that odd-numbered releases are development versions of the kernel. This is not to say that even-numbered releases are short-lived; quite the opposite: they are stable releases and continue to be maintained for years. However, in terms of development activity, most work occurs in the odd-numbered releases and hence they take up a much larger fraction of the time covered by the figure.

Of course, the size of the kernel distribution tells only a small part of the story. In the remainder of this section, we take a closer look at the history of Linux.

1.2.1 The early days

Linux started out as a computer science project by a Finnish student named Linus Torvalds. At the time, he was studying at the University of Helsinki and grew interested in operating systems, especially the UNIX operating system [9]. Unfortunately, UNIX was expensive. A license to just *run* UNIX could easily cost hundreds of dollars. Full source code licenses were even more expensive, easily costing US $100,000 or more! Unable to experiment with UNIX itself, Linus instead used MINIX [67]. This was a small, UNIX-like microkernel created by Andrew Tanenbaum, a professor at the Free University of Amsterdam. It was intended as a tool for teaching operating systems and was widely used at universities throughout the world. However, since it was intended *only* as a teaching tool, it had its limitations. One limitation was that it was designed for the Intel 8086 CPU. As such, it was unable to take advantage of the more sophisticated 32-bit memory model offered by the Intel 80386 CPUs [25]. This enhanced memory model turned out to be of particular interest to Linus, and since MINIX could not cope, he decided to start from ground up.

The first visible sign of this project appeared on July 3rd of 1991, when Linus posted an article to the comp.os.minix USENET newsgroup, asking for help in locating the POSIX standards documents. About two months later, Linux v0.01 was released to the world. Apparently, it did not work well yet and Linus was not too proud of it, so its distribution was limited to an inner circle of people [72]. This changed shortly afterward, with the release of v0.02.

Linus announced v0.02 with another article on comp.os.minix. The first part of this article is reprinted in Figure 1.3. In typical fashion, it started out with a humorous description as to why someone might be crazy enough to try writing his or her own operating system. While humorous, it captures nicely the motivation behind Linux: the desire to go out and explore operating system technology and to experiment with new ideas. The second paragraph of the article is interesting because it gives a brief description of the capabilities that Linux had at the time: Linux was limited to running on IBM AT compatible computers [59]. On the positive side, the kernel was sufficiently complete to support the tools needed to build a Linux kernel using Linux itself. As such, Linux was *self-hosting*, indicating that it had already passed the first major milestone of any operating system project.

With v0.02 out in the world, an increasing number of people started to take notice. Not only did they notice, but they tried it out, made their own improvements, and contributed their changes back to Linus. This process resulted in rapid enhancements, and after v0.12 was released in January of 1992, Linus felt that it had reached the point where it could be released as v1.0. To reflect this point, the next release carried a version number of 0.95, with the plan for v1.0 to follow shortly. What Linus did not count on was that the v0.9x series of

```
From: torvalds@klaava.Helsinki.FI (Linus Benedict Torvalds)
Newsgroups: comp.os.minix
Subject: Free minix-like kernel sources for 386-AT
Message-ID: <1991Oct5.054106.4647@klaava.Helsinki.FI>
Date: 5 Oct 91 05:41:06 GMT
Organization: University of Helsinki

Do you pine for the nice days of minix-1.1, when men were men and wrote
their own device drivers? Are you without a nice project and just dying
to cut your teeth on a OS you can try to modify for your needs? Are you
finding it frustrating when everything works on minix? No more all-
nighters to get a nifty program working? Then this post might be just
for you :-)
As I mentioned a month(?) ago, I'm working on a free version of a
minix-lookalike for AT-386 computers. It has finally reached the stage
where it's even usable (though may not be depending on what you want),
and I am willing to put out the sources for wider distribution. It is
just version 0.02 (+1 (very small) patch already), but I've successfully
run bash/gcc/gnu-make/gnu-sed/compress etc under it.
...
```

Figure 1.3. First part of the message announcing Linux v0.02.

Linux turned out to be so popular that many people just kept contributing more and more. One kernel enhancement followed the next, and the version numbers kept spinning, rapidly closing in on v1.0. In fact, Linus started to run out of version numbers. The solution? *Longer* version numbers. Version 0.99 was followed by v0.99.1, then even that was not enough, so v0.99.14 was followed by v0.99.14a. This went on until, finally, all the letters of the alphabet were exhausted and v0.9.14z had to be followed by v0.9.15. By this time, it was February of 1994 and many people started to wonder whether v1.0 would ever be released. But their patience was rewarded on March 13th, when Linus finally released the first official and stable version of Linux, version 1.0!

By all accounts, v1.0 was a capable operating systems with many useful applications both for desktop and small server environments. The only major issue was that it was still limited to IBM AT-compatible computers.

1.2.2   Branching out: Linux goes multiplatform

It did not take long before Linux started to get noticed outside the IBM AT world. Indeed, as early as 1992, Hamish Macdonald and Greg Harp started porting it to the Amiga, which was a popular home computer based on the Motorola 68000 CPU [38]. Similarly, around the same time Ralf Bächle started to work on a port to the MIPS architecture. However, Linus wanted to release a stable version of Linux before branching out to multiple platforms. As a result, these efforts remained separate from the main source tree. However, soon after v1.0 was finally released, the port for the MIPS RISC CPU was merged into the official source code (v1.1.45). More importantly, thanks to the efforts of Jon "maddog" Hall, Linus now was in possession of a Digital Alpha RISC computer [18]. This meant that Linus was interested not just in making Linux more portable, but also in making it 64-bit clean, so it could run on machines with huge amounts of memory. The subsequent efforts to improve portability of Linux were so successful that, in 1997, Linus was comfortable enough to graduate with a Master's thesis entitled "Linux: a Portable Operating System" [73]. Considering that by the end of that year Linux had been ported to more than seven different platforms (Digital Alpha, Intel 80386, Motorola 68000, IBM PowerPC, Sun SPARC, and a 64-bit version of SPARC), the title was certainly accurate, but it was probably just as much designed to lay to rest any lingering doubts about the portability of Linux.

1.2.3   IA-64 Linux

The Linux/ia64 project started at HP Labs in March of 1998 with the goal of creating a complete and optimized version of Linux for the IA-64 platform. The biggest challenge to getting this project started was the lack of a C compiler that could understand the GNU C dialect that the Linux kernel uses. In other words, before kernel development could start in earnest, an IA-64 version of the GNU toolchain (C compiler, assembler, and linker) had to be created. By November, the toolchain was working well enough that the first steps toward a Linux kernel could be taken. At the time, v2.1.126 was the current kernel version so the authors began to enhance this kernel step by step with the necessary IA-64 support.

By March of 1999, it was possible to boot the Linux/ia64 kernel into a simple command shell and execute a few commands. Since no hardware was available at the time, all of this had to be done on a simulator [49]. After the first public demonstration, the project widened to include several other companies, including Intel, and institutions such as CERN (European Organization for Nuclear Research). This resulted in close collaboration and fast-paced development activities, but since the architecture continued to be under nondisclosure, most of the work had to be done in secret.

Of course, the official Linux kernel did not stand still during this time, so as new kernels were released, the Linux/ia64 version had to be updated accordingly. Early in year 2000 the architecture was finally disclosed to the public and shortly after that, the IA-64 support was merged into the official Linux source tree with v2.3.43. Ever since then, development of Linux/ia64 has continued in the traditional Linux fashion, with people and companies from all over the world contributing enhancements.

1.2.4   Summary of Linux history

To summarize the discussion, Linux originally started out as an operating system that was closely tied to the IBM AT. However, portability of Linux improved quickly after the initial v1.0 release, and by the time v2.4.14 was released, Linux ranked among the most frequently ported operating systems. Not counting minor variations, this release supported 12 different architectures! A summary of the key attributes of various Linux platforms is shown in Table 1.1. The first row shows that Linux covers both little-endian and big-endian

Attribute	IA-64	IA-32	PA-RISC	Alpha	PowerPC	SPARC64
byte order	little	little	big	little	big	big
addressability	64 bits	32 bits	32 bits	64 bits	32 bits	64 bits
page size	4, 8, 16, or 64 Kbytes	4 Kbytes	4 Kbytes	8 Kbytes	4 Kbytes	8 Kbytes
addr. space	32 Pbytes	4 Gbytes	4 Gbytes	8 Tbytes	4 Gbytes	8 Tbytes

Table 1.1. Key attributes of Linux for various platforms.

platforms. The second row shows that Linux can support both traditional 32-bit platforms as well as 64-bit platforms. The final two rows show that Linux can accommodate a variety of page sizes and that the maximum virtual address space can range from just 4 Gbytes to over 32 Pbytes (1 Pbyte $= 2^{50}$ bytes)!

1.3 OVERVIEW OF THE LINUX KERNEL

The Linux kernel can be characterized as a modern implementation of the tried principles pioneered by UNIX. It is most directly influenced by System V and BSD UNIX [9, 39]. As such, it is a complete multiuser and multitasking system. Linux is modern in the sense that it has been extended with many abstractions that are not present in traditional UNIX (such as multithreading), is highly modular, and is written in the ANSI version of the C programming language [7]. The choice of ANSI C over traditional Kernighan & Ritchie C may seem like a minor implementation aspect, but the better type checking that it offers is an essential contributing factor to the success of Linux, especially considering its loosely knit and geographically dispersed development community [36].

Even though modular, Linux is a monolithic system, meaning that all kernel subsystems are linked together into a single piece of code with no protection between them. Modularity is supported in two ways. First, almost every aspect of Linux can be configured with compile-time options. For example, they can be used to select exactly which components should be built into the kernel and whether the target machine contains a single CPU or multiple CPUs. Second, most kernel components can be built as a *dynamically loadable kernel module (DLKM)*. Such modules are built separately from the main kernel and loaded into the kernel at runtime and on demand. This is often convenient because infrequently used components take up kernel memory only when they are really needed. Kernel modules also can be upgraded incrementally, meaning that it is often possible to improve the kernel at runtime without the need to reboot the machine. A final advantage is that they make it possible to build minimal kernels which, when run on a particular machine, will automatically adapt to the machine and load only those kernel components that are needed. In this sense, it is possible to build generic, yet small, kernels that will run on almost any machine.

Note that MINIX played a role in the practical aspects of getting Linux started, but from a design point of view, it had very little influence. Indeed, it almost served as the antithesis of Linux: MINIX was a microkernel, which isolated kernel subsystems into their

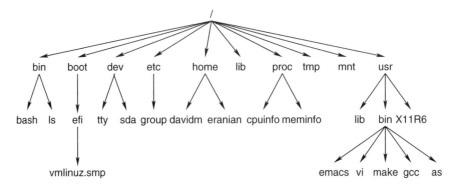

Figure 1.4. Portion of a typical Linux filesystem (namespace).

own protected domains and required message passing to communicate between them. Linus felt that microkernels often make simple things needlessly complicated and, overall, offered poorer performance, so Linux follows the more traditional, monolithic approach to implementing operating systems.

1.3.1   Key concepts

Let us briefly review some of the key concepts that provide the foundation of Linux. We derive these concepts from first principles and introduce necessary terminology along the way. We start at a high level and then quickly drill down into a few specific aspects of the Linux kernel that we need in later chapters.

Filesystem namespace

From the perspective of a computer user, the *filesystem* is one of the key abstractions of Linux. It provides a global, *hierarchical namespace* that contains various objects, including *regular files*, *directories*, *symbolic links*, and *special files*. The root of this namespace is denoted by a single slash character ("/"). The *absolute path* of an object is the names of its ancestors prepended to its name, using a slash character as a separator. For example, in the sample filesystem illustrated in Figure 1.4, the absolute path of the Linux kernel image called vmlinuz.smp is /boot/efi/vmlinuz.smp.

   Regular files consist of an unstructured (flat) sequence of 8-bit bytes. At the file level, their content is not interpreted in any fashion. Instead, interpretation is left to higher-level software. For example, Linux text files normally contain lines of ASCII characters, with a single linefeed character indicating the end of a line. Similarly, various applications interpret the Linux password file /etc/password as containing lines of fields that are separated by a colon character (":"). In contrast, directories are structured name/value pairs that describe the list of files contained within the directory. The value associated with each name is called an *inode number*, which can be thought of as a unique file number.

For example, in Figure 1.4, the directory at /usr would list the names lib, bin, and X11R6. Each of these names would be accompanied by the inode number that contains the content of the file (which may be a directory of its own). Symbolic links (or *symlinks*) are files whose content is interpreted as a path name. When translating a path, Linux handles sym-links by replacing the name of the symlink with its content. For instance, if /t was a symlink containing dev/tty, the path /t would be equivalent to /dev/tty. If the content of symlink starts with a slash character, it is treated as an absolute path. Special files refer to objects that generally have a side effect when accessed. For example, /dev/tty is a special file. Writing text to it has the side effect of printing the text on the terminal of the user. Similarly, /dev/sda is a special file representing the first SCSI disk. Reading from or writing to it has the side effect of directly accessing the corresponding disk blocks. Special files can also be used to perform arbitrary operations through the *ioctl()* system call. For example, on a special file representing a SCSI CD-ROM drive, the *ioctl()* request SCSI_IOCTL_DOORLOCK can be used to lock the door and prevent the user from removing a CD-ROM while the device is in use.

When Linux starts running, its filesystem consists of the *root filesystem*. This filesystem is normally stored on a disk drive partition that is selected by boot command-line options. The namespace provided by the root filesystem can be dynamically extended by *mounting* additional filesystems. Any directory can serve as a *mount point* and when a filesystem is mounted at such a point, the content of the mounted filesystem temporarily replaces the content of the mount point. If the filesystem is unmounted, the original content of the directory reappears.

The dynamic mounting of filesystems is useful for a number of reasons. For example, it can be used to manage disk space. Suppose /home was about to run out of disk space. This problem can be fixed with the purchase of a new disk drive, but the old filesystem cannot (normally) be extended to cover the new disk. Instead, the old content of /home can be copied to the new disk, and the filesystem on this new disk can then be mounted at /home. A second reason is interoperability: Linux supports over a dozen different filesystem formats, including the ISO-9660 CD-ROM format and the MS-DOS format. Mounting makes it possible to have portions of the global namespace be stored on different filesystems. For example, MS-DOS formatted floppy disks could be mounted at /mnt/floppy, or ISO-9660 formatted CD-ROMs could be mounted at /mnt/cdrom. A third reason is remote access: remote filesystem protocols such as Sun's *network file system (NFS)* or Microsoft's *server message block (SMB)* let multiple machines share a single filesystem across a network. Linux also supports a number of special filesystems. Like special files, they are of a more dynamic nature and tend to have side effects when accessed. The best example is procfs, a filesystem that is normally mounted at /proc. It is a virtual filesystem that provides access to and control over various aspects of Linux. For instance, /proc/meminfo contains detailed statistics on the current memory usage of Linux. Since it is a virtual file, its content changes as memory usage changes over time.

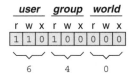

Figure 1.5. Linux file access rights.

Security and access control

To facilitate the safe sharing of a machine among multiple users, Linux associates security information with each file in the global filesystem namespace. Specifically, each file is owned by a *user* that is part of some *group*. Users and groups are identified by unique numbers called *user IDs (uid)* and *group IDs (gid)*, respectively. For convenience, the files /etc/passwd and /etc/group, respectively, associate symbolic names with these numeric IDs. In addition, the latter file defines group memberships: for each group, it contains a list of usernames that are part of that group.

Access to each object in the filesystem namespace is restricted according to a vector of *access rights*. This vector consists of the nine bits shown in Figure 1.5. Each vector specifies three access rights (r, w, and x) for user, group, and world. The r right represents the right to *read* a file, w the right to *write* to it, and x the right to *execute* it (run it as a program). For directories, r grants permission to obtain the list of files contained in the directory, w grants permission to create new entries in the directory, and x grants permission to traverse the directory when translating a path. When a file is accessed by the owner, the *user* bits determine whether the access is permitted. If it is accessed by another user that is in the same group, the *group* bits are used instead. Finally, if it is accessed by any other user (neither the owner nor a group member), the *world* bits are used for the access check. As shown in the figure, access rights are often represented as an octal number with three digits. The number 640 would grant read and write access to the user (owner) of the file, read access to group members, and no access at all to the rest of the world.

The user with ID zero is special and is normally called the *root user*, or simply *root*. For root, the normal access checks are bypassed. For example, with an access right of 640, root could still read and write the file. For this reason, root is sometimes called the *super-user*. There are several other occasions where Linux grants root special rights. The set of all these rights is collectively known as the *root privileges*. Having a single "superuser" is convenient, but for security-sensitive environments, it is often necessary to have finer-grained control over which user gets to do what. For this purpose, Linux also supports a capability-based security model. Capabilities divide the root privileges into a set of roughly 30 separate classes, and those rights can then be granted or denied to other users individually. As an example, the CAP_SYS_BOOT capability controls whether a user is allowed to reboot a machine.

When an application creates a new file, the owner is set to the user that is running the application. Similarly, the group is normally set to the user's default group, which is

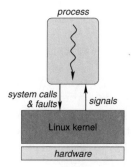

Figure 1.6. Linux process running on top of the kernel.

listed in the password file (/etc/passwd). The application can specify which access rights are turned on in the access rights vector. However, Linux determines the final vector by clearing all bits that are set in the *user mask*, or *umask*. For example, if an application attempts to create a new file with an access right vector of 666 and the *umask* is set to octal number 027, the final access right vector would be 640, i.e., the user could read and write the file, group could only read it, and world would have no access at all.

Applications

Users interact with Linux either through a *command-line shell* such as bash or through a graphical user interface such as GNOME or KDE. In either case, an *application* is started by invocation of a file that contains an *executable image* (sometimes called *binary*). In response, Linux creates a *process* with a single *thread of execution (thread)* that runs the desired application. As the application executes, it may create additional processes and threads of execution as needed.

So just what exactly are processes and threads and how do they relate to each other? A thread can be thought of as a virtual CPU: each thread has access to the register files and instruction set of a CPU. It is virtual in the sense that, independently of how many CPUs there are in a machine, an unlimited number of threads can be created (bounded only by memory). Processes can be thought of as being the containers in which threads execute. If threads are viewed as virtual CPUs, processes can be viewed as virtualizing the remainder of the machine: they provide the memory and the access to *input/output (I/O) devices* that threads need to execute. In particular, a process provides to a thread the illusion of having access to the entire memory address space of the machine. Since this is only an illusion, it is called *virtual memory*. Similarly, Linux virtualizes I/O devices and represents them as special files that are accessed through *file descriptors*. In other words, processes provide threads with an *execution environment*. This is illustrated in Figure 1.6, in which the process is the box with rounded corners. Inside, we find a wiggly line representing the thread.

The figure also shows the *Linux kernel* as the box beneath the process. The actual hardware of the machine is represented by the box at the bottom of the figure. A process can request various services from the kernel by *system calls*. For example, a process could use a system call to write a message to an I/O device, such as a terminal. Processes sometimes also invoke the kernel indirectly, due to *faults*. Some faults occur as a result of programming errors, such as a division by zero, but other faults occur during the normal course of execution and are used, e.g., to implement virtual memory. Depending on the nature of the fault, the kernel may (i) silently fix the problem that caused the fault, (ii) terminate the process, or (iii) send a *signal* to the process. As the arrows in the figure indicate, system calls and signals serve complementary purposes: system calls allow processes to call into the kernel, whereas signals allow the kernel to call into a process. We discuss both concepts in more detail a little later.

Protection

As we have seen so far, processes and threads are key to virtualizing a machine's hardware. Since they are virtual, multiple processes and threads can be run at the same time. To ensure the *secure* sharing of the underlying resources, Linux places each process and the kernel in their own *protection domain*. Processes are prevented from accessing *privileged* portions of the hardware, whereas the kernel has full access to the hardware. In general, the privileged portion of the hardware consists of those pieces that could bypass the security policies of the kernel. For example, any instruction that affects the virtual memory of a process must be privileged. To support this, CPUs typically use a privileged register that keeps track of the *current privilege level*: when the CPU executes a thread inside a process, the current privilege level is set to *user level* and only the unprivileged portions of the hardware are accessible. Attempts to violate this constraint trigger a fault and cause the kernel to be invoked. On the other hand, when the CPU executes inside the kernel, the current privilege level is set to *kernel level* and full access to the hardware is granted.

System calls

Linux provides about 200 different system calls. As shown in Table 1.2, they can be grouped loosely into six classes: filesystem, process, scheduling, System V *interprocess communication (IPC)*, socket, and miscellaneous. Among the filesystem-related system calls, we find classic UNIX calls such as *open()*, *write()*, and *close()*. Among the process-related system calls, we find *execve()*, *clone2()*, and *exit()*. To get a better sense of how system calls are used by processes, let us consider some examples:

```
#include <fcntl.h>
int main (int argc, char **argv) {
    int fd = open("/dev/tty", O_RDWR);
    write(fd, "hello world!\n", 13);
    exit(0);
}
```

In this example, the *open()* system call is used to open a special file called /dev/tty. This file represents the terminal or console device of the current process. Depending on the environment from which the program is invoked, this may be the actual Linux console or

Filesystem related:

access()	*fchown()*	*link()*	*pwrite()*	*stat()*
acct()	*fcntl()*	*lseek()*	*readahead()*	*symlink()*
chdir()	*flock()*	*lstat()*	*readlink()*	*truncate()*
chmod()	*fstatfs()*	*mkdir()*	*readv()*	*umask()*
chown()	*fstat()*	*mknod()*	*read()*	*umount()*
chroot()	*ftruncate()*	*mount()*	*rename()*	*unlink()*
close()	*getcwd()*	*open()*	*rmdir()*	*ustat()*
creat()	*getdents()*	*pivot_root()*	*select()*	*utimes()*
fchdir()	*ioctl()*	*poll()*	*sendfile()*	*writev()*
fchmod()	*lchown()*	*pread()*	*statfs()*	*write()*

Process related:

brk()	*getpgid()*	*mincore()*	*prctl()*	*setsid()*
capget()	*getpid()*	*mlockall()*	*ptrace()*	*setuid()*
capset()	*getppid()*	*mlock()*	*setfsgid()*	*sigaction()*
clone2()	*getpriority()*	*mmap()*	*setfsuid()*	*sigaltstack()*
dup2()	*getresgid()*	*mprotect()*	*setgid()*	*sigpending()*
dup()	*getresuid()*	*mremap()*	*setgroups()*	*sigprocmask()*
execve()	*getrlimit()*	*msync()*	*setpgid()*	*sigqueueinfo()*
exit()	*getrusage()*	*munlockall()*	*setpriority()*	*sigreturn()*
getegid()	*getsid()*	*munlock()*	*setregid()*	*sigsuspend()*
geteuid()	*gettid()*	*munmap()*	*setresgid()*	*sigtimedwait()*
getgid()	*getuid()*	*nanosleep()*	*setresuid()*	*wait4()*
getgroups()	*kill()*	*personality()*	*setreuid()*	
getpagesize()	*madvise()*	*pipe()*	*setrlimit()*	

Scheduling related:

sched_getparam()	*sched_get_priority_max()*	*sched_getscheduler()*	
sched_setparam()	*sched_get_priority_min()*	*sched_setscheduler()*	
sched_yield()	*sched_rr_get_interval()*		

Interprocess communication related:

msgctl()	*msgsnd()*	*semget()*	*shmat()*	*shmdt()*
msgget()	*semctl()*	*semop()*	*shmctl()*	*shmget()*
msgrcv()				

Socket (networking) related:

accept()	*getsockname()*	*recvmsg()*	*send()*	*socket()*
bind()	*getsockopt()*	*recv()*	*setsockopt()*	
connect()	*listen()*	*sendmsg()*	*shutdown()*	
getpeername()	*recvfrom()*	*sendto()*	*socketpair()*	

Miscellaneous:

adjtimex()	*getitimer()*	*query_module()*	*settimeofday()*	*sysinfo()*
create_module()	*gettimeofday()*	*quotactl()*	*swapoff()*	*syslog()*
delete_module()	*init_module()*	*reboot()*	*swapon()*	*times()*
fdatasync()	*pciconfig_read()*	*setdomainname()*	*sync()*	*uname()*
fsync()	*pciconfig_write()*	*sethostname()*	*sysctl()*	*vhangup()*
get_kernel_syms()	*perfmonctl()*	*setitimer()*	*sysfs()*	

Table 1.2. Linux system calls.

a terminal emulator running inside a graphical user environment. On success, the *open()* system call returns a non-negative file descriptor number that serves as a handle for the terminal. The second system call, *write()*, uses this file descriptor to write a short (13-byte) message ("hello world!") to the terminal. The third call, *exit()*, invokes the *exit()* system call and terminates the process. It automatically takes care of closing all open file descriptors, so there is no need to explicitly close the file descriptor returned by *open()*.

Of course, many, if not most, programs need to read or write to the terminal at some point during their execution. For this reason, when a program starts up, Linux automatically provides three standard file descriptors with numbers 0, 1, and 2. They, respectively, are the *standard input*, *standard output*, and *standard error* file descriptors. The first two can be used to read and write regular messages to the terminal, and standard error can be used to write error messages. Also, when returning from the main program, the *exit()* system call is invoked automatically. With this, the above example can be simplified to just a single system call:

```
int main (int argc, char **argv) {
    write(1, "hello world!\n", 13);
    return 0;
}
```

As alluded to earlier, a process can create additional threads or entire new processes. The traditional UNIX way of creating a new process is with *fork()*. This system call works by creating an identical copy of the calling process. The only major difference is that the new process gets its own unique numeric *process ID (pid)* so that the parent (the existing process) can be distinguished from the child (the new process). Once a new process has been created, it can be used to start a new application with the *execve()* system call. Suppose a process had to list the content of a directory by running the 1s command. Assuming this command is stored in file /bin/ls, it could be run with the help of *fork()* and *execve()* in the following fashion:

```
if (fork() == 0) {
    /* child... */
    char *ls_args[] = {"ls", "-l", 0};
    char *ls_env[] = {"HOME=/", 0};
    execve("/bin/ls", ls_args, ls_env);
}
/* parent... */
```

This code fragment begins by calling *fork()* to create a new process. In the parent, it will return the non-zero process ID of the child and the parent process will therefore skip execution of the **if**-body. In the child, *fork()* returns 0, so it will start executing the **if**-body. After defining two local variables, the child goes ahead and directly calls *execve()*. The first argument is the path to the executable image (/bin/ls), the second argument is a pointer to a list of argument strings. These strings are passed to the main program of 1s and serve as command-line arguments, except that the first element specifies the program name. In our case, the program name is set to ls, and the only command-line argument is -1, which will cause 1s to output a verbose (long) format of the directory listing. The third argument

Name	#	Description	Name	#	Description
SIGHUP	1	Terminal hangup	SIGCONT	18	Continue
SIGINT	2	Keyboard interrupt	SIGSTOP	19	Stop
SIGQUIT	3	Keyboard quit	SIGTSTP	20	Keyboard stop
SIGILL	4	Illegal instruction	SIGTTIN	21	Terminal read
SIGTRAP	5	Trace trap	SIGTTOU	22	Terminal write
SIGABRT	6	Abort	SIGURG	23	Urgent condition
SIGBUS	7	Bus error	SIGXCPU	24	CPU limit exceeded
SIGFPE	8	Floating-point exception	SIGXFSZ	25	File size limit exceeded
SIGKILL	9	Kill signal	SIGVTALRM	26	Virtual alarm clock
SIGUSR1	10	User-defined 1	SIGPROF	27	Profiling clock
SIGSEGV	11	Segmentation violation	SIGWINCH	28	Window size changed
SIGUSR2	12	User-defined 2	SIGIO	29	I/O now possible
SIGPIPE	13	Broken pipe	SIGPWR	30	Power failure
SIGALRM	14	Alarm clock	SIGSYS	31	Bad system call
SIGTERM	15	Termination	SIGRTMIN	32	*first real-time signal*
SIGSTKFLT	16	Stack fault	SIGRTMAX	63	*last real-time signal*
SIGCHLD	17	Child status changed			

Table 1.3. Linux signals.

to *execve()* is a pointer to a list of environment strings. Each string defines one *environment variable* as a name/value pair, separated by an equal sign ("="). In our case, only one environment variable, HOME, is passed, and its value is /, the path to the root directory.

Signals

Earlier, we said that the Linux kernel uses signals to notify a process of certain faults, such as a division by zero. The kernel may also use signals to notify the process of asynchronous events, such as when a device has data available for reading. Linux defines a total of 63 signals, each identifying a different cause or source of the signal. Table 1.3 lists the symbolic signal names, the associated numeric signal number, and a brief description. We should mention that the signal numbers listed in the table are valid for the IA-64 and IA-32 platforms; other platforms may use different numbers. There is no need to describe each signal in detail, but two representative examples are SIGINT and SIGSEGV. The former is a signal that is sent when a user attempts to stop a process by typing the interrupt key on a terminal. Typically, this key is bound to **Ctrl-C**. The SIGSEGV signal is generated when a process attempts to access memory that it has no right to access, either because it is an invalid address or because the access would violate memory protection, such as attempting to write to read-only memory.

Each signal has an associated *default action*. For example, the default action for SIGINT is to terminate the process. Similarly, the default action for SIGSEGV also terminates the process, but before doing so, Linux will create a *core dump* (memory dump). The core dump contains the complete state of the process (including all memory contents) at the time of the signal. Later on, a debugger could be used to analyze the core dump and track down the reason for the signal. If a process wants to customize the response to a signal, it can install a *signal handler* with the *sigaction()* system call. In Chapter 5, *Kernel Entry and Exit*, we explore this system call in more detail. Briefly, it lets a process specify a function that is to be executed whenever the signal occurs. For example, a program could install a handler for SIGINT to clean up (e.g., delete temporary files) before terminating the process.

Address-space layout of a process

Traditional UNIX executable images are stored in files with the *a.out* format. With such executable images, the initial address space of a process contains four primary segments: the *text segment*, *data segment*, *bss segment*, and *stack segment*. The text segment contains the executable code (instructions) of the application that the process is executing, the data segment contains static data initialized with application-specific values, and bss contains static data initialized to 0. The stack segment contains the chain of call frames required to keep track of nested function calls. Each thread requires its own stack, so if a process creates additional threads later on, additional stack segments need to be created in address space of the process. The end of the bss segment is marked by the *break value* of the process, and the end of the stack segment is marked by the *stack pointer*. Both segments can grow and shrink dynamically: the break value can be manipulated with the *brk()* system call and the stack pointer is manipulated as a result of function calls and returns, i.e., as a result of normal execution. Note that by increasing the break value, a process can allocate virtual memory dynamically. Memory allocated in this fashion is typically called the *heap* and, like the bss, it is initialized to 0.

Linux closely follows the traditional UNIX model, though most Linux platforms use the *executable and linking format (ELF)* instead of the **a.out** format. ELF is more flexible and not limited to three segments [60]. Also, ELF executables images are typically *dynamically linked* binaries. Such binaries are not self-contained and instead need to be linked with one or more *shared libraries* before they can be run. This linking is accomplished with the help of a *runtime loader*, sometimes called the *dynamic linker*. The *execve()* system call takes care of mapping the runtime loader into the address space of the process and invoking it before execution starts in the actual program. The runtime loader then takes care of loading the shared libraries needed by the program, linking them together, and, eventually, starting execution of the program by calling its *entry point* in the text segment.

To get a better sense of how this works in practice, let us take a look at the example illustrated in Figure 1.7. It illustrates the address-space layout of a process just before *execve()* transfers control it. The specific values illustrated assume that *execve()* was used to invoke the command ls -l on a Linux/ia64 machine. We can see that the executable image of the runtime loader starts at address 0x2000000000000000. The text segment of the program starts at address 0x4000000000000000. In the traditional **a.out** format, this would be followed immediately by the data and bss segments. However, the figure shows that ELF is more flexible and can accommodate gaps between the segments. In particular, on Linux/ia64, the data and bss segments start at address 0x6000000000000000. The stack segment for the initial thread occupies the upper portion of the address space. As

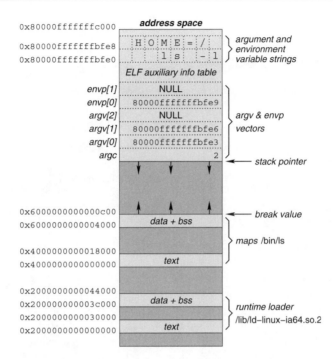

Figure 1.7. Address-space layout of a Linux/ia64 process running ls -l.

shown in the figure, Linux uses the initial (highest address) part of the stack not for call
frames, but to pass information about the program and how it was invoked. Specifically, it
uses the memory to store the argument vector, the environment variable vector, and associated strings that were passed to *execve()*. In addition, the *ELF auxiliary table* is stored
in this area. This table contains information about the executable image, such as a list of
shared libraries required for execution and the entry point of the program, i.e., the address
in the text segment at which execution should begin.

1.3.2 Hardware model

Before taking a closer look at the structure of the Linux kernel, we need to establish the
common hardware model for which Linux is designed. Considering that Linux runs on machines ranging from wristwatches, desktop computers, all the way to mainframe computers, there is of course no single model that accurately reflects all these different machines.
However, all of them do share the basic elements illustrated in Figure 1.8. As the figure
shows, the basic ingredients of a machine are CPUs, system memory, and I/O devices, all
connected by a shared system bus.

Linux can support machines with either one or several CPUs. If a machine contains just
a single CPU, it is called a *uniprocessor (UP)*; otherwise, it is called a *multiprocessor (MP)*.

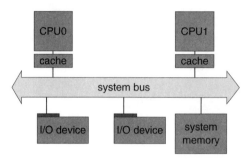

Figure 1.8. Basic hardware model assumed by Linux.

As we will see later in this book, certain problems require different solutions depending on whether the target is a UP machine or an MP machine. For this reason, the Linux kernel needs to be told what machine it should be built for, and the resulting kernel will be optimized accordingly. The CPUs are connected to the *system memory*, or *physical memory*, through the system bus. Accessing memory is relatively slow on modern machines, and for this reason Linux assumes that CPUs have *caches* that accelerate such accesses by storing frequently used data close to the CPU. Usually, some of the caches are directly built into the CPU. For example, the Itanium CPU model has three levels of caches: the first two levels are 32 Kbytes and 96 Kbytes in size, respectively, and are built directly onto the CPU chip. The third level is either 2 or 4 Mbytes in size and is built into the CPU cartridge (assembly). Linux supports arbitrary cache hierarchies, including *split caches*, where data is stored separately from instructions. Again, Itanium can serve as an example: its first-level cache is split into separate instruction and data caches of 16 Kbytes each. Linux requires that each CPU have an associated *memory management unit (MMU)* that provides the facilities needed to realize virtual memory. The reason the figure does not show separate boxes for the MMUs is that for modern CPU architectures, the MMU is integrated into the CPU itself.

Linux supports a wide variety of I/O devices. Generally, a machine contains nonvolatile storage devices, such as hard disks or flash ROM, a terminal-like I/O device, such as a serial-line interface or a graphics card with a separate keyboard, and so on. However, Linux does not *require* any particular device to be present. As long as Linux has some means to mount a root filesystem, it can work properly. For example, if there are no local nonvolatile storage devices, Linux could be configured to use a *network interface controller (NIC)* to mount the root filesystem from a remote machine.

1.3.3 Kernel components

We are now ready to take a closer look at how the Linux kernel is implemented. For this purpose, Figure 1.9 presents a refined version of the earlier diagram showing a process running on top of the Linux kernel. The figure shows several processes running on top

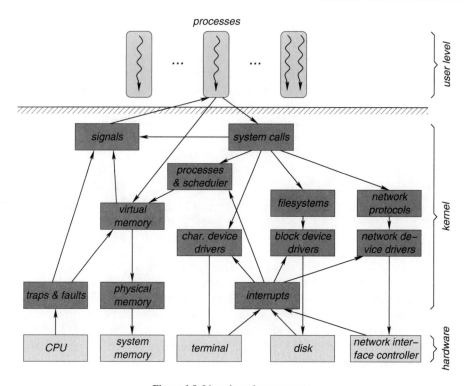

Figure 1.9. Linux kernel components.

of the Linux kernel. In contrast to the earlier diagram, the Linux kernel is now shown as a set of kernel components. The arrows connecting them indicate how they interact with each other. Similarly, the hardware is now shown divided into individual components, with arrows indicating which kernel component manages or uses the various pieces of hardware. Note that all processes and kernel-level components use the CPU, but to keep the figure simple, the corresponding arrows have been omitted.

Near the top of the kernel, we find the boxes representing the system call and signal facilities. As explained earlier, processes call into the kernel with system calls, and the kernel can call into a process with signals. The horizontal arrow from the system call facility to the signal facility indicates that system calls affect how signals are being delivered. For example, *sigaction()* can be used to establish a handler for a particular signal. We will be exploring all aspects related to crossing the boundary between user-level and kernel-level execution in Chapter 5, *Kernel Entry and Exit*. Just below the system call facility, we find the process facility, which creates and manages both processes and threads. It may seem strange that there is a single facility to implement both abstractions. As we see in Chapter 3, *Processes, Tasks, and Threads*, the reason is that they are both implemented in terms of a common abstraction called *tasks*. As such, processes and threads are merely two special cases of the general task abstraction. The figure also illustrates how the virtual memory system is built on top of the physical memory facility and the facility handling CPU traps and faults. Exactly how this works is the subject of Chapter 4, *Virtual Memory*. System calls also affect the operation of the filesystem and networking facilities. As illustrated by the figure, these are built on various device drivers and the interrupt facility. This is the topic of discussion in Chapter 7, *Device I/O*.

To get a more concrete sense of how Linux works internally, let us take a closer look at two key components, the Linux scheduler and the physical memory manager, as well as the key software caches that are used throughout the kernel.

The scheduler

The *Linux scheduler* (file kernel/sched.c) is responsible for virtualizing the CPUs. That is, it runs the threads of all the processes in the system. It does this by multiplexing, or *time slicing*, the one or more CPUs in the machine across the *runnable threads*. For this purpose, each CPU uses a *periodic timer interrupt*. Whenever this interrupt occurs, a CPU checks whether the currently running thread has exhausted its time slice and, if so, picks another thread for execution. A time slice is roughly 50 milliseconds long, so in a single second, up to 20 different threads may be running. On a human scale, this makes it appear as if a single CPU were able to run multiple threads concurrently. Of course, a single CPU really can do only one thing at a time, so this kind of apparent concurrency is called *pseudoconcurrency*. On MP machines, multiple CPUs execute multiple threads in a truly concurrent fashion. This is called *true concurrency*.

The Linux scheduler keeps track of runnable threads in a list called the *run queue*. Threads are selected from this queue according to a *scheduling policy* and a *scheduling priority*. Most threads use a *dynamic priority* policy that is similar to the classic UNIX scheduler. The basic idea is that threads are scheduled in order of decreasing priority. A lower-priority thread will be executed only if there are no higher-priority threads that are runnable. When a new thread is created, it starts out with a base priority. As it executes, the priority is adjusted dynamically, according to the thread behavior. Threads that block frequently (e.g., because they often have to wait for I/O devices to become ready) will have their priority gradually increased, whereas threads that always exhaust their time slice will have their priority gradually decreased. The net effect is that I/O-bound threads tend to have priority over CPU-bound threads. This is a useful policy because it tends to make the system more responsive to user interaction. That is, it achieves better *interactivity*. Users can influence the scheduling priority of a thread through its *nice value*. In effect, the nice value selects the base priority of the thread: larger values mean *less* priority, lower values mean *higher* priority. Valid nice values are in the range of −20 to +20. Nonprivileged users can only specify positive nice value, i.e., they can only decrease the scheduling priority.

Apart from the normal dynamic-priority policy, the Linux scheduler supports two real-time scheduling policies: *round-robin* and *FIFO* (first in, first out). They can be selected with the *sched_setscheduler()* system call. Both policies use static priority values in the range of 1 to 99. Real-time threads are executed strictly in order of decreasing static priority. All threads scheduled with the dynamic priority policy are treated as if they had a static priority of zero and will therefore execute only when there are no real-time threads that are runnable. The difference between the FIFO and round-robin policies is that within a static priority level, the former lets a thread run to completion, whereas the latter limits each thread to executing for up to one time slice and then switches to the next thread with the same static priority. For the FIFO policy, a thread needs to indicate completion by calling the *sched_yield()* system call. Due to the strict static priority, real-time threads can easily starve lower-priority threads from executing altogether. This creates security risks and for this reason, root privileges or the CAP_SYS_NICE capability are required for the selection of a real-time scheduling policy.

Memory management

Linux manages memory at several levels. At the lowest level is the *page allocator* (file mm/page_alloc.c). It manages physical memory as a pool of *page frames*. Each page frame has a platform-specific fixed size, such as 4 Kbytes or 16 Kbytes. The pool of page frames is managed with the *buddy system* [37], an efficient algorithm that enables memory allocation in groups of page frames that have a size that is an integral power of 2. The base-2 logarithm of the number of pages in a group is called the *allocation order*. An allocation order of zero corresponds to a single page, an order of four corresponds to sixteen pages, and so on. The maximum order is ten, such that a group of at most 1024 page frames can be allocated in a single call. The buddy system has the property that an allocation of order n will return physically contiguous memory that is aligned to a boundary of $2^n \cdot$ PAGE_SIZE bytes, where PAGE_SIZE is the size of a page frame. For example, with a page frame size of 4 Kbytes, an allocation of order four would return 64 Kbytes of memory aligned to a 64-Kbyte boundary.

A potential problem with the buddy system is that the longer a machine is running, the more fragmented physical memory may become. In extreme cases, it could happen that half the memory is free, but every other page frame is in use. This would make it impossible to satisfy any allocations with an order greater than zero, even though plenty of memory is available. In general, the higher the order of an allocation, the less likely it is to succeed. Kernel code should therefore avoid high-order allocations as much as possible and expect that non-zero order allocations may fail even when sufficient memory is available.

The primary kernel internal routine to allocate page frames is *alloc_pages()*. It takes two arguments: a *mask* and the *order* of the allocation. The mask consists of a set of flags that define exactly how the memory should be allocated. For example, the value GFP_KERNEL can be used to indicate that the allocation is used for general kernel purposes and that the allocator may block (sleep) for a while until the necessary memory becomes available. On the other hand, GFP_ATOMIC indicates that the memory is needed immediately, i.e., that the allocator may not block execution. When memory is no longer needed, it can be freed with *free_pages()*. This routine also takes two arguments: *addr*, the starting address of the memory and *order*, the order of the allocation. The latter must match the *order* value that was passed to the corresponding *alloc_pages()* call.

To better support kernel components that need to manage memory objects with a size that is not an integral number of page frames, Linux provides a *slab allocator* (file mm/-slab.c) [12]. This allocator provides the capability to create multiple *kernel memory caches*.

Each cache manages objects of a particular kind (and a fixed size). The slab allocator uses various clever tricks to make allocation and deallocation of individual objects extremely efficient. Like the page allocator, slab objects have a limit set on their maximum size. Normally, objects cannot be larger than 32 page frames (order five). Also, since the slab allocator is implemented on top of the page allocator, the same caveat applies regarding large allocations: the bigger the object, the more likely an allocation is to fail, even when plenty of memory is available. For convenience, the slab allocator also implements a pair of routines called *kmalloc()* and *kfree()*. They work like the standard C library routines *malloc()* and *free()* in the sense that they manage memory at a granularity of individual bytes. However, the same maximum size constraints apply as for normal slab allocations.

For large memory allocations, Linux provides the *vmalloc arena* (file mm/vmalloc.c). This is a region of virtual memory that works much like the ordinary process virtual memory. The major difference is that the vmalloc arena is owned by the kernel and not accessible from the user level. Memory can be allocated from this arena with *vmalloc()* and freed with *vfree()*. These routines have the same interfaces as the standard C library routines *malloc()* and *free()*. That is, they operate at a granularity of individual bytes rather than page frames. Unlike the standard *malloc()* routine, *vmalloc()* always returns memory that is aligned to a page-size boundary. Also, note that since the returned memory is virtual memory, the underlying page frames are not guaranteed to be physically contiguous.

The page cache

Reading data from a disk is typically orders of magnitudes slower than reading data from memory. For this reason, Linux caches disk data in memory as much as possible. The primary data structure for this purpose is the *page cache* (file mm/filemap.c). It contains all the filesystem data that is presently in memory. The information *about* each file, such as its size, last time of access, and so on is called *filesystem metadata*. This data is stored in a separate *buffer cache* (file fs/buffer.c). When processes use up more virtual memory than there is physical memory, some of the virtual memory must be stored on the disk. This disk area is called the *swap space*. Linux treats this space like a file, so its content, too, can be stored in the page cache. The collection of these pages is called the*swap cache*. The relationship between the three caches is illustrated in Figure 1.10. The buffer cache contains the metainformation about the file data cached in the page cache. The swap cache contains pages that are being written to the swap space.

An interesting property of Linux is that all virtual memory pages either are present in the page cache or are *anonymous memory*. The latter simply are virtual memory pages whose content is initially cleared to 0. That is, anonymous memory pages are not associated with any particular file, hence their name. Anonymous memory is created, e.g., when a process increases its break value by a call to *brk()*. The *mmap()* system call can also create anonymous memory with a special flag called MAP_ANONYMOUS. Although anonymous memory pages are normally not part of the page cache, they can be added to it through the swap cache. Specifically, if an anonymous page is written (dirtied) by a process and Linux is subsequently forced to save the anonymous page to swap space, it will be added to the page cache at that time.

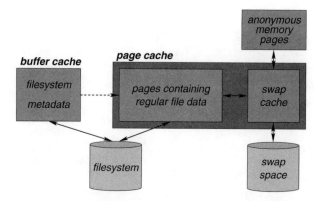

Figure 1.10. The buffer cache, page cache, and swap cache.

1.3.4   The kernel source code

This book is self-contained and there is no need to peruse the Linux source code in order to follow the book's content. However, for readers interested in exploring Linux in more detail or in gaining practical experience, the following description may be helpful in making the connection between this book and the actual source code. To further aid in this effort, this book also contains references to relevant portions of the Linux source code.

Before downloading the source code, it is useful to know how the Linux kernel versioning system works. Kernel development is split into two distinct phases: *development* kernels and *stable* kernels. Most development work happens in the former phase. Once a stable kernel has been released, the hope is that only minor bug fixes will be needed over time. However, this hope is not always realized. It is not unusual for early stable kernels to experience a fair amount of development until everything stabilizes. All kernels have a version number of the form $x.y.z$, where x is the major release number, y is the minor release number, and z is the step number. The major release number is incremented when there are significant changes to the kernel. For instance, when support for MP machines was introduced, the major version number changed from 1 to 2. Odd minor version numbers signify development kernels. Even minor numbers signify stable kernels. For example, v1.2.3 is a stable kernel because 2 is an even number. On the other hand, v2.3.4 is a development kernel because 3 is an odd number. The step number is simply a sequential number that increments each time a collection of improvements (patches) is released.

The Linux kernel source code can be downloaded from the following URL:

ftp://ftp.*cn*.kernel.org/pub/linux/kernel/

Here, *cn* should be replaced with the two-letter country code of the site downloading the kernel. For example, to download from a place in the USA, *cn* should be "us", from a place in Great Britain *cn* should "uk", and so on. The directory at this URL contains several subdirectories. For instance, there is one subdirectory per major kernel release. Directory v2.4/ contains the source code for all v2.4.*z* kernels, directory v2.2/ contains the v2.2.*z*

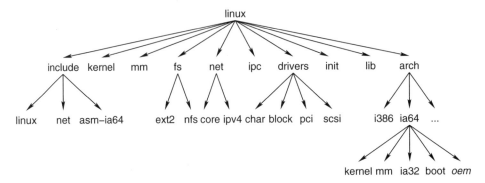

Figure 1.11. Organization of Linux source tree.

kernels, and so on. Linux/ia64-specific patches can be found in subdirectory ports/ia64/. To obtain a working Linux/ia64 kernel source tree, it is generally necessary to download both the official Linux kernel distribution and the matching IA-64 patch. For example, we could obtain the v2.4.14 kernel for Linux/ia64 by downloading v2.4/linux-2.4.14.tar.bz2 and ports/ia64/v2.4/linux-2.4.14-ia64-011105.diff.bz2 and executing the following commands:

```
$ bzcat linux-2.4.14.tar.bz2 | tar xvf -
$ cd linux
$ bzcat ../linux-2.4.14-ia64-011105.diff.bz2 | patch -p1
```

The resulting directory tree has the organization illustrated in Figure 1.11. Not shown in this tree are auxiliary directories such as Documentation/, which contains a loose assortment of documentation, and scripts/, which contains various commands and scripts needed to configure and build a kernel. Apart from these, the kernel contains the following major directories:

- **include/:** Public header files. Subdirectory linux/ contains most platform-independent header files, net/ contains headers related to the network subsystem. Each platform has its own subdirectory called asm-*plt*/, where *plt* is the name of the platform. For example, the IA-64 headers are in asm-ia64/, the headers for the IA-32 platform are in asm-i386/, and so on.

- **kernel/:** The source files that form the core kernel infrastructure, such as the process subsystem, the Linux scheduler, most system calls, and so on.

- **mm/:** The virtual memory system as well as the physical memory manager.

- **fs/:** Everything related to filesystems, including implementations of all filesystem-related system calls, e.g., *open()*, *read()*, and *write()*. In addition, there is one subdirectory for each supported filesystem. For example, ext2/ contains the native Linux filesystem, isofs/ contains the filesystem for ISO-9660–compliant CD-ROMs, and nfs/ contains an implementation of the Sun network file system (NFS).

- **net/:** Everything related to the network subsystem. This includes the socket infrastructure, all socket-related system calls, e.g., *socket()*, *bind()*, and *listen()*. In addition, it contains implementations of the actual network protocols. For example, the TCP/IP network stack is contained in subdirectory ipv4/.

- **ipc/:** The System V interprocess communication (IPC) facilities. This includes implementations of System V shared memory, semaphores, and message queues.

- **drivers/:** All device drivers. Most character device drivers are in subdirectory char/, and some block device drivers are in subdirectory block/. However, there are various other groupings. For instance, all SCSI-related drivers are in subdirectory scsi/, and network device drivers are in subdirectory net/.

- **init/:** Everything related to the main bootstrap procedure.

- **lib/:** Various support (library) routines, such as string, decompression, and check-summing routines.

- **arch/:** All platform-specific source code (other than the header files in include/asm-*plt/*). There is one subdirectory per platform. For example, the IA-64–specific code is in ia64/, IA-32–specific code in i386/, and so on. Each such directory has roughly the same structure as the top-level directory. For example, kernel/ contains general platform-specific kernel code, mm/ contains platform-specific code for the virtual memory system, and so on. In addition, ia64/ contains IA-32 emulation software in subdirectory ia32/ and several OEM-specific directories such as hp/ (HP specific) and sn/ (SGI specific).

It is interesting to note that the device drivers contained in the drivers/ subdirectory constitute the bulk of the kernel source code. For example, in v2.4.14, they took up 73 Mbytes or slightly more than half of the total kernel size of 142 Mbytes. In comparison, the top-level kernel/ directory took up less than half a megabyte. This is a good sign: even though the Linux source code has grown big over the years, most of the size is due to support for lots of different hardware, filesystems, and network protocols. The core kernel infrastructure itself has remained remarkably lean and manageable.

1.4 SUMMARY

In this chapter, we started out by describing the context that gave rise to Linux in general and Linux/ia64 in particular. Specifically, we began with a brief review of the history of microprocessor evolution and showed where IA-64 fits into this picture. Next, we looked at how Linux was created by Linus Torvalds in 1991 and then grew into a worldwide effort with dozens and hundreds of independent developers. With this context established, we moved on to a high-level overview of the Linux kernel. We described its key abstractions and introduced the major kernel components. Special emphasis was given to the Linux scheduler, kernel memory management, and the filesystem cache. As we will see in the following chapters, these facilities play a pervasive role throughout the Linux kernel. The chapter concluded with a brief description of the Linux source code. There is no need to refer to the source code to follow this book, but the fact that Linux is an Open Source system does provide the reader with the unique opportunity to browse, peruse, and experiment with its source code as desired.

Chapter 2

IA-64 Architecture

The IA-64 architecture can be thought of as a RISC CPU with massive register files. Like RISC, it employs a load/store model where data has to be loaded into a register before it can be operated on [19]. However, in contrast to RISC, IA-64 follows the EPIC (Explicitly Parallel Instruction Computing) paradigm, which means that parallelism is expressed explicitly at the level of individual instruction. Fundamentally, IA-64 CPUs assume that instructions can be executed in parallel. If a pair of instructions contains a sequential dependency that prevents their parallel execution, the instruction stream needs to explicitly express this constraint with a so-called stop bit. EPIC is motivated by the fact that *instruction-level parallelism (ILP)* is essential for achieving good performance on *any* modern architecture and the belief that, by making ILP explicit, a CPU can run more efficiently because it can spend more resources on the actual execution of instructions rather than on analyzing the instruction stream to discover any implicit parallelism [61].

The basic instruction format of IA-64 is RISC-like and involves three operands: two source operands and a destination (result) operand. The architecturally-visible state includes 128 general registers of 65 bits each and 128 floating-point registers of 82 bits each. IA-64 goes further than most previous mainstream architectures in splitting up register files on the basis of function. Beyond the usual general and floating-point register files, there are separate register files for boolean values (predicates) and for branch target addresses.

Apart from explicit parallelism and large register files, IA-64 provides several advanced hardware features that are designed to further improve performance, including *predication, control speculation, data speculation, stacked registers, rotating registers*, and *explicit hints*. We discuss each feature briefly in the next several paragraphs.

IA-64 is a *fully predicated* architecture, meaning that the execution of virtually every instruction can be controlled by one of 64 available predicates. A predicate is a one-bit register that can be either on or off. If the controlling predicate is on, the instruction is executed; otherwise, it is skipped. Predication can reduce the number of branches in IA-64 code and also simplifies instruction scheduling because instructions from different basic blocks can be interspersed at the level of individual instructions.

Control and *data speculation* are both aimed at hiding the latency of memory accesses. The goal here is to execute load instructions as early as possible, so that by the time the loaded value is needed, it has already arrived from the memory system. To achieve this goal, control speculation executes a load instruction long before it is known whether the address being accessed is valid. If the address turns out to be valid, the speculation was successful and performance is improved because some or all of the memory access latency was overlapped with other computation. But if the address turns out to be invalid, a fault could occur. To avoid this, IA-64 provides special *speculative load* instructions. These work like normal loads except that if the address is invalid, they set a special bit in the target register instead of raising a fault. Similarly, data speculation executes a load instruction ahead of earlier store instructions. This is safe only if the store instructions do not modify the data being read by the load. Sometimes, this can be verified ahead of time, but often it can be verified only at the very time the instructions are being executed. IA-64 solves this problem by providing special load instructions that can detect interfering stores.

Stacked registers are intended to accelerate nested function calls. They are similar to the fixed-size register windows found on some RISC architectures such as SPARC [75], but with two important differences: first, IA-64 allocates stacked registers dynamically so that each function can obtain exactly as many stacked registers as it needs, no more and no less (up to a limit of 96 registers). Second, the memory needed to back up the stacked registers is maintained in an area that is separate from the normal memory stack. Transfers between the stacked registers and this memory area are handled implicitly and automatically by the CPU. Indeed, they may even occur in a speculative fashion, e.g., whenever the CPU detects that there is available memory bandwidth.

Rotating registers provide the foundation for modulo-scheduled loops on IA-64. We will see an example of this later on in this chapter, but loosely speaking, modulo-scheduled loops provide the means to construct highly efficient, yet compact, loops.

Explicit hints are encoded into various instructions and provide additional information to the CPU's branch unit or the memory system. Hints to the former are intended to reduce branch penalties, whereas hints to the latter are designed to avoid or at least reduce memory stalls. While not a unique feature of IA-64, the hints it defines are unusual in the amount of information they can provide. For example, the prefetching instruction can not only control the exact cache level into which data should be placed but also indicates whether the data exhibits temporal or just spatial locality.

It should be noted that while these advanced features are useful on their own, they are really designed to work in combination. For example, the true power of rotating registers really comes to bear only when used in conjunction with predication, control speculation, and the extensive hints that the architecture provides.

IA-64 is backward compatible both with Hewlett-Packard's PA-RISC [35] and Intel's IA-32 [25] architectures. In many ways, the PA-RISC architecture can be viewed as a subset of IA-64. Because of this, backward compatibility can be achieved relatively easily with a software-only binary translator that converts PA-RISC machine code to IA-64 machine code on demand. The same is not true for IA-32: its architecture is so different that it can be difficult to achieve acceptable performance with a software-only approach. For this reason, IA-64 explicitly defines an interface that includes everything needed to run IA-32 machine code. Note that only the *interface* is part of the architecture: its implementation depends on the CPU model. It is expected that, initially, most CPU models will implement the interface in hardware, but as time progresses and the importance of IA-32 compatibility diminishes, more and more of the interface will be implemented in software.

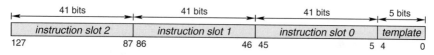

Figure 2.1. Instruction bundle format.

2.1 USER-LEVEL INSTRUCTION SET ARCHITECTURE

It is now time to explore IA-64 in more depth. Let us start with the user-level instruction set architecture.

2.1.1 Instruction format

IA-64 instructions are 41 bits wide. Groups of three instructions are packed into *bundles*, which are 128-bit large containers that are *naturally aligned* (i.e., aligned to 128 bits). Figure 2.1 illustrates the bundle format: the least significant 5 bits encode a *bundle template*; the next three fields, called *instruction slots*, provide space for one instruction each. Instruction bundles always use little-endian byte order so that instruction slot 0 occupies bits 5–45, slot 1 occupies bits 46–86, and slot 2 occupies bits 87–127.

The template field serves two purposes: first, it encodes the execution units needed by the three instructions and, second, it encodes which instructions can be executed in parallel. There are four kinds of execution units: integer units (I), memory units (M), floating-point units (F), and branch units (B). Most instructions can execute on just one particular unit, but some can execute on one of several units or even all of them. For example, most integer arithmetic instructions can execute both on M- and I-units. There are also a few special instructions that take up two instruction slots. Those instructions are said to execute on the X-unit, but this is really just a pseudo-unit: actual execution will occur on an I- or B-unit, depending on the instruction. Appendix C lists for each instruction the type of units it can execute on.

The template field encodes the available parallelism in the form of *stop bits*. In the absence of stop bits, an IA-64 CPU assumes that the three instructions in a bundle can be issued in parallel. Indeed, parallelism is not limited to a single bundle: as long as no stop bits are encountered, a CPU could continue to issue bundles for concurrent execution. A sequence of instructions that is separated by stop bits is called an *instruction group*. In an ideal world, every program would consist of a single instruction group that could be executed in a single cycle. Of course, this does not happen in reality for three reasons: (a) sequential dependencies, (b) branches, and (c) limited CPU resources. As an example of how sequential dependencies limit parallelism, consider that before the sum of two memory operands can be calculated, the operands need to be loaded from memory into registers. This implies that the two load and the add instructions needed to achieve this have to go into separate instruction groups. Similarly, any taken branch implicitly terminates an instruction group, so this further limits the amount of parallelism available in real programs. The other limiting factor is that, due to physical and cost constraints, a CPU can have only

Table 2.1. Execution units and stop bits encoded by the instruction templates.

Template	Slot 0	1	2	Template	Slot 0	1	2	Template	Slot 0	1	2
0x00	M	I	I	0x0a	M;;	M	I	0x12	M	B	B
0x01	M	I	I ;;	0x0b	M;;	M	I ;;	0x13	M	B	B ;;
0x02	M	I ;;	I	0x0c	M	F	I	0x16	B	B	B
0x03	M	I ;;	I ;;	0x0d	M	F	I ;;	0x17	B	B	B ;;
0x04	M	L	X	0x0e	M	M	F	0x18	M	M	B
0x05	M	L	X ;;	0x0f	M	M	F ;;	0x19	M	M	B ;;
0x08	M	M	I	0x10	M	I	B	0x1c	M	F	B
0x09	M	M	I ;;	0x11	M	I	B ;;	0x1d	M	F	B ;;

a relatively small number of execution units. When encountering an instruction group with more instructions than execution units, the CPU will be forced to execute the group in multiple cycles, even though in theory it could be executed in a single cycle. The net result is that instruction groups indicate the *maximum available parallelism* in a program and that the exact number of cycles necessary to execute a particular instruction group depends on the CPU model. For example, Itanium can issue at most two bundles, i.e., up to six instructions, in parallel.

Table 2.1 illustrates the available template codes and the bundle format that they correspond to. The bundle format is given by listing the execution unit for each slot and using a pair of semicolons to represent a stop bit. For example, template code 0x0a indicates that slots 0 and 1 contain instructions that can execute on an M-unit and that slot 2 contains an instruction that can execute on an I-unit. Furthermore, the double semicolon between slot 0 and 1 indicates that the CPU needs to wait for the results from the first instruction before issuing the instructions in slot 1 and 2 (and instructions from subsequent bundles). Some template codes such as 0x06 do not appear in the table—they are reserved for future extensions. Also note that template codes 0x04 and 0x05 correspond to bundle format MLX, but there is no L-unit! X-unit instructions take up two slots and L is simply a placeholder to indicate which instruction slot is used to encode the other half of such instructions.

To get a better idea of how instructions, bundles, templates, and instruction groups fit together, let us look at the example illustrated in Figure 2.2. It shows four bundles containing eleven instructions and three instruction groups. The first instruction group spans the instructions in the first bundle and the first instruction in the second bundle. The second group spans the next four instructions (lightly shaded), and the third group spans the remaining four instructions (dark shaded).

2.1.2   Instruction sequencing

The IA-64 instruction sequencing rules have been carefully crafted in such a way that it is possible to execute the instruction stream completely sequentially (one instruction at a time), completely in parallel (all instructions in a group at a time), or in some combination

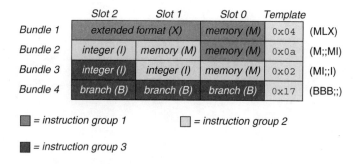

Figure 2.2. Example: Bundles, templates, and instruction groups.

(e.g., up to six instructions are issued in parallel). This flexibility is important for two reasons: first, it enables the building of CPUs with different cost/performance tradeoffs: a CPU that executes everything in sequence would not perform very well but would be cheap to build. On the other hand, a CPU that can issue six or more instructions in parallel might perform well but would be more expensive to build. Second, the ability to execute instructions one-by-one is important for debugging purposes so the effect of a program can be observed step-by-step. A related issue is that if an instruction faults for any reason, an operating system may need to resume execution in the middle of an instruction group once it handled the fault. For example, this situation occurs whenever a memory instruction causes a page fault.

The rule that enables this flexibility is that within an instruction group, all instructions must be independent of each other. Given a resource (e.g., a register or a memory location) and a pair of instructions that access this resource, there can be four classes of dependencies: read-after-write (RAW), write-after-write (WAW), read-after-read (RAR), and write-after-read (WAR). The class is determined by the order in which the instructions read or write the resource. For instance, a RAW dependency occurs when the second instruction reads the resource and the first instruction writes it. IA-64 requires that the following dependency rules be obeyed within an instruction group:

- WAW dependencies are generally not allowed for registers. In other words, it is not legal to write the same register more than once in an instruction group. There are some exceptions. For instance, later in this chapter we will see that writes to predicate register p0 are ignored and therefore this register can be written to multiple times.

- RAW dependencies are generally not allowed for registers. There are a few exceptions that allow compare-and-branch operations to execute in a single cycle.

- WAR dependencies are almost always permitted for registers. There is one rarely encountered exception involving modulo-scheduled loop branches, however (see the IA-64 architecture manual for details [26]).

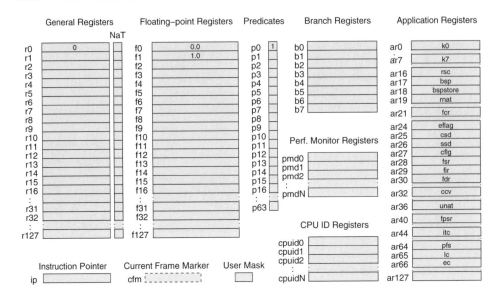

Figure 2.3. IA-64 user-level register files.

- RAR dependencies are always permitted for registers. This rule implies that it is permissible to read the same register multiple times within the same instruction group.

- All four dependencies (WAW, RAW, WAR, RAR) are allowed for memory accesses. For example, if a store is followed by a load from the same location, the load is guaranteed to observe the value that was written by the store, even if the two instructions appear in the same instruction group. In other words, memory accesses are always coherent.

The precise rules that determine when and where a stop bit is needed are fairly complex. Fortunately, for high-level languages, the compiler takes care that these rules are observed, and for programs in assembly language, the assembler will verify that the rules are being observed and warn the programmer of any violations.

2.1.3 Register files

The IA-64 user-level state is illustrated in Figure 2.3. It consists of five primary register files: the general, floating-point, predicate, branch, and application register files. In addition, several other registers serve miscellaneous purposes.

General register file

The general register file consists of 128 registers. Each register can store a 64-bit integer value plus an additional bit called the *NaT* bit (Not a Thing bit), which is used in con-

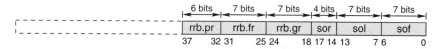

Figure 2.4. Format of current frame marker register (cfm).

junction with speculative execution. Specifically, this bit is set whenever a speculative load fails or when an input operand of an instruction has the NaT bit set already. For store instructions, an IA-64 CPU must raise the REGISTER NaT CONSUMPTION FAULT when attempting to store a register whose NaT bit is set.

The registers are partitioned into two subsets: the *static* and *stacked* registers. The former consists of registers r0–r31, and the latter of registers r32–r127. Register r0 is special in that it always reads as zero. Furthermore, it is not legal to write to r0; attempting to do so triggers an ILLEGAL OPERATION FAULT. The stacked registers are used to accelerate nested function calls and to provide an access window into a logically unbounded register stack. This register stack grows on nested function calls and shrinks when returning from a nested call. Each function call can allocate up to 96 stacked registers, which will be mapped starting at register r32. For example, if a function allocates eight stacked registers, it can access them through registers r32 to r39. A portion of the stacked registers can be marked as **rotating**, and those registers can then be used together with special loop branches to implement modulo-scheduled loops. Up to 96 registers can be marked **rotating** (in groups of eight) and also start at register r32. However, the number of rotating registers cannot exceed the number of allocated stacked registers.

The cfm register (current frame marker) defines the current register window configuration. In Figure 2.3, cfm is shown as a dashed box to reflect the fact that it cannot be accessed directly. Instead, cfm can be read or modified only indirectly as a side effect of other instructions. The register format is illustrated in Figure 2.4. As shown there, it is 38 bits wide and divided into six separate fields. The sof field (size of frame) specifies the number of stacked registers that have been allocated. Since at most 96 stacked registers can be allocated, this value must be in the range of 0 to 95. The sol field (size of locals) specifies the number of stacked registers that should be treated as local registers (more on this in Section 2.1.8). The number of rotating registers is specified in the sor field (size of rotating partition). Recall that this number must be an integer multiple of eight, so it can be encoded in just four bits: a value of 12 would indicate that all 96 stacked registers are rotating. The remaining fields are called rrb.gr, rrb.fr, and rrb.pr. They specify the register rename base for the general, floating-point, and predicate register files. User-level programs seldom need to worry about them. However, their values do have to be preserved across function calls, so they must be part of cfm.

Floating-point register file

The floating-point register file also consists of 128 registers, but each register is 82 bits wide and there are no NaT bits. Instead of setting a NaT bit, a speculation failure places a special value in the result register. This special value is called *NaTVal* (Not a Thing value). It consists of an 82-bit code that is otherwise unused (not a valid floating-point number). Attempting to store a floating-point register that contains a NaTVal will also raise a REGISTER NAT CONSUMPTION FAULT. Normal floating-point numbers are represented with a 64-bit significand, a 17-bit exponent, and a sign bit. The exponent is biased by 65535 (0xffff). Given a sign bit field value of *sign*, an exponent field value *exponent*, and a significand value of *significand*, the value of the floating-point number can be calculated as

$$(-1)^{sign} \cdot 2^{(exponent-65535)} \cdot significand/2^{63}.$$

Floating-point registers can also be used to store 64-bit integer values. In this case, the significand portion is used to hold the integer value, the sign bit is 0, and the exponent field is 0x1003e.

The floating-point register file is also divided into two subsets: registers f0 to f31 are called the *floating-point low partition*, and registers f32 to f127 are called the *floating-point high partition*. Registers f0 and f1 are special: the former always reads as floating-point constant 0.0, and the latter always reads as floating-point constant 1.0. Writing to these registers is illegal and attempting to do so triggers an ILLEGAL OPERATION FAULT. All registers in the high partition are rotating. For this reason, these registers are sometimes called the *rotating floating-point registers* and, in contrast, the registers in the low partition are sometimes called the *static floating-point registers*.

Predicate register file

One extraordinary aspect of IA-64 is that it provides 64 single-bit registers that are used as boolean values. A 0 in these registers corresponds to logical **false**, and a 1 to logical **true**. As their name suggests, these registers are used to predicate the execution of instructions. For this purpose, every instruction contains a 6-bit field that encodes the predicate register that controls whether or not the instruction should be executed. As a special case, predicate register p0 always reads as **true** and can therefore be used to unconditionally execute an instruction. Unlike r0, f0, or f1, predicate register p0 can be used as a destination operand. When the register is so used, the value written to p0 is simply discarded.

This register file is divided into two subsets: predicates p0–p15 are called the *static predicate registers*, and p16–p63 are called the *rotating predicate registers*. As the name suggests, the latter rotate when the modulo-scheduled loop branches are used.

It is also possible to read and write all 64 predicate registers at once. This is called *broadside access* and is done through register name pr. In other words, the predicate registers can be thought of either as 64 single-bit registers or as a single 64-bit register.

Branch register file

There are eight branch registers, each 64 bits wide. These registers hold the target addresses for *indirect branches*. This kind of branch computes the target address at runtime and commonly occurs on a return from a nested function call. In that case, a branch register supplies the address to which a function should return.

Figure 2.5. Format of previous function state register (pfs).

There are no NaT bits, and attempting to move a NaT value from a general register into a branch register triggers a REGISTER NAT CONSUMPTION FAULT.

Application register file

The application register file consists of 128 registers, each 64 bits wide. These registers are special-purpose data or control registers and are often used as implicit arguments to certain instructions. For example, application register ar65 serves as a loop counter and is an implicit operand to counted loop branches. Attempting to move a NaT value from a general register into an application register triggers a REGISTER NAT CONSUMPTION FAULT. Although the architecture provides up to 128 application registers, only 26 of them currently have a defined purpose. The remaining registers are either reserved for future use or are ignored when accessed. To ease assembly programming and debugging, each application register has a mnemonic name. For example, the loop count register has the mnemonic name ar.lc and this name can be used interchangeably with ar65. Table 2.2 briefly describes each application register and lists the mnemonic name associated with it. We should note that throughout this book, the "ar" prefix is dropped whenever the context makes it clear that an application register is meant. Of course, in assembly programs the prefix always needs to be specified.

The previous function state register, pfs, plays an important role during nested function calls. Its format is illustrated in Figure 2.5. As shown there, it is divided into five fields, two of them reserved for future use (**rv**); the others are called pfm (previous frame marker), pec (previous epilogue count), and ppl (previous privilege level). On a function call, the current frame marker cfm is saved in field pfm, the epilogue count ec is saved in field pec, and the privilege level at which the code is executing is saved in the 2-bit field ppl. Conversely, on return from a function call, the current frame marker, epilogue count, and privilege level are restored from these fields. The net effect is that pfs automatically preserves the current register stack configuration, epilogue count, and privilege level across one level of function calls. The content of pfs needs to be saved and restored explicitly if function calls are to be nested more than one level deep. In practice, this means that all nonleaf functions need to preserve the content of pfs around nested function calls.

Miscellaneous registers

Several special registers are used for miscellaneous purposes. Among them, the *instruction pointer (IP)* is the most important one. It is a 64-bit register that addresses the instruction bundle to be executed next. The instruction pointer cannot be written directly but, indirectly, it is updated whenever a branch is taken. The current content of the IP can be read

Table 2.2. Application registers.

Register	Name	Description
ar0–ar7	k0–k7	Kernel registers. These registers are readable at the user level but can be written only at the most privileged level. The exact use of these registers is operating-system-dependent; Linux uses them for various purposes.
ar16	rsc	Register stack configuration register. See Section 2.4 for details.
ar17	bsp	Backing store pointer. See Section 2.4 for details.
ar18	bspstore	Backing store write pointer. See Section 2.4 for details.
ar19	rnat	RSE NaT collection register. See Section 2.4 for details.
ar21	fcr	IA-32 floating-point control register.
ar24	eflag	IA-32 EFLAG register.
ar25	csd	IA-32 code segment descriptor. Reserved for future IA-64 use.
ar26	ssd	IA-32 stack segment descriptor. Reserved for future IA-64 use.
ar27	cflg	IA-32 combined CR0 and CR4 register.
ar28	fsr	IA-32 floating-point status register.
ar29	fir	IA-32 floating-point instruction register.
ar30	fdr	IA-32 floating-point data register.
ar32	ccv	Compare-and-exchange compare value register. This is an implicit operand to the compare-and-exchange instruction that implements atomic memory updates.
ar36	unat	User NaT collection register. This register collects the NaT bit when the entire content of a general register is saved (spilled) to memory. It also holds the NaT bit when a general register is restored (filled) from memory.
ar40	fpsr	Floating-point status register. It hosts the IEEE-754 arithmetic flags and various control flags that affect how floating-point arithmetic is performed.
ar44	itc	Interval time counter. This register increments at a fixed rate (such as the CPU clock rate) and can be used to obtain fine-grained time stamps.
ar64	pfs	Previous function state register. It is used to save information about the stacked registers on a nested function call and to restore the original stacked registers when on return from a function call.
ar65	lc	Loop count register. This is an implicit operand to counted loop branches and determines the number of loop iterations.
ar66	ec	Epilogue count register. This is an implicit operand to modulo-scheduled loop branch instructions and specifies the number of pipeline stages in a loop.

through register name ip. Instruction bundles must be 16-byte–aligned and therefore the least significant four bits in ip are 0 when IA-64 code is executed. However, when legacy IA-32 code is being executed, ip may contain arbitrary byte-aligned addresses.

The CPUID register file contains read-only information that helps identify the CPU model. There are at least five such registers. The first two contain an ASCII string that identifies the CPU vendor. The third register contains the architecture revision, family, model, and revision number of the CPU as well as a field for the total number of implemented CPUID registers. The fourth register contains a bit vector that identifies the architecture extensions supported by the CPU. The purpose of these registers is to make it possible to add extensions to the architecture without breaking backward compatibility. For this to work, software relying on the presence of a particular extension should first check whether the CPU implements the extension and, if not, fall back on an alternate implementation.

The performance monitor register file consists of several 64-bit registers that provide access to online CPU performance data. Both the number of these registers and their exact contents depend on the CPU model. Consequently, the architecture does not specify the details of how these registers work or what they measure. Itanium, for example, implements a sophisticated performance monitor that counts dozens of different events ranging from cache misses, number of instructions executed, all the way to the number of cycles for which the CPU was stalled because of branch mispredictions. More on this in Chapter 9, *Understanding System Performance*.

The user mask register um is logically a 6-bit register that provides two status flags, three control flags, and one reserved bit. The two status flags are called mfl (modified floating-point low partition) and mfh (modified floating-point high partition); they respectively indicate whether any register in the floating-point low or the floating-point high partition has been written since the flag was cleared last. The three control flags are called ac (alignment check), be (big-endian), and up (user performance monitor enable). The first flag controls how unaligned memory accesses are handled. If it is cleared, such accesses *may* generate an UNALIGNED DATA REFERENCE FAULT. If it is set, unaligned accesses *must* generate such a fault. For Linux applications, this flag is normally turned on to give the operating system a chance to warn about programs that issue unaligned accesses. However, if such warnings happen too frequently, clearing this flag can sometimes improve performance. The be flag controls the byte order that is used to access memory. If the flag is cleared, little-endian byte order is used; otherwise, big-endian byte order is used. On IA-64, Linux uses little-endian byte order, so this flag is normally cleared. However, with proper care, an application could temporarily or even permanently turn this flag on when dealing with big-endian data. The up flag controls whether user performance monitors are enabled. If cleared, the user performance monitors are turned off. We should note that even though the user mask is a separate register from the perspective of a user-level program, it really is just the user-level accessible portion of a much bigger register, called the processor status register (psr). For this reason, it is necessary to use the prefix psr to access individual user mask bits in assembly code. For example, psr.mfh would refer to the mfh flag. We describe register psr in more detail in Section 2.3.

2.1.4 Instruction set overview

In the following paragraphs, we provide an overview of the user-level instructions that
IA-64 implements. They fall into one of six major groups: integer, memory, branch, register
stack, control, and floating-point instructions. A complete instruction list can be found in
Appendix C, and detailed descriptions are available in the IA-64 architecture manual [26].

Throughout this chapter, we illustrate various instructions by using the IA-64 assembly
language [27]. The general instruction format for this language is as follows:

```
(qp)    mnemonic dst = src1, src2
```

Here, *qp* is the *qualifying predicate*, which controls whether the instruction is executed. It
can be any predicate register in the range of p0 to p63. If *qp* is equal to p0, the instruction is
executed unconditionally (since p0 is hardwired to **true**). As a convenience, the qualifying
predicate and the surrounding parentheses can be omitted in this case. For example, the
following two lines are equivalent:

```
(p0)    mnemonic dst = src1, src2  // always executed
        mnemonic dst = src1, src2  // equivalent short form
```

The *mnemonic* consists of the major opcode and zero or more suffixes, which together
determine the exact operation to be performed. For example, the opcode tbit is used for the
"test bit" instruction. Depending on the suffix, this instruction can test whether a particular
bit in a register is 0 (.z suffix) or 1 (.nz suffix). So the complete mnemonic to test a bit for
being non-zero would be tbit.nz.

The mnemonic is followed by the operands. The first one is the destination operand (*dst*)
and specifies the location in which the instruction should store the result. It is followed by
an equal sign and a list of source operands. Most instructions have one destination operand
and two source operands. However, some have no destination operand at all. For those
cases, *dst* and the equal sign are omitted. A few instructions produce two results, in which
case the two destination operands are separated by a comma. For example, the compare
instruction produces two results:

```
cmp.eq p8, p9 = r32, r33
```

This instruction compares general registers r32 and r33. If their contents are equal, p8 is set
to **true** and p9 to **false**, and vice versa.

There are three kinds of operands: constants, registers, and memory locations. A constant can be specified simply by listing its value as a literal constant. Similarly, a register
can be specified by its name. A memory location can be specified by square brackets around
the general register that contains its address. For example, the instruction:

```
ld8 r8 = [r32]
```

would read eight bytes from the address in register r32 and store the resulting value in register r8. Note that unlike many other architectures, IA-64 does not allow memory operands to
specify an offset. It is always necessary to calculate the final address of a memory location
in a register before it can be accessed.

2.1.5 Integer and SIMD instructions

The IA-64 architecture provides an extensive set of integer-related instructions, including arithmetic, logical, bit-field, and shift instructions. The arithmetic operations include addition, subtraction, and multiplication. An unusual aspect worth mentioning is that integer multiplication is implemented in the floating-point unit and therefore uses floating-point registers. For example, the instruction

```
xmpy.l f8 = f9, f10
```

multiplies the 64-bit signed integers contained in the least significant 64 bits of f9 and f10 and stores the resulting value in the least significant 64 bits of f8. Note that even though floating-point registers are used, the operands are treated as integers. The disadvantage of this approach is that integer values need to be moved to the floating-point register file before they can be multiplied. On the positive side, this approach is economical because much of the hardware needed for floating-point and integer multiplication can be shared. This has the welcome side effect that IA-64 CPUs can afford to implement integer multiplication in a fully pipelined fashion, meaning that a new multiplication can be started every cycle. Thus, while latency suffers a little, throughput is maximized.

Like most RISC architectures, IA-64 does not provide a division instruction. Instead, a reciprocal approximation instruction serves as the basis for both integer and floating-point division [43].

A challenge that all 64-bit architectures face is how to load large immediate constants into a register. IA-64 has an addl instruction that allows one source operand to be a 22-bit signed constant. Specifying r0 (hardwired to 0) as the other source operand allows the loading of an immediate constant in the range of $-2,097,152$ to $2,097,151$. For convenience, IA-64 assemblers allow the loading of such constants with the mov instruction. But this is only a pseudo-instruction that gets translated to the corresponding add instruction. For example, the following two lines are equivalent:

```
mov r8 = 99          // pseudo-instruction
addl r8 = 99, r0     // corresponding instruction
```

Loading an integer constant larger than the 22 bits that addl can accommodate requires a memory access, multiple add and shift instructions, or the special movl instruction. The last is special because it occupies two instruction slots and is therefore 82 bits wide. This provides enough space to encode a full 64-bit constant. The instruction can execute only on the X-unit, and the MLX template is the only one available for this purpose. In other words, movl is not just a very wide instruction but it is also difficult to schedule with surrounding code. For this reason, movl should be used only when the alternate code sequences would be more expensive.

The logical operations include bitwise **or**, **and**, **xor**, and various bit-field extraction and shifting instructions. There is no direct instruction to rotate the content of a register, though the shrp instruction shifts a pair of registers and can rotate a register by a constant number of bits.

Most integer instructions treat their operands either as 64-bit or 32-bit integers, but a number of SIMD (single instruction, multiple data) instructions treat the operands as a

vector of eight 8-bit integers or as a vector of four 16-bit integers (see Appendix C.6). For
example, instruction

```
padd2 r8 = r32, r33
```

would treat the three operand registers as vectors of four 16-bit integers, add the elements in
r32 and r33 individually, and store the resulting vector in r8. Different suffixes are available
to control the overflow behavior. For example, with the .uuu suffix, each vector element
is treated as an unsigned integer, and on overflow the result is saturated to the maximum
value (0xffff). Apart from accelerating multimedia applications, these instructions are
also useful in implementing character string and byte-order swapping operations.

2.1.6 Memory and semaphore instructions

IA-64 comes with a normal complement of load and store instructions. The smallest unit
of memory that they can access is a byte, and the largest is 16 bytes. Naturally-aligned
accesses execute atomically, i.e., there is no danger that an aligned load would ever observe
a partially executed aligned store. The same guarantee does not apply to unaligned accesses.
Indeed, the CPU does not have to support unaligned accesses at all. Instead, it can simply
generate an UNALIGNED DATA REFERENCE FAULT. It is then up to the operating system
to take the appropriate action, such as emulating the instruction in software or terminating
the program. Because of this, IA-64 programs should avoid unaligned memory accesses
as much as possible. That said, it is not uncommon for CPUs to have some support for
unaligned memory accesses. For example, the Itanium chip can execute them provided that
the access does not cross a cache-line boundary.

A complete list of memory-related instructions can be found in Appendix C.2; below
is an example of the typical usage of these instructions:

```
ld8 r16 = [r32], 8;; ld4 r17 = [r32];;
add r18 = r16, r17;;
st8 [r33] = r18                // store sum back to memory
```

In this example, the first instruction loads a 64-bit (8-byte) value from the address contained
in register r32, places the result in r16, and then increments the address by 8. The second
instruction loads four bytes from this updated address, zero-extends the value to 64 bits, and
then places the result in register r17. The third instruction adds the two values loaded from
memory and places the result in r18. The fourth and final instruction stores the resulting
sum in the memory location addressed by register r33. Note the stop bit between the first
and the second instruction. The stop bit is necessary because the post-increment implicitly
updates address register r32, so the second instruction cannot be executed concurrently with
the first one.

Speculative loads use the same syntax as ordinary loads, except that a suffix indicates
the type of speculation that is used. A suffix of .s indicates control speculation, .a indicates
data speculation, and .sa indicates the combination of control and data speculation.

Control speculative loads work exactly in the same way as ordinary loads except that
they produce a *NaT token* instead a fault when something goes wrong. For general registers,

producing a NaT token entails setting the NaT bit. For floating-point registers, it entails writing the special value NaTVal.

Data speculative (advanced) loads work like normal load instructions except that they take note of the destination register and the address range that is being read. This information is then recorded in a special hardware structure called the *advanced load address table (ALAT)*. Whenever a store is executed, the ALAT is searched and records with an address range that overlap the memory area written by the store are removed. This means that the presence of an ALAT record serves as an indicator of whether the corresponding data speculative load was successful: if the record is still present, there were no interfering stores and speculation was successful. On the other hand, if the record is missing, there may have been an interfering store and we must assume that speculation failed. IA-64 provides several "check" instructions to verify whether an ALAT record is still present. For example, the "check load" instruction (ld.c) verifies whether the ALAT record is still present and, if so, performs no operation (the destination register already contains the correct value). Otherwise, it reexecutes the memory access in a nonspeculative fashion. In the next section, we describe other "check" instructions that branch to recovery code in the case of a speculation failure.

As explained earlier, attempting to store a register that contains a NaT token normally triggers a REGISTER NAT CONSUMPTION FAULT. This is undesirable when the goal is to temporarily save the content of a register in memory. To handle such situations, IA-64 provides special *spill* and *fill* instructions. Specifically, st8.spill works like the normal st8 form except that it also copies the NaT bit to a bit in application register unat. The number of the unat bit used for this purpose is given by bits 3–8 of the memory address at which the register is being saved. For instance, if the memory address is 0x8100, then unat bit number 32 would be used. The complementary instruction is ld8.fill; it works like a normal ld8 instruction except that it also restores the NaT bit from the corresponding unat bit. Since the unat register is only 64 bits wide, its content must be saved before a register is spilled to an address that would overwrite an existing unat bit. Similarly, before ld8.fill is executed, it is necessary to ensure that unat contains the correct NaT bits. Floating-point registers can be spilled and filled with stf.spill and ldf.fill, respectively. Unlike in the integer case, there is no separate NaT bit and unat is not involved in the execution of these instructions. Instead, stf.spill simply saves the entire 82-bit floating-point register value in a 16-byte–aligned memory area. Correspondingly, ldf.fill restores the original register content from memory.

Since IA-64 is a load/store architecture, all calculations are normally performed on registers, not directly on memory locations. The semaphore instructions listed in Appendix C.3 are the exception to this general rule. They are provided to enable the efficient implementation of synchronization primitives. We see some examples in Chapter 3, *Processes, Tasks, and Threads*. There are three types of semaphore instructions, each performing one particular kind of atomic read-modify-write operation. The simplest is xchg, which atomically replaces the content of a register with the content of a memory location. A slightly more advanced instruction is fetchadd, which reads a memory location, adds a small signed integer constant to it, writes back the result to the memory location, and then places the old value in the destination register. The most powerful instruction is cmpxchg, which performs

Table 2.3. Effect of memory ordering semantics (O: ordered; −: no order implied).

First access	Second access		
	unordered	acquire	release
unordered	−	−	O
acquire	O	O	O
release	−	−	O

an atomic compare-and-exchange operation. Specifically, it reads a memory location, compares its content to the value in application register ccv and, if they match, writes the content of another register to the memory location. If they do not match, the memory location is not updated. In either case, the old value of the memory location is returned in the destination register. Since the semaphore instructions are guaranteed to execute atomically, they typically execute more slowly than the equivalent sequence of (nonatomic) instructions. For example, on Itanium, these instructions have a latency similar to a load instruction that misses in the first-level cache. For this reason, semaphore instructions should really be used only when atomicity is important.

To achieve maximum performance, IA-64 employs a *weakly ordered memory system* [2]. What this means is that the order in which data memory accesses are completed is not necessarily the same as the order in which they were issued. Data dependencies are honored, but other than that, a pair of memory accesses can be executed in any order. When device drivers or synchronization are handled, the order in which memory accesses are executed often matters. To enforce the required order, IA-64 provides special memory instructions that have **acquire** or **release** semantics. An instruction with **acquire** semantics is executed such that its effect is guaranteed to become visible before any subsequent data memory access. Conversely, an instruction with **release** semantics is executed such that all prior data memory accesses are guaranteed to have been completed before its effect becomes visible. The memory fence instruction (mf) combines the semantics of **acquire** and **release** and therefore acts as a barrier: earlier memory accesses are guaranteed to complete before the barrier takes effect, and all later memory accesses are guaranteed to execute after the barrier takes effect. In assembly language, the ordering requirements are expressed with suffixes: .acq denotes **acquire** semantics, .rel denotes **release** semantics, and if neither suffix is used, the memory access is unordered. Load instructions accept only the .acq suffix, and store instructions accept only the .rel suffix. Most semaphore instructions can accept either suffix, except that xchg is always executed with **acquire** semantics.

Table 2.3 summarizes the effect of the ordering semantics for pairs of memory accesses. "O" indicates that the first and second instruction are executed in order with respect to each other. A "−" indicates that no ordering is implied beyond what is required to satisfy data dependencies. For example, the second row shows that if the first access has **acquire** semantics, order is guaranteed, independently of the semantics of the second access.

To get an idea of the cost of ordered memory instructions, consider that the IA-64 memory model was defined such that executing every single load with **acquire** semantics and every single store with **release** semantics would yield a behavior that exactly matches the memory model used by traditional IA-32 CPUs. In other words, ordered memory instructions are not that expensive and usually execute considerably faster than do the semaphore instructions. On a related note, high-level languages usually provide support for generating ordered memory accesses. For example, in the C language, any data object declared **volatile** will be accessed with ordered memory accesses.

2.1.7 Branch instructions

IA-64 defines several branch instructions that can be used to change the flow of execution. They fall roughly into five classes: conditional, call-related, loop-related, instruction-set switching, and speculation check branches. The branch target is normally encoded as a 25-bit IP-relative offset, which provides a range of ± 16 Mbytes. For conditional and call-related branches, the target can also be a branch register or a 64-bit IP-relative offset. The former is known as an *indirect branch*, and the latter is known as a *long branch*. Just like movl, a long branch executes on the X-unit and takes up two instruction slots. The CPU ignores the least significant four bits of the branch target address; this behavior implies that execution always starts with the first instruction in a bundle.

The branch instructions accept several suffixes that encode various hints. For example, the "static predict taken" (.sptk) suffix indicates that a conditional branch should always be predicted **taken**, whereas the "dynamic predict taken" (.dptk) suffix indicates that it should be predicted **taken** unless the CPU's dynamic prediction hardware has information to the contrary. There are also **not taken** variants of these suffixes (.spnt and .dpnt). Another type of suffix can give hints to the CPU as to how many cache lines should be prefetched from the branch target: .few informs the CPU that it should stop prefetching after a few cache lines, whereas .many informs it to prefetch more lines. The exact number of lines that are prefetched is implementation specific. For example, a CPU could implement .few by prefetching only one cache line and .many by prefetching until it encounters another branch that is predicted **taken**.

An interesting aspect of IA-64 is that since it is a fully predicated architecture, conditional branches are actually just unconditional branches whose execution is controlled by the qualifying predicate. A few examples are shown below:

```
        br.cond.sptk.few label      // unconditional, IP-relative
(p0)    br.cond.sptk.few b6         // unconditional & indirect
(p6)    br.cond.sptk.few label      // conditional & IP-relative
(p6)    br.cond.sptk.many label     // same, but prefetch more
```

There are two call-related branches: br.call and br.ret. The former calls a function, and the latter returns to the caller. To streamline this operation, br.call automatically saves the return address in a branch register. The return address is defined to be the address of the bundle that follows the one containing the call instruction. Apart from modifying the flow of execution, these instructions have two side effects: they rename the stacked registers, which we describe in more detail later on, and they preserve some information on the caller's frame state in pfs. For example, pfs is used to save the content of ec (epilogue counter) and the current privilege level. Some examples of the call-related branches are shown below:

```
            br.call.sptk.few b0 = f    // call f(), save IP in b0
            br.ret.sptk.many b0        // return to address in b0
            br.call.sptk b0 = b6       // indirect call to addr. in b6
            brl.call.sptk b0 = f       // long call to f()
    (p6)    br.call.sptk b0 = f        // conditional call
    (p6)    br.ret.sptk b0 = f         // conditional return
```

Note that because of the way the return address is defined, a call instruction that appears in slot 0 or 1 of a bundle will skip the remaining instructions when returning from the call. The easiest way to avoid this problem is to follow the call instruction with a dummy label. This forces the start of a new bundle and ensures that no instructions are skipped accidentally.

The loop-related branches include br.cloop (counted loop branch), br.ctop (branch to top of counted loop), br.cexit (branch to exit of counted loop), br.wtop (branch to top of **while**-loop), and br.wexit (branch to exit of **while**-loop). The br.cloop instruction checks whether application register lc (loop count) is 0. If not, it decrements the register and branches to the target. If the register is 0, the instruction has no effect. We might wonder why a special instruction is needed when the same could be achieved with a general register (serving as a loop counter), a compare instruction, and a conditional branch. Obviously, one benefit is that br.cloop takes up just a single instruction slot, compared to the three that would be taken up by a decrement, compare, and branch sequence. However, the more important benefit is that br.cloop enables perfect loop prediction: the CPU can predict whether the branch will be taken by checking the content of lc.

The other loop-related branches are used to realize modulo-scheduled loops. Whether these branches are taken primarily depends either on the qualifying predicate or application register lc but is additionally qualified by the value in application register ec (epilogue count). When taken, they also rename the rotating registers. In Section 2.1.11 is an example of how modulo-scheduled loops work.

One branch instruction switches the instruction set from IA-64 to IA-32. It is called br.ia. Unlike the other branches, it supports only IP-relative addressing and unconditional execution (i.e., it cannot be predicated). Apart from changing the flow of execution, this branch has the side effect that the instructions at the target address will be interpreted and executed as IA-32 instructions. The IA-32 instruction set has been extended with the complementary instruction. There, the JMPE instruction can be used to switch the instruction set back from the IA-32 to IA-64.

In the speculation check class, we find instructions chk and fchkf. The former checks the result of a speculative load and branches to recovery code if the load failed for any reason. The latter checks the result of a floating-point calculation and branches to recovery code if the calculation generated an arithmetic trap. The chk instruction takes two operands: a register (general or floating-point) and an IP-relative offset. With a suffix of .s, the instruction checks whether the register contains a NaT token and, if so, branches to the bundle encoded by the IP-relative offset. If the register contains any other value, the instruction performs no operation. With a suffix of .a, the instruction checks the ALAT to see if the record created by an earlier advanced load is still present. If not, the instruction branches to the bundle encoded by the IP-relative offset; otherwise, it performs no operation. On some CPU models, the branching behavior of these instructions is unimplemented and instead triggers a SPECULATIVE OPERATION FAULT. The operating system is required to intercept this fault and emulate the missing functionality in software. To get a better idea of how the speculation check instruction can be used, let us take a look at a sample code fragment.

```
        ld8.s r8 = [r32];;      // control speculative load
        add r8 = 1, r8          // dependent calculation
        cmp.eq p6,p0 = r0, r32  // is r32 NULL?
(p6)    br.cond done            // guarding branch
        chk.s r8, recvr         // verify speculation success
cont:   st8 [r32] = r8          // store resulting value
done:   br.ret.sptk rp          // return to caller

recvr: ld8 r8 = [r32];;         // redo load nonspeculatively
       add r8 = 1, r8           // redo dependent calculation
       br.sptk cont             // resume normal execution
```

This example uses control speculation to load a memory word and increment its value before checking whether the address being accessed is valid (not a NULL pointer). If the conditional branch is not taken, we can be sure that the address was valid, but the speculative load may have failed for other reasons (e.g., a TLB miss). Thus, it is necessary to use a chk.s instruction to verify that the speculative calculation was successful. If it was, the code proceeds to store back the incremented value. If it was not, the CPU branches to the recovery code at label recvr. There, it reexecutes the load and the increment in a nonspeculative fashion and then resumes normal execution at label cont.

2.1.8   Register-stack-related instructions

The register stack is a mechanism that accelerates nested function calls. It is a dynamic register renaming facility that provides the illusion of containing an unbounded number of registers, so that each nested function call can get its own set of registers r32–r127. Of course, CPUs can implement only a fixed number of registers, and when the size of the register stack exceeds that number, some of the logical stacked registers have to be stored in memory. This memory area is called the *register backing store*. Later in this chapter, we describe how this memory area is being managed, but for now, we will ignore these details and treat the register stack as a truly infinite supply of stacked registers.

Stacked registers are allocated dynamically so that each function can request exactly as many registers as it needs. For example, Figure 2.6 illustrates a function that allocated five stacked registers. The function can access these registers as r32 through r36. The other stacked registers (r37 through r127) are outside the current register frame and should not be accessed. Now, whenever a program performs a nested function call, the current register frame is logically pushed onto the register stack. The called function can then obtain a fresh set of stacked registers by executing a special instruction. Conversely, when returning from a nested function call, the previous frame is restored from the register stack. In other words, the register stack grows taller with each nested function call and shrinks with each return.

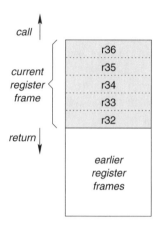

Figure 2.6. Logical view of a register stack.

When a function is called, usually one or more arguments must be passed to the callee. IA-64 supports this by making it possible to share some of the stacked registers between the caller and the callee. Specifically, a function can designate the last *n* stacked registers as *output registers*. On the next nested function call, these registers are renamed so that they become the first *n* stacked registers in the new register frame. A caller can therefore pass the *i*th argument simply by placing its value in the *i*th output register. The callee can then pick up the argument by reading the *i*th stacked register. The stacked registers that are not used as output registers are called *local registers*.

IA-64 CPUs use the cfm register to keep track of the shape of the current register frame. This register contains two 7-bit fields called sof (size of frame) and sol (size of locals). The former specifies the size of the current frame as a register count. A value of 0 means that no stacked registers have been allocated, and a value of 96 means that all stacked registers have been allocated. The sol field specifies the number of local registers. The number of output registers is implicitly given by the difference between sof and sol. As described earlier, cfm is a CPU-internal register that is not under direct program control. Instead, it is modified as a side effect of other instructions. The instruction with the most direct impact on cfm is alloc, because it allows allocation of (resizing) the current register frame. The synopsis for this instruction is as follows:

```
alloc r_s = ar.pfs,n_i,n_l,n_o,n_r
```

The effect of this instruction is to copy the current value of pfs into general register r_s, to resize the current register frame so it contains $n_i + n_l$ local registers and n_o output registers, and to treat the first n_r stacked registers as **rotating**. At this point, we might wonder why the number of local registers is specified as the sum of n_i and n_l. The reason is that the assembler distinguishes between *input registers* and *local registers*. From a hardware perspective, input registers are indistinguishable from local registers, but from a software perspective, input registers are different because they contain the input arguments on entry

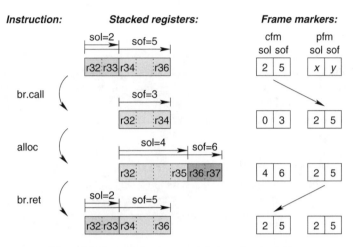

Figure 2.7. Example: Register stack during a function call.

to the function. Indeed, for programming convenience the assembler provides aliases of the form in$N$ for the first n_i stacked registers, loc$N$ for the next n_l stacked registers, and out$N$ for the final n_o stacked registers. For example, alloc r2 = ar.pfs,3,1,2,0 would cause the assembler to define the following aliases:

in0 = r32   in1 = r33   in2 = r34
loc0 = r35
out0 = r36   out1 = r37

Even though the real register names are sufficient for all programming tasks, the aliases are often more convenient to use because they make the three partitions more independent of each other. For example, the first output register is always called out0, no matter how many input and local registers there are.

Now, let us take a closer look at how the register stack operates during a function call. For this discussion, we adopt the hardware point of view and treat input registers as local registers. Let us assume that the CPU is currently executing a function with a register stack frame that contains two local and three output registers. This is illustrated by the top configuration in Figure 2.7. As we can see, r32 and r33 are the local stacked registers and r34, r35, and r36 are the output registers. Consequently, the sof and sol fields in cfm have a value of 5 and 2, respectively. The figure also illustrates pfm (previous frame marker), which is a part of application register pfs (previous function state). We will assume that its initial contents consist of x in sol and y in sof.

Suppose the function needs to perform a nested function call. It can do so by placing the outgoing arguments in the output registers (r34 and up) and then using the br.call instruction to branch to the target function. The effects of br.call are illustrated in the second configuration of Figure 2.7: the first effect is that cfm gets copied to pfm. Second, the local registers are saved on the register stack and then the stacked registers are renamed such that the local registers vanish from the current frame. Register r32 now refers to the first output register. In the final step, cfm is updated to reflect the current shape of the frame: sof is set to 3 and, since no local registers are remaining, sol is set to 0.

The target function may need a couple of stacked registers of its own. If so, it can resize the current register frame with the alloc instruction. For example, let us assume that the target function uses this instruction to allocate four local and two output registers. This is illustrated in the third configuration of Figure 2.7. As we can see, the only effect of this instruction is that cfm is updated such that sol has a value of 4 and sof a value of 6. It is important to note here that alloc merely resizes the current register frame—it does *not* trigger any register renaming. In other words, no matter how many alloc instructions are executed, r32 will continue to refer to the same physical register.

At this point, the target function is all set to execute and complete its job. Eventually, it will return to the caller by means of the br.ret instruction. When this happens, the following steps take place. First, the number of local registers specified in pfm.sol are restored from the register stack. Second, the registers are renamed such that the first of the restored registers becomes r32 again and, third, pfm is copied to cfm. As we can see from the last configuration illustrated it Figure 2.7, the end result is that after br.ret has been executed, the shape of the register stack is back to its original form. Note that while the *shape* is identical, the *contents* may not be. In particular, the output registers of the caller served as the first three local registers in the target function, and their contents may have changed. On the other hand, the two local registers in the caller were not part of the register frame of the target function, and their contents are therefore safe from modification. This is the property that gives local registers their name: their contents are protected from modification by nested function calls and they are, therefore, local to the caller.

On a final note, let us return to the topic of what happens when an attempt is made to access a stacked register that is not part of the current register frame. So far, we said that such registers should not be accessed. But what would happen if a program attempted to do so anyhow? First and foremost, IA-64 defines that any attempt to write such a register is an error condition that must be caught with an ILLEGAL OPERATION FAULT. On the other hand, reading such a register is permitted. However, the returned value is implementation dependent, so even though the action is permitted, it is generally not a useful thing to do.

2.1.9 Control instructions

The IA-64 architecture provides several instructions to control various aspects of the CPU. Unlike ordinary instruction, these do not produce a result directly but instead are useful primarily for their side effects. Many control instructions, such as cover or flushrs, affect the register stack; they are discussed in more detail later in this chapter. Others affect the memory system. For example, fc flushes a cache line, and lfetch prefetches a cache line. Two instructions set (sum) and reset (rum) individual bits in the user mask. As another example, the break instruction allows a program to call into the operating system. It takes a single operand, which must be an unsigned integer constant. This instruction has a wide range of applications, including system calls, software debug breakpoints, and error signaling.

2.1.10 Floating-point instructions

To support scientific applications, IA-64 provides an extensive set of floating-point instructions. While providing all the primitives needed to build high-performance floating-point applications, the instructions are minimal in the sense that instructions are provided only for those operations that cannot be implemented more efficiently in software. For example, there are instructions for floating-point addition, subtraction, and multiplication. More complex operations such as division, square root, or the trigonometric operations are implemented in software and provided in a library. However, IA-64 does provide all the primitives needed to efficiently implement division and square root. In particular, the frcpa instruction calculates an initial approximation of the reciprocal value of a number, and frsqrta calculates an initial approximation of the reciprocal square root of a number. The fma instruction (fused multiply-and-add) is also key to efficient implementation of many algorithms. It multiplies two floating-point operands and then adds a third operand. This instruction is powerful because the intermediate result of the multiplication is maintained in full precision, so it is more accurate than a multiplication and addition performed with separate instructions.

Another interesting aspect of IA-64 is the parallel floating-point instructions. These are similar to the integer multimedia instructions in the sense that they treat their operand registers as containing a pair of single-precision floating-point numbers. For example, the instruction

```
fpma f8 = f8, f9, f10
```

would treat the operand registers as pairs of single-precision floating-point numbers, multiply the pairs in f8 and f9, add the pair in f10, and then store the resulting pair in f8. These instructions are useful, e.g., for implementing single-precision complex arithmetic and for graphics applications that deal with a large amount of single-precision floating-point data.

2.1.11 Modulo-scheduled loops

Let us now take a closer look at how modulo-scheduled loops work. For this purpose, we use a toy problem that requires copying six data words from one memory area to another. We assume that at the start of the copy loop, the addresses of the source and destination memory areas are in registers r16 and r17, respectively. Figure 2.8 (a) uses IA-64 assembly code to illustrate how such a copy loop could be implemented in a traditional fashion. It uses the br.cloop instruction to realize a counted loop that iterates six times. The first instruction in the routine initializes the loop count register ar.lc with a value of 5. The reason a value of 5, instead of 6, is used is that br.cloop continues to iterate until ar.lc reaches a value of 0. In other words, if ar.lc were to be initialized with 0, the loop body would be executed once, with a value of 1, it would be executed twice, and so on. The loop body consists of the next three instructions: the ld8 instruction loads r18 with the data word at the address in r16 and then post-increments the address register by 8 (so it points to the next source word). The st8 instruction takes the word just loaded into r18, writes it to the address in r17, and then post-increments r17 by 8. Note that the load and the store instruction need to be separated by a stop bit (double semicolon) because otherwise there would be a RAW dependency on

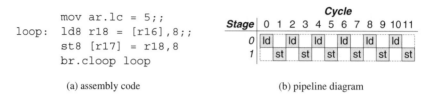

```
            mov ar.lc = 5;;
    loop:   ld8 r18 = [r16],8;;
            st8 [r17] = r18,8
            br.cloop loop
```

(a) assembly code   (b) pipeline diagram

Figure 2.8. Copy loop, traditional version.

r18, which is not allowed. At the end of the loop body, we find the br.cloop instruction, which takes care of branching back to label loop and repeating these steps until all six words have been copied.

From a correctness point of view, this traditional loop works perfectly well. But if we consider performance, we find some problems. Just by counting the number of instruction groups in the loop body, we see that it will take two cycles to execute (for this toy example we will ignore any additional delays that may be incurred by the memory accesses). This loop would therefore be able to copy one data word every two cycles, or 4 bytes/cycle. This may not seem so bad, but let us think of the load and the store instructions as separate stages in a manufacturing pipeline. With this analogy, the load instruction "manufactures" an item (the data word loaded from memory) and puts it on a conveyor belt. The conveyor belt moves the item to the next stage, where the store instruction picks it up and consumes the item (writes it to memory). With this interpretation, we can draw the pipeline diagram illustrated in Figure 2.8 (b). As shown there, in the first cycle, stage 0 loads a data word and puts it on the conveyor belt (r18). The conveyor belt then transports the data word to the next stage where, in cycle one, the store instruction picks it up and writes it to memory. In the remaining ten cycles, this sequence is repeated until all six words have been copied. Now, if we look at the resulting diagram, we immediately see a problem: both pipeline stages are idle half the time! If Henry Ford had built cars in this fashion, the factory workers would have been idle half the time and few people in the world would have ever been able to afford his Model T cars!

Clearly, it would be much better if we could keep the load and the store instructions busy at all times. In other words, we would like to keep the pipeline full as much as possible. Optimizing compilers can achieve this on any architecture with an approach called *software pipelining*. For our toy example, this approach would be reasonably straightforward, but for more realistic loops, it can be complicated and often results in a significant increase in code size. Fortunately, thanks to the IA-64 modulo-scheduled loop feature, software pipelined loops can be realized easily and without any significant increase in code size. In fact, we claim that the assembly code in Figure 2.9 (a) solves the problem and results in the pipeline diagram shown in Figure 2.9 (b). As this diagram shows, the pipeline is kept busy as much as possible and the six words can be copied in just seven cycles! The average throughput is therefore 6.9 bytes/cycle, almost twice that of the traditional loop.

As we might have guessed, the trick that makes this possible is the use of rotating registers as an automatic conveyor belt. Rotation is triggered by the loop-related branches

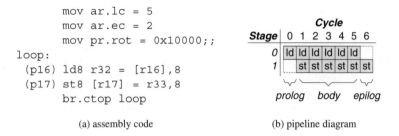

```
        mov ar.lc = 5
        mov ar.ec = 2
        mov pr.rot = 0x10000;;
    loop:
      (p16) ld8 r32 = [r16],8
      (p17) st8 [r17] = r33,8
            br.ctop loop
```

(a) assembly code

(b) pipeline diagram

Figure 2.9. Copy loop, modulo-scheduled version.

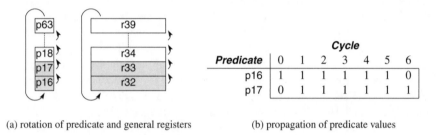

(a) rotation of predicate and general registers

(b) propagation of predicate values

Figure 2.10. Effect of br.ctop instruction.

br.ctop, br.cexit, br.wtop, and br.wexit. For our toy example, br.ctop is the right choice because we are dealing with a *counted* loop (the "c" in "ctop") and because we need to branch
to the *top* of the loop (as opposed to the exit of the loop). This type of branch basically acts
like an ordinary counted loop branch (br.cloop), except that when the branch is taken, it
also rotates the registers as illustrated in Figure 2.10 (a). As shown there, branches such
as br.ctop rotate registers by renaming each rotating register to the next higher-numbered
register and wrapping around the last one. For instance, in the rotating portion of the predicate registers, p16 becomes p17, and so on, up to p63, which becomes p16. Similarly, if
we assume that the routine used an alloc instruction to mark the first eight stacked registers
as **rotating**, r32 becomes r33, and so on, up to r39, which becomes r32.

The rotating portion of the stacked registers provides the conveyor belt we need to
transport the data words. Since our toy example contains only two pipeline stages, we can
choose any pair of consecutive registers for this purpose. Let us choose r32 and r33. The
load instruction can then load a data word into r32, and the next time br.ctop is executed, the
register will be renamed to r33, where the store instruction will write it back to destination
memory. In other words, we can use a loop body of the following form:

```
    loop:   ld8 r32 = [r16],8
            st8 [r17] = r33,8
            br.ctop loop
```

With this loop, each iteration will load a new data word and write back the data word from the previous iteration. If we look at Figure 2.9 (b), we can see that this will work fine for cycles one through five, but we have a problem for cycles zero and six: in the first cycle, the load needs to be executed, but there is no data word to consume yet, so the store must not be executed. Conversely, in the last cycle, all data words have been loaded already, so the load instruction must not be executed anymore, but the store instruction still needs to write back the last data word. The border condition that occurs when the pipeline is starting up is called the *prologue*, and the one that occurs when the pipeline is draining is called the *epilogue*. These conditions could be handled by extra code (e.g., with a load and a store before and after the loop body, respectively), but the nice part about modulo-scheduled loops is that they can also be handled with predication.

To support this, br.ctop takes the branch and decrements ar.lc until it becomes 0. While doing so, br.ctop will also set p63 to 1 right before it rotates the registers. Furthermore, when ar.lc becomes 0, it does not immediately exit the loop but instead continues to take the branch while the epilogue count in ar.ec is greater than 1. In this phase, br.ctop decrements ar.ec and sets p63 to 0 just before rotating the registers. If we initialize the epilogue count to the number of stages in the pipeline (2), p16 to 1, and p17 to 0, the net effect is that the loop will iterate seven times (ar.lc + ar.ec = 7) and p16 and p17 will have the values illustrated in Figure 2.10 (b). As shown there, in cycle zero the predicates have their initial values (1 and 0, respectively). In subsequent cycles, their contents are rotated and a new 1 bit is rotated in from p63. This continues until ar.lc becomes 0 in cycle five. At that point, p63 is set to 0 before the rotation, so that by the time cycle six starts, p16 contains 0. If we compare the resulting pattern in the predicates with the pipeline diagram in Figure 2.9 (b), we see that p16 is 1 whenever the load needs to execute, and p17 is 1 whenever the store needs to execute. Thus, instead of having to write separate prologue and epilogue code, we can fold them into the loop body as shown in Figure 2.9 (a) instead. This will have exactly the desired effect of executing only the load in the first iteration, executing both instructions in iterations two through six, and executing only the store in the last iteration.

Of course, before the loop is entered, the initial state needs to be established. Specifically, ar.lc needs to be set to 5 (number of iterations minus 1), ar.ec needs to be set to 2 (number of pipeline stages), p16 needs to be set to 1, and p17 to 0. The last two can be initialized with the single instruction mov pr.rot = 0x10000. This copies the source operand to the predicate registers with a broadside access, masking out the least significant 16 bits so that only the rotating predicates p16–p63 are modified. Because of these initializations, the code size of modulo-scheduled loops does increase slightly, but for more realistic cases this increase is insignificant compared to the size of the loop body.

In summary, the architectural features that IA-64 provides in support of modulo-scheduled loops enable the construction of highly efficient, yet compact, code sequences. Normally, optimizing compilers take care of generating such loops, but there are a few instances in the Linux kernel where such loops are implemented in assembly code. The *memory copy routine* (*memcpy()* in file arch/ia64/lib/memcpy.S) is an example of such a routine.

Table 2.4. Data model.

Type	Size [bytes]	Alignment [bytes]	Type	Size [bytes]	Alignment [bytes]
char	1	1	void *	8	8
short	2	2	float	4	4
int	4	4	double	8	8
long	8	8	long double	10 or 16	16
long long	8	8			

2.2 RUNTIME AND SOFTWARE CONVENTIONS

To ensure interoperability across different languages, compilers, and operating systems, a set of runtime and software conventions has been established for IA-64 [28]. The conventions cover such important aspects as data representation, register usage, procedure linkage (calling conventions), exception handling, and dynamic linking. For Linux, the IA-64–specific supplement of the UNIX System V Application Binary Interface is also of interest. It defines several additional aspects that are left unspecified in the general software conventions [32]. For this book, readers need not be familiar with all the details of these conventions, but it is useful to review the most important aspects, and we do so in this section.

2.2.1 Data model

The software conventions fundamentally define a 64-bit data model, which, depending on the operating system, may be based on little- or big-endian byte order. For Linux/ia64, the native byte order is little-endian because this improves backward compatibility with the IA-32 version of Linux. For the C programming language, the data model defined by the conventions is commonly known as LP64 because the C data types **long** and **void *** are both defined to be 64 bits wide. A complete list of the fundamental C data types, their sizes and alignment requirements is given in Table 2.4. This table is provided for information only: portable C programs should never rely on types such as **int** or **long** having a particular size. If types of a particular size are needed, it is better to use the facilities specifically designed for this purpose. For example, the ANSI C programming environment provides the stdint.h include file. It declares several types with names of the form **int$N$_t**, which correspond to integer types that are (at least) N bits wide. For example, **int32_t** is a type that is (at least) 32 bits wide. The Linux kernel provides similar types in the linux/types.h include file. Specifically, it declares several type names of the form **sN**. For example, **s32** is a type that is exactly 32 bits wide.

Looking at Table 2.4, we see that each type must be aligned according to its size. For example, a variable of type **long** always must start at an address that is an integer multiple of 8. This means that, on IA-64, fundamental data types must be naturally aligned. The table does not specify the exact formats used by the floating-point types. However, the software conventions require type **float** to use the IEEE single-precision format and type **double** to use the IEEE double-precision format [22]. The format of type **long double** is operating system dependent. Linux uses the 80-bit IEEE double-extended precision format, but other operating systems, such as HP-UX, may use the 128-bit IEEE quad-precision format instead. Note that while the 80-bit format is directly supported by IA-64, the 128-bit format must be emulated in software.

2.2.2   Register usage

To ensure interoperability between independently compiled functions, it is important to establish register usage conventions. For this purpose, IA-64 partitions registers into three classes: *scratch*, *preserved*, and *special*. A function can use registers in the first class without having to save them first. The flip side of this is that any function call can modify their contents. Said differently, if a caller wants to keep the content of a **scratch** register across a function call, the caller must save it before the call and restore it afterward. For this reason, **scratch** registers are sometimes called *caller-saved* registers. In contrast, **preserved** registers must not be used by a function unless it saves the old value before the first use and restores the original value before returning. Such registers are sometimes called *callee-saved* registers. The **special** class is used for registers that have special usage constraints. For example, read-only registers such as r0 and f0 never have to be saved and therefore are part of the **special** class.

Figure 2.11 illustrates the register usage established by the IA-64 software conventions: lightly shaded boxes are **scratch** registers, dark-shaded boxes are **preserved** registers, and white boxes are **special** registers. We can see that all static general registers except for r4–r7 and r12–r13 are **scratch** registers. Registers r32 through r127 are **special** because they are part of the register stack: effectively, input and local registers behave like **preserved** registers across function calls, whereas output registers behave like **scratch** registers. A function can therefore create as many preserved registers as it needs (up to a limit of 96) by allocating a suitable number of local registers. This property explains why it is sufficient for the static general register set to provide only four **preserved** registers. Registers r0, r1, r12, and r13 are **special**. Register r0 is read-only. Register r1 serves as the *global pointer*, which is used in addressing global data. Register r12 serves as the *memory stack pointer*, and r13 serves as the *thread pointer*. The last is intended for multithreaded programs where it is used to point to a *thread control block*. The IA-64 software conventions do not define the format of the thread control block, but they do require that register r13 be used only for this purpose. Indeed, even single-threaded programs *must not* write to this register. For convenience, IA-64 assemblers provide the register name aliases gp (global pointer), sp (stack pointer), and tp (thread pointer) for registers r1, r12, and r13, respectively.

For the floating-point register file, the low partition is about evenly divided between **scratch** and **preserved** registers: registers f6 through f15 are **scratch**, f0 and f1 are read-only and therefore **special**, and the remaining registers are **preserved**. The floating-point high partition (f32–f127) is entirely **scratch**. Since these registers can rotate, it makes sense to treat them all in the same fashion. Given the choice between making them all **scratch** or all **preserved**, the former makes more sense because it means that modulo-scheduled

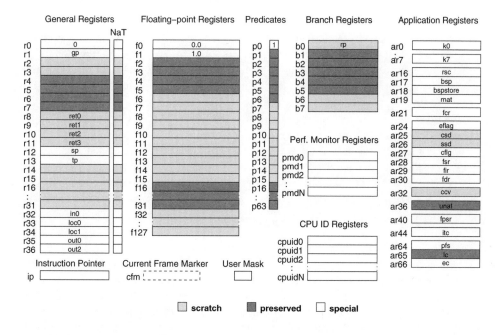

Figure 2.11. IA-64 register usage conventions.

loops that do not contain function calls (which is a common situation) never have to save any registers in the floating-point high partition. Indeed, the fact that the entire partition is **scratch** enables some interesting optimizations. For example, it often is a good idea to use the instruction:

```
rum psr.mfh  // reset ''modified floating-point high'' bit
```

at the end of a function that uses the high partition. The reason is that some operating systems (including Linux) check the psr.mfh flag to determine whether it is necessary to save the floating-point high partition on a context switch. By clearing this flag, a program indicates that the contents of the registers are no longer needed and thereby reduces the amount of work the operating system needs to perform in a context switch.

In the predicate register file, p7 through p15 are **scratch**, p0 is read-only and therefore **special**, and the other predicates are **preserved**. Note that predicates are normally saved and restored as a group through broadside accesses to register pr. This means that when *any* predicate register needs to be saved, *all* of them get saved. As we see later in this book, this property enables some interesting optimizations. Recall that registers p16 through p63 constitute the rotating partition. It may seem strange that these registers are **preserved** when we just argued that it is advantageous to treat the floating-point high partition as **scratch**. However, the situation is a little different here: first, saving all predicates requires just a single broadside access, so this can be done with little overhead. Second, it is often desirable to preserve control-flow decisions across function calls, meaning that there is a strong incentive for having as many **preserved** predicates as possible. Treating the rotating partition as **preserved** achieves this goal because it provides 48 additional **preserved** predicates.

In the branch register file, b1 through b5 are treated as **preserved** and the remaining registers are treated as **scratch**. While b0 is normally a **scratch** register, it serves a special purpose when a nested function is invoked or returns. During those times, b0 stores the return address. In IA-64, this address is known as the *return pointer* and for this reason the assembler defines the alias rp for this register.

Almost all other registers are **special** because they are read-only (ip, bsp, itc, k0–k7, cpuid0–cpuidN), automatically preserved (ec and rnat), or serve a special purpose (cfm, pfs, bspstore, pmd0–pmdN). The exceptions are application registers ar25, ar26, and ccv, which are **scratch**, and application registers unat and lc, which are **preserved**.

2.2.3 Procedure linkage

Let us now take a closer look at how a function can perform a nested function call while passing some arguments and, upon returning, receiving some return values. The software conventions require that up to eight stacked registers be used to pass integer arguments and that f8–f15 be used to pass float-point arguments. Arguments not passed in registers are passed on the memory stack. The exact rules defining how each argument is passed are complicated and described in the software conventions [28]. For our purposes, it is sufficient to know that, in preparation for a call, the outgoing arguments are placed in the output registers, starting with out0 and continuing up to out7. The function is then called with one of the two call instructions, br.call or brl.call. The call instruction has the effect of renaming the registers such that output register out0 becomes r32, out1 becomes r33, and so on, up to out7, which becomes r39. The callee can access the arguments directly through the renamed output registers but, more commonly, will employ an alloc instruction to define its own register frame. This instruction causes the argument registers to be treated as the input registers of the current frame, so that the callee can access them as in0–in7 (r32–r39).

Like arguments, results are returned in registers. For integer results, registers r8 through r11 are used; for floating-point results, registers f8 through f15 are used. Since most C functions return a single scalar value, r8 and f8 are by far the most commonly used return value registers, but multiple registers can be used for returning small structures. When returning large structures, the caller is responsible for allocating a suitable buffer and passing its address to the callee in register r8.

Now, when returning from a function, it is necessary to know where to return to. Register rp (b0) is used for this purpose. The software conventions require that upon entering a function, rp must contain the return address. Thus, a function can return to its caller with a br.ret instruction and specifying rp as the source operand. But what if a called function has to make another call? Since rp is a **scratch** register, the function would have to save the original content of rp before making the nested call and restore it before returning.

To see how this all works together, let us look at an example: Figure 2.12 illustrates the canonical call sequence with assembly code fragments. In the figure, we assume that *func1()* is a function that takes two integer arguments and returns an integer result. On the

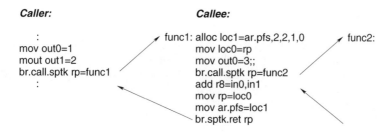

Caller:

```
        :
mov out0=1
mout out1=2
br.call.sptk rp=func1
        :
```

Callee:

```
func1: alloc loc1=ar.pfs,2,2,1,0
       mov loc0=rp
       mov out0=3;;
       br.call.sptk rp=func2
       add r8=in0,in1
       mov rp=loc0
       mov ar.pfs=loc1
       br.sptk.ret rp
```

func2:

Figure 2.12. Canonical calling sequence.

left side of the figure, we see how the caller sets up the arguments by placing the desired values in out0 and out1. It then invokes the function with a br.call instruction. Since the first operand specified is rp, the return address is placed in register rp, as required by the software conventions. Execution in the callee starts by allocating a suitable register window frame. In this particular case, the callee allocates two input registers, two local registers, and one output register. Since the callee will be making another nested call, it also uses the alloc instruction to save pfs in local register loc1. The next two instructions take care of saving the return address in loc0 and setting up output register out0. Another br.call instruction is then executed to invoke function *func2()*. This function will eventually return control to the instruction following br.call, and at that time the callee calculates a return value by adding in0 and in1 and placing the sum in r8. Note that the input and local registers are treated as **preserved** registers, so there is no danger of the call to *func2()* modifying the contents of these registers. Before returning to its caller, *func1()* needs to restore rp from loc0 and pfs from loc1. It then returns control by executing the br.ret.sptk instruction, specifying rp as the source operand of the instruction. The caller can then pick up the return value from r8 and process it as necessary.

One important point we have glossed over so far is the issue of how to pass integer arguments in registers when the argument is narrower than 64 bits. The IA-64 conventions require that all integers less than 32 bits wide be padded to 32 bits. This padded value is then placed in the least significant 32 bits of the register. The top 32 bits in the register remain undefined. For example, a **short** value would be sign-extended from 16 bits to 32 bits and then placed in a register. Similarly, a value of type **unsigned char** would be zero-extended from 8 to 32 bits. The fact that narrow integers are only padded to 32 bits implies that C programs need to be careful to use the same prototype in the caller and the callee. Otherwise, it could happen that a caller would pass a (possibly padded) 32-bit integer in a register and then the callee might try to interpret the register content as a 64-bit value. But since the top 32 bits would be undefined in such a case, the program might end up crashing or returning incorrect results. When using the C language, programmers should always declare function prototypes and ensure that each function is declared in one and only one place (preferably a header file).

2.2.4   Memory stack

IA-64 provides no special instructions for managing the memory stack. Instead, the layout and use of this stack is controlled entirely by the IA-64 software conventions. They require that register sp (r12) be used as the stack pointer and that the memory stack grow toward lower addresses. The stack pointer must be 16-byte–aligned at all times. The conventions also require that each interior (nonleaf) function allocate an extra 16-byte area at the top of the stack. This serves as a *scratch area* that may be used to accelerate the execution of certain functions. Specifically, a leaf function that requires at most 16 bytes of stack space can use this area and can thereby avoid having to allocate its own stack frame.

We should point out that it is never safe to use the memory immediately below the stack pointer, because its content may change unpredictably. In user-level applications, this may happen as the result of the delivery of a signal (see Chapter 5, *Kernel Entry and Exit*) and inside the Linux kernel this may happen, e.g., because of device interrupts.

2.2.5   Register stack

In contrast to the memory stack, the register stack is implemented in hardware and grows toward higher addresses. There is no explicit pointer to the top of the stack, but application register bsp always points to the memory location that would be used to save register r32, should that become necessary. Since the stacked registers are all 64 bits wide (ignoring the NaT bit), the address in bsp must be 8-byte–aligned at all times.

2.2.6   The global pointer

The *global pointer* (GP) points into the *short data segment*. This segment serves two purposes: first, it provides efficient access to globally accessible *small data* and, second, it provides a *linkage table* (sometimes called *global offset table*) that helps making executable code *position independent*. The latter is important because it simplifies the sharing of code, e.g., of shared libraries. The software conventions require that the global pointer be kept in register r1 (gp).

To see how the global pointer works, let us consider what the machine code would look like to load the global 32-bit integer variable *ctr* into register r3. The most obvious way to do this would be:

```
movl r2 = ctr;;            // load addr. of ctr into r2
ld4  r3 = [r2]             // load value of ctr into r3
```

Now what is the problem with this code? First, recall that the movl instruction occupies two slots in a bundle and that only the MLX template can accommodate it. Second, since the address of *ctr* is encoded as an immediate value in the movl instruction, the code changes whenever the address of *ctr* changes. This means that the code is not position-independent and therefore cannot easily be shared by multiple applications.

The short data segment lets us avoid these problems. Suppose that variable *ctr* is part of this segment and that its address happens to be equal to gp + 0xa50. We can then load the value of *ctr* with the following assembly code:

```
addl r2 = 0xa50, gp;;          // load addr. of ctr into r2
ld4 r3 = [r2]                  // load value of ctr into r3
```

This is better because the addl instruction occupies only a single slot. Furthermore, it can be executed both on M- and I-units and is therefore easier to accommodate in a bundle. Better still, the code is position independent: if the address of the short data segment changes, the content of gp needs to change accordingly, but the code itself remains the same!

Of course, it would be tedious if a programmer had to specify the GP-relative offset manually. To avoid this problem, IA-64 assemblers provide the @gprel directive. This directive translates a variable name into the corresponding GP-relative offset. For example, the previous code could also be written as:

```
addl r2 = @gprel(ctr), gp;;    // load addr. of ctr into r2
ld4 r3 = [r2]                  // load value of ctr into r3
```

GP-relative addressing works well, but there is one problem: the immediate value of the addl instruction is limited to a range of $-2,097,152$ to $2,097,151$. If we assume that gp points into the middle of the short data segment, this means that at most 4 Mbytes of data could be addressed in this fashion. To alleviate this problem, the IA-64 software conventions require that GP-relative addressing be used for small data only. Typically, data that is at most eight bytes in size is considered "small." For larger variables, the linkage table in the short data segment stores not the data itself, but a pointer to it. IA-64 assemblers support linkage-table-based addressing with the @ltoff directive. For example, if we assume *big* to be a large variable, we could load its first 32-bit word with the following code:

```
addl r2 = @ltoff(big), gp;;    // load pointer to addr. of big
ld8 r3 = [r2];;                // load addr. of big into r3
ld4 r8 = [r3]                  // load 1st word of big into r8
```

Here, @ltoff(big) returns the GP-relative offset of the linkage table entry in which the *address* of *big* is stored. The ld8 instruction then loads this address into register r3. In the last step, the ld4 instruction loads the first 32-bit word of the variable into r8.

When the size of small data is limited to eight bytes, the 4-Mbyte limit on the size of the short data segment implies that it can be used to address up to 524,288 distinct variables of *arbitrary* size! In practice, this is sufficient for all but the most extreme programs. And to make it possible to accommodate even those extreme programs, the calling conventions further require that there be a separate short data segment for each *load module*. A load module is defined to be a collection of code and data that can be loaded separately. For example, most applications consist of a main program and several shared libraries. Since the main program and the shared libraries are loaded separately, they are all considered separate load modules and they each come with their own short data segment. The concept of a load module is not limited to user-level applications. For example, operating systems such as Linux are usually divided into a main kernel and several dynamically loadable kernel modules. In such a scenario, the main kernel and the kernel modules are also separate load modules. With multiple short data segments, a programmer can avoid the 4-Mbyte limit simply by splitting up a program into multiple load units (e.g., by using shared libraries

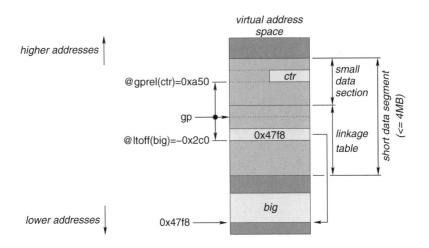

Figure 2.13. Global pointer and the short data segment.

or kernel modules). The downside is that when execution crosses from one load module to another, the value in gp needs to be updated. For this book, it is sufficient to know that a new gp value needs to be loaded when this crossover happens. The exact rules that achieve this update are spelled out in the IA-64 software convention manual [28].

Figure 2.13 is a graphical representation of the global pointer and the short data segment. In the example, register gp points into the middle of the short data segment, and the 32-bit variable *ctr* is located at an offset of 0xa50. Since we assumed variable *big* to be too large to be stored in the short data segment itself, the linkage table contains its address instead. The figure assumes that this address is 0x47f8 and that it is stored at GP-relative offset −0x2c0.

There are two points worth mentioning here: first, the global pointer does not have to point to the middle of the short data segment. The only requirement is that its value must be such that the entire segment can be addressed with the 22-bit immediate value that the addl instruction provides. Second, the addl instruction can be used only if the third operand is a general register in the range of r0 to r3. Fortunately, since register r1 serves the role of the global pointer, this constraint is met.

2.2.7 Programming in IA-64 assembly language

Because of the explicitly parallel nature of the IA-64 instruction set and because of instruction bundling, programming in assembly language can be quite different from traditional architectures. However, IA-64 assemblers can hide these differences by offering modes that provide automatic instruction group formation and automatic bundling. For example, the simplest way to write an assembly function that adds three 64-bit integers and returns the result is as follows:

```
        .proc add3
        .global add3
add3:   add r8 = r32,r33
        add r8 = r8,r34
        br.ret.sptk rp
        .endp
```

The **.proc** directive indicates the start of function *add3()*, and the **.global** directive declares label add3 as a global symbol. The latter ensures that the function can be called from other object files. The second line defines label add3 and contains the instruction to add the first two input registers (r32 and r33). The third line contains the instruction to add the third input register (r34), and the fourth line returns to the caller. In the last line, the **.endp** directive indicates the end of the function. Let us assume that this assembly code is stored in a file called ex1.s. We can then translate it into machine code by using an assembler such as the GNU assembler. The following command would achieve this:

```
$ as -xauto ex1.s -o ex1.o
```

To see what the assembler did, we can use the objdump utility to look at the resulting machine code:

```
$ objdump -d ex1.o
0000000000000000 <add3>:
  0: 0a 40 80 42 00 20    [MMI]  add r8=r32,r33;;
  6: 80 40 88 00 40 00           add r8=r8,r34
  c: 00 00 04 00                 nop.i 0x0
 10: 11 00 00 00 01 00    [MIB]  nop.m 0x0
 16: 00 00 00 02 00 80           nop.i 0x0
 1c: 00 00 84 00                 br.ret.sptk.few b0
```

In this output, the first column shows the code address, columns two through seven show the machine code one byte at a time, column eight shows the bundle template in square brackets, and the last column shows the disassembled code. From this output, we can see that the assembler took care of forming IA-64 bundles and inserting stop bits where necessary. For example, it placed the first two add instructions in an MMI bundle and filled it by inserting a nop instruction, which performs no operation. It also inserted a stop bit after the first add instruction. The stop bit is necessary because the second add instruction reads register r8, which is written by the first one (RAW dependency) and also because both instructions write to r8 (WAW dependency). In contrast, all remaining instructions are independent of each other, so the second add instruction, the three nop instructions inserted by the assembler and final branch instruction can all be executed in parallel and no further stop bits are needed.

Thanks to automatic bundling and instruction group formation, programming in IA-64 assembly language can be as easy as with traditional architectures. However, sometimes it is necessary for a programmer to maintain tight control over the exact code being generated. To support this, the automatic mechanisms can be overridden with manual annotations. In manual mode, the previous example could be written as:

```
        .proc add3; .global add3
add3:
    { .mmi                          // start of bundle, MMI template
        add r8 = r32,r33;;
        add r8 = r8,r34
        nop.i 0
    }                               // end of bundle
    { .mib                          // start of bundle, MIB template
        nop.m 0
        nop.i 0
        br.ret.sptk rp
    }
        .endp
```

As shown above, bundles are bracketed by curly braces: a left brace forces the start of a new bundle, and a right brace closes the bundle. The bundle template is selected with directives that consist of a dot followed by the desired template name (in lower case), and stop bits are represented by two consecutive semicolons. In manual mode, it is the programmer's responsibility to ensure that the assembly code is valid. In particular, it is imperative to insert enough stop bits to ensure that there are no dependency violations within an instruction group. To help with this, the GNU assembler provides the command-line option -x, which causes the assembler to check and report any violations. For example, if we were to remove the first stop bit in the above code we would get:

```
$ as -x ex1.s -o ex1.o
ex1.s: Assembler messages:
ex1.s:5: Warning: Use of 'add' violates RAW dependency
    'GR%, % in 1 - 127' (impliedf), specific resource number is 8
        :
        :
ex1.s:5: Warning: Use of 'add' violates WAW dependency
    'GR%, % in 1 - 127' (impliedf), specific resource number is 8
```

This output shows that the assembler found two dependency violations: the first warning says that the add instruction in line 5 creates a RAW dependency on r8. This clearly is true because the second instruction reads r8 right after it was written. The second warning reports a WAW violation, which means that the same register is written multiple times in the same instruction group. This is also true because both add instructions write to r8. Adding back the stop bit will fix both problems and the resulting code will be correct again.

Unwind information

An important aspect of IA-64 assembly language programming is that unwind information is *mandatory*. Loosely speaking, unwind information is needed to generate a stack back-trace and, traditionally, this has been used primarily for debugging or exception handling. But by unwind information being mandatory, other applications are enabled. For example, the Linux kernel takes advantage of unwind information to optimize performance-critical operations such as signal delivery. The flip side of this coin is that a routine with missing or incorrect unwind information is not just impossible to debug, but outright wrong and could indeed cause a program to crash. In Chapter 6, *Stack Unwinding*, we provide a more detailed description of the unwind information and the assembly language directives used to express it. For now, it is sufficient to remember that all assembly routines must include the necessary unwind directives.

Instruction labels and tags

IA-64 assemblers provide labels to refer to a particular bundle of instructions. As usual, the syntax for labels consists of a symbolic name followed by a colon. But since IA-64 executes instructions a bundle at a time, code labels can point *only* to the beginning of a bundle. The assembler enforces this rule by rejecting labels within a bundle or, in automatic bundling mode, by starting a new bundle whenever it encounters a code label.

The GNU assembler provides a local label extension that allows labels to consist of a decimal number followed by a colon. Local labels are very useful in macros because they can be redefined an arbitrary number of times. They can be referred to with constructs of the form nb or nf, where n is the decimal number of the local label. With suffix b, the assembler will search backward for the nearest local label matching number n, and with f, it will search forward. For example, the following code could be used to load the address of label number 2 into register r8:

```
1: {
       nop.m 0
       mov r8 = ip;;
       add r8 = 2f-1b, r8
   }
2:
```

The mov instruction reads the current IP (the address of the current instruction bundle) into r8, and the add instruction adds the difference between labels number 2 and 1, which is 16 bytes in this instance.

In some cases it is necessary to be able to refer to a particular instruction, rather than just the bundle containing it. For example, when exception handling information is encoded, this reference is needed so that the exact range of instructions to which a particular handler applies can be expressed. Similar needs arise when debug or unwind information is encoded (see Chapter 6, *Stack Unwinding*). To solve this problem, IA-64 assemblers provide *tags*. These work like code labels except that they identify a particular instruction. The two least significant bits of the tag value encode the instruction's slot number. Syntactically, tags are code labels enclosed in square brackets. For example, the code below defines one label and three tags:

```
L: {
   [taga:] nop.m 0
   [tagb:] nop.m 0
   [tagc:] nop.i 0
   }
```

The first tag is taga, and since it refers to the first instruction in the bundle (slot 0), its value is equal to the value of label L. The values of tagb and tagc are L+1 and L+2, respectively. The GNU assembler supports local tags in the same fashion as local labels.

2.3 SYSTEM INSTRUCTION SET ARCHITECTURE

The architecture described so far is sufficient for running user-level programs. However, an operating system needs additional facilities to support common abstractions such as virtual memory. IA-64 provides these facilities in the form of system register files and privileged instructions. The additional instructions and the system register files are privileged and can be accessed only by the operating system.

2.3.1 System register files

Figure 2.14 illustrates the system register files. They can be classified into four groups. The first group consists of the processor status register psr and the control register file. They are the most frequently used system registers and serve a variety of purposes. The second group consists of the region registers, protection key registers, and the *translation lookaside buffers (TLB)*. These provide the infrastructure needed to implement virtual memory; a more detailed discussion follows in Chapter 4, *Virtual Memory*. The third group is used for debugging and performance analysis; it consists of the instruction debug, data debug, and performance monitor registers. Recall that the user-level register state (Figure 2.3) also includes a performance monitor register file. The two are indeed closely connected: the system file consists of the *configuration* registers, whereas the user-level file consists of the *data* registers of the performance monitor. The configuration registers select *what* gets measured, and the data registers provide the actual measurement *values*. The net effect of this division is that applications need help from the operating system to set up performance monitoring, but once configured, they can access the measurement values directly. More on this in Chapter 9, *Understanding System Performance*.

A special aspect of the system register files is that many of its resources are not serialized automatically. This can improve performance but creates additional responsibilities for kernel programmers. Specifically, what this means is that after a system register is updated, an arbitrary amount of time may expire before the update actually takes effect. To force explicit serialization, IA-64 provides the srlz instruction, which stalls execution until all pending updates have taken effect. When the instruction is used with a suffix of .d (data), only resources related to the data stream are serialized. With a suffix of .i (instruction), serialization occurs both with respect to the data and the instruction streams. The exact serialization rules are described in the architecture manual [26], but for this book, it is sufficient to know that many system register files require explicit serialization.

Banked general registers

One aspect of the system register files that had to be omitted from Figure 2.14 for space reasons is that general registers r16 through r31 are *banked*. There are actually two sets of

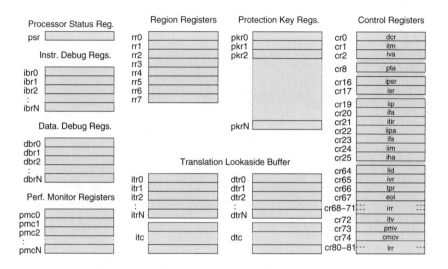

Figure 2.14. IA-64 system register files.

each of those registers. During normal execution, bank 1 (the second set) of the registers is active. However, as soon as an *interruption* occurs, e.g., due to a fault or a device interrupt, the CPU switches to the most privileged execution level and, at the same time, switches to bank 0 of the registers. This means that whenever an interruption occurs, the operating system immediately has access to 16 temporary registers. Moreover, in bank 0, registers r16 through r23 are guaranteed to retain their contents between different interruptions, so the registers can be used to store frequently used values, such as a pointer to the currently executing task. The same is not true for r24 through r31: they can be used by firmware, e.g., to recover from a correctable memory error. Their contents, therefore, are *volatile* and may change unpredictably between subsequent interruptions. In Chapter 5, *Kernel Entry and Exit*, we go into more detail of how the bank 0 registers are used in Linux/ia64.

Processor Status Register

The processor status register, psr, contains a mixture of status and control flags. Figure 2.15 illustrates its format. As shown there, psr contains two subsets called the *user mask* (least significant 6 bits) and the *system mask* (least significant 24 bits). The former can be manipulated with the unprivileged sum and rum instructions. The system mask can be manipulated with the privileged ssm and rsm instructions. In addition, a privileged version of the mov instruction can be used to set the least significant 32 bits of psr to the contents of a general register. The remaining bits of the psr can be modified only indirectly when execution modes are transitioned, e.g., when returning from an interruption.

Table 2.5 briefly describes each of the fields in the system mask, and Table 2.6 describes the fields outside the system mask. Of the many fields in this register, we encounter a

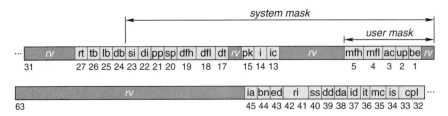

Figure 2.15. Format of processor status register (psr).

handful of them throughout this book. From an operating system perspective, one of the most important fields is cpl, which contains the current privilege level. Level 0 is the most privileged level and the only level that has access to the system register files and privileged instructions. Levels 1, 2, and 3 are increasingly less privileged. Linux distinguishes only between kernel-level and user-level execution, and for this reason it uses only privilege-level 0 (kernel level) and 3 (user level). However, operating systems designed to exploit multiple protection rings could use all four levels.

The i field in the system mask controls whether interrupts are enabled. As we see in Chapter 7, *Device I/O*, the IA-64 interrupt architecture is sophisticated and affords several ways to mask interrupt sources. When it is necessary to mask the delivery of *all* interrupts, the i bit provides the most efficient solution, however.

Three 1-bit fields in the psr determine whether memory references access physical or virtual memory. The fields are dt (data translation), rt (register stack translation), and it (instruction translation). They respectively control whether normal data references (load and store instruction), register stack references, and instruction fetches are accessing virtual memory. Note that instruction translation (it) occupies bit number 36 in the psr and cannot be manipulated directly. This is intentional because it eliminates difficult sequencing issues that would arise because instruction fetches are not under direct control of a program (unlike data memory references). Fortunately, this restriction is not an issue in practice because the bit can always be set to the desired value by execution of a dummy rfi instruction (return from interruption, see Section 2.3.2).

Another interesting pair of 1-bit fields are dfl and dfh. They control access to the low and the high partitions of the floating-point register file. A 0 in these bits disables the respective floating-point register partition, and any attempt to access a register in it will result in a DISABLED FLOATING-POINT REGISTER FAULT. Unlike the privilege-level- and virtual-memory-based protection, this facility is normally not used to implement security policies but instead is used to delay the saving and restoring of these registers as much as possible. Given the memory size of the floating-point high partition (96 registers of 16 bytes each, or 1.5 Kbytes), the benefit of reducing the number of times these registers have to be moved to and from memory can be significant.

Table 2.5. Processor status register: system mask fields.

Field	Bit	Description
be	1	**big-endian**. When 1, memory accesses are big-endian instead of little-endian.
up	2	**user performance monitor enable**. When 1, user monitors are enabled.
ac	3	**alignment check**. When 1, unaligned memory accesses *must* trigger an UN-ALIGNED DATA REFERENCE FAULT, when 0 the fault *may* occur.
mfl	4	**modified fp low partition**. Set to 1 if a register in the low partition (f2 to f31) has been written since this bit was cleared last.
mfh	5	**modified fp high partition**. Set to 1 if a register in the high partition (f32 to f127) has been written since this bit was cleared last.
ic	13	**interruption collection**. When 1, an interruption loads the current CPU state into the interruption control registers (iip, ipsr, iim, ifs, and others). When 0, these registers are not updated and speculative faults are always deferred.
i	14	**interrupt enable**. When 1, interrupts are enabled.
pk	15	**protection key enable**. When 1, protection keys are checked when virtual memory is accessed.
dt	17	**data address translation**. When 1, data references access virtual memory.
dfl	18	**disable fp low partition**. When 1, read or write accesses to the fp low partition result in a DISABLED FLOATING-POINT REGISTER FAULT.
dfh	19	**disable fp high partition**. When 1, read or write accesses to the fp high partition result in a DISABLED FLOATING-POINT REGISTER FAULT.
sp	20	**secure performance monitor**. When 1, user-level accesses to the performance monitor are disabled.
pp	21	**privileged perf. monitor enable**. When 1, privileged monitors are enabled.
di	22	**disable instruction set transition**. When 1, attempts to switch instruction sets through the IA-64 br.ia or IA-32 JMPE instructions result in a DISABLED INSTRUCTION SET TRANSITION FAULT. See Chapter 11, *IA-32 Compatibility*.
si	23	**secure interval timer**. When 1, attempts to read the interval time counter application register (itc) from the user level result in a PRIVILEGED OPERATION FAULT.

Control register file

The right part of Figure 2.14 illustrates the control register file. It is similar to the application register file in that it provides space for 128 registers, each 64 bits wide. Many of the registers are reserved for future use. The others can be classified roughly into three groups: registers cr0, cr1, and cr8 serve miscellaneous purposes, cr2 and cr16–cr25 are used during interruption handling, and cr64–cr81 are part of the IA-64 interrupt architecture. We describe the second group later in this chapter and return to the third group when describing the IA-64 interrupt architecture in Chapter 7, *Device I/O*.

For convenience, most control registers have a symbolic name that is recognized by the IA-64 assemblers. In Figure 2.14, these names are listed inside the box representing the register. For example, cr0 has the symbolic name dcr, and in assembly code it can be accessed either as cr0 or as cr.dcr.

Table 2.6. Processor status register: nonsystem mask fields.

Field	Bit	Description
db	24	**debug breakpoint enable**. When 1, data and instruction address breakpoints are enabled.
lp	25	**lower privilege transfer trap**. When 1, a LOWER PRIVILEGE TRANSFER TRAP occurs whenever a branch lowers the current privilege level.
tb	26	**taken branch trap**. When 1, a TAKEN BRANCH TRAP occurs whenever a branch is taken.
rt	27	**register stack translation**. When 1, memory accesses by the register stack engine access virtual memory.
cpl	32–33	**current privilege level**. Level 0 is the most privileged level; 3, the least privileged level.
is	34	**instruction set**. When 1, the IA-32 instruction set is executing; otherwise, the IA-64 instruction set is executing.
mc	35	**machine check abort mask**. When 1, machine check aborts are masked.
it	36	**instruction address translation**. When 1, instruction fetches access virtual memory.
id	37	**instruction debug fault disable**. When 1, instruction debug faults are disabled for the duration of one instruction.
da	38	**data access and dirty-bit fault disable**. When 1, data access and dirty-bit faults are disabled for the duration of one instruction.
dd	39	**data debug fault disable**. When 1, data debug faults are disabled for the duration of one instruction.
ss	40	**single step enable**. When 1, a SINGLE STEP TRAP occurs after successful execution of one instruction.
ri	41–42	**restart instruction**. When returning from an interruption, identifies the instruction slot number in the current bundle at which execution is to resume.
ed	43	**exception deferral**. When 1 and the instruction to be executed is a speculative load, a NaT token is loaded into the destination register.
bn	44	**bank number**. When 1, bank 1 of registers r16 to r31 is active; otherwise, bank 0 is active.
ia	45	**instruction access-bit fault disable**. When 1, instruction access-bit faults are disabled for the duration of one instruction.

rv	dd	da	dr	dx	dk	dp	dm	rv	lc	be	pp
	14	13	12	11	10	9	8		2	1	0

Figure 2.16. Format of default control register (dcr).

Of the miscellaneous control registers, cr0 plays an important role. It is known as the *default control register* (dcr) because it selects some of the default settings that are used when an interruption occurs. The format of the register is illustrated in Figure 2.16. The pp and be fields supply the default values for the psr bits of the same name. In addition, be also controls the byte order of the VHPT walker, which is a hardware accelerator for resolving TLB miss faults (see Chapter 4, *Virtual Memory*). The lc field controls how IA-32 atomic operations are to be handled if the memory being accessed is either unaligned or not fully cacheable. If lc is set to 1, such accesses are guaranteed to trigger an IA-32 LOCKED DATA REFERENCE FAULT. If it is set to 0, the CPU may try to handle the access on its own and raise the fault only if it is unable to handle the access. Bits 8 through 14 are known as the *deferral bits* because they control what type of faults are deferred when triggered by a speculative load instruction. For instance, dm controls whether TLB miss faults are deferred, and dp controls whether PAGE NOT PRESENT FAULTs are deferred. Setting any of these bits means that if a speculative load instruction triggers the corresponding fault, instead of taking the fault, the instruction writes a NaT token to the destination register. These bits can be used to tune performance optimally for a given fault behavior. For example, if speculative loads often end up accessing invalid memory, it is better to defer the faults because doing so would reduce the amount of unnecessary fault handling.

The second control register is cr1, known as the *interval timer match* register (itm). It is used in conjunction with the itc application register. Specifically, whenever the value in itc matches the value programmed into itm, the CPU raises an interval timer interrupt. This mechanism can be used as a basis for generating periodic interrupts or for implementing fine-grained timer interrupts.

The last miscellaneous control register is cr8, known as the *page table address* register (pta). It controls the base address of the virtual hash page table used by the VHPT walker and is described in more detail in Chapter 4, *Virtual Memory*.

2.3.2 Privileged instructions

Instructions that are in some way security-sensitive are considered privileged and can be executed only at privilege-level 0. Many of these instructions are related to virtual memory management. For example, several instructions manage the translation lookaside buffer (TLB), the region registers, and the protection key registers.

The control register file can be accessed with privileged move instructions. For example, the following code can be used to set bit 0 in the dcr register:

```
mov r8 = cr.dcr;;        // read cr.dcr into r8
or r8 = 1, r8;;          // set bit 0
mov cr.dcr = r8          // write new value to cr.dcr
```

Note that the control register has to be copied into a general register before bit 0 can be turned on. The reason is that arithmetic and logic instructions cannot operate directly on control registers.

Several instructions can change the current privilege level. The primary instruction is rfi (return from interruption). It returns execution to a previously interrupted context and as such can change the privilege level to any one of the four levels.

Since privileged instructions tend to have fairly complicated side effects, we describe them in more detail throughout the rest of this book as the need arises.

2.3.3 Interruptions

In IA-64 terminology, any event that causes the CPU to disrupt the normal flow of execution is called an *interruption*. There are four classes of interruptions:

- *abort*: Aborts occur in response to CPU-internal malfunctions (also known as *machine checks*) or because of hardware resets. They can be synchronous or asynchronous with respect to the instruction stream and can occur at an unpredictable location and with partially updated register or memory state. As a result, it is not always possible to resume execution after an abort. Aborts are normally handled by firmware, not by the operating system.

- *interrupt*: Interrupts are raised by any device that needs to asynchronously request attention from the CPU. Such devices include external I/O devices (such as a keyboard) or internal devices such as the interval timer implemented by application register itc and control register itm.

- *fault*: Faults are triggered by instructions that cannot or should not be carried out by the CPU. As such, these faults are synchronous with respect to the instruction stream. For example, attempting to access a register in the floating-point high partition when psr.dfh is cleared would trigger a fault. At the time a fault is taken, the CPU state reflects the state that existed *before* the instruction started execution.

- *trap*: Traps are triggered by instructions that started execution but need special assistance before they can complete. Traps are also synchronous with respect to the instruction stream, but unlike the case for faults, the CPU state reflects the state that exists *after* the instruction has begun execution. For example, turning on the tb (taken branch) bit in the psr and executing a branch instruction would result in a taken branch trap *after* the branch has been executed.

Except for aborts, all IA-64 interruptions are *precise* [19], meaning that there is an *interruption point* such that all instructions before this point have executed to completion and all instructions after that point have not started executing (or at least have not had any visible effect on the register or memory state). In this discussion, "before" and "after" refer to the order in which the instructions appear in the program. Notably, this rule applies even within an instruction group! This point is important because it means that even though an instruction group can be executed in parallel, the CPU is responsible for delivering interruptions in an order that is consistent with sequential execution. While this is more difficult to implement in a CPU, it greatly simplifies both the operating system and user-level programs because it means that restarting execution after an interruption has been handled simply requires resuming execution at a particular IP and instruction slot.

Interruptions are prioritized: aborts have higher priority than interrupts, which have higher priority than faults, which have higher priority than traps. Within each class, different interruption reasons also have unique priorities [26]. This ensures that if multiple interruptions are triggered during the same cycle, there is a total order in which the interruptions are delivered. Taking advantage of this total order can simplify an operating

Table 2.7. Interruption vectors.

#	Offset	Name	#	Offset	Name
0	0x0000	VHPT Translation vector	23	0x5300	Data Access Rights vector
1	0x0400	Instruction TLB vector	24	0x5400	General Exception vector
2	0x0800	Data TLB vector	25	0x5500	Disabled FP-Register vector
3	0x0c00	Alternate Instr. TLB vector	26	0x5600	NaT Consumption vector
4	0x1000	Alternate Data TLB vector	27	0x5700	Speculation vector
5	0x1400	Data Nested TLB vector	29	0x5900	Debug vector
6	0x1800	Instruction Key Miss vector	30	0x5a00	Unaligned Reference vector
7	0x1c00	Data Key Miss vector	31	0x5b00	Unsupported Data Ref. vector
8	0x2000	Dirty-Bit vector	32	0x5c00	Floating-point fault vector
9	0x2400	Instr. Access-Bit vector	33	0x5d00	Floating-point trap vector
10	0x2800	Data Access-Bit vector	34	0x5e00	Lower-Priv. Transfer Trap vec.
11	0x2c00	Break Instruction vector	35	0x5f00	Taken Branch Trap vector
12	0x3000	External Interrupt vector	36	0x6000	Single Step Trap vector
20	0x5000	Page Not Present vector	45	0x6900	IA-32 Exception vector
21	0x5100	Key Permission vector	46	0x6a00	IA-32 Intercept vector
22	0x5200	Instr. Access Rights vector	47	0x6b00	IA-32 Interrupt vector

system. For example, the DISABLED FLOATING-POINT REGISTER FAULT has higher priority than the UNALIGNED DATA REFERENCE FAULT. Because of this, an operating system handler that emulates unaligned memory accesses does not have to check whether the faulting instruction was attempting to access a disabled floating-point partition: by the time the unaligned handler gets called, access to the floating-point partition must have been established—otherwise, the higher-priority fault would have been raised instead.

The interruption vector table (IVT)

Interruptions are reported to the operating system through the *interruption vector table*. This table is 32 Kbytes in size and must be aligned to a 32-Kbyte boundary. The operating system establishes this table by writing its starting address to control register iva (interruption vector address). The table is divided into fixed-size entries that contain executable code. The first 20 entries are 64 bundles long (1024 bytes each), whereas remaining entries are 16 bundles long (256 bytes each). As Table 2.7 illustrates, each vector number has a name and an IVT-relative offset at which its entry starts. Note that some vector numbers do not appear in the table (e.g., 13–20 are missing). Those vectors are reserved for future use.

A given interrupt vector may handle more than one type of interruption. For example, the General Exception vector handles eight different faults, such as ILLEGAL OPERATION FAULT and RESERVED REGISTER/FIELD FAULT. However, this vector is an extreme case; most other vectors handle just one or two interruptions, and for those, there is usually a fairly direct correspondence between the vector name and the interruptions that trigger it. For example, the Instruction Access-Bit vector is invoked only as a result of the INSTRUCTION ACCESS BIT FAULT.

Interruption handling

Let us now look at how a CPU handles interruptions. From a high-level perspective, an interruption causes the CPU to switch to the most-privileged execution level (psr.cpl = 0) and to transfer control to the vector associated with the interruption. The exact sequence of steps that accomplish these goals is outlined below:

1. If psr.ic is 1, save critical state:

   - The content of psr is saved in control register ipsr (interruption processor status register). For traps, the value in psr.ri (restart instruction) at the time of the interruption is the slot number of the instruction that would have been executed if there had been no trap. For all other interruptions, the psr.ri contains the slot number of the instruction that caused the interruption.

   - The content of ip is saved in control register iip (interruption instruction pointer). For traps, the value saved is the address of the bundle containing the instruction that would have been executed next if there had been no trap. For all other interruptions, the value saved is the address of the bundle containing the instruction that caused the interruption.

   - The address of the bundle containing the last successfully executed instruction is saved in control register iipa (interruption instruction previous address).

   - Control registers ifa (interruption faulting address), iim (interruption immediate), iha (interruption hash address), and itir (interruption TLB insertion register) are written with information specific to the particular interruption taken.

   - Control register ifs (interruption function state) has two fields: bit 63 is known as the v field (valid), and the least significant 38 bits are known as the ifm field (interruption frame marker). On an interruption, ifs.v is cleared to zero and all other bits are undefined. As we will see later, this register is used in conjunction with the cover and rfi instructions to preserve the stacked registers.

2. Control register isr is written with information specific to the particular interruption taken. If the interruption was caused by a DATA NESTED TLB FAULT, this step is skipped.

3. All bits in psr are cleared to 0 except as follows:

   - Fields up, mfl, mfh, pk, dt, rt, mc, and it are left unchanged.

   - Field be is set to the value of dcr.be; field pp, to the value of dcr.pp.

4. The CPU calculates the address of the interruption handler by mapping the cause of the interruption to the appropriate vector number and adding the associated offset to the IVT base stored in iva.

5. The CPU performs an instruction serialization (equivalent to srlz.i) and jumps to the interruption handler address calculated in the previous step.

The exact values written to control registers isr, ifa, iim, iha, and itir depend on the cause of the interruption, but generally isr supplies several status bits. For example, for a TLB miss fault, isr provides three bits that indicate whether the fault was due to a read, write, or execute access. Registers ifa, iha, and itir are used primarily for virtual-memory-related faults and supply the faulting address, the VHPT walker hash address, and page size/protection key information, respectively. See Chapter 4, *Virtual Memory*, for details. The iim control register provides space for an immediate value that in some way is related to the cause of the interruption. For example, during a BREAK INSTRUCTION FAULT, iim is written with the immediate value encoded in the break instruction that triggered the fault.

Note that the interruption control registers (except for isr) are updated only if psr.ic is 1 at the time the interruption occurs. This property guarantees that once the CPU starts handling an interruption, the contents of these registers do not change unpredictably. Once the interruption handler has finished using them (either because it has handled the interruption or because it copied them to a safe location), the psr.ic bit can be turned back on. Of course, the converse implication is that an operating system generally must be careful not to trigger (or allow) another interruption to occur while psr.ic is 0. There are exceptions to this general rule, however, and in Chapter 4, *Virtual Memory*, we see how Linux/ia64 uses nested interruptions to resolve TLB misses.

Also, note that in the third step most bits in the psr are cleared to 0. In particular, fields cpl and bn are both cleared. This means that the CPU will start executing the interruption handler with privilege-level 0 (most privileged) and with bank 0 of registers r16 through r31 activated.

IA-64 provides the rfi instruction to return from an interruption. It basically reverses the steps taken to initiate interruption handling. Specifically, it restores the processor status register and the instruction pointer from control registers ipsr and iip, respectively, and then resumes execution with the instruction slot contained in psr.ri. If ifs.v is set, then rfi also restores the register frame, in accordance with the frame marker in ifs.ifm. The rfi instruction serves as an implicit serialization point and acts as if a srlz.i instruction had been executed.

2.4   THE REGISTER STACK ENGINE (RSE)

The register stack is an abstraction that provides an unlimited number of registers. It can be accessed in a LIFO (last in, first out) fashion with a window of up to 96 logical registers at a time. It is the job of the register stack engine (RSE) to implement this abstraction with the help of a fixed number of physical registers and memory. For example, Itanium uses 96 physical registers for this purpose. Figure 2.17 illustrates how the RSE can handle this job. The left portion of the figure shows the logical view: at the top of the register stack we have the current register frame. This portion of the register stack can be accessed with logical register names r32–r127. Below the current frame, we see the register frames of earlier (less deeply nested) functions.

Now, looking at the right portion of the figure, we see how this logical register stack is mapped to the physical registers and memory: the top portion of the register stack is kept in physical registers, and the lower portion is kept in memory. The memory reserved for

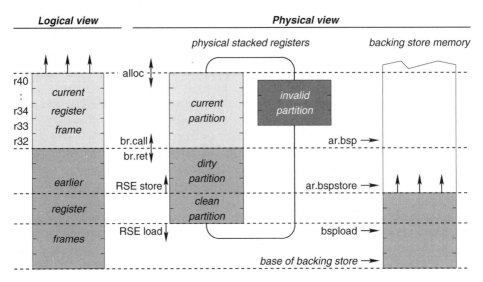

Figure 2.17. Logical view of the register stack and physical realization.

backing up the register stack is called the *register backing store* (or just *backing store*). The middle portion of the figure illustrates that the RSE maintains the physical registers as a ring of four partitions: the **current**, **dirty**, **clean**, and **invalid** partitions. As the name suggests, the **current** partition consists of the physical registers that hold the contents of the current register frame. The **dirty** partition consists of physical registers that are part of the logical register stack but whose contents have not yet been written to the backing store. The **clean** partition contains physical registers that are also part of the logical register stack but whose contents have already been written to backing store memory. Finally, the **invalid** partition consists of physical registers that are not currently used by the register stack. The contents of these registers are undefined.

So how does the RSE manage the four partitions? By definition, the current partition always needs to be exactly as big as the current register frame. Thus, if the size of the current register frame is increased (e.g., by an alloc instruction), the RSE takes the necessary registers from the **invalid** partition. If this partition does not contain enough registers, the RSE can also steal additional registers from the **clean** partition, and if even those are not enough, it can steal from the **dirty** partition. Before stealing from the **dirty** partition, the RSE has to store the contents of the needed registers to backing store. On the other hand, if the size of the current register frame shrinks, the RSE can simply release the extraneous registers into the **invalid** partition. As illustrated in the figure, the line between the **current** and **dirty** partitions moves upward as a result of nested function calls (br.call) and moves downward when returning from function calls (br.ret). When the latter happens, the RSE can usually simply adjust the size of the **current** and **dirty** partitions accordingly. But if the **current** partition grows beyond the bounds of the **clean** partition, the RSE needs to steal some registers from the **invalid** partition and load the contents of the logical registers from the backing store. Of course, the entire idea behind the RSE is to minimize the number of times registers have to be stored to the backing store or loaded from it. As long as the changes in the height of the register stack remain mostly within the number of available physical registers, the CPU can avoid most RSE memory traffic. On a final note, we should point out that the only way the **clean** partition can become nonempty is when the RSE decides to speculatively store or load stacked registers, ahead of their anticipated use.

In the right portion of Figure 2.17 we see that the RSE uses three registers to maintain the association between the active partitions and the backing store: application register bsp (backing store pointer) points to the backing store location that would be used to store the content of the physical register corresponding to r32 in the current register frame. Application register bspstore (backing store write pointer) points to the backing store location that will be written on the next RSE store. In other words, if the RSE needs to clean a register from the **dirty** partition, it simply writes that register to the address in bspstore and then increments the address. The lower boundary of the clean partition is maintained by an RSE internal register called bspload. The register is RSE internal in the sense that it is not part of the user-level (or even system) CPU state and there are no instructions that can directly read or write its content. Instead, the register is maintained entirely by the RSE. When the RSE needs to grow the clean partition in the downward direction, it simply loads the register content from the address in bspload and then decrements the address. Conversely, if the RSE needs to steal a register for the current partition, it simply increments bspload and then uses the freed physical register.

2.4.1 The register stack configuration register (rsc)

The RSE operates asynchronously to the CPU. Its operation is controlled by the application register rsc (register stack configuration). The format of this register is illustrated in Figure 2.18. The least significant two bits form the mode field, which controls how aggressive the RSE may be in issuing stores and loads. There are four modes:

- *enforced lazy* (rsc.mode $= 0$): In this mode, the RSE must not issue any RSE loads or stores unless they are mandatory. *Mandatory RSE stores* occur when the current register frame grows upward (e.g., as a result of an alloc) and the RSE needs to steal registers from the **dirty** partition. *Mandatory RSE loads* occur when the current register frame grows downward (e.g., as a result of a br.ret) beyond the registers covered by the **dirty** and **clean** partitions.

- *store intensive* (rsc.mode $= 1$): This mode is like **enforced lazy** mode, except that the RSE may issue stores speculatively (eagerly). Such speculative accesses could be used to take advantage of memory bus bandwidth that would otherwise go unused.

- *load intensive* (rsc.mode $= 2$): This mode is like **enforced lazy** mode, except that the RSE may issue loads speculatively (eagerly).

- *eager* (rsc.mode $= 3$): In this mode the RSE may issue both stores and loads speculatively.

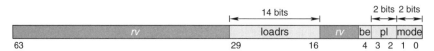

Figure 2.18. Format of register stack configuration register (rsc).

The mode field is treated as a hint, and the architecture does not require support for speculative RSE accesses. For example, the Itanium CPU model does not support them and effectively operates in **enforced lazy** mode at all times. The architecture also does not specify the exact policy used to decide whether or when to issue a speculative RSE access. This gives room to CPU designers to come up with policies that get as close as possible to the ideal case where the **clean** partition is managed such that the CPU never has to stall when calling or returning from a function. However, the architecture does require that speculative RSE accesses must not generate faults (such as TLB miss faults). In other words, if rsc.mode has a non-zero value, the RSE is at liberty to issue a speculative access, but if anything goes wrong, the access must be canceled and everything must appear as if it had never been issued. Another consequence of a non-zero value in rsc.mode is that the contents of rnat and bspstore can change unpredictably. To ensure that code does not accidentally rely on model-specific behavior, the architecture requires all instructions that read or affect these registers to be issued while the RSE is in **enforced lazy** mode. Violating this constraint triggers an ILLEGAL OPERATION FAULT.

The second field in the rsc register, pl, contains the privilege level that is used for RSE memory accesses. Attempting to write to this field a value that is numerically smaller than the value of the current privilege level (psr.cpl) has the effect of writing the current privilege level. In other words, a program may configure the RSE to run at the current privilege level or at any less-privileged (numerically higher) level, but never at a more-privileged (numerically lower) level. The third field, be, controls the byte order used for RSE accesses. As for psr.be, a 0 in this field indicates little-endian byte order, and a 1 indicates big-endian byte order. The third and last field, loadrs, is used as an implicit argument to the loadrs instruction. We describe this instruction in more detail later in this chapter.

2.4.2 Dealing with NaT bits

One important detail we have glossed over so far is that the stacked registers are 65 bits wide (because of the NaT bit), but the memory words in the backing store are, of course, only 64 bits wide. The RSE deals with this difference in the following fashion: when storing the content of a stacked register, it writes only the data portion of the register (bits 0 through 63) to memory and places the NaT bit in a temporary buffer. It keeps doing this until the 63rd NaT bit has been collected, and, at that point, it writes the collected NaT bits to the backing store and starts anew. The buffer that serves as the temporary storage area for the NaT bits is called the rnat register (RSE NaT collection register) and is part of the application register file. It is 64 bits wide, but since it contains at most 63 NaT bits, the most significant bit remains unused (it is ignored by the RSE).

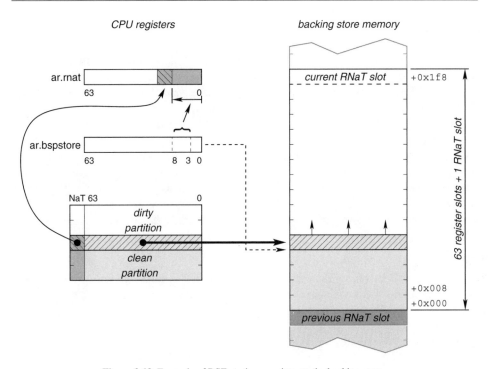

Figure 2.19. Example of RSE storing a register to the backing store.

Now, if we look at the pattern that the RSE generates in the backing store memory, we would find it divided into frames of 64 slots: the first 63 slots of each frame contain the data portion of saved registers, and the 64th slot contains the corresponding NaT bits. For brevity, we refer to the former as *register slots* and the latter as *RNaT slots*. The RSE assumes that each frame of 64 slots is aligned on a 512-byte boundary. This alignment is convenient because it means that the least significant nine bits of a backing store address can be used to determine whether the word at that address is an RNaT slot or a register slot. Furthermore, if it is a register slot, bits 3 through 8 of the address can be used as a bit index in the RNaT collection word to determine the corresponding NaT bit.

Figure 2.19 uses a simple example to show how this all works. Suppose the RSE decides that it is time to write a register from the **dirty** partition to the backing store. The stacked registers are illustrated in the lower-left portion of the figure. Since these registers operate as a ring buffer, the RSE would choose the first **dirty** register above the **clean** partition for writeback. In the figure, this register is represented as a shaded box. As explained earlier, the RSE would save the data portion of the register simply by writing it to the memory address contained in register bspstore. This step is illustrated by the bold arrow pointing to the right. At the same time, it would save the NaT bit by copying it to the rnat bit determined by bits 3 through 8 of bspstore. For example, if the address in bspstore ended in 0x000, bit 0 would be used; if it ended in `0x008`, bit 1 would be used; and so on up to `0x1f0`, which would correspond to bit 62. After saving the stacked register in this fashion, the RSE would then increment the address in bspstore by 8 and check whether the address now ends with `0x1f8`. If not, the RSE has finished saving the register. If the address does end with `0x1f8`, the RSE must write the content of rnat to the current RNaT slot (whose address is in bspstore now) and increment the address in bspstore by 8 again.

While the example illustrates only how stacked registers are saved to the backing store, it is easy to see how restoring a register would work: the data portion is restored from the register slot pointed to by bspload, and the NaT bit is restored by being copied from the corresponding bit in rnat. After restoring a register in this fashion, bspload is decremented by 8. If the new address ends in `0x1f8`, the RSE needs to load the RNaT collection word at that address into rnat and decrement bspload by 8 again.

2.4.3 RSE arithmetic

The fact that every 64th word on the register backing store is an RNaT slot introduces a discontinuity that makes it difficult to describe or reason about the RSE with ordinary linear arithmetic. To avoid this problem, we introduce three simple convenience operators:

$$\text{slot}(x) = \lfloor x/8 \rfloor \pmod{63}$$

$$x \oplus n = \begin{cases} x + 8n + 8\lfloor(\text{slot}(x)+n)/63\rfloor & \text{if } n >= 0 \\ x + 8n - 8\lfloor(62-\text{slot}(x)-n)/63\rfloor & \text{if } n < 0 \end{cases}$$

$$x \ominus y = (x-y)/8 - \left\lfloor \frac{\text{slot}(y)+(x-y)/8}{64} \right\rfloor \quad \text{for all } x > y$$

In these definitions, x and y are assumed to be naturally-aligned backing store addresses that point to register slots and n is assumed to be a register count. The first operator, $\text{slot}(x)$, returns the slot number of the register slot addressed by x. As the definition shows, the slot number is given simply by dividing the address by the size of a backing store word (8) and taking the integer part of this result modulo 63. In other words, the slot number is in the range of 0 to 62 and indicates the relative position of x within a backing store frame. The second operator, $x \oplus n$, returns the address of the register slot obtained after the backing store pointer x is advanced by n register slots. If n is positive, the backing store pointer is advanced toward higher addresses, simulating the effect of saving n registers to the backing store. Conversely, if n is negative, the backing store pointer is advanced toward lower addresses, simulating the effect of restoring n registers from the backing store. The definition for the case in which n is positive can be understood intuitively: x is advanced by the amount of space required for n registers ($8n$), and the expression $8\lfloor(\text{slot}(x)+n)/63\rfloor$ takes care of skipping any RNaT collection words that may be encountered as x is advanced. The definition for the case in which n is negative operates basically in the same way, except that it counts the number of RNaT collection words encountered by measuring the distance of the final slot from the *upper* end of the RSE frame. This calculation is illustrated in Figure 2.20 (for space reasons, this figure shows the backing store rotated right by 90 degrees so that memory addresses progress from left to right). The third operator, $x \ominus y$, returns the number of register slots between backing store pointers x and y. This operator is defined

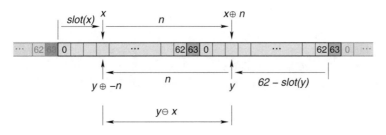

Figure 2.20. Effects of RSE operations.

only if $y < x$. The definition for this operator calculates the number of words between the two pointers $((x - y)/8)$ and then subtracts the number of RNaT collection words that lie between them.

The $\oplus$ and $\ominus$ symbols were chosen to help us remember their meaning: the former "adds" registers to the backing store and returns the new backing store pointer; the latter "subtracts" two backing store pointers and returns the number of register slots between them. However, this does not mean that the normal rules of addition and subtraction apply! For example, unlike ordinary addition, $\oplus$ is neither commutative nor associative. Fortunately, it is still possible to find a small number of rules that are sufficient to describe the RSE operations encountered in this book. These rules are given below:

$$(x \oplus n) \oplus -n = x \qquad (2.4.1)$$
$$(x \oplus n) \ominus x = n \qquad (2.4.2)$$
$$x \oplus (m + n) = (x \oplus m) \oplus n \qquad (2.4.3)$$
$$x \oplus (y \ominus x) = y \qquad (2.4.4)$$

Proving these rules correct is straightforward, but for this book it is sufficient if we can develop an intuitive idea of how they work. Rule (2.4.1) states that saving n registers starting at backing store pointer x and then restoring n registers yields the original backing store pointer x. Rule (2.4.2) states that advancing backing store pointer x by n register slots and then calculating the number of register slots between this pointer and x yields n again. Rule (2.4.3) states that advancing backing store pointer x by $(m + n)$ register slots gives the same result as advancing x first by m and then by n register slots. Finally, rule (2.4.4) is essentially the inverse of (2.4.2): it says that advancing a backing store pointer x by the number of register slots contained between another backing store pointer y and x yields y.

2.4.4 Convenience routines for RSE arithmetic

Operating systems frequently have to manipulate the RSE, and even user-level programs sometimes need to do so. For this reason, Linux/ia64 provides access to the operators we just introduced in an interface called the *RSE convenience routines* (file include/asm-ia64/rse.h). This interface is illustrated in Figure 2.21. As shown there, the first three rou-

unsigned long **ia64_rse_slot_num**(x);	/* *returns* slot(x) */
unsigned long *__ia64_rse_skip_regs__(x, n);	/* *returns* $x \oplus n$ */
unsigned long **ia64_rse_num_regs**(y, x);	/* *returns* $x \ominus y$ */
unsigned long **ia64_rse_is_rnat_slot**(x);	/* *returns* slot(x) = 63 */
unsigned long *__ia64_rse_rnat_addr__(x);	/* *returns* $x \oplus (62 - \text{slot}(x)) + 8$ */

Figure 2.21. RSE convenience routines.

Table 2.8. Instructions affecting the RSE (first part).

		Instruction		
Affected state	**alloc** r_1 = **ar.pfs**,*i,l,o,r*	**br.call**	**br.ret**	**rfi** (*if* ifs.v = 1)
r_1	pfs			
bsp		bsp $\oplus$ cfm.sol	bsp $\oplus$ −pfs.sol	bsp $\oplus$ −ifs.ifm.sof
pfs		pfm ← cfm pec ← ec ppl ← psr.cpl		
cfm	sof ← $i+l+o$ sol ← $i+l$ sor ← $r/8$ rrb ← 0	sof ← sof − sol sol ← 0 sor ← 0 rrb ← 0	pfs.pfm	ifs.ifm

tines are *ia64_rse_slot_num()*, *ia64_rse_skip_regs()*, and *ia64_rse_num_regs()*. They correspond directly to RSE arithmetic operators slot(), $\oplus$, and $\ominus$, respectively. Routine *ia64_rse_is_rnat_slot()* simply tests whether a given backing store address is an RNaT slot. Related to this is *ia64_rse_rnat_addr()*; it returns the address of the RNaT slot of a frame when given the address of any slot in that frame.

2.4.5 Instructions that affect the RSE

We now have all the machinery in place to make it easy to describe the effects that various instructions have on the RSE. These instructions include alloc, br.call, br.ret, rfi, cover, flushrs, loadrs, and the mov instruction that writes to application register bspstore. Their effects are summarized in Tables 2.8 and 2.9.

Let us start with alloc in Table 2.8. We already know that this instruction resizes the current register frame and that it takes six operands. As illustrated in the table, the instruction has the effect of saving the content of pfs in the destination operand (r_1). It also modifies the content of cfm by setting the sof (size of frame) field to the total number of registers desired ($i+l+o$), sol (size of locals) to the number of input and local registers ($i+l$), and sor (size of rotating partition) to the number of rotating registers (counted in groups of eight). The table uses the symbolic assignment of 0 to rrb to represent the fact that the instruction clears all rotating register bases to 0.

Table 2.9. Instructions affecting the RSE (second part).

Affected state	Instruction			
	cover	flushrs	loadrs	mov ar.bspstore=r_2
bsp	bsp $\oplus$ cfm.sof			$r_2 \oplus$ ndirty
bspstore		bsp	bsp $-$ rsc.loadrs	r_2
bspload		*CPU specific*	bsp $-$ rsc.loadrs	r_2
rnat		*updated*	*undefined*	*undefined*

ifs	*if* psr.ic $= 0$:
	    ifs.ifm $\leftarrow$ cfm
	    ifs.v $\leftarrow$ 1			

cfm	sof $\leftarrow 0$ sol $\leftarrow 0$ sor $\leftarrow 0$ rrb $\leftarrow 0$			

Observing the effect of br.call is rather interesting. As shown in Table 2.8, it works by advancing bsp by the number of local registers (including input registers) and using pfs to save the old content of cfm, the ec application register, and the current privilege level. The br.call instruction then establishes the shape of the new register frame in cfm by decrementing sof by the number of local registers and clearing sol, sor, and all rotating register bases. As we would expect, br.ret is simply the reverse of br.call: instead of advancing bsp, it decrements it; and instead of saving the old frame marker, it restores it from pfs.pfm. Of course, it also restores the original value of ec and the original privilege level, but those steps are not shown in the table. What may be more surprising is how similar the rfi instruction is to br.ret as far as the RSE is concerned. Basically, the two instructions have the same effect, except that rfi uses the ifs control register instead of the pfs application register and decrements bsp by the total size of the frame instead of just the size of the locals. The net effect is that rfi restores the entire register frame of the function that was active at the time of the interruption, which is the desired behavior.

From Table 2.9 we can see how the RSE-related control instructions work. The cover instruction can be used to push the entire current register frame into the **dirty** partition and allocate an empty frame (*NULL frame*). These actions are useful when an interruption is handled because they save the register frame that was active at the time of the interruption and protect it from accidental modification by the interruption handler. Looking at the table, we see that the instruction also has the side effect of saving cfm in control register ifs and marking its content valid. However, this step is omitted unless psr.ic is 0 at the time the instruction is executed.

The flushrs instruction is easy to understand. Its effect is to get rid of the **dirty** partition by forcing the RSE to save its contents to the backing store. Assuming the RSE is operating in **enforced lazy** mode, this means that after flushrs is executed, bspstore and bsp are guaranteed to contain the same value. As the name suggests, loadrs is the exact opposite:

it creates a **dirty** partition by forcing the RSE to load a certain number of bytes from the backing store. The number of bytes to load must be an integer multiple of 8 and is specified implicitly by the field loadrs in the rsc application register. A side effect of this instruction is that the **clean** partition is empty afterward. Because of this, using loadrs to load 0 bytes from the backing store can be used as a quick way to invalidate all registers outside the current register frame. Unlike flushrs, this instruction cannot be executed unless the RSE operates in **enforced lazy** mode. An additional constraint is that either the size of the current frame or the number of bytes loaded must be 0. This constraint may seem odd, but it is necessary to ensure that all IA-64 programs can execute on any CPU model, independently of the number of physical stacked registers that are implemented.

The last instruction in Table 2.9 is the mov instruction that writes to bspstore. It switches the backing store from one memory area to another. As we would expect, it writes the address in the second operand (r_2) to bspstore, but that is not its only effect. First, note that the table shows that bspload also gets set to this value. This means that the **clean** partition is empty afterward. In contrast, writing bspstore preserves the contents of the **dirty** partition. In the table, this is represented by the fact that bsp is set to $r_2 \oplus$ ndirty. Here, ndirty is the number of registers in the dirty partition. This implies that switching the backing store area by itself never causes the RSE to write any registers to memory.

2.5 SUMMARY

In this chapter, we introduced the IA-64 architecture in four steps. First, we described the user-visible portion of the architecture. This included the unprivileged register files, the instruction set, and the major architectural features such as speculation and modulo-scheduled loops. Second, we introduced the IA-64 software conventions. Here, we covered important issues such as the data model and the register usage model. A brief introduction into IA-64 assembly programming was also included. We then described the system architecture, which is key to implementing an operating system such as Linux. This part covered the privileged register files and the privileged instructions. In the last step, we described the register stack engine (RSE). Since this is an extraordinary feature of IA-64, we explored its operation in a fair amount of detail and defined a few rules that apply to RSE arithmetic. In Chapter 5, *Kernel Entry and Exit*, we take advantage of this arithmetic to describe how the Linux kernel manages the RSE.

Chapter 3

Processes, Tasks, and Threads

From the perspective of a user, the process is *the* key abstraction of UNIX-like operating systems such as Linux. A process primarily provides two virtualized resources: a virtual address space and a virtual CPU. The former lets the process allocate and manage memory as if it were the only process in the machine. Similarly, the virtual CPU makes it appear as if the process owned the CPU, even though it may actually be sharing the CPU with other processes. Virtual CPUs are usually called *threads of execution*, or simply *threads*. Traditional UNIX systems offered exactly one thread per process, but on modern systems, processes can create as many additional threads as needed. The facilities required to create and manage multiple threads of execution are usually contained in a separate library. The most popular library used for this purpose is the *pthread library*. The "p" in "pthread" comes from the fact that the library's interface is defined by a POSIX standard [50, 55]. This library provides the data structures and operations needed to create new threads, coordinate their execution, and terminate threads that are no longer needed.

Figure 3.1 illustrates the UNIX process model both for single- and multithreaded applications. On the left side, a single-threaded process is shown; the rounded box represents the address space of the process, and the wiggly line represents the single thread of execution. On the right side, a multithreaded process is shown. It looks identical, except that it has multiple wiggly lines, representing the multiple POSIX threads.

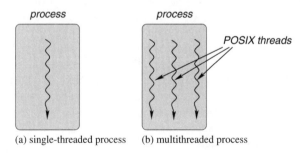

(a) single-threaded process (b) multithreaded process

Figure 3.1. UNIX process model.

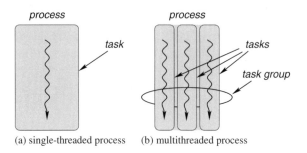

Figure 3.2. Linux process model.

Now, the reason we are so careful in defining the UNIX process model is that Linux uses a different model, which is compatible at the user level, but more flexible. The Linux model is centered around the *task* abstraction and is illustrated in Figure 3.2. The figure also illustrates single- and multithreaded processes. If we look at the left side, we see that there is virtually no difference compared to a single-threaded UNIX process. Indeed, the only difference is that in Linux, such a process is known as a *task*. However, if we look at the right side of the figure, we see that multithreaded processes are quite different. As shown in Figure 3.2, there is a separate task for each thread of execution. There is no kernel object that directly corresponds to the process. Instead, the process simply consists of a group of tasks that share the same address space. What this means is that Linux tasks share some of the properties of a UNIX process, but at the same time, they also share some of the properties of a POSIX thread. For example, Linux tasks have a unique task ID that serves the same function as a UNIX process ID. Each task also is associated with an address space, which provides the environment in which the task is executing. On the other hand, a task represents one and only one thread of execution, and in this sense, it is more like a POSIX thread. The reason Linux is using this model becomes clearer later in this chapter. The important thing to remember here is that tasks play the same role in Linux that single-threaded processes do in UNIX, yet they can also be used to realize multithreaded processes.

The Linux kernel represents each task with a kernel object known as the *task structure*. This structure consists of two major parts: a platform-independent part and a platform-specific part known as the *thread structure*. The thread structure contains the machine state (CPU state) needed to represents a single thread of execution. In contrast, the platform-independent part of the task structure provides the *environment* in which the thread executes. Loosely speaking, the thread structure corresponds to a wiggly line in Figure 3.2, and the remainder of the task structure corresponds to the box surrounding the line. This distinction is important because the platform-independent part of Linux takes care of handling virtually all task-related aspects, including the creation, execution, and termination of tasks. On the other hand, virtually all thread-related aspects are handled by platform-specific code. The two portions of the Linux kernel interact with each other through the *thread interface*. We need to emphasize here that this interface has nothing to do with the pthread library interface. The Linux-internal thread interface is much more primitive than the POSIX thread interface, but, unfortunately, both use the term *"thread"* for similar, but different, things. This collision of names is unfortunate but unavoidable. To eliminate confusion, this book consistently uses the term *"thread"* to refer to the Linux-internal notion of a thread. For any kind of POSIX-like thread, we use the term *"POSIX thread"* instead.

The primary goal of this chapter is to define the Linux thread interface, explain its role in the task infrastructure, and discuss its implementation for the IA-64 platform. Specifically, the chapter is organized as follows: the first section is an introduction to the Linux task infrastructure. It provides a brief description of the task data structure, the way in which tasks are created, and a historical perspective on how the task infrastructure evolved over time. The second section introduces the thread interface and describes its properties and implementation as realized for the IA-64 architecture. The discussion in this section focuses on individual threads. Of course, to be truly useful, threads have to interact with each other and with the external world, e.g., through I/O devices. Such interactions are enabled by the Linux *thread synchronization interface*, which is the subject of the third section. As we see there, Linux provides a variety of synchronization primitives, each tailored for a specific purpose. The final section concludes by highlighting and summarizing the most important points covered in this chapter.

3.1 INTRODUCTION TO LINUX TASKS

Linux tasks can be thought of as being equivalent to a single-threaded UNIX process. It is, therefore, not surprising that it is the most complex kernel data structure in existence. Fortunately, for this discussion it is not necessary to understand every nook and cranny of the task structure. A high-level understanding of its contents is sufficient. We can summarize the task structure as containing the following primary attributes:

- **Task info:** Consists of a unique task ID, as well as the inheritance tree information that defines the parent/child relationship among the tasks in the system. The task ID is similar to the UNIX process ID (*pid*), except that each task has its own ID. This attribute also includes a *task group ID* (*tgid*), which can be used to identify a group of tasks that belong to the same process.

- **Address space:** Defines the virtual address space of the task.

- **Scheduling info:** Contains the execution status of the task (runnable, blocked, stopped, etc.), the CPU scheduling policy, and scheduling parameters such as the dynamic priority. Also included is a flag called *need_resched*, which, when set, indicates that the task needs to invoke the Linux scheduler as soon as possible.

- **Executable info:** Identifies the file that provides the executable image for this task.

- **Signal info:** Consists of various signal-related information, such as the signal handler table, the pending signal mask, and a signal queue.

- **Credentials:** Determines the rights and privileges of the task. Example credentials are the user ID (*uid*), group IDs (*gids*), and the capability mask used to determine whether a specific resource, such as a device, may be accessed.

- **Accounting info:** Used to collect various per-task statistics, such as the time at which the task was created, how much time it has spent executing at the user and kernel level, how many page faults and page-swap operations it has encountered, etc.

- **Resource Limits:** Consists of various per-task limits, such as the core dump size limit, execution time limit, maximum number of open file descriptors, and so on.

- **Filesystem info:** Contains miscellaneous filesystem-related information, such as the default file permission mask (*umask*) and the current working directory.

- **Open file table:** Holds the table of files opened by the task.

- **Miscellaneous:** Consists of other minor attributes, such as a reference to the terminal associated with the task (*controlling terminal*).

Note that multithreaded processes contain one task for each POSIX thread. This means that the above information is replicated for each POSIX thread and, considering that each POSIX thread shares almost all process-related information, we may wonder whether this replication is wasteful. Yes, there is some duplication of information, but it is not nearly as bad as it may seem at first. The reason is that most task attributes are actually implemented as separate objects. Thus, the task structure usually does not store the entire attribute, but only a reference to it. For example, the filesystem info is stored in its own, reference-counted, *filesystem structure* (struct fs_struct in file include/linux/fs_struct.h), and the task structure contains only a pointer to this object. Even so, replication obviously does cost a little extra memory. However, we also need to consider that replication provides two important benefits. First, as we will see below, it enables fine-grained control over what attributes are to be shared when a new task is created. Second, it simplifies MP locking because the CPU that is executing on behalf of a task owns the corresponding task structure and hence does not need to acquire a lock before accessing it.

The kernel frequently needs to access the task structure associated with the currently executing task. For this purpose, Linux provides the *current task pointer* (*current* in file include/asm/current.h). On a UP machine, at most one task can be executing at any given time and *current* can be realized as a global variable. However, on an MP machine, each CPU executes a different task. A single *current* pointer therefore is not sufficient. Instead, each CPU must have its own version of the variable. The best way to realize that is with a CPU-local variable. With this approach, a CPU can use *current* to refer to the task that the CPU is currently executing. There are different ways to realize CPU-local variables (see Chapter 8, *Symmetric Multiprocessing*), but since *current* is so frequently used, most platforms dedicate a register to it. For example, on IA-64 register r13 is used for this purpose. The GNU C compiler supports the declaration of global register variables with the **asm** directive. For instance, on IA-64 the current pointer can be declared as follows:

```
register struct task_struct *current asm ("r13");
```

This declaration tells the compiler that it can assume that register r13 contains the value of variable *current*. Not only is this a convenient way for declaring a CPU-local variable, it is also efficient because it avoids the memory access that is normally needed to read a global variable. For this reason, most platforms use a dedicated register regardless of whether the kernel is intended for UP or MP machines.

3.1.1 Task creation

The *clone2()* system call is the fundamental primitive used to create new tasks. A user-level process normally invokes *fork()* to create a new process or invokes *pthread_create()* to create a POSIX thread. However, beneath the surface, both are using *clone2()* to get the job done. The interface for this system call is shown below:

```
int clone2(flags, ustack-base, ustack-size);
```

By default, this call behaves just like *fork()*. That is, *clone2()* creates a new task (the child) that is logically an identical copy of the caller (the parent). The only major difference between the two tasks is that the child has its own unique task ID. Since the call creates a copy of the parent task, it returns twice: in the parent it returns the child's task ID, and in the child it returns 0.

Note that *clone2()* by default makes a *copy* of the parent task. This means that the address space, filesystem info, and all the other task attributes start out with the identical values. However, once created, the child is independent of the parent and all modifications to the task structure affect only the child task. Similarly, changes in the parent task will not be reflected in the child task.

The versatility of the *clone2()* system call derives from the *flags* argument. The argument has two components: a signal field that specifies the signal that should be sent to the parent when the child terminates; and a set of 1-bit flags that specify the task attributes that should be shared between the parent and the child. Table 3.1 lists the names and descriptions for these flags. For example, if the CLONE_VM flag is set, the child shares the address space with the parent. Hence, all modifications the parent makes to the address space will be visible to the child, and vice versa.

This system call can be used to create a POSIX thread: the parent simply invokes the system call with flags CLONE_VM, CLONE_FS, CLONE_FILES, and CLONE_SIGNAL turned on. This yields a child task that executes in the same address space as the parent and also shares the filesystem info, open file table, pending signals, and signal handlers with the parent—just as expected for a POSIX thread.

There is just one complication: if the child task really is an identical copy of the parent and they both share the same address space, then their stacks will also share the same memory! This is, of course, not meaningful since it would quickly crash one or both tasks because of stack corruption. This is where the remaining system call arguments come into play: *ustack-base* and *ustack-size* allow the caller to specify the memory area that should be used for the stack in the child task. Thus, as long as the parent specifies a separate stack area when calling *clone2()* with the CLONE_VM flag turned on, the child will get its own stack and everything will work fine.

Table 3.1. *clone2()* flags.

Flag name	Description
CLONE_VM	If set, the address space is shared between the parent and the child.
CLONE_FS	If set, the filesystem info (current working directory, etc.) is shared between the parent and the child.
CLONE_FILES	If set, the open file table is shared between the parent and the child.
CLONE_SIGHAND	If set, the set of pending signals and the signal handler table are shared between the parent and the child.
CLONE_THREAD	If set, the child is part of the same task group as the parent.
CLONE_SIGNAL	Combines the effects of CLONE_SIGHAND and CLONE_THREAD.
CLONE_PTRACE	If set, the child also is being traced (run under the control of a debugger) if the parent is being traced.
CLONE_VFORK	If set, the parent does not get scheduled for execution until the child invoke the *execve()* system call.
CLONE_PARENT	If set, the new task becomes a sibling of the caller. That is, the caller and the new task share the same parent.
CLONE_PID	If set, the child has the same task ID as the parent. This creates various problems because there is no way to distinguish between the parent and the child task. For this reason, this flag should not normally be used (see Chapter 10, *Booting*, for an exception to this rule).

Note that *fork()* and *pthread_create()* are just the two extreme cases of task creation. The *clone2()* system call permits intermediate cases where some, but not all, task attributes are shared between the parent and the child. For example, an Internet server that deals with thousands of network connections might want to create tasks that share the address space but not the open file table.

How the kernel creates a new task

Now that we understand how user-level processes request the creation of a new task, let us take a closer look at what the kernel needs to do in response to a *clone2()* system call. Creating a new task involves the following steps:

1. Allocating memory for the new task.

2. Starting task initialization.

3. Creating a thread.

4. Finishing task initialization.

5. Entering the task in the run queue.

The first step may seem trivial, but memory allocation is relatively slow, so Linux takes great care to do this as efficiently as possible. Indeed, the kernel allocates a single block of physically contiguous memory that is then used to hold all task-related state, including the

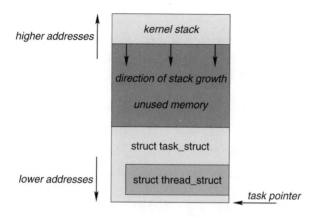

Figure 3.3. Typical task layout.

task structure and thread state. Some of the thread state is stored in the task structure itself. This state is called the *thread structure* (struct thread_struct in file include/asm/processor.h). Even though it is part of the task structure, the platform-independent part of the kernel cannot make any direct use of it, because its content is CPU specific. However, including the thread structure in the task structure provides platform-specific code a fast and convenient way to locate the thread state when given a task pointer.

How the allocated memory is used is somewhat platform specific. Figure 3.3 shows a typical layout. The task structure occupies the lowest part of the allocated memory. Included is the thread structure whose size is CPU-specific and can vary from a few bytes to more than a kilobyte. The memory above the task structure is typically used for the kernel stack. On most platforms, the stack grows toward lower addresses and the stack pointer is initialized to the top of the allocated memory. Note that if the kernel stack were to grow too large, it would overwrite the task structure and the kernel would quickly crash. This means the kernel needs to be careful not to put too much pressure on the stack. It is a common mistake by novice kernel programmers to declare large automatic variables, e.g., a temporary string buffer, or to use deeply nested recursive algorithms; both of these practices tend to cause kernel stack overflows. However, with a properly designed kernel, no stack overflow should ever occur (more on this in Chapter 7, *Device I/O*). Still, it is usually a smart choice to let the kernel stack grow toward the task structure. The reason is that this choice aids in debugging new code; if the code is faulty and causes a stack overflow, chances are that the task structure will be corrupted first. If so, the usual result is that the faulty task will crash but without taking down the entire kernel. Of course, there is no guarantee that this will always work, but in practice this heuristic is surprisingly useful.

The second step of task creation consists of initializing most of the task structure. This is where most of the task attributes are either copied or set up to be shared between the parent and the child.

The third step creates a new thread by calling the platform-specific *copy_thread()* routine. We describe this operation in the next section.

In the second-to-last step, the platform-independent task initialization is completed. In the final step, the new task is entered in the run queue and is thus now ready for execution. It should be noted that even though the child thread is created in the third step, it is entered into the run queue only in the last step. This is done to avert the danger of the child being scheduled for execution before the parent has initialized it.

3.1.2 Historical perspective

The process, task, and thread model described in this chapter was not incorporated into Linux right from the beginning. In fact, the initial version of Linux, released in 1991, employed the traditional UNIX process model, where each process has exactly one task and therefore one thread of execution [9]. This model, though old, is both powerful and elegant because it provides multiprocessing at the level of processes without exposing applications to the complexities of concurrent programming—the early UNIX application programmer never had to worry about concurrency, since it was all hidden within the kernel.

In the mid-1990s, shared-memory symmetric multiprocessor (SMP) machines became increasingly popular and with them came a desire to exploit multiple processors with algorithms that share data at a fine-grained level. For those algorithms to work effectively, the memory must be shared between multiple threads of execution. Thus, the concept of threads (also known as *lightweight processes*) was born, and the POSIX group eventually proposed the POSIX threads standard. This standard extended the UNIX process model by providing primitives to create and manage multiple threads of execution inside a single process.

It was clear that Linux also had to adapt to the new world. Perhaps it would have been most logical for Linux to adopt the POSIX standard and directly provide the necessary kernel primitives. However, Linus Torvalds, the creator of Linux, decided that the *resource fork*, or *rfork()*, system call invented for the Plan 9 operating system was more elegant and more flexible [54]. It seemed elegant because it would allow implementation of both *fork()* and *pthread_create()* with a single system call. It also promised to be more flexible because it permitted intermediate solutions between the extreme cases of the "copy everything" *fork()* and the "share everything" *pthread_create()*. Consequently, a stub for the *resource fork*-inspired *clone()* system call appeared as early as version 0.99.9 of kernel. At this point, the system call was not fully implemented, however. It simply was a synonym for the traditional *fork()* call. This situation did not change for a long time until in 1995, version 1.1.94 of the kernel added a full implementation of *clone()*. This system call operated like *clone2()*, except that the third argument (the size of the stack area, *ustack-size*) did not exist. The set of available clone flags was also slightly different.

Except for a few minor changes to the clone flags, this interface remained stable for about five years until version 2.3.99 of the kernel introduced *clone2()* to better support the IA-64 platform. Many other platforms continue to implement and use only the two-argument *clone()* system call. However, since *clone()* is identical to *clone2()* with the *ustack-size* argument value set to 0, it is reasonable to focus on *clone2()* in this book.

struct **pt_regs**;	/* thread's **scratch** registers */
struct **switch_stack**;	/* thread's **preserved** registers */
struct **thread_struct**;	/* miscellaneous thread state */
int **copy_thread**(nr, flags, ustack-base, ustack-size, task, regs);	
	/* create new thread */
struct task_structure ***switch_to**(prev,next);	/* switch context from prev to next */
start_thread(regs, ip, sp);	/* prepare thread for execve() */
flush_thread();	/* prepare thread for exit() */
exit_thread();	/* terminate thread */
release_thread(dead-task);	/* release thread's resources */

Figure 3.4. Thread interface.

3.2 THE THREAD INTERFACE

The previous section explained what a task is, how the Linux kernel creates tasks, and how it relies on the thread interface to abstract platform differences. With this background in place, we are now ready to take a closer look at the thread interface itself. Since the implementation of this interface is by definition platform specific, the actual implementations differ substantially from one architecture to another. However, the underlying principles are often similar, and this section focuses on describing these common principles. To give a concrete flavor of how these principles are realized in practice, we include a description of the IA-64 implementation. The two descriptions in combination should provide enough insights to make it easier to understand the thread implementations for the other platforms and should give many hints and ideas on how to implement it for a new platform.

The interface is outlined in Figure 3.4. It consists of three data structures and six routines. The data structures encapsulate the machine state of a single thread, and the routines let the kernel create, run, and terminate a thread as well as move a thread from one address space to another.

There are two unusual aspects to this interface: first, unlike most textbook implementations of threads [11, 64, 68, 69], Linux does *not* store the thread state in a single data structure. Instead, the state is distributed across three distinct structures called *pt-regs*, *switch-stack*, and *thread*. The pt-regs and switch-stack structures are stored on the thread's kernel stack, whereas the thread structure is part of the task structure. The second unusual aspect is that there is no function to create a pristine thread. Instead, Linux provides the *copy_thread()* function, which creates a copy, or *clone*, of the calling thread. In other words, each thread starts out as a copy of some other thread. The only exception is the initial thread. This thread is created in a special fashion at kernel boot time (see Chapter 10, *Booting*). All other threads are either direct or indirect descendants of the initial thread.

In the remainder of this section, we first describe each of the thread data structures and the way in which they combine to encapsulate the machine state. This discussion is followed by a detailed description of the six operations that the thread interface defines.

3.2.1 The pt-regs structure

Let us start with the *pt-regs structure* (struct pt_regs in file include/asm/ptrace.h). This structure encapsulates the minimum state that needs to be saved on entry to the kernel. The easiest way to determine what needs to be stored in this structure is to consider device interrupts. When a device interrupt occurs, enough state needs to be saved to make it possible to return from the interrupt handler and resume execution as if the interrupt had not happened at all (ignoring possible side effects of the interrupt handler). Naively, we might think it is necessary to save the entire machine state. Fortunately, if we consider the software conventions of any modern architecture, we find that there are two primary classes of registers: **preserved** and **scratch** (see Chapter 2, *IA-64 Architecture*). By definition, a function that is about to use a **preserved** register saves its value, e.g., on the memory stack, before overwriting it. When the function is done with the register, it restores the original value. Thus when the kernel is entered, it is generally not necessary to save **preserved** registers because any function called while executing in the kernel already takes care of preserving them. Consequently, pt-regs primarily needs to encapsulate the **scratch** registers.

It is important to keep pt-regs as small as possible because it is the most frequently used thread-related structure. To see this, consider that on every system call, interrupt, trap, or fault, the following sequence of events occurs:

1. Memory for the pt-regs structure is allocated on the kernel stack.

2. The **scratch** registers are saved in pt-regs.

3. The appropriate kernel handler is invoked.

4. The **scratch** registers are restored from pt-regs.

5. The memory for pt-regs is deallocated from the kernel stack.

Since both system calls and external interrupts can occur at arbitrarily high rates, keeping the size of pt-regs small minimizes the amount of state that needs to be saved on kernel entry and can provide a dramatic performance improvement.

Another important reason to keep this structure as small as possible is that several instances of the pt-regs structure may exist on the kernel stack at any given time because of nesting. On a platform where system calls, interrupts, traps, or faults can be nested up to N deep, the kernel stack needs to be at least as big as N times the size of the pt-regs structure. Thus, the smaller pt-regs, the smaller the kernel stack can be.

IA-64 implementation

As described in Chapter 2, *IA-64 Architecture*, IA-64 has a large number of **scratch** registers. Registers r1–r3, r8–r31, f6–f15, f32–f127 are just some of them, and altogether they amount to about 2 Kbytes of state. Saving and restoring all these registers upon every interrupt would be time consuming. For example, on a machine with a memory-write bandwidth of 2 Gbytes/s, entering the kernel would take upward of 1 μs.

Fortunately, the kernel never performs floating-point computations. In fact, on most platforms, the kernel never uses floating-point registers of its own, so there is no need to save them in the pt-regs structure. IA-64 is a bit unusual in this respect because even a pure integer program, such as the kernel, can execute more quickly if it has access to floating-point registers. For example, the IA-64 integer multiplication instruction does its work by using floating-point registers. Without access to floating-point registers, integer multiplications would have to be performed entirely in software, which would be substantially slower. Another example is that $\lfloor \log_2(i) \rfloor$, i.e., the integer base-two logarithm of i, can be calculated quickly with the normalization hardware present in the floating-point unit. The bottom line is that the IA-64 kernel benefits from having access to a few **scratch** floating-point registers. However, it does not need *all* of the more than 100 **scratch** registers defined by the software conventions. Instead, the kernel employs a modified convention where only registers f6 to f9 are permitted to be used as **scratch** registers. To enforce this convention, all kernel components are compiled with a special compiler option. This option marks **scratch** registers f10 to f16 and f32 to f127 as **fixed**, which tells the compiler not to use them. Since code generated by the compiler does not touch these registers, there is no need to save them in pt-regs. Of course, for this scheme to really work, manually written assembly code must also observe this special convention. Note that this restriction applies to **scratch** floating-point registers only. **Preserved** floating-point registers can still be used in a function if the compiler determines that their use would be beneficial to overall performance. The compiler simply has to save such registers on entry into the function and restore them at the end, as is usual for **preserved** registers.

Not having to save each and every floating-point **scratch** register reduces the size of pt-regs by about a factor of five: from 2 Kbytes down to about 400 bytes. On a machine with a write bandwidth of 2 Gbytes/s, saving this state would take just about 0.2 μs.

An IA-64–specific aspect of pt-regs that deserves special attention is how the NaT bits for the static general registers are handled. First, observe that the IA-64 software convention defines unat as a **preserved** register. Further note that on entry to the kernel, the static **scratch** registers, such as r2 and r3, have to be saved with a spill-form store (st8.spill). Each of these stores overwrites a particular bit in unat (see Chapter 2, *IA-64 Architecture*). Therefore, to avoid violating the software conventions, the kernel must save unat in pt-regs *before* spilling any static general registers. Fortunately, it is *not* necessary to save unat again *after* it has spilled the static general registers. The reason is that unat is a **preserved** register, so if another kernel function were to spill a register, it would take care of appropriately saving and restoring unat. The implication is that the unat value saved in the pt-regs is the unat value that was active when the kernel was entered. It does *not* contain the NaT bits of the static **scratch** registers saved in pt-regs. Determining where the latter bits are stored is, in general, quite difficult and usually requires inspection of the stack unwind information, as we describe in Chapter 6, *Stack Unwinding*.

3.2.2 The switch-stack structure

As the name suggests, the *switch-stack structure* (struct switch_stack in file include/asm-ptrace.h) is used whenever the kernel is about to switch execution from one thread to another. The switch-stack primarily contains the **preserved** registers. In combination, pt-regs and switch-stack encapsulate the minimal machine state that each thread requires for proper

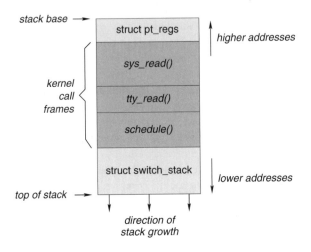

Figure 3.5. Kernel stack layout for blocked threads.

operation. This machine state is normally called the *eagerly managed state*, in contrast to *lazily managed state*. We will see some examples of the latter when discussing the thread structure.

To help us remember the purpose of the pt-regs and switch-stack structures, let us consider a specific example. Suppose a task wants to read a character from a terminal and invokes the *read()* system call for this purpose. If no input characters are available, the task will block execution. Once the task is blocked, the kernel stack might look as shown Figure 3.5: at the top of the figure, we can see the pt-regs structure that was created when the kernel was entered. Let us assume that the *read()* system call resulted in the invocation of function *sys_read()*, which in turn called *tty_read()*. Since we assumed that no input characters were available, *tty_read()* blocked the task by marking it as **blocked**, adding it to a wait queue, and forcing a context switch by calling *schedule()*. We can see this sequence of events by looking at the function call frames shown in the figure: right below the pt-regs structure is the call frame for *sys_read()*, which followed by the frame for *tty_read()*, which is followed by the frame for *schedule()*. Finally, at the bottom of the kernel stack, we see the switch-stack structure that was created by the context-switch routine.

Now, an interesting question is where the user-level machine state, i.e., the register values as they existed just before the kernel was entered, are saved. Since pt-regs encapsulates the user-level **scratch** registers and switch-stack encapsulates the **preserved** registers, it is tempting to think the two structures contain this state. Unfortunately, this is not always true. One of the kernel functions, say *tty_read()*, might have used a **preserved** register, in which case the user-level value of that register would have been saved in the call frame of that function and the value saved in switch-stack would be the value from *tty_read()*. In other words, unlike the pt-regs structure, the switch-stack structure often contains kernel values.

This means that, in general, the user-level values of **preserved** registers may be saved in the switch-stack itself or in any previous kernel call frame. Reconstructing the user-level values of **preserved** registers therefore requires finding the locations at which they were saved. On Linux/ia64, this reconstruction can be done reliably by means of the kernel stack unwind interface described in Chapter 6, *Stack Unwinding*.

Strictly speaking, Figure 3.5 is correct only for blocked threads that entered the kernel from user level. For kernel-only threads, pt-regs may or may not exist, depending on the platform Linux is running on. In the case of IA-64, pt-regs is guaranteed to exist because kernel-only threads maintain a dummy pt-regs structure. The kernel never actually reads anything from this dummy structure, but it does write to it sometimes. This is a small trick that makes the kernel stack layout more uniform and that can speed up execution of the context-switch routine, as we see on page 105.

IA-64 implementation

On IA-64, the switch-stack structure basically contains the **preserved** registers that are not already saved in the pt-regs structure. This includes general registers r4 to r7, floating-point registers f16 to f31, and branch registers b1 to b5, to name a few. There are, however, a few exceptions to this general rule.

The first exception is that the structure also contains registers f10 to f15, despite being **scratch** registers. As described earlier, the kernel never uses these registers and hence does not save them in pt-regs. However, since they are part of the eagerly managed state, the kernel must save them in the switch-stack. We might wonder what the point is of not saving them in pt-regs when they need to be saved in the switch-stack anyhow. Recall that pt-regs is used much more frequently, so keeping these registers in the switch-stack structure greatly reduces the frequency at which they need to be saved and restored.

The second exception is that the epilogue count register ec is not saved in the switch-stack, even though it is a **preserved** register. This is possible because the kernel follows two special rules. The first rule is that a root function must not modify ec. The second rule is that a routine that creates a switch-stack structure *must* be invoked like a regular function call. The first rule ensures that during execution in a root function, ec is guaranteed to contain the user-level value of the register. If a root function were to call another, more deeply nested kernel function, the IA-64 CPU would automatically copy the value of ec into the previous function state register pfs (see the description of br.call in Chapter 2, *IA-64 Architecture*). Since pfs is **preserved**, the user-level value of ec is also preserved. The second rule ensures that the value of ec is copied to pfs before a switch-stack structure is created, so that saving pfs also saves ec. Together the two rules guarantee that any value of the ec register, including the user-level value, can be reconstructed from one of the saved pfs values.

The third and final exception is that in some cases, a register is saved *both* in pt-regs and switch-stack. There are three principal reasons for this:

1. The Linux kernel short-circuits the return path of new threads (see page 108). For this to work, the kernel needs to be able to manipulate the address at which the new thread begins execution. This is most easily done by including the function return address

register in the switch-stack structure. On IA-64, register b0 (the return pointer) plays this role. Since this register is a **scratch** register, it also needs to be saved in pt-regs and it ends up being saved both in pt-regs and switch-stack.

2. Some **preserved** registers need to be modified on kernel entry. Before modifying them, the kernel must save their existing values in pt-regs. Since normal kernel execution may change the values in those registers again, it is also necessary to save them in the switch-stack. Registers bspstore, rnat, and unat are of this kind and are therefore saved both in pt-regs and switch-stack.

3. Predicate register pr provides broadside access to the sixty-four 1-bit predicates. Since some of the predicates are **scratch** and others are **preserved**, pr contains a mixture of **scratch** and **preserved** state and needs to be saved both in pt-regs and switch-stack. Note that it is safe to preserve what is normally considered a **scratch** predicate because, by definition, a **scratch** predicate has an undefined value after a function call, so preserving the previous value is certainly admissible. Similarly, saving the **preserved** predicates along with the **scratch** ones causes no harm and indeed enables some interesting optimizations. For example, the kernel entry/exit path (see Chapter 5, *Kernel Entry and Exit*) exploits this by using a **preserved** predicate to indicate whether or not the path is being executed because of a system call. This predicate does not have to be saved explicitly because it is saved in pt-regs along with all the **scratch** registers.

The unat register again needs some special consideration. Just as in the pt-regs case, the kernel must save the value in this register before it can spill the **preserved** static registers (r4–r7). In contrast to pt-regs, it is necessary to save unat *again* after those spills are done. Otherwise, the NaT bits for the **preserved** static registers could be lost during a context switch. This means that for a blocked thread such as the one shown in Figure 3.5, the unat register has been saved three times: the first value, in pt-regs, contains user-level NaT bits, the second value, in switch-stack, contains the NaT bits for the function that caused the thread to block, and the third value, also in switch-stack, contains the NaT bits of the static registers saved in the switch-stack.

3.2.3   The thread structure

The *thread structure* (struct thread_struct in file include/asm/processor.h) generally encapsulates lazily managed state. The major exception to this rule is the kernel stack pointer. By definition, this register points to the top of the stack. When a thread blocks, the last item allocated on the stack is the switch-stack structure and, for this reason, the stack pointer of a blocked thread always points to the switch-stack structure. This is illustrated in Figure 3.6, where it is assumed that the kernel stack pointer is saved in member *ksp* of the thread structure. Looking at the figure, the reason for saving the kernel stack pointer in the thread structure rather than the switch-stack structure should be quite clear: without it, there would be no way of determining *where* on the stack the switch-stack has been saved! Since the thread structure is part of the task structure, it has no such issue. And once the *ksp* value has been found, locating the switch-stack structure is trivial, too.

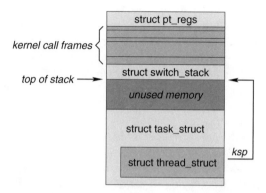

Figure 3.6. Using the saved kernel stack pointer (*ksp*) to locate the switch-stack structure.

A noteworthy point here is that in theory, the entire switch-stack structure could be made a part of the thread structure. However, this is usually not done because storing the switch-stack on the kernel stack is usually slightly more efficient.

Let us now turn attention to lazily managed state. In general, lazily managed state is switched not on every context switch, but only on demand, when it is clear that the new state really is needed. This approach results in a more efficient kernel if most threads do not use lazily managed state. To see this, suppose we have 100 round-robin scheduled threads in the system and only 5 of them use lazily managed state. Since the lazy state has to be switched only for the five threads that really use it, the kernel has to switch that state 20 times less frequently than the eagerly managed state! Considering that switching state takes time, lazily managed state can yield a significant increase in performance.

So what does it take to manage state lazily? In general, this trick can be used only if the kernel can precisely track when the registers in question are being accessed (read or written). For example, hardware breakpoint registers are typically privileged registers that are accessed only through the *ptrace()* system call. This makes it trivial for the kernel to keep track of which threads use the hardware breakpoint registers. Another example is the floating-point registers. Most CPUs permit access to these registers to be disabled. Attempting to access a disabled floating-point register causes a fault that the kernel can intercept. This "fault on access" scheme provides the basic mechanism that permits the kernel to track which threads are using the floating-point registers.

IA-64 implementation

On IA-64, the thread structure contains the kernel stack pointer, a flag word, and the lazily managed floating-point, debug register, and performance monitor state.

The flag word keeps track of the lazily managed state that the thread is using. It also contains a few minor control bits that influence the thread behavior. For example, two bits in the flag word control how unaligned memory accesses are handled.

The debug register state consists of the data and instruction breakpoint registers defined by the IA-64 architecture. These can be managed lazily because the only way the user level can access these registers is through the *ptrace()* interface. Specifically, whenever this system call is invoked to write an instruction- or data-debug register (through the PTRACE_POKEUSR request), a bit in the flag word of the target thread structure is set to indicate that, from now on, the debug register state needs to be switched on a context switch. Once this bit is on, it remains on until the thread terminates.

The performance monitor state is maintained only if per-thread performance monitoring is enabled. Just as with the debug register state, a bit in the thread structure's flag word indicates whether the performance monitor state is being maintained.

The final important piece of state that is managed lazily is the high partition of the floating-point register file, namely, registers f32–f127. Note that the low partition is managed eagerly because, on IA-64, even pure integer applications tend to use some floating-point registers. However, managing f32–f127 lazily has the potential to provide a big performance boost because the involved state is so large (1536 bytes) and because pure integer applications and even simple floating-point applications usually need no more than the 30 floating-point registers that the low partition provides.

The kernel uses the dfh and mfh bits in the psr (processor status register) to implement lazy management of the high partition. The idea is for the kernel to keep track of the thread that most recently used registers f32–f127. This thread is called the *fpu-owner* (*ia64_get_fpu_owner()* in file include/asm-ia64/processor.h). Whenever the fpu-owner is executing, access to f32–f127 is enabled, i.e., dfh is cleared. Conversely, when any thread other than the fpu-owner is executing, access to these registers is disabled, i.e., dfh is set. The mfh bit keeps track of whether the high partition has been modified since access to the high partition was last enabled.

The interesting question is, of course, what happens when a thread other than the fpu-owner attempts to access f32–f127. In this case, the CPU generates a fault, which the kernel intercepts in the *disabled floating-point register handler* (*disabled_fph_fault()* in file arch/-ia64/kernel/traps.c). When this handler is invoked, it is clear that the state in f32–f127 needs to be switched. The kernel switches the state by first saving the current values in f32–f127 in the thread structure of the fpu-owner. As an optimization, the kernel can skip saving these registers if mfh indicates that the registers have not been modified since they were loaded. Once the old state is out of the way, the kernel establishes the new state by loading registers f32–f127 from the thread structure of the currently executing thread. After this is done, the currently executing thread is the new fpu-owner and dfh can be cleared to grant access to f32–f127. Finally, execution is restarted with the instruction that caused the fault—apart from the slight additional delay caused by the fault, the thread will never notice that it did not have access to the registers when it started executing!

The algorithm described so far works well when running on a machine with a single CPU. On an MP machine, there is a problem: when the disabled floating-point register handler gets invoked, it is possible that the latest values for f32–f127 of the currently executing thread are stored in the high partition of *another* CPU. The fault handler would have to (a) determine which CPU has the needed register values and (b) fetch the values from that CPU. Although this approach could be implemented, Linux/ia64 adopts a much simpler solution: when switching execution away from a thread that modified the floating-point high partition, the kernel unconditionally saves the partition to the thread structure. With this trick, the fault handler can be assured that it can always find the latest values in the thread structure and does not have to worry about fetching registers from another CPU. Effectively, this means that the floating-point high state is *loaded* in a lazy fashion but *saved* in an eager fashion. The downside of this approach is that the registers may sometimes be saved to memory more often than strictly necessary.

3.2.4 IA-64 register stack

The discussion so far assumed that there is a single kernel stack. This assumption is true for most platforms, but not for IA-64. It defines a second stack, called the register stack. As explained in Chapter 2, *IA-64 Architecture*, the part of the register stack that is not stored in the CPU's stacked registers is kept on the register backing store. Now, where do we keep the memory needed for this second stack?

Recall that the kernel allocates one chunk of memory when creating a new task. As illustrated in Figure 3.7, the Linux/ia64 kernel initializes a new thread such that the kernel memory stack starts at the top end of this memory and the register backing store starts in the lower half, just above the task structure. Since the memory stack by convention grows toward lower addresses and the register backing store grows toward higher addresses, the two effectively share the same kernel stack memory. There is no fixed boundary between the two stacks. This is ideal because a function that makes heavy use of the register stack usually makes light use of the memory stack, and vice versa. Of course, if the two stacks were to collide, the thread would be corrupted and could cause a kernel crash. This is really no different from a stack overflow on platforms with a single stack, and, as explained earlier, on a properly designed kernel, this problem should never occur.

The register stack can be thought of as an example of a different kind of lazily managed state. The difference compared to the state in the thread structure is that it is managed entirely by the CPU. All the kernel needs to do is set up the appropriate registers (e.g., bsp) and hardware takes care of saving and restoring stacked registers as necessary. This is a powerful mechanism to automatically adjust the context-switch overhead according to the behavior of an application. To see this, consider that during a context switch, only the stacked registers that have been allocated or restored since the last context switch have to be saved. An application that switches context frequently is likely to have few stacked registers to save, giving it good context-switch performance. On the other hand, applications that tend to run for long periods of time experience longer context-switch times but also take full advantage of the large register file of IA-64.

Note that when the kernel is entered, the physical registers that back the stacked registers still contain user-level values. As the kernel executes, it may need additional stacked registers. If so, some or all of the user-level values may end up being saved on the kernel's register backing store. Thus, in general, the bottom of the kernel register backing store contains user-level data and the rest contains kernel data. Given this fact, could a malicious user damage the kernel by abusing the register stack to trigger a kernel stack overflow? The answer is no, because each IA-64 CPU implements a fixed number of physical stacked

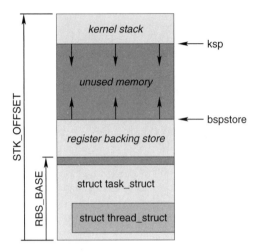

Figure 3.7. IA-64 task layout.

registers. For instance, Itanium implements 96 of these registers. This limits the number of values that have to be saved on behalf of the user. Hence, as long as the kernel stack is properly dimensioned, there is no danger of a user accidentally or maliciously causing a kernel stack overflow.

3.2.5 Summary of IA-64 thread state

Figure 3.8 summarizes the previous discussion with a picture of the IA-64 machine state. The figure shows where each register is saved. Note that the figure is *not* drawn to scale. In particular, r32–r127 and f32–f127 constitute the vast majority of the IA-64 machine state and there would not have been enough space to draw each of them individually.

As the figure shows, the static general registers, except for r4–r7, are saved in the pt-regs structure, as are floating-point registers f6–f9, branch register b6 and b7, as well as a few other miscellaneous registers. The switch-stack structure numerically contains fewer registers than pt-regs, but since it includes most of the eagerly managed floating-point registers, it ends up being slightly larger than pt-regs. The lazily managed state that is saved in the thread structure is by far the largest, primarily due to the floating-point high partition (f32–f127), which accounts for about 1.5 Kbytes of state all by itself. Finally, the stacked general registers (r32–r127) are saved on the register stack. Since it is necessary to save only those registers that have been used since the last context switch, the size of this state is variable.

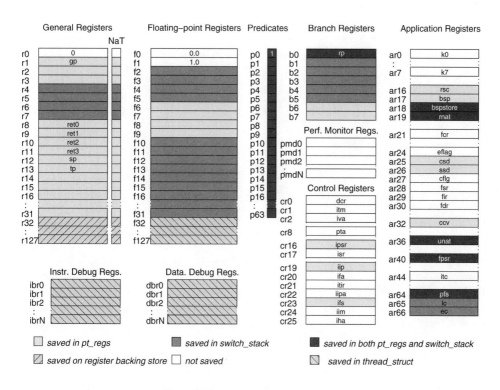

Figure 3.8. Summary of IA-64 thread state.

3.2.6 Running threads

The Linux kernel *scheduler* (*schedule()* in file kernel/sched.c) controls what thread gets to execute *when* and on *what CPU*. It is invoked periodically on each timer tick or whenever a thread blocks execution. When this happens, the scheduler inspects the queue of runnable threads and chooses the most suitable thread to execute next. To effect the switch to this new thread, the scheduler invokes the platform-specific *switch_to()* routine. In the kernel, this routine is implemented as a macro taking three arguments, but it is easier to think of it as a routine with the following prototype:

```
struct task_struct *switch_to(prev, next);
```

The job of this routine is to switch execution from thread *prev* to thread *next*. We should mention here that these arguments are pointers to task structures even though they are logically referring to threads. This is fairly common practice in the Linux kernel: since there is exactly one thread per task, the kernel often treats task pointers as synonyms for thread pointers. Since it is trivial to obtain a thread pointer from a task pointer, this practice does not cause any problems. The routine returns the thread that most recently executed on the

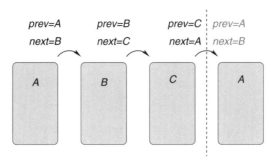

Figure 3.9. Effect of context switch on *prev* and *next* pointers.

current CPU. At this point, we might wonder why it even bothers to return a value. After all, if we switch execution from *prev* to *next*, the most recently executed thread is obviously *prev*! This is true at the point where *switch_to()* is *invoked*. However, when *returning* from it, the CPU is executing in the context that was active at the time *next* blocked execution. Thus, when the routine returns, *prev* and *next* actually contain stale values. This is illustrated in Figure 3.9. It shows three context switches from *A*, to *B*, to *C*, and then back to *A*. If we focus on the last context switch, we see that at the time *switch_to()* is called, *prev* points to *C* and *next* points to *A*. However, as soon as the machine state of *A* has been restored, *prev* and *next* will have the old values that existed during the first context switch (from *A* to *B*). But thanks to the return value of *switch_to()*, the kernel can keep track of the real predecessor (*C* in our example), so there is no problem. There is no need to use a similar trick for the *next* pointer because once the context switch has taken place, the *current* pointer can be used instead.

Two points about the context-switch code deserve special attention:

- There is one and only one place where the kernel invokes *switch_to()*. This is in the scheduler. As a result, the only way for a thread to block is through a call to *schedule()*, and the call frame for this routine appears last on the kernel stack, right above the switch-stack structure.

- Resuming execution of a blocked thread always returns control to the scheduler, right after the point where it calls *switch_to()*. However, a newly created thread starts execution in a special *return_from_clone()* routine. Such a thread therefore does not have a *schedule()* call frame above the switch-stack structure.

The implication of the first point is that *switch_to()* can be inlined even if it is large—since it is called exactly once, code size expansion is not an issue. Because of the second point, we must be careful not to assume that a call to *switch_to()* will return to the call site. This is *normally* true, but if the new thread has just been created by *clone2()*, execution instead continues in *return_from_clone()*.

IA-64 implementation

The IA-64 version of *switch_to()* breaks down into four major steps and handles eagerly managed and extra state separately. Extra state is a subset of the lazily managed state and includes, for example, the debug registers, but not the floating-point high partition. The four major steps of IA-64 context switching are described below.

1. Check the flags in the thread structure of the previously executing thread to see if it was using any extra state. If so, save it by calling the *extra state save routine* (*ia64_save_extra()* in file arch/ia64/kernel/process.c).

2. Check the flags in the thread structure of the new thread to see if it is using extra state. If so, load it by calling the *extra state load routine* (*ia64_load_extra()* in file arch/ia64/kernel/process.c).

3. Disable access to the floating-point high partition by clearing psr.dfh unless the new thread is the current owner of the partition.

4. Call the *IA-64 switch routine* (*ia64_switch_to()* in file arch/ia64/kernel/entry.S) to switch the eagerly managed state.

The reason for checking for extra state separately is that it is generally easier (and therefore faster) to check if *any* extra state is in use. If so, the kernel branches out of the fast path and handles the extra state in a separate routine. It is up to this routine to figure out exactly what state needs to be saved or loaded. Since this happens off the fast path of execution, performance is not as critical as for the rest of the context-switch routine. Thus, overall system performance should be good, even if the routines handling the extra state are relatively complex.

Note that the extra state of the new thread (if it has any) is loaded in the second step. Naively, we might expect this loading to be done as the last step. However, this would not work because the fourth step does not return to the caller if the new thread happens to be a thread that was just created by *clone2()*.

Step 3 ensures that when returning to the user level, the new thread does not have access to the floating-point high partition unless the thread already owns it. This is part of the lazy-state-saving logic explained in Section 3.2.3. Since dfh is stored in the pt-regs structure at the base of the kernel stack, this bit can be written only if the pt-regs structure exists on the kernel stack. Fortunately, this is always true for Linux/ia64 because it creates a dummy pt-regs structure if necessary (see Section 3.2.2).

In the last step, the eagerly managed state is switched by a call to the IA-64 switch routine. This routine has to be written in assembly language because it is performance-critical and because it needs to manipulate both the memory and the register stacks, which cannot be done safely in the C language. The assembly routine performs the following steps:

1. Saves the switch-stack state on the stack.

2. Saves the kernel stack pointer in the old thread structure.

3. Pins the task and stack memory of the new thread into the TLB.

4. Loads the kernel stack pointer from the new thread structure.

5. Sets the *current* pointer to the new thread's task structure.

6. Loads the switch-stack state structure from the stack.

Saving the switch-stack ensures that the **preserved** registers of the thread have been saved. It is not necessary to save **scratch** registers because they do not contain any interesting state. The context-switch routine gets invoked through a regular procedure call, so the calling convention guarantees that the **scratch** registers do not contain live values. In other words, the kernel always performs *synchronous* context switches. This is possible because kernel execution is never preempted. Of course, user-level execution is preemptable, so how can this work if the kernel context-switch routine never switches the **scratch** registers? Recall from Figure 3.5 that for a thread executing in the kernel, the first part of the kernel stack consists of a pt-regs structure. Thus, the kernel already saved the user-level **scratch** state when it was entered, so there is no need to save it again in the context-switch routine. In other words, always saving the pt-regs structure upon entry to the kernel is the trick that allows Linux to turn kernel-level synchronous context switches into user-level *asynchronous* context switches.

Steps two and four simply switch the kernel stack pointer from the old to the new thread. In the fifth step, the *current* pointer is set to the new thread's task structure, and in the final step, the **preserved** registers of the new task are restored by loading the switch-stack structure from the stack. The exact meaning of the third step will become clear in Chapter 4, *Virtual Memory*, but briefly, it ensures that a CPU can always access the task and stack memory of the currently executing thread without having to worry about triggering a virtual-memory-related fault (such as a TLB miss fault). As we will see later, this guarantee can be achieved with an IA-64 translation register.

It should be noted that none the above steps are performed with interrupts disabled. This is possible because, again, kernel execution is never preempted. However, it does imply that an interrupt handler could observe the *current* pointer and the register- and memory-stack pointers in an inconsistent state. For example, if an interrupt occurred between steps 5 and 6, the *current* pointer and the memory stack would point to the new thread, whereas the register backing store would still point to the old thread. This is usually not a problem because interrupt handlers must not rely on those pointers anyhow. About the only negative impact of a nonatomic context switch is that it becomes harder to check for a stack overflow in an interrupt handler. Since this cannot be done in a platform-independent fashion anyhow, this difficulty is not an issue in practice.

Switching the switch-stack state is mostly straightforward and consists primarily of storing and loading the **preserved** registers. It is interesting, however, to take a closer look at how the register backing store is handled. This handling is illustrated in Figure 3.10. Let us start in the upper-left corner. It shows the (fictional) state as it may exist upon entry to the context-switch routine. The left rectangle shows the old thread's backing store, the right rectangle shows the new thread's backing store, and, in the middle, we see the CPU state

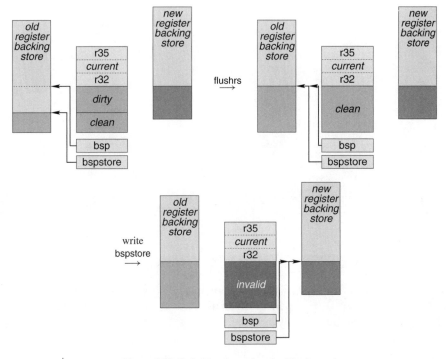

Figure 3.10. Switching the register backing store.

pertaining to the register stack. The figure shows that the current register frame is assumed to consist of registers r32–r35. Below the current frame are the stacked registers that are used by the old thread but are not currently accessible. These registers are divided into two partitions: the **clean** and the **dirty** partition. As the figure shows, the registers in the **clean** partition, by definition, already have been written to the old thread's backing store. As usual, the bspstore register marks the save location for the first **dirty** register, and the bsp register marks the save location for r32. Now, the first step in switching the backing store is to issue the flushrs instruction (see Chapter 2, *IA-64 Architecture*). This instruction forces the entire **dirty** partition onto the backing store and results in the configuration shown in the upper-right corner of the figure. As shown there, bspstore now has the same value as bsp, and the **dirty** partition has disappeared. Note that nothing from the current register frame has been written to the backing store.

We are now ready to complete the switchover. We achieve this by writing the new backing store pointer to bspstore. As explained in Chapter 2, *IA-64 Architecture*, writing this register also has an effect on bsp. In our case, since the **dirty** partition is empty, bsp and bspstore are set to the same value, resulting in the final configuration shown in the lower half of the figure. Note that another side effect of writing *bspstore* is that the formerly **clean** partition is now part of the **invalid** partition. This ensures that the CPU will restore

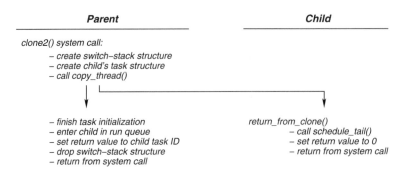

Figure 3.11. Relationship between task and thread creation.

the stacked registers from the new thread's backing store as it unwinds through its call stack. Let us again emphasize that the current register frame does not get saved or restored by the context-switch routine. This is not a problem, and is indeed desirable, because those registers are simply used to pass parameters to the context-switch routine itself, so they are not part of the machine state of either thread.

3.2.7   Creating threads

The Linux kernel creates a new thread only as part of creating a new task. The only way to create a new task is to call the *clone2()* system call. To understand how thread and task creation fit together, let us look at the steps that are executed in response to a *clone2()* system call. They are illustrated in Figure 3.11. As shown there, the first step of the *clone2()* system call handler creates a switch-stack structure on the kernel stack. This is done in a special assembly stub to ensure that the structure follows right below the pt-regs structure that is created when the kernel is entered. The significance of this layout will become clearer later on, but the primary motivation for this approach is to ensure that the entire machine state that existed at the time of the call to *clone2()* can be found in the pt-regs and switch-stack structures.

The assembly stub then calls a platform-independent task creation routine. For historical reasons, this routine continues to have the name *do_fork()*, even though *do_clone()* would be more appropriate. In this routine, the kernel creates a new task structure for the child and, eventually, creates a new thread by calling the platform-specific *copy_thread()* routine. Once this routine returns in the parent, the kernel finishes initializing the task structure, inserts the child in the run queue, sets the system call return value to the task ID of the child, and then returns to the assembly stub. There, the previously created switch-stack is simply dropped from the kernel stack (it is no longer needed), and, lastly, the stub returns from the system call.

Now, the purpose of the *copy_thread()* routine is to create a thread that is logically an identical copy of the parent, except that it must be set up such that the child thread will start execution in the *return_from_clone()* routine. As shown in the figure, this routine consists of a small stub that calls the platform-independent *schedule_tail()* routine and then directly returns from the *clone2()* system call with a value of zero. The call to the *schedule_tail()* routine is needed to ensure that the Linux scheduler gets notified when the new thread starts running for the first time.

Let us now take a closer look at how the *copy_thread()* routine works. From Figure 3.4 we may recall that it has the following prototype:

```
int copy_thread(nr, flags, ustack-base, ustack-size, task, regs);
```

By the time this routine is called, the child's task structure already exists and, for the most part, has been initialized. The kernel passes a pointer to this structure in the *task* argument. There is no need to explicitly pass a pointer to the parent's task structure because it is implicitly identified by the *current* pointer. The parent's pt-regs and switch-stack structures are passed with the *regs* pointer. The argument itself points to the pt-regs structure and, as explained earlier, the switch-stack structure is stored right below pt-regs. The *ustack-base* and *ustack-size* arguments determine the location of the user-level stack of the new thread. Specifically, the former specifies the starting address of the user-level stack area, and the latter specifies its size in bytes. The first two arguments, *nr* and *flags*, exist for historical reasons and are not needed anymore.

Figure 3.12 illustrates the effect of the *copy_thread()* routine with a hypothetical example. Part (a) shows the state as it exists when the routine is called, and part (b) shows the state after the routine returned.

Let us focus on part (a) first: it shows that the parent task belongs to some process identified as *process A*. At the top of the parent's kernel stack, we see the pt-regs structure. Directly below is the switch-stack structure, followed by one or more kernel call frames, the last one being the call frame for *copy_thread()*. The parent's user-level stack pointer, *usp*, is usually saved somewhere in the pt-regs structure and points to some place inside the parent's user-level stack area, which is part of process *A*'s virtual address space. The figure also shows the various arguments that are being passed to *copy_thread()*. The *regs* argument points to the pt-regs structure, *ustack-base* and *ustack-size* identify the area of the virtual address space that should be used for the child's stack, and *task* points to the partially initialized task structure for the child.

If we compare the two parts of the figure, it becomes clear what the routine needs to accomplish: first, it needs to copy the pt-regs and switch-stack structures from the parent to the child. This ensures that the child thread starts executing with the machine state as it existed when the parent invoked *clone2()*. It is important *not* to copy any call frames *below* the switch-stack structure, because the child does not follow the parent's return path and instead starts execution in *return_from_clone()*. Next, the thread structure needs to be initialized. This is platform specific, but typically consists of initializing the kernel stack pointer and a flag word. Recall that most state in this structure is lazily managed, so instead of actually copying the state, the routine can usually just initialize the flag word such that the lazily managed state is marked **unused**. The kernel stack pointer (*ksp* in the figure) is initialized to point to the switch-stack structure, as required for any task that is blocked. In the final step, the child's user-level stack needs to be set up. This again is platform

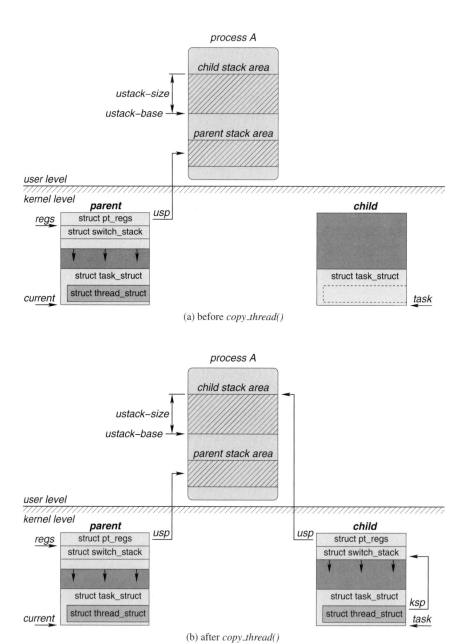

(a) before *copy_thread()*

(b) after *copy_thread()*

Figure 3.12. Environment before and after *copy_thread()*.

specific, but the expectation is that *copy_thread()* arranges for the new thread to use the virtual address range from *ustack-base* up to (but not including) *ustack-base + ustack-size*. As illustrated in Figure 3.12 (b), on platforms with a single stack that grows toward lower addresses, *copy_thread()* accomplished this by setting the user-level stack pointer (*usp*) to the top end of the stack area.

There are two special cases for user-level stack initialization. If *ustack-size* is 0, the user-level stack is expected to start at *ustack-base* without an a priori limit on the maximum stack size. Depending on the platform, the stack could grow toward lower addresses (e.g., IA-32), higher addresses (e.g., PA-RISC), or even in *both* directions (e.g., IA-64). The second special case occurs when *ustack-base* is 0. In this case, *ustack-size* is ignored and the child's user-level stack is initialized to be identical to that of the parent. Of course, this is meaningful only if the two threads do not share the address space, i.e., *clone2()* was invoked with the CLONE_VM flag cleared. Otherwise, the parent and child would end up using the same virtual memory for their stacks, and the likely result of this would be that both threads would crash with a segmentation violation or a similar fault. Note that this special case creates a subtle difference in the child: if *ustack-base* is non-zero, the child starts out with an empty stack. Thus, after returning from the *clone2()* system call, the child *must not* return, because there is no call frame to return to! In contrast, with a 0 *ustack-base*, the child starts out with the user-level stack it inherited from the parent, so returning to the caller of *clone2()* is perfectly valid and meaningful.

Thread creation inside the kernel

In a few instances, the kernel needs to create a thread for its own use. An example is the *kflush* daemon, which takes care of periodically writing modified filesystem data back to the disk. Such threads are created with the *kernel_thread()* function. This function is platform specific, but the essence of what it does can be expressed with the pseudocode below:

```
int kernel_thread (int (*fn)(void *), void *arg){
    int tid = clone2();
    if (tid == 0)
        exit((*fn)(arg));
    return tid;
}
```

As the pseudocode shows, the function first creates a child task by invoking the *clone2()* system call. In the parent, the system call returns the non-zero task ID of the new task, so the parent simply returns after creating the child task. In the child, the *clone2()* system call returns 0, so the child proceeds to call function *fn*. When that function returns, the child task terminates by calling the *exit()* system call.

Superficially, this may look identical to the user-level case of thread creation. However, an important difference is that, here, the kernel is already executing on the kernel stack when *clone2()* is invoked. By the time *copy_thread()* is called, the parent's task structure looks as shown in Figure 3.13. The crucial difference compared with Figure 3.12 is that the pt-regs and switch-stack structure are no longer at the base of the kernel stack. Instead, an arbitrary number of call frames may exist before the pt-regs structure, the last one being the

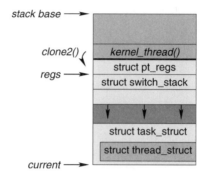

Figure 3.13. Stack layout while a kernel thread is created.

frame for the *kernel_thread()* routine. Since the child will begin execution inside the call frame of *kernel_thread()*, this frame must be present on the child stack as well. Otherwise, the child might crash as soon as *clone2()* returns. In theory, it would be sufficient to copy *just* this call frame, along with the pt-regs and switch-stack structures. However, since performance is not critical for this operation, it is usually much easier to simply copy *all* of the earlier call frames as well as the pt-regs and switch-stack structures. Besides being easier to implement, this also means that a backtrace of the child would show the call sequence that led to its creation. Knowing the sequence is useful for debugging. Finally, note that while this solution may not be optimal for creating kernel-only threads, it is optimal for the performance-critical case of creating threads from the user level.

IA-64 implementation

The most unusual part of the IA-64 implementation of *copy_thread()* is that it needs to deal with four stacks: the memory and register stacks for both kernel and user level. This is illustrated in Figure 3.14. At the top right, we see the user memory stack. Immediately below that is the user register backing store. Both are part of the parent stack area. At the kernel level, shown in the lower-left of the figure, we find the kernel memory stack at the top of the task area, the register backing store just below that, and, as usual, the task structure at the bottom.

To ensure proper operation of the child, *copy_thread()* needs to copy the relevant parts of the kernel stacks. As the figure shows, for the memory stack this requires copying the area from the top of the task memory down to the switch-stack structure. We find the top of the task memory by adding an offset of STK_OFFSET bytes to the *current* pointer.

Similarly, we find the start of the register backing store by adding an offset of RBS__OFFSET bytes to the *current* pointer. The end of the backing store area that needs to be copied is given by the value of the bsp register saved in the switch-stack structure.

For the user-level stacks, there are two cases: if *ustack-base* is zero, *copy_thread()* can simply copy the memory and register stack pointers that were saved in the pt-regs structure.

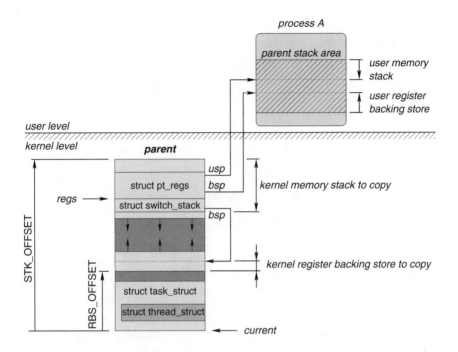

Figure 3.14. IA-64 version of *copy_thread()*.

If *ustack-base* is non-zero, the register stack pointer bspstore is initialized to *ustack-base* and the memory stack pointer *usp* is initialized to *ustack-base + ustack-size*. This leads to two possible user-level stack configurations, depending on whether or not *ustack-size* is 0. If non-zero, we get the configuration shown on the left-hand side of Figure 3.15. If 0, we get the configuration on the right-hand side. As the figure shows, at the user level we have a choice of whether we want to let the two stacks grow *toward* each other or whether to let them grow away from each other. The latter choice is particularly advantageous if *ustack-base* points to the middle of a page. This way, the memory stack and the register backing store can use up to half a page worth of memory and encounter only a single page fault or TLB fault (see Chapter 4, *Virtual Memory*). This approach can provide a nice performance boost if most threads tend to use relatively small amounts of stack space.

   Note that the *clone2()* system call only takes care of setting up the user-level stacks. It does *not* allocate any memory for those stacks, nor does it enforce the boundaries. It is up to the user level to do those jobs. This is the most flexible solution because it lets the application choose between allocating the memory statically, dynamically, or with *mmap()*. In the last case, the mapped memory may have the MAP_GROWSUP and/or MAP_GROWSDOWN flags set to allow the stack area to grow as needed. If desired, the user-level stack boundaries can be enforced with guard pages above and below the stack area.

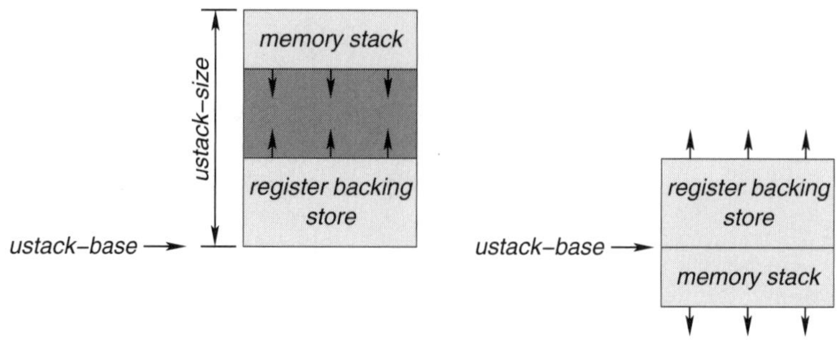

Figure 3.15. Possible IA-64 user stack configurations.

A final challenge for the IA-64 implementation of *copy_thread()* is that it must correctly propagate the NaT bits from the parent to the child. There are three places where NaT bits are being stored: the pt-regs structure, the switch-stack structure, and the register backing store. Let us start with the NaT bits in pt-regs: recall that the spill-form store instructions save in unat the NaT bit of the register being spilled. The unat bit number in which this bit is saved is taken from bits 3–8 of the *spill address*. After the spills are done, the unat register is saved in pt-regs. Now, when we copy pt-regs from the parent to the child, the spill addresses will of course change. Do we need to go through the saved unat value and adjust it for the new spill addresses? The answer, fortunately, is no. The task structure is guaranteed to at least be page aligned. Since the smallest supported page size is 4 Kbytes, we are assured that the spill addresses in the parent and the child are equal modulo 4096. Since only bits 3–8 influence the unat bit number, we are guaranteed that for each register that has been spilled, its unat bit number will be the same in the parent and the child. Thus, it is safe to simply copy the unat value in pt-regs. The same argument applies to the unat values saved in the switch-stack and to the rnat values saved in the switch-stack and on the register stack. Considering how slow and complicated it would be to fix up all these NaT collection words, the lesson from this discussion is that on IA-64, it really pays to align thread-related state at least to a 512-byte boundary!

3.2.8 Terminating threads

A thread is terminated as a result of terminating the task that it belongs to. The Linux kernel handles all aspects of task termination and then calls into platform-specific routines to terminate the underlying thread. As is usual for UNIX-like operating systems, task termination follows a two-phase protocol that, on Linux, is initiated with a call to the kernel's *do_exit()* routine. This routine releases most of the task's resources, including its address space, open files, and filesystem info. Once the resources have been released, the kernel calls the platform-specific *exit_thread()* routine. At this point, the task has become a *zombie*, i.e., a task that can no longer run. The only purpose of a zombie is to provide a place to hold the task's exit status until the parent collects it with the *wait4()* system call. After the exit status has been collected, the kernel calls the platform-specific *release_thread()* routine and then proceeds to free the task memory. At this point, both the thread and the task structure have ceased to exist. The interface for the two platform-specific thread-termination routines is shown below:

```
exit_thread();
release_thread(dead-task);
```

The *exit_thread()* routine takes no argument, because the task being terminated is the currently running task identified by the *current* pointer. In contrast, the *release_thread()* routine has a *dead-task* argument that is a pointer to the task that is being released. Remember that this routine is being called from the parent that is collecting the terminated task's exit status, so *current* cannot be used here.

IA-64 implementation

The IA-64 version of *exit_thread()* is simple and is used primarily to clean up architecture-specific state. For example, if per-thread performance monitoring was enabled, it will be turned off here (see Chapter 9, *Understanding System Performance*). Also, the routine checks whether the terminating thread owns the floating-point high partition and, if so, releases ownership. From a correctness point of view, this could be done equally well in *release_thread()*. However, releasing ownership in *release_thread()* would have the disadvantage that the dead floating-point state might be saved needlessly. For example, this would happen if another thread were to use the floating-point high partition after *exit_thread()* has been called but before *release_thread()* is called.

On IA-64, the *release_thread()* routine is used only for performance monitoring. Specifically, if performance monitoring was enabled for the dead task, then this routine frees up any memory that was allocated for this purpose. See Chapter 9, *Understanding System Performance*, for more information.

3.2.9   Moving threads across the address-space boundary

The final two routines in the thread interface permit the kernel to move a thread from one address space to another. These routines are *flush_thread()* and *start_thread()*, respectively; their prototypes are shown below:

```
flush_thread();
start_thread(regs, ip, sp);
```

Both routines are called by the kernel in response to an invocation of the *execve()* system call. As its name implies, the *flush_thread()* routine is expected to flush the thread state that belongs to the old address space. On most platforms, this means that lazily managed state, such as the floating-point state, can be dropped. The *flush_thread()* routine may also clear other registers so that the task starts execution in the new address space with a clean slate and no unwanted information is leaked from the old address space to the new one.

The *start_thread()* routine prepares the thread for execution in the new address space. The *regs* argument passed to this routine points to the thread's pt-regs structure. The routine is expected to initialize this structure such that when returning to user level, execution starts at the address passed in argument *ip* and with the stack pointer initialized to the address passed in argument *sp*.

It should be noted that there is no clear-cut line between what goes into *flush_thread()* and what goes into *start_thread()*. On most platforms, the work performed in *flush_thread()* could just as well be performed in *start_thread()*. However, since moving a thread into a new address space does logically consist of the two steps of leaving the old space and entering the new one, it is reasonable for Linux to provide separate hooks, even though for most platforms the division is more of a cleanliness than a correctness issue.

IA-64 implementation

On IA-64, the *flush_thread()* routine drops both the floating-point high state and the debug register state. It does this by clearing the appropriate bits in the flag word of the thread structure. The floating-point high state is dismissed because otherwise it would have to be cleared to 0. The debug registers must be turned off because otherwise the thread could experience unpredictable behavior. For example, suppose the debug registers contain a hardware breakpoint for address 0x4000000000000000. Since this address will refer to completely different memory in the new address space, it is not meaningful to preserve this breakpoint across an *execve()*. This routine would also be the logical place to clear the remaining machine state. However, it turns out that this would be difficult to do. Instead, Linux/ia64 clears the state in three other places:

1. The clearing of the **scratch** registers is deferred to *start_thread()*, where it is realized by clearing the appropriate members in the pt-regs structure passed in argument *regs*. For example, *start_thread()* clears register r3 by writing 0 to the pt-regs member of the same name. As an optimization, this clearing is performed only for security-sensitive cases, such as when a task with root privileges calls *execve()* to invoke an unprivileged executable image. Fortunately, it is easy to tell when such a case occurs: the kernel maintains a per-process flag called *dumpable* just for this purpose: if it is cleared, the *execve()* is security-sensitive and the registers need to be cleared. (The reason this flag is called *dumpable* is because, in the security-sensitive case, the kernel also must not create a core dump should the process crash.)

2. The **preserved** registers are cleared at the end of the *execve()* system call handler. Since system call handlers are root functions, the **preserved** registers are guaranteed to contain user-level state. If, instead, this clearing were done in the *flush_thread()* routine, the kernel stack unwind information would have to be consulted to determine the location of this state, which would be much slower.

3. The **invalid** partition of the stacked registers also needs to be cleared. But to avoid leaking kernel information to user level, this partition *always* needs to be cleared when returning to user level. Thus, this is taken care of in the normal kernel exit path. This path is described in more detail in Chapter 5, *Kernel Entry and Exit*.

Note that the second step clears the **preserved** registers unconditionally. In theory, this step also could be skipped if the *dumpable* flag is set. However, since this step directly clears the **preserved** registers, rather than memory holding their contents, it can be executed in a highly parallel fashion. For example, on Itanium, this step executes in less than 20 CPU cycles, so there is little point in trying to optimize it away.

Apart from clearing the **scratch** registers when necessary, the IA-64 version of *start-_thread()* also sets the instruction pointer in *regs* to the value passed in argument *ip* and clears the restart instruction slot field psr.ri. This ensures that upon return to user level, execution starts in the first slot of the bundle at address *ip*. The stack pointer is initialized according to the value passed in argument *sp*. Specifically, it is set to $sp - 16$. Subtracting 16 bytes from *sp* creates the scratch area required by the IA-64 software conventions (see Chapter 2, *IA-64 Architecture*).

It is less obvious how bspstore should be initialized. Different schemes are possible. For example, bspstore could be initialized to *sp*, which would give a configuration in which the user-level memory and register stacks grow away from each other. However, a better approach is to initialize bspstore to $sp - stacklimit$, where *stacklimit* is the user-level stack-size limit that is in effect for the current task. This limit corresponds to RLIM_STACK in the *setrlimit()* system call and, if it is set to RLIM_INFINITY, the kernel needs to choose a reasonably large value instead. Linux/ia64 uses a value of 4 Gbytes in this case. For all practical purposes, this indeed provides an unlimited amount of stack memory.

The *start_thread()* routine also clears psr.is to ensure that execution starts with the IA-64 instruction set (see Chapter 11, *IA-32 Compatibility*, for a description of how IA-32 executables are handled). The privilege level is set to the least privileged level 3 both in the processor status register (psr.cpl) and in the register stack configuration register (rsc.pl). The rsc.mode field is set to **eager** mode.

Finally, the register stack needs to be set up such that user-level execution will start with an empty register frame. This requires clearing the size of the user-level dirty partition and clearing pfs. Unfortunately, since pfs is a **preserved** register, it is not part of the pt-regs structure and cannot be accessed easily in *start_thread()*. Instead, its clearing is deferred to the *execve()* system call handler, just as is the clearing of all other **preserved** registers.

3.3 THREAD SYNCHRONIZATION

Threads are interesting only to the degree that they are able to share data with other threads or with I/O devices. For example, a thread that calculates the value of π to a hundred decimal places is useful only if the result can be printed on a terminal, saved in a file, or perhaps passed on to another thread for further processing. To facilitate data sharing, the Linux kernel defines a rich set of synchronization objects. These objects are all implemented on top of four thread synchronization interfaces that abstract the architectural differences among the various platforms Linux is running on. Each interface provides a different kind of synchronization primitive, namely, *interrupt masking*, *atomic operations*, *semaphores*, and *spinlocks*. We will see that each primitive has its own set of constraints and benefits.

We should note that the spinlock primitive has no effect on UP machines. We could defer its discussion to Chapter 8, *Symmetric Multiprocessing*, but to facilitate its comparison with the other thread synchronization primitives, we introduce it here. This is also in line with the kernel programming practice which dictates that new code should *always* be designed to be MP-safe. The reason is that it is usually much easier to *design* MP-safety into new code than to add it after the fact.

3.3.1 Concurrency model

The Linux kernel employs a model that recognizes two sources of concurrency: *multiple CPUs* and *interrupts*. An MP machine clearly has to deal with *true concurrency* since each CPU executes its own instruction stream independently and concurrently. In such an environment, proper synchronization is required to ensure that accesses to shared data are performed in a way that does not corrupt data integrity. Interrupts give rise to *pseudoconcurrency*. This occurs whenever data is shared between an interrupt handler and ordinary (noninterrupt) kernel code. The reason this is called *pseudo*concurrency is that, from the perspective of the CPU, it involves only sequential execution. Yet from the perspective of the interrupted code, it will appear as if interrupt handlers run concurrently. The shared data therefore needs to be protected with proper synchronization just as on an MP machine. However, while the two types of concurrency are similar in nature, they cannot always be treated in the same fashion. To keep this distinction clear and to emphasize their sources, the remaining discussion refers to true concurrency as *CPU concurrency* and to pseudo-concurrency as *interrupt concurrency*.

To get a better sense of the difference between the two sources of concurrency, let us consider an example. Suppose a data object needs to be updated atomically but is already in use (i.e., there is *contention* for the data object). With CPU concurrency, a CPU can simply wait for the object to become available and, once it is available, continue execution. With interrupt concurrency, waiting would be fatal. For example, suppose a thread had started to use a data object and then was interrupted. If the interrupt handler needs to access the same data object, it would find the object to be in use already. At this point it would have two choices: it could either block execution or it could enter a tight loop (*spinloop*), repeatedly checking whether the data object has become available. The Linux kernel does not permit interrupt handlers to block, so the first option is not feasible. Similarly, if the handler were to enter a spinloop, the interrupted thread could never make forward progress (because the CPU is busy executing the interrupt handler's spinloop) and the data object would never become available. In other words, the kernel would be stuck.

Because the two sources of concurrency are different, the Linux kernel uses separate primitives to handle them, as illustrated in Table 3.2. Interrupt masking is used to protect against interrupt concurrency, and spinlocks are used to protect against CPU concurrency. Note that the spinlock primitives have no effect on a UP machine. The table also shows the properties of the other two primitives: semaphores and atomic operations. Like spinlocks, semaphores protect against CPU concurrency and can be used to serialize access to a shared object. However, since they block the thread in case of contention, they cannot be used in interrupt handlers. The main advantage of semaphores over spinlocks is that they work the

Table 3.2. Thread synchronization primitives.

Primitive	Protects against	Limitation
interrupt masking	interrupt concurrency	
spinlocks	CPU concurrency	no effect on UP machines
semaphores	CPU concurrency	not for interrupt handlers
atomic operations	interrupt and CPU concurrency	only simple operations

same way on UP and MP machines. Semaphores are also often used for event signaling. The last row of the table shows that atomic operations have the benefit of protecting against both interrupt and CPU concurrency but are limited in the sense that they support only relatively simple operations, such as incrementing a counter or manipulating individual bits in a set.

From a theoretical point of view, atomic operations and semaphores are not necessary because they can be implemented with a combination of interrupt masking and spinlocks. But by defining them as separate primitives, Linux gives each platform the opportunity to implement them in a more optimized, platform-specific fashion.

3.3.2 Atomic operations

In concurrent programs, certain idioms occur frequently. For example, it is often necessary to atomically increment a shared counter. This, combined with the fact that many architectures provide special instructions for implementing atomic operations, provides sufficient incentive for Linux to abstract the most common operations so they can be exploited in platform-independent code. Atomic operations are also easy to use because they protect against both CPU and interrupt concurrency. Algorithms that are implemented exclusively with atomic operations are often called *lock-free* or *wait-free* algorithms [20, 44]. Because atomic operations do not involve any locks and, ideally, always complete in a bounded amount of time (e.g., there is no unlimited waiting for a data object to become available).

Linux divides the platform-specific atomic operations into three separate interfaces: system primitives, atomic counters, and bitset operations. Although these interfaces provide a large set of operations, it is normally not necessary for a platform to implement each operation from scratch. For example, atomic counters can easily be implemented with the *compare-and-exchange* operation provided by the system interface. However, because such a large number of operations are provided, each platform can choose the optimal way of implementing them.

Note that all operations discussed in this section execute atomically with respect to both interrupt and CPU concurrency. However, the operations make no guarantee about memory-access ordering. A memory access performed as part of an atomic operation could be executed out of order with respect to surrounding memory accesses. If a specific memory-access order is required, explicit memory barriers need to be used (see Chapter 7, *Device I/O*, and Chapter 8, *Symmetric Multiprocessing*).

xchg(*ptr*, *new*);	/* *exchange value* */
cmpxchg(*ptr*, *old*, *new*);	/* *compare & exchange (optional)* */

Figure 3.16. System primitives interface.

System primitives

Let us start with the interface for the *system primitives* (file include/asm/system.h). As shown in Figure 3.16, it consists of just two routines and one of them is even optional. Both routines are polymorphic in the sense that the *ptr* argument can point to a variable of type **int** or **long**. Since the C language does not support polymorphism, these routines are actually implemented as C macros.

The *xchg()* routine unconditionally replaces the value of the variable that *ptr* points to with the value passed in argument *new* and then returns the previous value of the variable.

The *cmpxchg()* routine is available only on certain platforms. Platform-independent code must check whether macro __HAVE_ARCH_CMPXCHG is defined and, if not, use an alternate algorithm that does not rely on *cmpxchg()*. The operation of this routine is as follows. If the value of the variable that *ptr* points to is not equal to *old*, nothing is done except that the current value of the variable is returned. If the two values match, then the variable is set to the value passed in *new* and the old value is returned (which is guaranteed to be the same as *old* in this case).

Compare and exchange caveat (ABA problem)

The *cmpxchg()* routine is a powerful primitive that can be used to implement other atomic operations. However, its power is sometimes a little deceptive and can easily lead to incorrect code. One trap that is particularly easy to fall into is thinking that it could be used to implement insertion into and removal from a singly linked list, such as a LIFO or stack data structure. For example, the seemingly obvious way to atomically remove an element from the head of a nonempty linked list would look like this:

```
struct stack {
    volatile struct stack *next;
    other fields...
} *head;

/* example of INCORRECT list removal code: */
struct stack *new, *old;
do
    old = head, new = head→next;
while (cmpxchg(&head, old, new) != old);
```

At first glance, this code looks correct: the body of the **do**-loop first copies the current value of the list *head* to *old*. It also copies a pointer to the second element in the list (*head→next*) to variable *new*. The code then attempts to atomically replace the list head pointer with the value in variable *new*. The code uses the *cmpxchg()* routine to ensure that this succeeds

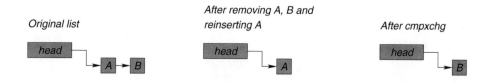

Figure 3.17. Example illustrating incorrect list removal with *cmpxchg()*.

only if the head pointer still has the same value as *old*. If the head pointer has changed by the time *cmpxchg()* is executed, it will not update the head pointer, and the **do**-loop will be repeated.

Eventually, the loop will execute without contention, at which point the loop is exited with variable *old* pointing to the list element that has just been removed.

Unfortunately, this code has a fatal flaw: *it does not work!* Suppose the linked list looked as shown in the left-hand side of Figure 3.17. After the two assignments in the **do**-loop body are executed, *old* points to element *A* and *new* points to element *B*. Now, suppose that before our CPU gets to execute *cmpxchg()*, another CPU sneaks in and first removes element *A*, then element *B*, and then reinserts element *A*. Now we have the configuration shown in the middle of the figure. At this point, our CPU may be able to finally execute *cmpxchg()*. It will find that *head* still points to *A* and hence the exchange operation will succeed. Since *new* still points to *B*, we will end up with the list shown on the right-hand side of the figure— instead of being empty, the list now contains element *B*! Since the sequence of events that leads to this failure involved removing *A* and *B*, and reinserting *A*, this problem is known as the *ABA problem* [45].

What went wrong? More careful analysis of the above code quickly reveals the culprit: the *cmpxchg()* routine protects us from *head* changing underneath us, but it does not protect us against a change of the *next* pointer in element *A*. In essence, the above code depends on *two* shared values, but since *cmpxchg()* can protect against a change in only one of them, the code cannot possibly be correct. This particular problem could be solved with a *compare-and-exchange-2* operation, which atomically checks and replaces two words [44]. The load-linked/store-conditional instructions that some CPU architectures provide also can solve this problem cleanly [56, 65]. However, since the Linux kernel does not define a separate LIFO stack interface, platform-independent code must play it safe and generally has to rely on explicit locking (e.g., with spinlocks) when implementing such a data structure.

So, when is it safe to use *cmpxchg()*? A simple and sufficient, but not a necessary, condition is that the *new* value that is being set by *cmpxchg()* must be either a *constant* or a value that is calculated from the value of *old* (such as *old* + 1). In the list removal code, *new* neither was a constant nor was it calculated from the value of *old*. The condition has been violated, and we cannot be sure that the use of *cmpxchg()* is correct. As the example showed, it was indeed incorrect.

typedef **atomic_t**;	/* opaque type for signed counter */
int **atomic_read**(c);	/* read the current counter value */
atomic_set(c, i);	/* set counter to i */
atomic_inc(c);	/* add 1 to the counter */
atomic_dec(c);	/* subtract 1 from the counter */
atomic_add(i, c);	/* add integer i to the counter */
atomic_sub(i, c);	/* subtract i from the counter */
int **atomic_inc_and_test**(c);	/* add 1, return true if result is $\neq 0$ */
int **atomic_dec_and_test**(c);	/* subtract 1, return true if result $= 0$ */
int **atomic_sub_and_test**(i, c);	/* subtract i, return true if result $= 0$ */
int **atomic_add_negative**(i, c);	/* add i, return true if result < 0 */

Figure 3.18. Atomic counter interface.

Atomic counter interface

The atomic counter interface revolves around the opaque type **atomic_t**, which contains a signed counter that is at least 32 bits wide (i.e., the value can be at least in the range of -2^{31} to $2^{31} - 1$). The only arithmetic operations defined for this type are addition and subtraction. The complete interface is shown in Figure 3.18.

The routines in this interface can be understood intuitively. Routine *atomic_read()* returns the current counter value, and *atomic_set()* sets the counter to the integer passed in *i*. The *atomic_add()* routine adds *i* to the counter value and *atomic_sub()* does the same for subtraction. For convenience, the *atomic_inc()* and *atomic_dec()* routines are equivalent to calling *atomic_add()* and *atomic_sub()* with a value of 1 in argument *i*. The next three routines, *atomic_inc_and_test()*, *atomic_dec_and_test()*, and *atomic_sub_and_test()*, also modify the counter value but in addition return an indication whether the resulting counter value was 0. The final routine, *atomic_add_negative()*, adds a value to the counter and returns **true** if the resulting counter value is negative.

Many platforms also provide the more generic *atomic_add_return()* and *atomic_sub_return()* routines, which modify the counter value and then return the updated value. This behavior permits the construction of arbitrary *modify-and-test* operations on atomic counters. However, since these routines are not universally implemented, platform-independent code cannot rely on their presence.

If this interface does not seem well thought out, it is because it was not. The interface started out with just the atomic increment and decrement routines, and over time more and more routines were added. Perhaps some day this interface will be cleaned up and made more orthogonal and complete. The problem is, of course, that this would almost unavoidably break existing source code, so this is not something that should be done without a good reason.

/* bitset pointers must be **long** aligned! */
set_bit(*nr*, *set*);   /* set bit nr in set */
clear_bit(*nr*, *set*);   /* clear bit nr in set */
change_bit(*nr*, *set*);   /* toggle bit nr in set */
int **test_bit**(*nr*, *set*);   /* return value of bit nr */
int **test_and_set_bit**(*nr*, *set*);   /* set bit nr and return previous value */
int **test_and_clear_bit**(*nr*, *set*);   /* clear bit nr and return previous value */
int **test_and_change_bit**(*nr*, *set*);   /* toggle bit nr and return previous value */

Figure 3.19. Bitset operations interface.

Bitset operations interface

The bitset interface provides the platform-independent part of Linux with the means to modify and test individual elements in an arbitrary-sized set of bits. In this interface, bitsets are represented simply as a void pointer, so the interface implementations cannot perform any range checks. It is thus up to the caller to make sure that it never attempts to modify or test a bit that is outside the set. Also, the caller must make sure that the bitset pointers are at least **long** aligned. The interface is shown in Figure 3.19.

The *set_bit()* routine sets bit number *nr* in the bitset that *set* points to. Similarly, *clear_bit()* clears the bit and *change_bit()* toggles the bit (changes it to 1 if it is 0, and vice versa). The *test_bit()* routine returns the current value of bit number *nr* in the set. The remaining three routines, *test_and_set_bit()*, *test_and_clear_bit()*, and *test_and_change_bit()*, modify a bit and return **true** if the bit was previously set (**false** otherwise). Note that these routines return the *old* value of the bit, which is different from the atomic counter routines, which return the *new* counter value.

IA-64 implementation

The primary instruction that the IA-64 architecture provides for implementing atomic operations is the cmpxchg instruction. This instruction has exactly the semantics required for the *cmpxchg()* routine defined in the system primitives interface. Indeed, all of the above interfaces can be implemented with this instruction alone. However, as an optimization, the IA-64 implementations also use the fetchadd and xchg instructions where appropriate. For example, if *atomic_inc_return()* is called with an increment value of ±1, ±4, ±8, or ±16, the IA-64 version automatically uses the fetchadd instruction instead of the more general (and slower) sequence required for cmpxchg.

In addition to the normal *cmpxchg()* routines, Linux/ia64 provides the *cmpxchg_acq()* and *cmpxchg_rel()* routines. These work like *cmpxchg()*, except that they have definite memory ordering semantics. The former has **acquire** semantics and the latter has **release** semantics (see Chapter 2, *IA-64 Architecture*). Since the routines are IA-64 specific, platform-independent code cannot take advantage of them. However, they are exported by the system primitives interface to enable more efficient implementation of some of the other thread synchronization interfaces.

struct **semaphore**;

down(*sem*);	/* acquire semaphore */
up(*sem*);	/* release semaphore */
int **down_interruptible**(*sem*);	/* acquire semaphore in interruptible state */
int **down_trylock**(*sem*);	/* acquire semaphore, if possible */

struct **rw_semaphore**;

down_read(*rwsem*);	/* acquire read semaphore */
up_read(*rwsem*);	/* release read semaphore */
down_write(*rwsem*);	/* acquire write semaphore */
up_write(*rwsem*);	/* acquire write semaphore */

Figure 3.20. Semaphore interface.

3.3.3 Semaphores

The semaphore is a flexible synchronization primitive that can be used to resolve contention for a shared data object as well as to signal events. Since semaphores block execution in the case of contention, they are well suited to protect accesses to data objects that take a long time to execute. The same property prevents semaphores from being used to resolve contention in interrupt handlers, because interrupt handlers cannot block execution.

That said, semaphores can be used in interrupt handlers as long as they are used only to *signal* the occurrence of an event. Signaling is allowed because the operation is guaranteed not to block. For example, a thread might use a semaphore to wait for the arrival of a disk data sector. When the data arrives, the disk controller generates an interrupt and the interrupt handler of the disk driver signals the arrival on the semaphore, thus waking up the waiting thread. This type of semaphore use is perfectly safe and indeed is common throughout the Linux kernel.

The semaphore interface provides both counting and read/write semaphores; it is illustrated in Figure 3.20. Both types of semaphores contain a counter value that determines their behavior. For counting semaphores, the *down()* routine decrements this counter and if it becomes negative, the calling thread blocks execution. Conversely, the *up()* routine increments the counter and if it was negative, it wakes up one of the blocked threads. The kernel does not impose a definite order in which blocked threads need to be woken up, though there is an expectation that, probabilistically, no thread will remain blocked indefinitely as threads are being woken up. The *down_interruptible()* routine is a variant of *down()* that will return immediately with a value of $-$EINTR should the thread receive a signal while it is blocked. On normal completion, *down_interruptible()* returns 0. Similarly, *down_trylock()* is a variant that never blocks. Instead, if the semaphore count becomes negative, it returns immediately with a non-zero value.

As their name implies, read/write semaphores can be used to solve the *Readers/Writers problem* [6]. This problem assumes that threads accessing a shared data object can be divided into *readers* and *writers*. The former only read the content of the object, whereas the latter may update it. Read/write semaphores regulate access to the object such that multiple readers can access it concurrently, but writers get exclusive access. With the interface shown above, a reader is expected to call *down_read()* before accessing the object and *up_read()* when it is done. Similarly, a writer is expected to call *down_write()* before updating the object and *up_write()* when it is done. Logically, *down_read()* and *up_read()* work exactly like *down()* and *up()* do for counting semaphores. However, *down_write()* and *up_write()* operate differently. A call to *down_write()* will block execution until the counter value becomes 0, i.e., until no other threads are left accessing the object. At that point, it sets the counter value to minus infinity to prevent any readers and other writers from accessing the object. When the writer is done, it calls *up_write()* to clear the counter value to 0 and wake up any readers or a single writer that may be waiting for access to the object.

Read/write semaphores must be implemented in a fashion that encourages fairness in the sense that if a semaphore is contested, access will roughly alternate between readers and writers. However, to avoid deadlock conditions, a reader must always be allowed to acquire a semaphore that is being used by other readers. This means that a constant stream of readers could starve writers, but this is not a problem because readers usually consume data produced by writers. In other words, if there is a prolonged period during which writers are locked out, the readers will eventually run out of work and, at that time, the writers will get a chance to acquire the semaphore. It is also desirable that accesses from multiple writers occur in first-come, first-served (FCFS) order.

The IA-64 instruction set provides no special instructions for implementing semaphores. Thus, the IA-64 implementation is based entirely on spinlocks and atomic operations. Indeed, it is virtually identical to the code used on other platforms and more or less follows the standard textbook algorithm for implementing semaphores [6, 11, 64].

3.3.4 Interrupt masking

Interrupt masking prevents contention on data objects that are shared between interrupt handlers and ordinary kernel code. When ordinary kernel code needs to access a shared object, it masks (disables) interrupts before starting the access and unmasks (enables) interrupts when it is done. Since interrupts cannot occur while they are masked, interrupt handlers will never experience any contention from ordinary kernel code and are guaranteed to be able to run to completion (of course, an interrupt handler may be interrupted by another, higher-priority, interrupt).

Linux distinguishes between hardware and software interrupts. Both can be masked separately, though masking hardware interrupts also masks software interrupts. Unlike other UNIX-like operating systems, Linux does not directly support hardware interrupt-priority levels. This reflects the school of thought which dictates that exposing interrupt levels in an operating system kernel is inherently nonportable and creates more problems than benefits. This does not mean, however, that Linux prevents a platform from exploiting interrupt-priority levels at the hardware-level. It simply means that if a thread wants to protect itself against interrupt concurrency, it will (briefly) disable all interrupt levels.

The kernel interface that abstracts platform differences in interrupt masking consists of the six operations shown in Figure 3.21. Routine *local_irq_disable()* disables and *local-*

local_irq_disable();	/* disable interrupts */
local_irq_enable();	/* enable interrupts */
unsigned long **local_irq_save**();	/* disable interrupts, return old flags */
local_irq_restore(*flags*);	/* restore flags */
local_bh_disable();	/* disable software interrupts */
local_bh_enable();	/* enable software interrupts */

Figure 3.21. Interrupt masking interface.

_irq_enable() enables both hardware and software interrupts. Besides just enabling and disabling interrupts, the kernel often needs to disable interrupts briefly and then restore the previous masking status. The *local_irq_save()* and *local_irq_restore()* routines serve this purpose. The former disables interrupts and returns the masking status that was previously in effect. The previous interrupt masking status can be restored by calling *local_irq_restore()* with the value returned by *local_irq_save()*. Note that the interrupt masking status is passed in a variable of type **unsigned long**. Why such a wide type when a single bit would do? The reason is that this type leaves room for each platform to implement these operations in the most efficient manner. For example, on the Alpha platform, *local_irq_save()* actually returns the *system priority level (SPL)* that was in effect at the time of the call. This trick extracts most of the benefits of hardware priority levels without complicating the kernel programming model. The final two routines, *local_bh_disable()* and *local_bh_enable()*, respectively disable and enable software interrupts only. The **bh** in the name for these routines comes from *bottom-half*, which derives from the fact that software interrupts used to be called bottom-half handlers.

We might also wonder why the names of these routine start with **local**. This prefix emphasizes that these operations affect only the *local* CPU, i.e., the CPU that is executing the operation in question. For backward compatibility, the kernel still supports a few global interrupt masking routines, namely, *cli()*, *sti()*, *save_flags()*, and *restore_flags()*. These correspond, respectively, to the first four routines in the interrupt masking interface, except that they affect interrupt masking on *all* CPUs. They were intended to make legacy device drivers safe for use in MP machines, even though such drivers were not designed with MP-safety in mind. However, global interrupt masking is implemented with a combination of a spinlock and interrupt masking. Because of that, it is slow and introduces needless serialization, so new code should avoid it as much as possible.

IA-64 implementation

The IA-64 versions of *local_irq_disable()* and *local_irq_enable()* are simple. The i bit in the processor status register controls the delivery of all interrupts, so clearing this bit (with the rsm instruction) implements *local_irq_disable()* and setting it (with the ssm instruction) implements *local_irq_enable()*.

The *local_irq_save()* routine reads the entire psr register, clears the i bit, and then returns the old content of psr. Correspondingly, *local_irq_restore()* works by writing the *flags*

struct **spinlock_t**;	/* platform-specific spinlock type */
spin_lock(*l*);	/* acquire spinlock l */
spin_unlock(*l*);	/* release spinlock l */
int **spin_is_locked**(*l*);	/* return true if l is locked */
int **spin_trylock**(*l*);	/* acquire lock if uncontended, return true if successful */
struct **rwlock_t**;	/* platform-specific read/write lock type */
read_lock(*rw*);	/* acquire read lock on rw */
read_unlock(*rw*);	/* release read lock on rw */
write_lock(*rw*);	/* acquire write lock on rw */
write_unlock(*rw*);	/* release write lock on rw */

Figure 3.22. Spinlock interface.

argument to psr. This is slightly more efficient than restoring just the i bit, but it does imply that changes to the psr register will not persist across a call to *local_irq_restore()*. Fortunately, portable kernel code has no knowledge of innards of the IA-64 psr register and will therefore never attempt to make such changes. On the other hand, platform-specific code can take advantage of this particular implementation and use the routines to obtain a copy of the psr register or to update it.

The software interrupt masking routines *local_bh_disable()* and *local_bh_enable()* are implemented with the help of a CPU-local counter variable. Essentially, the former increments the CPU-local counter and the latter decrements it. Since delivery of software interrupts is under control of the kernel (unlike the case with hardware interrupts), the kernel can simply check this CPU-local variable and suppress the delivery of any software interrupts while it has a non-zero value. See Chapter 7, *Device I/O*, for more details on software interrupts. This implementation is not IA-64 specific, and most other platforms use the same approach or a similar one.

3.3.5 Spinlocks

Spinlocks can be used to serialize access to shared data objects. Uncontended spinlocks can be acquired and released with very little overhead (compared with, say, semaphores). However, as their name implies, if a CPU attempts to acquire a spinlock that is already locked, it will enter a tight loop (spinloop) until the lock becomes available. Since the CPU will not be able to do anything else while executing the tight loop, spinlocks should be held only for short periods of time.

The interface that the Linux kernel uses to abstract platform differences in the implementation of spinlocks is shown in Figure 3.22. There are two basic flavors of spinlocks: ordinary spinlocks and read/write locks. Similar to read/write semaphores, the latter provide a spinlock-based solution to the Readers/Writers problem.

The interface can be understood intuitively: *spin_lock()* acquires an ordinary lock, spinning if necessary; the lock is released with *spin_unlock()*. In some rare cases, it is useful to be able to take different actions depending on whether or not a lock is available. For this purpose, *spin_is_locked()* can test whether a lock is available, and *spin_trylock()* can acquire a spinlock if available and do nothing otherwise (i.e., the operation never spins). The return value indicates whether the operation succeeded in acquiring the lock.

For read/write locks, *read_lock()* acquires and *read_unlock()* releases a read lock. Acquiring a read lock will succeed as long as there are only other readers. If a write lock is pending, *read_lock()* will spin until the write lock is released. Similarly, *write_lock()* acquires a write lock and, if necessary, spins as long as there are any other readers or writers. Finally, *write_unlock()* releases a write lock. The kernel expects the same fairness and dead-lock prevention rules from read/write locks as from read/write semaphores.

As mentioned earlier, spinlocks protect against CPU concurrency only and are useful for MP machines only. On UP machines, the above routines are implemented such that they have no effect. This is better than not implementing the spinlock routines at all, because it means that MP-safe code compiles and works correctly both on UP and MP machines. We should also say that, for historical reasons, the spinlock interface includes a *spin_unlock_wait()* routine. This routine stalls execution until a lock becomes available. This was sometimes used to implement read/write locks on top of regular spinlocks. However, since Linux now explicitly supports read/write locks, the routine is no longer needed and remains only for backward compatibility.

The IA-64 implementation of the spinlock interface is built on top of the *atomic_add()* and *cmpxchg()* atomic operations. However, since these routines are highly performance-critical, they are expressed as inline assembly code.

3.4 SUMMARY

In this chapter, we learned that even though the process is a key abstraction at the user level, Linux uses a slightly different model inside the kernel. This model is centered around the task abstraction, which is flexible enough to accommodate both single- and multithreaded processes. The chapter also described how tasks are created and how Linux relies on the thread interface to define a platform-independent notion of a thread of execution. Logically, tasks and threads are independent entities, yet physically, they are inseparable: one cannot exist without the other. Linux uses a fairly unconventional representation for the CPU machine state of a thread. Instead of a single data structure, it uses the pt-regs, switch-stack, and thread structures. While unconventional, this approach has the advantage of making it possible to finely tune which state gets saved when. The IA-64 implementation of the thread interface takes full advantage of this flexibility and, as a result, achieves good performance despite the large size of the IA-64 machine state.

The second half of the chapter focused on the concurrency model of Linux and the thread synchronization interfaces that are needed to cope with this concurrency. We have seen that these interfaces cover a broad range of different synchronization objects. Specifically, interrupt masking and atomic operations provide a foundation for building lock-free solutions, with the former covering only interrupt concurrency and the latter covering both interrupt and CPU concurrency. For lock-based solutions, the kernel provides semaphores and spinlocks. Both come in two flavors: ordinary locks and read/write locks. Semaphores are intended primarily for locks that are being held for extended periods of times. However, they can also be used for event signaling and they work both on UP and MP machines. In contrast, spinlocks are for MP machines only, and even there they should be used only for locks that are being held for brief periods of time.

Chapter 4

Virtual Memory

Linux processes execute in a virtual environment that makes it appear as if each process had the entire address space of the CPU available to itself. This virtual address space extends from address 0 all the way to the maximum address. On a 32-bit platform, such as IA-32, the maximum address is $2^{32} - 1$ or $\mathtt{0xffffffff}$. On a 64-bit platform, such as IA-64, this is $2^{64} - 1$ or $\mathtt{0xffffffffffffffff}$.

While it is obviously convenient for a process to be able to access such a huge address space, there are really three distinct, but equally important, reasons for using virtual memory.

1. *Resource virtualization.* On a system with virtual memory, a process does not have to concern itself with the details of how much physical memory is available or which physical memory locations are already in use by some other process. In other words, virtual memory takes a limited physical resource (physical memory) and turns it into an infinite, or at least an abundant, resource (virtual memory).

2. *Information isolation.* Because each process runs in its own address space, it is not possible for one process to read data that belongs to another process. This improves security because it reduces the risk of one process being able to spy on another process and, e.g., steal a password.

3. *Fault isolation.* Processes with their own virtual address spaces cannot overwrite each other's memory. This greatly reduces the risk of a failure in one process triggering a failure in another process. That is, when a process crashes, the problem is generally limited to that process alone and does not cause the entire machine to go down.

In this chapter, we explore how the Linux kernel implements its virtual memory system and how it maps to the underlying hardware. This mapping is illustrated specifically for IA-64. The chapter is structured as follows. The first section provides an introduction to the virtual memory system of Linux and establishes the terminology used throughout the remainder of the chapter. The introduction is followed by a description of the software and hardware structures that form the virtual memory system. Specifically, the second section describes the Linux virtual address space and its representation in the kernel. The third section describes the Linux page tables, and the fourth section describes how Linux manages

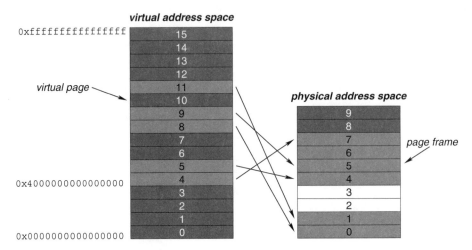

Figure 4.1. Virtual and physical address spaces.

the *translation lookaside buffer (TLB)*, which is a hardware structure used to accelerate virtual memory accesses. Once these fundamental structures are introduced, the chapter describes the operation of the virtual memory system. Section five explores the Linux page fault handler, which can be thought of as the engine driving the virtual memory system. Section six describes how memory coherency is maintained, that is, how Linux ensures that a process sees the correct values in the virtual memory locations it can access. Section seven discusses how Linux switches execution from one address space to another, which is a necessary step during a process context switch. The chapter concludes with section eight, which provides the rationale for some of the virtual memory choices that were made for the virtual memory system implemented on IA-64.

4.1 INTRODUCTION TO THE VIRTUAL MEMORY SYSTEM

The left half of Figure 4.1 illustrates the virtual address space as it might exist for a particular process on a 64-bit platform. As the figure shows, the virtual address space is divided into equal-sized pieces called *virtual pages*. Virtual pages have a fixed size that is an integer power of 2. For example, IA-32 uses a page size of 4 Kbytes. To maximize performance, IA-64 supports multiple page sizes and Linux can be configured to use a size of 4, 8, 16, or 64 Kbytes. In the figure, the 64-bit address space is divided into 16 pages, meaning that each virtual page would have a size of $2^{64}/16 = 2^{60}$ bytes or 1024 Pbytes (1 Pbyte $= 2^{50}$ bytes). Such large pages are not realistic, but the alternative of drawing a figure with several billion pages of a more realistic size is, of course, not practical either. Thus, for this section, we continue to illustrate virtual memory with this huge page size. The figure also shows that virtual pages are numbered sequentially. We can calculate the *virtual page number (VPN)* from a virtual address by dividing it by the page size and taking the integer portion of the result. The remainder is called the *page offset*. For example, dividing virtual address 0x40000000000003f8 by the page size yields 4 and a remainder of 0x3f8. This address therefore maps to virtual page number 4 and page offset 0x3f8.

Let us now turn attention to the right half of Figure 4.1, which shows the physical address space. Just like the virtual space, it is divided into equal-sized pieces, but in physical memory, those pieces are called *page frames*. As with virtual pages, page frames also are numbered. We can calculate the *page frame number (PFN)* from a physical address by dividing it by the page frame size and taking the integer portion of the result. The remainder is the *page frame offset*. Normally, page frames have the same size as virtual pages. However, there are cases where it is beneficial to deviate from this rule. Sometimes it is useful to have virtual pages that are larger than a page frame. Such pages are known as *superpages*. Conversely, it is sometimes useful to divide a page frame into multiple, smaller virtual pages. Such pages are known as *subpages*. IA-64 is capable of supporting both, but Linux does not use them.

While it is easiest to think of physical memory as occupying a single contiguous region in the physical address space, in reality it is not uncommon to encounter *memory holes*. Holes usually are caused by one of three entities: firmware, memory-mapped I/O devices, or unpopulated memory. All three cause portions of the physical address space to be unavailable for storing the content of virtual pages. As far as the kernel is concerned, these portions are holes in the physical memory. In the example in Figure 4.1, page frames 2 and 3 represent a hole. Note that even if just a single byte in a page frame is unusable, the entire frame must be marked as a hole.

4.1.1 Virtual-to-physical address translation

Processes are under the illusion of being able to store data to virtual memory and retrieve it later on as if it were stored in real memory. In reality, only physical memory can store data. Thus, each virtual page that is in use must be mapped to some page frame in physical memory. For example, in Figure 4.1, virtual pages 4, 5, 8, 9, and 11 are in use. The arrows indicate which page frame in physical memory they map to. The mapping between virtual pages and page frames is stored in a data structure called the *page table*. The page table for our example is shown on the left-hand side of Figure 4.2.

The Linux kernel is responsible for creating and maintaining page tables but employs the CPU's *memory management unit (MMU)* to translate the virtual memory accesses of a process into corresponding physical memory accesses. Specifically, when a process accesses a memory location at a particular virtual address, the MMU translates this address into the corresponding physical address, which it then uses to access the physical memory. This is illustrated in Figure 4.2 for the case in which the virtual address is 0x40000000000003f8. As the figure shows, the MMU extracts the VPN (4) from the virtual address and then searches the page table to find the matching PFN. In our case, the search stops at the first entry in the page table since it contains the desired VPN. The PFN associated with this entry is 7. The MMU then constructs the physical address by concatenating the PFN with the frame offset from the virtual address, which results in a physical address of 0x70000000000003f8.

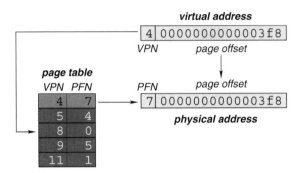

Figure 4.2. Virtual-to-physical address translation.

4.1.2 Demand paging

The next question we need to address is how the page tables get created. Linux could create appropriate page-table entries whenever a range of virtual memory is allocated. However, this would be wasteful because most programs allocate much more virtual memory than they ever use at any given time. For example, the text segment of a program often includes large amounts of error handling code that is seldom executed. To avoid wasting memory on virtual pages that are never accessed, Linux uses a method called *demand paging*. With this method, the virtual address space starts out empty. This means that, logically, all virtual pages are marked in the page table as **not present**. When accessing a virtual page that is not present, the CPU generates a *page fault*. This fault is intercepted by the Linux kernel and causes the page fault handler to be activated. There, the kernel can allocate a new page frame, determine what the content of the accessed page should be (e.g., a new, zeroed page, a page loaded from the data section of a program, or a page loaded from the text segment of a program), load the page, and then update the page table to mark the page as **present**. Execution then resumes in the process with the instruction that caused the fault. Since the required page is now present, the instruction can now execute without causing a page fault.

4.1.3 Paging and swapping

So far, we assumed that physical memory is plentiful: Whenever we needed a page frame to back a virtual page, we assumed a free page frame was available. When a system has many processes or when some processes grow very large, the physical memory can easily fill up. So what is Linux supposed to do when a page frame is needed but physical memory is already full? The answer is that in this case, Linux picks a page frame that backs a virtual page that has not been accessed recently, writes it out to a special area on the disk called the *swap space*, and then reuses the page frame to back the new virtual page. The exact place to which the old page is written on the disk depends on what kind of swap space is in use. Linux can support multiple swap space areas, each of which can be either an entire disk partition or a specially formatted file on an existing filesystem (the former is generally more efficient and therefore preferable). Of course, the page table of the process from which Linux "stole" the page frame must be updated accordingly. Linux does this update by marking the page-table entry as **not present**. To keep track of where the old page has been saved, it also uses the entry to record the disk location of the page. In other words, a page-table entry that is **present** contains the page frame number of the physical page frame that backs the virtual page, whereas a page-table entry that is **not present** contains the disk location at which the content of the page can be found.

Because a page marked as **not present** cannot be accessed without first triggering a page fault, Linux can detect when the page is needed again. When this happens, Linux needs to again find an available page frame (which may cause another page to be paged out), read the page content back from swap space, and then update the page-table entry so that it is marked as **present** and maps to the newly allocated page frame. At this point, the process that attempted to access the paged-out page can be resumed, and, apart from a small delay, it will execute as if the page had been in memory at all along.

The technique of stealing a page from a process and writing it out to disk is called *paging*. A related technique is *swapping*. It is a more aggressive form of paging in the sense that it does not steal an individual page but steals *all* the pages of a process when memory is in short supply. Linux uses paging but not swapping. However, because both paging and swapping write pages to swap space, Linux kernel programmers often use the terms "swapping" and "paging" interchangeably. This is something to keep in mind when perusing the kernel source code.

From a correctness point of view, it does not matter which page is selected for page out, but from a performance perspective, the choice is critical. With a poor choice, Linux may end up paging out the page that is needed in the very next memory access. Given the large difference between disk access latency (on the order of several milliseconds) and memory access latency (on the order of tens of nanoseconds), making the right replacement choices can mean the difference between completing a task in a second or in almost three hours!

The algorithm that determines which page to evict from main memory is called the *replacement policy*. The provably *optimal replacement policy (OPT)* is to choose the page that will be accessed farthest in the future. Of course, in general it is impossible to know the future behavior of the processes, so OPT is of theoretical interest only. A replacement policy that often performs almost as well as OPT yet is realizable is the *least recently used (LRU)* policy. LRU looks into the past instead of the future and selects the page that has not been accessed for the longest period of time. Unfortunately, even though LRU could be implemented, it is still not practical because it would require updating a data structure (such as an LRU list) on *every* access to main memory. In practice, operating systems use approximations of the LRU policy instead, such as the *clock replacement* or *not frequently used (NFU)* policies [11, 69].

In Linux, the page replacement is complicated by the fact that the kernel can take up a variable amount of (nonpageable) memory. For example, file data is stored in the page cache, which can grow and shrink dynamically. When the kernel needs a new page frame, it often has two choices: It could take away a page from the kernel or it could steal a page from a process. In other words, the kernel needs not just a replacement policy but also a *memory balancing policy* that determines how much memory is used for kernel buffers and how much is used to back virtual pages. The combination of page replacement and memory balancing poses a difficult problem for which there is no perfect solution. Consequently, the Linux kernel uses a variety of heuristics that tend to work well in practice.

To implement these heuristics, the Linux kernel expects the platform-specific part of the kernel to maintain two extra bits in each page-table entry: the **accessed** bit and the **dirty** bit. The **accessed** bit is an indicator that tells the kernel whether the page was accessed (read, written, or executed) since the bit was last cleared. Similarly, the **dirty** bit is an indicator that tells whether the page has been modified since it was last paged in. Linux uses a kernel thread, called the kernel swap daemon *kswapd*, to periodically inspect these bits. After inspection, it clears the **accessed** bit. If kswapd detects that the kernel is starting to run low on memory, its starts to proactively page out memory that has not been used recently. If the **dirty** bit of a page is set, it needs to write the page to disk before the page frame can be freed. Because this is relatively costly, kswapd preferentially frees pages whose **accessed** and **dirty** bits are cleared to 0. By definition such pages were not accessed recently and do not have to be written back to disk before the page frame can be freed, so they can be reclaimed at very little cost.

4.1.4   Protection

In a multiuser and multitasking system such as Linux, multiple processes often execute the same program. For example, each user who is logged into the system at a minimum is running a command shell (e.g., the Bourne-Again shell, `bash`). Similarly, server processes such as the Apache web server often use multiple processes running the same program to better handle heavy loads. If we looked at the virtual space of each of those processes, we would find that they share many identical pages. Moreover, many of those pages are never modified during the lifetime of a process because they contain read-only data or the text segment of the program, which also does not change during the course of execution. Clearly, it would make a lot of sense to exploit this commonality and use only one page frame for each virtual page with identical content.

With N processes running the same program, sharing identical pages can reduce physical memory consumption by up to a factor of N. In reality, the savings are usually not quite so dramatic, because each process tends to require a few private pages. A more realistic example is illustrated in Figure 4.3: Page frames 0, 1, and 5 are used to back virtual pages 1, 2, and 3 in the two processes called `bash 1` and `bash 2`. Note that a total of nine virtual pages are in use, but thanks to page sharing, only six page frames are needed.

Of course, page sharing cannot be done safely unless we can guarantee that none of the shared pages are modified. Otherwise, the changes of one process would be visible in all the other processes and that could lead to unpredictable program behavior.

This is where the page *permission bits* come into play. The Linux kernel expects the platform-specific part of the kernel to maintain three such bits per page-table entry. They are called the R, W, and X permission bits and respectively control whether read, write, or execute accesses to the page are permitted. If an access that is not permitted is attempted, a *page protection violation* fault is raised. When this happens, the kernel responds by sending a segmentation violation signal (SIGSEGV) to the process.

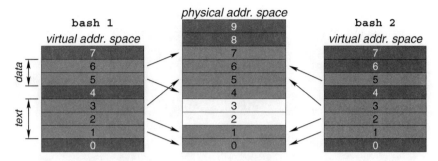

Figure 4.3. Two processes sharing the text segment (virtual pages 1 to 3).

The page permission bits enable the safe sharing of page frames. All the Linux kernel has to do is ensure that all virtual pages that refer to a shared page frame have the W permission bit turned off. That way, if a process attempted to modify a shared page, it would receive a segmentation violation signal before it could do any harm.

The most obvious place where page frame sharing can be used effectively is in the text segment of a program: By definition, this segment can be executed and read, but it is never written to. In other words, the text segment pages of all processes running the same program can be shared. The same applies to read-only data pages.

Linux takes page sharing one step further. When a process forks a copy of itself, the kernel disables write access to *all* virtual pages and sets up the page tables such that the parent and the child process share all page frames. In addition, it marks the pages that were writable before as *copy-on-write (COW)*. If the parent or the child process attempts to write to a copy-on-write page, a protection violation fault occurs. When this happens, instead of sending a segmentation violation signal, the kernel first makes a private copy of the virtual page and then turns the write permission bit for that page back on. At this point, execution can return to the faulting process. Because the page is now writable, the faulting instruction can finish execution without causing a fault again. The copy-on-write scheme is particularly effective when a program does a *fork()* that is quickly followed by an *execve()*. In such a case, the scheme is able to avoid almost all page copying, save for a few pages in the stack- or data-segment [9, 64].

Note that the page sharing described here happens automatically and without the explicit knowledge of the process. There are times when two or more processes need to cooperate and want to explicitly share some virtual memory pages. Linux supports this through the *mmap()* system call and through System V shared memory segments [9]. Because the processes are cooperating, it is their responsibility to map the shared memory segment with suitable permission bits to ensure that the processes can access the memory only in the intended fashion.

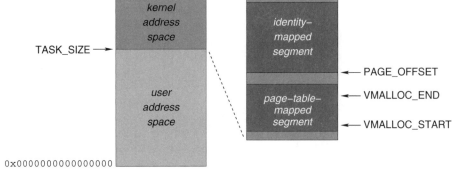

Figure 4.4. Structure of Linux address space.

4.2 ADDRESS SPACE OF A LINUX PROCESS

The virtual address space of any Linux process is divided into two subspaces: kernel space and user space. As illustrated on the left-hand side of Figure 4.4, user space occupies the lower portion of the address space, starting from address 0 and extending up to the platform-specific *task size limit* (TASK_SIZE in file include/asm/processor.h). The remainder is occupied by kernel space. Most platforms use a task size limit that is large enough so that at least half of the available address space is occupied by the user address space.

User space is private to the process, meaning that it is mapped by the process's own page table. In contrast, kernel space is shared across all processes. There are two ways to think about kernel space: We can either think of it as being mapped into the top part of each process, or we can think of it as a single space that occupies the top part of the CPU's virtual address space. Interestingly, depending on the specifics of CPU on which Linux is running, kernel space can be implemented in one or the other way.

During execution at the user level, only user space is accessible. Attempting to read, write, or execute kernel space would cause a protection violation fault. This prevents a faulty or malicious user process from corrupting the kernel. In contrast, during execution in the kernel, both user and kernel spaces are accessible.

Before continuing our discussion, we need to say a few words about the page size used by the Linux kernel. Because different platforms have different constraints on what page sizes they can support, Linux never assumes a particular page size and instead uses the platform-specific *page size constant* (PAGE_SIZE in file include/asm/page.h) where necessary. Although Linux can accommodate arbitrary page sizes, throughout the rest of this chapter we assume a page size of 8 Kbytes, unless stated otherwise. This assumption helps to make the discussion more concrete and avoids excessive complexity in the following examples and figures.

4.2.1   User address space

Let us now take a closer look at how Linux implements the user address spaces. Each address space is represented in the kernel by an object called the *mm structure* (struct mm_struct in file include/linux/sched.h). As we have seen in Chapter 3, *Processes, Tasks, and Threads*, multiple tasks can share the same address space, so the mm structure is a reference-counted object that exists as long as at least one task is using the address space represented by the mm structure. Each task structure has a pointer to the mm structure that defines the address space of the task. This pointer is known as the *mm pointer*. As a special case, tasks that are known to access kernel space only (such as kswapd) are said to have an *anonymous address space*, and the mm pointer of such tasks is set to NULL. When switching execution to such a task, Linux does not switch the address space (because there is none to switch to) and instead leaves the old one in place. A separate pointer in the task structure tracks which address space has been borrowed in this fashion. This pointer is known as the *active mm pointer* of the task. For a task that is currently running, this pointer is guaranteed not to be NULL. If the task has its own address space, the active mm pointer has the same value as the mm pointer; otherwise, the active mm pointer refers to the mm structure of the borrowed address space.

Perhaps somewhat surprisingly, the mm structure itself is not a terribly interesting object. However, it is a central hub in the sense that it contains the pointers to the two data structures that are at the core of the virtual memory system: the page table and the list of virtual memory areas, which we describe next. Apart from these two pointers, the mm structure contains miscellaneous information, such as the mm context, which we describe in more detail in Section 4.4.3, a count of the number of virtual pages currently in use (the *resident set size*, or *RSS*), the start and end address of the text, data, and stack segments as well as housekeeping information that kswapd uses when looking for virtual memory to page out.

Virtual memory areas

In theory, a page table is all the kernel needs to implement virtual memory. However, page tables are not effective in representing huge address spaces, especially when they are sparse. To see this, let us assume that a process uses 1 Gbytes of its address space for a hash table and then enters 128 Kbytes of data in it. If we assume that the page size is 8 Kbytes and that each entry in the page table takes up 8 bytes, then the page table itself would take up 1 Gbyte/8 Kbytes · 8 byte = 1 Mbyte of space—an order of magnitude more than the actual data stored in the hash table!

To avoid this kind of inefficiency, Linux does not represent address spaces with page tables. Instead, it uses lists of *vm-area structures* (struct vm_area_struct in file include/-linux/mm.h). The idea is to divide an address space into contiguous ranges of pages that can be handled in the same fashion. Each range can then be represented by a single vm-area structure. If a process accesses a page for which there is no translation in the page table, the vm-area covering that page has all the information needed to install the missing page. For our hash table example, this means that a single vm-area would suffice to map the entire hash table and that page-table memory would be needed only for recently accessed pages.

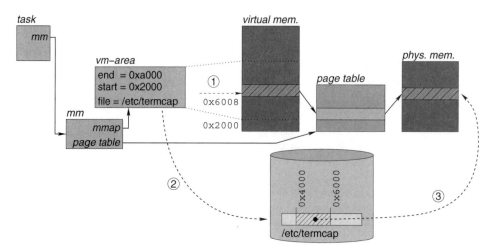

Figure 4.5. Example: vm-area mapping a file.

To get a better sense of how the kernel uses vm-areas, let us consider the example in Figure 4.5. It shows a process that maps the first 32 Kbytes (four pages) of the file /etc/termcap at virtual address 0x2000. At the top-left of the figure, we find the task structure of the process and the mm pointer that leads to the mm structure representing the address space of the process. From there, the mmap pointer leads to the first element in the vm-area list. For simplicity, we assume that the vm-area for the mapped file is the only one in this process, so this list contains just one entry. The mm structure also has a pointer to the page table, which is initially empty. Apart from these kernel data structures, the process's virtual memory is shown in the middle of the figure, the filesystem containing /etc/termcap is represented by the disk-shaped form, and the physical memory is shown on the right-hand side of the figure.

Now, suppose the process attempts to read the word at address 0x6008, as shown by the arrow labeled (1). Because the page table is empty, this attempt results in a page fault. In response to this fault, Linux searches the vm-area list of the current process for a vm-area that covers the faulting address. In our case, it finds that the one and only vm-area on the list maps the address range from 0x2000 to 0xa000 and hence covers the faulting address. By calculating the distance from the start of the mapped area, Linux finds that the process attempted to access page 2 ($\lfloor 0x6008 - 0x2000/8192 \rfloor = 2$). Because the vm-area maps a file, Linux initiates the disk read illustrated by the arrow labeled (2). We assumed that the vm-area maps the first 32KB of the file, so the data for page 2 can be found at file offsets 0x4000 through 0x5fff. When this data arrives, Linux copies it to an available page frame as illustrated by the arrow labeled (3). In the last step, Linux updates the page table with an entry that maps the virtual page at 0x6000 to the physical page frame that now contains the file data. At this point, the process can resume execution. The read access will be restarted and will now complete successfully, returning the desired file data.

As this example illustrates, the vm-area list provides Linux with the ability to (re-)create the page-table entry for any address that is mapped in the address space of a process. This implies that the page table can be treated almost like a cache: If the translation for a particular page is present, the kernel can go ahead and use it, and if it is missing, it can be created from the matching vm-area. Treating the page table in this fashion provides a tremendous amount of flexibility because translations for clean pages can be removed at will. Translations for dirty pages can be removed only if they are backed by a file (not by swap space). Before removal, they have to be cleaned by writing the page content back to the file. As we see later, the cache-like behavior of page tables provides the foundation for the copy-on-write algorithm that Linux uses.

AVL trees

As we have seen so far, the vm-area list helps Linux avoid many of the inefficiencies of a system that is based entirely on page tables. However, there is still a problem. If a process maps many different files into its address space, it may end up with a vm-area list that is hundreds or perhaps even thousands of entries long. As this list grows longer, the kernel executes more and more slowly as each page fault requires the kernel to traverse this list. To ameliorate this problem, the kernel tracks the number of vm-areas on the list, and if there are too many, it creates a secondary data structure that organizes the vm-areas as an AVL tree [42, 62]. An AVL tree is a normal binary search tree, except that it has the special property that for each node in the tree, the height of the two subtrees differs by at most 1. Using the standard tree-search algorithm, this property ensures that, given a virtual address, the matching vm-area structure can be found in a number of steps that grows only with the logarithm of the number of vm-areas in the address space.[1]

Let us consider a concrete example. Figure 4.6 show the AVL tree for an Emacs process as it existed right after it was started up on a Linux/ia64 machine. For space reasons, the figure represents each node with a rectangle that contains just the starting and ending address of the address range covered by the vm-area. As customary for a search tree, the vm-area nodes appear in the order of increasing starting address. Given a node with a starting address of x, the vm-areas with a lower starting address can be found in the lower ("left") subtree and the vm-areas with a higher starting address can be found in the higher ("right") subtree. The root of the tree is at the left end of the figure, and, as indicated by the arrows, the tree grows toward the right side. While it is somewhat unusual for a tree to grow from left to right, this representation has the advantage that the higher a node in the figure, the higher its starting address.

First, observe that this tree is not perfectly balanced: It has a height of six, yet there is a missing node at the fifth level as illustrated by the dashed rectangle. Despite this imperfection, the tree does have the AVL property that the height of the subtrees at any node never differs by more than one. Second, note that the tree contains 47 vm-areas. If we were to use a linear search to find the vm-area for a given address, we would have to visit 23.5 vm-area structures on average and, in the worst case, we might have to visit all 47 of them. In con-

---

[1]In Linux v2.4.10 Andrea Arcangeli replaced AVL trees with Red-Black trees [62]. Red-Black trees are also balanced, but can be implemented more efficiently.

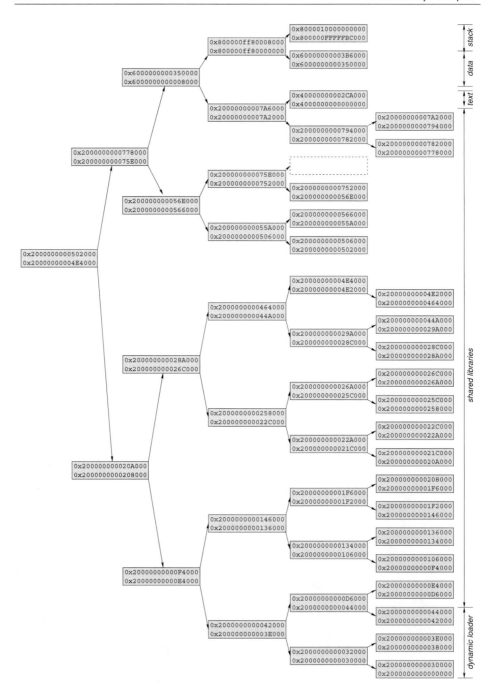

Figure 4.6. AVL tree of vm-area structures for a process running Emacs.

trast, when the AVL tree is searched, at most six vm-areas have to be visited, as given by the height of the tree. Clearly, using an AVL tree is a big win for complex address spaces. However, for simple address spaces, the overhead of creating the AVL tree and keeping it balanced is too much compared to the cost of searching a short linear list. For this reason, Linux does not create the AVL tree until the address space contains at least 32 vm-areas. Let us emphasize that even when the AVL tree is being maintained, the linear list continues to be maintained as well; this provides an efficient means to visit *all* vm-area structures.

Anatomy of the vm-area structure

So far, we discussed the purpose of the vm-area structure and how the Linux kernel uses it, but not what it looks like. The list below rectifies this situation by describing the major components of the vm-area:

- **Address range:** Describes the address range covered by the vm-area in the form of a start and end address. It is noteworthy that the end address is the address of the first byte that is *not* covered by the vm-area.

- **VM flags:** Consist of a single word that contains various flag bits. The most important among them are the access right flags VM_READ, VM_WRITE, and VM_EXEC, which control whether the process can, respectively, read, write, or execute the virtual memory mapped by the vm-area. Two other important flags are VM_GROWSDOWN and VM_GROWSUP, which control whether the address range covered by the vm-area can be extended toward lower or higher addresses, respectively. As we see later, this provides the means to grow user stacks dynamically.

- **Linkage info:** Contain various linkage information, including the pointer needed for the mm structure's vm-area list, pointers to the left and right subtrees of the AVL tree, and a pointer that leads back to the mm structure to which the vm-area belongs.

- **VM operations and private data:** Contain the *VM operations pointer*, which is a pointer to a set of callback functions that define how various virtual-memory-related events, such as page faults, are to be handled. The component also contains a private data pointer that can be used by the callback functions as a hook to maintain information that is vm-area–specific.

- **Mapped file info:** If a vm-area maps a portion of a file, this component stores the file pointer and the file offset needed to locate the file data.

Note that the vm-area structure is not reference-counted. There is no need to do that because each structure belongs to one and only one mm structure, which is already reference-counted. In other words, when the reference-count of an mm structure reaches 0, it is clear that the vm-area structures owned by it are also no longer needed.

A second point worth making is that the VM operations pointer gives the vm-area characteristics that are object-like because different types of vm-areas can have different handlers for responding to virtual-memory-related events. Indeed, Linux allows each filesystem, character device, and, more generally, any object that can be mapped into user

space by *mmap()* to provide its own set VM operations. The operations that can be provided in this fashion are *open()*, *close()*, and *nopage()*. The *open()* and *close()* callbacks are
invoked whenever a vm-area is created or destroyed, respectively, and is used primarily to
keep track of the number of vm-areas that are currently using the underlying object. The
nopage() callback is invoked when a page fault occurs for an address for which there is no
page-table entry. The Linux kernel provides default implementations for each of these callbacks. These default versions are used if either the VM operations pointer or a particular
callback pointer is NULL. For example, if the *nopage()* callback is NULL, Linux handles the
page fault by creating an *anonymous page*, which is a process-private page whose content
is initially cleared to 0.

4.2.2   Page-table-mapped kernel segment

Let us now return to Figure 4.4 and take a closer look at the kernel address space. The right-
hand side of this figure is an enlargement of the kernel space and shows that it contains two
segments: the identity-mapped segment and the page-table-mapped segment. The latter
is mapped by a kernel-private page table and is used primarily to implement the kernel
vmalloc arena (file include/linux/vmalloc.h). The kernel uses this arena to allocate large
blocks of memory that must be contiguous in virtual space. For example, the memory
required to load a kernel module is allocated from this arena. The address range occupied
by the vmalloc arena is defined by the platform-specific constants VMALLOC_START and
VMALLOC_END. As indicated in the figure, the vmalloc arena does not necessarily occupy
the entire page-table-mapped segment. This makes it possible to use part of the segment
for platform-specific purposes.

4.2.3   Identity-mapped kernel segment

The identity-mapped segment starts at the address defined by the platform-specific constant
PAGE_OFFSET. This segment contains the Linux kernel image, including its text, data, and
stack segments. In other words, this is the segment that the kernel is executing in when in
kernel mode (unless when executing in a module).

    The identity-mapped segment is special because there is a direct mapping between a vir-
tual address in this segment and the physical address that it translates to. The exact formula
for this mapping is platform specific, but it is often as simple as *vaddr* − PAGE_OFFSET.
This one-to-one (identity) relationship between virtual and physical addresses is what gives
the segment its name.

    The segment could be implemented with a normal page table. However, because there is
a direct relationship between virtual and physical addresses, many platforms can optimize
this case and avoid the overhead of a page table. How this is done on IA-64 is described in
Section 4.5.3.

    Because the actual formula to translate between a physical address and the equivalent
virtual address is platform specific, the kernel uses the interface in Figure 4.7 to perform
such translations. The interface provides two routines: _*pa()* expects a single argument,
vaddr, and returns the physical address that corresponds to *vaddr*. The return value is un-

unsigned long __**pa**(*vaddr*);	/* *translate virtual address to physical address* */
void *__**va**(*paddr*);	/* *translate physical address to virtual address* */

Figure 4.7. Kernel interface to convert between physical and virtual addresses.

defined if *vaddr* does not point inside the kernel's identity-mapped segment. Routine __*va()* provides the reverse mapping: it takes a physical address *paddr* and returns the corresponding virtual address. Usually the Linux kernel expects virtual addresses to have a pointer-type (such as **void ***) and physical addresses to have a type of **unsigned long**. However, the __*pa()* and __*va()* macros are polymorphic and accept arguments of either type.

A platform is free to employ an arbitrary mapping between physical and virtual addresses provided that the following relationships are true:

$$\_\_va(\_\_pa(vaddr)) \quad = \quad vaddr \quad \text{for all } vaddr \text{ inside the identity-mapped segment}$$

$$paddr_1 < paddr_2 \quad \Rightarrow \quad \_\_va(paddr_1) < \_\_va(paddr_2)$$

That is, mapping any virtual address inside the identity-mapped segment to a physical address and back must return the original virtual address. The second condition is that the mapping must be monotonic, i.e., the relative order of a pair of physical addresses is preserved when they are mapped to virtual addresses.

We might wonder why the constant that marks the beginning of the identity-mapped segment is called PAGE_OFFSET. The reason is that the page frame number *pfn* for an address *addr* in this segment can be calculated as:

$$pfn \quad = \quad (addr - \text{PAGE\_OFFSET})/\text{PAGE\_SIZE}$$

As we will see next, even though the page frame number is easy to calculate, the Linux kernel does not use it very often.

Page frame map

Linux uses a table called the *page frame map* to keep track of the status of the physical page frames in a machine. For each page frame, this table contains exactly one *page frame descriptor* (struct page in file include/linux/mm.h). This descriptor contains various housekeeping information, such as a count of the number of address spaces that are using the page frame, various flags that indicate whether the frame can be paged out to disk, whether it has been accessed recently, or whether it is dirty (has been written to), and so on.

While the exact content of the page frame descriptor is of no concern for this chapter, we do need to understand that Linux often uses page frame descriptor pointers in lieu of page frame numbers. The Linux kernel leaves it to platform-specific code how virtual addresses in the identity-mapped segment are translated to page frame descriptor pointers, and vice versa. It uses the interface shown in Figure 4.8 for this purpose.

Because we are not concerned with the internals of the page frame descriptor, Figure 4.8 lists its type (struct page) simply as an opaque structure. The *virt_to_page()* routine can be

struct **page**;	/* page frame descriptor */
struct page *virt_to_page(vaddr);	/* return page frame descriptor for vaddr */
void *page_address(page);	/* return virtual address for page */

Figure 4.8. Kernel interface to convert between pages and virtual addresses.

used to obtain the page frame descriptor pointer for a given virtual address. It expects one argument, *vaddr*, which must be an address inside the identity-mapped segment, and returns a pointer to the corresponding page frame descriptor. The *page_address()* routine provides the reverse mapping: It expects the *page* argument to be a pointer to a page frame descriptor and returns the virtual address inside the identity-mapped segment that maps the corresponding page frame.

Historically, the page frame map was implemented with a single array of page frame descriptors. This array was called *mem_map* and was indexed by the page frame number. In other words, the value returned by *virt_to_page()* could be calculated as:

$$\&mem\_map[(addr - \mathsf{PAGE\_OFFSET})/\mathsf{PAGE\_SIZE}]$$

However, on machines with a physical address space that is either fragmented or has huge holes, using a single array can be problematic. In such cases, it is better to implement the page frame map by using multiple partial maps (e.g., one map for each set of physically contiguous page frames). The interface in Figure 4.8 provides the flexibility necessary for platform-specific code to implement such solutions, and for this reason the Linux kernel no longer uses the above formula directly.

High memory support

The size of the physical address space has no direct relationship to the size of the virtual address space. It could be smaller than, the same size as, or even larger than the virtual space. On a new architecture, the virtual address space is usually designed to be much larger than the largest anticipated physical address space. Not surprisingly, this is the case for which Linux is designed and optimized.

However, the size of the physical address space tends to increase roughly in line with Moore's Law, which predicts a doubling of chip capacity every 18 months [57]. Because the virtual address space is part of an architecture, its size cannot be changed easily (e.g., changing it would at the very least require recompilation of all applications). Thus, over the course of many years, the size of the physical address space tends to encroach on the size of the virtual address space until, eventually, it becomes as large as or larger than the virtual space.

This is a problem for Linux because once the physical memory has a size similar to that of the virtual space, the identity-mapped segment may no longer be large enough to map the entire physical space. For example, the IA-32 architecture defines an extension that supports a 36-bit physical address space even though the virtual address space has only 32 bits. Clearly, the physical address space cannot fit inside the virtual address space.

unsigned long **kmap**(*page*);	/* *map page frame into virtual space* */
kunmap(*page*);	/* *unmap page frame from virtual space* */

Figure 4.9. Primary routines for the highmem interface.

The Linux kernel alleviates this problem through the *highmem interface* (file include/-linux/highmem.h). *High memory* is physical memory that cannot be addressed through the identity-mapped segment. The highmem interface provides indirect access to this memory by dynamically mapping high memory pages into a small portion of the kernel address space that is reserved for this purpose. This part of the kernel address space is known as the *kmap segment*.

Figure 4.9 shows the two primary routines provided by the highmem interface: *kmap()* maps the page frame specified by argument *page* into the kmap segment. The argument must be a pointer to the page frame descriptor of the page to be mapped. The routine returns the virtual address at which the page was mapped. If the kmap segment is full at the time this routine is called, it will block until space becomes available. This implies that high memory cannot be used in interrupt handlers or any other code that cannot block execution for an indefinite amount of time. Both high and normal memory pages can be mapped with this routine, though in the latter case *kmap()* simply returns the appropriate address in the identity-mapped segment.

When the kernel has finished using a high memory page, it unmaps the page by a call to *kunmap()*. The *page* argument passed to this routine is a pointer to the page frame descriptor of the page that is to be unmapped. Unmapping a page frees up the virtual address space that the page occupied in the kmap segment. This space then becomes available for use by other mappings. To reduce the amount of blocking resulting from a full kmap segment, Linux attempts to minimize the amount of time that high memory pages are mapped.

Clearly, supporting high memory incurs extra overhead and limitations in the kernel and should be avoided where possible. For this reason, high memory support is an optional component of the Linux kernel. Because IA-64 affords a vastly larger virtual address space than that provided by 32-bit architectures, high memory support is not needed and therefore disabled in Linux/ia64. However, it should be noted that the highmem *interface* is available even on platforms that do not provide high memory support. On those platforms, *kmap()* is equivalent to *page_address()* and *kunmap()* performs no operation. These dummy implementations greatly simplify writing platform-independent kernel code. Indeed, it is good kernel programming practice to use the *kmap()* and *kunmap()* routines whenever possible. Doing so results in more efficient memory use on platforms that need high memory support (such as IA-32) without impacting the platforms that do not need it (such as IA-64).

Summary

Figure 4.10 summarizes the relationship between physical memory and kernel virtual space for a hypothetical machine that has high memory support enabled. In this machine, the identity-mapped segment can map only the first seven page frames of the physical address

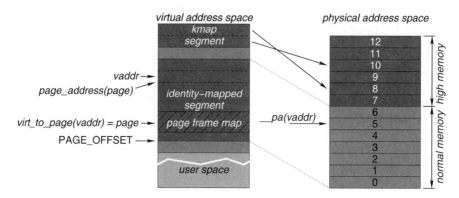

Figure 4.10. Summary of identity-mapped segment and high memory support.

space—the remaining memory consisting of page frames 7 through 12 is high memory and can be accessed through the kmap segment only. The figure illustrates the case in which page frames 8 and 10 have been mapped into this segment. Because our hypothetical machine has a kmap segment that consists of only two pages, the two mappings use up all available space. Trying to map an additional high memory page frame by calling *kmap()* would block the caller until page frame 8 or 10 is unmapped by a call to *kunmap()*.

Let us now turn attention to the arrow labeled *vaddr*. It points to the middle of the second-last page mapped by the identity-mapped segment. We can find the physical address of *vaddr* with the *__pa()* routine. As the arrow labeled *__pa(vaddr)* illustrates, this physical address not surprisingly points to the middle of page frame 5 (the second-to-last page frame in normal memory).

The figure illustrates the page frame map as the diagonally shaded area inside the identity-mapped segment (we assume that our hypothetical machine uses a single contiguous table for this purpose). Note that this table contains page frame descriptors for *all* page frames in the machine, including the high memory page frames. To get more information on the status of page frame 5, we can use *virt_to_page(vaddr)* to get the *page* pointer for the page frame descriptor of that page. This is illustrated in the figure by the arrow labeled *page*. Conversely, we can use the *page* pointer to calculate *page_address(page)* to obtain the starting address of the virtual page that contains *vaddr*.

4.2.4   Structure of IA-64 address space

The IA-64 architecture provides a full 64-bit virtual address space. As illustrated in Figure 4.11, the address space is divided into eight *regions* of equal size. Each region covers 2^{61} bytes or 2048 Pbytes. Regions are numbered from 0 to 7 according to the top three bits of the address range they cover. The IA-64 architecture has no a priori restrictions on how these regions can be used. However, Linux/ia64 uses regions 0 through 4 as the user address space and regions 5 through 7 as the kernel address space.

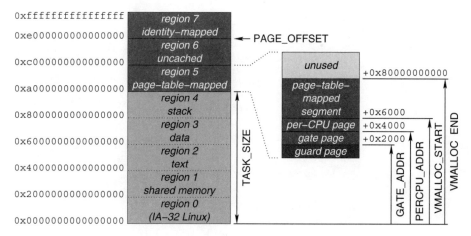

Figure 4.11. Structure of Linux/ia64 address space.

There are also no restrictions on how a process can use the five regions that map the
user space, but the usage illustrated in the figure is typical: Region 1 is used for shared
memory segments and shared libraries, region 2 maps the text segment, region 3 the data
segment, and region 4 the memory and register stacks of a process. Region 0 normally
remains unused by 64-bit applications but is available for emulating a 32-bit operating
system such as IA-32 Linux.

In the kernel space, the figure shows that the identity-mapped segment is implemented
in region 7 and that region 5 is used for the page-table mapped segment. Region 6 is
identity-mapped like region 7, but the difference is that accesses through region 6 are not
cached. As we discuss in Chapter 7, *Device I/O*, this provides a simple and efficient means
for memory-mapped I/O.

The right half of Figure 4.11 provides additional detail on the anatomy of region 5. As
illustrated there, the first page is the *guard page*. It is guaranteed *not* to be mapped so that
any access is guaranteed to result in a page fault. As we see in Chapter 5, *Kernel Entry
and Exit*, this page is used to accelerate the permission checks required when data is copied
across the user/kernel boundary. The second page in this region serves as the *gate page*. It
assists in transitioning from the user to the kernel level, and vice versa. For instance, as we
also see in Chapter 5, this page is used when a signal is delivered and could also be used
for certain system calls. The third page is called the *per-CPU page*. It provides one page
of CPU-local data, which is useful on MP machines. We discuss this page in more detail
in Chapter 8, *Symmetric Multiprocessing*. The remainder of region 5 is used as the vmalloc
arena and spans the address range from VMALLOC_START to VMALLOC_END. The exact
values of these platform-specific constants depend on the page size. As customary in this
chapter, the figure illustrates the case in which a page size of 8 Kbytes is in effect.

63   61   IMPL_VA_MSB   0

| vrn | *unimplemented* | *implemented* |

Figure 4.12. Format of IA-64 virtual address.

+0x1ffffffffffffff

+0x1ff8000000000000

unimplemented

+0x0007ffffffffffff

+0x0000000000000000

Figure 4.13. Address-space hole within a region with IMPL_VA_MSB = 50.

Virtual address format

Even though IA-64 defines a 64-bit address space, implementations are not required to fully support each address bit. Specifically, the virtual address format mandated by the architecture is illustrated in Figure 4.12. As shown in the figure, bits 61 through 63 must be implemented because they are used to select the virtual region number (vrn).

The lower portion of the virtual address consists of a CPU-model-specific number of bits. The most significant bit is identified by constant IMPL_VA_MSB. This value must be in the range of 50 to 60. For example, on Itanium this constant has a value of 50, meaning that the lower portion of the virtual address consists of 51 bits.

The unimplemented portion of the virtual address consists of bits IMPL_VA_MSB + 1 through 60. Even though they are marked as **unimplemented**, the architecture requires that the value in these bits match the value in bit IMPL_VA_MSB. In other words, the unimplemented bits must correspond to the sign-extended value of the lower portion of the virtual address. This restriction has been put in place to ensure that software does not abuse unimplemented bits for purposes such as type tag bits. Otherwise, such software might break when running on a machine that implements a larger number of virtual address bits.

On implementations where IMPL_VA_MSB is less than 60, this sign extension has the effect of dividing the virtual address space within a region into two disjoint areas. Figure 4.13 illustrates this for the case in which IMPL_VA_MSB = 50: The sign extension creates the unimplemented area in the middle of the region. Any access to that area will cause the CPU to take a fault. For a user-level access, such a fault is normally translated into an illegal instruction signal (SIGILL). At the kernel level, such an access would cause a kernel panic.

Although an address-space hole in the middle of a region may seem problematic, it really poses no particular problem and in fact provides an elegant way to leave room for future growth without impacting existing application-level software. To see this, consider an application that requires a huge data heap. If the heap is placed in the lower portion of the

Figure 4.14. Format of IA-64 physical address.

region, it can grow toward higher addresses. On a CPU with IMPL_VA_MSB $= 50$, the heap could grow to at most 1024 Tbytes. However, when the same application is run on a CPU with IMPL_VA_MSB $= 51$, the heap could now grow up to 2048 Tbytes—without changing its starting address. Similarly, data structures that grow toward lower addresses (such as the memory stack) can be placed in the upper portion of the region and can then grow toward the CPU-model-specific lower bound of the implemented address space. Again, the application can run on different implementations and take advantage of the available address space without moving the starting point of the data structure.

Of course, an address-space hole in the middle of a region does imply that an application must not, e.g., attempt to sequentially access all possible virtual addresses in a region. Given how large a region is, this operation would not be a good idea at any rate and so is not a problem in practice.

Physical address space

The physical address format used by IA-64 is illustrated in Figure 4.14. Like virtual addresses, physical addresses are 64 bits wide. However, bit 63 is the uc bit and serves a special purpose: If 0, it indicates a cacheable memory access; if 1, it indicates an uncacheable access. The remaining bits in a physical address are split into two portions: implemented and unimplemented bits. As the figure shows, the lower portion must be implemented and covers bits 0 up to a CPU-model-specific bit number called IMPL_PA_MSB. The architecture requires this constant to be in the range of 32 to 62. For example, Itanium implements 44 address bits and therefore IMPL_PA_MSB is 43. The unimplemented portion of a physical address extends from bit IMPL_PA_MSB $+ 1$ to 62. Unlike a virtual address, a valid physical address must have all unimplemented bits cleared to 0 (i.e., the unimplemented portion is the zero-extended instead of the sign-extended value of the implemented portion).

The physical address format gives rise to the physical address space illustrated in Figure 4.15. As determined by the uc bit, it is divided into two halves: The lower half is the cached physical address space and the upper half is the uncached space. Note that physical addresses x and $2^{63} + x$ correspond to the same memory location—the only difference is that an access to the latter address will bypass all caches. In other words, the two halves alias each other.

If IMPL_PA_MSB is smaller than 62, the upper portion of each half is unimplemented. Any attempt to access memory in this portion of the physical address space causes the CPU to take an UNIMPLEMENTED DATA ADDRESS FAULT.

Recall from Figure 4.11 on page 149 that Linux/ia64 employs a single region for the identity-mapped segment. Because a region spans 61 address bits, Linux can handle IMPL-_PA_MSB values of up to 60 before the region fills up and high memory support needs to

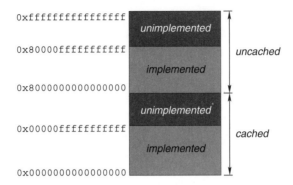

Figure 4.15. Physical address space with IMPL_PA_MSB = 43.

be enabled. To get a back-of-the-envelope estimate of how quickly this could happen, let us assume that at the inception of IA-64 the maximum practical physical memory size was 1 Tbytes (2^{40} bytes). Furthermore, let us assume that memory capacity doubles roughly every 18 months. Both assumptions are somewhat on the aggressive side. Even so, more than three decades would have to pass before high memory support would have to be enabled. In other words, it is likely that high memory support will not be necessary during most of the life span, or even the entire life span, of the IA-64 architecture.

4.3 PAGE TABLES

Linux maintains the page table of each process in physical memory and accesses a page table through the identity-mapped kernel segment. Because they are stored in physical memory, page tables themselves cannot be swapped out to disk. This means that a process with a huge virtual address space could run out of memory simply because the page table alone uses up all available memory. Similarly, if thousands of processes are running, the page tables could take up most or even all of the available memory, making it impossible for the processes to run efficiently. However, on modern machines, main memory is usually large enough to make these issues either theoretical or at most second-order. On the positive side, keeping the page tables in physical memory greatly simplifies kernel design because there is no possibility that handling a page fault would cause another (nested) page fault.

Each page table is represented as a multiway tree. Logically, the tree has three levels, as illustrated in Figure 4.16. As customary in this chapter, this figure shows the tree growing from left to right: at the first level (leftmost part of the figure), we find the *global directory* (*pgd*); at the second level (to the right of the global directory), we find the *middle directories* (*pmd*); and at the third level we find the *PTE directories*. Typically, each directory (node in the tree) occupies one page frame and contains a fixed number of entries. Entries in the global and middle directories are either **not present** or they point to a directory in the next level of the tree. The PTE directories form the leaves of the tree, and its entries consist of *page-table entries (PTEs)*.

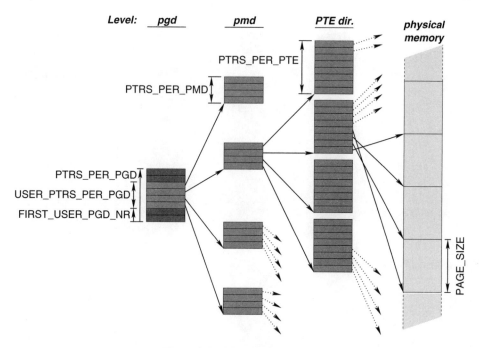

Figure 4.16. Linux page-table tree.

The primary benefit of implementing a page table with a multiway tree instead of a linear array is that the former takes up space that is proportional only to the virtual address space actually *in use*, instead of being proportional to the *maximum* size of the virtual address space. To see this, consider that with a 1-Gbyte virtual address space and 8-Kbyte pages, a linear page table would need storage for more than 131,000 PTEs, even if not a single virtual page was actually in use. In contrast, with a multiway tree, an empty address space requires only a global directory whose entries are all marked **not present**.

Another benefit of multiway trees is that each node (directory) in the tree has a fixed-size (usually a page). This makes it unnecessary to reserve large, physically contiguous regions of memory as would be required for a linear page table. Also, because physical memory is managed as a set of page frames anyhow, the fixed node size makes it easy to build a multiway tree incrementally, as is normally done with demand paging.

Going back to Figure 4.16, we see that the size and structure of the directories is controlled by platform-specific constants. The number of entries in the global, middle, and PTE directories are given by constants PTRS_PER_PGD, PTRS_PER_PMD, and PTRS-_PER_PTE, respectively. The global directory is special because often only part of it can be used to map user space (the rest is either reserved or used for kernel purposes). Two additional parameters define the portion of the global directory that is available for user space. Specifically, FIRST_USER_PGD_NR is the index of the first entry, and USER_PTRS-

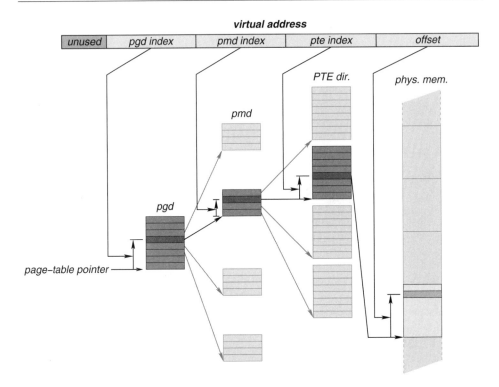

Figure 4.17. Virtual-to-physical address translation using the page table.

_PER_PGD is the total number of global-directory entries available to map user space. For the middle and PTE directories, all entries are assumed to map user space.

So how can we use the page table to translate a virtual address to the corresponding physical address? Figure 4.17 illustrates this. At the top, we see that a virtual address, for the purpose of a page-table lookup, is broken up into multiple fields. The fields used to look up the page table are pgd index, pmd index, and pte index. As their names suggest, these fields are used to index the global, middle, and PTE directories, respectively. A page-table lookup starts with the page-table pointer stored in the mm structure of a process. In the figure, this is illustrated by the arrow labeled *page-table pointer*. It points to the global directory, i.e., the root of the page-table tree. Given the global directory, the pgd index tells us which entry contains the address of the middle directory. With the address of the middle directory, we can use the pmd index to tell us which entry contains the address of the PTE directory. With the address of the PTE directory, we can use the pte index to tell us which entry contains the PTE of the page that the virtual address maps to. With the PTE, we can calculate the address of the physical page frame that backs the virtual page. To finish up the physical address calculation, we just need to add the value in the offset field of the virtual address to the page frame address.

Note that the width of the pgd index, pmd index, and pte index fields is dictated by the number of pointers that can be stored in a global, middle, and PTE directory, respectively. Similarly, the width of the offset field is dictated by the page size. Because these fields by definition consist of an integral number of bits, the page size and the number of entries stored in each directory all must be integer powers of 2. If the sum of the widths of these fields is less than the width of a virtual address, some of the address bits remain unused. The figure illustrates this with the field labeled **unused**. On 32-bit platforms, there are usually no unused bits. However, on 64-bit platforms, the theoretically available virtual address space is so big that it is not unusual for some bits to remain unused. We discuss this in more detail when discussing the IA-64 implementation of the virtual memory system.

4.3.1   Collapsing page-table levels

At the beginning of this section, we said that the Linux page tables *logically* contain three levels. The reason is that each platform is free to implement fewer than three levels. This is possible because the interfaces that Linux uses to access and manipulate page tables have been carefully structured to allow collapsing one or even two levels of the tree into the global directory. This is an elegant solution because it allows platform-independent code to be written as if each platform implemented three levels, yet on platforms that implement fewer levels, the code accessing the unimplemented levels is optimized away completely by the C compiler. That is, no extra overhead results from the extraneous logical page-table levels.

The basic idea behind collapsing a page-table level is to treat a single directory entry as if it were the entire directory for the next level. For example, we can collapse the middle directory into the global directory by treating each global-directory entry as if it were a middle directory with just a single entry (i.e., PTRS_PER_PMD = 1). Later in this chapter, we see some concrete examples of how this works when a page table is accessed.

4.3.2   Virtually-mapped linear page tables

As discussed in the previous section, linear page tables are not very practical when implemented in physical memory. However, under certain circumstances it is possible to map a multiway tree into virtual space and make it appear as if it were a linear page table. The trick that makes this possible is to place a *self-mapping* entry in the global directory. The self-mapping entry, instead of pointing to a middle directory, points to the page frame that contains the global directory. This is illustrated in Figure 4.18 for the case where the global-directory entry with index 7 is used as the self-mapped entry (labeled SELF). Note that the remainder of the global directory continues to be used in the normal fashion, with entries that are either not mapped or that point to a middle directory.

To make it easier to understand how this self-mapping works, let us consider a specific example: Assume that page-table entries are 8 bytes in size, pages are 8 Kbytes in size, and that the directories in the page tree all contain 1024 entries. These assumptions imply that the page offset is 13 bits wide and that the pgd, pmd, and pte indices are all 10 bits wide. The virtual address is thus 43 bits wide. A final assumption we need to make is that the

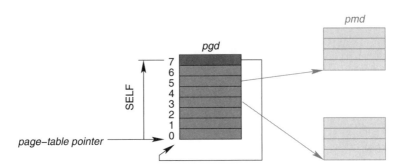

Figure 4.18. Self-mapping entry in the global directory.

format of the entries in the pgd and pmd directories is identical to the format used in the PTE directories.

Assuming the self-mapping entry has been installed in the global-directory entry with index SELF, we claim that the equations below for $L3(va)$, $L2(va)$, and $L1(va)$ are the virtual addresses at which we can find, respectively, the PTE-directory entry, middle-directory entry, and global-directory entry that correspond to virtual address va:

$$L3(va) = \text{SELF} \cdot 2^{33} + 8 \cdot \lfloor va/2^{13} \rfloor$$
$$L2(va) = \text{SELF} \cdot 2^{33} + \text{SELF} \cdot 2^{22} + 8 \cdot \lfloor va/2^{23} \rfloor$$
$$L1(va) = \text{SELF} \cdot 2^{33} + \text{SELF} \cdot 2^{22} + \text{SELF} \cdot 2^{13} + 8 \cdot \lfloor va/2^{33} \rfloor$$

For example, if we assume that $\text{SELF} = 1023 = \text{0x3ff}$, we could access the page-table entry for virtual address $va = \text{0x80af3}$ at virtual address 0x7fe00000200.

The effect of the self-mapping entry can be observed most readily when considering how the above equations affect the virtual address. Figure 4.19 illustrates this effect. The first line shows the virtual address va broken up into the three directory indices va_pgd_idx, va_pmd_idx, va_pte_idx and the page offset va_off. Now, if we consider the effect of equation $L3(va)$, we see that the page offset was replaced by $8 \cdot va\_pte\_idx$ (the factor of 8 comes from the fact that each page-table entry is assumed to be 8 bytes in size). Similarly, the pte index has been replaced with va_pmd_idx, and the pmd index has been replaced with va_pgd_idx. Finally, the pgd index has been replaced with SELF, the index of the self-mapping entry. When we look at the effects of $L2(va)$ and $L1(va)$, we see a pattern emerge: At each level, the previous address is shifted down by 10 bits (the width of an index) and the top 10 bits are filled in with the value of SELF.

Now, let us take a look at what the operational effect of $L1(va)$ is when used in a normal three-level page table lookup. We start at the global directory and access the entry at index SELF. This lookup returns a pointer to a middle directory. However, because this is the self-mapping entry, we really get a pointer to the global directory. In other words, the global directory now serves as a fake middle directory. So we use the global directory

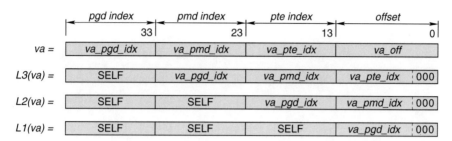

Figure 4.19. Effect of self-mapping entry on virtual address.

again to look up the pmd index, which happens to be SELF again. As before, this lookup returns a pointer back to the global directory but this time the directory serves as a fake PTE directory. To complete the three-level lookup, we again use the global directory to look up the pte index, which again contains SELF. The entry at index SELF is now interpreted as a PTE. Because we are dealing with the self-mapping entry, it once again points to the global directory, which now serves as a fake page frame. The physical address that $L1(va)$ corresponds to is thus equal to the address of global directory plus the page offset of the virtual address, which is $8 \cdot va\_pgd\_idx$. Of course, this is exactly the physical address of the global-directory entry that corresponds to address va—just as we claimed!

For equations $L2(va)$ and $L3(va)$ the same logic applies: Every time SELF appears as a directory index, the final memory access goes one directory level higher than it normally would. That is, with SELF appearing once, we "remove" one directory level and thus access the PTE instead of the word addressed by va, and so on.

Another way to visualize the effect of the self-mapping entry is to look at the resulting virtual address space. Unfortunately, it would be impossible to draw the space to scale with the 1024-way tree we assumed so far. Thus, Figure 4.20 illustrates the address space that would result for a machine where each of the three indices is only 2 bits wide and the page offset is 4 bits wide. In other words, the figure illustrates the address space for a three-level 4-way tree with a 16-byte page size and page-table entries that are 4 bytes in size. The value of SELF is assumed to be 2; i.e., the second-last entry in the global directory is used for the self-mapping entry.

The figure illustrates how the virtually-mapped linear page table occupies the address space from 0x200 to 0x2ff. Not surprisingly, this is the quarter of the address space that corresponds to the global-directory entry occupied by SELF. Most of the linear page table is occupied by page-table entries. However, its third quadrant (0x280 to 0x2df) is occupied primarily by the middle-directory entries. The global-directory entries can be found in the tiny section covering the address range from 0x2a0 to 0x2af. Note how the pmd (and pgd) entries create a hole in the linear page table that corresponds exactly to the hole that the page table creates in the virtual address space. This is necessarily so because otherwise there would be virtual memory addresses for which there would be no PTE entries in the linear page table!

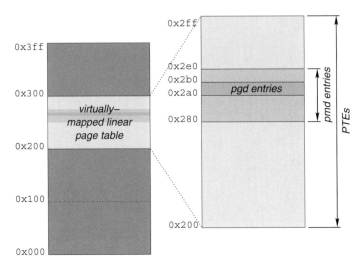

Figure 4.20. Effect of self-mapping entry on virtual address space.

Note that with a more realistic 1024-way tree, the virtual address space occupied by the virtually-mapped linear page table is less than 0.1 percent of the entire address space. In other words, the amount of space occupied by the linear page table is minuscule.

Applications of virtually-mapped linear page tables

A virtually-mapped linear page table could be used as the primary means to manipulate page tables. Once the self-mapping entry has been created in the global directory, all other directory entries can be accessed through the virtual table. For example, to install the page frame of the middle directory for virtual address *va*, we could simply write the new global-directory entry to address $L1(va)$. While this would work correctly, it is usually more efficient to walk the page table in physical space. The reason is that a virtual access involves a full page-table walk (three memory accesses), whereas a page-directory access in physical space would take just one memory access.

The true value of a linear virtual page table derives from the fact that because it is a linear table, special hardware that accelerates page-table lookups can easily be built for it. We see an example of this in Section 4.4.1.

4.3.3   Structure of Linux/ia64 page tables

On IA-64, the Linux kernel uses a three-level page-table tree. Each directory occupies one page frame and entries are 8 bytes in size. With a page size of 8 Kbytes, this implies that the page table forms a 1024-way tree. The global- and middle-directory entries contain the physical address of the next directory or 0 if the entry is not mapped. In contrast, the PTE-directory entries follow the PTE format that we describe in Section 4.3.4.

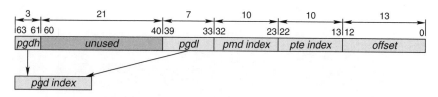

Figure 4.21. Format of user-space virtual address (with 8-Kbyte pages).

Figure 4.21 illustrates the user-space virtual address format. Corresponding to a page size of 8 Kbytes, the page offset occupies the lowest 13 bits. Similarly, because each directory level has 1024 ways, each index is 10 bits wide. As the figure shows, the PTE-directory index (pte index) occupies bits 13 to 22, and the middle-directory index (pmd index) occupies bits 23 to 32. What is unusual is that the global-directory index is split into a 7-bit low part (pgdl) and a 3-bit high part (pgdh) that covers bits 33 to 39 and 61 to 63, respectively. Bits 40 to 60 are unused and must be 0.

The global-directory index is split into two pieces to make it possible to map a portion of the virtual space of each IA-64 region. This provides room for future growth. For example, an application could place its data segment in region 3 and the stacks in region 4. With this arrangement, the starting addresses of the data segment and the stacks would be separated by 2^{61} bytes and the application would be virtually guaranteed that, no matter how much data the application will have to process in the future, its data segment will never collide with the stacks. Of course, the size of the data segment would still be limited by the amount of space that can be mapped within a region, but by using separate regions the application isolates itself from having to know this implementation detail. In other words, as future machines can support more memory, future Linux kernels can implement a larger virtual address space per region and the application will be able to take advantage of this larger space without requiring any changes.

It should be noted that the Linux kernel normally expects directory indices to take up consecutive bits in a virtual address. The exception to this rule is that discontiguities are permitted in the global-directory index *provided* that no vm-area structure maps an address range that would overlap with any of the unimplemented user-space areas. On IA-64, this means that all vm-areas must be fully contained within the first 2^{40} bytes of a region (assuming 8-Kbyte pages, as usual). Linux/ia64 checks for this constraint and rejects any attempts to violate it.

Recall from Figure 4.11 on page 149 that regions 5 through 7 are reserved for kernel use. A process therefore is not permitted to map any addresses into user space for which pgdh would be greater than or equal to 5. The Linux/ia64 kernel enforces this by setting parameters FIRST_USER_PGD_NR to 0 and USER_PTRS_PER_PGD to $5 \cdot 2^7 = 640$. This implies that the top three octants of each global directory remain unused. Apart from wasting a small amount of memory, this does not cause any problems.

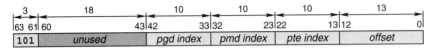

Figure 4.22. Format of kernel virtual address for region 5 (with 8-Kbyte pages).

Table 4.1. Summary of Linux/ia64 virtual memory and page-table parameters.

Parameter	Page size			
	4 Kbytes	8 Kbytes	16 Kbytes	64 Kbytes
total user address space	320 Gbytes	5 Tbytes	80 Tbytes	20 Pbytes
address space per region	64 Gbytes	1 Tbyte	16 Tbytes	4 Pbyte
width of directory index	9 bits	10 bits	11 bits	13 bits
PTRS_PER_PGD	512	1024	2048	8192
PTRS_PER_PMD	512	1024	2048	8192
PTRS_PER_PTE	512	1024	2048	8192
FIRST_USER_PGD_NR	0	0	0	0
USER_PTRS_PER_PGD	320	640	1280	5120

Kernel page table

The kernel uses a separate page table to manage the page-table-mapped kernel segment. In contrast to user space, where there is one page table per process, this page table belongs to the kernel and is in effect independent of which process is running.

On IA-64, this segment is implemented in region 5; the structure of virtual addresses in this region is illustrated in Figure 4.22. We can see that it is identical to Figure 4.21, except that the global-directory index is no longer split into two pieces. Instead, it occupies bits 33 to 42. As required for region 5 addresses, the region number bits 61 to 63 have a fixed value of 5 or, in binary notation, 101.

Summary

Table 4.1 summarizes key virtual-memory and page-table parameters as a function of the Linux/ia64 page size. With a page size of 8 Kbytes, the total mappable user address space is 5 Tbytes (five regions of 1 Tbyte each). Larger page sizes yield correspondingly larger spaces. With the smallest page size of 4 Kbytes, "only" 320 Gbytes of user address space are available. The other extreme is a page size of 64 Kbytes, which yields a mappable user address space of 20 Pbytes ($20 \cdot 2^{50}$ bytes!). By almost any standard, this can only be described as *huge*.

Because Linux/ia64 uses the same index width in each of the three levels of the page table, the three parameters PTRS_PER_PGD, PTRS_PER_PMD, and PTRS_PER_PTE have the same value. With a page size of 8 Kbytes, they are all equal to 1024, and with a page size of 64 Kbytes, they increase to 8192. The value for USER_PTRS_PER_PGD simply reflects the fact that the last three-eights of the address space is occupied by kernel space.

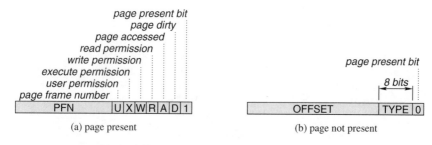

Figure 4.23. Logical format of a page-table entry (PTE).

4.3.4 Page-table entries (PTEs)

Linux assumes that page-table entries (PTEs) have one of two possible logical formats, depending on whether or not a virtual page is present in physical memory. If it is present, the PTE has the logical format shown in Figure 4.23 (a). If a virtual page is not present, the PTE has the format shown in Figure 4.23 (b). Comparing the two, we see that the **page present** bit is common, and, as the name suggests, it determines which format is in effect. A value of 1 indicates that the PTE has the **present** format, and a value of 0 indicates the PTE has the **not present** format.

Let us first take a closer look at Figure 4.23 (a). As it shows, the bit next to the **present** bit is the **dirty** (D) bit. It indicates whether there has been a write access to the virtual page since the bit was cleared last. The next bit is called the **accessed** (A) bit. It indicates whether the virtual page has been accessed at all (read, written, or executed) since the bit was cleared last. As explained earlier, the A and D bits are related in that they both play a role in implementing the page replacement and writeback policies. The next three bits are the permission bits; they control whether read (R), write (W), or execute (X) accesses to the page are permitted. A value of 1 indicates that accesses of that type are permitted, and a value of 0 prohibits such accesses. The permission bits are followed by a related bit, the **user** (U) bit. This bit controls whether the page is accessible from the user level. If it is 0, only the kernel can access the page. If it is 1, both the kernel and the user level can access the page in accordance with the permission bits. The last field in the Linux PTE contains the page frame number (PFN). The width of this field is platform specific, since it depends on the maximum amount of physical memory that the platform can support.

If the **present** bit is off, the PTE has the much simpler format shown in Figure 4.23 (b). Apart from the **present** bit, there are just two fields: TYPE and OFFSET. These fields record the disk location where a virtual page has been stored. Specifically, TYPE specifies the swap device (or swap file) and OFFSET specifies the swap block number. The TYPE field must be 8 bits wide, which implies that up to 256 distinct swap devices or files can be supported. There is no minimum width for the OFFSET field—Linux uses whatever number of bits are available on a particular platform. However, since its width determines the maximum block number, OFFSET determines the maximum size of a swap device or file, so it is generally a good idea to make this field as wide as possible.

The PTE manipulation interface

It is important to realize that the two formats depicted in Figure 4.23 are only *logical* formats. Linux never directly manipulates fields in a PTE. Instead, it manipulates them indirectly through the *PTE manipulation interface* (file include/asm/pgtable.h) shown in Figure 4.24. This interface gives each platform the flexibility to map the logical PTE format to a real format that best suits the requirements of the platform.

The interface defines three types, called **pte_t**, **swp_entry_t**, and **pgprot_t**. The first one is an opaque type that represents a PTE in the platform-specific format. The second type, **swp_entry_t** represents PTE values for which the **present** bit is off. The reason Linux requires a separate type for this case is that limitations in the page out code require that such PTEs must fit into a variable of type **unsigned long**. No such limitation exists for PTEs that have the **present** bit on, so **pte_t** could be a much larger type. However, the two types are related in the sense that it must be possible to convert a value of type **swp_entry_t** to a value of type **pte_t** without loss of information. The reverse also must be true for PTE values that have the **present** bit off.

The third type, **pgprot_t**, is also a platform-specific opaque type and represents the PTE bits other than the PFN field. Its name derives from the fact that values of this type contain the page permission bits. However, a platform is free to represent any other PTE bits in this type, so it generally contains more than just the permission bits. Associated with **pgprot_t** are several manifest constants that define the fundamental permission bit settings that the Linux kernel uses. Table 4.2 describes the available constants. The first column gives the name of the constant, the second column provides the logical permission bit settings (R, W, and X) as well as the value of the U bit that the constant encodes (see Figure 4.23), and the third column describes how the constant is used by the kernel. Constants whose name begins with PAGE represent protection values that are commonly used throughout the kernel. In contrast, the _P*xwr* and _S*xwr* constants translate the protection and sharing attributes of the *mmap()* system call to suitable protection values. Specifically, if the MAP_PRIVATE flag is specified in the system call, modifications to the mapped area should remain private to the process and Linux uses one of the _P*xwr* constants. If MAP_PRIVATE is not specified, the kernel uses one of the _S*xwr* constants instead. The specific constant used depends on the protection attributes specified in the system call. In the name of the constant, *r* corresponds to PROT_READ, *w* to PROT_WRITE, and *x* to PROT_EXEC. For example, for an *mmap()* system call with MAP_PRIVATE, PROT_READ, and PROT_WRITE specified, the kernel would use _P011. As the table illustrates, the major difference between the _P*xwr* and the _S*xwr* constants is that the former always have the W bit turned off. With write permission turned off, Linux can use the copy-on-write scheme to copy only those privately-mapped pages that really are modified by the process.

Comparing PTEs

The first routine in the interface is *pte_same()*, which compares two PTEs for equality. The routine expects two arguments *pte1* and *pte2* of type **pte_t** and returns a non-zero value if the two PTEs are identical.

```
/* PTE-related types: */
typedef pte_t;                              /* page-table entry (PTE) */
typedef unsigned long swp_entry_t;          /* swap space entry */
typedef pgprot_t;                           /* page protections */

/* comparing PTEs */
int pte_same(pte1, pte2);                   /* check for PTE equality */

/* converting between page frame descriptors and PTEs: */
pte_t mk_pte(page, prot);                   /* create PTE from page & prot. bits */
pte_t mk_pte_phys(addr, prot);              /* create PTE from addr. & prot. bits */
struct page *pte_page(pte);                 /* get page frame descriptor for PTE */

/* manipulating the accessed/dirty bits: */
pte_t pte_mkold(pte);                       /* mark PTE as not recently accessed */
pte_t pte_mkyoung(pte);                     /* mark PTE as recently accessed */
pte_t pte_mkclean(pte);                     /* mark PTE as not written */
pte_t pte_mkdirty(pte);                     /* mark PTE as written */

int pte_young(pte);                         /* PTE marked as accessed? */
int pte_dirty(pte);                         /* PTE marked as written? */

/* manipulating protection bits: */
pte_t pte_modify(pte, prot);                /* set protection bits in PTE */
pte_t pte_wrprotect(pte);                   /* mark PTE as not writable */
pte_t pte_mkwrite(pte);                     /* mark PTE as writable */
pte_t pte_mkexec(pte);                      /* mark PTE as executable */

int pte_read(pte);                          /* PTE marked as readable? */
int pte_write(pte);                         /* PTE marked as writable? */
int pte_exec(pte);                          /* PTE marked as executable? */

/* modifying PTEs atomically: */
int ptep_test_and_clear_dirty(pte_ptr);     /* test and clear dirty bit */
int ptep_test_and_clear_young(pte_ptr);     /* test and clear accessed bit */
ptep_mkdirty(pte_ptr);                      /* mark PTE as written */
ptep_set_wrprotect(pte_ptr);                /* mark PTE as not writable */
pte_t ptep_get_and_clear(pte_ptr);          /* get and clear PTE */

/* manipulating swap entries: */
swp_entry_t pte_to_swp_entry(pte);          /* extract swap entry from PTE */
pte_t swp_entry_to_pte(swp_entry);          /* convert swap entry to PTE */
unsigned long SWP_TYPE(swp_entry);          /* extract TYPE from swap entry */
unsigned long SWP_OFFSET(swp_entry);        /* extract OFFSET from swap entry */
swp_entry_t SWP_ENTRY(type, offset);        /* convert type & offset to swap entry */
```

Figure 4.24. Kernel interface to manipulate page-table entries (PTEs).

Table 4.2. Page protection constants.

Constant	UXWR	Description
PAGE_NONE	1 0 0 0	Protection value to use for a page with no access rights.
PAGE_READONLY	1 0 0 1	Protection value to use for a read-only page.
PAGE_SHARED	1 0 1 1	Protection value to use for a page where modifications are to be shared by all processes that map this page.
PAGE_COPY	1 1 0 1	Protection value to use for a copy-on-write page.
PAGE_KERNEL	0 1 1 1	Protection value to use for a page that is accessible by the kernel only.
__Pxwr	1 x 0 r	Protection value to use on a page with access rights xwr when modifications to the page should remain private to the process. There are eight such constants, one for each possible combination of the execute (x), write (w), and read (r) bits. For example, constant __P001 defines the value to use for a page that is only readable.
__Sxwr	1 x w r	Protection value to use on a page with access rights xwr when modifications to the page should be shared with other processes. There are eight such constants, one for each possible combination of the xwr access bits.

Converting between page frame descriptors and PTEs

The second set of routines in the interface provides the ability to convert page frame pointers to PTEs, and vice versa. Routine *mk_pte()* expects two arguments: a pointer *page* to a page frame descriptor and a protection value *prot* that specifies the page protection as a platform-specific **pgprot_t** value. The routine calculates the page frame number of *page* and combines it with *prot* to form a PTE that is returned in the form of a value of type **pte_t**. Routine *mk_pte_phys()* provides the same functionality, except that the first argument is a physical address instead of a page frame descriptor. This routine is used to map a page frame for which there is no page frame descriptor—a case that usually arises for memory-mapped I/O pages. The *pte_page()* routine provides the reverse operation. It expects the single argument *pte*, which must be a PTE, and returns a pointer to the page frame descriptor that corresponds to *pte*. The operation of this routine is undefined if *pte* maps a physical address for which no page frame descriptor exists.

Manipulating the accessed/dirty bits

The third set of routines provides the ability to manipulate and test the **accessed** (A) and **dirty** (D) bits in the PTE. They all expect the single argument *pte*, which must be a PTE of type **pte_t**. The routines that modify the PTE also return a value of that type. The routines that test a bit in the PTE simply return the current value of the bit. The *pte_mkold()* routine clears the A bit in the PTE, and *pte_mkyoung()* sets it. Similarly, *pte_mkclean()* clears the D bit in the PTE, and *pte_mkdirty()* sets it. The *pte_young()* and *pte_dirty()* routines can be used to query the current settings of the A and D bits, respectively.

Manipulating protection bits

The fourth set of routines provides the ability to manipulate the protection bits in a PTE. The first argument to these routines is always a PTE of type **pte_t**. Those routines that modify the PTE also return a value of that type, whereas the routines that test a particular permission bit return a non-zero value if the bit is set and 0 if the bit is cleared. The *pte_modify()* routine can be used to replace the protection bits with the value passed in the second argument, *prot*. This argument must be of type **pgprot_t** and contain a protection value in the platform-specific format. The *pte_wrprotect()* routine can be used to clear the W bit in a PTE, and *pte_mkwrite()* can be used to set it. Similarly, *pte_mkexec()* can be used to set the X bit. No routines directly manipulate the R bit. The current setting of the R, W, and X permission bits can be queried with *pte_read()*, *pte_write()*, and *pte_exec()*, respectively.

Modifying PTEs atomically

The fifth set of routines provides routines for atomically modifying existing PTEs. These routines need to be used to avoid potential race conditions when PTEs that are marked **present** in a page table are modified. For example, consider a machine with two CPUs. If one CPU performs a write access to a page just as the other CPU attempts to clear the **dirty** bit, the bit could end up with the wrong value if it is not cleared atomically. To avoid such problems, the interface provides *ptep_test_and_clear_dirty()* to atomically read and then clear the D bit. The routine expects one argument, *pte_ptr*, which must be a pointer to the PTE to be modified. The return value is non-zero if the D bit was set and 0 otherwise. Similarly, *ptep_test_and_clear_young()* can be used to atomically test and clear the A bit. The *ptep_mkdirty()* and *ptep_set_wrprotect()* routines are atomic variants of *pte_mkdirty()* and *pte_wrprotect()*, respectively. The last atomic routine, *ptep_get_and_clear()* is a catch-all routine in the sense that it can be used to atomically modify any bits in the PTE. It works by atomically reading and then clearing the PTE pointed to by *pte_ptr*. It is a catch-all because once the PTE is cleared, its **present** bit is off and all future accesses by other CPUs will cause a page fault. In the page fault handler, the other CPUs will have to follow the normal MP-locking protocol to avoid any potential race conditions. In other words, the other routines to atomically modify PTEs are not strictly needed—they could all be emulated with *ptep_get_and_clear()*. However, providing specialized routines for the most common operations makes sense because such routines are generally more efficient than implementations based on *ptep_get_and_clear()*.

Manipulating swap entries

The final set of PTE-related routines provides the means to support moving virtual pages to swap space and back. Specifically, *pte_to_swp_entry()* converts a PTE to the corresponding swap entry. The PTE is specified by argument *pte*, and the return value is the corresponding swap entry. This operation is meaningful only if *pte* has the **present** bit turned off, i.e., the PTE must already be in the format illustrated in Figure 4.23 (b). The *swp_entry_to_pte()* routine provides the reverse operation and translates the swap entry passed in argument *swp_entry* to an equivalent PTE. The TYPE and OFFSET fields can be extracted from a

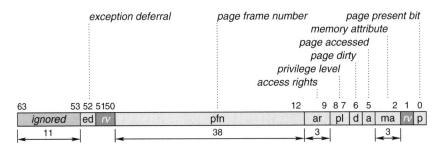

Figure 4.25. Format of IA-64 PTE when **present** bit is set (p = 1).

swap entry with *SWP_TYPE()* and *SWP_OFFSET()*, respectively. Conversely, *SWP_EN-TRY()* can be used to construct a swap entry in accordance with the values of the *type* and *offset* arguments.

Note that no routine directly translates a PTE in the **present** format to a PTE in the **not present** format. Instead, Linux uses the following canonical sequence to move a page out to swap space:

1. Call *ptep_get_and_clear()* to read the old PTE and then clear it.

2. Reserve swap space for the page; the swap space location reserved determines the value of the TYPE and OFFSET fields.

3. Write the page frame to swap space.

4. Build the swap entry by calling *SWP_ENTRY()*.

5. Call *swp_entry_to_pte()* to translate the swap entry into the corresponding PTE.

6. Install the new PTE in the page table.

Similarly, when a page is moved from disk to memory, the corresponding steps happen in reverse. In other words, when a virtual page is moved from memory to disk, or vice versa, the old PTE is essentially "thrown away" and a new one is constructed from ground up, which is why there is no need for routines that explicitly manipulate the **present** bit.

IA-64 implementation

Figure 4.25 illustrates the PTE format used by Linux/ia64. To help distinguish the logical PTE format in Figure 4.23 from the IA-64–specific format shown here, the figure uses lowercase names for the field names. The figure illustrates that there is a **present** bit p, an **accessed** bit a, a **dirty** bit d, and a page frame number field pfn just as in the logical format. These bits serve exactly the same purpose as the corresponding bits in the logical format.

The IA-64 PTE format does not have separate permission bits. Instead, it uses the 2-bit privilege-level field pl and the 3-bit access-rights field ar to determine the protection

Table 4.3. IA-64 page access rights.

ar	kernel	user pl = 0	user pl = 3	ar	kernel	user pl = 0	user pl = 3
0	R	–	R	4	RW	–	R
1	RX	–	RX	5	RWX	–	RX
2	RW	–	RW	6	RW	–	RWX
3	RWX	–	RWX	7	RX	XP0	X

status of a page. IA-64 supports four privilege levels, but Linux uses only two of them: 0 is the most-privileged level and is used for accesses by the kernel; 3 is the least-privileged level and is used for user accesses. Table 4.3 shows how the different values for ar and pl affect the rights for kernel and user-level accesses. Note that for the kernel, the access rights are determined solely by ar; pl has no influence. For user-level accesses, pl = 0 generally means that the page is owned by the kernel and therefore inaccessible. However, something interesting happens when ar = 7. In the table, this entry is marked XP0, which should be read as *execute, promote to privilege-level 0*. This means that the page is executable even at the user level. Furthermore, if an epc (enter privileged code) instruction is executed in such a page, the privilege level is raised to privilege-level 0 (kernel). This mechanism can be used to implement system calls and, as we see in Chapter 5, *Kernel Entry and Exit*, is also useful for signal handling. The gate page described in Section 4.2.4 is mapped in this fashion, and the IA-64–specific constant PAGE_GATE can be used to map other pages in this way.

Another interesting aspect of the IA-64 protection scheme is that there is no way to grant write permission without also granting read permission. Fortunately, for the R and X permission bits, Linux allows platform-specific code to grant the access right even if it was not set in the logical protection value (this is *not* true for the W bit, of course). Thus, Linux/ia64 simply maps logical protection values that have only the W bit set to privilege-level and access-right values that grant both read and write permission.

The IA-64 PTE defines two fields, ma and ed, that have no equivalent in the logical format. The ma field specifies the *memory attribute* of the page. For all normal memory pages, this value is 0, indicating that accesses to the page are cacheable. However, to support memory-mapped I/O, this field can be used to select different types of uncached accesses. For example, ma = 4 marks the page as **uncacheable**. A value of ma = 6 marks the page as **write coalescing**, which is similar to **uncacheable**, except that consecutive writes can be coalesced into a single write transaction. As a special case, ma = 7 marks a page as a **NaT Page**. Speculative loads from such a page will deposit a NaT token in the target register. Other memory accesses, such as nonspeculative loads or stores, will trigger a NAT PAGE CONSUMPTION FAULT. The ed bit is also related to speculation. It is meaningful only for pages that are executable. For such pages, the bit indicates the speculation model that is in effect. A value of 1 indicates the **recovery** model, and a value of 0 indicates the **no-recovery** model. See the discussion on page 199 for more details on the speculation model. Linux supports only the **recovery** model, so this bit should always be 1.

Figure 4.26. Format of IA-64 PTE when **present** bit is cleared ($p = 0$).

Finally, note that some bits in the IA-64 PTE are marked **rv**. These bits are reserved
for future architectural uses. Attempting to set them will result in a RESERVED REGIS-
TER/FIELD FAULT when the PTE is loaded into the CPU. In contrast, the most significant
11 bits of the PTE are defined as **ignored**. These bits are completely ignored by the CPU
and are available for use by the operating system. Linux/ia64 uses bit 63 to mark a page
that has no access rights. Because such a page is inaccessible, there is no need to back it
with a physical page frame. Thus, such a page can be considered to be present even if the p
bit in the PTE is turned off.

Figure 4.26 shows the IA-64 PTE format when the present bit p is cleared. In this case,
the bits other than the present bit are all ignored by the CPU and are available for use by
the operating system. Linux uses bits 1 through 8 to encode the swap entry TYPE field and
bits 9 through 62 to encode the swap entry OFFSET field. Bit 63 is again used to mark a
page with no access rights. Note that if this bit is set, Linux considers the page present even
though bit p is cleared.

Given the IA-64 PTE format, it is clear that types **pte_t** and **pgprot_t** must be wide
enough to hold a 64-bit word. They could be defined as being equivalent to **unsigned long**.
However, to take advantage of C type-checking rules, both types are declared as separate
structures that contain just one 64-bit word each. This is a compiler trick that makes it easier
to detect programming errors early on because passing a PTE where a protection value is
expected (or vice versa) results in a type violation that can be reported by the C compiler.

The IA-64 implementations of the many PTE manipulation routines defined in Figure 4.24 are straightforward; most of them involve just simple bit manipulation in PTE
or protection values. The PTE manipulation routines that need to execute atomically are
all implemented with the cmpxchg8 instruction that we already encountered in Chapter 3,
Processes, Tasks, and Threads.

4.3.5   Page-table accesses

Just like PTEs, Linux never directly manipulates directory entries. Instead, it manipulates
them through the interface shown in Figure 4.27. In this interface, all virtual address arguments are called *addr* and must be values of type **unsigned long**. Global- and middle-
directory entries are represented by types **pgd_t** and **pmd_t**, respectively. As we have seen
already, PTE-directory entries are represented by type **pte_t**. All types usually occupy one
machine word, but for some platforms, they are more complex structures occupying multiple words.

typedef **pgd_t**;	/* global-directory entry */
typedef **pmd_t**;	/* middle-directory entry */
unsigned long **pgd_index**(*addr*);	/* extract pgd index from addr */
pgd_t ***pgd_offset**(*mm, addr*);	/* get pgd entry pointer for addr */
pgd_t ***pgd_offset_k**(*addr*);	/* get kernel pgd entry pointer for addr */
pmd_t ***pmd_offset**(*pgd_entry_ptr, addr*);	/* get pmd entry pointer for addr */
pte_t ***pte_offset**(*pmd_entry_ptr, addr*);	/* get PTE pointer for addr */
int **pgd_none**(*pgd_entry*);	/* check if pgd_entry is mapped */
int **pgd_present**(*pgd_entry*);	/* check if pgd_entry is present */
int **pgd_bad**(*pgd_entry*);	/* check if pgd_entry is invalid */
int **pmd_none**(*pmd_entry*);	/* check if pmd_entry is mapped */
int **pmd_present**(*pmd_entry*);	/* check if pmd_entry is present */
int **pmd_bad**(*pmd_entry*);	/* check if pmd_entry is invalid */
int **pte_none**(*pte*);	/* check if pte is mapped */
int **pte_present**(*pte*);	/* check if pte is present */

Figure 4.27. Kernel interface to access page tables.

The first routine in this interface, *pgd_index()*, simply extracts the global-directory index from virtual address *addr* and returns it.

The *pgd_offset()* routine looks up the global-directory entry for a user-space address. Argument *mm* specifies the mm structure (address space), and *addr* specifies the virtual address to look up. Similarly, *pgd_offset_k()* can be used to look up the global-directory entry for a kernel-space address. Because there is only one kernel page table, this routine needs just one argument: the virtual address *addr*, which must point inside the page-table-mapped kernel segment.

Once the global-directory entry has been found, *pmd_offset()* can be used to find the middle-directory entry of a virtual address. This routine expects two arguments, namely, *pgd_entry_ptr*, which must be a pointer to the global-directory entry found previously, and *addr*, the virtual address being looked up. This routine can be used both for user-space and kernel-space addresses.

Once the middle-directory entry has been found, *pte_offset()* can be used to find the PTE-directory entry of a virtual address. This routine again expects two arguments, namely, *pmd_entry_ptr*, which must be a pointer to the middle-directory entry found previously, and *addr*, the virtual address being looked up. This routine also can be used both for user-space and kernel-space addresses.

The final eight routines in the interface check the validity of a directory entry. The 3-character prefix of the routine name indicates the page-table level at which the check is used (**pgd** for global-, **pmd** for middle-, and **pte** for PTE-directory entries). Routines whose names end in **none** check whether the entry corresponds to a mapped portion of the address space. Routines whose names end in **present** check whether the entry corresponds to a portion of the address space that is present in physical memory. Because Linux page tables are not paged themselves, they are never stored in the swap space and the *pgd_present()* and *pmd_present()* routines always return the complement of *pgd_none()* and *pmd_none()* (an entry is present if it is mapped, and vice versa). Routines whose name end in **bad** check whether the entry is invalid. These routines are intended to make it easier to detect page table corruptions as early as possible but are not strictly required for the correct operation of Linux. Thus, on platforms that cannot (easily) distinguish valid and invalid entries, these routines can always return **false**. Also, note that *pte_bad()* does not exist, so there is no means to check whether a PTE is invalid.

The page-table access interface has been designed to support two primary access methods: address-driven and range-driven accesses. The former starts with a virtual address and, level by level, determines the global-, middle-, and PTE-directory entries that correspond to this address. In contrast, range-driven accesses visit all directory entries that fall into a certain address range. It is best to illustrate each method with an example. We do so next.

Example: Printing physical address of a virtual address

A good way to illustrate address-driven accesses is to look at how a user-space virtual address can be translated into the corresponding physical address. The code below implements a function called *print_pa()* that accomplishes this translation. It expects two arguments: a pointer, *mm*, to an mm structure and a virtual address, *va*. The function attempts to translate the virtual address by using the page table associated with *mm*. If the translation exists, the function prints the virtual address and the physical address it maps to. If no translation exists, nothing is printed.

```
print_pa (struct mm_struct *mm, unsigned long va) {
    pgd_t *pgd = pgd_offset(mm, va);
    if (pgd_present(*pgd)) {
        pmd_t *pmd = pmd_offset(pgd, va);
        if (pmd_present(*pmd)) {
            pte_t *pte = pte_offset(pmd, va);
            if (pte_present(*pte))
                printk("va 0x%lx -> pa 0x%lx\n",
                       va, page_address(pte_page(*pte));
        }
    }
}
```

Taking a closer look at the function, we see that it first uses *pgd_offset()* to obtain a pointer *pgd* to the global-directory entry for the virtual address. Then it uses *pgd_present()* to check whether the entry is present, i.e., to check whether the middle directory exists. If it exists, the function descends to the next level of the page-table tree where it uses *pmd_offset()* and *pmd_present()* to accomplish the equivalent steps for the middle directory. The page-table traversal is completed by a call to *pte_offset()*. This call accesses the middle directory and returns a pointer to the PTE. The function uses *pte_present()* to check whether the PTE maps a page that is present in physical memory. If so, it uses *pte_page()* to translate the PTE into the corresponding page frame descriptor. In the final step, the function uses *page_address()* to obtain the physical address of the page frame and prints both the virtual and physical addresses with a call to *printk()*.

Let us emphasize that the above three-level lookup works correctly regardless of how many levels are actually implemented on a platform. For example, on a platform that has the middle level collapsed into the global level, *pmd_offset()* would return the value of *pgd* after casting it to a pointer to a middle-directory entry (**pmd_t**) and routine *pmd_present()* would always return **true**. This behavior not only ensures proper operation but also lets the compiler optimize away the middle-directory access completely. Thus, even though logi-cally a three-level lookup is being used, it would perform exactly like a two-level lookup.

Example: Counting the number of present pages

The kernel uses the range-driven access method when it needs to perform a certain op-eration on the directory entries that correspond to a given address range. For example, in response to a *munmap()* system call, the kernel needs to remove the page-table directory entries that fall in the range specified by the system call.

To see how this access method works, let us consider the simple example of counting the number of pages that are present in a given address range. This is what the *count_pages()* function below implements. It expects three arguments: a pointer, *mm*, to an mm structure and two user-space addresses, *start* and *end*, that specify the starting and ending point of the address range in which to count present pages (*end* points to the first byte *beyond* the desired range; both *start* and *end* are assumed to be global-directory aligned).

```
count_pages (struct mm_struct *mm, long start, long end) {
    int i, j, k, num_present = 0;
    pgd_t *pgd = pgd_offset(mm, 0);
    for (i = pgd_index(start); i < pgd_index(end); ++i)
        if (pgd_present(pgd[i]) {
            pmd_t *pmd = pmd_offset(pgd + i, 0);
            for (j = 0; j < PTRS_PER_PMD; ++j)
                if (pmd_present(pmd[j])) {
                    pte_t *pte = pte_offset(pmd + j, 0);
                    for (k = 0; k < PTRS_PER_PTE; ++k)
                        if (pte_present(pte[k]))
                            ++num_present;
                }
        }
    printk("%d pages present\n", num_present);
}
```

The function calls *pgd_offset()* to obtain a pointer *pgd* to the global-directory *page*. The first argument to this function is the *mm* pointer as usual. However, the second argument is 0. This causes *pgd_offset()* to return a pointer to the very first entry in the global direc-tory. Since we know that the directory contains PTRS_PER_PGD entries, we can equally well treat this value as a pointer to the global directory itself and use array indexing to access particular entries. This is what the first **for**-loop does: It iterates variable *i* over the global-directory indices that correspond to the starting and ending addresses. Note how *pgd_index()* is used to extract these indices from the corresponding addresses. In the loop body, *pgd_present()* checks whether the *i*th entry in the directory is present. If not, the entry is skipped. If it is present, the function descends to the next level of the tree (the middle directory). Here the same basic steps are repeated: *pmd_offset()* obtains a pointer, *pmd*, to the middle directory, and a **for**-loop iterates over each index *j* in the middle directory (0 to PTRS_PER_PMD − 1). In the third level, the analogous steps are repeated for the PTE directory. In the body of the third **for**-loop, the function iterates *k* over the indices in the PTE directory (0 to PTRS_PER_PTE − 1); if the indexed entry refers to a page frame that is present in physical memory, the function increments the counter *num_present*. After iterating over the entire address range, the function prints the resulting page count by calling *printk()*.

There are two points worth emphasizing: First, just as in the previous example, the above code works properly (and efficiently) when one or more levels of the page-table tree are collapsed into a higher level of the tree; second, note that given the global-, middle-, and PTE-directory indices *i, j, k*, there is no platform-independent way to construct a virtual address that would yield these indices. Thus, in the above example it would not be possible, e.g., to print the virtual address of each page that has been found to be present. There is nothing fundamentally difficult about providing such an operation, but because Linux does not need it, there is little point in defining it.

IA-64 implementation

Given the IA-64 page-table structure described in Section 4.3.3, it is straightforward to see how the page-table access interface is implemented. In fact, all operations are so simple that they are implemented either as macros or as inlined functions. The directory entry types (**pgd_t, pmd_t**, and **pte_t**) can all be thought of as being equivalent to a 64-bit word. However, to take advantage of C type-checking rules, each type has its own structure declaration. This ensures that if, say, a pmd entry is accidentally used when a pte entry is expected, the C compiler can detect the problem and issue a suitable error message.

The IA-64 implementation of *pgd_index()* simply extracts the *pgdh* and *pgdl* components (see Figure 4.21 on page 159) from the virtual address, concatenates them, and returns the result. Similarly, the implementations of *pgd_offset()*, *pgd_offset_k()*, *pmd_offset()*, and *pte_offset()* extract the relevant address bits from the virtual address to form an index and then use this value to index the directory identified by the first argument passed to these routines.

In all three levels of the directory, Linux/ia64 uses a value of 0 to indicate an entry that is not mapped. Thus, routines *pgd_none()*, *pmd_none()*, and *pte_none()* simply test whether the directory entry passed to the routine is equal to 0. Similarly, *pgd_present()* and *pmd_present()* test whether the directory entry is not 0. Because virtual pages can be paged out to disk, *pte_present()* is different and checks the **present** bit in the PTE. As a special case, a virtual page with no access rights is always considered present. Finally, on IA-64 the *pgd_bad()* and *pmd_bad()* routines verify the validity of a directory entry by checking whether they contain a valid physical address. Specifically, they check whether any of the unimplemented physical address bits are non-zero and return **true** if so.

pgd_t ***pgd_alloc**();	/* allocate global directory */
pmd_t ***pmd_alloc_one**();	/* allocate middle directory */
pte_t ***pte_alloc_one**();	/* allocate PTE directory */
pgd_free(*pgd_ptr*);	/* free a global directory */
pmd_free(*pmd_ptr*);	/* free a middle directory */
pte_free(*pte_ptr*);	/* free a PTE directory */
pmd_t ***pmd_alloc_one_fast**();	/* nonblocking allocate middle dir. */
pte_t ***pte_alloc_one_fast**();	/* nonblocking allocate PTE dir. */
int **do_check_pgt_cache**(*low, high*);	/* free cached directory pages */
pgd_populate(*pgd_entry_ptr, pmd_entry_ptr*);	/* set global-directory entry */
pmd_populate(*pmd_entry_ptr, pte_ptr*);	/* set middle-directory entry */
set_pte(*pte_ptr, pte*);	/* set PTE */
pgd_clear(*pgd_entry_ptr*);	/* clear global-directory entry */
pmd_clear(*pmd_entry_ptr*);	/* clear middle-directory entry */
pte_clear(*pte_ptr*);	/* clear PTE */

Figure 4.28. Kernel interface to create page tables.

4.3.6   Page-table directory creation

Now that we understand how page tables can be accessed, we are ready to explore how they can be created in the first place. Figure 4.28 shows the interface Linux uses to abstract platform differences in how this creation is accomplished. The first three routines can be used to create directories at each of the three levels of the page-table tree. Specifically, *pgd_alloc()* creates a global directory, *pmd_alloc_one()* creates a middle directory, and *pte_alloc_one()* creates a PTE directory. The routines return a pointer to the newly created directory or NULL if they fail for any reason. The newly created directory is initialized such that its entries are marked as **not mapped**. The memory needed for the directory is normally obtained from the page allocator. This implies that if the page allocator is short on memory, the routines can block execution temporarily.

Once a directory is no longer needed, it can be freed by a call to one of *pgd_free()*, *pmd_free()*, or *pte_free()*, depending on whether it is a global, middle, or PTE directory, respectively. To reduce allocation and deallocation overheads, most platforms maintain a cache of free directories. This is usually done by implementing these routines such that they add the newly freed directory to a list of unused directories, instead of returning their memory to the page allocator. Access to this cache is provided through two separate allocation routines: *pmd_alloc_one_fast()* and *pte_alloc_one_fast()*. These work exactly like the normal middle-, and PTE-directory allocation routines, except that they guarantee not to block execution. The cache is particularly effective because it avoids not just the normal page allocator overheads but also the overhead of initializing the directory. To see this, consider that before a directory is freed, Linux removes all existing mappings from it, meaning that by the time *pgd_free()*, *pmd_free()*, or *pte_free()* is called, the directory is guaranteed to have all entries marked as **not mapped**. Thus, when a directory is taken from the cache, it is already initialized and can be returned directly, without the need to clear its content again. While the cache generally improves performance, it could create problems if it grew too large. To prevent this, the interface defines the *do_check_pgt_cache()* routine to make it possible to reduce or limit the size of the cache. The routine takes two arguments, *low* and *high*, which are both page counts that are interpreted as follows: if the cache occupies more than *high* pages, then the routine should free up directories until the cache occupies no more than *low* pages.

The final six routines set or clear directory entries. The *pgd_populate()* routine sets the pmd identified by argument *pmd_entry_ptr* as the new value for the pgd entry pointed to by argument *pgd_entry_ptr*. In contrast, *pgd_clear()* marks the entry pointed to by *pgd_entry_ptr* as **not mapped**. After this operation, *pgd_none()* would return **true** for this entry. The *pmd_populate()*, *pmd_clear()*, *set_pte()*, and *pte_clear()* routines implement the equivalent operations for middle- and PTE-directory entries. Backward compatibility is the only reason why *set_pte()* is not called *pte_populate()*.

IA-64 implementation

The IA-64 implementation of the page-table creation interface is straightforward, largely because each directory occupies one page frame. Memory management of directory nodes is therefore particularly easy because the normal page allocator can be used to allocate and free directories. Like most other platforms, Linux/ia64 implements the nonblocking versions of the directory allocation routines by maintaining a cache of unused directories.

4.4 TRANSLATION LOOKASIDE BUFFER (TLB)

Every time the CPU accesses virtual memory, a virtual address must be translated to the corresponding physical address. Conceptually, this translation requires a page-table walk, and with a three-level page table, three memory accesses would be required. In other words, every virtual access would result in four physical memory accesses. Clearly, if a virtual memory access were four times slower than a physical access, virtual memory would not be very popular! Fortunately, a clever trick removes most of this performance penalty: modern CPUs use a small associative memory to cache the PTEs of recently accessed virtual pages. This memory is called the *translation lookaside buffer (TLB)*.

The TLB works as follows. On a virtual memory access, the CPU searches the TLB for the virtual page number of the page that is being accessed, an operation known as *TLB lookup*. If a TLB entry is found with a matching virtual page number, a *TLB hit* occurred and the CPU can go ahead and use the PTE stored in the TLB entry to calculate the target physical address. Now, the reason the TLB makes virtual memory practical is that because it is small—typically on the order of a few dozen entries—it can be built directly into the CPU and it runs at full CPU speed. This means that as long as a translation can be found in the TLB, a virtual access executes just as fast as a physical access. Indeed, modern CPUs often execute *faster* in virtual memory because the TLB entries indicate whether it is safe to access memory speculatively (e.g., to prefetch instructions).

But what happens if there is no TLB entry with a matching virtual page number? This event is termed a *TLB miss* and, depending on the CPU architecture, is handled in one of two ways:

- **Hardware TLB miss handling:** In this case, the CPU goes ahead and walks the page table to find the right PTE. If the PTE can be found and is marked **present**, then the CPU installs the new translation in the TLB. Otherwise, the CPU raises a page fault and hands over control to the operating system.

- **Software TLB miss handling:** In this case, the CPU simply raises a *TLB miss fault*. The fault is intercepted by the operating system, which invokes the TLB miss handler in response. The miss handler then walks the page table in software and, if a matching PTE that is marked **present** is found, the new translation is inserted in the TLB. If the PTE is not found, control is handed over to the page fault handler.

Whether a TLB miss is handled in hardware or in software, the bottom line is that miss handling results in a page-table walk and if a PTE that is marked **present** can be found, the TLB is updated with the new translation. Most CISC architectures (such as IA-32) perform TLB miss handling in hardware, and most RISC architectures (such as Alpha) use a software approach. A hardware solution is often faster, but is less flexible. Indeed, the performance advantage may be lost if the hardware poorly matches the needs of the operating system. As we see later, IA-64 provides a hybrid solution that retains much of the flexibility of the software approach without sacrificing the speed of the hardware approach.

TLB replacement policy

Let us now consider what should happen when the TLB is full (all entries are in use) and the CPU or the TLB miss handler needs to insert a new translation. The question now is, Which existing entry should be evicted (overwritten) to make space for the new entry? This choice is governed by the *TLB replacement policy*. Usually, some form or approximation of LRU is used for this purpose. With LRU, the TLB entry that has not been used the longest is the one that is evicted from the TLB. The exact choice of replacement policy often depends on whether the policy is implemented in hardware or in software. Hardware solutions tend to use simpler policies, such as *not recently used (NRU)*, whereas software solutions can implement full LRU or even more sophisticated schemes without much difficulty.

Note that if TLB miss handling is implemented in hardware, the replacement policy obviously also must be implemented in hardware. However, with a software TLB miss handler, the replacement policy can be implemented either in hardware or in software. Some architectures (e.g., MIPS) employ software replacement, but many newer architectures, including IA-64, offer a hardware replacement policy.

Removing old entries from the TLB

A final challenge in using a TLB is how to keep it synchronized (or *coherent*) with the underlying page table. Just as with any other cache, care must be taken to avoid cases where the TLB contains stale entries that are no longer valid. Stale entries can result from a number of scenarios. For example, when a virtual page is paged out to disk, the PTE in the page table is marked **not present**. If that page still has a TLB entry, it is now stale (because we assumed that the TLB contains only **present** PTEs). Similarly, a process might map a file into memory, access a few pages in the mapped area, and then unmap the file. At this point, the TLB may still contain entries that were inserted when the mapped area was accessed, but because the mapping no longer exists, those entries are now stale. The event that by far creates the most stale entries occurs when execution switches from one process to another. Because each process has its own address space, the *entire* TLB becomes stale on a context switch!

Given the number and complexity of the scenarios that can lead to stale entries, it is up to the operating system to ensure that they are flushed from the TLB before they can cause any harm. Depending on the CPU architecture, different kinds of TLB flush instructions are provided. Typical instructions flush the entire TLB, the entry for a specific virtual page, or all TLB entries that fall in a specific address range.

Note that a context switch normally requires that the entire TLB be flushed. However, because this is such a common operation and because TLB fault handling is relatively slow, CPU architects over the years have come up with various schemes to avoid this problem. These schemes go by various names, such as *address-space numbers*, *context numbers*, or *region IDs*, but they all share the basic idea: The tag used for matching a TLB entry is expanded to contain not just the virtual page number but also an address-space number that uniquely identifies the process (address space) to which the translation belongs. The CPU is also extended to contain a new register, asn, that identifies the address-space number of the currently executing process. Now, when the TLB is searched, the CPU ignores entries whose unique number does not match the value in the asn register. With this setup, a context switch simply requires updating the asn register—no flushing is needed anymore. Effectively, this scheme makes it possible to share the TLB across multiple processes.

4.4.1   The IA-64 TLB architecture

The IA-64 architecture uses an interesting approach to speed up virtual-to-physical address translation. Apart from the basic TLB, there are three other hardware structures, two of which, the *region registers* and the *protection key registers*, are designed to increase the effectiveness of the TLB. The third, the *virtual hash page table walker (VHPT walker)* is designed to reduce the penalty of a TLB miss.

Figure 4.29 illustrates how an IA-64 CPU translates a virtual address to a physical address. Let us start in the upper-right corner of the figure. There, we find a virtual address that has been divided into the three fields: the virtual region number vrn, the virtual page number vpn, and the page offset field offset. As usual, the page offset does not participate in the translation and is copied straight to the offset field of the physical address at the lower-right corner of the figure. In contrast, the 3-bit region number vrn is first sent to the region registers in the upper-left corner. Here, the region register indexed by vrn is read, and the resulting *region ID* value is sent to the TLB. At the TLB, the region ID is combined with the virtual page number vpn and the resulting region ID/vpn key is used to search the TLB. If an entry matches the search key, the remaining fields of the entry provide the information

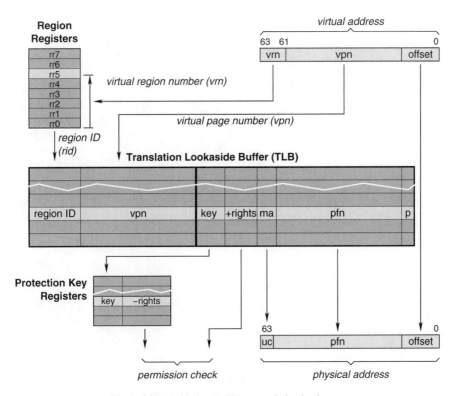

Figure 4.29. IA-64 virtual address translation hardware.

necessary to complete the address translation. Specifically, the pfn field provides the page
frame number associated with the virtual page number. This field, too, can be copied down
to the corresponding field in the physical address. The memory attribute field ma determines whether or not the memory access can be cached. If it can, the uc field (bit 63) of
the physical address is cleared; otherwise, it is set. The final two fields, +rights and key, are
used to check whether the memory access is permitted. The +rights field provides a set of
positive rights that control what kind of accesses (read, write, or execute) are permitted at
what privilege level (user and/or kernel). The key field is sent to the protection key registers. There, the register with a matching key value is read, and its -rights field supplies the
negative rights needed to complete the permission check. Specifically, any kind of access
specified in the -rights field is prohibited, even if it would otherwise be permitted by the
+rights field. If there is no register matching the key value, a KEY MISS FAULT is raised.
The operating system can intercept this fault and decide whether to install the missing key
or take some other action (such as terminate the offending process). At this point the CPU
has both the physical address and the information necessary to check whether the memory
access is permitted, so the translation is complete.

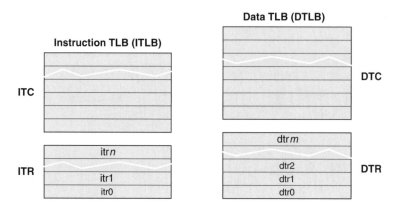

Figure 4.30. IA-64 TLB structure.

A somewhat unusual aspect of IA-64 is that the **present** bit is also part of the TLB entry. The Linux kernel never inserts a translation for a page that is not present, but the VHPT walker may do so.

TLB structure and management policies

As Figure 4.30 illustrates, the IA-64 TLB is divided into four logically separate units. On the left side is the *instruction TLB (ITLB)*, which translates instruction addresses; on the right side is the *data TLB (DTLB)*, which translates data addresses. Both the ITLB and the DTLB are further subdivided into *translation registers (ITR and DTR)* and *translation caches (ITC and DTC)*. The difference between the two lies in where the replacement policy is implemented: for the translation caches, the hardware (CPU) implements the replacement policy, whereas for translation registers, the replacement policy is implemented in software. In other words, when a TLB entry is inserted into a translation register, both the TLB entry and the translation register name (e.g., itr1) have to be specified. In contrast, insertion into a translation cache requires specification of only the TLB entry—the hardware then picks an existing entry and replaces it with the new one.

The architecture guarantees that the ITC and DTC have a size of at least one entry. Of course, a realistic CPU typically supports dozens of entries in each cache. For example, Itanium implements 96 ITC entries and 128 DTC entries. Even so, to guarantee forward progress the operating system must never assume that more than one entry can be held in the cache at any given time. Otherwise, when inserting two entries back to back, the hardware replacement policy may end up replacing the first entry when inserting the second one. Thus, the operating system must be written in a way that ensures forward progress even if only the second entry survives.

Both ITR and DTR are guaranteed to support at least eight translation registers. However, the IA-64 architecture leaves hardware designers the option to implement translation registers in the form of translation cache entries that are marked so that they are never con-

Figure 4.31. Format of IA-64 page table address register pta.

sidered for replacement by the hardware. With this option, the more translation registers used, the fewer entries available in the translation cache. For this reason, it is generally preferable to allocate only as many translation registers as are really needed and to allocate them in order of increasing register index.

Linux/ia64 uses translation registers to pin certain critical code sections and data structures. For example, one ITR entry is used to pin the TLB fault handlers of the kernel, and another is used to map firmware code that cannot risk taking a TLB miss fault. Similarly, the kernel uses a DTR entry to pin the kernel stack of the currently running process.

The VHPT walker and the virtually-mapped linear page table

One question we have glossed over so far is what happens when there is no matching TLB entry for a given region ID/vpn pair, i.e., when a TLB miss occurs. On IA-64, this event can be handled in one of two ways: if enabled, the VHPT walker becomes active and attempts to fill in the missing TLB entry. If the VHPT walker is disabled, the CPU signals a TLB miss fault, which is intercepted by the Linux kernel. The details of how a TLB miss is handled in software is described in Section 4.5. For now, let us focus on the case where the TLB miss is handled by the VHPT walker.

First, let us note that the use of the VHPT walker is completely optional. If an operating system decides not to use it, IA-64 leaves the operating system complete control over the page-table structure and the PTE format. In order to use the VHPT walker, the operating system may need to limit its choices somewhat. Specifically, the VHPT walker can support one of two modes: hashed mode or linear-page-table mode. In hashed mode, the operating system should use a hash table as its page table and the PTEs have a format that is known as the *long format*. With the long format, each PTE is 32 bytes in size. In linear-page-table mode, the operating system needs to be able to support a virtually-mapped linear page table and the PTEs have a format known as the *short format*. The short format is the one Linux uses. As shown in Figure 4.25, this type of PTE is 8 bytes in size.

The VHPT walker configuration is determined by the *page table address* control register pta. This register is illustrated in Figure 4.31. Bit ve controls whether or not the VHPT walker is enabled. The operation of the VHPT walker is further qualified by a control bit in each region register. Only when a TLB miss occurs in a region for which this control bit *and* pta.ve are both 1 does the VHPT walker become active. The second control bit in pta is vf; it determines whether the walker operates in hashed (long-format) or virtually-mapped linear page table (short-format) mode. A value of 1 indicates hashed mode. Let us assume that ve is 1 (enabled) and that vf is 0 (virtually-mapped linear page table mode). With this configuration, the base and size fields define the address range that the linear page table

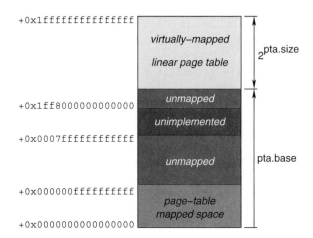

Figure 4.32. Virtually-mapped linear page table inside a Linux/ia64 region.

occupies in each region. The base field contains the 49 most significant bits of the region-relative offset at which the table starts, and the size field contains the number of address bits that the table spans (i.e., the table is $2^{pta.size}$ bytes long).

Note that while the VHPT walker can be disabled separately in each region (by a bit in the region registers), for those regions in which it is enabled, the linear page table is mapped at the same relative address range in each region. Given this constraint, the location at which the linear page table is placed needs to be chosen carefully.

Figure 4.32 illustrates the solution that Linux/ia64 is using. Two factors influence the placement of the linear page table. First, so that virtual address space is not wasted, it is preferable for the page table to not overlap with the normal space mapped by the page table. The latter space is illustrated in the figure by the rectangle at the bottom of the region. As usual, the addresses listed next to it are valid for the case in which a three-level page table is used with a page size of 8 Kbytes. Second, the page table also may not overlap with the address-space hole in the middle of the region that exists if the CPU does not implement all address bits (as determined by the IMPL_VA_MSB parameter). This hole is illustrated in the figure by the dark-shaded rectangle in the middle of the region. The addresses listed next to it are valid for the case where IMPL_VA_MSB = 50. With these two factors in mind, Linux/ia64 sets up the pta register such that the linear page table is mapped at the top end of the region, as illustrated by the lightly shaded rectangle. Note that for certain combinations of page sizes and IMPL_VA_MSB, the page-table-mapped space might either cross over into the unimplemented space or might overlap with the virtually-mapped linear page table (when IMPL_VA_MSB = 60). The Linux kernel checks for this at boot time, and if it detects an overlap condition, it prints an error message and halts execution.

Now, let us take a look at how the VHPT walker operates. When a TLB miss occurs for virtual address va, the walker calculates the virtual address va' of the PTE that maps va.

Using the virtually-mapped linear page table, this address is given by:

$$va' = \lfloor va/2^{61} \rfloor \cdot 2^{61} + \text{pta.base} \cdot 2^{15} + 8 \cdot \left(\lfloor va/\text{PAGE\_SIZE} \rfloor \bmod 2^{\text{pta.size}} \right)$$

That is, va' is the sum of the region's base address, the region offset of the linear page table, and the offset of the PTE within the linear page table. In the last summand, the factor of 8 is used because each PTE has a size of 8 bytes, and the modulo operation truncates away the most significant address bits that are not mapped by the page table. The VHPT walker then attempts to read the PTE stored at this address. Because this is again a virtual address, the CPU goes through the normal virtual-to-physical address translation. If a TLB entry exists for va', the translation succeeds and the walker can read the PTE from physical memory and install the PTE for va. However, if the TLB entry for va' is also missing, the walker gives up and requests assistance by raising a VHPT TRANSLATION FAULT.

Let us emphasize that the VHPT walker *never* walks the Linux page table. It could not possibly do so because it has no knowledge of the page-table structure used by Linux. For example, it does not know how many levels the page-table tree has or how big each directory is. But why use the VHPT walker at all given that it can handle a TLB miss only if the TLB entry for the linear page table is already present? The reason is spatial locality of reference. Consider that the TLB entry that maps a particular PTE actually maps an entire page of PTEs. Thus, after a TLB entry for a page-table page is installed, all TLB misses that access PTEs in the same page can be handled entirely by the VHPT walker, avoiding costly TLB miss faults. For example, with a page size of 8 Kbytes, each page-table TLB entry maps 8 Kbytes/8 = 1024 PTEs and hence 1024 · 8 Kbytes = 8 Mbytes of memory. In other words, when accessing memory sequentially, the VHPT walker reduces TLB miss faults from one per page to only one per 1024 pages! Given the high cost of fielding a fault on modern CPUs, the VHPT walker clearly has the potential to dramatically increase performance.

On the other hand, if memory is accessed in an extremely sparse pattern, the linear page table can be disadvantageous because the TLB entries for the page table take up space without being of much benefit. For example, again assuming a page size of 8 Kbytes, the most extreme case would occur when one byte is accessed every 8 Mbytes. In this case, each memory access would require two TLB entries: one for the page being accessed and one for the corresponding page-table page. Thus, the effective size of the TLB would be reduced by a factor of two! Fortunately, few applications exhibit such extreme access patterns for prolonged periods of time, so this is usually not an issue.

On a final note, it is worth pointing out that the virtually-mapped linear page table used by Linux/ia64 is *not* a self-mapped virtual page table (see Section 4.3.2). The two are very similar in nature, but the IA-64 page table does not have a self-mapped entry in the global directory. The reason is that none is needed: The self-mapped entry really is needed only if the virtual page table is used to access global- and middle-directory entries. Since Linux/ia64 does not do that, it needs no self-mapping entry. Another way to look at this situation is to think of the virtual page table as existing in the TLB only: If a page in the virtual page table happens to be mapped in the TLB, it can be used to access the PTE directory, but if it is not mapped, an ordinary page-table walk is required.

Linux/ia64 and the region and protection key registers

Let us now return to Figure 4.29 on page 177 and take a closer look at the workings of the region and protection key registers and how Linux uses them. Both register files are under complete control of the operating system; the IA-64 architecture does not dictate a particular way of using them. However, they clearly were designed with a particular use in mind. Specifically, the region registers provide a means to share the TLB across multiple processes (address spaces). For example, if a unique region ID is assigned to each address space, the TLB entries for the same virtual page number vpn of different address spaces can reside in the TLB at the same time because they remain distinguishable, thanks to the region ID. With this use of region IDs, a context switch no longer requires flushing of the entire TLB. Instead, it is simply necessary to load the region ID of the new process into the appropriate region registers. This reduction in TLB flushing can dramatically improve performance for certain applications. Also, because each region has its own region register, it is even possible to have portions of different address spaces active at the same time. The Linux kernel takes advantage of this by permanently installing the region ID of the kernel in rr5–rr7 and installing the region ID of the currently running process in rr0–rr4. With this setup, kernel TLB entries and the TLB entries of various user-level processes can coexist without any difficulty and without wasting any TLB entries.

Whereas region registers make it possible to share the entire TLB across processes, protection key registers enable the sharing of *individual* TLB entries across processes, even if the processes must have distinct access rights for the page mapped by the TLB entry. To see how this works, suppose that a particular TLB entry maps a page of a shared object. The TLB entry for this page would be installed with the access rights (+rights) set according to the needs of the owner of the object. The key field would be set to a value that uniquely identifies the shared object. The operating system could then grant a process restricted access to this object by using one of the protection key registers to map the object's unique ID to an appropriate set of negative rights (-rights). This kind of fine-grained sharing of TLB entries has the potential to greatly improve TLB utilization, e.g., for shared libraries. However, the short-format mode of the VHPT walker cannot take advantage of the protection key registers and, for this reason, Linux disables them by clearing the pk bit in the processor status register (see Chapter 2, *IA-64 Architecture*).

4.4.2   Maintenance of TLB coherency

For proper operation of the Linux kernel to be guaranteed, the TLB must be kept coherent with the page tables. For this purpose, Linux defines an interface that abstracts the platform differences of how entries are flushed from the TLB. The interface used for this purpose, shown in Figure 4.33, is called the *TLB flush interface* (file include/asm/pgalloc.h).

The first routine in this interface is *flush_tlb_page()*. It flushes the TLB entry of a particular page. The routine takes two arguments, a vm-area pointer *vma* and a virtual address *addr*. The latter is the address of the page whose TLB entry is being flushed, and the former points to the vm-area structure that covers this page. Because the vm-area structure contains a link back to the mm structure to which it belongs, the *vma* argument indirectly also identifies the address space for which the TLB entry is being flushed.

flush_tlb_page(*vma*, *addr*);	/* *flush TLB entry for virtual address addr* */
flush_tlb_range(*mm*, *start*, *end*);	/* *flush TLB entries in address range* */
flush_tlb_pgtables(*mm*, *start*, *end*);	/* *flush virtual-page-table TLB entries* */
flush_tlb_mm(*mm*);	/* *flush TLB entries of address space mm* */
flush_tlb_all();	/* *flush the entire TLB* */
update_mmu_cache(*vma*, *addr*, *pte*);	/* *proactively install translation in TLB* */

Figure 4.33. Kernel interface to maintain TLB coherency.

The second routine, *flush_tlb_range()*, flushes the TLB entries that map virtual pages inside an arbitrary address range. It takes three arguments: an mm structure pointer *mm*, a start address *start*, and an end address *end*. The *mm* argument identifies the address space for which the TLB entries should be flushed, and *start* and *end* identify the first and the last virtual page whose TLB entries should be flushed.

The third routine, *flush_tlb_pgtables*, flushes TLB entries that map the virtually-mapped linear page table. Platforms that do not use a virtual page table do not have to do anything here. For the other platforms, argument *mm* identifies the address space for which the TLB entries should be flushed, and arguments *start* and *end* specify the virtual address range for which the virtual-page-table TLB entries should be flushed.

The fourth routine, *flush_tlb_mm()*, flushes all TLB entries for a particular address space. The address space is identified by argument *mm*, which is a pointer to an mm structure. Depending on the capabilities of the platform, this routine can either truly flush the relevant TLB entries or simply assign a new address-space number to *mm*.

Note that the four routines discussed so far may flush more than just the requested TLB entries. For example, if a particular platform does not have an instruction to flush a specific TLB entry, it is safe to implement *flush_tlb_page()* such that it flushes the entire TLB.

The next routine, *flush_tlb_all()*, flushes the entire TLB. This is a fallback routine in the sense that it can be used when none of the previous, more fine-grained routines are suitable. By definition, this routine flushes even TLB entries that map kernel pages. Because this is the only routine that does this, any address-translation-related changes to the page-table-mapped kernel segment or the kmap segment must be followed by a call to this routine. For this reason, calls to *vmalloc()* and *vfree()* are relatively expensive.

The last routine in this interface is *update_mmu_cache()*. Instead of flushing a TLB entry, it can be used to proactively install a new translation. The routine takes three arguments: a vm-area pointer *vma*, a virtual address *addr*, and a page-table entry *pte*. The Linux kernel calls this routine to notify platform-specific code that the virtual page identified by *addr* now maps to the page frame identified by *pte*. The *vma* argument identifies the vm-area structure that covers the virtual page. This routine gives platform-specific code a hint when the page table changes. Because it gives only a hint, a platform is not required to do anything. The platform could use this routine either for platform-specific purposes or to aggressively update the TLB even before the new translation is used for the first time. However, it is important to keep in mind that installation of a new translation generally displaces an existing entry from the TLB, so whether or not this is a good idea depends both on the applications in use and on the performance characteristics of the platform.

IA-64 implementation

On Linux/ia64, *flush_tlb_mm()* is implemented such that it forces the allocation of a new address-space number (region ID) for the address space identified by argument *mm*. This is logically equivalent to purging all TLB entries for that address space, but it has the advantage of not requiring execution of any TLB purge instructions.

The *flush_tlb_all()* implementation is based on the ptc.e (purge translation cache entry) instruction, which purges a large section of the TLB. Exactly how large a section of the TLB is purged depends on the CPU model. The architected sequence to flush the entire TLB is as follows:

```
long flags, i, j, addr = BASE_ADDR;
local_irq_save(flags);                    /* disable interrupts */
for (i = 0; i < COUNT0; ++i, addr += STRIDE0) {
    for (j = 0; j < COUNT1; ++j, addr += STRIDE1)
        ptc_e(addr);
}
local_irq_restore(flags);                 /* reenable interrupts */
```

Here, BASE_ADDR, COUNT0, STRIDE0, COUNT1, and STRIDE1 are CPU-model-specific values that can be obtained from PAL firmware (see Chapter 10, *Booting*). The advantage of using such an architected loop instead of an instruction that is guaranteed to flush the entire TLB is that ptc.e is easier to implement on CPUs with multiple levels and different types of TLBs. For example, a particular CPU model might have two levels of separate instruction and data TLBs, making difficult to clear all TLBs atomically with a single instruction. However, in the particular case of Itanium, COUNT0 and COUNT1 both have a value of 1, meaning that a single ptc.e instruction flushes the entire TLB.

All other flush routines are implemented with either the ptc.l (purge local translation cache) or the ptc.ga (purge global translation cache and ALAT) instruction. The former is used on UP machines, and the latter is used on MP machines. Both instructions take two operands—a start address and a size—which define the virtual address range from which TLB entries should be purged. The ptc.l instruction affects only the local TLB, so it is generally faster to execute than ptc.ga, which affects the entire machine (see the architecture manual for exact definition [26]). Only one CPU can execute ptc.ga at any given time. To enforce this, the Linux/ia64 kernel uses a spinlock to serialize execution of this instruction.

Linux/ia64 uses *update_mmu_cache()* to implement a cache flushing that we discuss in more detail in Section 4.6. The routine could also be used to proactively install a new translation in the TLB. However, Linux gives no indication whether the translation is needed for instruction execution or for a data access, so it would be unclear whether the translation should be installed in the instruction or data TLB (or both). Because of this uncertainty and because installing a translation always entails the risk of evicting another, perhaps more useful, TLB entry, it is better to avoid proactive installation of TLB entries.

int **init_new_context**(*task*, *mm*);	/* *force new address-space number for mm* */
get_mmu_context(*mm*);	/* *allocate address-space number if necessary* */
reload_context(*mm*);	/* *activate address-space number of mm* */
destroy_context(*mm*);	/* *free address-space number* */

Figure 4.34. Kernel interface to manage address-space numbers.

4.4.3   Lazy TLB flushing

To avoid the need to flush the TLB on every context switch, Linux defines an interface that abstracts differences in how address-space numbers (ASNs) work on a particular platform. This interface is called the *ASN interface* (file include/asm/mmu_context.h), shown in Figure 4.34. Support for this interface is optional in the sense that platforms with no ASN support simply define empty functions for the routines in this interface and instead define *flush_tlb_mm()* in such a way that it flushes the entire TLB.

Each mm structure contains a component called the *mm context*, which has a platform-specific type called the *mm context type* (mm_context_t in file include/asm/mmu.h). Often, this type is a single word that stores the ASN of the address space. However, some platforms allocate ASNs in a CPU-local fashion. For those, this type is typically an array of words such that the ith entry stores the ASN that the address space has on CPU i.

When we take a look at Figure 4.34, we see that it defines four routines. The first routine, *init_new_context()*, initializes the mm context of a newly created address space. It takes two arguments: a task pointer *task* and an mm structure pointer *mm*. The latter is a pointer to the new address space, and the former points to the task that created it. Normally, this routine simply clears the mm context to a special value (such as 0) that indicates that no ASN has been allocated yet. On success, the routine should return a value of 0.

The remaining routines all take one argument, an mm structure pointer *mm* that identifies the address space and, therefore, the ASN that is to be manipulated. The *get_mmu-_context()* routine ensures that the mm context contains a valid ASN. If the mm context is already valid, nothing needs to be done. Otherwise, a free (unused) ASN needs to be allocated and stored in the mm context. It would be tempting to use the process ID (pid) as the ASN. However, this does not work because the *execve()* system call creates a new address space without changing the process ID.

Routine *reload_context()* is responsible for activating on the current CPU the ASN represented by the mm context. Logically, this activation entails writing the ASN to the CPU's asn register, but the exact details of how this is done are, of course, platform specific. When this routine is called, the mm context is guaranteed to contain a valid ASN.

Finally, when an ASN is no longer needed, Linux frees it by calling *destroy_context()*. This call marks the ASN represented by the mm context as available for reuse by another address space and should free any memory that may have been allocated in *get_mmu_con-text()*. Even though the ASN is available for reuse after this call, the TLB may still contain old translations with this ASN. For correct operation, it is essential that platform-specific code purges these old translations before activating a reused ASN. This is usually achieved by allocating ASNs in a round-robin fashion and flushing the entire TLB before wrapping around to the first available ASN.

IA-64 implementation

Linux/ia64 uses region IDs to implement the ASN interface. The mm context in the mm structure consists of a single word that holds the region ID of the address space. A value of 0 means that no ASN has been allocated yet. The *init_new_context()* routine can therefore simply clear the mm context to 0.

The IA-64 architecture defines region IDs to be 24 bits wide, but, depending on CPU model, as few as 18 bits can be supported. For example, Itanium supports just the architectural minimum of 18 bits. In Linux/ia64, region ID 0 is reserved for the kernel, and the remaining IDs are handed out by *get_mmu_context()* in a round-robin fashion. After the last available region ID has been handed out, the entire TLB is flushed and a new range of available region IDs is calculated such that all region IDs currently in use are outside this range. Once this range has been found, the *get_mmu_context()* continues to hand out region IDs in a round-robin fashion until the space is exhausted again, at which point the steps of flushing the TLB and finding an available range of region IDs are repeated.

Region IDs are 18 to 24 bits wide but only 15 to 21 bits are effectively available for Linux. The reason is that IA-64 requires the TLB to match the region ID and the virtual page number (see Figure 4.29 on page 177) but not necessarily the virtual region number (vrn). Thus, a TLB may not be able to distinguish, e.g., address 0x2000000000000000 from address 0x4000000000000000 unless the region IDs in rr1 and rr2 are different. To ensure this, Linux/ia64 encodes vrn in the three least significant bits of the region ID.

Note that the region IDs returned by *get_mmu_context()* are shared across all CPUs. Such a global region ID allocation policy is ideal for UP and small to moderately large MP machines. A global scheme is advantageous for MP machines because it makes possible the use of the ptc.ga instruction to purge translations from all TLBs in the machine. On the downside, global region ID allocation is a potential point of contention and, perhaps worse, causes the region ID space to be exhausted faster the more CPUs there are in the machine. To see this, assume there are eight distinct region IDs and that a CPU on average creates a new address space once a second. With a single CPU, the TLB would have to be flushed once every eight seconds because the region ID space has been exhausted. In a machine with eight CPUs, each creating an address space once a second, a global allocation scheme would require that the TLB be flushed once every second. In contrast, a local scheme could get by with as little TLB flushing as the UP case, i.e., one flush every eight seconds. But it would have to use an interprocessor interrupt (IPI, see Chapter 8, *Symmetric Multiprocessing*) instead of ptc.ga to perform a global TLB flush (because each CPU uses its own set of region IDs). In other words, deciding between the local and the global scheme involves a classic tradeoff between smaller fixed overheads (ptc.ga versus IPI) and better scalability (region ID space is exhausted with a rate proportional to total versus per-CPU rate at which new address spaces are created).

On IA-64, *reload_context()* has the effect of loading region registers rr0 to rr4 according to the value in the mm context. As explained in the previous paragraph, the value actually stored in the region registers is formed by shifting the mm context value left by three bits and encoding the region's vrn value in the least significant bits.

The IA-64 version of *destroy_context()* does not need to do anything: *get_mmu_context()* does not allocate any memory, so no memory needs to be freed here. Similarly, the range of available region IDs is recalculated only after the existing range has been exhausted, so there is no need to flush old translations from the TLB here.

4.5   PAGE FAULT HANDLING

A page fault occurs when a process accesses a virtual page for which there is no PTE in the page table or whose PTE in some way prohibits the access, e.g., because the page is not present or because the access is in conflict with the access rights of the page. Page faults are triggered by the CPU and handled in the *page fault handler*.

Because Linux uses demand paging and page-fault-based optimizations such as copy-on-write, page faults occur during the normal course of operation and do not necessarily indicate an error. Thus, when the page fault handler is invoked, it first needs to determine whether the page fault is caused by an access to a valid page. If not, the page fault handler simply sends a segmentation violation signal to the faulting process and returns. Otherwise, it takes one of several possible actions:

- If the page is being accessed for the first time, the handler allocates a new page frame and initializes it, e.g., by reading its content from disk. Page faults caused by first-time accesses are called *demand page faults*.

- If the page has been paged out to swap space, the handler reads it back from disk into a newly allocated page frame.

- If the page fault occurred because of a page-fault-based optimization (such as copy-on-write), the handler takes the appropriate recovery action (such as performing the delayed page copy).

Each of these actions results either in a new or updated page, and the handler must accordingly either create or update the PTE in the page table. Because the page-table tree is also created on demand, installing a new PTE may require allocating and initializing a middle and a PTE directory (the global directory is guaranteed to exist already). The page fault handler can use the *pmd_alloc()* and *pte_alloc()* routines from Section 4.3.6 for this purpose. Before the handler installs the PTE, it updates the **accessed** and **dirty** bits as well. Since the page fault itself is an indication that the page is being accessed, the handler uses *pte_mkyoung()* to unconditionally turn on the **accessed** bit. On the other hand, the **dirty** bit is turned on by *pte_mkdirty()* only if the page fault is the result of a write access. After updating the page table, the page fault handler returns and execution resumes in the faulting process. There, the instruction that previously faulted is restarted and, thanks to the updated page table, it can now complete execution.

The above description glanced over two important questions: how does the kernel determine whether an access is valid and, if it is, how does it determine what action to take?

To verify the validity of an access, the page fault handler must search the vm-area list (or the AVL tree if it exists) for the vm-area that covers the page being accessed. If the vm-area exists and its access right flags (VM_READ, VM_WRITE, and VM_EXEC) permit the access, then the access is valid. The answer to the second question is determined primarily by the state of the page table as it exists on entry to the handler:

1. The handler can determine whether it is dealing with a demand page fault by checking whether the PTE exists in the page table. If either *pmd_none()* or *pte_none()* returns **true**, then the PTE does not yet exist and the fault is a demand page fault. The exact action to be taken for such a fault depends on the vm-area that covers the page. If this vm-area defines its own *nopage()* callback, the handler deals with the fault by invoking the callback; otherwise, it handles the fault by creating an anonymous page. The *nopage()* handler often ends up reading the content of the page from a file, but more complex actions, such as reading the page from a remote machine, are also possible.

2. The **present** bit of the PTE tells the handler whether a page has been paged out to swap space. If the bit is cleared (*pte_present()* returns **false**), the handler knows that it is dealing with a page that has been paged out. The appropriate action is for the handler to read the page back in from swap space.

3. Finally, page-fault-based optimizations manifest themselves as differences between the PTE and the vm-area for the page. For example, a copy-on-write page can be identified by the fact that the PTE disallows write accesses (*pte_write()* returns **false**), yet the vm-area permits them (the VM_WRITE access right is enabled). The appropriate action to handle such faults depends on the exact optimization that is being performed. For a copy-on-write page, the handler would have to perform the delayed page copy.

The discussion so far illustrates that page fault handling is a complex operation: it may involve reading a page from swap space, from an arbitrary filesystem, or even from a remote machine. Fortunately, as we see in Section 4.5.2, the platform-specific part of the kernel only has to handle those aspects that are unique to the platform, because all other work is taken care of by the Linux page fault handler.

4.5.1 Example: How copy-on-write really works

To get a better idea of how the page fault handler coordinates its work with the rest of the kernel, let us look at how Linux handles copy-on-write pages. Let us assume a process *A* with a single region of virtual memory that is writable and that occupies the address range from 0x8000 to 0xe000. Let us further assume that only the page at address 0xa000 is resident in the virtual memory. Figure 4.35 (a) illustrates this case. At the top left, we find the task structure labeled *task A*. The task structure contains a pointer to the mm structure that represents the address space of this process. In the box labeled *mm*, we find a pointer to the vm-area list, labeled *mmap*, and a pointer to the page table, labeled *pgd*. In reality, *pgd* points to the global directory of the page table. However, for simplicity the figure represents

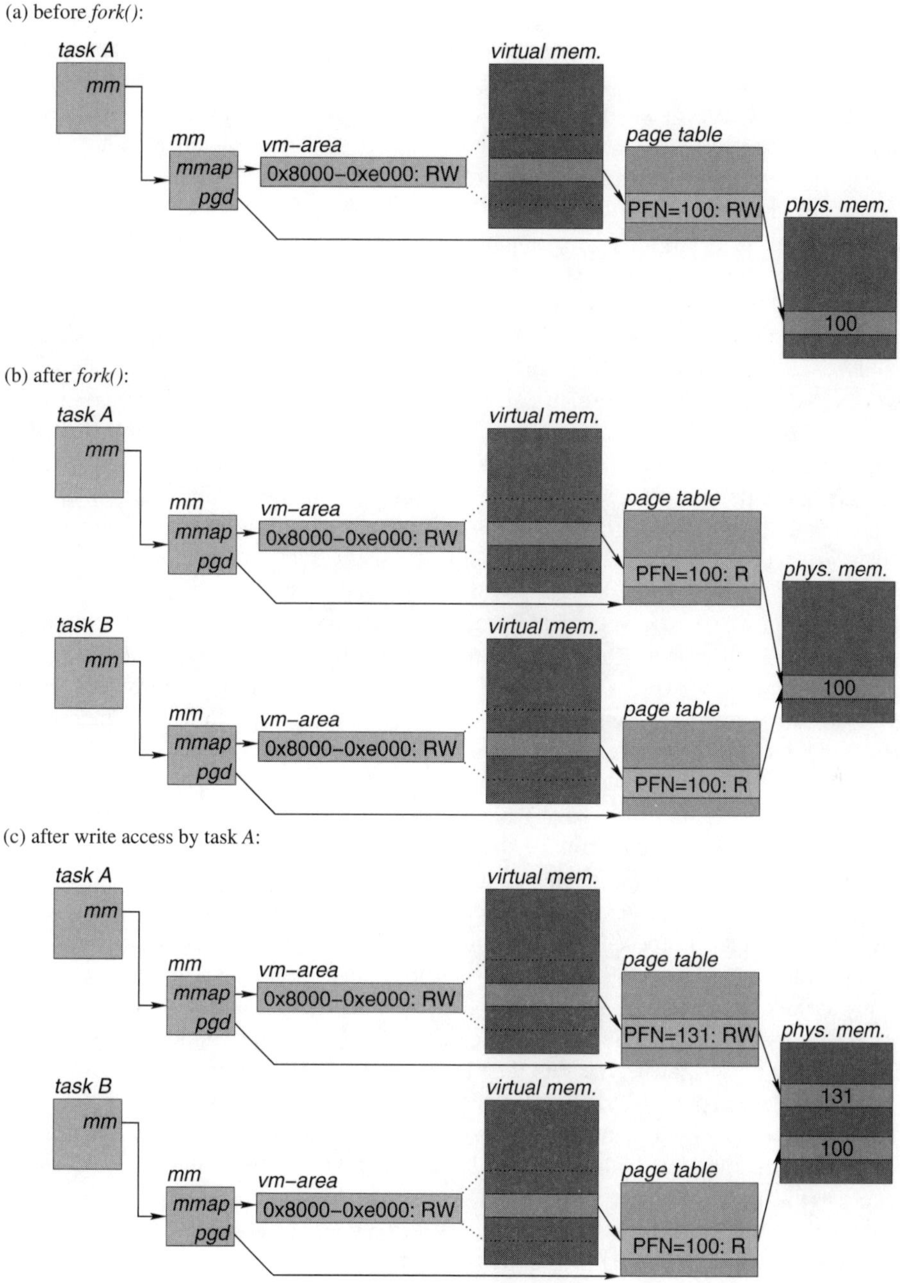

(a) before *fork()*:

(b) after *fork()*:

(c) after write access by task *A*:

Figure 4.35. Example of a copy-on-write operation.

the page table as the linear table labeled *page table*. Because the process has only a single region mapped in the virtual memory, the vm-area list has just a single entry, represented by the box labeled *vm-area*. To keep the complexity of the figure within reason, the vm-area shows only the starting and ending address of the region and the access rights (RW, for read and write access). Because we assumed that the page at 0xa000 is resident, it has an entry in the page table and maps to some page frame. In the figure, we assumed that the virtual page is backed by physical page frame 100. Since the page is both readable and writable, the PTE for this page has the permission bits set to RW.

Now let us assume that process *A* invokes the *clone2()* system call without specifying the CLONE_VM flag. In a traditional UNIX system, this would be equivalent to calling *fork()* and has the effect of creating a new process that is a copy of the caller. The state as it would exist after *clone2()* returns is illustrated in Figure 4.35 (b). As the figure shows, the new process has its own task structure, labeled *task B* and its own copies of *mm*, *vm-area*, and *page table*. The two processes are identical, but note how *clone2()* turned off write permission in the PTEs of both the parent and the child. It does this for every writable PTE in an attempt to delay the copying of writable pages as long as possible. Turning off write permission in the PTEs of writable pages is the first step of a copy-on-write; it ensures that neither process can write to the page without first causing a page fault. Note that the access permissions in the vm-area structures remain unchanged at RW.

So what happens when one of the processes attempts to write to the virtual page at 0x8000? Suppose process *A* writes to the page first. Because the PTE allows only read accesses, this write triggers a page fault. The page fault handler goes through the steps described in the previous section and first locates the matching vm-area. It then checks whether the vm-area permits write accesses. Because the vm-area in process *A* still has the access rights set to RW, the write access is permitted. The page fault handler then checks whether the PTE exists in the page table and whether the PTE has the **present** bit on. Because the page is resident, both of these checks pass. In the last step, the page fault handler checks whether it is dealing with a write access to a page whose PTE does not permit write accesses. Because this is the case, the handler detects that it is time to copy a copy-on-write page. It proceeds by checking the page frame descriptor of page frame 100 to see how many processes are currently using this page. Because process *B* is also using this page frame, the count is 2 and the page fault handler decides that it must copy the page frame. It does this by first allocating a free page frame, say, page frame 131, copying the original frame to this new frame, and then updating the PTE in process *A* to point to page frame 131. Because process *A* now has a private copy of the page, the access permission in the PTE can be set to RW again. The page fault handler then returns, and at this point the write access can complete without any further errors. Figure 4.35 (c) illustrates the state as it exists at this point.

Note that the PTE in process *B* still has write permission turned off, even though it is now the sole user of page frame 100. This remains so until the process attempts a write access. When that happens, the page fault handler is invoked again and the same steps are repeated as for process *A*. However, when checking the page frame descriptor of page frame 100, it finds that there are no other users and goes ahead to turn on write permission in the PTE without first making a copy of the page.

4.5.2   The Linux page fault handler

The Linux kernel provides a platform-independent *page fault handler* (*handle_mm_fault()* in file mm/memory.c) that takes care of handling most aspects of page fault handling. Platform-specific code is responsible for intercepting any virtual-memory-related faults that a CPU may raise and invoking the handler as necessary. The interface of the Linux page fault handler is shown below:

```
int handle_mm_fault(mm, vma, addr, access_type);
```

The routine takes four arguments: *mm* is a pointer to the mm structure of the address space in which the fault occurred, *vma* is a pointer to the vm-area that covers the page that is being accessed, *addr* is the virtual address that caused the fault, and *access_type* is an integer indicating the type of access (read, write, or execute). The return value is an indication of how the page fault was handled. A return value of 1 signifies that the fault was handled successfully and that it should be counted as a *minor fault*. This means that the page installed was already in memory, e.g., because the page is in use by another process as well. A return value of 2 signifies that the fault was also handled successfully, but that it should be counted as a *major fault* because the page had to be read from disk, e.g., from a file or swap space. A value of 0 signifies that the page fault could not be handled properly and that the kernel should send a bus error signal (SIGBUS) to the process. Finally, a negative return value signifies that the kernel is completely out of memory and that the faulting process should be terminated immediately.

Before invoking *handle_mm_fault()*, platform-specific code must perform these steps:

1. Determine the virtual address *addr* that triggered the fault.

2. Determine the access type (read, write, or execute).

3. Verify that the fault occurred in user mode and, if so, get the mm structure pointer *mm* of the currently running process (task).

4. Find the vm-area structure that covers the page being accessed.

5. Verify that the access type is permitted by the vm-area structure.

If all of these steps are completed successfully, the Linux page fault handler can be invoked. After the handler returns, the platform-specific code is responsible to account the fault either as a minor or a major fault, depending on whether the return value was 1 or 2, respectively (this accounting info is stored in the task structure described in Chapter 3, *Processes, Tasks, and Threads*). If the return value is 0, a bus error signal must be sent to the process and if it is negative, the process must be terminated immediately (as if it had called *exit()*).

What should the platform-specific code do if one of the above steps fails? The answer depends on exactly *which* step failed. The first two steps (determining the fault address and access type) usually cannot fail.

If the third step fails, the page fault occurred in kernel mode. This is normally an indication of a kernel bug and results in a panic (kernel stops execution). However, the Linux kernel may legitimately cause page faults while copying data across the user/kernel boundary. Thus, when a page fault happens in kernel mode, platform-specific code must check whether it was the result of such a copy and, if so, initiate an appropriate recovery action. We describe in Chapter 5, *Kernel Entry and Exit*, exactly what this entails.

If the fourth step fails, there is no vm-area that covers the page being accessed; this is normally an indication of an attempt to access nonexistent virtual memory. If this failure occurs, the platform-specific code sends a segmentation violation signal to the process. There are two special cases, however: If the page accessed is just above a vm-area with the VM_GROWSUP flag set or just below a vm-area with the VM_GROWSDOWN flag set, the platform-specific code must expand the corresponding vm-area to include the page being accessed and then use this expanded vm-area to finish processing the page fault in the normal fashion. This mechanism is intended for automatic stack expansion and is permitted only if the resulting stack size does not exceed the stack size limit (RLIMIT_STACK) or the virtual-address-space limit (RLIMIT_AS) established by the *setrlimit()* system call.

If the fifth and last step fails, the process attempted to access the address space in an illegal fashion (e.g., it tried to execute a read-only page) and the platform-specific code again sends a segmentation violation signal to the process.

4.5.3   IA-64 implementation

When a virtual-memory-related fault occurs on IA-64, the interruption handling described in Chapter 2, *IA-64 Architecture*, is initiated. Recall that, among other things, this handling switches the CPU to the most-privileged execution level (level 0), turns off the interruption collection (ic is cleared in psr), activates bank 0 of registers r16 to r31, and then hands over control to the appropriate handler in the interruption vector table (IVT).

The architecture defines a total of 13 virtual-memory-related faults, each with its own handler. A set of six faults handles TLB misses and another set of seven faults handles PTE-related faults. Three primary control registers pass information to these handlers:

- The *interruption status register* (isr) contains various flag bits that indicate the type of access that caused the fault. For example, three bits indicate whether the fault occurred as a result of a read, write, or execute access.

- The *interruption faulting address* (ifa) register contains the virtual address that caused the fault.

- The *interruption hash address* (iha) register is used when a TLB miss occurs as a result of the VHPT walker attempting to access the virtually-mapped linear page table. When this happens, the iha register contains the virtual address that the VHPT walker was attempting to access.

The fault handlers first read these control registers to determine how to handle the fault. The bank 0 registers are active at that time, so the handlers can use registers r16 to r31 for this purpose. Doing so avoids the need to save CPU state to memory. Indeed, whenever possible, the handlers attempt to complete the entire fault handling with only the bank 0 registers. However, because the bank 0 registers are available only while ic is off, more complicated

Table 4.4. IA-64 TLB miss faults.

Fault	Description
ITLB FAULT	Instruction access missed in the instruction TLB.
DTLB FAULT	Data access missed in the data TLB.
VHPT TRANSLATION FAULT	VHPT access missed in the data TLB.
ALTERNATE ITLB FAULT	Instruction access missed in the instruction TLB and the VHPT walker is disabled.
ALTERNATE DTLB FAULT	Data access missed in the data TLB and the VHPT walker is disabled.
DATA NESTED TLB FAULT	Data access missed in the TLB during execution with ic off.

fault handling, in particular any fault handling that requires invoking the Linux page fault handler, forces the handlers off the fast path and also forces them to save the essential CPU state in a pt-regs structure in memory (see Chapter 3, *Processes, Tasks, and Threads*). Once this state has been saved, control can be handed over to the Linux page fault handler.

TLB miss handlers

Table 4.4 lists the six types of TLB-related misses. As the table shows, IA-64 breaks down TLB faults according to the cause of the miss. There are separate handlers for misses triggered by instruction fetches (execute accesses), data accesses (read or write accesses), and VHPT walker accesses. The alternate ITLB and DTLB miss handlers are triggered when the VHPT walker is disabled for the region being accessed (as controlled by a bit in the region register) or when the walker is disabled completely (as controlled by the page table address register bit pta.ve). The DATA NESTED TLB FAULT is triggered when a TLB miss occurs while interruption collection is disabled (ic bit is off), i.e., while another fault is being handled. Ordinarily, a nested fault would indicate a kernel bug. However, as we will see below, Linux/ia64 uses nested TLB misses to support nonspeculative accesses to the virtually-mapped linear page table.

Nested DTLB miss handler

Let us start by taking a look at how the handler for the DATA NESTED TLB FAULT works. It is effectively a helper routine that translates a virtual address *addr* to the physical address *pte_paddr* at which the corresponding PTE can be found. Because this fault is triggered only while ic is off, the CPU does not update the control registers and they instead continue to.contain the information for the *original* fault. Unfortunately, the information in the control registers is not sufficient for the nested DLTB miss handler to complete its job. Thus, Linux/ia64 uses three bank 0 registers to pass additional information between the handler of the original fault and the nested DTLB miss handler. The first register is used to pass the virtual address *addr*, and the second is used to pass the address *rlabel* to which execution should return once the nested DTLB handler is done. The third register serves as the result register and is used to return *pte_paddr*.

The nested DTLB miss handler operates by turning off the data translation bit psr.dt and then walking the three-level page table. Because physical data accesses are used during the page-table walk, there is no danger of triggering further TLB misses. The starting point of the page-table walk is determined by the region that *addr* is accessing. If it accesses region 5, the kernel page table is used; otherwise (access to region 0 to 4), the page table of the currently running process is used. If the walk is completed successfully, the physical address of the found PTE is placed in the result register and control is returned to the original handler by a jump to address *rlabel*. If any error is encountered during the page-table walk (e.g., because the virtual address is not mapped), control is transferred to the Linux page fault handler instead.

ITLB/DTLB miss handler

With the operation of the nested DTLB miss handler explained, it is straightforward to describe the ITLB and DTLB miss handlers. In a first step the TLB miss handlers read the ifa control register to determine the faulting address *addr*. In a second step, the bank 0 registers are set up so that the nested DTLB handler can find the necessary information in case execution later triggers a DATA NESTED TLB FAULT. Specifically, the faulting address *addr* and the return address *rlabel* are placed in the bank 0 registers used for this purpose. In the third step, the actual work can begin: The handlers use the thash instruction to translate the faulting address *addr* to *pte_vaddr*, the address in the virtually-mapped linear page table at which the PTE for *addr* can be found. The handlers then attempt to read the PTE by loading the word at this address. If the TLB entry for *pte_vaddr* exists, the load succeeds and the PTE can be installed either in the ITLB (for an ITLB miss) or in the DTLB (for a DTLB miss). Conversely, if the TLB entry for *pte_vaddr* is missing, a DATA NESTED TLB FAULT is triggered and the CPU hands over control to the nested DTLB miss handler. As described previously, this handler walks the page table in physical mode and, if a mapping exists for *addr*, places the physical address *pte_paddr* of the PTE in the result register. The nested miss handler then returns control to the original handler with the data translation bit dt still turned off. The original handler now has the physical address *pte_paddr* of the PTE, and because data accesses are still done in physical mode, the handler can directly load the word at this address, without the risk of causing any further faults. This procedure again yields the desired PTE, which can then be installed in the appropriate TLB (ITLB or DTLB).

The elegance of handling TLB misses in this fashion derives from the fact that both the virtual and physical access cases use exactly the same instruction sequence once the PTE address has been determined. The only difference is whether loading the PTE occurs in physical or in virtual mode. This means that the address *rlabel* can be the address of the same load instruction that attempts to read the PTE from the virtually-mapped linear page table. If the virtual access fails, the load instruction is reexecuted after the nested DTLB miss handler returns, but now in physical mode. Note that, for this technique to work, the address register of the load instruction must be the same as the result register that the nested DTLB handler uses to return the physical address of the PTE.

VHPT miss handler

When a TLB miss occurs in a region for which the VHPT walker has been enabled, the walker first attempts to handle the miss on its own. Conceptually, it does this by using the thash instruction to translate the faulting address *addr* to *pte_vaddr*, the address in the virtually-mapped linear page table at which the PTE for *addr* can be found. If the TLB entry for *pte_vaddr* is present in the TLB, the VHPT walker (usually) can handle the miss on its own. On the other hand, if this TLB entry is also missing, the CPU raises a VHPT TRANSLATION FAULT and passes *addr* in control register ifa and *pte_vaddr* in iha.

Once the VHPT miss handler starts executing, it extracts the original faulting address *addr* from ifa and then traverses the page table in physical mode, just like the nested DTLB miss handler. Once the physical address of the PTE has been found, the PTE is loaded and installed in the appropriate TLB (DTLB if the original access was a data access, ITLB otherwise). In addition, the VHPT constructs and inserts into the DTLB a translation that maps the address contained in iha. This ensures that future TLB misses to nearby addresses can be handled through the virtually-mapped linear page table.

Because this handler inserts two translations in the TLB, care must be taken to ensure that the CPU can make forward progress, even if only one of the two translations survives. Fortunately, in this particular case, the order of insertion does not matter because the CPU can make forward progress either way: If the translation for the original faulting address survives, the access that caused the fault can obviously complete without further TLB misses. Conversely, if translation for the virtually-mapped linear page table survives, the VHPT walker is either able to handle the reoccurrence of the TLB miss for the original faulting address on its own or the CPU raises a regular ITLB or DTLB FAULT, which would also resolve the fault.

Note that with a perfect VHPT walker, the CPU would only raise VHPT TRANSLATION FAULTs—regular ITLB or DTLB FAULTs would never be raised. However, the IA-64 architecture leaves CPU designers the option of implementing an imperfect VHPT walker or of omitting it completely. This flexibility is achieved by the requirement that if a VHPT walker cannot handle a particular TLB miss, the CPU must raise an ITLB or DTLB FAULT instead. In the most extreme case of a nonexistent VHPT walker, this means that instead of VHPT TRANSLATION FAULTs, only ITLB or DTLB FAULTs would occur. In a more realistic scenario, the VHPT walker would be able to handle most TLB misses except that in certain corner cases, it would have to resort to raising an ITLB or DTLB FAULT. For example, the Itanium VHPT walker can handle virtual page-table accesses as long as the PTE can be found in the second-level cache. If the PTE is not cached, the walker gives up and raises an ITLB or DTLB FAULT instead.

Alternate ITLB/DTLB miss handler

The CPU dispatches to the alternate ITLB and DTLB handlers when a TLB miss occurs and the VHPT walker is disabled. Because regions 6 and 7 of the virtual address space of Linux/ia64 are identity-mapped, they have no associated page table and the VHPT walker has to be disabled for those regions. In other words, TLB misses caused by accesses to regions 6 and 7 always result in the one of the alternate TLB miss handlers being invoked.

For the other regions, the VHPT walker is normally enabled. However, for performance measurements and debugging purposes, it is sometimes useful to turn off the VHPT in these regions as well. The bottom line is that accesses to region 6 and 7 are always handled by the alternate miss handlers, and accesses to region 0 to 5 are only sometimes handled here. Thus, before doing anything else, the alternate TLB miss handlers first check whether the faulting access is to region 6 or 7. If not, the miss is redirected to the normal ITLB/DTLB miss handler described earlier. If it is, the handler can calculate the necessary PTE directly from the address being accessed. That is, there is no need to walk a page table. The PTE calculated in this fashion permits read, write, and execute accesses by the kernel only and maps to the physical address that is equal to the least significant 61 bits of the virtual address. The **dirty** and **accessed** bits are set to 1, and the memory attribute is derived from the region being accessed: For region 6 the **uncacheable** attribute is used, and for region 7 the **cacheable** attribute is used.

Calculating the PTE is straightforward, but a few corner cases need to be taken care of. First, user-level accesses to regions 6 and 7 have to be intercepted and redirected to cause a segmentation fault. This may seem strange because the permission bits in the translations that would be inserted in response to such accesses would prevent user-level accesses at any rate. However, the reason the redirection is necessary is that the IA-64 architecture does not permit the same physical address to be mapped with conflicting memory attributes. Suppose an application accessed a particular physical address first through region 6 and then through region 7. Both accesses would trigger a segmentation violation signal, but the application can intercept those and skip over the faulting instruction. Now, if user-level accesses were not intercepted, the two accesses would result in the same physical address being mapped both cached and uncached, which violates the architecture and could cause a failure on some CPUs. Because this is an unacceptable risk, the alternate TLB miss handlers must prevent such translations from being inserted in the first place. This is most easily achieved by rejecting all user-level accesses to regions 6 and 7.

A related problem arises from speculative loads in the kernel. If TLB misses are not deferred (dcr.dm is 0), a speculative load inside the kernel may cause a TLB miss to an arbitrary address. If that address happens to fall inside region 6 or 7, the speculative load would trigger an alternate TLB fault. This again poses the risk of inserting a translation with conflicting memory attributes. To prevent this, the alternate DTLB miss handler also checks whether the faulting access was caused by a speculative load and, if so, turns on the exception deferral bit (ed in psr) instead of installing a translation. The net effect of this method is that all speculative loads to region 6 and 7 produce a NaT value, unless the translation for the page being accessed happens to be in the TLB already. This solution may sometimes produce a NaT unnecessarily, but apart from a small performance impact, does not affect the correct operation of the kernel. This solution also has the advantage that speculative loads cannot pollute the TLB with unnecessary translations.

PTE fault handlers

Let us now turn our attention to the PTE-related faults. As Table 4.5 shows, there are seven such faults. The INSTRUCTION ACCESS-BIT FAULT and DATA ACCESS-BIT FAULTS are

Table 4.5. IA-64 PTE faults.

Fault	Description
INSTR. ACCESS-BIT FAULT	Instruction fetch to a page with the **accessed** bit cleared.
DATA ACCESS-BIT FAULT	Data (read or write) access to a page with the **accessed** bit cleared.
DIRTY-BIT FAULT	Write access to a page with the **dirty** bit cleared.
PAGE NOT PRESENT FAULT	Access to a page with the **present** bit cleared.
INSTR. ACCESS RIGHT FAULT	Instruction fetch to a page with no execute access right.
DATA ACCESS RIGHTS FAULT	Data (read or write) access to page violates access rights.
KEY PERMISSION FAULT	Access to a page violates protection key permissions.

raised if an instruction fetch or a data access is performed to a page with the **accessed** (A) bit turned off in the PTE. Linux uses this bit to drive its page replacement algorithm, and the handlers for these faults turn on this bit in the PTE, update the TLB entry, and then return. Just like the DTLB/ITLB miss handlers, they use the virtually-mapped linear page table to access the PTE and fall back on the nested DTLB miss handler if necessary.

The DIRTY-BIT FAULT is raised on a write access to a page with the **dirty** (D) bit turned off in the PTE. This fault is handled exactly like the DATA ACCESS-BIT FAULT except that it turns on both the **dirty** and the **accessed** bits. Turning on just the **dirty** bit would also work correctly but would be suboptimal because as soon as the handler returned, the lower-priority DATA ACCESS-BIT FAULT would be raised. In other words, by turning on both bits in this handler, the work of two faults can be accomplished with a single fault, which results in better performance.

The PAGE NOT PRESENT fault, INSTRUCTION ACCESS RIGHT fault, and DATA ACCESS RIGHTS FAULT are raised when the **present** bit is cleared in a PTE or when a page is accessed in a way that violates the permission bits in the PTE. None of these faults can be handled in the IVT itself. Consequently, the handlers for these faults unconditionally transfer control to the Linux page fault handler, where the appropriate action is taken. This action often has the effect of changing the PTE. If so, Linux normally takes care of flushing the old TLB entry. However, Linux assumes that PTEs with the **present** bit cleared are never installed in the TLB, so it does not flush the TLB after turning on the **present** bit on a page that was paged in. Because IA-64 violates this assumption, the PAGE NOT PRESENT FAULT handler must flush the TLB entry before calling the Linux page fault handler.

The final PTE-related fault is the KEY PERMISSION FAULT. This fault can only be raised if protection key checking is enabled (psr.pk is 1). Because Linux/ia64 does not use protection key registers, this checking is disabled and hence the fault cannot occur.

Multiprocessor considerations

The combination of a global TLB purge instruction and software TLB miss handling creates a subtle race condition. Suppose there are two CPUs, P_0 and P_1, with P_0 accessing virtual address a, and P_1 updating the page-table entry for this address. We could then get the sequence of events illustrated in Figure 4.36. P_0 accesses virtual memory address a, and

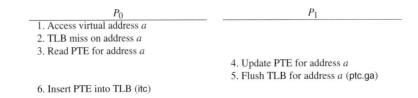

Figure 4.36. Example race condition between TLB miss handling on CPU P_0 and TLB flush on CPU P_1.

this might trigger a TLB miss. The TLB miss handler would then start executing and read the corresponding PTE from the page table. Right after that, P_1 might update this PTE and, to ensure that all CPUs are aware of this modification, it would use ptc.ga to flush the TLB entries for the page at address a. On P_0, this instruction would have no effect, because the TLB entry for address a is not yet present. However, right after the TLB flush has completed, P_0 might finish the TLB miss handling and execute an itc instruction to insert the PTE it read in step 3. This means that after step 6, the TLB of P_0 would contain a stale translation: address a would be mapped according to the old PTE read in step 3, not according to the updated PTE written in step 4!

To avoid this problem, the TLB miss handler can reread the PTE from the page table after step 6 and check to see if it changed. If it did change, there are two options: the handler can either restart miss handling from the beginning or it can return after flushing the entry inserted in step 6. In the latter case, the memory access will be reexecuted, and because the translation for address a is still missing, the TLB miss handler will be invoked again. Eventually, the miss handler will be able to execute without encountering a race condition, and at that point the correct PTE for address a will be inserted into the TLB.

Note that even though we used a TLB miss to illustrate the race condition, it can arise with any fault handler that inserts a TLB translation based on the content of a page table. Also note that the race condition arises from the fact that the fault handling is not atomic with respect to the ptc.ga instruction. If global TLB flushes were implemented with interprocessor interrupts instead, the fault handling would be atomic and the PTE rechecking would not be necessary.

Dispatching to the Linux page fault handler

The previous discussion of the fault handlers makes it amply clear that there are many cases in which the assistance of the Linux page fault handler is required. However, before the platform-independent *handle_mm_fault()* can be invoked, the IA-64–specific code must locate the appropriate vm-area structure and verify that the access does not violate the access rights in the vm-area structure. Because these actions must be performed whenever control is transferred to the Linux page fault handler, they are implemented in a common routine called *ia64_do_page_fault()*. Most actions performed by this routine are straightforward and follow the steps outlined at the beginning of this section. However, two interesting IA-64–specific aspects warrant further discussion.

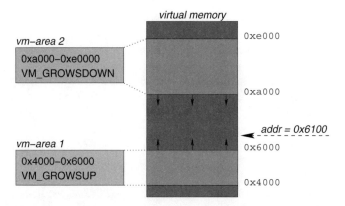

Figure 4.37. Ambiguity caused by vm-areas with different growth directions.

First, note that the platform-specific code is responsible for supporting automatic expansion of vm-areas with the flag VM_GROWSUP or VM_GROWSDOWN set. For most platforms, stacks grow either toward higher or lower addresses, and consequently these platforms support just the flag that corresponds to the stack growth direction. IA-64 is special in that it needs to support both growth directions as the register stack grows toward higher addresses and the memory stack grows toward lower addresses. As Figure 4.37 illustrates, this requirement introduces a potential ambiguity. Suppose *vm-area 1* covers the address range 0x4000 to 0x6000 and grows toward higher addresses and *vm-area 2* covers the range 0xa000 to 0xe000 and grows toward lower addresses. Now, if a process accesses address 0x6100, should *vm-area 1* or *vm-area 2* be expanded? Without knowing the intent of the process there is no way to resolve this ambiguity in a way that is guaranteed to be correct. However, because the register stack engine (RSE) accesses the register backing store in a strictly sequential fashion, Linux/ia64 adopts the policy that a vm-area with the VM_GROWSUP flag set is expanded only if the page fault was caused by an access to the word immediately above the end of the vm-area. This implies that the case illustrated in the figure would be resolved in favor of expanding *vm-area 2*. Only if address 0x6000 were to be accessed would *vm-area 1* be expanded. This policy is guaranteed to make the right choice provided VM_GROWSUP is used only to map register backing store memory.

The second question is how faults caused by speculative loads should be treated (see Chapter 2, *IA-64 Architecture*, for more information on speculation). The IA-64 architecture defines two speculation models: **recovery** and **no-recovery** [76]. The **recovery** model requires that speculative loads are always accompanied by corresponding recovery code. As the name suggest, the **no-recovery** model does not require recovery code. For this model to work, speculative faults must not produce a NaT unless it is *guaranteed* that a nonspeculative load to the same address would also fail.

Linux/ia64 does not support the **no-recovery** model at the user level because it could cause unexpected application failures. To see why, consider an application that implements a distributed shared memory system (DSM) by using segmentation violation signals to detect which pages need to be fetched from a remote machine. The TreadMarks DSM is an example of such a system [3]. If this application performed a speculative load to unmapped memory and the offending code uses the **no-recovery** model, the Linux page fault handler would be faced with the difficult choice of returning a NaT or sending a segmentation violation signal. If it were to return a NaT, it would have made an error if the speculative load was to a DSM page that the signal handler would have fetched from the remote machine. On the other hand, if it were to deliver the signal, then it would have made an error if the speculative load was accessing an address that was indeed illegal. This problem could be solved if the application knew about speculative loads and could decide on its own whether a NaT should be produced. However, because this would result in an application that is not portable to other architectures, Linux/ia64 does not support the **no-recovery** model.

The **recovery** model does not suffer from this problem because the presence of the recovery code ensures that it is always safe to return a NaT. This behavior also answers how page faults caused by speculative loads should be handled: Because Linux/ia64 does not support the **no-recovery** model, it handles such accesses by setting the ed bit in the processor status register (psr) of the interrupted process. This action instructs the CPU to place a NaT value in the target register when the speculative load is restarted after returning from the page fault handler. In our DSM example, this might cause the application's recovery code to be invoked unnecessarily at times, but other than a slight performance degradation, there are no ill effects.

4.6 MEMORY COHERENCY

A given memory location is said to be *coherent* if all CPUs and I/O devices in a machine observe one and the same value in that location. Modern machines make aggressive use of memory caches and thereby introduce many potential sources for incoherence. For example, to maximize performance, caches usually delay stores by the CPU as long as possible and write them back to main memory (or the next level in the cache hierarchy) only when absolutely necessary. As a result, the same memory location may have different values in the various caches or in main memory. Modern machines also often use separate caches for instructions and data, thereby introducing the risk of the same location being cached both in the instruction and data cache, but with potentially different values.

A particularly insidious source of incoherence arises from *virtually-tagged* caches that tag the cache contents not with the memory location (physical address) but with the virtual address with which the location was accessed. Consider the scenario where the same location is accessed multiple times with different virtual addresses. This is called *virtual aliasing* because different virtual addresses refer to the same memory location. Linux frequently does this and with virtually-tagged caches, the memory location may end up being cached multiple times! Moreover, updating the memory location through one virtual address would not update the cache copies created by the aliases, and we would again have a situation where a memory location is incoherent.

flush_cache_all();	/* make all kernel data coherent */
flush_icache_range(*start*, *end*);	/* make range in i- and d-caches coherent */
flush_cache_mm(*mm*);	/* make data mapped by mm coherent */
flush_cache_range(*mm*, *start*, *end*);	/* make data in address range coherent */
flush_cache_page(*vma*, *addr*);	/* make data page in vma coherent */
flush_dcache_page(*pg*);	/* make page cache page coherent */
clear_user_page(*to*, *uaddr*, *pg*);	/* clear page and maintain coherency */
copy_user_page(*from*, *to*, *uaddr*, *pg*);	/* copy page and maintain coherency */

Figure 4.38. Kernel interface to maintain memory coherency.

I/O devices are yet another source of incoherence: a device may write a memory location through DMA (see Chapter 7, *Device I/O*) and this new value may or may not be observed by the memory caches.

We would like to emphasize that, by itself, an incoherent memory location is not an issue. A problem arises only if an incoherent value is *observed*, e.g., by a CPU or an I/O device. When this happens, the result is usually catastrophic. For example, suppose we are dealing with a platform that uses separate instruction and data caches. If the operating system reads a page of code from the text section of an executable file and copies it to the user space of a process, the data cache will be updated but the instruction cache will remain unchanged. Thus, when the process attempts to execute the newly loaded code, it may end up fetching stale instructions and the process may crash. To avoid such problems, memory locations must be made coherent before a stale value can be observed. Depending on the platform architecture, maintaining coherency may be the responsibility of hardware or software. In practice, the two often share the responsibility, with the hardware taking care of certain sources of incoherence and the software taking care of the rest.

4.6.1   Maintenance of coherency in the Linux kernel

To accommodate the wide variety of possible memory coherence schemes, Linux defines the interface shown in Figure 4.38. Every platform must provide a suitable implementation of this interface. The interface is designed to handle all coherence issues except DMA coherence. DMA is handled separately, as we see in Chapter 7, *Device I/O*.

The first routine in this interface is *flush_cache_all()*. It must ensure that for data accessed through the kernel address space, all memory locations are coherent. Linux calls this routine just before changing or removing a mapping in the page-table-mapped kernel segment or the kmap segment. On platforms with virtually-tagged caches, the routine is usually implemented by flushing all data caches. On other platforms, this routine normally performs no operation.

The second routine, *flush_icache_range()*, ensures that a specific range of memory locations is coherent with respect to instruction fetches and data accesses. The routine takes two arguments, *start* and *end*. The address range that must be made coherent extends from *start* up to and including *end* − 1. All addresses in this range must be valid kernel or mapped user-space virtual addresses. Linux calls this routine after writing instructions to memory. For example, when loading a kernel module, Linux first allocates memory in the page-table-mapped kernel segment, copies the executable image to this memory, and then calls *flush_icache_range()* on the text segment to ensure the d-caches and i-caches are coherent before attempting to execute any code in the kernel module. On platforms that do not use separate instruction or data caches or that maintain coherency in hardware, this routine normally performs no operation. On other platforms, it is usually implemented by flushing the instruction cache for the given address range.

The next three routines are all used by Linux to inform platform-specific code that the virtual-to-physical translation of a section of a (user) address space is about to be changed. On platforms with physically indexed caches, these routines normally perform no operation. However, in the presence of virtually indexed caches, these routines must ensure that coherency is maintained. In practice, this usually means that all cache lines associated with any of the affected virtual addresses must be flushed from the caches. The three routines differ in the size of the section they affect: *flush_cache_mm()* affects the entire address space identified by mm structure pointer *mm*; *flush_cache_range()* affects a range of addresses. The range extends from *start* up to and including *end* − 1, where *start* and *end* are both user-level addresses and are given as the second and third arguments to this routine. The third routine, *flush_cache_page()*, affects a single page. The vm-area that covers this page is identified by the *vma* argument and the user-space address of the affected page is given by argument *addr*. These routines are closely related to the TLB coherency routines *flush_tlb_mm()*, *flush_tlb_range()*, and *flush_tlb_page()* in the sense that they are used in pairs. For example, Linux changes the page table of an entire address space *mm* by using code that follows the pattern shown below:

```
flush_cache_mm(mm);
...change page table of mm...
flush_tlb_mm(mm);
```

That is, before changing a virtual-to-physical translation, Linux calls one of the *flush_cache* routines to ensure that the affected memory locations are coherent. In the second step, it changes the page table (virtual-to-physical translations), and in the third step, it calls one of the *flush_tlb* routines to ensure that the TLB is coherent. The order in which these steps occur is critical: The memory locations need to be made coherent *before* the translations are changed because otherwise the flush routine might fault. Conversely, the TLB must be made coherent *after* the translations are changed because otherwise another CPU might pick up a stale translation after the TLB has been flushed but before the page table has been fully updated.

The three routines just discussed establish coherence for memory locations that may have been written by a user process. The next three routines complement this by providing the means to establish coherence for memory locations written by the kernel.

The first routine is *flush_dcache_page()*. The Linux kernel calls it to notify platform-specific code that it just dirtied (wrote) a page that is present in the page cache. The page is identified by the routine's only argument, *pg*, which is a pointer to the page frame descriptor of the dirtied page. The routine must ensure that the content of the page is coherent as far as any user-space accesses are concerned. Because the routine affects coherency only in regards to user-space accesses, the kernel does not call it for page cache pages that cannot possibly be mapped into user space. For example, the content of a symbolic link is never mapped into user space. Thus, there is no need to call *flush_dcache_page()* after writing the content of a symbolic link. Also, note that this routine is used only for pages that are present in the page cache. This includes all non-anonymous pages and old anonymous pages that have been moved to the swap cache.

Newly created anonymous pages are not entered into the page cache and must be handled separately. This is the purpose of *clear_user_page()* and *copy_user_page()*. The former creates an anonymous page, which is cleared to 0. The latter copies a page that is mapped into user space (e.g., as a result of a copy-on-write operation). Both routines take an argument called *pg* as their last argument. This is a pointer to the page frame descriptor of the page that is being written. Apart from this, *clear_user_page()* takes two other arguments: *to* and *uaddr*. The former is the kernel-space address at which the page resides, and *uaddr* is the user-space address at which the page will be mapped (because anonymous pages are process-private, there can be only one such address). Similarly, *copy_user_page()* takes three other arguments: *from*, *to*, and *uaddr*. The first two are the kernel-space addresses of the source and the destination page, and *uaddr* is again the user-space address at which the new page will be mapped. Why do these two routines have such a complicated interface? The reason is that on platforms with virtually indexed caches, it is possible to write the new page and make it coherent with the page at *uaddr* without requiring any explicit cache flushing. The basic idea is for the platform-specific code to write the destination page not through the page at address *to*, but through a kernel-space address that maps to the same cache lines as *uaddr*. Because anonymous pages are created frequently, this clever trick can achieve a significant performance boost on platforms with virtually indexed caches. On the other hand, on platforms with physically indexed caches, these operations normally perform no operation other than clearing or copying the page, so despite having rather complicated interfaces, the two routines can be implemented optimally on all platforms.

4.6.2 IA-64 implementation

The IA-64 architecture guarantees that virtual aliases are supported in hardware but leaves open the possibility that on certain CPUs there may be a performance penalty if two virtual addresses map to the same memory location and the addresses do not differ by a value that is an integer multiple of 1 Mbyte. This implies that Linux can treat IA-64 as if all caches were physically indexed, and hence *flush_cache_all()*, *flush_cache_mm()*, *flush_cache_range()*, and *flush_cache_page()* do not have to perform any operation at all. To avoid the potential performance penalty, Linux/ia64 maps shared memory segments at 1-Mbyte–aligned addresses whenever possible.

While IA-64 generally requires that coherence is maintained in hardware, there is one important exception: When a CPU writes to a memory location, it does not have to maintain coherence with the instruction caches. For this reason, the IA-64 version of *flush_icache_range()* must establish coherence by using the flush cache (fc) instruction. This instruction takes one address operand, which identifies the cache line that is to be written back (if it is dirty) and then is evicted from all levels of the cache hierarchy. This instruction is broadcast to all CPUs in an MP machine, so it is sufficient to execute it on one CPU to establish coherence across the entire machine. The architecture guarantees that cache lines are at least 32 bytes in size, so the routine can be implemented by executing fc once for every 32-byte block in the address range from *start* to *end* − 1. Care must be taken not to execute fc on an address that is outside this range; doing so could trigger a fault and crash the kernel.

Is implementing *flush_icache_range()* sufficient to guarantee coherence between the data and instruction caches? Unfortunately, the answer is no. To see this, consider that Linux calls this routine only when it positively knows that the data it wrote to memory will be executed eventually. It does not know this when writing a page that later on gets mapped into user space. For this reason, *flush_dcache_page()*, *clear_user_page()*, and *copy-_user_page()* logically also must call *flush_icache_range()* on the target page. Given that there are usually many more data pages than code pages, this naive implementation would be prohibitively slow. Instead, Linux/ia64 attempts to delay flushing the cache with the following trick: The Linux kernel reserves a 1-bit field called PG_arch_1 in every page frame descriptor for platform-specific purposes. On IA-64, this bit indicates whether or not the page is coherent in the instruction and data caches. A value of 0 signifies that the page *may not* be coherent and a value of 1 signifies that the page is *definitely coherent*. With this setup, *flush_dcache_page()*, *clear_user_page()*, and *copy_user_page()* can be implemented so that they simply clear the PG_arch_1 bit of the dirtied page. Of course, before mapping an executable page into user space, the kernel still needs to flush the cache if the PG_arch_1 bit is off. Fortunately, we can use the platform-specific *update_mmu_cache()* for this purpose. Recall from Section 4.4.2 that this routine is called whenever a translation is inserted or updated in the page table. On IA-64, we can use this as an opportunity to check whether the page being mapped has the execute permission (X) bit enabled. If not, there is no need to establish coherency with the instruction cache and the PG_arch_1 bit is ignored. On the other hand, if the X bit is enabled and the PG_arch_1 bit is 0, coherency must be established by a call to *flush_icache_range()*. After this call returns, the PG_arch_1 bit can be turned on, because it is now known that the page is coherent. This approach ensures that if the same page is mapped into other processes, the cache flush does not have to be repeated again (assuming it has not been dirtied in the meantime).

There is just one small problem: Linux traditionally maps the memory stack and memory allocated by the *brk()* system call with execute permission turned on. This has a devastating effect on the delayed i-cache flush scheme because it causes all anonymous pages to be flushed from the cache even though usually none of them are ever executed. To fix this problem, Linux/ia64 is lazy about turning on the X bit in PTEs. This works as follows: When installing the PTE for a vm-area that is both writable and executable, Linux/ia64 does *not* turn on the X bit. If a process attempts to execute such a page, a protection violation fault is raised by the CPU and the Linux page fault handler is invoked. Because the vm-area permits execute accesses, the page fault handler simply turns on the X bit in the PTE and then updates the page table. The process can then resume execution as if the X bit had been turned on all along. In other words, this scheme ensures that for vm-areas that are

---

activate_mm(*prev_mm*, *next_mm*);   /* *activate new address space* */
switch_mm(*prev_mm*, *next_mm*, *next_task*, *cpu*);   /* *switch address space* */

Figure 4.39. Kernel interface to switch address spaces.

mapped both executable and writable, the X bit in the PTEs will be enabled only if the page experiences an execute access. This technique has the desired effect of avoiding practically all cache flushing on anonymous pages.

The beauty of combining the delayed i-cache flush scheme with the lazy execute bit is that together they are able to not just delay but completely avoid flushing the cache for pages that are never executed. As we see in Chapter 7, *Device I/O*, the effectiveness of this pair is enhanced even further by the Linux DMA interface because it can be used to avoid the need to flush even the executable pages. The net effect is that on IA-64 it is virtually never necessary to explicitly flush the cache, even though the hardware does not maintain i-cache coherence for writes by the CPU.

4.7 SWITCHING ADDRESS SPACES

In Chapter 3, *Processes, Tasks, and Threads*, we discussed how Linux switches the execution context from one thread to another. We did not discuss how the address space is switched. The reason is that Linux treats context switching and address-space switching as separate operations. This makes sense because a context switch triggers an address-space switch only if the old and the new thread do not share the same address space. Conversely, there are occasions, such as an *execve()* system call, where the address space is switched but the currently executing thread remains the same. In other words, not every context switch causes an address-space switch, and vice versa—a good indication that these are fundamentally separate operations.

4.7.1 Address-space switch interface

Linux uses the *address-space switch interface* (file include/asm/mmu_context.h) in Figure 4.39 to abstract platform differences in how an address-space switch can be effected. The *activate_mm()* routine switches the address space of the currently executing thread. It takes two arguments, *prev_mm* and *next_mm*, which are pointers to the mm structure of the old and the new address space, respectively. Similarly, *switch_mm()* is called when the address space is switched as part of a context switch. The first two arguments have the same meaning as for *activate_mm()*, but this routine receives two additional arguments: *next_task* and *cpu*. The *next_task* argument is a pointer to the task structure of the thread that will be executed next. As usual, the currently running thread is implicitly identified by global variable *current*. The *cpu* argument is the unique ID of the CPU that is performing the address-space switch (see Chapter 8, *Symmetric Multiprocessing*).

In an ideal world, *switch_mm()* would not be necessary and *activate_mm()* could be used instead. However, Linux provides separate routines to accommodate platforms that inextricably (and incorrectly) tie together context switching and address-space switching. On those platforms, an address-space switch can be effected only through a context switch, and *activate_mm()* must implicitly perform a dummy context switch. This means that if *activate_mm()* were used in place of *switch_mm()*, the dummy context switch would almost immediately be followed by a real context switch, which would be inefficient. In other words, *switch_mm()* can be thought of as a version of *activate_mm()* that is optimized for the case where it is known that the address-space switch will quickly be followed by a context switch. Of course, on all other platforms, *switch_mm()* can be implemented directly in terms of *activate_mm()*.

4.7.2 IA-64 implementation

On Linux/ia64, switching the address space involves three simple steps:

1. Set current page-table pointer to the global directory of the new address space.

2. Ensure that the new address space has a valid ASN (region ID) by calling *get_mmu-_context()*.

3. Load the region ID of new address space into region registers by calling *reload_context()*.

The first step is necessary only because Linux/ia64 maintains the physical address of the global directory of the current address space in kernel register k6. This simplifies the TLB fault handler slightly and also lets it run more efficiently.

   The IA-64 architecture leaves context and address-space switching entirely to software, so there is no problem in keeping the two operations separate. Thus, *switch_mm()* can be implemented simply as a call to *activate_mm()*, passing the first two arguments, *prev_mm* and *next_mm*, and dropping the remaining three arguments.

4.8 DISCUSSION AND SUMMARY

Let us close this chapter by discussing the rationale behind some of the virtual memory choices of Linux/ia64.

   First, there is the question of page size. The IA-64 architecture supports a large number of different page sizes including at least 4 Kbytes, 8 Kbytes, 16 Kbytes, 256 Kbytes, 1 Mbyte, 4 Mbytes, 16 Mbytes, 64 Mbytes, and 256 Mbytes. Linux uses a three-level page table, so the page size it uses directly affects the amount of virtual memory that a page table can map. For example, with a page size of 4 Kbytes, only 39 virtual address bits can be mapped. Thus, even though IA-64 can support pages as small as 4 Kbytes, from the perspective of Linux it is much better to pick a larger page size. Indeed, each time the page size is doubled, the amount of virtual memory that can be mapped increases 16 times! With a page size of 64 Kbytes, for example, 55 virtual address bits can be mapped.

   Another consideration in choosing a page size is that programs should perform no worse on a 64-bit platform than on a 32-bit platform. Because pointers are twice as big on IA-64 as on a 32-bit platform, the data structures of a program may also be up to twice as big (on average, the data size expansion factor is much smaller: on the order of 20–30 percent [47]). Given that IA-32 uses a page size of 4 Kbytes, this would suggest a page size of 8 Kbytes for IA-64. This size would guarantee that data structures that fit on a single page on IA-32 would also fit on a single page on IA-64. But we should also consider code size. Comparing the size of the text section of equivalent IA-32 and IA-64 programs, we find that IA-64 code is typically between two to four times larger. This would suggest a page size of 16 Kbytes.

The optimal page size depends heavily on both the machine and the applications in use. Taking all these factors into account, it is clear that any single page size cannot be optimal for all cases. Consequently, Linux/ia64 adopts the pragmatic solution of providing a kernel compile-time choice for the page size. In most cases, a choice of 8 Kbytes or 16 Kbytes would be reasonable, but under certain circumstances a page size as small as 4 Kbytes or as large as 64 Kbytes could be preferable. Of course, this solution implies that applications must not rely on Linux/ia64 implementing a particular page size. Fortunately, this is not a problem because the few applications that really do need to know the page size can obtain it by calling the *getpagesize()* library routine. Another approach to dealing with the page size issue is to put intelligence into the operating system to detect when a series of pages can be mapped by a single page of larger size, i.e., by a superpage. Superpage support can often mitigate some of the performance problems that occur when the page size is too small for a particular application. However, it does introduce additional complexity that could slow down all programs. More importantly, because superpages do not change the mapping granularity, they do not increase the amount of virtual memory that a page table can map.

Second, the choice with perhaps the most dramatic consequences is the structure of the address space that Linux/ia64 supports. The IA-64 architecture leaves the operating system designer almost complete freedom in this respect. For example, instead of the structure described in this chapter, Linux/ia64 could have implemented a linear address space whose size is determined by the amount of memory that can be mapped by a page table. This approach would have the disadvantage of placing everything in region zero. This would imply that the maximum distance by which different program segments can be separated is limited by the amount of virtual memory that can be mapped by the smallest supported page size (4 Kbytes). This is a surprisingly serious limitation, considering that a page size of 4 Kbytes limits virtual memory to just 2^{39} bytes. In contrast, designers can exploit the region support in IA-64 and separate segments by 2^{61} bytes, no matter what the page size.

A third choice that is closely related to the address-space structure is the format of the page-table entries. The short format is the most natural choice for Linux/ia64 because it makes possible the use of the VHPT walker by mapping the Linux page table into virtual space. On the downside, the short-format PTEs cannot take advantage of all the capabilities provided by IA-64. For example, with the long format, it would be possible to specify a separate protection key for each PTE, which in turn could enable more effective use of the TLB. Although Linux/ia64 directly maps its page table into the virtually-mapped linear page table, the IA-64 architecture does not require this to be the case. An alternative would be to operate the VHPT walker in the long-format mode and map it to a separate cache of recently used translations. This cache can be thought of as a CPU-external (in-memory)

TLB. With this, Linux could continue to use a compact 8-byte long page-table entry and still take full advantage of operating the VHPT walker in long-format mode. Of course, the cost of doing this would be that the cache would take up additional memory and extra work would be required to keep the cache coherent with the page tables.

In summary, the IA-64 architecture provides tremendous flexibility in implementing the virtual memory system. The virtual memory design described in this chapter closely matches the needs of Linux, but at the same time it represents just one possible solution in a large design space. Because the machines that Linux/ia64 is running on and the applications that use it change over time, it is likely that the virtual memory system of Linux/ia64 will also change from time to time. While this will affect some of the implementation details, the fundamental principles described in this chapter should remain the same.

Chapter 5

Kernel Entry and Exit

The Linux kernel attempts to stay out of the way of user-level tasks as much as possible. But every so often, tasks relinquish control to the kernel either voluntarily, because they need to invoke a kernel service through a system call, or involuntarily, because the kernel needs to handle an event such as a device interrupt or a page fault. Whenever user-level execution is stopped and the kernel is entered, we say that an *interruption* has occurred; the point at which user-level execution was stopped is called the *interruption point*. System calls can also be thought of as a type of interruption, but they are different because they are accompanied by a set of system call arguments that define the type of service that the task is requesting from the kernel (such as opening a file). The major sources of interruptions are listed below.

- **Device interrupts:** When an I/O device needs the attention of the kernel, it raises an interrupt, which preempts execution at the user level and transfers control to the device-specific interrupt handler in the kernel.

- **Instruction emulation faults:** It is not uncommon for CPUs to omit implementing particular instructions or hard-to-implement features of specific instructions. Instead, when a task attempts to execute such an instruction, the CPU triggers an interruption that will give the kernel a chance to emulate the missing functionality in software. For example, most RISC CPUs do not support unaligned memory accesses in hardware and instead emulate them in the kernel. Also, it is not uncommon for CPUs to forego hardware implementation of the nonfinite arithmetic required by the IEEE floating-point standard [22]. On such CPUs, any arithmetic operation that would produce a nonfinite result such as $+\infty$ would also trigger an interruption that would have to be emulated in software (see Chapter 10, *Booting*).

- **Virtual memory faults:** As described in Chapter 4, *Virtual Memory*, Linux exploits virtual memory faults to implement its virtual memory system.

- **Software errors:** Occasionally, applications contain programming errors that can cause a task to perform an illegal operation, such as attempting to divide an integer by zero, accessing nonexistent memory, or executing an invalid instruction. Such errors trigger an interruption, and the kernel normally responds to them by sending a signal to the task or by terminating it.

- **Hardware errors:** Just like software, hardware can fail at times. In extreme cases, such as a complete loss of power, a failure can be catastrophic and the system will crash without giving the kernel a chance to recover from the failure. In more benign cases, such as a parity or ECC error in the system memory, the CPU will raise an interruption. Such hardware-induced interruptions are called *machine checks* because they give the kernel (or firmware) a chance to check the health of the machine and to recover from the error if possible. For example, parity errors can be transient in nature, so rereading the faulty memory location often fixes the problem.

This list illustrates the variety of the sources for interruptions. Fortunately, while the actual handling of each source is specialized, the steps required to get from the user level to the kernel's interruption handler and back tend to be the same for all of them. Even system calls follow the same basic protocol, though the details are slightly different.

System calls enable tasks to call into the kernel but, at times, the kernel needs to do just the opposite: call from the kernel into a task. In Linux, this capability is supported by the *signal facility*. This facility enables the kernel to invoke any one of a fixed number of process-specific *signal handlers*. This is called *delivering a signal* and, just as for system calls, is accompanied by a set of arguments that describe the reason for the call. It is interesting to note that signal delivery is the only time that a user/kernel boundary crossing is initiated from within the kernel.

Both system calls and signals are accompanied by data (arguments). Passing such data in registers is usually not a problem. However, care needs to be taken when some or all of the data are passed through memory. Because the user level does not have the right to access kernel memory, such data necessarily have to be passed through user memory. Even though the kernel is privileged to access user memory, it still needs to be careful because some of that memory may not be mapped. Similarly, because the access is performed by the kernel with all its rights and privileges, the kernel must be careful not to allow the user level to trick it into accessing memory to which the user level should not have access. For these reasons, the Linux kernel uses a *user memory access facility* to ensure safe access to user memory and consistent enforcement of its security policies.

All of the above aspects are related to crossing the user/kernel boundary, and the remainder of this chapter is structured accordingly: The first three sections explore how *execution* crosses this boundary, and the fourth and last section is focused on how to move *data* across it. Specifically, the first section describes how the kernel handles interruptions. This includes a discussion of the steps taken to enter the kernel, invoke an interruption handler, and return to the user level. It also serves as the foundation for the second and third sections, which, respectively, describe how system calls and signals work on Linux. The fourth section explores the approach Linux takes to safely and efficiently access user memory data, as may be required during a system call or signal delivery.

5.1 INTERRUPTIONS

Whenever an interruption occurs, the CPU transfers control to the kernel, where it begins interruption handling by executing the normal kernel entry path. This path establishes a new execution environment, which permits the kernel to run without corrupting the CPU state that existed at the interruption point. Once the new environment is established, the kernel determines the cause of the interruption and dispatches to the appropriate handler. For example, if the interruption was triggered by an unaligned memory access, the kernel would invoke a handler that emulates the unaligned access in software. After the handler returns, the kernel finishes interruption handling by executing the exit path. The primary purpose of this path is to restore the original CPU state and return execution to the interruption point. In the remainder of this section, we take a closer look at how the entry and exit paths operate and how they are realized on Linux/ia64.

5.1.1   Kernel entry path

The major steps taken on the kernel entry path are illustrated in the upper part of Figure 5.1. As shown there, the first step is to check whether the interruption occurred at the user or the kernel level. This distinction is important because it affects how the new execution environment has to be established. If the interruption occurred at the user level, the CPU stack needs to be switched to the kernel stack of the current task. As the figure illustrates, this happens in the second step. On the other hand, if the interruption occurred at the kernel level, the CPU is already using the kernel stack, so this step can be skipped. The third step allocates a pt-regs structure on the kernel stack and saves the **scratch** registers in it. As discussed in Chapter 3, *Processes, Tasks, and Threads*, this is sufficient to ensure that the kernel does not corrupt the CPU state at the interruption point: all other registers are **preserved** registers and, by definition, are saved and restored by the routines that use them. With the **scratch** state safely stored away on the kernel stack, the entry path is complete and the kernel is ready to invoke the interruption handler.

5.1.2   Kernel exit path

After the interruption handler is done, it returns and the exit-path processing is initiated. This is illustrated in the lower part of Figure 5.1. The exit path starts with a series of decisions. The first one checks whether execution is returning to the user level. If not, the kernel can proceed straight to restoring the CPU state, deallocating the pt-regs structure and resuming execution at the interruption point. On the other hand, if execution returns to the user level, the kernel needs to check whether the task to which it is returning needs to be rescheduled, e.g., because another task with higher priority has become runnable or because the time slice of the currently executing task is exhausted. The kernel maintains a flag, called *need_resched*, in the task structure for this purpose: If the flag is non-zero, the task needs to be rescheduled by calling the kernel scheduler. After the scheduler returns, the exit path must recheck this flag and if it is set, call the scheduler again. In other words, the scheduler needs to be called until a task is found whose *need_resched* flag is cleared. Note that whenever the scheduler is invoked, the current task is bound to change. This means that the CPU may not immediately return to the interruption point of the task that was running on entry to the kernel—instead, it will return to the interruption point of the newly selected task. This is not a problem because, eventually, the old task will be scheduled for execution

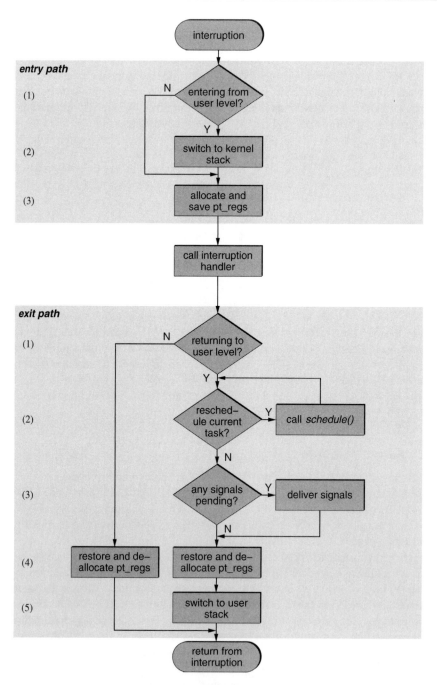

Figure 5.1. The kernel entry and exit paths.

again and the CPU will return to the old task's interruption point at that time. Once task selection is complete, the exit path proceeds to step three, where the kernel needs to check whether the current task has any signals pending. If so, the kernel must deliver them, which is in itself a fairly complicated operation that we discuss in more detail in Section 5.3. Then, in steps four and five, the exit path is finally able to return execution to the user level by restoring the task's **scratch** CPU state from the pt-regs structure, switching the CPU back to the user-level stack and resuming execution at the interruption point.

5.1.3   Discussion

If we compare the upper and lower parts of Figure 5.1, we see that the entry path is substantially shorter than the exit path. This is largely because of the nature of the two paths, but it is also a desirable property because a shorter entry path translates into lower interruption handling *latency*. In other words, if a particular action could be performed either in the entry path or in the exit path, it would be preferable to perform it in the latter. Of course, the choice does not matter as far as processing *throughput* is concerned, but reducing interruption handling latency could mean the difference between meeting or missing a deadline. For example, low-cost I/O controllers often have limited buffering capacity, and for such devices, low interruption latency is important to avoid buffer overruns that could lead, e.g., to dropped network packets (in the case of a network interface controller) or dropped characters (in the case of a serial-line adapter).

Because the entry and exit paths are executed on every interruption, there is a large incentive to optimize them as much as possible. The risk here is that the two paths look so deceptively simple. Indeed, each individual step is quite innocuous, but there are subtle aspects to the order in which they need to be executed. The risk is compounded by the fact that the paths need to work properly under widely different circumstances, including entry from the user level, entry from the kernel level, execution with different interrupt masking status, and so on. For instance, consider what would happen if, in the exit path, the order of step one (check for returning to the user level) and two (rescheduling check) was reversed. Even though this may look harmless on the surface, it would make the difference between a kernel that is preemptive and one that is not. Because the Linux kernel is *not* preemptable, simply flipping the order of these two steps would make the difference between a working and a nonworking kernel.

One of the easiest mistakes to make when optimizing the exit path is to assume that the task that is the current one at the beginning of the exit path is also the current one at the end of it. While this is true most of the time, it is clearly wrong whenever the scheduler gets invoked, i.e., whenever the task flag *need_resched* is non-zero.

Another issue that needs careful attention is interruption nesting. Since the third step of the entry path always allocates a pt-regs structure and the interruption handler generally also consumes some stack space, there is a risk of overflowing the kernel stack if there are too many nested interruptions. Fortunately, on most platforms, interruptions seldom nest more than a few levels deep. For example, on IA-64, an unaligned memory access in the kernel would invoke the unaligned interruption handler and this handler could trigger a TLB miss fault, leading to a total nesting depth of three. The major exceptions to this rule are interruptions caused by device interrupts. Without proper care, these could easily lead the kernel to be reentered dozens or even hundreds of times. As we see in Chapter 7, *Device I/O*, a properly designed kernel bounds the number of times the kernel can be reentered because of device interrupts; this makes it possible to use a fixed-size stack and still guarantee the absence of kernel stack overflows. But even so, the kernel exit path needs to be careful not to violate any assumptions made by the I/O subsystem. For example, if the exit path were to enable interrupts at the wrong time, that could easily void any efforts by the I/O subsystem to limit the maximum nesting depth.

5.1.4   IA-64 implementation

On IA-64, all interruptions are handled through the *interruption vector table (IVT)* (file arch/ia64/kernel/ivt.S). This table must be aligned to a 32-Kbyte boundary, and its starting address must be placed in control register iva (interruption vector address). Each entry in the table corresponds to a particular IA-64 interruption vector and consists of a short piece of code. As described in Chapter 2, *IA-64 Architecture*, when an interruption occurs, the CPU initiates interruption handling with the following steps:

1. The CPU saves its most critical state in control registers. Specifically, the instruction pointer ip is saved in iip (interruption instruction pointer), and the processor status register psr is saved in ipsr (interruption processor status register). Other control registers, such as ifa (interruption faulting address), are also set up to supply additional information on where and why the interruption occurred.

2. Most bits in psr are cleared to 0. Among others, these bits include the following: the register bank bit, psr.bn; the current privilege-level bits, psr.cpl; the interruption collection bit, psr.ic, and the interrupt bit, psr.i. This implies that the CPU will execute with privilege-level 0 (most privileged), with bank 0 of registers r16–r31 selected, and with both device interrupts and interruption collection disabled. The notable exceptions are the data translation bit, psr.dt, instruction translation bit, psr.it, and the RSE translation bit, psr.rt, which are not modified. This means that the CPU continues to run in virtual address space. Of course, the kernel may later on switch to physical address space by clearing the translation bits as necessary, but because most IA-64 CPUs run slower that way, the kernel attempts to avoid this as much as possible.

3. The CPU determines the vector that is associated with the interruption, looks up the offset O of the vector, and starts executing the code at address iva $+ O$. For example, when the CPU detects an unaligned memory access, it triggers an UNALIGNED DATA REFERENCE FAULT. This interruption maps to the *Unaligned Reference vector*. As described in Chapter 2, *IA-64 Architecture*, this is the 30th entry in the IVT and starts at offset 0x5a00. If we looked in arch/ia64/kernel/ivt.S, we would find the *unaligned_access()* routine at this offset. In other words, any unaligned memory access would cause the CPU to dispatch execution to address iva $+$ 0x5a00, and therefore control would be handed over to *unaligned_access()*.

Once control is handed over to the code in the IVT, the interruption can be handled with either the *general* or the *bank 0* interruption handling model. The former follows the steps outlined in Figure 5.1 and can support arbitrarily complex interruption handlers. The latter is a more constrained, IA-64–specific model that allows simple handlers to execute more rapidly than with general interruption handling. Below, we describe each in turn.

Bank 0 interruption handling

Bank 0 interruption handling occurs directly in the execution environment that the CPU establishes in response to an interruption. In that environment, only bank 0 of registers r16–r31 are available for immediate use. All other registers still contain the CPU state that existed at the interruption point, so a bank 0 handler has to explicitly preserve their contents if it needs them. For example, if a handler needs to use one or more predicate registers, it would first have to save pr in a bank 0 register or in memory. Then, before returning, the handler would have to restore pr to its original content.

Another restriction of bank 0 interruption handling is that the interruption collection bit (psr.ic) must remain turned off. The reason is that otherwise another interruption could occur and overwrite the bank 0 registers and the control registers. Unfortunately, the implications of having to leave interruption collection turned off are rather severe:

- The handler must not encounter any other interruption while it is executing. This means that device interrupts also must be left disabled, i.e., psr.i must remain cleared.

- No memory access can be performed unless it can be guaranteed that the memory access does not trigger a TLB miss fault.

Because device interrupts must remain disabled, the execution time of bank 0 interruption handlers directly affects the worst-case interrupt response latency of the kernel. To keep this latency low, such handlers should avoid lengthy processing.

With all these restrictions, is bank 0 interruption handling good for anything at all? The answer is, yes. Fortunately, some of the most performance-critical operations can be handled with this model. In particular, many of the virtual-memory-related faults, such as TLB misses and some of the page-table-related faults fall into this class. Also, the model is sufficiently powerful to support emulation of certain unimplemented instructions. For example, some IA-64 CPUs have no hardware support to branch to recovery code when one of the speculation check instructions (chk.a, chk.s, and fchkf) detects a speculation failure. Instead, those CPUs raise a SPECULATIVE OPERATION FAULT, and a bank 0 interruption handler can be used to emulate the missing hardware functionality.

It should also be noted that some of the restrictions can be worked around. For example, it is perfectly legitimate to access memory through the physical address space, because doing so will not trigger any TLB miss faults. Similarly, because the kernel memory and register stacks of the currently running task are pinned with a translation register (see Chapter 3, *Processes, Tasks, and Threads*), they can be accessed in virtual mode without any problem. For the register stack, this means that an alloc instruction can be executed without the risk of a resulting mandatory RSE store triggering a TLB miss fault. There is also one exception to the general rule prohibiting nested interruptions: as long as the protocol described in Chapter 4, *Virtual Memory*, is followed, an access to the virtually-mapped linear page table may trigger a DATA NESTED TLB FAULT. This means that a bank 0 interruption handler can access the virtually-mapped linear page table.

In summary, bank 0 interruption handling clearly is useful in its own right. But as we see next, the single biggest reason for its existence is that it is a necessary feature to support general interruption handling on IA-64. In this sense, bank 0 interruption handling is simply a clever technique to exploit hardware resources that must exist in the CPU anyway.

General interruption handling

On IA-64, general interruption handling directly follows the steps outlined in Figure 5.1, but several interesting aspects warrant additional discussion. First, Linux/ia64 does not use a single entry path. Instead, most IVT entries that require general interruption handling have their own copy. This replication minimizes the number of taken branches encountered en route to the interruption handler and also enables customization of the entry path according to the needs of the handler. For example, the IA-64 page fault interruption handler requires the content of just three of the control registers, so it makes sense to customize the entry path so it reads those three control registers but none of the ones that may be needed by other handlers. In contrast, the *normal exit path* (*leave_kernel()* in file arch/ia64/kernel/entry.S) is shared for virtually all interruptions. The reason this sharing is possible is that the actions taken during exit-path processing depend more on the current state of the system than on the particulars of the interruption. Sharing the exit path reduces the size of the kernel and increases the likelihood that the exit path stays cached.

The IA-64 entry path consists of two phases. In the first phase, bank 0 interruption handling is used to switch to the kernel stack (if necessary) and to save enough state in the pt-regs structure to permit switching to bank 1 of registers r16–r31 and, hence, to turn interruption collection back on. Because this code is replicated many times in the IVT, it is implemented by a macro called the *save-min macro* (DO_SAVE_MIN in file arch/ia64/-kernel/minstate.h). Of course, for IA-64, switching to the kernel stack requires switching both the memory and the register stacks. Switching the former is easy, but switching the register stack is sufficiently complex to require a discussion of its own, so we will return to this topic a bit later. Note that even though the save-min macro is executed during bank 0 interruption handling, it can access the pt-regs structure through virtual address space because the structure resides on the kernel memory stack, which is pinned into the TLB with a translation register. The first phase usually also allocates and sets up the register stack frame needed to call the interruption handler. The reason this is done so early is that most interruption handlers get their arguments directly from the contents of one or more of the control registers. Because the interruption-related control registers retain their contents only while psr.ic is off, setting up the call frame here makes it possible to directly copy the control registers to the appropriate argument registers.

After the first phase is over, the CPU is executing in the kernel with interruption collection turned back on. The second phase starts with the entry path saving the remaining **scratch** state (primarily r16–r31) to the pt-regs structure. Because this code also is replicated many times throughout the IVT, another macro, called the *save-rest macro* (SAVE-_REST in file arch/ia64/kernel/minstate.h), is used for this purpose. The remainder of the second phase is specific to each IVT entry and is responsible for calling the appropriate interruption handler. For those handlers that use the shared exit path, this is done in a special way to ensure that the handler returns directly to the exit path.

Once the interruption handler returns, the exit path starts executing. The first three steps and much of the fourth step of Figure 5.1 are executed in normal kernel mode. After restoring as much of the pt-regs state as possible, the fourth step turns off the interruption collection bit psr.ic and switches back to bank 0 interruption handling. Registers r16–r31 of bank 0 provide the temporary storage needed to restore the remaining **scratch** registers, switch back to the user stacks (if returning to the user level), and execute the rfi instruction needed to resume execution at the interruption point.

5.1.5   Switching the IA-64 register stack

It is now time to discuss how Linux/ia64 handles the register stack. Table 5.1 describes this with a step-by-step description of all instructions relating to the register stack engine (RSE) that are executed during kernel entry and exit. This table lets us track the register stack during interruption handling. It also let us prove that the entry path correctly switches the stack from the user to the kernel backing store and that after the exit path is executed, the register stack is back to the original state as it existed at the interruption point.

The first column of the table lists the instruction being executed, along with a line number in parentheses. Because the RSE-related instructions are relatively complex and tend to have several side effects, it is easiest to understand their operation by watching the effect they have on the RSE-related state. In the table, the most important part of this state is shown to the right of the instruction column: The second and third columns show the values of the backing store write pointer, bspstore, and the backing store pointer, bsp, respectively. Column four shows the value in the current frame marker register, cfm; column five shows the value in the previous frame marker field, pfs.pfm, which is part of the previous function state application register, and column six shows the interruption frame marker field, ifs.ifm, which is part of the interruption function state control register.

The table displays the frame marker values as pairs of the form $s \mid l$, where s is the "size of frame" (sof) field, which gives the size of the register frame, and l is the "size of locals" (sol) field, which gives the number of local registers in the frame. The frame markers also include the information required for register rotation, but for brevity we omit those fields. Similarly, to enhance readability we list register values only in those positions where they are being written. For example, the bsp column is empty in line (19) because the loadrs instruction does not write the bsp register. To find its current value, we would have to search that column for the most recent entry in the table. In our case, this would be in line (14), where bsp is being written with B_1. From this, we can infer that in line (19) register bsp also has the value B_1.

Note that lines (1) through (13) are executed as part of the entry path, line (14) as part of the interruption handler, and lines (15) through (24) as part of the exit path. We describe each of these parts in turn.

Table 5.1. Register stack during normal kernel entry and exit.

Instruction	bspstore	bsp	cfm sof sol	pfs.pfm sof sol	ifs.ifm sof sol
user level					
(1) ⟨interruption⟩	?	b_1	$s_t \mid s_l$	$o_t \mid o_l$	?
(2) $P_{pfs} \leftarrow$ pfs					
(3) $P_{rsc} \leftarrow$ rsc					
(4) rsc $\leftarrow$ 0	b_0				
(5) cover		$b_1 \oplus s_t$	$0 \mid 0$		$s_t \mid s_l$
(6) $P_{ifs} \leftarrow$ ifs		b'_1			
(7) $P_{bspst} \leftarrow$ bspstore					
(8) bspstore $\leftarrow B_0$	B_0	$B_0 \oplus (b'_1 \ominus b_0)$			
(9) $d \leftarrow$ bsp $- B_0$					
(10) rsc.mode $\leftarrow$ 3	?	B_1			
(11) psr.ic $\leftarrow$ 1					?
(12) alloc r_1=ar.pfs,0,h_l,h_a,0			$h_a + h_l \mid h_l$		
(13) br.call *handler*		$B_1 \oplus h_l$	$h_a \mid 0$?	$h_a + h_l \mid h_l$	
⋮					
(14) br.ret		B_1	$h_a + h_l \mid h_l$		
(15) psr.ic $\leftarrow$ 0					
(16) rsc.mode $\leftarrow$ 0					
(17) alloc r_1=ar.pfs,0,0,0,0			$0 \mid 0$		
(18) rsc.loadrs $\leftarrow d$	B_0				
(19) loadrs	$B_1 - d$				
(20) bspstore $\leftarrow P_{bspst}$	b_0	$b_1 \oplus s_t$			
(21) pfs $\leftarrow P_{pfs}$				$o_t \mid o_l$	
(22) rsc $\leftarrow P_{rsc}$	?				
(23) ifs $\leftarrow P_{ifs}$					$s_t \mid s_l$
(24) rfi		b_1	$s_t \mid s_l$		?
user level					

RSE during entry path

At the beginning of Table 5.1, we assume that the CPU was executing somewhere at the user level and then an interruption occurred in line (1). At the point of the interruption, registers bsp, cfm, and pfs.pfm have certain values, which we call b_1, $s_t \mid s_l$, and $o_t \mid o_l$, respectively. While we do not know *what* those values are, we know that they are frozen, in the sense that they do not change on their own. Register ifs also has a frozen value, but since it is a control register, it is not part of the user-level state and we do not care about it. In the table, we represent this with a question mark (?). The bspstore register is special because it may not be frozen at this point: depending on the value in the register stack configuration registers rsc, the RSE may be operating in one of the eager modes (**load intensive, store intensive**, or **eager**), meaning the value in this register could change whenever the RSE decides to store a dirty register. For this reason, we also mark the table entry for this register with a question mark. With this, we have established the initial RSE-related state. Of course, the interruption also affects various other bits in the CPU. In particular, the psr.ic control bit is turned off, which will be important because it affects the behavior of the cover instruction.

A graphical representation of the initial RSE-related state can be found at the top-left of Figure 5.2. It shows the bsp and bspstore registers, along with the current register frame (r32 and up) and the **dirty** and **clean** partitions of the RSE. The user and kernel register backing stores are represented by the boxes to the left and right of the registers, respectively. As the figure shows, both bsp and bspstore initially point to the user register backing store.

Now, continuing in Table 5.1, we see that the kernel first saves a few registers. Specifically, in line (2), the current value of pfs ($o_t \mid o_l$) is copied to p_{pfs}, which is part of the pt-regs structure. In other words, the kernel saves the user-level value of pfs to the kernel memory stack. Similarly, in line (3), the kernel saves the user-level value of rsc in p_{rsc}, which is also part of the pt-regs structure. With this state saved away, the kernel can now reconfigure the RSE according to its own needs. It does this in line (4) by writing 0 to rsc. This ensures that the RSE is operating in **enforced lazy** mode and that all RSE accesses are performed at privilege-level 0 and with little-endian byte order, as required for execution in the Linux/ia64 kernel. Putting the RSE in **enforced lazy** mode effectively freezes the value in bspstore. As the table shows, we label this frozen value b_0. All RSE-related state is now frozen, and the resulting configuration is illustrated at the top-right of Figure 5.2. Compared with the previous configuration, the difference is that the RSE has stored a few dirty registers and hence bspstore now has the slightly larger value b_0.

At this point, the current register frame still contains the user-level frame that existed at the time of interruption. To protect it from being modified by the interruption handler, the kernel executes a cover instruction in line (5). Intuitively, we can understand this operation by looking at Figure 5.2 and comparing the top-right configuration with the next one labeled "(5) cover": the cover instruction increments bsp such that the **dirty** partition grows large enough to completely cover the current register frame. More formally, we can trace the effect of the RSE-related instructions by looking them up in Tables 2.8 and 2.9 of Chapter 2, *IA-64 Architecture*, and applying the state modifications described there to the current RSE state. For example, if we look up the cover instruction in Table 2.9, we find that it does the following:

1. Sets bsp to bsp $\oplus$ cfm.sof.

2. Sets ifs.ifm to cfm and ifs.v to 1 (since psr.ic is 0).

3. Sets all fields in cfm to 0.

If we apply these modifications to the current RSE state in Table 5.1, we arrive at the values shown in line (5) of the table. Note that bsp now has the value $b_1 \oplus s_t$, because the size of the user-level frame was assumed to be s_t. For convenience, we will call this new bsp value b_1'. Similarly, ifs.ifm now contains the previous value of cfm which was $s_t \mid s_l$. In line (6), this value is saved in p_{ifs}. As shown in line (7), the kernel also saves the user-level value of bspstore (namely b_0) in p_{bspst}. Both p_{ifs} and p_{bspst} are part of the pt-regs structure.

The kernel is now ready to switch the RSE from the user register backing store to the kernel register backing store. Let us assume that the kernel register backing store starts at

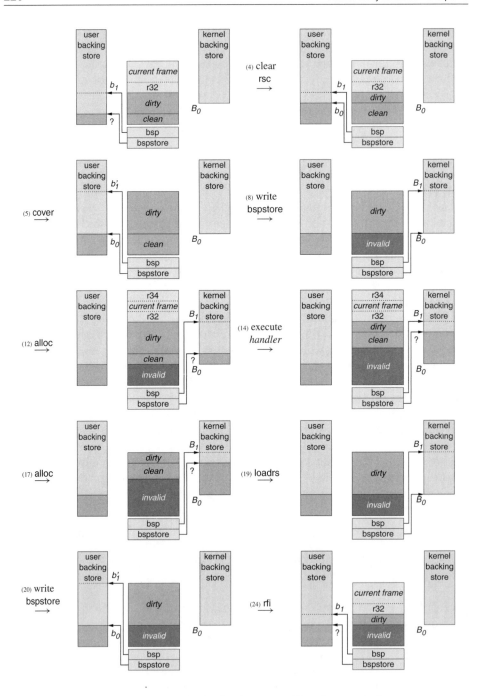

Figure 5.2. Register stack switching during normal kernel entry and exit.

address B_0. The kernel achieves the switch by writing this address to bspstore as shown in line (8) of the table. We can again use Table 2.9 to look up the effect of writing this register. We find that just like the cover instruction, writing the register has several side effects.

First, it writes the new address not just to bspstore, but also to bspload—the register that determines the start of the **clean** partition. Second, it writes bsp with the new address and then advances it by ndirty register slots, where ndirty is the number of registers in the **dirty** partition. Given the RSE state in Table 5.1, ndirty can be calculated as $(b'_1 \ominus b_0)$, so the new value of bsp is $B_0 \oplus (b'_1 \ominus b_0)$. For convenience, we will call this new value B_1.

In Figure 5.2, the configuration labeled "(8) write bspstore" summarizes the effect of writing bspstore with B_0: It switches bspstore over to the kernel backing store, and since bspload is written with the same value, the **clean** partition is emptied. This means that the stacked registers that were formerly in the **clean** partition are effectively being discarded and marked **invalid**. Because their contents have already been written to the user-level register backing store, no data is lost. In contrast, the registers in the **dirty** partition cannot just be discarded because their values may not exist anywhere else. Writing them to the user-level register backing store is not a viable option because it would be slow and could trigger other interruptions, such as a page fault.

Fortunately, setting bsp to B_1 avoids these issues: It preserves the user-level **dirty** partition by turning it into the initial kernel **dirty** partition. The kernel calculates the byte size of this **dirty** partition by subtracting B_0 from the new value of bsp and, as shown in line (9), saves it in variable d for later use. As usual, this variable is also part of the pt-regs structure and stored on the memory stack. It might be tempting to calculate d from the user backing store addresses (e.g., by calculating $b'_1 - b_0$), but this would be wrong: The user and kernel register backing stores may be aligned differently, and hence saving the dirty registers on the kernel backing store may save a different number of NaT collection words than would be the case if the registers were saved on the user backing store. Put another way, switching the register backing store preserves the *number of register slots* but *not* necessarily the number of bytes in the **dirty** partition.

At this point, the RSE has been switched over from the user to the kernel register backing store. All that is left to do is for the kernel to select its preferred RSE mode. It does this in line (10) by writing a value of 3 to the rsc.mode field of the register stack configuration register. This puts the RSE in **eager** mode so it can use available memory bandwidth to speculatively save or restore stacked registers. As shown in line (11), the kernel also turns the psr.ic bit back on. This means that the interruption-related control registers no longer have a defined (frozen) value. Accordingly, the table shows a question mark for the content of ifs.ifm.

RSE during execution of the interruption handler

The exact sequence of RSE-related instructions needed to invoke the interruption handler depends somewhat on the type of the interruption being handled. Usually, the kernel allocates a new register frame with an alloc instruction, as shown in line (12) of Table 5.1. As described earlier, this instruction is often executed while the psr.ic is still cleared, but as far as the RSE-related state is concerned, this makes no difference. The register frame created by alloc contains a certain number, h_l, of local registers and a certain number, h_a, of output registers that are used to pass the handler arguments. If the kernel has no need to preserve values across the handler invocation, it does not have to allocate any local registers and h_l can be 0. As the table shows, the only state affected by the alloc instruction is the cfm register, and it is set to $h_a + h_l \mid h_l$. Figure 5.2 shows the graphical representation of this RSE state in the configuration labeled "$_{(12)}$ alloc".

Once the output registers are allocated and set up, the kernel invokes the actual interruption handler with the br.call instruction shown in line (13) of the table. By definition, this instruction advances bsp by h_l register slots and reduces both the size of the register frame and the size of locals by h_l. Consequently, the value of bsp is $B_1 \oplus h_l$, and the value of cfm is $h_a \mid 0$. The instruction also saves the previous value of cfm ($h_a + h_l \mid h_l$) in pfs.pfm.

The interruption handler can be an arbitrary kernel function written in C, and it can call other functions as necessary. Thus, we cannot trace the RSE state in this phase. However, because the handler must follow the IA-64 software conventions, we know that before returning to its caller, it will restore pfs to the value that was present on entry to the function [28]. Therefore, we know that during execution of the br.ret instruction in line (14), the content of pfs.pfm is equal to $h_a + h_l \mid h_l$. If we use Table 2.8 to look up the effect of br.ret, we find that br.ret sets cfm to pfs.pfm and that it restores the number of registers specified by pfs.sol from the backing store. This implies that cfm will be restored to $h_a + h_l \mid h_l$ and that bsp will be restored to B_1, so that the RSE state in line (14) will be the same as in line (12). This is illustrated in Figure 5.2 by the configuration labeled "$_{(14)}$ execute *handler*". Note that during the execution of the handler, the RSE may have saved some of the user registers on the kernel backing store and may have invalidated some of the registers previously in the **clean** partition. The former may happen because the RSE is in **eager** mode, and the latter may happen when the RSE runs out of physical stacked registers, which forces it to reuse some of the user registers for kernel purposes. The bottom line is that after returning from the handler, bspstore can point anywhere inside the region from B_0 to B_1 and some or even all of the user stacked registers can be part of the **invalid** partition.

RSE during exit path

As soon as the interruption handler returns, the kernel starts executing the exit path. As far as the RSE-related instructions are concerned, this path starts at line (15) of Table 5.1. As we can see there, the kernel starts by clearing psr.ic. Then, in line (16), it puts the RSE in **enforced lazy** mode by writing 0 to psr.mode.

At this point, the kernel would like to simply abandon the kernel register backing store and resume using the user register backing store instead. However, the configuration labeled "$_{(14)}$ execute *handler*" in Figure 5.2 shows that we have a small problem: Some of the user registers may have been written to the kernel register backing store after the alloc instruction was executed in line (12). Before the kernel register stack is dropped, it is necessary to ensure those values have been loaded back into the stacked registers. This is the purpose of the loadrs instruction. The operation of this instruction is defined only when the current register frame is empty. Thus, before executing the instruction, the kernel needs to drop the current register frame. It can do so by executing a dummy alloc instruction that resizes the current frame to be empty. This is shown in line (17) of the table and illustrated in Figure 5.2 by the configuration labeled "$_{(17)}$ alloc".

Next, the kernel needs to write to the rsc.loadrs field the number of bytes the loadrs instruction should load, starting from the point just below the current value of bsp, which is B_1. Because the kernel wants to ensure that no user registers are left on the kernel register backing store, it needs to ensure that all bytes in the range from B_0 to B_1 are loaded. Of course, $(B_1 - B_0)$ is just the value that was saved in variable d of the pt-regs structure, so all the kernel needs to do is read this variable and store its value in rsc.loadrs, as shown in line (18) of the table.

With this setup in place, the kernel can now execute the loadrs instruction shown in line (19). The purpose of this instruction is to ensure that the number of bytes specified in rsc.loadrs has been loaded into the stacked registers and to set bspstore to $bsp - rsc.loadrs$. With the current RSE state, this means that bspstore is set to $(B_1 - d)$, which is equal to B_0. The resulting RSE state is illustrated graphically in Figure 5.2 by the configuration labeled "$_{(19)}$ loadrs". Note that while it is necessary to tell the loadrs instruction to ensure that all $d = (B_1 - B_0)$ bytes have been loaded, only the bytes above B_0 that correspond to registers in the **invalid** partition actually have to be loaded from the register backing store. This means that if the RSE did not have to reuse any of the user registers while executing the interruption handler, the loadrs instruction does not have to access memory at all.

With the user registers restored, the kernel can now load the user-level value of bspstore from p_{bspst} and write it to the bspstore register. Because this value is equal to b_0, both bspstore and bspload are set to b_0. The resulting value for bsp is a bit harder to calculate, but we claim that it is equal to $b_1 \oplus s_t$ (a proof follows later). With these values, the RSE is essentially back to the state that existed after execution of the cover instruction. However, by looking at Figure 5.2 and comparing the configurations labeled "$_{(5)}$ cover" and "$_{(20)}$ write bspstore", we discover an important difference: the stacked registers that before formed the **clean** partition are now marked **invalid**. From a correctness point of view there is no harm in this because the RSE will automatically reload those registers from memory when needed. But of course it does mean that the interruption could slow down execution at the user level a little because the RSE might have to restore registers from the backing store that before were in the **clean** partition.

In the next three steps, the kernel restores the remaining RSE-related user-level state. Specifically, line (21) restores pfs with the value saved in variable p_{pfs}. In our case, this is $o_t \mid o_l$. Similarly, line (22) restores rsc with the user-level register stack configuration that was saved in variable p_{rsc}. Because this may put the RSE into one of the eager modes, the value of bspstore is unpredictable after this instruction has been executed. The table illustrates this in line (22) by marking the value of bspstore with a question mark. Line (23) sets ifs to the value saved in p_{ifs}, which is the value returned by the cover instruction, i.e., $s_t \mid s_l$.

With these registers restored, the kernel in a final step executes the rfi instruction shown in line (24). By definition, this loads the number of registers specified in ifs.ifm.sof from the backing store and copies the value in ifs.ifm to cfm. In our case, this means that s_t registers are loaded from the backing store. Because bsp was previously at $b_1 \oplus s_t$, it is now at b_1 and the value in cfm is $s_t \mid s_l$. If we compare the values of bsp, cfm, and pfs as they existed in line (1) and line (24), we see that they are identical. We can also see this by looking at Figure 5.2 and comparing the top-left configuration with the bottom-right configuration. The two are identical, except for the position of bspstore and the fact that the **clean** partition and some of the previously **dirty** user registers have been invalidated. Of course, the **dirty** registers were saved to the backing store before being invalidated, so from a correctness point of view, this is not an issue. The net effect is that, apart from a small delay, the interruption is transparent to the user level.

Correctness proof

We claimed that writing b_0 to bspstore in line (20) of Table 5.1 will cause bsp to be set to the value $b_1 \oplus s_t$. This is not entirely self-evident and warrants a more formal analysis. Fortunately, the analysis is not difficult. First, observe that, by definition, writing bspstore sets bsp to bspstore $\oplus$ ndirty. In our case, bspstore is written with b_0 and the number of registers in the **dirty** partition, ndirty, is given by:

$$\text{ndirty} = \text{bsp} \ominus \text{bspstore} = B_1 \ominus B_0$$

Now, the value of B_1 was defined as $B_0 \oplus (b_1' \ominus b_0)$, so if we substitute this into the equation for ndirty and apply RSE arithmetic rule (2.4.2) from Chapter 2, *IA-64 Architecture*, we get:

$$\text{ndirty} = \{\underbrace{B_0}_{x} \oplus \underbrace{(b_1' \ominus b_0)}_{n}\} \ominus \underbrace{B_0}_{x} \overset{(2.4.2)}{=} (b_1' \ominus b_0)$$

We can now use this expression for ndirty in the formula for calculating the new bsp value and apply rule (2.4.4) to get:

$$\text{bsp} = \text{bspstore} \oplus \text{ndirty} = \underbrace{b_0}_{x} \oplus (\underbrace{b_1'}_{y} \ominus \underbrace{b_0}_{x}) \overset{(2.4.4)}{=} b_1' = b_0 \oplus s_t$$

This proves that in line (20), register bsp is set to the value $b_0 \oplus s_t$, just as we claimed.

Clearing the invalid partition

The discussion so far has focused on proving that the kernel entry and exit paths properly preserve the contents of the user-level stacked registers. Another equally important aspect is to ensure that an interruption does not create the potential for leaking arbitrary kernel data to the user level. This is not an issue for the static registers or the stacked registers that are in use (dirty) at the time of interruption. But what about the registers in the **invalid** partition? If the interruption handler were to use one or more stacked registers, it might have stored kernel data in them and at the time the rfi instruction is executed, that data would still be present. This could leak arbitrary kernel data to the user level and would pose an unacceptable security risk. To avoid this, Linux/ia64 clears the contents of the registers in the **invalid** partition whenever lowering the privilege level, that is, whenever returning to the user level. This must be done with interrupts disabled; otherwise, a nested interruption could occur partway through the clearing, and then the already cleared registers could be tainted with kernel data again. For this reason, the best place to perform this operation is at the beginning of step five of the normal exit path shown in Figure 5.1. This step is executed with bank 0 interruption handling and is therefore protected from nested interruptions. Note that the clearing of the **invalid** partition could trigger mandatory RSE traffic. Fortunately, this is not a problem because the kernel register backing store is pinned with a translation register, so there is no danger of this traffic triggering a TLB miss fault.

5.2   SYSTEM CALLS

Let us now turn our attention to how system calls work on Linux. Every system call has a *name* and an associated *number*. The mapping from system call name to system call number is defined in the platform-specific header include/asm/unistd.h by macros of the form __NR_*name*, where *name* is the system call name. For example, on IA-64 the macro __NR_open maps to 1028, meaning that the *open()* system call is identified by this number. While the assignment of system call numbers is platform specific and fairly arbitrary, once a system call number has been defined, it is virtually impossible to change it ever again— this number is the sole factor that determines the semantics of the system call. In other words, if the numbering changed, existing applications might stop working.

The exact sequence of actions required to invoke a system call is platform specific but generally involves the following six steps:

1. The application places both the system call number and the system call arguments in agreed-upon places, typically in CPU registers or on the memory stack.

2. The application executes a special instruction that has the effect of interrupting execution at the user level and transferring control to the kernel. Depending on the platform, this instruction may be called the *software interrupt*, *trap*, *break*, or *syscall* instruction.

3. The kernel extracts the system call number and uses it as an index into the *system call table* to determine the appropriate *system call handler*. The Linux kernel uses the convention of implementing a system call with name *x* in a system call handler with name *sys_x*. For example, the *open()* system call is implemented in the kernel function *sys_open()*.

4. The kernel extracts the system call arguments and uses them to invoke the system call handler. After the system call handler returns, the kernel arranges for the system call result value and error status to be returned to the user level in agreed-upon places, typically in specific CPU registers.

5. The kernel executes a special *return from interruption* instruction to return control to the user level, where the application resumes execution.

6. The application extracts the error status and the result value. If the error status indicates that the system call failed, the application initiates the appropriate error handling; otherwise, it uses the result and continues execution.

Given the strong dependency on the specifics of a particular platform, it would be cumbersome and unportable if applications had to directly invoke system calls. Instead, the runtime systems of the various high-level languages provide *system call stubs* that make it appear as if system calls were ordinary function calls. For example, an application written in C can open an existing file for read access by invoking the *open()* system call in the following manner:

```
#include <fcntl.h>
    ⋮
int fd = open("/etc/motd", O_RDONLY);
```

The *open()* function being called here is actually a system call stub implemented in the C runtime system (libc); it takes care of invoking the kernel with the appropriate system call number (__NR_open) and arguments. Upon returning from the kernel, the stub also takes care of extracting the error status and result values and, if the system call failed, setting the C runtime system variable *errno* to the appropriate error code.

From the perspective of the kernel, a system call is not unlike any other interruption. In fact, a system call follows exactly the steps outlined in Figure 5.1. Of course, in this case the "interruption handler" corresponds to code that extracts the system call arguments, invokes the system call handler, and then arranges for the result value and the error status to be returned. Still, compared to an ordinary interruption, the only major difference is that system calls can directly pass data from the user level to the kernel and back. Passing scalar values, such as a file descriptor number, is relatively easy. More complex objects, such as the timeval structure used by the *gettimeofday()* system call, create some special challenges, which we discuss in more detail in Section 5.4. Actually, performance considerations make even the passing of scalar values a less than trivial issue. The reason is that system calls can be invoked at very high rates—often at rates that are orders of magnitudes higher than those for other interruptions. For example, on a machine with a reasonably well-designed I/O system, it is rare for devices to raise interrupts at a rate higher than, say, 100,000 times a second. But a task can easily execute millions of system calls a second. For this reason, close attention needs to be paid to the system call execution path, and there is a big incentive to streamline as much as possible the mechanism used to pass the system call arguments.

5.2.1 Signaling errors

From a logical point of view, every system call returns two values: a scalar result of type **long** and an error code. An error code of 0, indicates that the system call executed successfully and that the result value is valid. If the error code is non-zero, the system call failed for some reason and the result value is undefined. The reason for the failure can be determined from the value of the error code. The platform-specific header file include/asm/errno.h defines manifest constants for this purpose. For example, the IA-64 version of this file defines constant ENOMEM to map to error code 12, and this code is returned whenever a system call fails because the kernel is out of memory. Even though this header file is platform specific, all platforms must define the same set of manifest constants and the error codes must all fall in the range of 1 to 511. This does not leave a whole lot of flexibility, but it is sufficient to make it possible for each platform to adhere to the UNIX ABI standard that may exist for it. For example, on the IA-32 platform, the Intel386 Binary Compatibility Specification requires error code 9 to represent EBADF, i.e., the code must indicate that a system call failed because of a bad file descriptor number [23].

Occasionally, the kernel encounters internal error conditions that can be resolved before returning to the user level. The kernel uses a separate set of error codes to signal such conditions. Because these codes are never returned to the user level, there are no ABI compatibility issues and they can be defined in the platform-independent header file include/linux/errno.h. To avoid collisions with the platform-specific error codes, only values greater than 511 are used for this purpose.

It would be awkward and often inefficient if every kernel function that can be called from a system call handler had to return both a result value and an error code. To avoid this, the Linux kernel uses a single return value of type **long** to encode both the result value and the error code: On success, a non-negative result value is returned; and on failure, the negative value of the error code is returned. This means that the sign bit of the returned value can be used to determine whether or not a call was successful: negative values indicate failure, non-negative values indicate success.

So far, so good, but what if a system call needs to return a negative value on success? For example, *mmap()* might map a memory segment at such a high address that the resulting address would have a negative value when interpreted as a value of type **long**. Fortunately, error codes have relatively small values (e.g., less than 1000), and because the highest part of the address space is occupied by the kernel, it is always possible to distinguish the largest valid user-space address from a negative error code. Assuming the largest error code is e_{max}, this discrimination can be done simply by checking whether the returned value is smaller than $-e_{max}$. If so, the value clearly is not a negated error code and the call was successful.

This takes care of virtually all system calls, but there are still a few cases where a small negative value needs to be returned on success. The most noteworthy instance is *ptrace()*. For example, the PTRACE_PEEKDATA request reads an arbitrary machine word from the target task, and if that word happens to contain a small negative value, it must still be possible to return it successfully. How such cases are handled is platform specific, but one possibility would be to use a special system call stub for *ptrace()* that passes to the system call a pointer to a word as an additional, implicit argument. The handler could use this implicit argument to return the result value, and the handler's return value could be used exclusively to encode the error code (or 0 on success) so that there would be no risk of confusing small negative result values with error codes.

5.2.2   Restarting system call execution

System calls raise an interesting question: What should the kernel do if a signal occurs in the middle of system call execution? Most system calls execute quickly and without blocking, so the kernel can simply ignore the signal until the system call handler returns. On the way back to the user level, the exit path will take care of checking for and delivering any pending signals. But what if the system call takes a long time to complete and, in particular, what if the system call suspended execution and is waiting, e.g., for some data to arrive on a socket? The obvious answer is to say that the kernel should deliver the signal immediately and finish execution of the system call afterward. But doing so would require switching to the user level when the kernel stack is not empty, which is not possible in Linux. Furthermore, even if this were possible, we would be facing the problem that the system call would have to relinquish any locks it may be holding and, afterward, it would have to reacquire the locks and revalidate all system call arguments.

To avoid these kinds of issues, traditional UNIX systems have supported one of two behaviors: the System V behavior or the BSD behavior [9, 39]. The System V behavior causes a system call handler that is interrupted by a signal to fail immediately with error code EINTR. With BSD behavior, a system call handler that is interrupted by a signal also returns immediately so that the exit path can deliver the signal. The difference is that after the signal has been delivered, the original system call is automatically restarted from the beginning so that the signal delivery is transparent to the user level (apart from any side effects that the signal might have had). The System V behavior is true to the UNIX spirit of solving problems in the simplest possible way. However, for an application programmer, it creates an unwanted burden because the programmer needs to memorize which system calls can potentially return EINTR and explicitly restart them if necessary (or deal with the situation in some other fashion). What is worst about this is that a single missed check for EINTR could cause the application to fail intermittently. Note that the meaning of EINTR is qualitatively different from other error codes: normally, a system call fails only when there is no possibility of successful execution, given the current task state. In contrast, EINTR indicates that the system call was executing fine, except that it was unfortunate enough to be interrupted by a signal. That is, there was nothing wrong with the system call per se—it just failed to finish execution because of an external event. The BSD behavior does not have this problem and for this reason application programmers often prefer it over the System V behavior. However, it should be noted that even with BSD behavior, the *select()* system call may return EINTR, so it does not completely obviate the need to check for this error code.

Regardless of which behavior is in effect, the kernel needs to be careful not to return EINTR or restart a system call after partially executing a *non-idempotent* system call (a system call with side effects). For example, if a *write()* system call is interrupted after writing the first 10 bytes of data to a TCP socket, it would be wrong to restart it from the beginning because that would cause the first 10 bytes to appear twice on the TCP connection! Instead, the kernel handles this situation by forcing an early system call return, indicating that 10 bytes were written successfully. For *write()*, this particular situation is known as a *short write*, and the general technique of forcing an early, but successful, system call return neatly eliminates the need for restarting partially executed, non-idempotent system calls.

The Linux kernel originally implemented only the BSD behavior. Because this is generally the behavior preferred by application programmers, this choice made sense. However, there was a serious downside: It was rather difficult to port applications to Linux that were designed with the System V behavior in mind. To see this, consider the simple example shown in Figure 5.3. The intended purpose of this program is to wait until one character is entered on standard input or until the user sends a keyboard interrupt signal (SIGINT, normally sent when the user presses **Ctrl-C**). Although the program may look innocuous at first, it does rely on the fact that each time a SIGINT signal is delivered to the applica-

```
#include <signal.h>
#include <stdio.h>

static volatile sig_atomic_t signaled;
static struct sigaction act;

void handler (int signum) {
    signaled = 1;
}

int main (int argc, char **argv) {
    char ch;
    act.sa_handler = handler;
    sigaction(SIGINT, &act, NULL);
    while (read(0, &ch, 1) != 1 && !signaled) /* skip */;
}
```

Figure 5.3. Example of a program that fails with automatic system call restarting.

tion, the expression in the **while**-loop is reevaluated. With System V behavior, this is true because *read()* will return with an error code of EINTR when this happens. In contrast, with BSD behavior, the *read()* system call will be restarted automatically, so the **while** expression does not get reevaluated, meaning that a keyboard interrupt would have no effect other than setting *signaled* to 1!

Of course, this particular program easily can be fixed. For example, we could add the call *close(0)* to *handler()*. This would force the restarted *read()* system call to fail because file descriptor 0 would no longer be valid after the signal handler returns. Another solution would be to use *siglongjmp()* in *handler()* to return control to the main program. However, both solutions have side effects which, in a more complex program, would have to be studied carefully before we could guarantee that the modified program still works as intended. For example, the *siglongjmp()* approach raises reentrancy issues: what if *read()* was actually called through a library routine that acquired a lock? In such a case, the *siglongjmp()* might cause the library routine to fail to release the lock, thus introducing the potential for *deadlock* (see Chapter 8, *Symmetric Multiprocessing*).

The net effect of these considerations was that Linux eventually had to support System V behavior also. The choice of the behavior is left to the application (or its libraries) on a signal-by-signal basis and can be selected when a signal handler is installed with *sigaction()*. As we will see later, this system call involves a *sigaction structure* that contains a flag called SA_RESTART. If the flag is set, BSD behavior is used. Otherwise, Linux defaults to the System V behavior. We discuss the details of how Linux implements system call restarting in Section 5.3. For the time being, we just need to keep in mind that, occasionally, a system call may need to be restarted and therefore platform-specific code has to support this operation.

Table 5.2. Usage of break operand.

Range	Usage
0x000000–0x03ffff	ABI specific
0x040000–0x07ffff	application specific
0x080000–0x0fffff	debugger specific
0x100000–0x1fffff	operating system specific

5.2.3   Invoking system calls from the kernel

A curiosity of Linux is that the kernel itself can invoke system calls. This happens relatively rarely and is more a convenience than a strict requirement. But the reason this capability is useful is that it is sometimes easier to invoke a system call than to directly call the corresponding system call handler. This is true in particular for *clone2()* because the *sys_clone2()* handler needs the pt-regs structure that is created in kernel entry path. If the kernel were to call *sys_clone2()* directly, it would have to find some other means to create this structure. Not all platforms can support system calls from within the kernel. For example, the Alpha architecture does not permit execution of the special system call instruction at the kernel level [65]. Such platforms have to implement special routines to emulate the system calls needed by the kernel. Fortunately, only a handful of system calls are used in this fashion, so this emulation does not pose a serious problem. Still, it is clearly preferable to support kernel-level system calls wherever possible. IA-64 can readily support this capability.

5.2.4   IA-64 implementation

The first platform-specific choice regarding system calls is what instruction is to be used to enter the kernel. On IA-64, a natural choice is the break instruction. This instruction takes a single operand, a 21-bit integer constant that indicates the reason for entering the kernel. The IA-64–specific supplement to the UNIX System V ABI divides the available operand values into the four ranges described in Table 5.2 [32]. The first range is reserved for ABI-specific purposes. For example, an operand value of 1 is defined to indicate that the application attempted to perform an integer division by zero. The second and third ranges are reserved for application- and debugger-specific purposes. The fourth range is reserved for operating-system-specific use; Linux uses the first value in this range, 0x100000, for system calls. In theory, the low-order bits of this constant could be used to encode the system call number, but since this would make it more difficult to support *indirect system calls*, where the system call number is determined by a runtime value, Linux/ia64 instead uses **scratch** register r15 to encode the system call number.

The next question is how the system call result value and the error code should be returned from a system call. Recall from Chapter 2, *IA-64 Architecture*, that the software conventions define registers r8–r11 to be used as return registers [28]. Because multiple return registers are available, there is no need to cram both the error code and the result value into a single register, as is the case for kernel-internal error signaling. Linux/ia64

```
#include <asm/unistd.h>

open:   mov r15 = __NR_open          // place syscall number in r15
        break 0x100000               // call into the kernel
        cmp.eq p6,p0 = -1,r10        // did the system call fail?
(p6)    br.cond __syscall_error      // yes, jump to error handler
        br.ret rp                    // no, return to caller
```

Figure 5.4. Linux/ia64 system call stub for *open()*.

uses registers r8 and r10 for this purpose. Register r10 is an error indicator: a value of 0 indicates the system call executed successfully, whereas a value of -1 indicates that the system call failed. Correspondingly, register r8 is used to return the result value on success and the (non-negative) error code on failure. The advantage of this scheme is that system call stubs can uniformly test the value in r10 to reliably determine whether the system call failed—independently of whether the system call returns a file descriptor, a user address, or even an arbitrary 64-bit value as might be returned by *ptrace()*.

Because the kernel internally uses a different error signaling scheme, the IA-64–specific system call exit path must convert the kernel internal return values to the correct settings of r8 and r10. This can be done approximately by setting r10 to the sign bit of the system call handler's return value r (-1 if $r < 0$ and 0 otherwise) and setting r8 to the absolute value of r. To allow a system call handler to return a negative result value without triggering a system call failure, this scheme is extended in the following fashion: on entry to the kernel, the system call entry path clears a special *force_success* flag in the pt-regs structure and, on return, the system call exit path checks this flag before converting the return value. If the flag is still cleared, the normal return value conversion described previously is used. However, if the flag is set, the exit path clears register r10, irrespective of the value in register r8. Thus, a system call handler needing to return a negative value can force a successful return by setting the *force_success* flag in the pt-regs structure. For convenience, the header file include/asm-ia64/ptrace.h provides the *force_successful_return()* routine for this purpose.

The last question we need to consider is how system call arguments should be passed into the kernel. As explained earlier, system calls are performance critical, so it is worthwhile to use the most efficient argument-passing scheme available. Given that IA-64 uses stacked registers r32 and up to pass arguments to functions, it would be ideal if those registers could be used directly to invoke the system call handler in the kernel. This is indeed exactly what Linux/ia64 does. While the principle of passing on the user level system call arguments may sound simple, great care needs to be taken to ensure that the scheme really does work correctly, securely, and under all possible circumstances.

Before delving into this topic, let us summarize the discussion so far by taking a look at how system calls are typically invoked on Linux/ia64. Figure 5.4 illustrates the system call stub for *open()*. The figure shows that the assembly stub first includes header file asm/unistd.h to obtain the manifest constants that define the IA-64 system call numbers.

The first instruction in the stub moves the system call number __NR_open into register r15. The second instruction calls the kernel with the break instruction. Upon returning from the kernel, execution resumes after the break instruction where the stub checks register r10 to see if the system call failed. If r10 contains −1, it did fail and the stub branches off to an error handler (__syscall_error). Typically, this error handler would set global variable *errno* to the error code returned in r8 and then return to the caller. If the system call did not fail, then the stub executes the br.ret instruction, which will return control directly to the caller. Note that, apart from the time spent in the kernel, this code can execute in as little as two cycles because the first two and the last three instructions can be executed in a single cycle each. Also note how the system call stub does not have to touch the system call argument registers. In fact, the system call stub is completely oblivious to the number and the types of the system call arguments!

Register stack during system call

As discussed earlier, the system call path follows the same steps during kernel entry and exit that any other interruption follows. In particular, on a system call the register stack also needs to be switched from the user register backing store to the kernel register backing store. The register stack switch follows the same basic pattern as during normal kernel entry and exit, but with one important difference: The system call arguments need to be preserved across the register stack switch so they can be passed directly to the system call handler without register copying and without being passed through memory. The technique that makes this possible is described in Table 5.3. If we compare it to Table 5.1, we see that the sequence of instruction is very similar to the normal entry and exit paths. The main differences are these:

- There are no alloc instructions in the system call entry and exit paths.

- The cover instruction has moved from the entry path to the exit path, i.e., it is not executed until after the system call handler has returned.

- The size d of the **dirty** partition is calculated only in the exit path, after the cover instruction has been executed.

The combined effect of these relatively minor changes is that the system call arguments are being passed directly from the user level to the respective system call handler. To see how this works, let us consider some of the key points in Table 5.3.

Suppose that an application is running at the user level and is about to make a system call. At that point, the current register frame will consist of a certain number s_l of local registers and a number s_a of output (argument) registers. The application will then place the system call arguments in the output registers and invoke the system call stub with the br.call instruction, shown in line (1) of the table. At the time of the call, the bsp register will have a certain value, b_1, and cfm will have the value $s_a + s_l \mid s_l$. As usual, the br.call instruction pushes the local registers into the **dirty** partition and advances the bsp register by s_l register slots, so that by the time control reaches the system call stub, bsp has the

Table 5.3. Register stack during a system call.

Instruction	bspstore	bsp	cfm sof sol	pfs.pfm sof sol	ifs.ifm sof sol
user level	?	b_1	$s_a + s_l \mid s_l$	?	?
(1) br.call *sys_stub*		$b_1 \oplus s_l$	$s_a \mid 0$	$s_a + s_l \mid s_l$	
(2) break 0x100000		b_1'			
(3) $P_{pfs} \leftarrow$ pfs					
(4) $P_{rsc} \leftarrow$ rsc					
(5) rsc $\leftarrow 0$	b_0				
(6) $P_{bspst} \leftarrow$ bspstore					
(7) bspstore $\leftarrow B_0$	B_0	$B_0 \oplus (b_1' \ominus b_0)$			
(8) rsc.mode $\leftarrow 3$	?	B_1			?
(9) psr.ic $\leftarrow 1$		B_1			
(10) br.call *sys_handler*		B_1	$s_a \mid 0$?	$s_a \mid 0$	
$\vdots$					
(11) br.ret		B_1	$s_a \mid 0$		
(12) psr.ic $\leftarrow 0$					?
(13) rsc.mode $\leftarrow 0$					
(14) cover		$B_1 \oplus s_a$	$0 \mid 0$		$s_a \mid 0$
(15) $d \leftarrow$ bsp $- B_0$	B_0				
(16) rsc.loadrs $\leftarrow d$					
(17) loadrs	$(B_1 \oplus s_a) - d$				
(18) bspstore $\leftarrow P_{bspst}$	b_0	$(b_1 \oplus s_l) \oplus s_a$			
(19) pfs $\leftarrow P_{pfs}$				$s_a + s_l \mid s_l$	
(20) rsc $\leftarrow P_{rsc}$	?				
(21) rfi		$b_1 \oplus s_l$	$s_a \mid 0$		?
(22) br.ret		b_1	$s_a + s_l \mid s_l$		
user level					

value $b_1 \oplus s_l$ and cfm has the value $s_a \mid 0$. This means that the current frame now consists of the output registers, i.e., the system call arguments only.

The system call stub then triggers an interruption by executing the break instruction shown in line (2). The interruption is intercepted in the IVT where the kernel switches the RSE from the user register backing store to the kernel register backing store as usual, except that it does not execute a cover instruction. By the time the kernel invokes the system call handler in line (10), cfm contains $s_a \mid 0$ just as it did when the system call stub was invoked. In other words, the current frame still contains the system call arguments.

Now, when the system call handler returns, the kernel starts switching the RSE back to the user-level backing store. In line (14) it allocates the empty register frame required by the loadrs instruction. However, this time, it uses cover instead of alloc. This has the effect that instead of the current frame being dropped, it is pushed into the **dirty** partition. The system call arguments are therefore now part of the **dirty** partition.

The kernel then calculates the size d of this expanded **dirty** partition in line (15) and then executes the loadrs instruction in line (17) to ensure that all user registers have been loaded from the kernel register backing store. At this point, the RSE is in the same configuration as after executing loadrs in the normal exit path, and the remaining steps are the same. In particular, after the rfi instruction in line (21) is executed, control returns to the system call stub, which returns to the caller with the br.ret instruction shown in line (22).

If we compare the values of bsp and cfm in line (22) with the initial state at the beginning of the table, we see that they are identical. The value of pfs.pfm has been restored to the value that existed on entry to the system call stub, which is the same behavior as during a normal function call. In other words, as far as the application is concerned, the system call stub behaved like an ordinary function call even though it ended up calling the kernel!

For the most part, it is straightforward to track the effect that the instructions in Table 5.3 have on the RSE-related state. As usual, the exception is where the register stack is switched back to the user register backing store. Let us start with line (17) where we claim that after loadrs has finished execution, bspstore contains the value B_0. Observe that line (15) sets d to $(B_1 \oplus s_a) - B_0$, so by applying the rules of normal arithmetic we get:

$$\text{bspstore} = (B_1 \oplus s_a) - d = (B_1 \oplus s_a) - ((B_1 \oplus s_a) - B_0) = B_0$$

Thus, after loadrs has finished executing, bspstore is indeed equal to B_0.

Now, in line (18) we claimed that writing bspstore with b_0 sets bsp to $(b_1 \oplus s_l) \oplus s_a$. By definition, writing bspstore sets bsp to the value bspstore $\oplus$ ndirty. In our case, ndirty, the number of registers in the **dirty** partition, is given by:

$$\text{ndirty} = \text{bsp} \ominus \text{bspstore} = (B_1 \oplus s_a) \ominus B_0$$

In line (7), the value of B_1 was defined as $B_0 \oplus (b_1' \ominus b_0)$, so if we substitute this into the equation for ndirty and apply RSE-arithmetic rules (2.4.3) and (2.4.2) from Chapter 2, *IA-64 Architecture*, we get:

$$\text{ndirty} = \left[\underbrace{B_0}_{x} \oplus \underbrace{(b_1' \ominus b_0)}_{m} \oplus \underbrace{s_a}_{n} \right] \ominus B_0 \overset{(2.4.3)}{=} \left[\underbrace{B_0}_{x} \oplus \underbrace{\{(b_1' \ominus b_0) + s_a\}}_{n} \right] \ominus \underbrace{B_0}_{x}$$

$$\overset{(2.4.2)}{=} (b_1' \ominus b_0) + s_a$$

In the final step, we can use the expression for ndirty in the formula for calculating the value of bsp:

$$\text{bsp} = \text{bspstore} \oplus \text{ndirty} = \underbrace{b_0}_{x} \oplus \{\underbrace{(b_1' \ominus b_0)}_{m} + \underbrace{s_a}_{n}\}$$

$$\overset{(2.4.3)}{=} \{ \underbrace{b_0}_{x} \oplus (\underbrace{b_1'}_{y} \ominus \underbrace{b_0}_{x})\} \oplus s_a \overset{(2.4.4)}{=} b_1' \oplus s_a = (b_0 \oplus s_l) \oplus s_a$$

This proves that after writing bspstore in line (18), the value in bsp is the same as if the initial bsp value had been advanced first by s_l and then by s_a register slots, just as the table claims.

Restarting system calls

Passing the system call arguments directly from the user level to the system call handler is beneficial from a performance perspective but poses a problem when a system call needs to be restarted. To see this, consider that when the system call handler is called, the arguments occupy registers r32 and up and are therefore treated as ordinary local registers. The system call handler, therefore, could modify their contents during the course of normal execution. This implies that by the time the system call handler returns, the argument registers may have different values and if the system call were to be restarted, the wrong values would be passed to the system call handler. The result of this would be spurious failures in applications, where a system call would sometimes fail for no apparent reason. Clearly, this is not acceptable. To avoid the problem, Linux/ia64 uses a special register usage convention which says that a system call handler may not modify any of the registers used to pass arguments. The GNU C language supports this special convention through a function attribute called syscall_linkage. This attribute has the effect that the compiler will treat the eight integer argument registers r32–r39 as **preserved**, even though they are normally treated as **scratch**. An example of how this attribute can be used is shown below:

```
__attribute__ ((syscall_linkage)) long
f (a, b, c, d) {
    return a + b + c + d;
}
```

Function *f()* simply calculates the sum of the four integer arguments. These arguments are passed in registers r32–r35, and normally, it would be entirely possible that the compiler would reuse some of them as temporary storage. The syscall_linkage attribute prevents this and ensures that on exit from the function, registers r32–r35 hold the same values as they did on entry to the function. The attribute also ensures that the compiler does not use r36–r39 in this function. The reason this is done is to avoid tainting them with arbitrary kernel data, which would create the risk of leaking security-sensitive data back to the user level.

While this attribute solves the technical aspect of the problem, there is still a practical issue: It clearly would be undesirable to mark every system call handler in the Linux kernel with an IA-64–specific attribute. Fortunately, it is not unusual to employ (slightly) different calling conventions for C functions that are called from interruption handlers. Indeed, Linux uses a macro called asmlinkage to mark all such functions. Thus, Linux/ia64 can define this macro to expand into the syscall_linkage attribute. This solution is not perfect, because it ends up declaring functions with the syscall_linkage attribute that are never called during system call execution. Fortunately, the performance effect of this attribute is so small that it is negligible. The bottom line is that as long as at least all the system call handlers are declared with the asmlinkage macro, the system call handlers will not corrupt the system call arguments and restarting a system call will not pose any problem. Of course, any assembly code executed along the system call entry and exit paths also must observe this convention and must not modify the system call argument registers.

```
            alloc r2 = ar.pfs,6,0,0,0  // make r32-r37 writable
            tnat.nz p8,p0 = r32
            tnat.nz p9,p0 = r33
            tnat.nz p10,p0 = r34
            tnat.nz p11,p0 = r35
            tnat.nz p12,p0 = r36
            tnat.nz p13,p0 = r37;;
(p8)        mov r32 = -1          // set r32 to -1 if it was a NaT
(p9)        mov r33 = -1          // set r33 to -1 if it was a NaT
(p10)       mov r34 = -1          // set r34 to -1 if it was a NaT
(p11)       mov r35 = -1          // set r35 to -1 if it was a NaT
(p12)       mov r36 = -1          // set r36 to -1 if it was a NaT
(p13)       mov r37 = -1          // set r37 to -1 if it was a NaT
            br.ret.sptk.many rp
```

Figure 5.5. Routine to filter out NaT arguments.

Guarding against NaT arguments

Another effect of directly passing system call arguments in registers is that the kernel must be careful to avoid crashing if an application either accidentally or maliciously passes a NaT value in one of the argument registers. Without proper care, a NaT argument could trigger a REGISTER NAT CONSUMPTION FAULT inside the kernel and crash the machine.

This problem could be avoided by forcing all system call handlers to check the arguments for NaT values before using them, but this solution would be both arduous and error prone. A much better solution, and the one adopted by Linux/ia64, is to filter out NaT arguments on the system call entry path. This can be done with an assembly subroutine along the lines of the one shown in Figure 5.5. This routine first uses the alloc instruction to ensure that r32–r37 are allocated, then tests the NaT bit of each of those registers and uses the test results to replace the value of those registers that do contain a NaT value with −1. Because the Linux kernel has no system call that takes more than six arguments, this procedure ensures that no NaT argument survives this filter routine.

There are a few points worth making about this routine. First, note that the argument checking is a highly parallel operation: The routine has just one stop bit, so an IA-64 CPU could execute it in as little as two cycles. Second, the routine has no knowledge of how many arguments are actually being passed to the system call handler. This means that the alloc instruction is absolutely essential. Otherwise, if fewer than six arguments were being passed, some of the registers accessed by the routine could lie outside the current register frame and attempting to write them would raise an ILLEGAL OPERATION FAULT. Note that even if the routine knew how many arguments are expected by the kernel system call handler, it would not help because the routine could not rely on user-level code to allocate the required number of arguments. That is, without the alloc instruction, a malicious application could invoke a system call with fewer than the expected number of arguments and cause a kernel crash. Fortunately, placing the alloc instruction in the routine neatly bypasses all these issues and works correctly and independently of how many arguments are expected or passed. A final point is whether it is acceptable to silently replace a NaT value with -1. The answer is yes: The behavior of system calls is completely undefined in the presence of a NaT argument. A system call could legitimately emulate the behavior of a REGISTER NAT CONSUMPTION FAULT and raise an illegal instruction (SIGILL) signal, it could terminate the offending task with extreme prejudice, or it could even delete all the files owned by the user running the application! Clearly, this leaves open the possibility of replacing NaT with -1 or indeed any other non-NaT value. The value -1 was chosen because it increases the likelihood that a system call will fail when an application passes a NaT argument by accident. For example, -1 is not a valid file descriptor number, user-space address, user ID, or a valid process ID.

Using epc to speed up system calls

The IA-64 architecture provides the special epc instruction (enter privileged code) to accelerate system call execution. This instruction works in conjunction with virtual pages that are mapped with the access right XP0 (see Chapter 4, *Virtual Memory*). At the user level, such pages are executable, but not readable or writable. When the CPU is executing on such a page and encounters an epc instruction, it will raise (promote) the current privilege level to the kernel level, i.e., the psr.cpl field will be set to 0. Once the CPU is executing at privilege-level 0, it can execute privileged instructions and access the kernel address space so, for all practical purposes, it has entered the kernel and can therefore perform the same actions as if the kernel had been entered through an interruption. In particular, it could execute any system call handlers.

Why is this beneficial? The main advantage of epc over break is that because it does not trigger the normal interruption processing, it can be executed with a smaller overhead. In particular, a break instruction forces the CPU to wait until all pending instructions have been executed before executing any new instructions. Because modern CPUs can have many instructions in flight at any given time, this stall can amount to a significant performance penalty. In contrast, epc does not disrupt the execution pipeline of the CPU and, in that sense, provides a much smoother and faster entry into the kernel.

The Linux kernel does not take advantage of epc, though no major reason would prevent it from doing so. For example, the kernel could place a slightly modified version of the system call entry path on the gate page and place an epc instruction in front of it. As described in Chapter 4, *Virtual Memory*, the gate page is mapped with the XP0 access right so that jumping to the epc instruction would have an effect similar to invoking a system call with break, except that it would run faster. However, the performance improvement from simply using the epc instruction would be relatively minor because it would still be necessary to perform all the usual kernel entry and exit processing.

To take full advantage of epc, it would really be necessary to couple it with *lightweight system calls*, which are system calls that can be performed without switching to the kernel stacks. For example, simple system calls such as *getpid()* and *gettimeofday()* could be implemented as lightweight system calls. Because of their simplicity, these system calls could be executed right after epc has raised the privilege level and thereby could avoid almost all of the normal entry and exit processing of ordinary system calls. Clearly, this would dramatically speed-up the execution of lightweight system calls.

If Linux were to take advantage of epc, it would introduce a subtle change to the kernel because the current privilege level (psr.cpl) would no longer be an accurate indication as to whether the CPU is executing on the kernel stacks. The reason is that even if the gate page disabled interrupts (and interruption collection) right after executing the epc instruction, there would still be a small window during which execution could be interrupted. If so, the interruption would observe the CPU at privilege-level 0 even though the CPU would still be using the user-level stacks. Conversely, disabling interrupts *before* executing epc is not an option either, because interrupt masking is a privileged operation. The net result is that epc introduces a new state of execution where the CPU is halfway between executing at the user level and executing at the kernel level.

Another consideration is that lightweight system calls would have to be careful to provide a faithful emulation of normal system call behavior. For example, while it would be fastest to execute lightweight system calls like ordinary user-level function calls, they would still have to check for and deliver pending signals, reschedule the CPU if necessary, and support system call tracing through the *ptrace()* interface. Not doing so would change the semantics of the lightweight system calls in ways that could break existing applications.

In summary, the potential performance benefit of epc and lightweight system calls have to be weighed carefully against the additional complexity they would introduce in the kernel. In this evaluation, it is important not to succumb to the temptation of optimizing micro-benchmarks that have little or no impact on real applications. For example, with epc it is trivial to implement a fast version of the *getpid()* system call. But the performance of this system call is not critical to any application other than artificial benchmark programs, so optimizing *getpid()* would produce great benchmark results but few real-world benefits. This is not to say that epc is not a useful instruction. Quite the opposite: When used properly, epc should be able to provide dramatic performance benefits even for real-world applications.

5.3   SIGNALS

Signals can be thought of as being the complementary facility to system calls: The latter let an application call into the kernel (*downcall*), and the former allow the kernel to call into an application (*upcall*). As with system calls, each signal has a *signal name* and an associated *signal number*. The mapping between signal name and number is defined in the platform-specific header file include/asm/signal.h. For example, on Linux/ia64, this header file maps the keyboard interrupt signal SIGINT to signal number 2. The Linux kernel uses 31 standard UNIX signals and provides for up to 32 POSIX.4 real-time signals [17]. All signal numbers must be in the range of 1 to 63 and the real-time signals must occupy the consecutive range from SIGRTMIN to SIGRTMAX. Within those constraints, signal numbers can be assigned to suit the needs of the platform.

The kernel uses signals to notify a task of error conditions and asynchronous events. An example of the former is the segmentation violation signal (SIGSEGV), which is raised whenever a task attempts to access nonexistent (unmapped) virtual memory. An example

int **sigaction**(*signum, newactionp, oldactionp*);	/* set handler for signal signum */
int **kill**(*pid, signum*);	/* send signal to a task */
int **sigprocmask**(*op, newsetp, oldsetp*);	/* mask/unmask signals */
int **sigpending**(*sigsetp*);	/* return set of pending signals */
int **sigsuspend**(*sigsetp*);	/* wait for signal to occur */
int **sigaltstack**(*newstackp, oldstackp*);	/* establish alternate signal stack */

Figure 5.6. Signal-related system calls.

of the latter is the keyboard interrupt signal, which is sent whenever a user decides to type **Ctrl-C**. The asynchronous nature of signals introduces pseudoconcurrency at the task level. To control this concurrency, the task must have a way to temporarily mask the delivery of specific signals. The kernel supports this by maintaining a *signal mask* in the task structure. This mask consists of a bitset that represents the set of signals whose delivery is blocked. The fact that signals are raised asynchronously and that their delivery can be masked and unmasked means that signals can also be viewed as being the Linux virtual machine equivalent of device interrupts.

Several system calls enable a task to control how and when signals are delivered. It turns out that most of these system calls require no special support from the platform-specific code. In contrast, the actual delivery of a signal is a platform-specific operation and the main topic of this section. However, before exploring this issue, let us review the signal-related system calls so we can understand how they affect signal delivery.

5.3.1 Signal-related system calls

The Linux kernel provides six primary system calls to control signal delivery. The interface of these system calls is shown in Figure 5.6.

The first and most important system call is *sigaction()*. It lets an application define what action the kernel should take when a particular signal occurs. It takes three arguments: *signum*, *newactionp*, and *oldactionp*. The *signum* argument specifies the signal number whose action should be defined. The *newactionp* and *oldactionp* arguments are pointers to a *sigaction structure* (struct sigaction in file include/asm/signal.h). The former specifies the new action for the signal, and the latter (if not NULL) returns the action that was previously in effect. A sigaction structure contains the member *sa_handler*, which is a pointer to the signal handler function that should be called when the signal occurs, and *sa_flags*, which is a set of flags that control various details of signal delivery. For example, setting the SA_RESTART flag requests that the kernel use BSD instead of System V behavior when a system call is interrupted by signal *signum*. Another useful flag is SA_ONSTACK. As we see later when discussing *sigaltstack()*, this flag controls whether signal *signum* will be delivered on an alternate signal stack.

The function pointer stored in *sa_handler* can be set to the special values SIG_IGN or SIG_DFL. The former indicates that the signal should be ignored, and the latter indicates that the default action should be taken. Depending on the signal number *signum*, the default action may cause the task to be stopped or terminated (in some cases, after creating a core dump), or may cause the signal to be ignored, as if SIG_IGN had been specified. If *sa_handler* contains a proper function pointer, the corresponding signal handler is normally declared as a function that takes a single argument *signum*. This argument contains the number of the signal that is being delivered. However, this declaration is primarily for compatibility with the ANSI C standard [7]. The Linux kernel actually passes three arguments to a signal handler, as illustrated by the prototype below:

```
void sighandler(signum, siginfo, sigcontext);
```

In addition to the signal number, Linux passes the *siginfo* and *sigcontext* arguments. The former is a pointer to a *siginfo structure* (siginfo_t in file include/asm/siginfo.h) and is used to pass additional information about the signal as defined by the POSIX.4 standard [17]. For example, when a segmentation violation signal occurs, the kernel passes, in the *si_addr* member of siginfo, the virtual address that triggered the signal. The *sigcontext* argument is a pointer to a *sigcontext structure* (struct sigcontext in file include/asm/sigcontext.h). This structure is platform specific and encapsulates the CPU state that existed at the time the signal occurred. For portability, the *siginfo* and *sigcontext* arguments should be declared only when they are really needed. ANSI C-compliant programs should declare only the first argument. Programs that follow the POSIX.4 standard may need the second argument and usually declare the third argument as a **void** pointer. Finally, programs that use the third argument are not just Linux specific but also platform specific.

The second system call, *kill()*, allows a task to send a signal to another task (or even itself). It takes two arguments: *pid*, the ID of the task to send the signal to and *signum*, the number of the signal to send. The POSIX.4 standard defines a related *sigqueue()* system call that provides the same capability, except that an additional word of data can be passed along with the signal. Linux also implements this system call, but because it provides the same basic functionality as *kill()*, we do not discuss it separately in this book.

The third system call, *sigprocmask()*, manipulates the signal mask that the kernel maintains for each task. It can add or remove signals from the signal mask or set it to a particular value. It takes three arguments. The first one, *op*, controls how the signal mask is to be modified and can be one of SIG_BLOCK, SIG_UNBLOCK, or SIG_SETMASK. The second and third arguments, *newsetp* and *oldsetp*, are both pointers to a *signal set* (sigset_t in file include/asm/signal.h); *newsetp* specifies which signals are to be manipulated, *oldsetp* (if not NULL) returns the signal mask that was previously in effect. Specifically, if *op* is SIG_BLOCK, the signals in *newsetp* are *added* to the signal mask. In contrast, if *op* is SIG_UNBLOCK, the signals in *newsetp* are *removed* from the signal mask. In the third case, *op* is SIG_SETMASK, and the signal mask is set precisely to the value of *newsetp*, meaning that only the signals that are present in this set are masked and all others are unmasked.

The *sigpending()* system call queries the set of signals that have been raised but not yet delivered. It takes a single argument, *sigsetp*, which is a pointer to the signal set used to return the result. A related system call is *sigsuspend()*. A task can call it to block (suspend) execution until a signal is delivered. It takes a single argument, *sigsetp*, which is a pointer to a signal set. The system call atomically sets the signal mask to this value before suspending execution and restores the original signal mask before returning.

The last signal-related system call is *sigaltstack()*. It is key to enabling the reliable delivery of signals, especially of the SIGSEGV signal. As we see later in this discussion, when the kernel delivers a signal to an application, it needs to allocate a signal frame on the user-level stack. This implies that if the user-level stack is invalid, e.g., because it is out of memory or because the stack pointer is corrupted, it would be impossible to deliver a signal. To prevent this problem, *sigaltstack()* can be used to establish an *alternate signal stack*. Once it is established, signal handlers registered with the SA_ONSTACK flag turned on will be invoked on this alternate stack. This ensures that the kernel can invoke the signal handler no matter what the state of the normal user-level stack happens to be at the time.

As shown in Figure 5.6, *sigaltstack()* takes two arguments: *newstackp* and *oldstackp*. Both are pointers to a *stack structure* (stack_t in file include/asm/signal.h). The former defines the new alternate signal stack, and the latter (if not NULL) is used to return the alternate signal stack that was previously in effect (if any). The stack structure defines a stack as a fixed-size memory area. Specifically, member *ss_sp* specifies the starting address (lowest address) of the memory area, and member *ss_size* specifies its size in bytes. A third member, *ss_flags*, consists of two flags SS_ONSTACK and SS_DISABLE. If the latter is set in *newstackp*, use of the alternate signal stack is disabled. Similarly, if the flag is set in *oldstackp*, it indicates that the alternate signal stack was disabled previously. SS_ONSTACK has no effect in *newstackp*, but for *oldstackp* it indicates whether the task is currently running on the alternate signal stack.

Example: Intercepting the segmentation violation signal

To see how some of the signal-related system calls are typically used and how they affect signal delivery, let us take a look at a particular example. Figure 5.7 contains a simple program that illustrates the use and handling of the segmentation violation signal. The sample program starts by including a few header files and then defines a signal handler function, called *sighandler()*. All this function does is terminate the program by calling *_exit()* with a status of −1. The second function is *doit()*; all it does is store an ASCII NUL character at the address passed in argument *cp*. The main program is implemented in the third function. It declares a sigaction structure called *act*, which it uses to establish *sighandler()* as the handler for the SIGSEGV signal by calling *sigaction()*. Afterward, the main program calls *doit()* with a NULL pointer. Because NULL is not a valid address, *doit()* will trigger a page fault when attempting to store the NUL character at this address.

The Linux page fault handler will determine that the address being accessed is not valid and will raise the segmentation violation signal. When returning from the page fault handler, the kernel exit path will find the SIGSEGV signal to be pending and, consequently, arranges for this signal to be delivered to the application. This is done in such a way that when the application resumes execution, it will appear as if *sighandler()* had been called by *doit()*. That is, if we looked at the function call chain when *sighandler()* is running, we would see that *main()* called *doit()* and that it called *sighandler()* just at the point where it attempted to store the NUL character. Suppose the IA-64 assembly code for *doit()* looked as shown in Figure 5.8. With this code, the call chain would show that *doit()* called *sighandler()* just as the st1 instruction started to execute.

```
#include <signal.h>
#include <stdlib.h>
#include <string.h>

void sighandler (int signum) {
    _exit(-1);
}

void doit (char *cp) {
    *cp = 0;
}

int main (int argc, char **argv) {
    struct sigaction act;
    act.sa_handler = sighandler;
    sigaction(SIGSEGV, &act, 0);
    doit(NULL);
    return 0;
}
```

Figure 5.7. Example of a program that intercepts SIGSEGV.

```
doit:   st1 [r32] = r0          // store ASCII NUL character
        nop.i 0x0
        br.ret rp               // return to caller
```

Figure 5.8. IA-64 assembly code for *doit()* function.

The important point here is that the call to *sighandler()* is far from an ordinary function call. Normally, the compiler ensures that when another function is called, none of the **scratch** registers contain live values. But because the compiler did not know that the st1 instruction will cause a signal handler to be invoked, it assumed that executing the instruction does not affect the values in the **scratch** registers. Indeed, if we look at the assembly code again, we see that the br.ret instruction uses register rp, which is a **scratch** register. Thus, unlike the case of ordinary function calls, the **scratch** registers must be saved before the signal handler can be invoked and restored afterward.

When a signal handler returns, the kernel automatically restores the execution environment that was active before the signal occurred. In our example program, this would mean that the st1 instruction would be reexecuted as soon as the signal handler returns. Because the NULL pointer would still be an invalid address, the page fault would occur again. In other words, if *sighandler()* simply returned, the segmentation violation signal would occur repeatedly and the program would fail to make any progress. To avoid this, *sighandler()* instead calls _exit() to terminate the program as soon as the signal occurs for the first time.

5.3.2 Signal delivery

Recall from Figure 5.1 on page 212 that step three of the kernel exit path checks whether any signals are pending and, if they are, delivers them. This is achieved by a call to a platform-specific routine called *do_signal()*. Apart from the exit path, the only other point from which this function is called is the *sigsuspend()* system call handler. This special case is needed because *sigsuspend()* has to restore the original signal mask before returning to the user level. This means that the check for signal delivery normally done in the kernel exit path is too late because the signal that causes *sigsuspend()* to return may be blocked by the original signal mask.

The *do_signal()* routine is responsible for dequeuing a pending signal, looking up the sigaction structure that the task established for it, and processing it accordingly. If sigaction member *sa_handler* has one of the special values SIG_IGN or SIG_DFL, the routine can process the signal immediately either by ignoring it or by performing the default action, such as creating a core dump and terminating the task. If the default action causes the task to be terminated, *do_signal()* returns immediately because there is no point in processing any of the signals that may still be pending. If the signal is ignored, the routine starts from the beginning and dequeues the next pending signal. This repeats until there are no more pending signals or until a signal is found that requires invoking a signal handler.

To invoke a signal handler, the kernel needs to modify the task state such that when the CPU returns to the user level, execution starts in the signal handler as if it had been called by the user-level function that was running last. We use the example in Figure 5.9 to illustrate how this can be achieved. The left part illustrates the task state at the time the *do_signal()* routine is called: at the top of the kernel stack, we find the pt-regs structure that contains the **scratch** state of the task. For our example, the instruction pointer ip stored in the pt-regs structure would point to the st1 instruction that caused the page fault. The stack pointer sp would point to the top of the user-level stack, which consists of the frame for *main()* and the frame for *doit()* right beneath it.

Now, to make it appear as if *sighandler()* had been called, *do_signal()* needs to modify the task state such that it looks as illustrated in the middle part of Figure 5.9. This involves four steps. First, the routine needs to allocate a new user-level stack frame to make space for the sigcontext and siginfo structures. Normally, this frame is allocated right beneath the stack frame of the user-level function that was running last (*doit()* in our example). However, if an alternate signal stack has been established, this frame is allocated at the top of that stack instead. Second, *do_signal()* uses the sigcontext structure to save the existing user-level state such that it can resume execution after the signal handler returns. As illustrated in the figure by the dashed arrow, this at a minimum requires copying the **scratch** state from the pt-regs structure to sigcontext, though many platforms also save the **preserved** CPU state in sigcontext. Third, the siginfo structure can be filled in with the auxiliary signal-related information mandated by POSIX. In the fourth and final step, the fake call to the signal handler needs to be set up. Specifically, in the pt-regs structure, the instruction pointer ip needs to be set to the address of the signal handler's entry point and the stack pointer sp needs to be set to the new top of the user-level stack. The three signal handler arguments, *signum*, *siginfo*, and *sigcontext* need to be passed according to

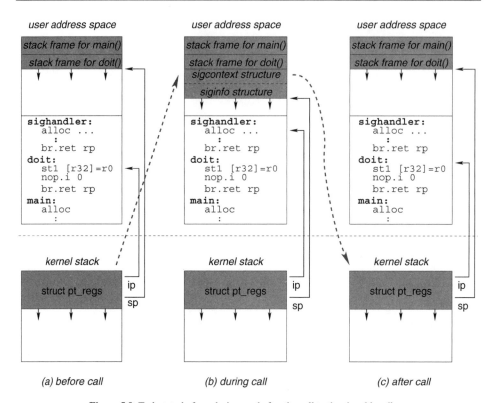

Figure 5.9. Task state before, during, and after the call to the signal handler.

the calling conventions of the platform. They may need to be stored on the user stack or in the pt-regs structure. Also, *do_signal()* needs to arrange for execution to return to the kernel once the signal handler returns. Linux provides the *sigreturn()* system call for this purpose, so the return can be arranged by setting the return pointer rp to the system call stub for *sigreturn()*. The question is of course where to place this stub. There are several possibilities. The stub could be generated dynamically on the user-level stack, e.g., as part of the stack frame allocated for sigcontext and siginfo. Another option is to let the application specify where this stub can be found. Linux supports this option through a special *sa_restorer* member in the sigaction structure. It lets the application specify the address of the *sigreturn()* stub at the time *sigaction()* is invoked (this is normally done by the C library and is therefore transparent to application programmers). On some platforms, e.g., IA-64, it is also possible to map the stub at a fixed address in virtual space, so that rp can simply be set to this address. As far as the kernel is concerned, the exact choice does not matter as long as platform-specific code ensures that *sigreturn()* is invoked in *some* fashion.

At this point, the task is ready for execution and the *do_signal()* routine can return control to the kernel exit path. There, the task's **scratch** state will be restored from the modified pt-regs structure, and control is returned to the user level where execution will start in the signal handler. In our example, this would mean that control would be handed over to function *sighandler()*. This function immediately calls *_exit()* and therefore terminates the task as soon as the signal occurs.

Let us explore what would happen if *sighandler()* did return: As previously arranged, the *sigreturn()* system call would be invoked at that point. When execution reaches the *sigreturn()* system call handler, the user stack would again look as illustrated in the middle part of Figure 5.9, except that on the kernel stack we would now find the pt-regs structure containing the current user-level values of the **scratch** registers. Because the signal handler has finished execution, the goal is to restore the task state such that execution can resume at the original place, as if the signal had never happened (apart from side effects). To achieve this, we need to bring the task back to the state shown in the right part of the figure. As illustrated by the dashed arrow, this means that the **scratch** state has to be restored from the sigcontext structure and copied back to the pt-regs structure. This would mean that the instruction pointer ip would be set back to the st1 instruction that originally triggered the signal and the stack pointer sp would be set back to point to the stack frame of the *doit()* function. Of course, all other **scratch** registers, and in particular the return pointer rp, would also be restored. Once pt-regs has been reconstructed, the *sigreturn()* system call handler can return. The kernel exit path will then restore the original **scratch** state from the pt-regs structure and resume execution at the point where the signal occurred, just as desired.

Several points related to signal handler execution are worth emphasizing:

- A signal handler can access the sigcontext structure through the *sigcontext* argument and can inspect or even modify the content of this structure. For example, a signal handler could modify the instruction pointer ip in this structure to skip execution of the instruction that triggered the signal.

- A signal handler can use *siglongjmp()* to jump outside the signal handler and return control directly to a point established with *sigsetjmp()*. However, this routine may not be used to switch stacks, so it can be used only if the current stack and the stack of the *siglongjmp()* target are the same. This is usually the case except for applications that use the *sigaltstack()* system call to establish an alternate signal stack.

- It is not necessary to save the **preserved** state when invoking a signal handler because the software conventions already ensure that the signal handler will preserve the contents of such registers. In other words, the sigcontext structure is to signal delivery what the pt-regs structure is to the kernel entry path.

The signal handler invocation mechanism described previously automatically takes care of these points. However, when evaluating alternative implementation approaches, it is important to consider them to avoid breaking existing applications.

Handling interrupted system calls

The *do_signal()* routine is also responsible for restarting system calls whose execution is interrupted by a signal. System calls that can be interrupted in this fashion are called *inter-*

ruptible system calls. They work by periodically checking whether a signal is pending for delivery and, if so, returning immediately with one of the following error codes.

- **EINTR:** This error code is returned if the system call is interruptible but not restartable. This means that *do_signal()* must not restart the system call. Instead, the system call will fail with EINTR as the error code.

- **ERESTARTNOHAND:** This error code is returned if the system call is both interruptible and restartable but the system call should be restarted only if the task did not specify its own signal handler. Otherwise, *do_signal()* should arrange for the system call to fail with error code EINTR. Because the special signal handler values SIG_IGN and SIG_DFL cause the signal to be ignored or the task to be terminated, the explanation is equivalent to saying that ERESTARTNOHAND should restart the system call only the signal is invisible to the task. From the perspective of a system call handler, this means that this error code should be returned for system calls that must return EINTR if there is any chance at all that the task could have observed the occurrence of the signal. An example of a system call treated in this fashion is *select()*, which needs to return EINTR even for signals for which the BSD behavior is in effect.

- **ERESTARTSYS:** This error code is returned if the system call is both interruptible and restartable and the system call should be restarted if BSD behavior is in effect (as controlled by the sigaction flag SA_RESTART). If System V behavior is in effect, the interrupted system call should be handled as for ERESTARTNOHAND, i.e., the system call should be restarted only if the signal is invisible to the task.

- **ERESTARTNOINTR:** This error code is returned if the system call is both interruptible and restartable but the system call is not permitted to return error code EINTR. In other words, *do_signal()* must always restart system calls that return this code. This error code is used, for example, by the *automount filesystem* (file fs/autofs/root.c) to enable termination (interruption) of a task that may be stuck trying to execute *open()* on a file that resides on an unreachable (or slow) remote filesystem. Because *open()* may not return EINTR, autofs returns ERESTARTNOINTR to unconditionally restart the system call.

These descriptions show that *do_signal()* needs to be able to determine whether a signal interrupted the execution of a system call. If so, it also needs to be able to check the error code that the system call handler returned and, if indicated, arrange for the system call to be restarted. These steps are all platform specific. Next, we describe how they work on IA-64.

5.3.3   IA-64 implementation

By and large, the Linux/ia64 version of *do_signal()* (*ia64_do_signal()* in file arch/ia64/-kernel/signal.c) delivers signals in the fashion just described. Two aspects warrant further discussion: The first involves the mechanics of restarting a system call, and the second involves the handling of the register stack during signal handler invocation.

```
#include <asm/unistd.h>

open:   mov r15 = __NR_open           // place syscall number in r15
        break 0x100000                // call into the kernel
  →     cmp.eq p6,p0 = -1,r10         // did the system call fail?
  (p6)  br.cond __syscall_error       // yes, jump to error handler
        br.ret rp                     // no, return to caller
```

Figure 5.10. Example: Restarting the *open()* system call.

Let us start by taking a look at system call restarting. By convention, the callers of *do_signal()* pass it an argument that indicates whether it is being called from the system call exit path. If it is not called from the system call exit path, no restart is necessary. Otherwise, a restart may be necessary. To find out, the routine has to check the content of the pt-regs structure: if the member that corresponds to register r10 contains -1, the member for r8 contains an error code. The final determination of whether a restart is necessary is based on this error code and the task state, as explained previously. For instance, if the error code is ERESTARTNOINTR, the system call would have to be restarted.

To restart a system call, *do_signal()* needs to modify the pt-regs structure that was created on entry to the kernel. Let us consider a concrete example. Suppose the *open()* system call had to be restarted. As illustrated by the arrow in Figure 5.10, at the time *do_signal()* is invoked, the user-level IP saved in the pt-regs structure would point to the instruction following the break instruction. So, basically, *do_signal()* just needs to adjust the saved IP value so that it points to the break instruction again. Because IA-64 instructions are grouped into bundles, this adjustment is more complicated than simply decrementing the IP value. On Linux/ia64, it is implemented in a special *decrement IP routine* (*ia64_decrement_ip()* in file arch/ia64/kernel/ptrace.c), which *do_signal()* uses for this purpose.

Of course, it is also necessary to ensure that the system call argument registers and the system call number register r15 still have their original contents. As explained in Section 5.2.4, the system call entry and exit paths and the system call handlers themselves are careful not to modify the argument registers. Thus, no special actions have to be taken to restore their contents. As for register r15, it is saved in the pt-regs structure in the system call entry path and restored in the exit path, so it is preserved as well. In other words, on IA-64, adjusting the saved IP value is all that is needed to restart a system call!

Let us now take a look at the register stack. First, we need to decide what to do when an alternate signal stack has been established with *sigaltstack()*. Because the alternate signal stack occupies a fixed-size memory area, it makes sense to employ the usual convention of placing the register backing store at the low end and the memory stack at the high end of the memory area. The two stacks then grow toward each other. This is indeed the solution that Linux/ia64 uses. Second, we need to consider how *do_signal()* can deal with the register stack. This turns out to be a thornier issue: When it is necessary to invoke a signal handler, it is not easy for *do_signal()* to set up the task state to make it appear as if the handler had been invoked with the three arguments *signum*, *siginfo*, and *sigcontext*. To see why, let us take another look at Figure 5.2 on page 220.

The configuration labeled "$_{(14)}$ execute *handler*" shows the state of the register stack at the time *do_signal()* gets invoked. As we can see, up to the point labeled B_1, the stacked registers contain user-level state; directly above that is the first kernel register frame, in our case, the register frame of *do_signal()*. This means that creating the register frame for the signal handler would require somehow inserting three additional stacked registers between the last **dirty** register and the first stacked register of the *do_signal()* frame.

Although we could do this, a little trick bypasses the issue completely: Because it is so difficult to deal with the register stack while executing in the kernel, why not simply defer dealing with it until execution is back at the user level? To achieve this, the kernel enlists the help of a small stub called the *signal trampoline* (*ia64_sigtramp()* in file arch/ia64/kernel/gate.S). This routine sets up the register stack, calls the signal handler, and returns control to the kernel through the *sigreturn()* system call. The only problem is that kernel code is normally not accessible from user level. Here is where the gate page comes into play. As described in Chapter 4, *Virtual Memory*, this page is mapped with access right XP0, which means that it is executable at the user level. Of course, the kernel still needs to find a way to pass the three signal handler arguments to the trampoline routine, but because the trampoline consists of kernel code, it is trivial to use a special calling convention. For example, the kernel could pass the arguments either on the user memory stack or in a couple of **scratch** registers. It turns out that passing them on the stack simplifies the implementation of user-level stack unwinders (see Chapter 6, *Stack Unwinding*). For this reason, Linux/ia64 passes them in the lowest three 64-bit words of the signal handler frame.

The net effect of the trampoline routine is that *do_signal()* can use the following three steps to arrange for the invocation of a signal handler:

1. Allocate a signal handler frame on the user memory stack with space for the siginfo and sigcontext structures and any other information that may have to be passed on the user memory stack (e.g., the signal handler arguments). If an alternate signal stack is in use, then this frame is allocated on that stack.

2. Set up the signal handler frame by copying the **scratch** state in the pt-regs structure to the sigcontext structure and by initializing the siginfo structure with the relevant information.

3. Modify the pt-regs structure on the kernel stack such that when the kernel returns, execution will begin at *ia64_sigtramp()* in the gate page. This entails setting the saved IP value to the address of *ia64_sigtramp()*.

Once these steps are accomplished, *do_signal()* can simply return. The kernel exit path takes care of restoring the modified user-level state from the pt-regs structure. The rfi instruction executed at the end of this path then returns execution to the user level and passes control to the signal trampoline.

It is important to understand that when execution starts in the signal trampoline, the register frame has *exactly* the shape and content that it had when the signal occurred. In our example from Figure 5.8, this would mean that the register frame would look exactly like it did when the st1 instruction started executing in routine *doit()*. The trampoline therefore has to be careful not to step on any of the registers in the current frame. To prevent this, it executes a cover instruction early on. This instruction moves the old register frame out of the way by pushing it into the **dirty** partition. If necessary, the register stack can be switched over to the alternate signal stack at this point.

Next, the trampoline can allocate its own register frame and copy the signal handler arguments to the appropriate output registers. This point also provides a convenient place to perform other actions. For example, instead of having *do_signal()* set up the sigcontext structure all by itself, it is possible to defer saving some of the **scratch** registers until here. Indeed, would it not be elegant if *all* **scratch** registers could be saved here? After all, this would turn the signal trampoline into the user-level equivalent of the kernel entry path. Of course, this is not really possible because, unlike the kernel entry path, the trampoline does not have access to the bank 0 registers. Thus, *do_signal()* unavoidably has to save at least a few **scratch** registers so that the trampoline has the temporary storage needed to get its job done. But any additional **scratch** registers, such as floating-point registers f10–f15, can be saved by the trampoline.

Once everything is ready, the signal handler is invoked with the normal calling conventions. Accordingly, when the handler is done, it can return with the usual br.ret instruction and transfer control back to the trampoline routine. As soon as that happens, preparations can begin for restoring the original task state. In particular, if the alternate signal stack is in use, the register stack has to be switched back to the original stack and any **scratch** registers that were saved by the trampoline have to be restored. In the last step, the signal trampoline invokes the kernel with the *sigreturn()* system call. The IA-64–specific *sigreturn() system call handler* (*sys_rt_sigreturn()* in file arch/ia64/kernel/entry.S) then finishes restoring the task state from the sigcontext structure and returns control to the user level, thereby completing the delivery of the signal.

Discussion

We would like to point out that even though there is no good reason to explicitly save the **preserved** registers before invoking a signal handler, most platforms other than IA-64 do so. This has two implications for Linux/ia64. First, suppose a signal handler needs to access the value of a **preserved** register as it existed at the time the signal occurred. Because the register is not saved in the sigcontext structure, its value could be in a number of different places: It could still be in the register itself, or it may have been saved on the memory stack or in a stacked register, for example. To find out, it would be necessary to decode and interpret the IA-64 unwind information (see Chapter 6, *Stack Unwinding*). While this is not particularly difficult, it is different from other platforms and relatively slow. For applications that need to do this frequently, another approach might be preferable: They could install a *shim signal handler* that saves the **preserved** registers before calling the real signal handler and restores them afterward. To facilitate this solution, Linux/ia64 declares the sigcontext structure to be large enough to hold the entire CPU state. This means that the shim signal handler can use the sigcontext structure itself to save the **preserved** registers.

BSD version (does not work):

```
void func (void *ctx) { ...; sigreturn(ctx); }
void sighandler (int signum, void *siginfo, void *ctx) {
    func(ctx);
}
```

UNIX 98 version (does not work):

```
void func (void *ctx) { ...; setcontext(ctx); }
void sighandler (int signum, void *siginfo, void *ctx) {
    func(ctx);
}
```

Portable version (does work):

```
void func (void *jb) { ...; siglongjmp(jb, 1); }
void sighandler (int signum) {
    jmp_buf jb;
    if (sigsetjmp(jb)) return;
    func(jb);
}
```

Figure 5.11. Short-circuiting out of a signal handler on Linux/ia64.

Indeed, the shim layer approach could be implemented in a way that is completely transparent to the application. For example, a compatibility library could provide a wrapper for *sigaction()* that would maintain its own sigaction table and arrange signal handling to always start in the shim signal handler. With this approach, applications that frequently need to access the **preserved** state could simply be linked against this compatibility library and, from their perspective, it would look as if the kernel had saved the entire CPU state in sigcontext. In other words, not saving the **preserved** registers in the kernel provides optimal performance for the vast majority of applications that do not access them, yet still leaves open the possibility of also supporting the other applications in near optimal fashion.

The second implication of not saving the **preserved** registers in the kernel is that the sigcontext structure cannot be used to execute a *short-circuit return* from a function called by a signal handler. BSD UNIX supported this as illustrated in the top part of Figure 5.11. In this example, the signal handler *sighandler()* invokes a subroutine called *func()*. This function can then force an immediate return from the signal handler by calling the *sigreturn()* system call on the *ctx* pointer that it received as an argument. Even though Linux/ia64 implements a system call of the same name, a direct call to *sigreturn()* does not work because *sighandler()* and *func()* may have modified some of the **preserved** registers. Short-circuiting execution with *sigreturn()* would fail to restore the original contents of these registers and would likely cause the application to crash as soon as execution returns from the signal handler.

This issue is not just a BSD compatibility issue, because UNIX 98 provides equivalent functionality with the *setcontext()* system call [52]. This is illustrated in the middle part of Figure 5.11. If we compare the UNIX 98 version with the BSD UNIX version, we see that the only difference is the name of the system call. This also would not work on Linux/ia64 because it implements *setcontext()* not as a system call but as a library routine that can be used only for synchronous context switching.

Given that Linux/ia64 supports neither the BSD nor the UNIX 98 approach, what should an application do? The solution is simple and illustrated in the bottom part of Figure 5.11. As we can see there, *sighandler()* declares a local jump buffer variable *jb*, calls *sigsetjmp()* on it, and, if it returns a non-zero value, returns immediately. When this function is called by the signal handler, it saves the **preserved** registers in the jump buffer and returns with a value of 0. Execution then continues normally and *func()* is invoked. Now, to perform a short-circuit return, this function can call *siglongjmp()*, passing it the pointer to the previously initialized jump buffer, *jb*. This has the effect of restoring the **preserved** registers and making *sigsetjmp()* return a second time, but this time with a non-zero return value, so that the signal handler will return immediately. In other words, the overall effect is identical to the BSD *sigreturn()* and the UNIX 98 *setcontext()* system call.

If we compare the *sigsetjmp()* solution with the other two, we see that the structure of the code is nearly identical. The only major difference is that the signal handler has to invoke *sigsetjmp()* before calling any other function. Even this small difference could be hidden with a shim signal handler. The idea would be to add wrappers for *sigreturn()* and *setcontext()* to a compatibility library such that their behavior would match the corresponding BSD and UNIX 98 system call. However, because the *sigsetjmp()* approach is more portable, it could make more sense to avoid the compatibility issues altogether and modify the application to directly use the *sigsetjmp()* approach. This is especially true given that beyond being portable, it also performs well: The kernel saves only the **scratch** registers, and *sigsetjmp()* saves only the **preserved** registers, so there is no duplication of work.

5.4   KERNEL ACCESS TO USER MEMORY

When calls are made across the user/kernel boundary, it is almost always necessary to pass along some data. Most of the time, this data is passed in registers, which is unproblematic apart from the minor complication of IA-64 NaT values (see Section 5.2.4). However, when data is passed through memory, providing safe and efficient access to this data can be quite tricky. First, let us observe that it is always the kernel that accesses user-space memory. For safety reasons, the user level does not have access to kernel space and therefore could not possibly copy data to or from kernel space. However, even the kernel has to be careful when accessing user space: if the kernel were to attempt to write to a user page that is mapped read-only, a fatal page fault could occur inside the kernel. Similarly, if the user were to pass a bogus pointer, dereferencing that pointer could cause a fatal page fault because the memory at that address may not be mapped at all. Even worse, if the bogus pointer happened to be a kernel address, dereferencing it could access memory that the user level has no right to access or could cause the machine to crash.

```
/* checking validity of user memory area: */
#define VERIFY_READ                    /* check for read access */
#define VERIFY_WRITE                   /* check for write access */
int access_ok(type, addr, size);       /* check if memory area is inaccessible */
int verify_area(type, addr, size);     /* return −EFAULT if area inaccessible */

/* accessing data in user memory: */
int put_user(val, ptr);                /* copy a single value to user memory */
int get_user(var, ptr);                /* copy a single value from user mem. */
long copy_to_user(to, from, count);    /* copy memory area to user memory */
long copy_from_user(to, from, count);  /* copy memory area from user mem. */
long clear_user(to, count);            /* zero user memory area */
long strlen_user(str);                 /* return length of string in user mem. */
long strnlen_user(str, count);         /* return length of bounded user string */
long strncpy_from_user(to, from, count); /* copy bounded string from user mem. */

/* enabling and disabling validity checking: */
typedef mm_segment_t;                  /* segment descriptor type */
#define KERNEL_DS                      /* kernel data segment */
#define USER_DS                        /* user data segment */
mm_segment_t get_fs();                 /* get active data segment */
set_fs(ds);                            /* set active data segment */
int segment_eq(a, b);                  /* test two segment for equality */
```

Figure 5.12. Kernel interface to copy data across user/kernel boundary.

To prevent such problems, the kernel always accesses user space through the *user memory access interface* (file include/asm/uaccess.h). This interface, shown in Figure 5.12, provides all the facilities needed to access user-space memory safely and efficiently. The interface is implemented by platform-specific code to make possible its tight integration with the particular features and requirements of each CPU architecture. The basic idea behind this interface is that the validity of a pointer passed to the kernel from the user level can be verified in two steps: First, verify that the memory area identified by the pointer lies entirely inside user space. Second, if the memory area is inside user space, check the vm-area lists of the virtual memory system (see Chapter 4, *Virtual Memory*) to verify that the memory area corresponds to valid (mapped) memory and that the memory is accessible (readable or writable). The challenge is, of course, to implement these steps as efficiently as possible and without race conditions.

Before getting into implementation aspects, let us take a closer look at the definition of the user memory access interface. As Figure 5.12 shows, the first part of the interface supports checking the validity of user memory areas. For this purpose, it defines two platform-specific flags, VERIFY_READ and VERIFY_WRITE, which are used in conjunction with the *access_ok()* and *verify_area()* routines. The former checks whether a user-space memory area is valid for read or write access. It expects three arguments. The first is *type*, which must be VERIFY_READ to check for read access only or VERIFY_WRITE to check for both read and write access. The second argument, *addr*, is the starting address of the user memory area, and the third argument, *size*, is the size of the area in bytes. The routine returns **false** if the memory area is *definitely* invalid and **true** if it *may* be valid. The routine may sometimes return **true** even though the memory area may not be completely accessible. For this reason, even after the memory area is checked with *access_ok()*, it is critical to use only the routines discussed below to access user space. Put differently, the kernel must *never* access user space directly by dereferencing a pointer, even after checking the pointer with *access_ok()*. It is easiest to think of *access_ok()* as being the routine that implements the first step of verifying the validity of user memory: It simply checks that the memory area lies completely within user space. The *verify_area()* routine works like *access_ok()*, except that it returns −EFAULT instead of **false** if the memory is inaccessible and 0 otherwise.

The second portion of the interface shown in Figure 5.12 consists of the routines that actually access user memory. Those routines are called the **checked** versions because they implicitly call *access_ok()* to verify that the memory area being accessed is valid. For each of these routines there is also an **unchecked** version with the same name except for a prefix of two underscore characters. For example, the **unchecked** version of *put_user()* is called *__put_user()*. The **checked** versions are safer to use because there is no danger of forgetting to call *access_ok()* first. However, to access large user memory areas, it is often more efficient to use a single call to *access_ok()* to check the validity of the entire memory area and then use the **unchecked** access routines to read or write individual components of the area.

Let us now turn our attention to the individual access routines. The *put_user()* routine deposits a value in user memory. The first argument, *val*, contains the value to deposit, and the second argument, *ptr*, determines both the type and address of the user memory location at which the value is to be stored. The type of the memory location can be arbitrary as long as it has a size of 1, 2, 4, or 8 bytes (on 32-bit platforms, the maximum size is limited to 4 bytes). The routine returns 0 on success and −EFAULT if the value could not be deposited for some reason. Because *put_user()* is polymorphic, it necessarily has to be implemented as a C preprocessor macro. The complementary routine to *put_user()* is *get_user()* because it reads a value from user memory. The first argument must be the variable that is to receive the value read from user memory. The second argument, *ptr*, again determines both the type and address of the user memory location from which the value is read. Like *put_user()*, the location can have any type that fits in 1, 2, 4, or 8 bytes.

The *get_user()* and *put_user()* routines would in theory be sufficient to copy arbitrary user memory areas. However, they would be inefficient for copying large amounts of memory. For this reason, the interface also provides *copy_to_user()* and *copy_from_user()*. As their names suggest, the former copies data from kernel to user memory, and the latter copies data from user to kernel memory. Both routines expect three arguments: The address of the target memory area is passed in argument *to*, and the address of the source memory area is passed in argument *from*. The number of bytes to copy is passed in the third argument, *count*. One peculiarity of these routines is that they return the number of bytes that *failed* to get copied. That is, on success, these routines return 0. Another is that if *copy_from_user()* fails to read part of the user memory area, it fills the remainder of the kernel memory area with zeroes. This is a safety measure and ensures that the kernel does not inadvertently read uninitialized kernel memory that might still contain sensitive data, such as a password that belongs to another task.

The next specialized routine is *clear_user()*. It provides an efficient means for zeroing large user memory areas and takes two arguments: The first one, *to*, is the starting address of the user memory area, and the second one, *count*, is the number of bytes to clear. As with the *copy* routines, the return value specifies the number of bytes that failed to get cleared so that, on success, 0 is returned.

The kernel frequently needs to access ASCII NUL-terminated strings in user memory. To support strings efficiently, the interface provides three additional routines: *strlen_user()*, *strnlen_user()*, and *strncpy_from_user()*. The first two can be used to determine the length of the user memory string at the address passed in the first argument, *str*. For *strnlen_user()*, a second argument, *count*, limits the maximum string length: If a NUL terminator is not found within the first *count* bytes of the string, *strnlen_user()* returns the value *count*. The *strncpy_from_user()* routine can be used to copy a bounded string from user memory. It expects three arguments: *to*, the address of the kernel memory buffer to copy the string to; *from*, the starting address of the user memory string; and *count*, the maximum length of the string. On success, it returns the length of the string copied (not counting the terminating NUL character if there is one), and on failure it returns −EFAULT.

5.4.1   Example: How *gettimeofday()* returns the timeval structure

To get a better idea of how the user memory access interface works, let us look at how the *gettimeofday()* system call handler could be implemented. In this example, we focus on how the *timeval structure* (struct timeval in file include/linux/time.h) is returned and ignore the fact that this system call can also be used to obtain time-zone information.

The code below shows the safest and perhaps most obvious way of implementing this fictitious version of the *gettimeofday()* system call handler:

```
long sys_gettimeofday (struct timeval *tv) {
    struct timeval now = get_current_time();
    if (   put_user(now.tv_sec, &tv->tv_sec) != 0 ||
           put_user(now.tv_usec, &tv->tv_usec) != 0)
        return -EFAULT;
    return 0;
}
```

We can see that the handler obtains the current time by calling *get_current_time()* and storing the result in the local variable *now*. This variable is a timeval structure, so it contains two members, *tv_sec* and *tv_usec*, which give the current time in seconds and microseconds since the epoch. Both values need to be copied to the user address passed in argument *tv*. Because both values are 8 bytes in size (on a 64-bit platform), the copying can be achieved through two separate calls to *put_user()*. If either call returns a value other than 0, the address passed in *tv* is invalid for some reason and the handler returns with −EFAULT. On the other hand, if both calls succeed, the handler returns 0, indicating successful completion.

While the above version would work fine, it is inefficient in the sense that the two *put_user()* calls will implicitly result in two separate calls to *access_ok()*. Because the members *tv_sec* and *tv_usec* are adjacent, we can avoid the double calls by calling *access_ok()* explicitly to check the entire timeval structure and using the **unchecked** version of *put_user()* to access the individual members. The method is illustrated below.

```
long sys_gettimeofday (struct timeval *tv) {
    struct timeval now = get_current_time();
    if (    !access_ok(VERIFY_WRITE, tv, sizeof(*tv)) ||
            __put_user(now.tv_sec, &tv->tv_sec) != 0 ||
            __put_user(now.tv_usec, &tv->tv_usec) != 0)
        return -EFAULT;
    return 0;
}
```

An even more efficient version is possible if we are willing to copy the entire timeval structure from kernel to user memory. This is illustrated by the third and final version of the *gettimeofday()* system call handler:

```
long sys_gettimeofday (struct timeval *tv) {
    struct timeval now = get_current_time();
    if (copy_to_user(tv, &now, sizeof(*tv)) != 0)
        return -EFAULT;
    return 0;
}
```

This version is not only efficient to execute, but it is also shorter than the previous two versions. This is not unusual; *copy_to_user()* and *copy_from_user()* are often preferred for these reasons. However, there is one caveat for *copy_to_user()*: The routine copies each and every byte of the memory area, so there is a danger of leaking kernel data to user space if a structure with padding is copied. For example, on most modern platforms, the structure

```
struct struct_with_padding {
    char ch;
    int l;
};
```

would contain 3 bytes of padding between the members *ch* and *l*. The padding ensures that *l* is aligned to a 4-byte boundary.

To avoid leaking bits because of padding, the kernel normally explicitly declares any padding that might be necessary and then initializes that padding to 0 before copying it to user space. When this is not possible, an alternative solution is for the kernel to clear the entire structure, e.g., with a call to *memset()*, before setting the contents of the structure members. This also ensures that all padding will have a harmless value of 0. A third solution is, of course, not to use *copy_to_user()* at all and instead use an approach similar to the one used in the first two versions of *sys_gettimeofday()*. Because each of the three solutions has its strengths and weaknesses, they are all used throughout the kernel.

5.4.2   Disabling validity checking

The last portion of the interface shown in Figure 5.12 consists of routines that make it possible to use the interface for accessing kernel memory. On the surface, this may sound silly: By definition, the kernel can access its own memory so there should be no need to go through this interface, right? It turns out that this argument is flawed: In practice, several system call handlers need to be called from within the kernel itself. Indeed, as described in Section 5.2, the kernel sometimes even performs system calls on its own. In both cases, system call arguments that normally contain user memory pointers may now contain kernel pointers. Of course, the user memory access interface ordinarily rejects such pointers, meaning that the system call handler would fail to execute properly. For example, suppose a piece of kernel code wanted to open the file /etc/motd. We naively might think we could do this simply by calling the *open()* system call handler as shown below:

```
int fd = sys_open("/etc/motd", O_RDONLY, 0);
```

Unfortunately, this would not work because the string "/etc/motd" would have an address inside the identity-mapped kernel segment and would therefore be rejected when *sys_open()* attempts to access it with the user memory access interface.

To avoid this kind of problem, the Linux kernel implements a concept called *segments*. There are two segments: the *user segment* and the *kernel segment*, and for each task, the kernel maintains a variable in the task structure to keep track of which segment the task is currently operating in. If a task is operating in the user segment, the user memory access interface operates normally, as described previously. However, when a task operates in the kernel segment, the user memory access interface performs no validity checks at all. That is, it effectively trusts the caller to pass only valid arguments.

From the perspective of the user access memory interface, segments are simply a means to turn on or off the validity checking of user memory areas. However, segments can have additional, platform-specific meaning. For example, on the IA-32 platform, segments also play a role in the virtual memory system (see Chapter 11, *IA-32 Compatibility*). For this reason, the data type of a segment and the values used for the kernel and data segments are platform specific, and Figure 5.12 does not provide concrete values for them. Instead, it simply lists the segment type with the name **mm_segment_t** and the kernel and user segments with the names KERNEL_DS and USER_DS, respectively.

The interface defines three routines to manipulate segments: *get_fs()*, *set_fs()*, and *segment_eq()*. The *get_fs()* routine obtains the segment that the currently executing task is operating in. The return value is either USER_DS (user segment) or KERNEL_DS (kernel segment). For activation of a particular segment for the current task, *set_fs()* can be used. It expects a single argument, *ds*, the segment that should be activated. The third routine, *segment_eq()*, compares two segments for equality. With these routines, a correct version of the kernel code trying to open file /etc/motd could look like this:

```
int fd; mm_segment_t old_segment = get_fs();
set_fs(KERNEL_DS);
fd = sys_open("/etc/motd", O_RDONLY, 0);
set_fs(old_segment);
```

This code temporarily disables address checking by calling *set_fs()* to activate the kernel segment for the currently running task. The return value is saved in the local variable *old_segment*. With validity checking disabled, *sys_open()* can be called and, assuming the file /etc/motd really does exist and is readable, will succeed now. In the last step, the code restores the previously active segment by calling *set_fs()* again, this time passing it *old_segment*. It is important not to forget this step because otherwise the user level would end up with unrestricted access to kernel memory!

5.4.3   IA-64 implementation

Each platform has a fair amount of flexibility in deciding how and where the validity checking is implemented. In extreme cases, it could be implemented entirely in *access_ok()* or entirely in the actual access routines, such as *put_user()*. Neither extreme is ideal: The former would require visiting the vm-area list to ensure that each and every byte is mapped with the appropriate access rights. Moreover, the routine would have to protect itself against race conditions and would have to ensure that the vm-area list does not change between the time *access_ok()* is called and the time user memory is accessed. Conversely, deferring validity checking until user memory is accessed is not ideal because it would often cause the same checks to be executed over and over again.

The compromise adopted by Linux/ia64 is to use *access_ok()* to perform a quick check to verify that the memory area being accessed lies within the space selected by the active segment (user space if the segment is USER_DS, and kernel space otherwise). If this check succeeds, the user memory access routines will go ahead and access user memory, optimistically assuming that the accessed memory is indeed valid. But what happens if the memory turns out to be invalid, e.g., because it is not mapped? In that case, a page fault would occur and, because the memory is invalid (not mapped) and the access is performed from within the kernel, would normally cause a kernel panic. To prevent this, the user memory access routines inform the page fault handler when they are about to access user memory. Should an access trigger a page fault due to invalid memory, the page fault handler checks whether the fault was caused by an access to user space and, if so, executes a recovery action instead of panicking the kernel. The advantage of this middle-ground solution is that it can access user memory with little overhead, provided the memory is valid. Usually, the memory *is* valid, which means that the scheme is highly efficient in practice.

Implementing *access_ok()*

Now that we know what *access_ok()* should do, let us explore how to implement it efficiently. When the active segment is the kernel segment, the job of *access_ok()* is easy: Any address is valid, and hence the routine can simply return **true**. The check is more complex when the user segment is active. Consider the address-space layout illustrated in Figure 5.13. If we assume that the user segment (USER_DS) extends from address 0 to TASK_SIZE $- 1$, checking whether the *len* bytes starting at *addr* are contained entirely in the user segment requires evaluating the expression

$$(addr < \text{TASK\_SIZE}) \wedge (len \leq \text{TASK\_SIZE}) \wedge (addr + len \leq \text{TASK\_SIZE}).$$

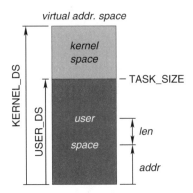

Figure 5.13. Checking whether memory area is inside a segment.

This would mean that each call to *access_ok()* would require at least six operations: three comparisons, an addition, and two conjunctions. To simplify this, the IA-64 version of this routine exploits the fact that the kernel always accesses user memory sequentially and in order of increasing addresses. Recall from Chapter 4, *Virtual Memory*, that Linux/ia64 places a *guard page* at the beginning of the kernel space, i.e., at address TASK_SIZE. This page is guaranteed not to be mapped, and hence any access to it would result in a page fault. This makes it possible to simplify the previous expression to just

$$addr < \text{TASK\_SIZE}.$$

This check alone ensures that the first memory access is within user space. All subsequent accesses will go toward increasingly high addresses. If the memory area is invalid, this could eventually lead to an access inside kernel space. However, because user memory is accessed sequentially, it is guaranteed that the first such access would hit in the guard page, trigger a page fault, and cause the access to fail. In other words, even though the IA-64 version of *access_ok()* checks only that the starting address of the user memory area lies within user space, the combination of the kernel accessing memory sequentially and the presence of the guard page still ensures proper validity checking.

The last trick is to pick suitable values for the kernel and user segments. Given that Linux/ia64 does not use segments for any other purpose, it is possible to base the choice solely on the needs of *access_ok()*. To this effect, Linux/ia64 adopts the convention that the segment value simply represents the maximum address that is valid for the given segment. Accordingly, the constants KERNEL_DS and USER_DS are defined as follows:

```
#define KERNEL_DS    0xffffffffffffffff
#define USER_DS      (TASK_SIZE - 1)
```

With these definitions, the IA-64 version of *access_ok()* could look like this:

```
#define access_ok(type,addr,size) ((addr) <= get_fs())
```

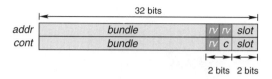

Figure 5.14. Format of Linux/ia64 exception table entry.

If the active segment is the kernel segment (KERNEL_DS), the IA-64 version of *access_ok()* will accept any address; if the active segment is the user segment (USER_DS), this version will accept any address in the range from 0 to TASK_SIZE − 1, just as desired.

One problem remains, however: This version of *access_ok()* would grant user-level access to the virtually-mapped linear page table and to unimplemented virtual addresses (see Chapter 4, *Virtual Memory*). Both could be fatal for the kernel! To guard against this, *access_ok()* also needs to verify that when the user segment is active, the region offset of *addr* is within the region's page-table-mapped space. With this additional check, *access_ok()* is safe and will return **true** if and only if address *addr* is a valid address for the active segment.

Using poor man's exception handling to efficiently access user memory

As described earlier, the user memory access routines assume that accesses to user memory succeed and, if they fail unexpectedly, recover with assistance from the page fault handler. For this assumption to work out, the page fault handler needs to know when a user memory access is about to occur. In principle, this could be achieved by implementing the user memory access routines such that they register their intent to access user memory before actually performing the access. This intent could be recorded in any data structure that the page fault handler has access to, such as the task structure. This scheme would work but would be needlessly slow. Instead, Linux/ia64 uses a more streamlined implementation that is based on the *poor man's exception handling* mechanism that was first implemented in 1996 by Richard Henderson for Linux v2.1.7. The basic idea behind this mechanism is to mark every instruction that accesses user memory in a special *exception table* and to associate a recovery action with each such instruction. If an instruction triggers a page fault because it is accessing invalid memory, the page fault handler searches the exception table and, if an entry for the faulting instruction is found, executes the associated recovery action instead of causing a kernel panic.

In the case of Linux/ia64, exception table entries have the format shown in Figure 5.14. Each entry consists of two signed 32-bit words: The first one, *addr*, specifies the address of the instruction that may cause a page fault; the second one, *cont*, specifies the address of the instruction at which execution should resume after a page fault. So that they fit in 32 bits, they are expressed as global-pointer relative addresses. In both words, the instruction address is expressed as a bundle address and a slot number. The bundle address occupies the top 28 bits, the slot number the least significant 2 bits. In both words, bits 2 and 3 are available to encode other information. Three are reserved (shown as **rv** in the figure), and bit 2 of the second word is the c bit that affects how the recovery action is executed.

```
get_user_int:
[l1:]  ld4 r8 = [r32]          // this instruction may fault
[l2:]  br.ret rp

       .section "__ex_table"
       data4 @gprel(l1)        // encode addr word
       data4 @gprel(l2)        // encode cont word
```

Figure 5.15. Assembly code to read 32-bit value from user memory.

When a page fault is triggered by an instruction with an entry in the exception table, the page fault handler executes a recovery action that has the following three effects at the point of the fault:

- Register r8 is set to −EFAULT.

- If the c bit is set, register r9 is cleared to 0.

- Execution is resumed at the instruction address encoded in the *cont* word.

Because registers r8 and r9 as well as the instruction pointer ip are all registers that are saved in the pt-regs structure created when the kernel is reentered because of the page fault, executing this recovery action in the page fault handler requires just simple manipulation of the pt-regs structure.

With the format of the exception table defined, the next question is how this table can be built. At first, it may seem difficult to reliably gather all the instructions that access user memory and create exception table entries for them. Fortunately, the ELF object file format used by Linux offers an elegant solution: ELF supports an arbitrary number of sections, and Linux uses a separate section called __ex_table just to hold the exception table. This makes it possible to construct the exception table entries incrementally, as the instructions that access user memory are built into the kernel.

To see how this all fits together, let us look at a concrete example. Suppose we wanted to write an assembly routine called *get_user_int()* that reads an unsigned 32-bit word from the user memory address passed in r32. If successful, the routine should return the word in register r8. If the access fails for any reason, the routine should return −EFAULT in r8. With the Linux/ia64 poor man's exception handling mechanism, this could be accomplished with the code shown in Figure 5.15.

This routine obviously has the desired effect when it is called with a valid user address in r32: The first instruction (ld4) will read the 32-bit value into r8 (and zero-extend it to 64 bits), and the second instruction (br.ret) will return control to the caller. Of course, the interesting part in this code comprises the three directives that follow the second instruction. The first directive (.**section**) switches the current section to the exception table section (__ex_table). The two **data4** directives encode the exception table entry for the ld4 instruction: The first one adds the global-pointer relative address of the ld4 instruction to the exception table, and the second one encodes the continuation point as the address of the return instruction br.ret. In these directives, **@gprel** (*l*) is an assembler expression that calculates the global-pointer relative address ($l - gp$), and the **data4** directive truncates away the top 32 bits of the resulting value and places the truncated value in the current section. If the routine needed to clear register r9 on a fault, it could request that by encoding the value **@gprel (12) +4** in the second word. Note that labels 11 and 12 are surrounded by square brackets. The brackets tell the assembler to treat the labels as tags that encode the bundle address in the top 60 bits and the instruction slot number in the least significant 2 bits—just the format needed for the exception table!

The example demonstrates how an individual entry can be placed in the exception table but does not answer the question of how the final table is built. The final table is created automatically by the ELF linker: When the linker builds the final kernel image, it gathers all the __ex_table sections from the individual object files and merges them into a single output section of the same name. What is even better, the linker merges the sections in order of increasing addresses, meaning that the final table will be sorted by address. This means that the page fault handler can use a binary search to efficiently locate the exception table entry for any given address.

Now, let us see what happens when *get_user_int()* is called with an invalid user address: The ld4 instruction will cause a page fault, and the page fault handler will search the exception handler table for an entry for address 11. The entry created by the first **data4** directive will match, and as soon as the page fault handler finds this entry, it executes the recovery action encoded in the second word. In our example, this action will have the effect of setting r8 to −EFAULT and resuming execution at 12. Because the c bit is cleared, the value in r9 will not be modified. The overall effect is just what we wanted: In case the access fails, the routine returns with error code −EFAULT in register r8.

With the poor man's exception handling mechanism explained, it is straightforward to see how the various user memory access routines can be realized on Linux/ia64. However, it is worth noting that the *get_user()* and *put_user()* routines can be implemented with inline assembly code directives. This means that not only the *access_ok()* routine but also the actual user memory access can be inlined entirely at the call site. The net effect is that a call to *get_user()* or *put_user()* has an overhead of just a handful of extra instructions when the access succeeds. Of course, when the access fails, the resulting page fault, exception table search, and recovery are quite costly, but applications normally do not do this (not intentionally at least), so performance in the case of failure is not an issue. Put differently, the poor man's exception handling mechanism makes it possible to access user memory almost as efficiently as accessing ordinary kernel memory and without introducing the complexity of the more general exception handling mechanisms that are provided by higher-level languages such as C++ or Java [8, 66].

5.5 SUMMARY

This chapter explored the key issues related to crossing the user/kernel boundary. In particular, the first section described the basic mechanisms used to enter the kernel on an interruption and to exit it once the interruption is handled. The second section introduced the facilities needed for handling system calls and described the implementation used by Linux/ia64. Signals were discussed in the third section. As described there, they can be viewed as an upcall facility that lets the kernel invoke user-level signal handlers. With the mechanisms that move *execution* across the user/kernel boundary explained, the fourth section described how *data* can be transferred across this boundary. In addition to security, performance is a major concern for these transfers. Linux/ia64, like several other Linux platforms, solves this problem with an elegant and fast solution based on poor man's exception handling.

Chapter 6

Stack Unwinding

When a task enters the kernel from the user level, it begins executing some handler, such as a system call handler or an interrupt handler. To get its job done, this handler typically needs to call other kernel functions, and those may call their own helper functions. Each time a new function is called, a *call frame* is pushed onto the kernel stack. Thus, at any given time the task can be characterized by the sequence of call frames that caused the current function to be invoked. This sequence is called the *call chain* or the *backtrace* of the task. Occasionally, the kernel needs to determine the backtrace of a task; to do this, it has to *unwind* its kernel stack. Why the kernel needs this functionality and how it can be realized on IA-64 is the subject of this chapter.

Before diving into the mechanics of stack unwinding, let us take a look at why the kernel may have to unwind a stack.

- When a task crashes while executing in the kernel, Linux prints an error message and then terminates the offending task. The error message includes a backtrace that shows the sequence of function calls that led to the crash.

- Linux defines the *wait channel* of a blocked task to be the kernel function that was executing last before the task blocked. The name of this function can give an idea as to what the task was doing at the time it blocked. This is often useful for debugging. At the user level, the ps lax command can be invoked and in the resulting output, the wait channel is listed in column WCHAN.

- To aid debugging, the kernel has a few places at which it uses a platform-specific function called *thread_saved_pc()* to determine the instruction pointer in the second-last call frame of a blocked task.

- Kernel debuggers such as kdb need to be able to access and display various information about the call frames of blocked tasks [41].

In each of the above cases, the kernel needs to be able to unwind the call chain. For backtraces, it is usually necessary to unwind all the way to the beginning of the call chain, but for some operations, such as displaying the wait channel, it may only be necessary to unwind one or two levels of the chain.

To get a better sense of what is involved in stack unwinding, let us start by taking a look at the call frames used by traditional CISC architectures, such as IA-32. CISC architectures

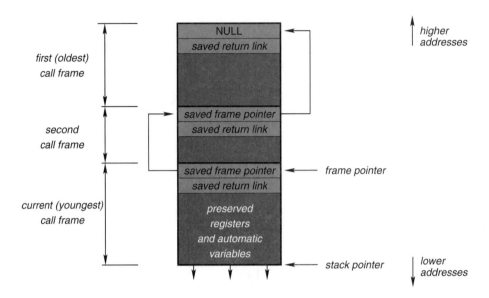

Figure 6.1. Typical example of a traditional call chain.

tend to use a rigid, hardware-defined format for call frames. While the details of the format differ from one architecture to another, they generally all look similar to the one illustrated in Figure 6.1. The figure assumes that the stack grows toward lower addresses. The stack pointer defines the lowest address in the call frame of the currently executing function. Since the stack pointer can vary as the function is executing, a separate *frame pointer* identifies the beginning (highest address) of the current call frame. Unlike the stack pointer, its value is guaranteed to remain the same while the function is executing.

Now, the figure shows that at the beginning of each frame, two words are used to store the *saved frame pointer* and the *saved return link*, respectively. The first word gives us the frame pointer value of the previous call frame. By following this pointer, we can unravel the call chain level by level. The start of the call chain is normally indicated with a NULL value in the saved frame pointer word of the first (oldest) call frame. The saved return link in each frame gives us the return address of function that created the frame. With this type of call frame format, printing the backtrace of a task simply requires traversing the frame pointer chain (youngest to oldest) and printing the return link of each frame encountered along the way.

On modern architectures, stack unwinding is not so simple. To achieve the best possible performance, the software conventions for these architectures avoid performing any unnecessary work and provide as much flexibility as possible. For example, on IA-64, the frame pointer is maintained only when strictly needed, and even then it can be stored wherever convenient: on the memory stack, in a stacked register, a static **preserved** register, or, under certain circumstances, even in a **scratch** register.

Clearly, the old approach of simply following the frame pointer chain no longer works. In some cases, it is possible to reverse-engineer the frame pointer chain by reading and interpreting the machine code of the functions that are being unwound. Unfortunately, this tends to be both fragile and slow. IA-64 takes a different approach that guarantees safe and relatively efficient stack unwinding. It is based on the idea of attaching a separate data structure to each function. This data structure is called the *unwind descriptor list* and contains all the information that may be required to unwind a particular function. Indeed, the information is complete enough to permit reconstruction of the *entire* **preserved** CPU state. Of course, this completeness comes at a price: though faster than code inspection, decoding the unwind information is complicated and quite slow.

Given that the Linux kernel uses stack unwinding only to improve a few error messages and to provide debug information such as wait channels, the question arises whether it is really worthwhile to introduce the complexity of full stack unwinding into the Linux/ia64 kernel. The answer is not obvious. However, what tips the balance in favor of full unwind support is that it helps simplify and, indeed, greatly speed up some performance-critical paths such as the one used to deliver a signal (see Chapter 5, *Kernel Entry and Exit*). This speedup occurs because with full unwind support, the kernel can avoid creating a switch-stack structure when delivering a signal. In other words, Linux/ia64 uses unwind information not just for debugging but also to speed up kernel execution.

The remainder of this chapter is divided into five sections. The first section briefly describes how the IA-64 unwind information is stored in ELF object files such as the kernel image or kernel modules. The next section describes the unwind interface that is implemented by the Linux/ia64 *kernel unwinder*. A few examples illustrating its use are also presented. The third section introduces the assembler directives that must be used in handwritten assembly code. Without these directives, it would not be possible to unwind through handwritten assembly code, so assembly programmers need to be familiar with the material presented here. The fourth section describes how the kernel unwinder is implemented and introduces the techniques that permit the kernel to unwind stack frames efficiently, despite the complexity involved. The last section provides a summary and some concluding remarks.

6.1   IA-64 ELF UNWIND SECTIONS

The IA-64 software conventions require that each function in a program be accompanied by a list of descriptors that specify the information required for stack unwinding. This information is normally generated automatically by a compiler and placed in a pair of special ELF sections, called .IA_64.unwind and .IA_64.unwind_info, respectively [32]. The structure of these sections and their relationship are illustrated in Figure 6.2.

The section called .IA_64.unwind contains the *unwind table*. Each entry in this table has a fixed size of 24 bytes and associates a range of instruction addresses with a pointer to additional unwind information. Functions that consist of a single block of consecutive instructions have one entry in this table. Functions with multiple discontiguous instruction blocks may have multiple entries. The first word in an unwind table entry (start) gives the

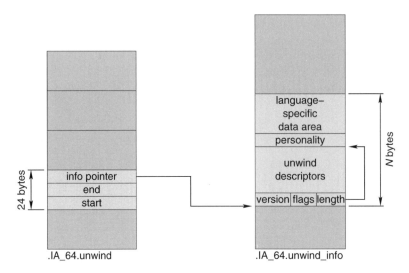

Figure 6.2. Format of IA-64 ELF unwind sections.

starting address of the address range covered by this entry, and the second word (end) gives
its end address. The third word is a pointer to an *unwind information block*, which is a
variable-sized data structure stored in the .IA_64.unwind_info section. All three addresses
are specified as text-segment relative addresses, and the table entries are sorted in order of
increasing start address.

Each unwind information block in the .IA_64.unwind_info section starts with a header
word that contains sundry information such as a version code, a flag word, and a length
field. The header word is followed by a list of unwind descriptors that contain all the information required for stack unwinding. This list is followed by a personality word and a
language-specific data area. Both are needed for exception handling purposes only. Since
the Linux kernel is written in C, a language that does not support exception handling, the
personality word is always NULL and the language-specific data area is empty. The format
of the unwind descriptors is defined by the IA-64 software conventions [28]. We will see
some examples later in this chapter. Occasionally it is useful to be able to inspect them. On
Linux/ia64, the `readelf` program can be used for this purpose. For example, the command `readelf -u vmlinux` would display the unwind descriptors contained in the
ELF file called vmlinux.

Although all the information required for reliable stack unwinding is present in the
unwind sections, directly using that information would be difficult and inefficient because it
is stored in a tightly encoded format. To solve this problem, the Linux/ia64 kernel provides
an unwind interface that abstracts the complexities of the encoding format and provides a
convenient way to unwind a stack at runtime. We describe this interface next.

unw_init();	/* initialize unwinder */
void ***unw_add_unwind_table**(*str*, *base*, *gp*, *start*, *end*);	/* add unwind table */
unw_remove_unwind_table(*handle*);	/* remove unwind table */

Figure 6.3. Linux/ia64 kernel interface to manage unwind tables.

6.2 THE KERNEL UNWIND INTERFACE

The Linux/ia64 kernel unwind interface consists of three groups of routines. The first group, shown in Figure 6.3, manages unwind tables. The second, shown in Figure 6.4, provides routines to navigate a call chain. The third group, shown in Figure 6.5, provides accessor routines that permit reading and writing the CPU state represented by a call frame. Each group of routines is described in more detail below. It should be noted that the unwind interface presented here is available only on IA-64. Other Linux platforms continue to use ad hoc methods for stack unwinding.

6.2.1 Managing unwind tables

The first routine in Figure 6.3 is *unw_init()*. As its name suggests, it takes care of initializing the kernel unwinder. Apart from initializing various bits, the main purpose of this function is to register the kernel's own unwind table. The routine is called as early as possible in the bootstrap procedure to ensure that a backtrace can be printed in case something goes wrong and the kernel crashes (see Chapter 10, *Booting*, for a description of the Linux bootstrap procedure). To enable such an early call, the routine must not allocate memory dynamically. Otherwise, it could not be called until one of the Linux kernel memory allocators has been initialized.

When a kernel module is loaded, its unwind table must be registered. The *unw_add-_unwind_table()* routine serves this purpose. Argument *str* is a character string that contains the name of the kernel module, *base* is the base address of the module's text segment, and *gp* is the global pointer (GP) of the module (see Chapter 2, *IA-64 Architecture*). The final two arguments, *start* and *end*, point to the beginning and the end of the module's .IA_64.unwind section. If the routine fails for any reason (e.g., because the kernel is out of memory), it returns a NULL pointer. Otherwise, it returns a handle that uniquely identifies the module's unwind information.

When a module is removed from the kernel, its unwind table is no longer needed and can be removed with *unw_remove_unwind_table()*. The only argument to this routine is the handle that was returned by *unw_add_unwind_table()* when the module was registered.

6.2.2 Navigating through the call chain

Figure 6.4 illustrates the group of unwind routines that permit navigation of the call chain. The current position in the call chain is tracked by a *frame info structure* (struct unw_frame-_info in file include/asm-ia64/unwind.h). Its initial position is determined when the frame

struct **unw_frame_info**;	/* encapsulates current frame info */
unw_init_frame_info(*info*, *task*, *sw*);	/* initialize frame info structure */
unw_init_from_blocked_task(*info*, *task*);	/* initialize frame info for blocked task */
unw_init_running(*callback*, *arg*);	/* initialize frame info for running task */
int **unw_unwind**(*info*);	/* unwind to the previous frame */
int **unw_unwind_to_user**(*info*);	/* unwind to user level */

Figure 6.4. Linux/ia64 kernel interface to navigate call frames.

info is initialized with a call to *unw_init_frame_info()*. Once the initial position has been selected, the stack can be navigated in only one direction: toward older, less deeply nested call frames.

As the figure shows, *unw_init_frame_info()* expects three arguments. The first one, *info* is a pointer to the frame info structure to be initialized. The *task* argument is a pointer to the task structure whose stack is to be unwound. The third and most important argument, *sw*, points to a switch-stack structure on the memory stack. This switch-stack defines the position in the stack at which unwinding begins. Why a switch-stack structure instead of just a stack pointer address? Recall that stack unwinding on IA-64 reconstructs, and indeed requires, the entire **preserved** CPU state. Since the switch-stack structure encapsulates this state (see Chapter 3, *Processes, Tasks, and Threads*), it contains exactly the information needed for this purpose. Using a switch-stack is also convenient because blocked tasks already store such a structure as the last item on their memory stacks.

For convenience, the IA-64 unwind interface defines two additional frame info initialization routines. The *unw_init_from_blocked_task()* routine initializes the frame info for a task that is blocked. It takes the same arguments as *unw_init_frame_info()*, except that the switch-stack pointer is missing. There is no need to pass this pointer because, for a blocked task, the switch-stack structure is identified by the kernel stack pointer value saved in the thread structure (see Chapter 3, *Processes, Tasks, and Threads*). The more intriguing convenience function is *unw_init_running()*; it permits unwinding the currently running task right from the point at which it is called. This function is different from the previous ones in that it does not take a frame info pointer argument. Instead, it expects two other arguments. The first argument, *callback*, is a pointer to a callback function that does the actual unwinding. The second one, *arg*, is an arbitrary value that is passed unmodified to the callback function. The prototype of the callback function is as follows:

> void *unwind_callback*(*info*, *arg*);

When a callback is invoked, *arg* has the value that was passed as the second argument to *unw_init_running()*. Argument *info* points to a frame info structure that has been initialized such that the unwinding starts at the call site of *unw_init_running()*.

To better understand the limitations of *unw_init_running()*, let us consider how it works. When called, it first creates a switch-stack structure on the current memory stack. It then allocates a frame info structure, also on the memory stack, and initializes it with a call to *unw_init_frame_info()*. In this call, it passes pointers to the newly created frame info and switch-stack structures as the first and third arguments. A pointer to the current task structure is passed as the second argument. In the last step, *unw_init_running()* invokes the callback function, passing it both the frame info pointer and the *arg* value. The implication of all this is that the *info* pointer passed to the callback routine is valid only as long as the callback routine is executing. Also, since a switch-stack structure is created on-the-fly, *unw_init_running()* is relatively slow to execute. Provided these limitations are kept in mind, *unw_init_running()* provides a convenient and elegant way to unwind the current task at any point in time.

Once the frame info is initialized, it is possible to traverse the call chain. This can be done one frame at a time by a call to *unw_unwind()*. Its only argument is *info*, the pointer to the current frame info. The function inspects the frame info and then updates it to reflect the CPU state as it existed in the previous call frame. The routine returns 0 on success. If it fails for any reason, a negative value is returned. In the absence of kernel bugs, the routine fails only when there are no more call frames to unwind, i.e., when the beginning of the call chain has been reached. The unwind interface also provides *unw_unwind_to_user()*, which is a convenience function that repeatedly calls *unw_unwind()* until the return address in the current frame is in user space. This provides a convenient way to reconstruct the user-level CPU state and is used extensively in the IA-64 implementation of the *ptrace()* system call.

6.2.3   Accessing the CPU state of the current frame

So far, we have seen how to start the unwinding and how to navigate a call chain frame by frame. However, this is uninteresting unless we can access the CPU state represented by each call frame. Here the accessor routines shown in Figure 6.5 come into play: they allow us to inquire about or modify the state in the current frame. Looking at the figure, we see a couple of routines with a name starting with *unw_get* and most others with names starting with *unw_access*. The former group can be used to access frame-related values that are read-only, and the latter are used to access frame-related values that can be both read and written. The arguments passed to each routine and the return value have the same meaning across these routines: the *info* argument is a pointer to the current frame info. Argument *valp* is a pointer to the value that the routine reads or writes. This is normally a pointer to a 64-bit word, except for *unw_access_fr()*, where it is a pointer to a 128-bit word that contains a value in the 82-bit floating-point register format. Argument *reg* specifies the register number that is being accessed, and argument *write* indicates whether the register is being read or written. A non-zero value indicates a write access. Finally, argument *natp* passes the NaT bit when a general register is accessed. It must be a pointer to a byte. A non-zero value in this byte indicates a NaT bit value of 1. The accessor routines all return 0 on success and a negative value on failure.

Throughout the remainder of this section, we use Figure 6.6 to help explain the meaning of the values returned by the accessor routines. It illustrates the case where a task entered the kernel, performed nested calls to functions *funcA()*, *funcB()*, *funcC()*, and then blocked execution. The frame info values shown in the figure represent the state as it would exist after it is initialized with a call to *unw_init_from_blocked_task()* and the most recent frame is

int **unw_is_intr_frame**(*info*);	/* *true if in an interruption frame* */
int **unw_get_ip**(*info*, *valp*);	/* *return instruction pointer* */
int **unw_get_rp**(*info*, *valp*);	/* *return return link* */
int **unw_get_sp**(*info*, *valp*);	/* *return stack pointer* */
int **unw_get_psp**(*info*, *valp*);	/* *return previous stack pointer* */
int **unw_get_bsp**(*info*, *valp*);	/* *return backing store pointer* */
int **unw_access_gr**(*info*, *reg*, *valp*, *natp*, *write*);	/* *access general register* */
int **unw_access_br**(*info*, *reg*, *valp*, *write*);	/* *access branch register* */
int **unw_access_fr**(*info*, *reg*, *valp*, *write*);	/* *access floating-point register* */
int **unw_access_ar**(*info*, *reg*, *valp*, *write*);	/* *access application register* */
int **unw_access_pr**(*info*, *valp*, *write*);	/* *access predicate register* */
int **unw_access_cfm**(*info*, *valp*, *write*);	/* *access current frame register* */

Figure 6.5. Linux/ia64 kernel interface to access frame info.

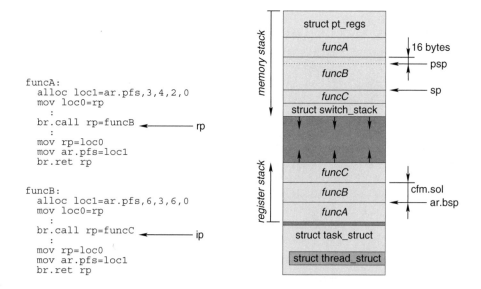

Figure 6.6. Frame info when *funcB()* is the current frame.

unwound with a call to *unw_unwind()*. In other words, the figure illustrates the case where the call frame of *funcB()* is the current frame. Now let us look at the values that the accessor routines would return in this scenario.

- **unw_get_ip()** returns the address of the instruction bundle that would be executed next when control returns to *funcC()*. In the figure, this address points to the first bundle after br.call rp=funcC, as illustrated by the arrow labeled ip (instruction pointer).

- **unw_get_rp()** returns the address of the instruction bundle that would be executed once control returns from *funcB()*. Since *funcB()* was called by *funcA()*, this address points to the first bundle after br.call rp=funcB, as illustrated by the arrow labeled rp (return pointer). This value is also known as the *return link* of the current frame.

- **unw_get_sp()** returns the value of the stack pointer register (sp) as it would exist when control returns from *funcC()*. The stack pointer is the lowest address in the memory stack frame of *funcB()*, as illustrated by the arrow labeled sp. Note that the stack pointer can change as execution progresses, so the returned value is not guaranteed to be valid for any instruction other than the one identified by *unw_get_ip()*.

- **unw_get_psp()** returns the value of the previous stack pointer psp, which is defined to be the value of the stack pointer register (sp) at the time *funcB()* was called. In other words, the returned value corresponds to the frame pointer of *funcB()* minus 16. The 16-byte offset is due to the scratch area required by the IA-64 software conventions. In the figure, the value returned by this routine is represented by the arrow labeled psp: it points to 16 bytes below the top end of the memory stack frame of *funcB()*. Unlike the stack pointer, this value is fixed during execution in *funcB()*.

- **unw_get_bsp()** returns the value of the register stack backing store pointer register (ar.bsp) as it would exist during execution of *funcB()*. The backing store pointer is the base of the register stack frame of *funcB()*, as illustrated by the arrow labeled ar.bsp.

- **unw_access_cfm()** provides access to the value of the current frame marker register cfm as it would exist when control returns from *funcC()*. As illustrated by the arrow labeled cfm.sol, this value can be used to determine the size of the local register stack partition allocated by *funcB()*.

- **unw_access_gr()** provides access to the values of **preserved** general registers r4–r7 and r32–r127. The register to be accessed is identified by argument *reg*: 4 corresponds to r4, 32 to r32, and so on. If the current frame is an interruption frame as indicated by *unw_is_intr_frame()*, then **scratch** registers r1–r3 and r8–r31 can also be accessed. Register r0 has a hardwired value of 0 and can never be accessed through this routine. The value accessed by this routine corresponds to the value that is present in the register when *funcB()* is entered or exited. That is, it is usually *not* the value that is present in the register when the instruction at address *unw_get_ip()* is executing. That value can be obtained from the frame info for *funcC()*.

Table 6.1. Manifest constants used to access application registers.

Register	Manifest constant	Register	Manifest constant
bsp	UNW_AR_BSP	bspstore	UNW_AR_BSPSTORE
unat	UNW_AR_UNAT	rnat	UNW_AR_RNAT
lc	UNW_AR_LC	ec	UNW_AR_EC
pfs	UNW_AR_PFS	rsc	UNW_AR_RSC
ccv	UNW_AR_CCV	fpsr	UNW_AR_FPSR

- *unw_access_br()* provides access to the values of **preserved** branch registers b1–b5. The register to be accessed is identified by argument *reg*: 1 corresponds to b1, 5 to b5, and so on. If the current frame is an interruption frame as indicated by *unw_is_intr_frame()*, then **scratch** registers b0, b6, and b7 can also be accessed. The value accessed by this routine corresponds to the value that is present in the register when *funcB()* is entered or exited.

- *unw_access_fr()* provides access to the values of **preserved** floating-point registers f2–f5 and f10–f127. The register to be accessed is identified by argument *reg*: 2 corresponds to f2, 5 to f5, and so on. If the current frame is an interruption frame as indicated by *unw_is_intr_frame()*, then **scratch** registers f6–f9 can also be accessed. Registers f0 and f1 are hardwired to a floating-point value of 0.0 and 1.0, respectively, and can never be accessed through this routine. For registers f2–f31, the value accessed by this routine corresponds to the value that is present in the register when *funcB()* is entered or exited. For registers f32–f127, the value accessed is the user-level value of the register.

- *unw_access_ar()* provides access to the values of **preserved** application registers. The register to be accessed is identified by argument *reg* and can be one of the manifest constants listed in the Table 6.1. The value accessed by this routine corresponds to the value that is present in the register when *funcB()* is entered or exited. Reading the value of UNW_AR_BSP normally returns the same value as *unw_get_bsp()*. However, if a function switches backing store pointers, this function returns the ar.bsp value *before* the switch, whereas *unw_get_bsp()* returns the value *after* the switch.

- *unw_access_pr()* provides broadside access to **preserved** predicate registers p1–p5 and p16–p63. Bit *n* corresponds to p*n*. If the current frame is an interruption frame, as indicated by *unw_is_intr_frame()*, the bits corresponding to **scratch** predicate registers p6–p15 are also meaningful. The predicate values accessed by this routine correspond to the value that is present when *funcB()* is entered or exited.

A careful look at the interface in Figure 6.5 shows a curious asymmetry. For the memory stack, there are separate routines to get the current and previous stack pointer values. In contrast, for the register stack there is only *unw_get_bsp()*, which returns the register backing store pointer ar.bsp of the current frame. There is no routine that returns a pointer to the top of the register stack frame. However, as shown in Figure 6.6, this pointer can be calculated from the size of the local register partition as stored in the current frame marker register cfm. However, we cannot just add the size of the local partition to ar.bsp to obtain this pointer, because every 64th word in the register stack contains an RNaT collection word. In other words, calculating this pointer requires skipping zero, one, or more RNaT slots. This is most easily accomplished with the expression:

$$ia64\_rse\_skip\_regs(bsp, sol)$$

As described in Chapter 2, *IA-64 Architecture*, this calculation adds the size of the local partition *sol* to the register stack pointer *bsp*, skipping any intervening RNaT slots, and returns the desired address.

6.2.4   Using the unwind interface

Let us look at some concrete examples of how the unwind interface can be used. The goal here is to demonstrate that it is easy to use this interface even though the machinery behind it is rather complex.

Printing a backtrace

First, suppose we wanted to print a backtrace of a blocked task. The following routine would accomplish this:

```
show_stack (struct task_struct *t) {
    struct unw_frame_info info; long ip, sp, bsp;
    printk("        ip                  sp               bsp\n");
    unw_init_from_blocked_task(&info, t);
    do {
        unw_get_ip(&info, &ip);
        unw_get_sp(&info, &sp); unw_get_bsp(&info, &bsp);
        printk("%016lx %016lx %016lx\n", ip, sp, bsp);
    } while (unw_unwind(&info) >= 0);
}
```

The routine first declares *info* as a frame info variable and then initializes it with the state of the last call frame of blocked task *t*. It does this by calling *unw_init_from_blocked_task()*. The routine then enters a loop that reads the instruction pointer, memory stack pointer, and register stack pointer values and prints them to the Linux console, using *printk()*. After the current values are printed, the call chain is unwound to the previous frame through a call to *unw_unwind()*. As long as this call returns a non-negative value, there are more stack frames to print and the loop continues. If there are no more call frames, a negative value is returned and the loop stops.

   The output produced by this function might look like the example shown below. In this example, the function printed the backtrace for the init process (see Chapter 10, *Booting*). For convenience, the output below also includes the name of the function that corresponds to the printed ip value.

```
        ip                  sp                  bsp
 e00000000055d590 e00000003f137d70 e00000003f130dd8  schedule()
 e00000000055cbe0 e00000003f137d90 e00000003f130da8  schedule_timeout()
 e0000000005c82c0 e00000003f137dd0 e00000003f130ce0  do_select()
 e0000000005c8ae0 e00000003f137df0 e00000003f130c20  sys_select()
 e0000000005155c0 e00000003f137e60 e00000003f130c20  ia64_ret_from_syscall
```

The first output line shows the stack frame for the function that was running before the
task blocked. This frame was created by *schedule()*, the only function in the Linux kernel
that can block execution. Following the trace further, we see that *schedule()* was invoked
with *schedule_timeout()*, *do_select()*, and *sys_select()*. This indicates that the init process
invoked the *select()* system call and is waiting for a *select()*-related event or a timeout to
occur. The last line in the output corresponds to the pt-regs structure that exists at the beginning of the memory stack. It lists *ia64_ret_from_syscall* as the function name. In reality,
this is not a proper function but an assembly stub that returns execution to the user level.

Looking at the sp column, we see that the stack pointer address increases as we go
farther down in the output. Since the later lines correspond to earlier stack frames, this is
what we would expect for a stack that grows toward lower addresses. For the bsp column,
the opposite is true as the register stack grows toward higher addresses. Note that for some
functions, the memory stack frame, the register stack frame, or both may be empty. In
the output above, the bsp value for *ia64_ret_from_syscall* and *sys_select()* are identical,
indicating that the former has an empty register stack frame.

Accessing user-level register values

As explained in Chapter 3, *Processes, Tasks, and Threads*, it is usually difficult to take a
blocked task and reconstruct the user-level CPU state as it existed at the time the kernel
was entered. The unwind interface makes this easy. Suppose we wanted to print the user-
level values of registers r4 and ar.lc of the currently running task. Although this particular
example may not have much practical value, it serves to illustrate two important aspects of
the unwind interface: how to unwind the currently running task and how to reconstruct user-
level state. We will need to use *unw_init_running()*. This requires implementing a callback
function. In our example, it needs to unwind the call chain to the user level and, once that
point is reached, print the desired user-level values. This is shown below:

```
show_regs_callback (struct unw_frame_info *info, void *arg) {
    struct unw_frame_info info; long r4, lc; char r4_nat;
    unw_unwind_to_user(info);
    unw_access_gr(&info, 4, &r4, &r4_nat, 0);
    unw_access_ar(&info, UNW_AR_LC, &lc, 0);
    printk("r4:%c%016lx, lc:%016lx\n", r4_nat?'*':' ', r4, lc);
}
```

When this callback is invoked, *info* points to the frame info structure created by *unw_init-
_running()*. Argument *arg* is unused in our example. The first thing the callback does is
unwind the stack all the way to the user level by calling *unw_unwind_to_user()*. It then uses
the accessor routines to read the user-level value of r4, its NaT bit, and the value of ar.lc. In

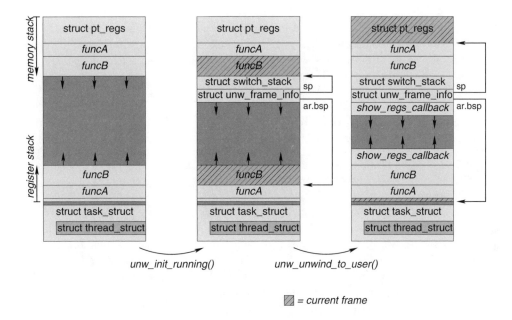

Figure 6.7. Effects of *unw_init_running()* and *unw_unwind_to_user()*.

the last step, it calls *printk()* to print the values. Note that if the NaT bit is set, the printed value of r4 starts with an asterisk (*), which is a common way of indicating NaT values.

With the callback in place, we can print the user-level values of r4 and ar.lc of the current task by invoking *unw_init_running()* in the following fashion:

```
unw_init_running(show_regs_callback, 0);
```

The easiest way to understand how this works is to look at the effect that the major operations have on the task's stacks and the frame info structure. This is illustrated in Figure 6.7. The leftmost part of the figure shows the task memory as it might exist for a task that entered the kernel and then called functions *funcA()* and *funcB()*. We can see the memory and register stacks and the call frames for the two functions as well as the pt-regs structure on the memory stack that is created when the kernel is entered. Let us now assume that *funcB()* calls *unw_init_running()*. The middle part of the figure shows the resulting configuration as it exists just before the callback is invoked: *unw_init_running()* created its own stack frame that consists of a switch-stack structure and a frame info structure. The latter is initialized such that the call frame of *funcB()* is the current frame. When the callback invokes *unw_unwind_to_user()*, the stack is unwound frame by frame until the pt-regs structure is reached, as shown in the rightmost part of the figure. At this point, the register values of the current frame correspond to the user-level values, which is just what we wanted.

We should note that the unwind interface never accesses memory in user space. Since the user-level stacked registers reside primarily in that space, the unwind interface cannot be used to access user-level registers r32–r127. Of course, the interface *can* be used to obtain the user-level value of ar.bsp and, with that, the user-level backing store can be accessed directly, so this is not a serious limitation.

6.3   EMBEDDING UNWIND INFORMATION IN ASSEMBLY CODE

When writing programs in a higher-level language such as C, the compiler takes care of generating unwind information for each function. However, when writing programs in assembly language, this information must be supplied by the programmer in the form of *unwind directives* [27]. These directives tell the assembler if and how each of the instructions in a function affects the frame state. This may sound frighteningly complicated at first. Fortunately, for the vast majority of assembly routines, adding the necessary unwind directives is straightforward. In fact, most leaf functions do not require any unwind directives at all. Even complicated interior functions seldom require more than a couple of directives.

For the purpose of unwinding, a program (text segment) is viewed as a sequence of *procedures*, each consisting of a contiguous sequence of machine instructions. Usually, each procedure corresponds to one assembly routine. However, a routine that consists of multiple discontiguous code sequences would correspond to multiple procedures, and this is why the remainder of this chapter is careful to distinguish between the two. Unwind directives are specified at the granularity of individual IA-64 instructions and treat each bundle as containing exactly three instructions. For bundles with the MLX template, the last slot is treated as if it contained an instruction that has no effect.

The *frame state* tracks the state of the call frame throughout a procedure. Specifically, given the CPU state in effect at a particular instruction, the frame state for that instruction contains all the information necessary to restore the **preserved** CPU state that was in effect at the time the procedure was called. To achieve this, the frame state needs to track information about two types of registers: the frame registers and the **preserved** registers. The frame registers describe the current call frame and consist of the stack pointer (sp), the previous stack pointer (psp), the register backing store pointer (ar.bsp), the current frame marker register (cfm), and the instruction pointer (IP). At the beginning of a procedure, the frame state has an initial value that corresponds to a call frame in which all of the following are true:

- The register stack frame has the shape described by the current frame marker (cfm).

- No memory stack frame has been allocated (apart from the 16-byte scratch area).

- The return link is in branch register b0 (also known as rp).

- The previous function state is in ar.pfs.

- No **preserved** registers have been saved.

Any change to the initial frame state must be marked with one or more of the unwind directives listed in Table 6.2 on page 279. Since the frame state tracks only frame registers and **preserved** registers, only instructions that affect those registers require unwind directives. It is not necessary, and in fact impossible, to use an unwind directive for an instruction that affects an ordinary **scratch** register, for example. A large class of assembly functions never modify the initial frame state and hence require no unwind directives. This includes leaf functions that use at most 16-bytes of stack space, provided they do not modify ar.pfs, sp, or b0.

To understand how the unwind directives work, we need to consider where a **preserved** register can be saved. Fundamentally, there are three possibilities. A **preserved** register can be saved in one of the following locations:

1. In another **preserved** register.

2. In a **scratch** register.

3. On the memory stack.

The first two cases may sound paradoxical. After all, what could the point be of saving a **preserved** register to yet another **preserved** register? Similarly, why would it be possible to save a register to a **scratch** register which, by definition, is *not* preserved across function calls? Let us look at each case in more detail.

The first case is actually very common and occurs whenever a **preserved** register is copied to a stacked register. Once the copy is in a stacked register, the register stack engine takes care of automatically preserving the value. If necessary, it will do so by writing the value to the backing store and restoring it when needed. Of course, it would also be legal to save a **preserved** register to a static **preserved** register, such as r5. However, doing so would require saving the value of r5 first. Often, this does not make much sense, but there are certainly occasions where this is useful.

The second case is possible only if no other function is called while the preserved value lives in the **scratch** register. This most commonly occurs in leaf functions. For example, if a leaf function uses the counted loop branch instruction (br.cloop), it has to preserve the loop-counter register ar.lc. It makes sense to use a **scratch** register for this purpose. However, saving a **preserved** register in a **scratch** register is not limited to leaf functions. Even an inner function can use this approach provided that the preserved value is copied out of the **scratch** register and saved in some other place before the next function call.

For the third case, saving a **preserved** register to the memory stack, the unwind descriptors provide three addressing modes: *stack pointer relative addressing, frame pointer relative addressing*, and *implicit addressing*. With stack pointer relative addressing, the memory address at which the register is saved is given as a non-negative offset relative to the stack pointer. In Figure 6.8, register ar.lc is addressed in this mode. With frame pointer relative addressing, the memory address is given by psp + 16 − *pspoff*, i.e., the offset is relative to the frame pointer (psp + 16). The figure shows ar.pfs addressed in this mode. The final addressing mode, implicit, can be used only for general registers r4–r7 and the **preserved** branch and floating-point registers. It is based on a spill area that, by default, is

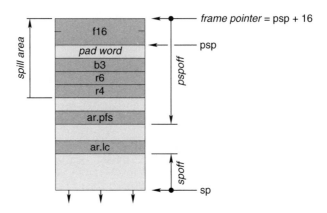

Figure 6.8. Addressing modes for memory stack frame.

located at the beginning of the memory stack frame. The spill area is just large enough to contain the registers saved in it plus an 8-byte pad word that may be necessary to ensure that saved floating-point registers are 16-byte aligned. Registers are allocated to this spill area from lower to higher addresses. General registers are allocated first, branch registers are allocated second, and floating-point registers are allocated last. Within a register class, the spill locations are allocated in accordance with the index of the register: the lowest index receives the lowest spill address. Figure 6.8 illustrates the case where registers r4, r6, b3, and f16 have been saved to the spill area. This addressing mode is called implicit because the register name implicitly determines the memory location in which the register is saved.

6.3.1   Region directives

We are now ready to explore the first set of directives in Table 6.2. Recall from the introduction to this section that a procedure consists of a contiguous sequence of instructions. The **.proc** and **.endp** directives mark the beginning and end of such a procedure, respectively. Both directives take an assembly symbol as an argument; the symbol should correspond to the name of the procedure. As far as unwind information is concerned, the procedure name has no effect.

The instructions in a procedure are partitioned into prologue and body *regions*. The **.prologue** directive starts a *prologue region*, and **.body** starts a *body region*. Prologue regions describe the *prologue* of a procedure, which takes care of establishing the procedure's call frame. Body regions cover the remaining instructions during which the call frame remains unchanged (with some exceptions, as we see later). A body region can also contain an instruction sequence that restores the original CPU state and returns execution to the caller of the procedure. Such an instruction sequence is called an *epilogue*. A region

Table 6.2. Summary of assembler unwind directives.

Region directives

`.proc` *sym*	marks start of procedure *sym*
`.prologue` [*mask gr*]	starts a prologue region
`.body`	starts a body region
`.endp` [*sym*]	marks end of procedure *sym*

Prologue directives

`.altrp` *br*	return link is in branch register *br* instead of b0
`.fframe` *imm*	fixed memory stack frame of *imm* bytes
`.vframe{,sp,psp}` *l1*	variable memory stack frame; previous sp in *l1*
`.save.{g,f,b}` *mask* [*gr*]	register set *mask* is saved in spill area or register *gr*
`.save.gf` *mask$_1$* *mask$_2$*	register sets *mask$_1$* & *mask$_2$* are saved in spill area
`.save{,sp,psp}` *sr l1*	register *sr* is saved in *l1*
`.spill` *off*	spill area starts at offset *off*
`.unwabi` *os imm*	ABI-specific directive

Body directives

`.label_state` *imm*	saves current frame state under label *imm*
`.copy_state` *imm*	restores frame state labeled *imm*
`.restore sp` [*imm*]	marks instruction that restores sp

General directives

`.spill{reg,sp,psp}` *r l2*	register *r* is saved in *l2*
`.spill{reg,sp,psp}.p` *qp r l2*	if predicate *qp* is **true**, register *r* is saved in *l2*
`.restorereg` *reg*	register *r* is restored
`.restorereg.p` *qp reg*	if predicate *qp* is **true**, register *r* is restored

Legend

ar = ar.fpsr | ar.bsp | ar.bspstore | ar.rnat | ar.pfs | ar.unat | ar.lc

gr = r1–r127	*fr* = f2–f127		*br* = b0–b7
tr = *gr* | *fr* | *br*	*sr* = *ar* | rp | pr | @priunat		*r* = *tr* | *sr*
imm = unsigned constant	*off* = sp or psp relative offset		*mask* = register mask
sym = procedure name	*l1* = *gr* | *off*		*l2* = *off* | *tr*

starts with the first instruction following the region directive and ends at the next region directive. Empty regions are allowed.

The frame state at any given point in a procedure can be determined as follows:

- On entry to a region, the current frame state is equal to the exit state of the previous region (the frame state as it existed at the end of the previous region). For the first region in a procedure, the entry state is equal to the initial frame state (no memory stack frame, no registers saved, return link in b0, previous function state in ar.pfs). For body regions, special directives can be used to set the entry state equal to the entry state of an earlier body region (see `.copy_state` in Section 6.3.3).

- On entry to a prologue region, a copy of the current frame state is pushed onto a stack called the *frame state stack*.

- Within a prologue region, the current frame state is modified according to the directives that occur in the region.

- Within a body region, the frame state is constant. However, general unwind directives can be used to break this general rule. If a body region contains general unwind directives, the frame state is modified accordingly.

- A body region may contain an epilogue. If it does, one or more entries are popped from the frame state stack and then the entry at the top of the stack is restored as the current frame state.

To permit more efficient encoding of the unwind information, the `.prologue` directive can optionally take two arguments: a 4-bit register *mask* and a general register *gr*. The register mask indicates whether the prologue region saves rp, ar.pfs, psp, and pr in consecutive registers starting with *gr*. Bit three corresponds to rp, bit two to ar.pfs, and so on. If a bit is set, the corresponding register is saved. For example, the directive `.prologue 0xc r35` would indicate that the prologue region saves rp and ar.pfs in registers r35 and r36, respectively.

6.3.2 Prologue directives

Prologue directives may be specified only inside prologue regions. As Table 6.2 shows, they form the largest set of unwind directives. This is not surprising considering that prologue regions describe the portion of a procedure responsible to set up the call frame.

The first directive in the table, `.altrp`, declares an alternate branch register as the one containing the return link on entry to the region. It takes a single argument, *br*, that names the branch register containing the return link. If this directive does not appear, register b0 is assumed to contain the return link.

The `.fframe` directive defines a fixed-size memory stack frame. It must appear immediately before the instruction that decrements the stack pointer sp; it takes a single argument that specifies the stack size in bytes. This directive may occur once per prologue region. When a fixed-size stack frame is in effect, a body region must not modify the stack pointer, except possibly to restore it to its original value (see `.restore` in Section 6.3.3).

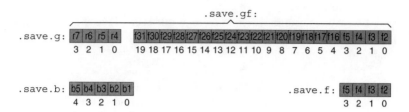

Figure 6.9. Register masks for `.save` directives.

The `.vframe` directive defines a variable-sized memory stack frame. It must appear immediately before the instruction that saves the old stack pointer value. The old stack pointer value is known as the previous stack pointer value (psp). The directive takes a single argument, ll, which specifies the location at which psp is saved. For `.vframe`, the location is a general register, such as r35. For `.vframesp` and `.vframepsp`, the location is a memory stack address expressed as a stack pointer or frame pointer relative offset, respectively.

Instructions that save a **preserved** general register, branch register, or floating-point register must be preceded by a `.save.g`, `.save.b`, or `.save.f` directive, respectively. The first argument to these directives is a register mask indicating which registers are being saved. The encoding of these masks is illustrated in Figure 6.9. If N bits are set in this mask, it is assumed that the next N instructions save the registers in order of increasing index. By default, the registers are saved to the memory stack spill area, with the implicit addressing mode described earlier. If the optional second argument gr is specified, it must be a general register and it means that the registers mentioned in the mask are saved in consecutive registers starting with register gr. Since floating-point registers are too big to be stored in general registers, only the one-argument form of the `.save.f` directive is valid. Also, this directive can be used only for registers f2–f5.

The `.save.gf` directive combines and extends the functionality of `.save.g` and `.save.f`. The two arguments are masks that specify which general and floating-point registers are saved. Unlike the case with `.save.f`, the floating-point mask of this directive is wide enough to cover all **preserved** floating-point registers, including registers f16–f31.

Directives `.save`, `.savesp`, and `.savepsp` indicate that the next instruction saves a special register in a general register, a stack pointer relative location, or a frame pointer relative location, respectively. These directives can be used only for **preserved** registers that are not general, branch, or floating-point registers. For example, the directives can be used for application registers fpsr and unat or for the predicate registers (pr). Note that when specifying a register name of `ar.unat`, the directive indicates where the procedure saved the value of ar.unat that existed on entry to the procedure. If the procedure needs to spill any general registers (with st8.spill) and subsequently save the resulting UNaT collection word, the location of this word must be marked with the special register name `@priunat` (primary UNaT).

The .spill directive declares an alternative location for the spill area. It takes a single argument, off, which specifies the psp relative offset at which the spill area starts. As described earlier, by default the spill area is allocated such that it ends at the highest address of the memory stack frame.

The final prologue directive, .unwabi, provides an escape code to include ABI-specific information in the unwind information (ABI stands for *application binary interface*). The first argument specifies the ABI under which this directive should be interpreted. Three ABIs are defined: **@svr4** (UNIX SVR4), **@hpux** (HP-UX), and **@nt** (Windows NT). The second argument is a 1-byte constant with ABI-specific meaning. The Linux kernel uses directive

```
.unwabi @svr4 'i'
```

to mark interruption frames, which are call frames created on entry to the kernel. These frames consist of a pt-regs structure and require special handling because they contain **scratch** registers, which cannot be expressed with IA-64 unwind directives.

6.3.3   Body directives

Body directives may be specified only inside body regions. As Table 6.2 shows, there are only three such directives. The first two, .label_state and .copy_state, handle cases in which the frame state does not flow sequentially from one region to the next. Both directives take an unsigned number *imm* as their only argument. The number serves as a label for the frame state. Directive .label_state makes a copy of the entry state of the current region and stores it under label *imm*. Later on, .copy_state can be used to set the entry state of the current region equal to the one associated with label *imm*. The .label_state directive must always appear before any matching .copy_state directives. Label numbers can in theory be arbitrarily large. However, most toolchains limit them in some fashion. For example, the GNU toolchain limits them to 64 bit numbers.

The third body directive, .restore sp, indicates that the current body region contains an epilogue that undoes the effect of the most recent prologue region. If the epilogue undoes the effect of the *N* most recent prologue regions, the programmer can specify this by passing *N* as the optional second argument. In operational terms, this parameter specifies the epilogue count, which is the number of entries that should be popped from the frame state stack when the end of the body region is reached (see Section 6.3.1). The directive must appear immediately before the instruction that restores the stack pointer or anywhere in the region if no memory stack frame has been allocated. Except for the registers saved on the memory stack, the epilogue must keep the register save locations valid throughout the epilogue. For example, if the return link has been saved in r35, that register must continue to hold the return link even once the epilogue has started. Note that this directive marks the instruction that restores the stack pointer, *not* the beginning of the epilogue.

6.3.4   General directives

General directives may be specified both in prologue and body regions. They are more general in the sense that they can be used to describe conditional prologue/epilogue code that is executed only if a particular predicate register is **true**. From a practical point of view, they are more convenient to use because the register to be saved is expressed with its regular name instead of a register mask. The downside is that, compared to the other directives, general directives take up more space in the unwind sections. However, while unwind information encoding efficiency is generally a big concern, it does not matter for the handful of assembly routines that are present in the Linux/ia64 kernel. Thus, despite their taking up more space, it is often better to use these directives in handwritten assembly code since they improve readability and maintainability.

As shown in Table 6.2, there are two types of general directives: spill and restore. Both types come in unconditional and predicated forms and must appear immediately before the instruction they are describing. The unconditional form of the spill directives can be used to describe an instruction that saves **preserved** register r to another register or the memory stack. For saving to another register, the `.spillreg` directive is used. In this case, argument $l2$ is the register name of the save location. For saving to the memory stack, the `.spillsp` directive is used for stack pointer relative addressing and `.spillpsp` is used for frame pointer relative addressing. In this case, argument $l2$ is the stack pointer or frame pointer relative offset of the save location, respectively. The predicated form of the spill directive works exactly like the unconditional one, except that there is an additional argument called qp, which specifies the predicate register that controls whether the directive should take effect. If the predicate register has a value of 0 (**false**), the directive has no effect.

The second type of general directives, `.restorereg` and `.restorereg.p`, mark instructions that restore the value of a **preserved** register. The unconditional form always takes effect, whereas the predicated form takes effect only if the predicate register specified by argument qp has a value of 1 (**true**). There is no need to specify the location from which a value is restored, so these directives can be used to reverse the effect of all spill directives, not just `.spillreg` or `.spillreg.p`.

The predicated forms of the general unwind directives require that the controlling predicate must remain valid between the spill directive and the matching restore directive. A **preserved** predicate must be used if there are any function calls in this range.

6.3.5 Examples

To ensure that unwinding works reliably, assembly programs must contain proper unwind directives. It is, however, equally important to understand when unwind directives are not needed. To emphasize this point, let us take a look at a trivial assembly routine:

```
        .proc add
  add:  add r8 = r32, r33
        br.ret.sptk b0
        .endp add
```

This routine adds the two numbers passed in registers r32 and r33 and returns the sum in register r8. Since the routine does not modify any **preserved** registers, there is no need to specify any unwind directives other than `.proc` and `.endp`. In fact, such simple routines do not even require an entry in the unwind table because the initial frame state is valid throughout the entire routine.

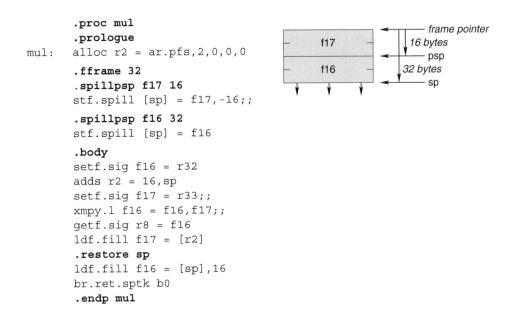

```
          .proc mul
          .prologue
mul:      alloc r2 = ar.pfs,2,0,0,0

          .fframe 32
          .spillpsp f17 16
          stf.spill [sp] = f17,-16;;

          .spillpsp f16 32
          stf.spill [sp] = f16

          .body
          setf.sig f16 = r32
          adds r2 = 16,sp
          setf.sig f17 = r33;;
          xmpy.l f16 = f16,f17;;
          getf.sig r8 = f16
          ldf.fill f17 = [r2]
          .restore sp
          ldf.fill f16 = [sp],16
          br.ret.sptk b0
          .endp mul
```

Figure 6.10. Using unwind directives in assembly code.

The second example is slightly more complicated. The assembly code on the left side
of Figure 6.10 shows a routine that multiplies two integer numbers passed in registers r32
and r33 and returns the result in register r8. Since the IA-64 integer multiplier lives in the
floating-point unit, we need to transfer the input values to floating-point registers before we
can multiply them. Normally, such a routine would use a pair of **scratch** registers, such as
f8 and f9. However, to illustrate memory-stack-related unwind directives, the example uses
preserved registers f16 and f17 in lieu of **scratch** registers and saves the original register
values on the memory stack. In our example, the memory stack frame has the layout shown
on the right side of the figure: f16 is saved at the end of the stack frame, and f17 is saved
just before that. Note that the software conventions ensure that on entry to the routine, the
caller already has allocated a 16-byte scratch area. The routine uses this space to save f17.

Now, let us take a look at the unwind directives. The `.proc` and `.endp` directives
enclose the routine, as usual. The `.prologue` directive marks the beginning of the prologue region. The first stf.spill instruction in the prologue serves two purposes: it saves f17
and it allocates the 16 bytes of stack space required in addition to the 16 bytes of scratch
space that the caller already allocated. To describe this, we need two separate unwind directives: the first one, `.fframe 32`, signifies that the memory stack frame has a fixed
size of 32 bytes (the 16 bytes the instruction allocates plus the 16 bytes that the caller allocated). The second, `.spillpsp f17 16`, signifies that register f17 is being saved at a
frame pointer relative offset of 16 bytes. The second stf.spill instruction saves register f16;

directive `.spillpsp f16 32` is used to describe this instruction. Since this is the last instruction that saves a **preserved** register, the prologue region is complete. The start of the body region is indicated with directive `.body`. In the body, the actual multiplication is performed, but the frame state remains unchanged. However, toward the end of the routine, registers f17 and f16 are restored. These are the epilogue instructions. Fortunately, there is no need to describe the effect of each epilogue instruction, except for the one that restores the stack pointer. In the example, this is the second ldf.fill instruction because it restores the original stack pointer by adding 16 to register sp. Consequently, this instruction is marked by the directive `.restore sp` placed just in front of it.

As the above examples demonstrate, annotating an assembly routine with unwind directives is not difficult. The primary point to keep in mind is that unwind directives need to be used only for instructions that affect frame registers or **preserved** registers.

6.4 IMPLEMENTATION ASPECTS

Let us now look at how the unwind interface is implemented in the Linux/ia64 kernel. As explained in Section 6.1, the ELF unwind sections are optimized to take up as little space as possible. The encoding used for the unwind descriptors is indeed quite effective: measurements of the Linux/ia64 kernel show that unwind sections take up just about seven percent of the text segment. On average, a procedure that requires unwind information typically consumes about 30 bytes of space in the .IA_64.unwind_info section. The flip side of this tight encoding is that decoding is complicated and time consuming. For example, on an early IA-64 machine, the time required to parse the unwind descriptors for a single procedure averaged about 160 μs. This may not seem terribly slow at first; however, consider that for most procedures, unwinding a frame requires no more than restoring the stack pointer, the return link, the previous function state register, and perhaps a handful of **preserved** registers. Clearly, 160 μs is a long time to execute what is effectively no more than a handful of assignment operations. Fortunately, the techniques presented in this chapter accelerate unwinding to such a degree that it takes less than 10 μs to unwind a frame—a speedup of more than an order of magnitude!

6.4.1 The frame info structure

The key data structure of the unwind interface is the frame info structure. To a user of this interface, the structure is opaque. Internally, it consists of three components: the first tracks the frame registers, the second tracks the locations at which the **preserved** registers have been saved, and the third contains auxiliary information that we describe below.

A register value can be saved on the memory stack, the register stack, or in some other register. This seems to make tracking the register save locations difficult, because some **preserved** registers may have been saved to memory whereas others may still reside in a CPU register. To avoid this difficulty, the kernel unwind interface requires that the unwind starting point be given by a switch-stack structure (see *unw_init_frame_info()* in Figure 6.4). When the switch-stack structure is created, the **preserved** registers that may contain values required during the unwind are forced into memory. Thus, using a switch-stack structure as

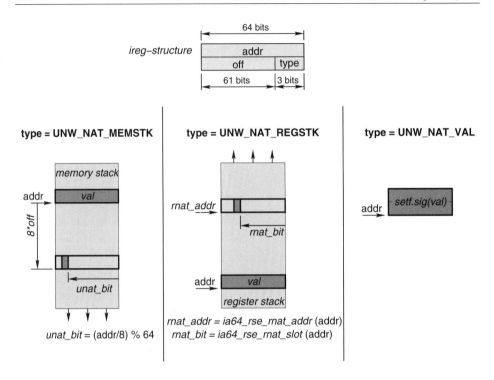

Figure 6.11. I-reg structure used to track **preserved** static registers.

the unwind starting point is not just convenient but also ensures that all save locations can be found in memory.

For most registers, tracking their save location simply requires knowing the address at which they were saved. Thus, for each of those registers, the unwind frame info maintains a separate pointer that contains the address at which the register was saved.

Tracking the save location for registers r4–r7 is not quite so simple because the NaT bit of those registers is often saved in a different place than bits 0–63. For each of these registers, the frame info maintains a separate *i-reg structure* (struct unw_ireg in file include/asm-ia64/unwind.h). This structure permits tracking the save locations of both the register value and the NaT bit, as illustrated in Figure 6.11. The upper part of the figure shows the i-reg structure, which consists of two words. The first word, addr, is the address of the memory word that contains bits 0–63 of the saved register value. The second word describes where the saved NaT bit can be found and consists of a 3-bit type field and a 61-bit offset field (off). As the lower part of the figure shows, there are three primary cases. The type field indicates which case is in effect:

- **type = UNW_NAT_MEMSTK:** The register was saved on the memory stack with the st8.spill instruction. Consequently, the NaT bit can be found in a UNaT collection word. The address of this UNaT collection word is given by $\mathsf{addr} + 8 \cdot \mathsf{off}$. Since the offset field off is scaled by a factor of 8, it can address any word in the 64-bit address space, even though it is only 61 bits wide. The number of the bit in the UNaT word that contains the saved NaT bit (*unat_bit*) is given by $\mathsf{addr}/8$ modulo 64.

- **type = UNW_NAT_REGSTK:** The register was saved on the register stack, so the NaT bit can be found in an RNaT collection word. The address of the RNaT collection word, *rnat_addr*, and the NaT bit number, *rnat_bit*, can be calculated as follows:

$$rnat\_addr = ia64\_rse\_rnat\_addr(\mathsf{addr})$$
$$rnat\_bit = ia64\_rse\_rnat\_slot(\mathsf{addr})$$

  If the resulting RNaT address points beyond the end of the register backing store, the RNaT word can be found in the RNaT collection word saved in the switch-stack structure. The bit number remains the same. The off field is unused in this case.

- **type = UNW_NAT_VAL:** The register was saved to a floating-point register with the setf.sig instruction. In this case, there is no separate NaT bit. Instead, the instruction translates a set NaT bit into the special NaTVal floating-point value. The accessor routine *unw_access_gr()* takes care of translating NaTVal to a NaT bit, and vice versa. The off field is unused in this case.

Note that, unlike the NaT bit, bits 0–63 need not distinguish between an integer value that was saved in integer format versus one that was saved in floating-point format. The reason is that Linux/ia64 uses the little-endian byte order. With that byte order, the first 64 bits of a floating-point value that was saved to memory in the 82-bit floating-point register format correspond exactly to the 64 bits that are written by the setf.sig instruction.

Now that we have described the first two components of the frame info structure, let us look at the third component: the auxiliary information. Most of it is used to accelerate certain unwind operations. For example, the switch-stack pointer is stored in the frame info structure to enable the lazy initialization optimization described in Section 6.4.4. The rest of the auxiliary information describes the address ranges of the current memory and the register stacks. These ranges are checked to verify that a given address points to a valid stack location before that address is accessed. In theory, a correctly operating kernel does not need these safety checks. However, they do not cost much and since they help guard both against kernel bugs and hardware failures, it is worthwhile to keep them.

6.4.2 Unwind descriptor processing

Given a frame info structure, unwinding it to the previous frame requires (a) restoring the frame registers and (b) determining which registers the previous frame saved where. The information required to complete these two steps can be found in the unwind descriptors associated with the procedure that created the previous frame. The return link (rp) in the current frame points inside that procedure. We can use this IP value to locate the unwind descriptors as follows.

First, recall that at boot time, the call to *unw_init()* registered the unwind table for the kernel's text segment. Similarly, whenever a kernel module is loaded, the corresponding unwind table is registered with a call to *unw_add_unwind_table()*. We can check each registered table in turn to locate the one whose instruction address range includes the IP value of the return link. As described in Section 6.1, this table contains entries that give the instruction address range that each procedure occupies. Since the table is sorted by starting address, we can perform a binary search to locate the procedure that contains IP. This entry provides us not just with the starting and ending address of the procedure, but also with a pointer to the unwind descriptor list we were looking for.

Now that we have found the descriptor list, we just need to decode it and then we are all set to update the current frame info structure. Unfortunately, the decoding step is quite complicated and a detailed description is beyond the scope of this book. However, it is easy to explain the ideas behind the descriptor list with an example. Suppose that the return link of the current frame points to the second stf.spill instruction in the integer multiplication routine shown in Figure 6.10. The unwind descriptor list for this routine might look like this:

```
prologue(rlen=3)
    fframe(t=1,size=32)
    spillpsp(t=1,reg=f17,off=16)
    spillpsp(t=2,reg=f16,off=32)
body(rlen=8)
    restore_sp(elen=2)
```

This list should be interpreted as follows. The first descriptor is prologue(rlen=3), which tells us that the first region in the procedure is a prologue region that is three instructions long. The second descriptor, fframe(t=1,size=32), says that the procedure uses a fixed memory stack frame of 32 bytes. The t=1 parameter says that the descriptor applies to instruction number 1 in the region. The first instruction in a region is numbered 0, so this descriptor applies to the instruction that saves f17. The next two descriptors, spillpsp(t=1,reg=f17,off=16) and spillpsp(t=2,reg=f16,off=32), mean that register f17 is saved by instruction 1 at psp relative offset 16 and f16 is saved by instruction 2 at psp relative offset 32. The fifth descriptor, body(rlen=8), starts a body region that is 8 instructions long. There is only one descriptor in this region, namely, restore_sp(elen=2), which signifies that the region contains an epilogue. The elen=2 parameter indicates that the second instruction from the end of the region is the one that restores the stack pointer.

Unwind descriptors are processed sequentially, in the order in which they appear in the descriptor list. This processing can stop as soon as the end of the region that contains the IP value is reached. In our case, in which we assumed IP points to the second stf.spill instruction, we can stop as soon as we find the body descriptor. Thus, we need to consider only the first four descriptors to determine how to update the frame info state. The first descriptor, prologue, serves no other use than to tell us how big the region is. The second descriptor, fframe, tells us that the memory stack frame is 32 bytes large. The third and fourth descriptors indicate that registers f16 and f17 were saved on the memory stack. The t parameters associated with these descriptors specify when they take effect. A t parameter of 0 corresponds to the first instruction in the region, 1 to the second, and so on. Only descriptors whose t value is smaller than the t value of the IP are in effect. In our example, we assumed that IP points to the spill instruction that saves f16, which is the third instruction in the procedure. Thus, the t value of IP is 2, and only descriptors with a t value less than 2 are in effect. This means that the frame descriptor and the first spillpsp descriptor are in effect and that we should ignore the second spillpsp descriptor.

After processing all the relevant descriptors, we now know that by the time the procedure reached the second stf.spill instruction, it had created a fixed memory stack frame of 32 bytes and saved f17 at a frame pointer relative offset of 16 bytes. Thus, we can now update the frame info structure to reflect this: the psp value can be set to sp plus 32 bytes, and the save address of register f17 can be set to psp (recall that a frame pointer relative offset of *off* corresponds to address psp $+ 16 - off$).

6.4.3   Unwind scripts

In the previous example, we had to process four unwind descriptors just to find out how to adjust two values in the frame info structure. This is a recurring theme: each procedure tends to have many, often complicated, unwind descriptors, yet the resulting actions on the frame info are usually few and always simple. Moreover, the kernel tends to unwind the same procedures over and over again. For example, every call to *ptrace()* potentially unwinds the stack of the traced task. Each time this happens, the exact same sequence of procedures needs to be unwound. Clearly, these are properties worth exploiting.

The kernel does so through *unwind scripts*. Each unwind script is associated with a particular IP value. If the return link in the current frame info has the same value as the IP associated with an unwind script, then executing that script has the same effect as interpreting the corresponding unwind descriptors, except that it will be much faster to execute. To exploit the fact that the same procedures tend to be unwound repeatedly, the kernel maintains a cache of such unwind scripts. When the kernel unwinds an IP location for the first time, it builds a script and puts it in the unwind script cache. On subsequent unwinding of the same location, the kernel simply reuses the cached script and thereby saves the cost of having to interpret the unwind descriptors again.

Unwind scripts consist of a sequence of unwind instructions that are executed sequentially and unconditionally. The instruction format is illustrated in Figure 6.12: each instruction is 32 bits wide and contains a 4-bit opcode field (opc), a 9-bit destination field (dst), and a 19-bit value field (val). These instructions treat the frame info as a linear array of 64-bit words. The destination field specifies the index of the 64-bit word in the frame info that is to be updated by the instruction. For example, suppose the stack pointer value were stored in the sixth 64-bit word of the frame info structure, then an instruction that updates the stack pointer would have a dst value of 5.

Table 6.3 lists the possible opcodes and their formal operation. A more detailed description follows below:

- **ADD:** Adds val to the destination word. The instruction can be used, for example, to adjust the stack pointer in a procedure that uses a fixed-size memory stack frame.

Figure 6.12. Format of unwind script instructions.

Table 6.3. Unwind instruction opcodes.

Opcode	Operation
ADD	s[dst] += val
LOAD	s[dst] = *s[val]
ADD_PSP	s[dst] = (psp + val)
ADD_SP	s[dst] = (sp + val)
MOVE	s[dst] = s[val]
MOVE2	s[dst] = s[val]; s[dst+1] = s[val+1]
MOVE_STACKED	s[dst] = ia64_rse_skip(ar.bsp, val)
SETNAT_TYPE	s[dst+1] = val
SETNAT_MEMSTK	s[dst+1] = (pri_unat - s[dst])	MEMSTK

- **LOAD:** Takes the address in the frame info word with index val, loads the 64-bit value at that address, and stores the resulting value in the destination word. The instruction can be used, for example, to adjust the stack pointer for a variable-sized memory stack frame.

- **ADD_PSP:** Adds val to the previous stack pointer value stored in the frame info and stores the result in the destination word. The instruction can be used to update the save location of a register that was saved with frame pointer relative addressing.

- **ADD_SP:** Same as ADD_PSP, except that it uses stack pointer relative addressing.

- **MOVE:** Copies the frame info word with index val to the destination word. The instruction can be used to update the save location of a register that was saved to another register.

- **MOVE2:** Same as MOVE, except that it moves two consecutive words. The instruction can be used to copy an entire i-reg structure (see Figure 6.11), as is necessary when updating the save location of a **preserved** static register (r4–r7) that was saved to another **preserved** static register.

- **MOVE_STACKED:** Sets the destination word to the register backing store address of the stacked register with index 32 + val. The register backing store address of r32 is given by the value of ar.bsp in the current frame info. The instruction can be used when a register is saved to a stacked register.

Table 6.4. Sample unwind script and its effect on the frame info.

Unwind instructions			Frame info (partial)				
opc	dst	val	ip	sp	psp	f17	
			mul+2	0x9f80	0x9f80	0x1230	*(initial state)*
ADD	psp	32	mul+2	0x9f80	0x9fa0	0x1230	
ADD_PSP	f17	0	mul+2	0x9f80	0x9fa0	0x9fa0	*(final state)*

- **SETNAT_TYPE:** Sign-extends val to 64 bits and writes the resulting value to the second word in the i-reg structure specified by dst. The instruction can be used to set the type field of the i-reg structure, as is necessary when a **preserved** static register is saved in a stacked register or a floating-point register.

- **SETNAT_MEMSTK:** Sets the second word in the i-reg structure specified by dst. In this word, the type field is set to UNW_NAT_MEMSTK and the off field is set to the difference between the save location of the primary UNaT collection word and the value in the addr field of the i-reg structure. The instruction can be used when a **preserved** static register is saved on the memory stack.

Let us now return to our example from the previous section. There, we saw that unwinding the integer multiplication routine at the point where the second stf.spill instruction is about to be executed requires processing four of the six unwind descriptors. These descriptors can be translated into the unwind script shown in the left half of Table 6.4. Just two unwind instructions are required to describe the frame at that point. The operation of these instructions is most easily understood by considering how they affect the frame info. Suppose the initial frame info was as shown in the first row of the right half of the table. IP points to the third instruction in the procedure (mul+2), and the stack pointer sp has the hypothetical value 0x9f80. In the absence of other information, the memory stack frame is assumed to be empty, so the initial value of the previous stack pointer psp is also 0x9f80. Furthermore, we assume that register f17 has been saved at address 0x1230. For example, this might be the address in the switch-stack structure at which f17 has been saved.

The first instruction in the unwind script is ADD psp 32, which has the effect of updating psp to 0x9fa0. The second instruction is ADD_PSP f17 0, which has the effect of setting the save location of f17 to 0x9fa0. That is all!

Now, if we take a look at the last line of the frame info table, we see that at instruction address mul+2, the stack pointer had a value of 0x9f80 and the previous stack pointer had a value of 0x9fa0. Furthermore, at that point the value of f17 that was in effect on entry to the procedure can be found at address 0x9fa0. Note that there is an important difference between the frame registers (such as sp and psp) and the register save locations in the frame info: the former contains the values that are in effect *at the current IP*, whereas the latter contain the save locations for the values that are in effect *on entry to the procedure*. If we wanted to know the values of the **preserved** registers at the current IP instead, we would have to use the save locations in the frame info *before* executing the unwind script. In our example, the value of f17 that was in effect at mul+2 can be found at address 0x1230.

Dealing with predication

The discussion so far has ignored the fact that certain unwind descriptors are predicated, i.e., take effect only if a particular predicate register has a value of 1 (**true**). Perhaps the most obvious way of dealing with this would be to extend the script language to support some form of conditional execution, either with predication or conditional jumps. Unfortunately, both approaches are likely to significantly slow script execution. They would also destroy another useful property of unwind scripts: without conditional execution, the length of each script is bound by a (small) constant. With conditional execution, there would be no such bound, which would complicate management of the script cache.

For these reasons, the Linux/ia64 kernel uses a different approach. When building a script for a procedure that contains predicated unwind descriptors, the kernel collects the list of the predicate registers mentioned in the unwind descriptors. This list is called the script's *qualifying predicates*. The kernel then uses the value of the predicate register pr from the current frame info to build a script that is tailored to the case in which the script's qualifying predicates have the values given by pr. After the script has been built, the kernel puts it in the cache and tags it not just with the IP, but also with a 64-bit mask that represents the script's qualifying predicates and the value of pr. For example, a script that is valid only if p2 is 0 (**false**) and p5 is 1 (**true**) would have a predicate mask of 0x24 and could have any pr value for which bit 2 is cleared and bit 5 is set. A value of 0x21 would meet this constraint. Note that bit 1 is set in this value. This does not matter because its value is filtered out by the predicate mask.

The effect of qualifying scripts with a predicate mask/value pair is that the script cache may end up containing multiple scripts that have the same IP value, but different values for the qualifying predicates. This dilutes the effectiveness of the script cache. However, the effect of this dilution is usually small because it is likely that when a particular IP location is unwound, the qualifying predicates are usually the same.

6.4.4   Lazy initialization and script hinting

While unwind scripts are the primary means for the kernel to achieve good unwind performance, the kernel employs two additional techniques that further increase speed: *lazy frame info initialization* and *script hinting*. The former is intended to speed up initialization of the frame info structure. Conceptually, a call to *unw_init_frame_info()* must set the save location of each **preserved** register to the address in the switch-stack structure at which that register was saved. This is a fair amount of work. Considering that most of the time few of the **preserved** registers will ever be accessed, we end up with a fair amount of wasted work. To avoid this, a call to *unw_init_frame_info()* simply stores the address of the switch-stack structure in the frame info and clears the save locations to NULL pointers. Later on, if a particular **preserved** register is accessed, the kernel first checks to see if the save location is NULL. If so, the kernel performs the delayed initialization and sets the save location to the address in the switch-stack structure at which the register was saved. Once the save location has been updated, the access can proceed normally. Lazy initialization is a worthwhile optimization as long as the cost of the additional NULL pointer checks is less than the amount of time saved when initializing the frame info. This is true for the kernel because robustness considerations make it desirable to perform NULL pointer checks any-way. These checks reduce the likelihood that a corrupt frame info structure could cause the kernel to crash. In other words, since the NULL pointer checks need to be done anyway, lazy initialization incurs no extra overhead.

The final optimization, script hinting, is based on the observation that the commonly encountered kernel backtraces contain mostly unique IP values. Especially after the first one or two frames are unwound, the current IP value becomes an accurate predictor for the IP value in the next frame. It therefore makes sense to include in each unwind script a pointer to the unwind script that is most likely to be executed next. Of course, there is no guarantee that this hint is correct, so before using it, the kernel has to verify that the predicted IP value (and predicate mask/value) is indeed correct. Provided the hint is correct, the kernel does not have to search the cache for the script, which is normally done with a hash table lookup. Viewed from a different angle, script hinting ensures efficient operation even if the hash table contains a fair number of collisions.

6.4.5 Putting it all together

We now have all the pieces in place to describe how the two key routines *unw_init_frame_info()* and *unw_unwind()* work.

When the former is called, it first clears the frame info structure to all zeroes. In a second step, it initializes the auxiliary information by copying the switch-stack pointer to the frame info and calculating the extents of the memory and register stacks. In the third step, it initializes the frame registers to reflect the state of the procedure that was active before the switch-stack was created. In the last step, the routine determines the save locations of the procedure by running the unwind script that matches the current IP and predicate values. If necessary, the routine builds a new script, using the procedure's unwind descriptors, and puts it in the script cache before running it.

When *unw_unwind()* is called, the following steps take place: first, the frame registers are restored. For example, the stack pointer value sp is restored to the value in the previous stack pointer psp, the IP value is restored to the value in the save location of the return link rp, the backing store pointer ar.bsp is restored in accordance with the value of the previous function state register ar.pfs, and so on. Once the frame registers have been updated, the cache is searched for a script that matches the new IP and predicate values. If such a script does not exist yet, the routine builds one from the unwind descriptors of the procedure that contains IP, puts the script in the cache, and then runs it. After the script has finished executing, the frame info reflects the state of the new frame and the routine is done.

The script cache used by *unw_unwind()* has a fixed size and uses the *least recently used (LRU)* replacement policy. For the Linux/ia64 kernel, it is usually sufficient if the cache can hold about a hundred scripts. Each script is about 256 bytes in size, so with 128 entries, the cache would take up about 32 Kbytes of memory. Cache lookups are implemented by means of a small hash table so that, in the absence of collisions, scripts can be found with a single access. If multiple scripts hash to the same entry in the table, a linked list is used to chain together these scripts.

6.5 SUMMARY

In this chapter, we explored the topic of stack unwinding. Traditionally, stack unwinding is used primarily for debugging, e.g., to print a backtrace or perhaps to print the name of the function that caused a task to block. On most other platforms, stack unwinding is implemented by ad hoc methods that are often unreliable and may involve rigid stack frame conventions or code inspection, which tends to be slow. In contrast, the IA-64 software conventions define a clean and comprehensive set of rules that guarantee reliable and efficient stack unwinding without significantly restricting code optimizations and without requiring code inspection. The Linux/ia64 kernel takes advantage of these rules by implementing a kernel stack unwinder. This unwinder can be used not just to obtain the backtraces that the Linux kernel occasionally needs to print, but also to reconstruct the **preserved** CPU state as it existed at any point in a call chain. Thanks to the latter, the kernel entry and exit paths can often be simplified and the performance-critical operation of delivering a signal can be speeded up greatly.

The chapter described in four sections the kernel unwinder and its implementation. The first section presented some background material on where the IA-64 unwind information is stored and how it can be accessed. The second section described the interface of the kernel unwinder. In the third section, we explored how directives can used to annotate assembly programs with unwind information. Assembly programmers need to be familiar with these directives because IA-64 programs are neither complete nor correct without proper unwind information. In the last section, we looked at some of the implementation aspects of the kernel unwinder. In particular, we described how unwind scripts can speed up stack unwinding.

Chapter 7

Device I/O

A computer that consisted of just a CPU and system memory could function perfectly well but would be of little or no practical value because it would have no way of interacting with the outside world. For this reason, all interesting machines also contain one or more *input/output devices (I/O devices)*, sometimes called *peripherals*, and this chapter explores how such devices are supported by Linux. We should caution that I/O in itself is an extremely rich topic and covering it completely would be well beyond the scope of this book. However, the goal here is to provide sufficient detail so that the reader can understand how the platform-specific I/O support works in Linux.

Specifically, after a brief introduction into the I/O hardware organization of modern machines, we explore the mechanisms supporting programmed I/O in the second section, direct memory access (DMA) in the third section, and device interrupts in the fourth section. As in previous chapters, IA-64 is used as a running example to illustrate how the various interfaces can be implemented.

7.1 INTRODUCTION

From a logical perspective, most machines can be thought of as having the classic bus-based organization illustrated in Figure 7.1. At the top of this figure, we find the CPU connected to the *system bus*. The bus, in turn, is connected to the system memory and all the I/O devices. In the figure, only two I/O devices are shown: a graphics card that connects to a graphics display and a peripheral controller that connects to a keyboard and a mouse.

The system bus typically consists of three types of signal lines: *control lines*, *data lines*, and *address lines*. When the CPU needs to access system memory, it places the address of the desired memory location on the address bus, sets the control lines to indicate whether it wants to read or write the location, and then uses the data lines to actually transfer the data to or from memory.

I/O devices are accessed in the same fashion, except that devices implement *I/O control registers* instead of normal memory locations. When the CPU accesses an I/O control register, the access is called a *programmed I/O* access and usually has a side effect. For example, writing the ASCII code 0x2a to the graphics card may have the effect of placing an asterisk character (*) on the display. Depending on the CPU architecture, the I/O control registers may be part of the normal memory address space or may be part of a separate I/O

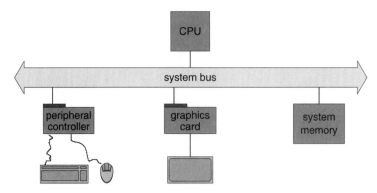

Figure 7.1. Typical bus-based machine organization.

address space. The former is known as *memory-mapped I/O*, and the latter is known as *port I/O*. With port I/O, a separate control line on the bus is used to indicate whether a CPU access is addressing memory space or I/O space.

Historically, the motivation for having a separate I/O space was to reduce hardware costs: since a machine typically has a far greater number of memory locations than I/O control registers, fewer address bits can be used for the latter. For example, some early CPUs supported a 32-bit memory address space but only a 16-bit I/O address space. This meant that I/O devices could be built more cheaply, needing only a 16-bit address decoder. In modern machines, the cost of address decoding is no longer a major concern and, combined with the fact that I/O-space accesses usually execute more slowly than memory-mapped I/O accesses, means that separate I/O address spaces are slowly falling out of favor.

Device I/O can occur in one of two modes: *polled mode* or *interrupt-driven mode*. In polled mode, the CPU periodically polls each I/O device to see whether it has any I/O pending or whether it completed an I/O operation. In contrast, in interrupt-driven mode the I/O device actively requests attention from the CPU by raising a *device interrupt*. Depending on the platform architecture, device interrupts are transmitted through one or more dedicated *interrupt request lines* or through special *interrupt transactions* on the system bus. In either case, when the CPU receives an interrupt, it stops its current activity, starts the interruption processing described in Chapter 5, *Kernel Entry and Exit*, and then executes a device-specific *interrupt handler*. Once the device-specific processing is complete, the CPU resumes executing the previous activity.

Servicing an I/O device often involves transferring large amounts of data between system memory and the device. With programmed I/O, this transfer is relatively inefficient because each data word has to cross the bus twice: once to get from the device to the CPU and once to get from the CPU to system memory (or vice versa). *Direct memory access (DMA)* avoids this inefficiency by copying data directly from the device to system memory (or vice versa). This is achieved through a *DMA engine*, which may be a separate controller attached to the system bus or may be part of the I/O device itself. Independently of where the DMA engine is implemented, the CPU uses programmed I/O to set it up and initiate a transfer. Upon completion, the DMA engine typically notifies the CPU by raising an interrupt.

7.1.1   Organization of modern machines

The bus-based machine organization discussed so far provides a convenient logical view of modern machines but in reality, they are much more complex. The primary reason is that a system bus that operates at several hundred megahertz necessarily has to be relatively short (because of signal propagation delays) and can support only a limited number of connection points (because of signal quality issues). Because of these constraints, modern machines generally use the system bus only to connect the CPUs, the system memory, and one or two *I/O bridges*. The actual I/O devices are then connected through secondary buses that are directly or indirectly connected to these bridges. This makes it possible to limit the physical dimension of the system bus and to maintain the high signal quality that is necessary to make a high-frequency system bus work reliably.

A secondary reason for the complexity of modern machines is that no single bus is perfect for connecting all I/O devices. Indeed, sometimes a bus is not appropriate at all, and other *I/O interconnect technologies*, such as high-speed point-to-point links between pairs of devices, are more suitable. This is exacerbated by the fact that it takes a long time to create and establish an I/O interconnect technology and, once popular, it is difficult to drop support for it, even if it is obsolete. This means that modern machines have to support several generations of I/O interconnect technologies. For example, some machines still support the original ISA bus, even though from a technical point of view, it is hopelessly obsolete [5]. Similarly, the PCI bus will be supported for a long time, even as its performance falls behind more scalable point-to-point interconnect technologies [53].

The net effect is that modern machines often have a highly complex organization. For example, a more realistic, but still simplified, view of a modern machine is illustrated in Figure 7.2. As the figure shows, there is still a system bus, but there are many important differences compared with Figure 7.1. First, instead of just one CPU, there are four CPUs. Second, the system bus is used only to connect the CPUs, system memory, and the I/O bridges—no I/O device is directly connected to the system bus.

In the figure, three I/O bridges are shown: two PCI host bridges and an InfiniBand channel adapter. As shown in the lower left of the figure, the first PCI host bridge connects the system bus to PCI local bus 0. On this bus, we find the graphics adapter and a USB controller. USB itself is a fairly complicated serial interconnect technology that typically connects low- to medium-bandwidth devices such as keyboards, mice, and audio speakers. To the right, the figure shows an *InfiniBand channel adapter* that connects the system bus to the *InfiniBand fabric*. This interconnect is not based on a bus but instead on switched point-to-point links, so the fabric is illustrated as a network cloud. This fabric connects to various I/O devices known as *InfiniBand nodes*. In the figure, only two nodes are shown, but in reality there could be dozens, hundreds, or even thousands of such nodes, each of which could be a simple device such as a disk or a network interface controller, a more autonomous device such as a network-attached storage component, or even an entire machine

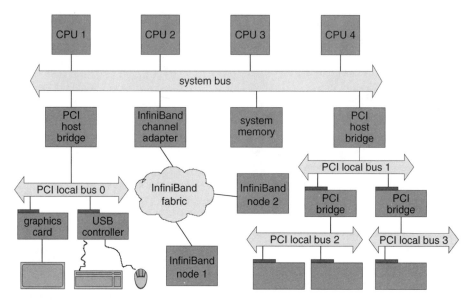

Figure 7.2. Simplified view of modern machine.

of its own. Finally, the lower-right of the figure shows that it is also not unusual for modern machines to provide for multiple PCI-type buses that are connected in a tree. While each PCI bridge adds a little latency, the advantage of such a scheme is that it makes the machine more expandable, often providing for dozens or hundreds of PCI expansion slots.

7.1.2   Software support for I/O on modern machines

While the complexity of modern machines can be quite daunting, the good news is that, at the lowest level, device I/O continues to be based on programmed I/O, DMA, and device interrupts. For example, once initialized, PCI bridges are transparent and all devices connected to a PCI bus can be accessed through ordinary programmed I/O, regardless of how many bridges there are between the CPU and the devices. Similarly, message-oriented interconnects such as USB and InfiniBand are accessed through software layers that use ordinary programmed I/O, DMA, and interrupts to manage a USB controller or an InfiniBand channel adapter, respectively. This is an important observation because it means that I/O device support can be broken up into two separate components: an *interconnect-specific component* (e.g., PCI vs. USB) and a *platform-specific component* (e.g., IA-32 vs. IA-64). Since Linux provides interfaces to abstract differences in the latter component, this means that Linux device drivers are interconnect specific, but not platform specific. For example, a properly implemented Linux device driver for a PCI network interface controller works correctly whether it happens to run on an IA-32, PA-RISC, or IA-64 machine.

void ***ioremap**(*paddr, size*);	/* map I/O area */
void ***ioremap_nocache**(*paddr, size*);	/* map I/O area uncacheable */
iounmap(*ioaddr*);	/* unmap I/O region */
io_remap_page_range(*uaddr, paddr, size, prot*);	/* map I/O area in user space */
unsigned char **readb**(*ioaddr*);	/* read byte (8 bits) */
unsigned short **readw**(*ioaddr*);	/* read word (16 bits) */
unsigned int **readl**(*ioaddr*);	/* read longword (32 bits) */
unsigned long **readq**(*ioaddr*);	/* read quadword (64 bits) */
writeb(*val, ioaddr*);	/* write byte (8 bits) */
writew(*val, ioaddr*);	/* write word (16 bits) */
writel(*val, ioaddr*);	/* write longword (32 bits) */
writeq(*val, ioaddr*);	/* write quadword (64 bits) */
rmb();	/* read memory barrier */
wmb();	/* write memory barrier */
mb();	/* full memory barrier */

Figure 7.3. Memory-mapped I/O interface.

7.2 PROGRAMMED I/O

Linux supports programmed I/O through two separate interfaces: one for memory-mapped I/O and one for port I/O. Memory-mapped I/O is generally more efficient and is therefore the preferred mechanism for newer device drivers. However, older devices or low-cost devices sometimes still make use of port I/O, and for this reason, Linux needs to continue to support it as well.

7.2.1 Memory-mapped I/O

Figure 7.3 illustrates the *memory-mapped I/O interface* (file include/asm/io.h) that Linux uses to abstract differences in how platforms support memory-mapped I/O. The interface consists of three sets of routines. The first set supports mapping and unmapping of device control registers. The second set provides routines to access the control registers, and the third set provides the means to order device accesses with respect to ordinary memory accesses. We describe each in more detail below.

Before the I/O control registers of a device can be accessed, they have to be mapped into kernel space with a call to *ioremap()*. This routine expects two arguments: the physical base address *paddr* of the control registers and the *size* of the control registers, measured in bytes. The routine maps the control registers into kernel space and then returns the kernel address at which control registers have been mapped. When the control registers are no longer needed, the mapped area can be released again by a call to *iounmap()*, passing it the address that was returned by *ioremap()*.

Sometimes it is necessary to map I/O control registers into user space. The interface supports this with the *io_remap_page_range()* routine. It is similar to *ioremap()* except that the control registers at physical address *paddr* are mapped directly at the user-space address specified by argument *uaddr*. Furthermore, the caller can use the *prot* argument to specify the exact page protection value with which the control registers are mapped. This argument has the platform-specific type **pgprot_t**, which we described in Chapter 4, *Virtual Memory*. Note that protection can be enforced only at the granularity of a page size. Before calling this routine, a caller therefore needs to verify that the user-level mapping would not have unintended side effects. In general, a user-level mapping is safe if the mapped control registers are aligned to a page boundary and occupy the entire physical address range that is being mapped. On the other hand, if some of the physical address range is occupied by control registers that belong to another device, the mapping almost certainly is unsafe and could seriously compromise the security of the entire machine. Just imagine what would happen if those other control registers could be used to reset the machine!

For portability, it is not possible to access I/O control registers directly, even after they are mapped into kernel space. Instead, they *must* be accessed indirectly with the special *I/O area access routines*. The *readb()*, *readw()*, *readl()*, and *readq()* routines can be used to read a control register. These routines read one byte (8 bits), one word (16 bits), one longword (32 bits), or one quadword (64 bits), respectively. They expect a single argument, *ioaddr*, which must be a naturally-aligned address inside the mapped area returned by *ioremap()*. For example, the call readb(*ioc*+3) would read the third byte of the control registers mapped at address *ioc*. Analogously, a control register can be written with one of *writeb()*, *writew()*, *writel()*, or *writeq()*. These routines expect two arguments, *val*, the value to be written, and *ioaddr*, the naturally-aligned address of the control register that is to be written. On 32-bit platforms, support for the *readq()* and *writeq()* routines is optional.

The I/O area access routines always use *little-endian byte order*. For machines that normally use big-endian byte order, this means that *readw()*, *readl()*, and *readq()* need to swap the byte order of the data returned from the control register. Similarly, the corresponding write routines have to swap the byte order of the data before placing it in the control register. In some cases, it is necessary to be able to access control registers without the byte swapping that normally takes place on big-endian machines. To support this, the memory-mapped I/O interface provides secondary versions of the access routines. The names of these routines start with a prefix of "__raw_". For example, __raw_readl() works like *readl()*, except that it never swaps the byte order of the 32-bit word returned from the control register.

The I/O area access routines guarantee that the control registers will be accessed in a coherent fashion. For example, data written to a control register with *writel()* is guaranteed to automatically become visible to the device. Correspondingly, data read, e.g., with *readl()*, is guaranteed to automatically return the value that the control register had at the time of the call. The exact way in which the I/O area access routines achieve coherency is platform specific. On many platforms, including Linux/ia64, *ioremap()* simply returns a mapping that is **uncacheable** (see Chapter 4, *Virtual Memory*). Since accesses through such a mapping bypass all caches, this automatically ensures coherency with the control registers. However, while uncached mappings are one way to guarantee coherency, it is not necessarily the only way. Platforms are free to use other approaches as long as they meet the coherency requirement. In a few rare cases, it is necessary to ensure that a mapping is not just coherent, but definitely **uncacheable**. For this purpose, the memory-mapped I/O interface provides a routine called *ioremap_nocache()*. This routine works exactly like *ioremap()*, except that it guarantees that accesses to the returned mapping are **uncacheable**.

A final aspect of the I/O area access routines is that they guarantee that the CPU will execute them in the order in which they are called. For example, if a device driver calls *writel()* and then *readl()*, the driver can be certain that the CPU will execute the former before the latter. In other words, calls to the I/O area access routines will not be reordered. However, when one of the write routines is called, there is no guarantee that the data will have arrived at the control register by the time the call returns. The only way to ensure this is to follow the write with a dummy read of a control register on the *same* device. This technique is sometimes called *read around write*.

Although the I/O area access routines are guaranteed to execute in order, there is still a potential ordering issue: drivers for DMA-capable devices often have to ensure that accesses to I/O control registers are ordered not just with respect to other accesses to control registers, but also with respect to ordinary memory accesses. This is the purpose of the last three routines: *rmb()* implements a read memory barrier, *wmb()* a write memory barrier, and *mb()* a full memory barrier. A read memory barrier ensures that the CPU finishes executing all previous read accesses before initiating any subsequent read accesses. For the purpose of the read barrier, both ordinary load instructions and the accesses performed by *readb()*, *readw()*, *readl()*, and *readq()* are counted as read accesses. Similarly, a write memory barrier ensures that the CPU finishes executing all previous write accesses before initiating any subsequent write accesses. For the purpose of the write barrier, both ordinary store instructions and the accesses performed by *writeb()*, *writew()*, *writel()*, and *writeq()* are counted as write accesses. The full memory barrier combines the effects of a read and a write barrier: the CPU finishes executing all previous accesses before initiating any subsequent accesses.

Example: Accessing the VGA framebuffer

To get a better sense of the memory-mapped I/O interface, let us consider how to access the framebuffer of a VGA-compatible graphics card. Normally, the VGA framebuffer resides at the fixed physical address 0xb8000 and contains 24 lines of 80 characters of text. Each character is represented as a 16-bit word: the lower 8 bits contain the ASCII code of the character to be displayed, and the upper 8 bits contain the character attribute. This attribute controls the foreground and background colors of the character, whether it is blinking, and whether it is displayed in brighter-than-normal intensity. For example, an attribute value of 0x87 would display a normal-intensity, blinking character in white on black. Given these assumptions, the following code could be used to print a blinking "X" character in the upper-left corner of the display:

```
display (void) {
    void *fbuf = ioremap(0xb8000, 2*80*24);
    writew('X' | (0x87<<8), fbuf);
    iounmap(fbuf);
}
```

As we can see, the first line calls *ioremap()* to map the physical memory range from `0xb8000` to `0xb8c700` into kernel space and saves the returned kernel address in *fbuf*. The second line writes the character `'X'` with attribute `0x87` to this address, which normally corresponds to the upper-left corner of the display. In the third and last line, the memory-mapped I/O area is released again by a call to *iounmap()*.

Of course, this example is not terribly realistic, since it would be inefficient to call *ioremap()* and *iounmap()* on each call to the function. Also, whether the example really works depends on the machine having a VGA graphics adapter installed and also depends on the exact state of the VGA graphics controller. Still, the example does illustrate the general usage of the memory-mapped I/O interface.

The example also raises an important question: just how does a driver know the physical address range that a given device occupies? The answer depends on the bus that the device is connected to. For legacy devices that were originally designed for the ISA bus (such as VGA), the address range is usually hardcoded. More modern buses, such as PCI, assign the address range dynamically at boot time or at runtime when a device is plugged into a machine. We discuss this in more detail in Chapter 10, *Booting*.

IA-64 implementation

The Linux/ia64 implementation of *ioremap()* is trivial thanks to region 6. As described in Chapter 4, *Virtual Memory*, this region provides uncached, identity-mapped access to the physical address space. This means that an uncached access to physical address *paddr* can be performed by an access to the kernel virtual address:

$$0\text{xc}000000000000000 + paddr$$

In other words, all that *ioremap()* has to do is to add *paddr* to the starting address of region 6 (`0xc000000000000000`) and return the resulting address. Since *ioremap()* returns uncached mappings, it can be used to implement *ioremap_nocache()* as well. The implementation of *iounmap()* is even easier: it does not have to do anything at all! Similarly, *io_remap_page_range()* can be implemented simply by a call to *remap_page_range()*. The latter is a platform-independent kernel function that maps an arbitrary physical address range into user virtual memory. This works on IA-64 because the only difference between mapping ordinary memory and mapping an I/O area is the memory attribute with which the address range is mapped, and since the caller of *io_remap_page_range()* is responsible for encoding the correct memory attribute in the *prot* argument, there is really no difference between the Linux/ia64 versions of *io_remap_page_range()* and *remap_page_range()*.

The fact that region 6 provides uncached access to the physical address space also makes it straightforward to implement the I/O area access routines. For example, *readb()* and *writeb()* could be realized as shown below:

```
#define readb(a)     (*(volatile unsigned char*)(a))
#define writeb(v,a)  (*(volatile unsigned char*)(a) = (v))
```

The address passed in argument *a* is already inside region 6, so it can be dereferenced directly. However, the routines must be careful to ensure that the accesses are performed in order, as required by the memory-mapped I/O interface. This is the reason the above routines use **volatile** pointers to perform the accesses. The first effect of using the **volatile** qualifier is that it stops the compiler from reordering or optimizing away the memory accesses. On IA-64, the qualifier has a second effect: it ensures that the compiler generates resulting load instructions with **acquire** semantics and resulting store instructions with **release** semantics (see Chapter 2, *IA-64 Architecture*). For example, the compiler would generate the ld1.acq instruction for *readb()* and the st1.rel instruction for *writeb()*.

Overall, the **volatile** keyword achieves the desired effect that neither the compiler nor the CPU will reorder the resulting memory access. Strictly speaking, it would be possible to use ordinary loads and stores here because the IA-64 architecture guarantees that uncached memory accesses are never reordered with respect to other uncached accesses. However, the **volatile** qualifier is still needed to ensure the compiler does not reorder or eliminate the access. Furthermore, IA-64–specific code can take advantage of the additional ordering guarantees that the ordered loads and stores provide: they guarantee that the I/O area access routines are ordered not just with respect to other I/O area accesses, but also with respect to *any other* memory access. The bottom line is that it is rarely necessary to use explicit memory barriers in IA-64–specific code. However, for portability, it is still necessary to implement the barrier routines *rmb()*, *wmb()*, and *mb()*. IA-64 provides the mf instruction (memory fence) for this purpose. The instruction realizes a full barrier. Because there are no special instructions for read or write barriers, mf is used to implement not just *mb()* but also *rmb()* and *wmb()*.

Ordering memory accesses on IA-64

The ordering requirements imposed by the memory-mapped I/O interface unfortunately match poorly with the memory model implemented by IA-64. It is therefore important to distinguish between the ordering guarantees that the memory-mapped I/O *interface* requires and the ordering guarantees that the Linux/ia64 *implementation* provides. When writing platform-independent code, it is essential to follow the former, whereas when writing IA-64–specific code, following the latter is slightly more efficient.

Let us consider a couple of examples. Suppose we had a DMA-driven serial-line controller that allowed us to output a string by placing it in the DMA buffer at address *dmabuf* and writing the length of the string to the DMA control register at address *dmactl*. Given this hypothetical serial-line controller, we could use the following code to write the string "hello" to the serial line:

```
memcpy(dmabuf, "hello", 5);
wmb();
writel(5, dmactl);
```

If we follow the ordering rules of the memory-mapped I/O *interface*, it is important to separate the call to *writel()* from the call to *memcpy()* by at least a write memory barrier (a full barrier would work, too). Otherwise, it could happen that on some platforms the *writel()* call is executed before the string written by *memcpy()* has arrived in the memory from which the DMA engine would read it. Thus, without *wmb()*, the output on the serial line might get garbled on some platforms. On the other hand, when we follow the ordering rules of the Linux/ia64 *implementation*, we could omit the call to *wmb()* because the store instruction that is issued as a result of the call to *writel()* will have **release** semantics. By definition, this will ensure that all previous memory accesses, in particular the ones that resulted from the call to *memcpy()*, are completed first.

Given the previous example, we might be tempted to think that it is never necessary to use the barrier routines on IA-64. This is not true, however. To see this, let us assume that we have a slightly different serial-line controller that initiates a DMA operation as soon as the I/O control register *dmactl* is read. For this case, let us assume that the first byte in the DMA buffer at *dmabuf* contains the length of the string to be output and the remaining bytes contain the string itself. We could output the string "hello" with the following code:

```
dmabuf[0] = 5; memcpy(dmabuf + 1, "hello", 5);
mb();
readl(dmactl);
```

In this example, the full barrier *mb()* is needed even on Linux/ia64. The reason is that *readl()* will perform a memory access with **acquire** semantics, which ensures that no subsequent memory access is issued until after *readl()* has completed, but it has no effect on prior memory accesses. In particular, it does not order the memory accesses that were issued by the call to *memcpy()*. Now, we should point out that this kind of controller is very unusual, and in the vast majority of cases, Linux/ia64 does not need any explicit barriers. However, since Linux/ia64 needs to be able to work properly even in the presence of such strange hardware, this example clearly demonstrates that barriers cannot be implemented as routines that have no effect.

The discussion so far illustrates that it very difficult to implement the memory-mapped I/O interface so that it fits perfectly with the memory model and ordering instructions provided by IA-64. This is indeed a common theme: there are just too many differences between the memory models of different platforms to make it possible to define a reasonable memory-mapped I/O interface that could be implemented optimally on each platform. Despite this, the interface at least does recognize the existence of weakly ordered memory systems, and this is much more important than the small performance penalty that a few extraneous memory barriers may incur.

7.2.2 Port I/O

Linux defines the *port I/O interface* (file include/asm/io.h) to abstract differences in how various platforms access control registers that reside in I/O space. Compared to the memory-mapped I/O interface, the major difference is that port I/O has much stricter ordering (consistency) requirements. Because of this, port I/O tends to be substantially slower than memory-mapped I/O. For instance, consider that on a 733 MHz Itanium workstation, writing a 32-bit word via memory-mapped I/O space takes just one cycle (from the perspective of the CPU). In contrast, writing the same control register via port I/O takes on the order of 100 cycles! Another important difference is that port I/O is often limited to a small address space. Most platforms implement a 16-bit I/O address space, meaning that there are a total of only 65,536 I/O ports. Together, these two limitations are sufficient to strongly

#define IO_SPACE_LIMIT	/* largest valid port number */
unsigned char **inb**(*ioport*);	/* input byte (8 bits) */
unsigned short **inw**(*ioport*);	/* input little-endian word (16 bits) */
unsigned int **inl**(*ioport*);	/* input little-endian longword (32 bits) */
outb(*val, ioport*);	/* output byte (8 bits) */
outw(*val, ioport*);	/* output little-endian word (16 bits) */
outl(*val, ioport*);	/* output little-endian longword (32 bits) */
insb(*ioport, dst, count*);	/* input string of bytes */
insw(*ioport, dst, count*);	/* input string of words */
insl(*ioport, dst, count*);	/* input string of longwords */
outsb(*ioport, src, count*);	/* output string of bytes */
outsw(*ioport, src, count*);	/* output string of words */
outsl(*ioport, src, count*);	/* output string of longwords */

Figure 7.4. Port I/O interface.

discourage the use of port I/O in modern machines. Unfortunately, even modern platforms cannot entirely avoid port I/O because there continue to be low-cost and ill-designed PCI devices that place some control registers in I/O space only. On the positive side, as long as a machine uses only well-designed I/O devices, there is no need to ever use port I/O and such a machine would not be affected by the poor performance of port I/O.

The port I/O interface is illustrated in Figure 7.4. It exports a platform-specific constant IO_SPACE_LIMIT that defines the largest I/O port number (address) that the interface can support. Many platforms implement a 16-bit I/O space and define this constant as 0xffff.

Six primary routines provide the ability to read or write a byte (8 bits), word (16 bits), or longword (32 bits). The routines that read from I/O space are called *inb()*, *inw()*, and *inl()* and read a byte, word, or longword, respectively. They take a single argument, *ioport*, which is the port number (address) that should be read. The routines that write to I/O space are called *outb()*, *outw()*, and *outl()*, respectively. The value to be written is passed in the first argument, *val*, and the port number is passed in the second argument, *ioport*. Like the memory-mapped I/O access routines, these routines always use little-endian byte order.

A secondary set of six routines provide the ability to read or write strings (sequences) of bytes, words, or longwords from or to I/O space. These routines are called *insb()*, *insw()*, *insl()*, *outsb()*, *outsw()*, and *outsl()*. Unlike the previous routines, these never perform any byte swapping. The routines all share the same basic interface: they expect the I/O port number in the first argument, *ioport*, the address of a kernel buffer in the second argument, *dst* or *src*, and a count in the third argument, *count*. In the case of the input routines, the kernel buffer stores the values that are read from the I/O port; in the case of the output routines, the kernel buffer contains the values that are to be written to the I/O port.

As alluded to earlier, the I/O-space accesses must adhere to strict ordering rules. Specifically, all accesses must be performed in order and must be ordered with respect to all other memory accesses by the same CPU. Indeed, I/O-space accesses should also ensure that

Figure 7.5. IA-64 sparse I/O port encoding used to access the legacy I/O space.

they are *accepted* by the I/O device in order. What this means is that all previous accesses should have returned data before initiating an I/O-space access and that the I/O space access should have arrived at the I/O device before initiating any subsequent accesses.

IA-64 implementation

The IA-64 architecture provides no special instruction to access I/O space, but for backward compatibility, it defines a single 64-Kbyte I/O space. This I/O space is called the *legacy I/O space* and targets two separate issues: first, it provides access to legacy *devices* that implement some control registers in I/O space only, and, second, it provides compatibility for legacy *applications* that perform direct I/O from the user level and assume that certain devices reside at specific I/O ports. For example, a legacy display-tuning utility might expect that a VGA graphics controller has its graphics control registers mapped at I/O ports 0x3ce and 0x3cf.

Since there are no special I/O instructions, IA-64 implements the legacy I/O space by mapping it into a 64-Mbyte memory-mapped region. Accesses to this region are then translated into corresponding I/O-space accesses either by the CPU itself or by a bus bridge. The base address of the region is called *iobase*. It must be aligned to 64 Mbytes, i.e., the least significant 26 bits of the address must be 0. Linux/ia64 maintains the address of this region in kernel register ar.k0 (see Chapter 10, *Booting*).

Now, why does the 64-Kbyte legacy I/O space take up 64 Mbytes in the memory space? The reason is that the I/O port numbers are *sparsely encoded*. Figure 7.5 illustrates how this encoding works: the least significant 12 bits of the I/O port number are encoded in bits 0–11 of the memory address, and bits 2–15 of the I/O port are encoded in bits 12–25. This means that bits 2–11 of the I/O port are encoded twice, and the double encoding of these 10 bits means that the size of the legacy I/O space is inflated by a factor of 1024 in the memory space. This encoding implies that I/O port 0 can be accessed through memory address *iobase* + 0, port 3 through address *iobase* + 3, port 4 through address *iobase* + 0x1004, and so on, up to port 65535, which can be accessed through address *iobase* + 0x3ffffff. As we can see, the effect is that each 4-Kbyte page corresponds to four I/O ports. This is handy because it means that the normal page protection mechanism can be used to implement fine-grained access control to the I/O port space. For instance, suppose a Linux application uses the *ioperm()* system call to request access to I/O ports 0x3cc to 0x3cf. With the sparse encoding, this access can be granted by mapping a 4-Kbyte page into user space that maps to physical address *iobase* + 0xf3000.

Accessing the 64-Mbyte legacy I/O space through uncached space ensures that I/O-space accesses are performed in the proper order, but it does not ensure that each access has been accepted by the device before executing the next one. IA-64 provides the special mf.a instruction (memory fence, acceptance form) for this purpose. Executing this instruction ensures that no subsequent data memory access is initiated by the CPU until (a) all previous reads from uncached memory have returned data and (b) all previous writes to uncached memory have been accepted by the target i.e., the I/O device. Linux/ia64 provides with the _ia64_mf_a() routine a convenient way for generating this instruction.

Given the discussion so far, it is clear that Linux/ia64 can implement the I/O interface on top of the memory-mapped I/O interface. For example, the kernel can map the 64-Mbyte legacy I/O space at boot time with a call along the lines of:

```
unsigned long kiobase = ioremap(iobase, 0x4000000);
```

With this setup in place, *outb()* could be implemented as shown below:

```
static inline void outb (unsigned char v, unsigned long p) {
    writeb(v, kiobase + ((p & 0xfff) | ((p >> 2) << 12));
    __ia64_mf_a();
}
```

That is, on Linux/ia64 we can write the byte v to I/O port p by using *writeb()* to write the byte to sparsely encoded legacy I/O space address that corresponds to port p. After this access, the mf.a instruction is executed to ensure that the access has been accepted before the CPU executes any subsequent memory accesses. The other port I/O routines can be implemented analogously.

Given the 64-Kbyte legacy I/O space, we might assume that Linux/ia64 defines IO-_SPACE_LIMIT as 0xffff, but this is not the case. Instead, Linux/ia64 pretends to implement a full 64-bit I/O space and defines the constant as 0xffffffffffffffff. This is done for a simple reason: large machines can easily have dozens or even hundreds of separate I/O buses. If each of these buses needed to support just a handful of legacy devices, the 64-Kbyte legacy I/O space could easily be exhausted. For this reason, Linux/ia64 leaves open the possibility of supporting multiple I/O spaces. The first 65,536 ports always map to the legacy I/O space, but ports above that range can map to additional I/O spaces in a machine-specific fashion. For example, the higher-order bits of the 64-bit I/O port number could be used to select which I/O space is being addressed. The additional I/O spaces would not be available to legacy applications because they cannot deal with port numbers above 0xffff, but the Linux kernel itself and most device drivers do not suffer from this limitation and could therefore readily support legacy I/O devices mapped in these spaces.

The implementation of multiple I/O spaces is facilitated by ACPI v2.0 (see Chapter 10, *Booting*). In the ACPI namespace, each bus object provides a control method called *current resource settings (_CRS)*, which returns a list of resources implemented by the bus. In this list, resources of type **I/O resource** are used to describe I/O spaces. Each **I/O resource** specifies the size, base address, and encoding scheme of an I/O space. In ACPI, these three values are known by the names _LEN (**length**), _TRA (**translation offset**), and _TRS (**translation sparse**), respectively. The encoding scheme indicates whether the I/O space uses dense or sparse encoding. If _TRS is non-zero, the same sparse encoding scheme is used as for the legacy I/O space. If _TRS is 0, a dense (one-to-one) mapping is used, where memory address $\_\mathrm{TRA} + p$ corresponds to I/O port number p. The bottom line is that ACPI v2.0 provides all the information needed to enumerate and access all I/O spaces implemented by a machine.

7.3 DIRECT MEMORY ACCESS (DMA)

Direct memory access (DMA) occurs whenever a device reads or writes system memory directly, i.e., without the involvement of the CPU. When data flows from memory to the device, this is called *outbound DMA*, and when it flows from the device to the memory, it is called *inbound DMA*. Although the DMA transfer itself occurs under direct control of the device, the CPU controls the device and thereby ultimately has control over when and where DMA operations take place. Conceptually, it is simple for the CPU to initiate a DMA transfer: for an outbound DMA transfer, it places the data somewhere in system memory and then informs the device of the location and size of that data and that it should start the transfer. Upon completion of the transfer, the device typically raises an interrupt and sets a completion bit in one of its control registers. For inbound DMA, the same basic steps occur except that the flow of data is reversed: the CPU informs the device of the location and size of an empty data buffer and that it can start the transfer whenever the device is ready. Once the transfer has completed, the device raises an interrupt and at that point the CPU can read the new data from system memory.

Unfortunately, this simplicity is marred by two factors:

1. Memory caches raise coherency issues: data written by the CPU may end up in a cache and may not be written to system memory immediately. Conversely, data written by the device ends up in system memory and may not update or invalidate the caches. Both scenarios introduce the potential of the CPU and the device observing different values for one and the same memory location, and such incoherency would prevent DMA from working correctly.

2. Some devices have limited DMA controllers that can address only a portion of the physical address space. For example, 32-bit devices can address only the first 4 Gbytes of the physical address space found in 64-bit platforms.

The first factor is, fortunately, seldom an issue because modern platforms provide *cache-coherent DMA*. This means that hardware automatically handles the cases where a DMA transaction hits a memory location that is currently cached. But on platforms that are not cache-coherent, the CPU must take care of explicitly flushing or invalidating its caches before initiating a DMA transaction.

The second factor is more serious. Suppose we have a machine with 64 Gbytes of memory and a disk controller that can use DMA only for addresses below 4 Gbytes. In such a machine, most of the disk I/O could not take advantage of DMA because if we assume uniformly distributed data buffers, there is only 1 chance in 16 (6.25%) that a given buffer will be below 4 Gbytes. Alternatively, instead of not using DMA at all, such a machine could reserve a few *bounce buffers* below 4 Gbytes, which are then used as intermediate buffers. This way the device can use DMA to move the data to or from the bounce buffer, and the

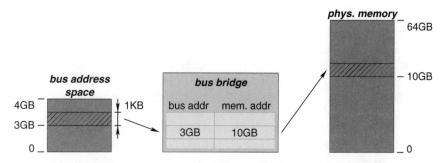

Figure 7.6. Using the I/O TLB to translate bus addresses.

CPU can take care of copying the data to or from the original buffer. While DMA is still being used, bounce buffers negate the primary benefit of DMA entirely: with programmed I/O, data has to cross the interconnect twice, but with DMA through a bounce buffer, data has to cross the interconnect three times! However, because programmed I/O is uncached, it is often still faster to use DMA through a bounce buffer than to resort to programmed I/O. Either way, because of the high cost of limited addressability, many platforms provide special hardware called the *I/O translation lookaside buffer (I/O TLB)*. On some platforms, the hardware is known as the *I/O memory management unit (IOMMU)*. However, since it is used to map *I/O space* rather than real memory, we prefer to use the term I/O TLB throughout this book.

I/O TLBs work like the CPU's virtual memory TLB, except that they translate bus addresses into physical memory addresses. This translation is also page based, though the page size does not necessarily have to be the same as for the virtual memory system. Just as for normal TLBs, a wide range of implementation options are available for I/O TLBs. For example, the replacement policy could be implemented in hardware or in software. In the former case, an *I/O page table* is associated with the I/O TLB that supplies translations for addresses that miss in the I/O TLB. Some I/O TLB implementations even support protection bits that allow the operating system to protect itself from errant DMA transactions that might be generated by a faulty device or a faulty driver.

To see how the I/O TLB hardware works, let us consider the example illustrated in Figure 7.6. It shows a machine with a single 32-bit I/O bus (e.g., a PCI bus) that is connected to 64 Gbytes of system memory through a bus bridge. The bus address space is represented by the leftmost rectangle, the bridge by the middle rectangle, and the physical memory by the rightmost rectangle. Now, suppose we had to transfer 1 Kbyte of data from an I/O device to a memory buffer at address 10 Gbyte. Since the I/O bus is only 32 bits wide, the buffer cannot be reached directly by the DMA controller. Instead, we can install an I/O TLB entry in the bus bridge, which then maps an otherwise unused bus address, say 3 Gbyte, to the buffer's address. Once this I/O TLB entry is installed, the CPU can go ahead and instruct the I/O device to use DMA to send its data to address 3 Gbyte. Whenever the I/O device writes some data to an address mapped by the I/O TLB entry at 3 Gbyte, the bus bridge will take care of automatically translating the address to the corresponding address in the memory buffer. The overall effect is that the I/O TLB neatly solves the problem of DMA controllers with limited addressing capability.

As this discussion illustrates, DMA is in practice a rather complicated issue. The coherency and I/O TLB differences alone make the problem challenging, but even this complexity is multiplied many times once we consider that different platforms have widely differing machine organizations ranging from simple single-bus machines to machines with hundreds of buses that may reside behind multiple and often different bridges. Not surprisingly, the result was that Linux historically supported DMA with various ad hoc interfaces. But as Linux started to be used on larger and more complex machines, these interfaces increasingly became a liability and in 1999 a group of kernel developers led by David Miller fixed the problem by introducing a high-level interface called the PCI DMA interface. Even though the interface is technically PCI specific, its abstractions and operations are sufficiently general that it can be used for many other I/O interconnect technologies as well. For this reason, the remainder of this section focuses on the PCI DMA interface.

7.3.1   PCI DMA interface

The *PCI DMA interface* (file include/asm/pci.h) is illustrated in Figure 7.7. As shown there, the interface defines a single, platform-specific type: **dma_addr_t**. This type must be wide enough to hold any bus address. On a 64-bit platform that supports only 32-bit PCI buses, this type could be just 32 bits wide. On the other hand, if the platform can support DMA controllers that can address more than 32 bits, a correspondingly wider type should be used.

The first routine provided by the interface is *pci_dma_supported( )*. It can be used to determine whether the DMA controller implemented by a given device can be supported by the platform. If the answer is negative, it would be necessary to operate the device with programmed I/O only (if possible) or to disable the device completely. The routine takes two arguments: *dev*, a pointer to a *PCI device structure* (struct pci_dev in file include/linux/pci.h) that corresponds to the device that the caller is inquiring about and *mask*, a DMA address mask that indicates the address bits that the DMA controller of the device can support. Each bit that is set in the mask corresponds to an address bit that is supported by the DMA controller. For example, for a DMA controller that can only address the first 64 Kbytes of data, the mask argument would be set to 0xffff. The integer result returned by the function indicates whether the platform can support the device: a non-zero value indicates success (device can be supported), and 0 indicates failure.

The remainder of the interface is divided into two parts: the first consists of just two routines and supports *coherent DMA*. The second consists of ten routines and supports *streaming DMA*. Both sets of routines can be called from an interrupt handler and therefore must not block execution under any circumstance.

Coherent DMA handles cases in which a data structure needs to be shared between the CPU and a device and the content of that structure changes frequently and incrementally.

In contrast, streaming DMA is intended for data that, once created, does not change until its entire content has been transferred through DMA. This distinction fits naturally with the queue-centric model that most modern DMA-capable devices employ. For example,

typedef **dma_addr_t**;	/* DMA address type */
int **pci_dma_supported**(*dev*, *mask*);	/* check if DMA is supported */
/* coherent DMA: */	
void *****pci_alloc_consistent**(*dev*, *size*, *baddr_ptr*);	/* allocate coherent memory */
pci_free_consistent(*dev*, *size*, *baddr*);	/* free coherent memory */
/* streaming DMA: */	
#define PCI_DMA_TODEVICE	/* DMA to device */
#define PCI_DMA_FROMDEVICE	/* DMA from device */
#define PCI_DMA_BIDIRECTIONAL	/* DMA in both directions */
#define PCI_DMA_NONE	/* invalid DMA direction */
dma_addr_t **pci_map_single**(*dev*, *buf*, *size*, *dir*);	/* map contiguous buffer */
dma_addr_t **pci_map_page**(*dev*, *pg*, *off*, *size*, *dir*);	/* map buffer by page */
pci_unmap_single(*dev*, *baddr*, *size*, *dir*);	/* unmap contiguous buffer */
pci_unmap_page(*dev*, *baddr*, *size*, *dir*);	/* unmap buffer by page */
pci_dma_sync_single(*dev*, *baddr*, *size*, *dir*);	/* synchronize buffer */
int **pci_map_sg**(*dev*, *sg_tbl*, *sg_len*, *dir*);	/* map vector of buffers */
pci_unmap_sg(*dev*, *sg_tbl*, *sg_len*, *dir*);	/* unmap vector of buffers */
pci_dma_sync_sg(*dev*, *sg_tbl*, *sg_len*, *dir*);	/* synchronize vector of buffers */
sg_dma_address(*sg_entry_ptr*);	/* get bus address of buffer */
sg_dma_len(*sg_entry_ptr*);	/* get length of buffer */

Figure 7.7. PCI DMA interface.

many network interface controllers (NICs) define a descriptor table that implements two ring buffers: a send and a receive ring buffer. Each entry in the descriptor table represents either a send buffer or a receive buffer and contains a pointer to the actual data buffer (the content of the network packet) and housekeeping information, such as whether the buffer is currently owned by the CPU or the NIC. For such a device, coherent DMA could be used for the descriptor table, and streaming DMA could be used for the data buffers.

Though we used the example of an NIC, the same distinction between descriptor tables and data buffers is natural to many other types of I/O devices, including disk controllers. In cases in which it is less clear whether a given transfer should be performed with coherent or streaming DMA, it helps to consider who allocates and owns the memory whose content is being transferred: for coherent DMA, the memory is allocated by the PCI DMA interface itself, and for streaming DMA, the memory is allocated by the caller. Coherent DMA therefore typically requires an extra copy to get the data into the DMA buffer. For this reason, it is almost always preferable to use streaming DMA to transfer large amounts of data.

Coherent DMA

Coherent DMA is easy to use. It requires that a coherent DMA buffer be allocated by a call to *pci_alloc_consistent()* and that the DMA controller be informed of the location (address) of this buffer. After that, both the CPU and the device share the buffer and they can both access the buffer directly. In particular, if CPU writes to the buffer, the writes will be visible to the device immediately. The same is true for the reverse direction: if the device writes to the buffer, the new data will be immediately visible to the CPU. In other words, the buffer is coherent with respect to writes from both the CPU and the device. This property is, of course, what gives coherent DMA buffers their name. On platforms where DMA is not cache-coherent, the implication is that coherent DMA buffers must be mapped uncached. It is therefore advisable to assume that CPU accesses to coherent DMA buffers are relatively slow. When a buffer is no longer needed, it can be freed by a call to *pci_free_consistent()*.

At this point we might wonder why the names of these routines end with a suffix of "consistent" instead of "coherent." This is unfortunately a historical misnomer: a memory system is said to be **consistent** when it is both coherent (each memory location has one and only one value at any given time) and the order in which memory accesses are being observed follows a certain set of consistency rules [2]. But coherent DMA buffers do *not* provide any automatic guarantees about the order in which memory accesses are being observed between the CPU and the device. Instead, memory ordering still needs to be enforced explicitly by calls to one of the barrier routines *rmb()*, *wmb()*, or *mb()*. Since coherent DMA buffers guarantee only coherency, not consistency, it is misleading and indeed wrong to use "consistent" in the routine names, but as long as this discrepancy is kept in mind, it is just a minor blemish.

Looking at Figure 7.7, we see that both the allocation and the deallocation routines take three arguments. The first one, *dev*, is a pointer to the PCI device structure for which the coherent DMA buffer is being allocated or freed, and the second argument, *size*, is the size of the buffer in bytes. The *pci_alloc_consistent()* routine returns two values. The first value is returned as the result value of the routine and is a kernel pointer to the newly allocated buffer. The second value is returned through the third argument, *baddr_ptr*, which must be a pointer to a DMA address. The value returned through this pointer is the DMA (bus) address through which the device can access the buffer. For example, in the case illustrated in Figure 7.6, the kernel pointer returned by the routine would be equal to *__va(*10 Gbytes) and the value returned through *baddr_ptr* would be equal to 3 Gbytes (see Chapter 4, *Virtual Memory*, for a description of the *__va()* routine). The DMA address is guaranteed to be suitably aligned for use by the DMA controller. For example, the DMA controllers found on ISA buses often limit transfers to at most 64 Kbytes of data that cannot cross a 64-Kbyte alignment boundary. Thus, when a coherent memory buffer is allocated for a device using such a controller, the DMA address is guaranteed not to cross a 64-Kbyte boundary. For *pci_free_consistent()*, the third argument, *baddr*, plays the analogous role: it specifies the DMA address of the buffer being freed. This argument must be equal to the DMA address that was returned by the corresponding call to *pci_alloc_consistent()*.

Streaming DMA

Streaming DMA is used to transfer data between an existing memory buffer and a device. To indicate the direction of the transfer, the interface defines four platform-specific constants: PCI_DMA_TODEVICE, PCI_DMA_FROMDEVICE, PCI_DMA_BIDIRECTIONAL, and PCI_DMA_NONE. The first is used for outbound DMA, the second for inbound DMA, the third is used when the same buffer is transferred more than once and in potentially different directions, and the fourth is an invalid direction used as a debugging aid to catch initialization or memory corruption errors.

Streaming DMA can be used to transfer an individual buffer or multiple buffers. The latter is known as *scatter/gather DMA* because inbound DMA scatters the incoming data into multiple buffers and outbound DMA gathers the data from multiple buffers.

Let us first take a look at the routines that handle individual buffers. The *pci_map-_single()* routine prepares a buffer for transfer by streaming DMA. The exact steps required here are platform specific but typically involve setting up a mapping in the I/O TLB hardware. The routine takes four arguments: *dev* is the PCI device pointer, *buf* is the kernel address of the data buffer, *size* is the buffer size in bytes, and *dir* is the direction in which the transfer is to take place. If the DMA controller used for device *dev* has any alignment constraints, the address passed in *buf* must already be suitably aligned. That is, unlike coherent DMA, streaming DMA requires that the caller take care of properly aligning the buffer. The routine returns a single value, which is the DMA address through which the device can access the buffer. This address can then be used to program the DMA controller. When a streaming DMA buffer is no longer needed, it can be unmapped by a call to *pci-_unmap_single()*. This routine expects the same arguments as *pci_map_single()*, except that the second argument, *baddr*, needs to be the buffer's DMA address instead of its kernel address. The routine takes care of freeing all the resources (e.g., I/O TLB entries) that were allocated during the corresponding call to *pci_map_single()*.

Linux v2.4.13 introduced an alternative pair of routines to handle individual buffers: *pci_map_page()* and *pci_unmap_page()*. They work exactly like *pci_map_single()* and *pci-_unmap_single()*, except that when a mapping is created, the address of the data buffer is specified by arguments *pg* and *off* instead of argument *buf*. The *pg* argument is a pointer to the descriptor of the page frame that contains the first byte of the data buffer, and *off* is the page offset of that byte. These routines are more general because they can be used to handle data buffers that reside in high memory (see Chapter 4, *Virtual Memory*). Indeed, they can be used to emulate the original versions with two trivial macros along the following lines:

```
#define pci_map_single(d,b,sz,dir) \
    pci_map_page(d, virt_to_page(b), b & (PAGE_SIZE - 1), sz, dir)
#define pci_unmap_single(d,a,sz,dir) pci_unmap_page(d, a, sz, dir)
```

In other words, the original routines are not really needed any longer, so we will not discuss them any further.

A streaming DMA mapping can be used for multiple transfers but, unlike the case for coherent DMA, coherency must be established manually whenever the buffer's content changes. This can be achieved with a call to *pci_dma_sync_single()*, passing the same arguments as for *pci_unmap_page()*, except that the transfer direction argument *dir* cannot be

Table 7.1. Coherency effect of streaming DMA operations.

op	DMA transfer direction		
	PCI_DMA_TODEVICE	**PCI_DMA_FROMDEVICE**	**PCI_DMA_BIDIRECTIONAL**
map	makes CPU data visible	no effect	makes CPU data available
unmap	no effect	makes device data visible	makes device data available
sync	makes CPU data visible	makes device data visible	*invalid*

PCI_DMA_BIDIRECTIONAL. The exact rules of when and how coherency is established for streaming DMA buffers are listed in Table 7.1.

As the table shows, the three operations *pci_map_page()* (*map*), *pci_unmap_page()* (*unmap*), and *pci_dma_sync_single()* (*sync*) establish coherency as a function of the direction of the DMA transfer. For example, the entry in the row labeled *map* and column labeled PCI-_DMA_TODEVICE reads "makes CPU data visible." This means that, for outbound DMA, mapping a buffer ensures that all writes performed by the CPU become visible to the device. In the second column, we see that, for inbound DMA, mapping the buffer has no effect on coherency; instead, it is the unmap operation that establishes coherency by ensuring that all writes by the device become visible to the CPU. The third column shows that for buffers mapped for bidirectional transfers, both mapping and unmapping the buffer causes coherency to be established. This means that bidirectional buffers generally have a higher overhead; because of this, they should be used only when absolutely necessary. Also note that it is invalid to call *pci_dma_sync_single()* with a direction of PCI_DMA-_BIDIRECTIONAL. The reason is that the routine would have no way of telling whose writes (CPU or device) the caller is trying to make visible.

For scatter/gather DMA, the three primary routines are *pci_map_sg()*, *pci_unmap_sg()*, and *pci_dma_sync_sg()*. These work exactly like *pci_map_page()* and so on, except that the data buffer is specified as a vector of scatter/gather entries. Specifically, the *sg_tbl* argument is a pointer to an array of *scatter list entries* (struct scatterlist in file include/asm/scatter-list.h), and *sg_len* is the number of entries in this table. Each entry specifies a linear memory region in the form of an address/length pair. The *pci_map_sg()* routine takes care of setting up the hardware such that DMA to these memory regions is possible. Since each region may require its own entry in the I/O TLB, it is no longer possible to return a single DMA address. Instead, the routine stores the DMA addresses in a platform-private section of the scatter/gather entry. The *sg_dma_address()* routine retrieves these addresses in a portable fashion. A specialty of *pci_map_sg()* is that it can coalesce scatter/gather entries if they are physically contiguous. Thus, the number of DMA buffers that have to be transferred may be smaller than *sg_len*. This is the reason *pci_map_sg()* returns an integer result: it specifies the number of DMA buffers that need to be transferred. If no coalescing takes place, the returned value is equal to *sg_len*. In the extreme case where all entries can be coalesced, the returned value is 1. Note that while *pci_map_sg()* may coalesce scatter list entries, it may not split them. The value returned by the routine is therefore never greater than *sg_len*. The sizes of the (possibly coalesced) buffers can be obtained with *sg_dma_len()*.

```
(1)  u32 *ctrlreg;
(2)  struct {
(3)    volatile u32 nsegments;
(4)    struct { u32 addr; u32 len; } seg[4];
(5)  } *mbox;

(6)  init (struct pci_dev *dev) {
(7)    dma_addr_t busaddr;
(8)    mbox = pci_alloc_consistent(dev, sizeof(*mbox), &busaddr);
(9)    ctrlreg = ioremap(0x1000, 4);
(10)   writel(busaddr, ctrlreg);
(11) }

(12) sendpacket (struct pci_dev *dev, void *hdr, size_t hdr_len,
(13)                void *data, size_t len) {
(14)   struct scatterlist sg[2]; int i, n;
(15)   sg[0].address = hdr; sg[0].length = hdr_len;
(16)   sg[1].address = data; sg[1].length = len;
(17)   n = pci_map_sg(dev, sg, 2, PCI_DMA_TODEVICE);
(18)   for (i = 0; i < n; ++i) {
(19)     mbox->seg[i].addr = sg_dma_address(sg + i);
(20)     mbox->seg[i].len = sg_dma_len(sg + i);
(21)   }
(22)   wmb(); mbox->nsegments = n;
(23)   while (mbox->nsegments); /* wait for DMA to finish... */
(24)   pci_unmap_sg(dev, sg, 2, PCI_DMA_TODEVICE);
(25) }
```

Figure 7.8. Using the PCI DMA interface to send a network packet.

7.3.2   Example: Sending a network packet

To get a better feeling for how the PCI DMA interface works, let us consider how to send a network packet with a hypothetical network interface controller (NIC). We will assume that the NIC has a single 32-bit control register that is memory-mapped at address 0x1000 and that it contains the address of a *mailbox* data structure used to coordinate the work between the NIC and the CPU. We will assume that the mailbox contains a 32-bit segment count followed by four segment descriptors consisting of a 32-bit start address and a 32-bit length each. Furthermore, we will assume that as soon as the CPU sets the segment count to a non-zero value n, the NIC will start to use DMA to access the first n segments and begin transmitting a network packet that contains the data in the segments. After the segments have been transferred, we will assume that the NIC clears the segment count back to zero.

Given these assumptions, we could send an arbitrary network packet as illustrated in Figure 7.8. The program fragment shown there first declares global variables *ctrlreg* and *mbox* to keep track of the memory-mapped control register and the address of the mailbox, respectively. This is followed by functions *init()* and *sendpacket()*. The former sets up the mailbox area and the latter actually sends a network packet. Specifically, in line (8) we can see that *init()* calls *pci_alloc_consistent()* to allocate a coherent DMA buffer for the mailbox data structure. This is ideal because the CPU and the NIC are constantly sharing the mailbox structure, so streaming DMA would be unsuitable. The DMA address of the coherent buffer is returned in variable *busaddr* and the kernel address of the buffer is saved in variable *mbox*. In line (9), the program calls *ioremap()* to map the control register and in line (10) it calls *writel()* to write the DMA address of the coherent DMA buffer to the control register. The NIC at this point knows the location of the mailbox structure and therefore is ready for operation.

Now, suppose we wanted to send a network packet. Typically, such a packet consists of a header and the actual data. In the *sendpacket()* function shown in line (12), we assume that the header and the data are passed separately as address/length pairs. Specifically, the header address is passed in argument *hdr*, its byte size in *hdr_len*, and the data address is passed in *data* and its length in argument *len*. This means that we need to use DMA for two memory areas that may not be contiguous. Thus, it is best to use the scatter/gather DMA routines.

The *sendpacket()* function starts by declaring a scatterlist array with two elements in line (14). In lines (15) and (16) the scatterlist is initialized with the header and the data portions. In line (17), the program prepares for streaming DMA by calling *pci_map_sg()*. As expected, it passes the PCI device pointer, the address of the scatterlist array, the length of the array (2), and PCI_DMA_TODEVICE as the DMA direction. The function then returns the number n of DMA buffers that are needed to map the data in the scatterlist array. Of course, in our example it is very unlikely that the header and the data portions are physically contiguous, but this could happen and in that case, the value returned by the function would be 1 instead of 2. In either case, after the function returns, the program loops over the number n of DMA buffers. In lines (19) and (20) it fills the location and size of these buffers into the mailbox segments.

Line (22) starts by calling *wmb()* and ends by setting the segment count of the mailbox to n. The write memory barrier ensures that the writes to the mailbox segments become visible to the NIC before the segment count is written. Once the NIC detects that the segment count is no longer 0, it reads the segment descriptors from the mailbox and starts to transfer the content of the DMA buffers.

The program waits in line (23) for the NIC to indicate that it is done with the transfer, which it will do by clearing the segment count back to 0. As soon as that happens, line (24) unmaps the DMA buffers by calling *pci_unmap_sg()*. Note that exactly the same arguments are being passed as in line (17). In particular, the scatterlist array length is still 2, not n. This is correct because the unmap routine needs to know how big the scatterlist array is, not how many DMA buffers were used during the transfer.

While this example illustrates how the PCI DMA interface can be used, we caution that the hypothetical NIC is grossly simplified. In particular, real NICs typically represent entire send and receive queues in the mailbox data structure and would, of course, be interrupt driven. But still, the principle of how scatter/gather streaming DMA is used remains the same.

7.3.3 IA-64 implementation

The IA-64 architecture provides for cache-coherent DMA. This means that no special actions need to be taken to ensure coherency between CPU writes and device writes. In particular, normal cached memory can be used for coherent DMA buffers. Note that DMA is coherent even with respect to the i-cache, even though it is *not* guaranteed to be coherent with respect to writes by the CPU, which go to the d-cache. Fully coherent DMA is advantageous because it means that executable code read with DMA will automatically update (or invalidate) the i-cache, thus obviating the need to flush the cache explicitly. As described in Chapter 4, *Virtual Memory*, Linux/ia64 uses the PG_arch_1 bit in the page frame descriptors to keep track of which physical page frames are definitely coherent with the i-cache. Since DMA is cache-coherent, this bit can be turned on whenever a page is read entirely through DMA. Loading an executable image through DMA therefore avoids the cache flushing that is necessary when programmed I/O is used. Since all modern disk controllers are DMA driven, this means that Linux/ia64 practically never has to flush the caches to establish coherency.

As described earlier, many platforms support some form of I/O TLB. However, the IA-64 architecture does not define such a mechanism, and it is up to the individual chipsets to provide such functionality. This implies that the IA-64 implementation of the PCI DMA interface varies, depending on the chipset that is in use in a given machine. For example, Intel's 80460GX chipset for Itanium has no I/O TLB [33], whereas the chipsets from other vendors typically support some form of hardware I/O TLBs. This raises an interesting question: what should happen when an I/O device is asked to use DMA to transfer data to a memory location that is out of its reach, but there is no I/O TLB? Linux/ia64 solves this problem in an elegant fashion: on machines that have no or only incomplete I/O TLB support, it provides a *software I/O TLB* implementation that uses DMA bounce buffers to emulate the PCI DMA interface.

Software I/O TLB

The idea behind the software I/O TLB implementation of the PCI DMA interface is to emulate a hardware I/O TLB by means of low memory and bounce buffers. Low memory is simply memory with a physical address that is small enough that any DMA controller in the machine can reach it. Normally, all memory below 4 Gbytes is considered to be low memory, but the exact boundary is determined at boot time by the *low memory threshold variable* (MAX_DMA_ADDRESS in file arch/ia64/mm/init.c). The software I/O TLB can allocate memory from this pool by passing the GFP_DMA flag to the kernel's page allocator. Low memory makes it straightforward to implement *pci_alloc_consistent()*: if a device's DMA controller cannot support the entire address space, the routine simply allocates low memory instead of normal memory. This ensures that coherent DMA buffers are always within reach of the device.

Streaming DMA is more complicated: the PCI DMA interface has no control over the location of the data buffers. It can therefore easily happen that the buffer is out of reach of the DMA controller. To fix this situation, the software I/O TLB uses bounce buffers that are located in low memory. In particular, when *pci_map_page()* or *pci_map_sg()* detects that a

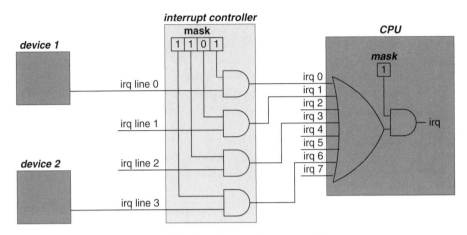

Figure 7.9. Linux hardware interrupt model.

data buffer is out of reach of the DMA controller, they allocate a bounce buffer from low memory and use the coherency rules illustrated in Table 7.1 to copy the data between the bounce buffer and the original buffer as necessary. Specifically, for those cases listed as "makes CPU data visible," the software I/O TLB copies the data from the original buffer to the bounce buffer; for the cases listed as "makes device data visible," the data is copied in the reverse direction. Note that the PCI DMA routines *must not* block execution. To ensure this, the software I/O TLB implementation reserves the necessary memory at boot time, when low memory is still plentiful. It attempts to reserve enough memory so that there is no risk of running out of bounce buffers in the middle of a DMA operation. If this statically reserved memory turns out to be insufficient later on, the implementation could also fall back on GFP_ATOMIC (nonblocking) memory allocation, but this should be thought of as a last-resort solution because, at that point, there is no guarantee that a sufficient amount of low memory is available anymore.

The net effect of the software I/O TLB implementation is that drivers can assume that any device in an IA-64 machine can use DMA to access any physical memory location, even though not all chipsets support a hardware I/O TLB. In other words, the PCI DMA interface is a powerful abstraction that greatly simplifies device drivers because it removes from them the burden of having to explicitly manage bounce buffers.

7.4   DEVICE INTERRUPTS

The platform-independent part of Linux uses a simple model to abstract differences in the interrupt system of each platform. This model is illustrated in Figure 7.9. As shown there, devices connect through an interrupt controller to the CPU: devices connect through *interrupt lines* to the interrupt controller which, in turn, connects to the CPU's interrupt pins. The figure also shows two levels of interrupt masking. In the CPU itself is a bit that masks the delivery of all interrupts. The second level of masking controls the delivery of interrupts from individual interrupt lines. This is illustrated with the 4-bit mask register in the interrupt controller. The Linux kernel does not actually care where the second level of masking bits is implemented: it could be inside the CPU, inside the interrupt controller (as illustrated), or any place else. The only constraint is that there is *some* means to mask individual interrupt lines. Note that most devices also offer the ability to mask interrupts in the device itself. However, this is a device-driver-specific aspect, so Linux does not provide a general interface for such masking.

Operationally, Linux uses interrupts in the following fashion. When the kernel detects a device, e.g., at boot time, it looks up the associated driver and asks it to initialize the device. If the device is interrupt driven, the driver looks up the irq number that is associated with the device and registers its *interrupt handler* with the kernel. For example, in Figure 7.9, the driver for device 2 would register its handler for irq number 6, since that is the pin the device will use to interrupt the CPU. Now, whenever the device needs service from the driver, it will assert its interrupt line. Assuming the line is enabled and the CPU has interrupt delivery unmasked, this assertion will cause the CPU to stop executing its current task and to dispatch execution to the interrupt handler that has been registered by the device driver. The driver then services the device (e.g., by reading a newly arrived network packet) and then returns so that the CPU can resume execution at the previous point.

But just what exactly is the context in which the interrupt handler is invoked? The answer is that Linux actually offers three different choices, depending on the *mode* selected by the interrupt handler. We call these modes **critical**, **noncritical**, and **deferred**. Each mode offers a different tradeoff between performance and execution-time restrictions.

In **critical** mode, the CPU executes the interrupt handler with interrupt delivery masked and uses the kernel stack of whatever task happened to be running at the time of the interrupt. This ensures that interrupt handling is initiated and completed in the minimum amount of time possible. In other words, **critical** mode minimizes interrupt response time. However, since it completely masks interrupt delivery, this mode should be used judiciously. In particular, it should be used only for devices that have little latency tolerance, and even then it should be used only if the handler can finish execution quickly. The exact definition of "quickly" depends on the details of the machine in use. An upper bound is that the sum of the execution times of *all* **critical** interrupt handlers must not exceed the minimum latency tolerance of *any* device in the machine. Fortunately, on modern machines, it is seldom necessary to use this mode because modern I/O controllers have sufficient buffering capacity to tolerate fairly large interrupt response times. Older devices, however, may have such small buffers that **critical** mode is unavoidable. For example, the original NS-16550 serial-line controller found in early PCs has a receive buffer than can hold just a single byte of data [59]. When operating at high line speeds, this buffer can easily overflow. To reduce the chance of this happening, **critical** mode would be appropriate.

To avoid the execution-time limit that comes with **critical** mode, device drivers should use the **noncritical** mode whenever possible. It works in the same way as **critical** mode, except that only the line of the device that caused the interrupt is masked while the handler is executing. This means that interrupts from other devices can still occur and can, therefore, preempt execution of **noncritical** interrupt handling.

Unfortunately, in some cases the processing required in response to an interrupt can be so lengthy that masking *any* interrupts for that period of time would cause problems. For such situations, Linux provides **deferred** mode, which is implemented by means of software interrupts. Software interrupts work like hardware interrupts, except that hardware interrupt delivery remains unmasked while a software interrupt is being handled. Another important difference is that software interrupt handlers are not invoked in response to hardware interrupts. Instead, they are raised by software. Typically, the way this is used is that the interrupt handler for a device will perform a minimal amount of work in **critical** or **noncritical** mode. If additional processing is required, the handler raises a software interrupt to finish the processing in **deferred** mode. For example, device drivers for network interface controllers use **noncritical** mode to extract a newly arrived network packet from the device and then raise a software interrupt to push the packet through the network stack (e.g., TCP/IP).

7.4.1   IA-64 hardware interrupt architecture

Before continuing, it is worthwhile to consider what a real-world hardware interrupt architecture might look like. Using IA-64 as an example, we will see that real hardware interrupt architectures are wildly more complex than the abstract model that Linux defines. Fortunately, the abstract model was designed to be flexible enough to accommodate the real world while presenting a nice, clean interface to the platform-independent part of Linux, including its many device drivers.

The IA-64 hardware interrupt architecture is called *SAPIC*, which stands for *streamlined advanced programmable interrupt controller*. This mouthful of an acronym reflects the history of PC-style interrupt controllers: the original PC used an Intel 8259 *programmable interrupt controller (PIC)*. When PCs with multiple CPUs started to appear, this PIC was replaced by a backward-compatible, but MP-capable, *advanced programmable interrupt controller (APIC)*. This controller was versatile, but because it had to be backward compatible with the original PIC, it carried a large amount of legacy hardware. IA-64 presented an opportunity to clean up this legacy hardware, and hence was born the *streamlined* version of the APIC, or SAPIC. Apart from removing the legacy hardware, SAPIC also incorporates various other enhancements, such as support for more CPUs (256 instead of 15) and faster interrupt delivery. Curiously, if we looked inside an IA-64 machine, we would not be able to find a chip called "SAPIC"—because SAPIC refers to the entire interrupt architecture. The actual implementation is divided into two halves: the CPU-local half and the I/O half. The former is called *LSAPIC* for *local SAPIC* and the latter is called *I/O SAPIC*. In line with this split, let us start by describing the CPU-internal aspects of SAPIC.

CPU-internal architecture

The IA-64 interrupt architecture is built around 8-bit *interrupt vectors* that identify the source (or type) of an interrupt. This means that, per CPU, up to 256 different interrupt sources can be supported. The first 16 vectors (0–15) are reserved and are used for special purposes such as the nonmaskable interrupt (NMI, vector 2). The remaining 240 vectors have no fixed meaning and can be used by an operating system as needed. The vectors are

Figure 7.10. Format of control register tpr (task priority register).

prioritized in order of increasing vector number. For example, interrupt vector 226 could interrupt (preempt) the handling of interrupt vector 224, but not vice versa.

When an interrupt occurs, a CPU initiates the normal interruption handling described in Chapter 2, *IA-64 Architecture*, and dispatches execution to the external interrupt vector at offset 0x3000 in the interruption vector table (IVT). There, the operating system can read the vector of the highest-priority pending interrupt from control register ivr (external interrupt vector register). In the case of a *spurious interrupt*, i.e., when this register is read when no interrupt is pending, a value of 15 is returned. Once the vector has been obtained, the operating system can look up and invoke the associated interrupt handler. After this handler returns, the operating system must signal the completion of the interrupt handling by writing control register eoi (end of external interrupt) so that the CPU can unmask the delivery of lower-priority interrupts that may be pending. The value written to this register is ignored: the write implicitly acknowledges the highest-priority interrupt vector.

In addition to vector-priority-based qualification, interrupt delivery can also be masked through the processor status register bit psr.i and control register tpr (task priority register). As described in Chapter 2, *IA-64 Architecture*, clearing psr.i masks the delivery of all external interrupts (including the nonmaskable interrupt, NMI). That is, if it is 0, no external interrupts are delivered to the CPU. In contrast, tpr provides finer-grained control over what interrupts are masked. The format of this register is illustrated in Figure 7.10. The 1-bit mmi field is used to mask (disable) all maskable interrupts. Turning it on will mask the delivery of all external interrupts, except the nonmaskable interrupt (NMI). On the other hand, if this bit is cleared, the 4-bit mic field controls what interrupt vectors are masked. For this purpose, the 256 interrupt vectors are divided into 16 classes of 16 vectors each: vectors 16 to 31 are in class one, 32 to 47 in class two, and so on. Writing a value of n to mic will mask delivery of all interrupts in classes 1 through n. Remember that vectors 0–15 are special, so class zero is never affected by mic. This means that setting mic to 0 will unmask all external interrupts and setting it to 15 will mask all interrupts except NMI. Note that the four least significant bits in tpr are ignored. This is convenient because it means that the effect of writing a vector number n to tpr is (a) to mask the delivery of all interrupts in the same or any lower class (i.e., mic is set to $\lfloor n/16 \rfloor$) and (b) to turn off the masking of all maskable interrupts (i.e., mmi is cleared).

It is important not to confuse vector priorities with interrupt classes. The former work at the level of individual vectors, and the latter work at the level of groups of 16 vectors. For example, vector priorities ensure that vector 226 can interrupt vector 224, but not vice versa. However, writing vector 224 to tpr will mask the *entire class* of vector 224, and since 226 is in that same class, its delivery will be masked, too. As we see later in this chapter, interrupt classes can be useful in preventing kernel stack overflows.

Each IA-64 CPU has three internal interrupt sources: the interval timer, correctable machine check, and performance monitoring unit (PMU) interrupt. Each source has its own control register that stores the 8-bit interrupt vector that is to be raised when the interrupt occurs. Specifically, the itv (interval timer vector) contains the vector number that is raised when the interval timer match interrupt is raised, cmcv (correctable machine check vector) contains the vector number that is raised when the CPU detects a correctable machine check (such as a memory parity error), and pmv (performance monitoring vector) contains the vector number that is raised when the PMU interrupt occurs (e.g., because of a performance counter overflow, see Chapter 9, *Understanding System Performance*). The CPU can mask delivery of these interrupts individually by setting bit 16 of the respective control register.

Platform interrupt architecture

Let us now consider how device interrupts are signaled to the CPU. Devices normally trigger interrupts in one of two ways: by *edge-triggering* or *level-triggering*. With the former, an interrupt line is briefly asserted and it is the *change* (i.e., the edge) in the signal that triggers the actual interrupt. In contrast, with level-triggered interrupts, a device asserts an interrupt line and then keeps it asserted until the interrupt has been handled by a CPU. Level-triggered interrupts are generally preferred in modern machines because they are less susceptible to noise and because they facilitate interrupt line sharing. For example, on the PCI bus, all interrupt lines are level-triggered. However, for backward compatibility with older devices, many IA-64 machines also support edge-triggered interrupt lines.

Now that we understand how interrupts are generated at the source (device), how do they get transmitted to the CPU? Perhaps the obvious way to do this would be for the CPU to provide a separate pin for each interrupt line. Each interrupt pin could then be mapped to one of the 240 available interrupt vectors that IA-64 provides. But since there are so many vectors, this would not be economical. Instead, the interrupt lines are wired to one or more I/O SAPICs, which translate interrupt requests from devices into *interrupt transactions* that are transmitted to the CPU over the normal system bus. On the system bus, an interrupt transaction looks very much like a regular read or write transaction, except that the transmitted data encodes an interrupt vector number rather than the address and content of a memory location. On MP machines, more than one CPU is connected to the system bus. To send an interrupt to a particular CPU, it is therefore necessary to also encode a CPU identifier in the transaction. IA-64 uses a 16-bit *local ID* for this purpose. When a machine boots (see Chapter 10, *Booting*), firmware assigns a unique local ID to each CPU and writes that ID to a special CPU control register called lid (local ID). During an interrupt transaction, the lid of the target CPU is encoded along with the interrupt vector number. The pair uniquely identifies what interrupt vector should be raised on which CPU.

Figure 7.11 illustrates the IA-64 interrupt architecture. It shows a dual-CPU machine with two bus bridges, two I/O SAPICs, and two separate PCI buses with two slots each. Note that the relative ratio between the number of CPUs, I/O SAPICs, PCI buses, and slot numbers is largely independent. The figure illustrates a pair of each simply to keep the complexity of the figure reasonable. In reality, a dual-CPU machine would most likely use just a single I/O SAPIC that supports two or three PCI buses with four to five slots each.

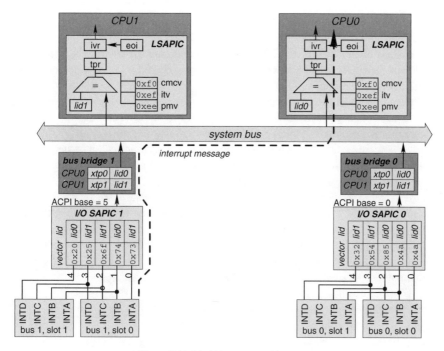

Figure 7.11. IA-64 interrupt architecture.

Looking at the two rectangles at the top of the figure, we see that each CPU contains an LSAPIC. Inside this controller, we find all the registers discussed so far: ivr to report the current highest-priority vector, eoi to acknowledge the completion of an interrupt, tpr to mask interrupts until the operation system is ready to handle them, and the CPU-internal vector registers cmcv, itv, and pmv. We can also see that the local ID register lid is connected to a comparator that filters out interrupt transactions targeted at other CPUs.

At the bottom of the figure we find four rectangles representing the four PCI slots. PCI provides four level-triggered interrupt lines per slot, labeled INTA, INTB, INTC, and INTD. A PCI device raises an interrupt by pulling one of these lines to the low signal-level. Each PCI interrupt line is wired to one of several I/O SAPIC interrupt pins. The figure illustrates only five interrupt pins per I/O SAPIC, but in reality, a single I/O SAPIC typically provides on the order of 64 interrupt pins. The I/O SAPIC contains a table that maps interrupt pins to interrupt transactions. This table is indexed by the interrupt pin number and has two columns specifying the vector number and the local ID that should be used for the interrupt transaction. For example, in the figure we see that INTB of slot 1, bus 1 (lower-left corner) is wired to pin 2 of I/O SAPIC 1. Since the corresponding table entry contains vector 0x6f and local ID *lid1*, asserting this interrupt line will result in an interrupt transaction for vector 0x6f targeted at *CPU1*. Most I/O SAPICs also contain other configuration bits that control miscellaneous aspects of interrupt generation. For example, there may be bits that control the physical aspects of the interrupt line, such as whether the line is edge- or level-triggered.

If we take a closer look at the interrupt line wiring and the I/O SAPIC tables, we see that interrupt sharing is possible at two levels. Level-triggered interrupt lines can be shared physically by multiple interrupt lines wired to the same pin. For example, pin 1 of I/O SA-PIC 0 is shared by INTB of slot 0 and INTA of slot 1 (lower-right corner of figure). Logical interrupt sharing is also possible by assignment of the same vector number to different interrupt pins. For example, in I/O SAPIC 0, we can see that pins 0 and 1 both map to interrupt vector 0x4a. As far as the IA-64 interrupt architecture is concerned, both types of sharing are legal. However, operating systems may have their own constraints on sharing.

Once an interrupt transaction has been formed by an I/O SAPIC, it is sent upstream, toward the system bus. On the way there, it may cross one or more bus bridges. Eventually, the transaction arrives at the final bridge and at that point one of two actions takes place: the bridge can either directly broadcast the transaction on the system bus or it can *re-steer* the transaction. With re-steering, the bus bridge replaces the local ID in the interrupt transaction with a different value before broadcasting it on the system bus. This gives the bridge a chance, e.g., to load-balance interrupts across different CPUs. Re-steering support in the bus bridge is optional and, even if implemented, a bridge may re-steer a transaction only if a special *interrupt redirection* bit in the interrupt transaction is turned on.

Looking again at Figure 7.11, we can see how re-steering is implemented. As shown there, each bridge implements a table with one row per CPU and two columns. The first column contains an xtp (*external task priority*) value, and the second column contains a local ID. If re-steering is enabled on an incoming interrupt transaction, the bus bridge searches this table for the row with the smallest xtp value. If there are multiple such rows, the bus bridge picks one of them in an unspecified fashion (e.g., the first one) and then replaces the local ID in the transaction with the local ID found in the selected row. As we see later, the xtp values are under the control of the operating system, and therefore re-steering provides a simple but flexible mechanism to implement dynamic interrupt load distribution policies.

Example: Tracing the path of an interrupt

At this point it may be helpful to review the discussion by looking at how an interrupt is raised and transmitted through an IA-64 machine.

Suppose that in Figure 7.11, the PCI device on bus 1, slot 0 asserts interrupt line INTA. I/O SAPIC 1 will detect this and since this line is connected to pin 0, it will access the corresponding entry in the I/O SAPIC table. This entry contains vector 0x73 and local ID *lid1*, so the I/O SAPIC will send an interrupt transaction with these values to bus bridge 1.

Let us further assume that re-steering is enabled for this transaction. Once the transaction arrives at the bridge, it will inspect its own table to determine a new target CPU for the transaction. If we assume that xtp0 contains a smaller value than xtp1, the bridge will re-steer the interrupt message toward the CPU with local ID *lid0*. The updated interrupt message is then broadcast on the system bus. The LSAPIC in both CPUs will receive this message, but since the local ID is *lid0*, only *CPU0* accepts the interrupt and marks it as **pending**. Since the interrupt has been accepted by the CPU, it is now only a question of *when* the interrupt will actually be processed by the CPU. For this to happen, the value in tpr needs to be low enough to let interrupt vector 0x73 through.

The final hurdle is that vector 0x73 needs to become the highest-priority pending interrupt. Once that happens, it is posted in ivr and, provided psr.i is enabled, the CPU dispatches execution to offset 0x3000 in the IVT. The operating system then reads the vector number from ivr and invokes the corresponding interrupt handler. Once the handler returns, the operating system writes the eoi register, thus completing the processing of the interrupt.

Interprocessor interrupts (IPIs)

In an MP machine, the operating system needs to coordinate its operation across the multiple CPUs that are in the machine. This is usually achieved through *interprocessor interrupts* (IPIs) and IA-64 is no different. The IPI facility of IA-64 is implemented in the LSAPIC in the form of a *processor interrupt block*. This block occupies a 2-Mbyte range in the physical memory address space. By default, its base address is 0xfee00000. This block serves two primary purposes: first, it can send an interrupt message to any other CPU in the machine and, second, it can set the xtp value of the local CPU. On machines with legacy 8259 interrupt controllers, this block serves a third purpose: it can generate legacy interrupt acknowledgment (INTA) cycles. Linux/ia64 has no need to use this feature.

The nice thing about transaction-based interrupts is that IPIs work exactly like ordinary device interrupts. If a CPU wants to send an interrupt to another CPU, all it needs to do is look up the local ID of the target CPU, combine it with the vector number it wants to send, and write the resulting value to the processor interrupt block. The LSAPIC will then generate an interrupt message on the system bus just like any bus bridge would, and the target CPU will process the incoming interrupt vector in the normal fashion.

Note that a CPU can send an IPI to *any* CPU, including itself. The latter can be useful for delaying the handling of an interrupt. For example, if an operating system received an interrupt at an inopportune time, it could simply record the fact that the vector had occurred and otherwise ignore it. Later, when the operating system is ready to handle the interrupt, it could *replay* the original interrupt by sending the previously ignored vector to itself with an IPI. The CPU and operating system can then handle the replayed interrupt as usual.

The fact that IPIs are indistinguishable from device interrupts is also useful. For example, if a CPU receives an interrupt and later on finds that it would be better to handle the interrupt on another CPU, it can forward the interrupt by posting an IPI to the other CPU.

Obtaining the machine configuration

The discussion so far illustrates that the IA-64 interrupt architecture is both flexible and powerful. But for an operating system to be able to take advantage of this architecture, it needs to have three distinct pieces of information:

- The local ID of each CPU in the machine.

- The number, type, and base address of each I/O SAPIC in the machine.

- The interrupt routing (wiring) that connects the interrupt lines to the I/O SAPIC pins.

#define NR_IRQS	/* max. irq number + 1 */
#define SA_INTERRUPT	/* latency-critical interrupt */
#define SA_SHIRQ	/* sharable interrupt */
#define SA_SAMPLE_RANDOM	/* randomness source */
int **request_irq**(*irq, handler, flags, name, dev_ptr*);	/* register interrupt handler */
free_irq(*irq, dev_ptr*);	/* cancel interrupt handler */
enable_irq(*irq*);	/* enable interrupt */
disable_irq(*irq*);	/* disable interrupt */
disable_irq_nosync(*irq*);	/* disable intr. immediately */
unsigned long **probe_irq_on**();	/* start probing for irq number */
int **probe_irq_off**(*cookie*);	/* return triggered irq */

Figure 7.12. Device interrupt interface.

All of this can be obtained from ACPI (see Chapter 10, *Booting*). Specifically, the *multiple APIC description table (MADT)* contains the information needed for the first two items: it describes both the LSAPICs and I/O SAPICs that are installed in the machine. The LSAPIC entries specify the local ID of the CPU, among other things. The I/O SAPIC entries primarily provide the type, base address, and number of interrupt pins. Obtaining the interrupt routing information is more complicated; Chapter 10, *Booting*, describes this in more detail. Loosely speaking, ACPI provides a list that describes how the four interrupt lines of each PCI slot are wired to the I/O SAPIC pins. There is only one problem: since there can be multiple I/O SAPICs, there must be a way to uniquely identify the interrupt pin of each I/O SAPIC. ACPI achieves this by assigning a *base interrupt line number* in the MADT entry of each I/O SAPIC. A machinewide *global interrupt line number* can then be obtained by adding the I/O SAPIC pin number to this base number. For instance, Figure 7.11 on page 323 shows that ACPI assigned a base value of 0 to I/O SAPIC 0 (ACPI base = 0) and a base value of 5 to I/O SAPIC 1 (ACPI base = 5). The global interrupt line number for pin three of I/O SAPIC 1 would therefore be 8.

7.4.2 Device interrupt interface

Now that we have seen a real-world hardware interrupt architecture, we are in a better position to appreciate the simplicity and elegance of the Linux device interrupt interface. This interface is illustrated in Figure 7.12. It is centered around the concept of the *irq number*. Loosely speaking, an irq number corresponds to an interrupt line connected to a CPU. Linux assumes that these numbers occupy the range of 0 to NR_IRQS − 1, where NR_IRQS is a platform-specific constant. Ideally, each interrupt source would have its own irq number, but since this is not always possible, Linux does allow multiple devices to share the same irq number. Sharing interrupts imposes a performance penalty, but compared to not being able to support all the devices in a given machine, this approach is still preferable.

A device driver, or indeed any interrupt-driven kernel code, can install (register) an interrupt handler by calling *request_irq()*. This routine takes five arguments: the first is *irq*, the irq number for which the handler should be installed. The second argument, *handler*, is a pointer to the interrupt handler (see Section 7.4.3), and the third argument, *flags*, specifies additional information about the interrupt handler and is expressed as the bitwise-**or** of the platform-specific constants SA_INTERRUPT, SA_SHIRQ, and SA_SAMPLE_RANDOM.

The SA_INTERRUPT flag indicates whether the handler should be executed in **critical** or **noncritical** mode. If it is set, **critical** mode is used, i.e., the handler is executed with all interrupts disabled. Most device drivers do not (and should not) set this flag. The SA_SHIRQ flag signals that the handler can share the irq number with other devices. This means that the handler must be able to detect and gracefully handle the situation where it gets called even though its underlying device did not request the interrupt. All device drivers that can support shared interrupts should set this flag to ensure that Linux will work properly on machines with a small number of irq numbers. The third flag, SA_SAMPLE_RANDOM, is only a hint; it does not affect correctness of operation. When it is set, it indicates that the device is a good source of randomness. This randomness is collected and made available by the kernel's random number generator (normally accessed through /dev/random or /dev/urandom). A device qualifies as a good source of randomness if the time between interrupts is highly variable and unpredictable. Note, however, that for most classes of devices, higher-level software already takes care of collecting available randomness, so there is often little or no point in setting this flag. For instance, the time between the completion of SCSI device requests is sampled by the SCSI layer so a SCSI device driver does not need to set SA_SAMPLE_RANDOM.

The last two arguments to *request_irq()* are used for identification purposes. Specifically, the fourth argument, *name*, is a pointer to a string that provides a human-readable name for the interrupt handler. This name is printed in the last column of the output of /proc/interrupts, for example. In contrast, the fifth argument, *dev_ptr* is used for kernel-internal identification purposes: it must be a non-NULL pointer that uniquely identifies the device for which this handler is being installed. For PCI devices, a pointer to the PCI device structure could be passed. However, the device interrupt interface does not interpret this pointer on its own; so as long as the pointer is unique, any other value can be passed. The return value of *request_irq()* is an integer error code: a value of 0 indicates success. In the case of failure, the routine returns the negative value of the error code indicating the reason of the failure. For example, calling this routine for an irq number that already has a nonsharable interrupt handler installed results in an error code of −EBUSY.

Once installed, an interrupt handler gets called whenever an interrupt is requested for the corresponding irq number. For interrupt handlers sharing a single irq number, this means that each handler gets called every time any one of the devices requests an interrupt. With N interrupt handlers, this usually means that $N - 1$ of the interrupt handlers will find that there is no work to do, so the time they spend to determine this is effectively wasted. For maximum performance, *machines* should therefore be designed to avoid interrupt sharing as much as possible. However, *device drivers* should always try to support interrupt sharing and, if they can, register their interrupt handler with the SA_SHIRQ flag set. Otherwise, the driver may render the device unusable on a machine that requires interrupt sharing.

When an interrupt handler is no longer needed, its registration can be canceled by a call to *free_irq()*. This routine takes two arguments, *irq* and *dev_ptr*. Argument *irq* is the irq number under which the handler was registered, and *dev_ptr* must be the unique pointer identifying the exact device for which the handler was registered.

Sometimes it is necessary to temporarily disable (mask) the delivery of interrupts from a given irq number. For this purpose, the interface provides the *disable_irq()* and *enable_irq()* routines. Both expect a single argument, *irq*, the irq number that should be disabled or enabled, respectively. Interrupts that are triggered for an irq number that is disabled remain pending until *enable_irq()* is called and are delivered at that time. Calls to these routines can be nested, and interrupt delivery is enabled only when the number of calls to *enable_irq()* is equal to the number of calls to *disable_irq()*. Calling *enable_irq()* without first calling *disable_irq()* is illegal; attempting to do this will result in a warning message. On MP machines, *disable_irq()* does not return until all interrupt handling that may currently be in progress for the irq number has finished execution. Of course, in a situation where an interrupt handler would have to disable its own irq number, this would result in a deadlock (see Chapter 8, *Symmetric Multiprocessing*). For this reason, the interface also provides a routine called *disable_irq_nosync()* which works exactly like *disable_irq()* except that it returns immediately.

Note that *disable_irq()* and *enable_irq()* are quite different from the *local_irq_disable()* and *local_irq_enable()* routines from Chapter 3, *Processes, Tasks, and Threads*: the last two affect interrupt delivery on the local CPU for all devices, whereas the first two affect interrupt delivery for a particular irq number on all CPUs. Also note that for shared irq numbers, *disable_irq()* will affect interrupt delivery for *all* devices that share this irq number. For this reason, device drivers should avoid using *disable_irq()* and instead mask interrupts directly in the device if that is possible.

The device interrupt interface also provides a facility to autodetect the irq number that a particular device is using. This facility is heuristic in nature so there is no guarantee that it works at all times and under all possible circumstances. Fortunately, on modern machines, the devices themselves (e.g., PCI devices) or firmware (e.g., ACPI) provides the irq number so autodetection is generally not needed anymore. Still, drivers for older devices may continue to use this facility, so Linux needs to continue to support it.

Autodetecting the irq number for a particular device works as follows: first, the device needs to be initialized so no interrupts are pending. Next, *probe_irq_on()* is called, and the device is then manipulated such that it will generate an interrupt. In the third and last step, *probe_irq_off()* is called. If everything worked right, the facility will have detected the interrupt that was generated by the device and will return the corresponding irq number. If no interrupt was detected, 0 is returned; if multiple interrupts were detected, the negative value of the smallest detected irq number is returned. The *probe_irq_on()* routine takes no arguments but returns a value that should be passed unmodified as the *cookie* argument to *probe_irq_off()*. Note that it is not possible to autodetect irq number 0 since this would be indistinguishable from the case where no interrupt was detected. Another limitation is that the facility cannot be used to autodetect shared irq numbers.

struct irq_desc ***irq_desc**(*irq*);	/* get irq descriptor for irq */
u8 **irq_to_vector**(*irq*);	/* get IA-64 vector from irq number */
unsigned int **local_vector_to_irq**(*vector*);	/* get irq number for local vector */

Figure 7.13. Linux/ia64 interrupt vector interface.

IA-64 implementation

Linux/ia64 associates each irq number with an *irq descriptor* (struct irq_desc in file include/-linux/irq.h). This descriptor consists of the following major components:

- **Action list:** The list of interrupt handlers that have been registered for this irq number. If multiple devices share the irq number, this list contains one entry per device.

- **Interrupt controller:** A pointer to an interrupt controller structure that defines how the irq number is to be managed. For example, the structure defines how to disable or enable the irq number, how to acknowledge an interrupt, and so on.

- **Status:** Various flags that describe the current status of the irq number, e.g., whether an interrupt is pending or whether the interrupt handler is currently running.

Now, how many irq numbers do we need for IA-64? Or asked differently, what should the value of NR_IRQS be? Since interrupt vector numbers are 8 bits wide, a value of 256 seems reasonable. For many machines, this is indeed a good choice. However, large machines contain multiple, independent system buses and since interrupt vectors are transmitted over the system bus, each system bus may have its own vector number space. In other words, on large machines, NR_IRQS may have to be set to the number of system buses times 256. It is even conceivable to build machines where each CPU would have its own 8-bit vector space. In such cases, there would no longer be a direct correspondence between the IA-64 interrupt vector and the Linux irq number. Instead, the mapping would become entirely machine specific. Another effect would be that NR_IRQS could become very large, which could make impractical the representation of the irq descriptor table as a single array of irq descriptors. To keep all this manageable, Linux/ia64 defines a simple *interrupt vector interface* (file include/asm-ia64/hw_irq.h) that abstracts such differences.

This interface is illustrated in Figure 7.13. The first routine, *irq_desc()*, returns a pointer to the irq descriptor that corresponds to the irq number passed in argument *irq*. The second routine, *irq_to_vector()*, maps the irq number passed in argument *irq* to the IA-64 interrupt vector it corresponds to. The third and final routine, *local_vector_to_irq()*, maps the local interrupt vector passed in argument *vector* to the corresponding irq number. Here, "local" means that the routine performs the translation in accordance with the CPU that is calling the routine.

For small- to medium-sized machines, 256 irq numbers are plenty, and in those cases implementing this interface is trivial: *irq_to_vector()* and *local_vector_to_irq()* can be identity functions, i.e., they directly return the value being passed in the argument. Similarly, with just 256 irq numbers, there is no problem with using a single array to represent the irq descriptor table, so *irq_desc()* can simply index this array and return a pointer to the appropriate entry. On larger machines, this interface would have to be implemented in a way that matches the needs and the organization of the actual machine.

The Linux/ia64 interrupt vector interface makes it possible to accommodate a wide range of schemes to map IA-64 vectors to irq numbers (and vice versa). However, one constraint must be observed by all implementations: interrupt sources that share the same irq number also must share the same interrupt controller. The reason is that the pointer to the interrupt controller is stored in the irq descriptor and hence there can be only one controller per irq number. This implies that different interrupt controllers cannot share the same IA-64 vector number unless they map to distinct irq numbers.

On Linux/ia64, each type of interrupt controller is represented by an *interrupt controller structure* (struct hw_interrupt_type in file include/linux/irq.h). It consists of a string and several callback function pointers. The string provides a human-readable name that identifies the type of the interrupt controller. For example, this string is printed in the second-last column of the output from /proc/interrupts. The primary callback functions are *startup()*, *shutdown()*, *enable()*, *disable()*, *ack()*, and *end()*. They all take a single argument, the irq number that should be affected by the call. As its name suggests, *startup()* is called when the irq number is used for the first time. The routine enables the interrupt line and performs any other controller-specific initialization that might be necessary. Conversely, *shutdown()* is called when the irq number is no longer in use, and the routine should disable the interrupt line as well as perform any other operations that might be necessary at that point. The *disable()* and *enable()* callbacks can temporarily disable the interrupts for a given irq number. The final two callbacks, *ack()* and *end()*, are called at beginning and end of interrupt handling. Their exact operation depends on the interrupt controller. Next, we see examples of how the callbacks can be used.

Linux/ia64 provides at least four types of interrupt controllers, known by their names **none**, **LSAPIC**, **IO-SAPIC-level**, and **IO-SAPIC-edge**.

- **none:** This is a *dummy interrupt controller* (file arch/ia64/kernel/irq.c) that is used for irq numbers not in use. The callbacks perform no operation except that *ack()* prints a warning message indicating that the irq number triggered unexpectedly.

- **LSAPIC:** The *LSAPIC interrupt controller* (file arch/ia64/kernel/irq_lsapic.c) represents the local SAPIC that is built into each IA-64 CPU. Since the interrupt sources managed with this controller are built into the CPU itself, no external hardware needs to be managed and none of the callbacks perform any real work.

- **IO-SAPIC-level:** The *level-triggered interrupt controller* (file arch/ia64/kernel/iosapic.c) is used for interrupt lines that are connected to I/O SAPIC pins that are level-triggered. For this controller, both *startup()* and *enable()* program the I/O SAPIC to unmask interrupt delivery for the corresponding interrupt pin. Callbacks *shutdown()* and *disable()* perform the complementary operation. The *ack()* callback performs no operation, but *end()* sends an end-of-interrupt transaction to the I/O SAPIC to let it know that the Linux kernel has finished handling an interrupt (this transaction is independent of the CPU-internal eoi register).

- **IO-SAPIC-edge:** The *edge-triggered interrupt controller* (file arch/ia64/kernel/iosa-pic.c) is used for interrupt lines that are connected to an I/O SAPIC pin that is edge-triggered. The *startup()*, *enable()*, *shutdown()*, and *disable()* callbacks work the same as for the level-triggered case. In contrast to the level-triggered case, the *end()* call-back performs no operation because with edge-triggered interrupt sources, there is no need to inform the I/O SAPIC of the completion of interrupt handling. On the other hand, since there is no explicit end-of-interrupt transaction, the kernel needs to be protected from the flood of interrupts that could result from a faulty or uninitialized device that constantly triggers interrupts. The *ack()* callback achieves this protection by checking whether this interrupt line has been triggered before and whether it is (still) disabled. If so, *ack()* calls *disable()* to mask the line either permanently or until a device driver registers an interrupt handler for it.

Note that some I/O SAPICs allow each individual interrupt pin to be configured to operate either in level- or in edge-triggered mode. Since Linux/ia64 uses different interrupt controller structures to represent these modes, it is possible that the irq descriptors for a single I/O SAPIC may point to different interrupt controller structures, even though they share the same physical I/O SAPIC.

With the interrupt vector interface and the interrupt controller abstraction explained, we can now take a look at how the remainder of the device interrupt interface is implemented. Let us start by considering the interrupt flags SA_INTERRUPT, SA_SHIRQ, and SA_SAMPLE_RANDOM. It turns out that their exact values are not critical (as long as they are unique), and Linux/ia64 simply uses the values that most other platforms use.

The Linux/ia64 implementation of *request_irq()* first looks up the irq descriptor with *irq_desc()* and then checks whether the desired irq number is still available. This is the case if no other interrupt handler has been registered yet (descriptor's action list is empty) or if the previously registered handlers as well as the new handler are all sharable, as indicated by the SA_SHIRQ flag. If the irq number is not available, the routine returns with error code −EBUSY. Otherwise, it allocates a new irq action structure, fills in the info for the new handler, and then appends it to the action list in the irq descriptor. In the final step, the routine checks whether this is the first time a handler has been registered for this irq number and, if so, it calls the *startup()* callback of the associated interrupt controller.

The *free_irq()* routine is complementary in that it cancels an interrupt handler with the following steps. First, it checks whether this is the last interrupt handler that has been registered for the irq number. If so, it calls the *shutdown()* callback of the associated interrupt controller. Second, it atomically removes the irq action structure that corresponds to the interrupt handler and frees the associated memory.

Linux/ia64 implements the *enable_irq()* and *disable_irq_no_sync()* routines by looking up the irq descriptor and invoking the associated interrupt controller's *enable()* or *disable()* callback, respectively. The *disable_irq()* routine works the same as *disable_irq_no_sync()*, except that after disabling the irq number, it waits until all interrupt handling that may currently be in progress for this irq number has completed.

Automatic irq number probing is implemented by *probe_irq_on()* and *probe_irq_off()* as follows. The former iterates over each irq descriptor and for those descriptors that are unused (do not have an interrupt handler installed), it enables them temporarily by calling the interrupt controller's *startup()* callback and marking the descriptor with the special flags IRQ_AUTODETECT and IRQ_WAITING. It does this *without* installing an interrupt handler. Now, when an interrupt occurs for which there is no handler, Linux/ia64 clears the IRQ_WAITING flag and masks the irq number by calling the interrupt controller's *disable()* routine. Thus, *probe_irq_off()* can detect which interrupt fired by looking for an irq number whose descriptor has the IRQ_AUTODETECT flag set and the IRQ_WAITING flag cleared. If autodetection works properly, there is exactly one such irq number and the routine will return this number as the result value. If there are multiple irq numbers, the routine returns the negative value of the smallest irq number that triggered. Note that it is not possible to autoprobe for shared interrupt lines that are already in use. This is because *probe_irq_on()* completely ignores descriptors that already have one or more interrupt handlers installed, independently of whether they are marked with the SA_SHIRQ flag. This is not an issue in practice because autoprobing is needed only for old edge-triggered devices, which are not sharable for electrical reasons.

It is worthwhile to point out that this implementation is almost platform independent. Indeed, since Linux/ia64 already uses the interrupt vector interface to abstract the mapping from irq number to interrupt descriptor and the interrupt controller structure to manage irq numbers, it would be straightforward to design a generic implementation of the device interrupt interface that would be completely portable. Indeed, this is expected to happen at some point during the evolution of the Linux kernel.

7.4.3   Interrupt handling

When an interrupt occurs, the CPU stops its current task and starts executing a platform-specific, low-level interrupt handler. It is the job of the low-level interrupt handler to execute the kernel entry path as usual (Chapter 5, *Kernel Entry and Exit*), to determine the irq number of the interrupt that just occurred, and to invoke the device driver handlers that have been registered for the irq number. Once all handlers have been executed, the kernel needs to check whether any software interrupts are pending and, if so, handle them by calling the platform-independent *software interrupt handler* (*do_softirq()* in file kernel/softirq.c). The prototype of the interrupt handlers is as follows:

```
void irqhandler(irq, dev_ptr, pt_regs);
```

Here, *irq* is the irq number, and *dev_ptr* is the unique pointer that was passed in the argument of the same name when the handler was registered by *request_irq()*. The third argument, *pt_regs*, is a pointer to the pt-regs structure that the kernel entry path created in response to the interrupt. This argument is normally not needed by device drivers, but it is sometimes useful for debugging.

Two important questions around interrupt handling concern *interrupt serialization* and *interrupt nesting*.

Interrupt serialization relates to the question of how much concurrency an interrupt handler needs to cope with. The answer is that Linux normally serializes interrupt handler execution on the basis of irq numbers. That is, for any given irq number, at most one interrupt handler is running at any given time. As a special case, some platforms, including Linux/ia64, support an IRQ_PER_CPU flag in the interrupt descriptor. If this flag is turned on, the registered handlers are invoked immediately when an interrupt occurs, regardless of whether another CPU may be executing the handler already. This prevents needless serialization when interrupt handling is completely local to the CPU that is fielding the interrupt. In the case of Linux/ia64, this flag is used for virtually all interrupts generated by the LSAPIC, including the interval timer and the performance monitor unit interrupts.

Interrupt nesting relates to the question as to whether and how deep interrupt handlers can be nested. Interrupt nesting can occur whenever the underlying hardware supports interrupt priorities or when a **noncritical** interrupt handler (the normal case for Linux) is running. Allowing interrupt nesting is generally a good idea because it improves response time and ensures that higher-priority interrupts are not delayed by lower-priority ones. But if interrupts nest too deeply, there is a danger of overflowing the kernel stack, leading to memory corruption and perhaps kernel crashes. To prevent this, each platform needs some mechanism to limit nesting depth. Since the hardware interrupt architectures vary widely among different platforms, each typically requires its own specialized solution. In the next section, we examine the solution employed by Linux/ia64.

IA-64 implementation

As far as Linux/ia64 is concerned, interrupt handling starts at offset 0x3000 in the interruption vector table (IVT). There, the kernel executes the normal kernel entry path, extracts the interrupt vector number by reading control register ivr, and then calls the *external interrupt handler (ia64_handle_irq()* in file arch/ia64/kernel/irq_ia64.c). This handler uses *local_vector_to_irq()* to map the vector number to the corresponding irq number and then invokes the device interrupt handlers that have been registered in the action list of the irq descriptor. Once the interrupt has been handled, the kernel informs the CPU that it is finished with the current interrupt by writing the eoi register (end of external interrupt register). The handler then rereads ivr to see if another interrupt is already pending. If not, ivr returns the value 15 (spurious interrupt). Otherwise, it returns the vector of the new interrupt, which the routine then processes in the same fashion as the original interrupt. This batch-style processing of pending interrupts increases efficiency by reducing the number of times the kernel entry and exit paths are executed for back-to-back interrupts.

Now let us look at how Linux/ia64 avoids kernel stack overflows. Recall, that IA-64 external interrupts are prioritized in order of vector number (higher numbers have higher priority), meaning that once an interrupt at vector n occurred, there is no risk of getting a nested interrupt of a priority-level below n. However, since there are 256 vectors, this leaves open the possibility of getting hundreds of nested interrupts on the same kernel stack! Even if handling an interrupt took only 1 Kbyte of stack space on average, the kernel stack would have to be a quarter of a megabyte in size to avoid the potential for stack overflows! Since each task has its own kernel stack, such a large size would not be practical. To avoid this problem, Linux/ia64 uses tpr (task priority register) to limit nesting depth. Specifically, when the external interrupt handler starts executing, it saves the current value of tpr in a local variable. Then, it writes the vector number of the current interrupt to tpr.

As explained in Section 7.4.1, such a write masks interrupt delivery for all interrupts in the same or any lower interrupt class. After device interrupt handling is done, the original tpr value is restored. Since there are only 16 priority classes, a stack size of just 32 Kbytes would guarantee that stack overflows can be avoided, provided each interrupt uses no more than about 2 Kbytes of stack space on average.

But what would happen if another interrupt occurred either before tpr is written with the new value or after the original value is restored? Of course, this would defeat the scheme for limiting nesting depth we just described. To avoid this, the kernel turns off the interrupt bit in the processor status register (psr.i) during those times when the tpr does not protect it from nested device interrupts. Specifically, the external interrupt handler is invoked with this bit turned off and, before restoring tpr, the handler clears the bit again with a call to *local_irq_disable()*. This ensures that the kernel entry and exit paths are executed with interrupt delivery disabled, save for one exception: if software interrupts are pending, the handler needs to call *do_softirq()*. This function may reenable interrupt delivery by calling *local_irq_enable()*. Fortunately, this is not a problem because *do_softirq()* checks the current interrupt nesting depth before doing anything else. If the depth is greater than 1, the routine returns immediately. In other words, software interrupts are processed only at nesting depth 1, and the net effect is that they increase maximum nesting depth by just one level (e.g., from 16 to 17). This can be compensated for easily by slightly increasing the size of the kernel stack.

In summary, when interrupt handling starts, the fact that psr.i is cleared ensures that no nested interrupts occur. Once the tpr has been written with the current vector number, psr.i can be turned back on and from then on, tpr limits nesting depth. Toward the end of interrupt handling, psr.i is turned off again and the original value of tpr is restored. After that point, the kernel exit path needs to be careful not to turn psr.i back on again. The only exception to this rule occurs in *do_softirq()*, but since this routine enables interrupt delivery only after verifying that the kernel is not already in the middle of executing an interrupt handler, this exception adds at most one level of nesting depth.

7.4.4   Managing the IA-64 interrupt steering logic

A final interrupt-related question that is specific to IA-64 is how to manage the interrupt steering logic provided by SAPIC. Recall that this logic consists of two parts: a static part and a dynamic part. The I/O SAPICs implement a table that statically provides a local ID for each interrupt pin. The re-steering logic that is optionally implemented in the bus bridges provides a dynamic means to steer interrupts according to the settings of the xtp (external task priority) value of each CPU.

Linux/ia64 has almost complete freedom over the policies used to assign local IDs in the I/O SAPICs and to manage the xtp. It could use a completely static distribution policy by programming the I/O SAPICs to never allow re-steering, or it could rely entirely on dynamic re-steering (provided the bridges support it).

An example of a dynamic policy would be to always set xtp to the same value as tpr. With this policy, interrupts would be steered toward CPUs that are either not processing interrupts or that are processing lower-priority interrupts. This scheme makes sense from a interrupt load balancing point of view. On the other hand, from an interrupt-affinity point of view, it might make sense to assign increasingly large xtp values to the different CPUs in an MP machine. That way, a few CPUs would handle most of the interrupt load, and the interrupt handler code of the CPU with the lowest xtp value would be used so frequently that it would be more likely to remain cached.

A static policy can make sense when it is advantageous to handle certain interrupts on particular CPUs. For example, suppose a denial-of-service attack was launched against a machine. Linux/ia64 could protect itself against such an attack by disabling re-steering of the interrupts from the network interface controllers and statically steer those interrupts to one CPU designated to handle such loads. That way, the other CPUs in the machine would not be exposed to the excessive interrupt load generated by the attack and would be available to do other work, such as letting a system administrator log in to the console to analyze, and perhaps even correct, the situation.

Clearly, many policies are possible, and depending on circumstances, one or another may be more favorable. The policy that Linux/ia64 implements assumes that it is desirable to distribute the interrupt load as much as possible. For this reason, Linux/ia64 enables re-steering for all I/O SAPIC interrupt sources. But since the xtp is implemented in the bridge chips (i.e., outside of the CPU), accesses to it are relatively slow. Thus, instead of changing the xtp every time the tpr is updated, Linux/ia64 uses only three xtp-priority values: **low**, **medium**, and **high**. The **medium** value is used during normal execution. Whenever a CPU executes its idle task, it reduces the priority to **low** and therefore actively solicits more work by drawing interrupts to itself. On the other hand, when a CPU is about to be stopped through a call to *stop_this_cpu()* (see Chapter 8, *Symmetric Multiprocessing*), it raises the xtp value to **high** to avoid receiving any further interrupts.

7.5 SUMMARY

In this chapter we investigated various aspects related to device I/O. After the first section introduced the organization of modern machines, the second section described the programmed I/O interfaces that Linux provides. Both memory-mapped and port I/O are supported, and we discussed their implementation in the context of IA-64. The third section introduced the concept of DMA and described the PCI DMA interface that Linux defines for this purpose. The fourth section described how Linux deals with device interrupts. We have seen that even though Linux uses a simple model to abstract device interrupts, the model is sufficiently flexible to work well with the sophisticated interrupt architectures provided by modern machines such as IA-64.

Chapter 8

Symmetric Multiprocessing

In this chapter we explore how Linux supports machines with multiple CPUs. It is quite a challenge to build an operating system that supports such machines in the most efficient manner possible, especially when the goal is to do so without sacrificing performance of smaller machines. The reason for this difficulty is that *multiprocessor (MP)* support is not something that can be added with a self-contained subsystem. Instead, MP support affects almost every single aspect of the operating system, including virtual memory, process management, device drivers, and so on. For this reason, this book discusses MP issues along the way, as the need arises in each chapter. For example, Chapter 3, *Processes, Tasks, and Threads*, introduces the synchronization primitives that MP support is built upon; Chapter 4, *Virtual Memory*, discusses some race conditions in the TLB miss handler that need to be taken into consideration; and Chapter 10, *Booting*, discusses how to boot an MP machine. Because of this, Chapter 8 discusses only those MP aspects that are not covered elsewhere already.

Specifically, the first section discusses what kinds of MP machines Linux is designed to run on and what facilities are needed to support them. In this section, we also encounter the important concepts of *MP-safety* and *MP-scalability*. The second section discusses the philosophy and principles behind the locking approach that Linux uses to ensure both correctness and scalability, followed by a section describing the routines needed to abstract differences in how various platforms support MP machines. The next section explores the topic of how to support CPU-private data. This is an important issue because accesses to such data are performance-critical and because CPU-private data can often reduce the amount of locking needed in the kernel. In the fifth section, we switch gears a little and look into the issue of how to measure wall-clock time with high resolution. We discuss this topic because although solving the problem for UP machines is utterly trivial, it is still a real challenge for MP machines. The chapter concludes with a summary of the covered topics and references to further reading.

8.1 INTRODUCTION TO MULTIPROCESSING ON LINUX

When it was conceived in 1991, Linux was designed for machines with a single CPU. This was a logical choice given how rare multiprocessors were at the time. However, the world has changed dramatically since then: ten years later the prices of CPUs have fallen to the

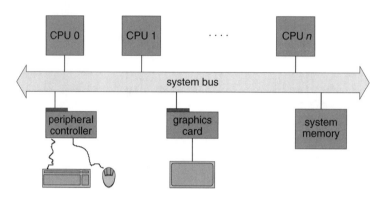

Figure 8.1. Typical organization of an SMP machine.

point where dual-CPU machines are the most economic choice from a price/performance ratio perspective. Accordingly, Linux evolved over time to support multiple processors. To be more precise, Linux has been enhanced to run on *shared memory symmetric multiprocessor (SMP)* machines. The typical organization of such a machine is illustrated in Figure 8.1. As shown there, such a machine has a number of CPUs connected to a shared system bus. System memory and all I/O devices are also connected to this bus. The fact that system memory is shared by all CPUs is why such machines are called *shared memory* SMPs. While common, this is by no means the only way to design a multiprocessor. For example, *massively parallel processor (MPP)* machines can contain hundreds or even thousands of CPUs, each with their own system memory. Such machines coordinate their work through *message passing* instead of shared memory and are not supported by Linux.

The reason the organization in Figure 8.1 is called "symmetric" is that from the perspective of each CPU, the machine looks the same: each CPU sees the same I/O devices, memory, interrupt lines, and so on. Early multiprocessors often were asymmetric designs where certain jobs could be performed only by certain CPUs. Their asymmetric nature made it difficult to support them with a general-purpose operating system such as Linux, and for this reason they fell out of favor (with the notable exception of computer game consoles, which are often still asymmetric in design). Even though Linux was designed with symmetric machines in mind, it is not limited to machines that are 100 percent symmetric. For example, Linux/ia64 can support machines that have separate interrupt lines for each CPU. Also, Linux can run on SMP machines with asymmetric memory access latencies. These are called *cache-coherent nonuniform memory access (cc-NUMA)* machines and generally consist of multiple nodes that are connected by a high-speed switch. Each node may contain some system memory and one or more CPUs. Accessing node-local memory is fast, but accessing system memory on a remote node requires crossing the switch and is often two or three times slower. Thus, even though system memory is still shared, the large difference in access latency means that good performance can be achieved only if the operating system places frequently used data structures in local memory. A more detailed discussion of asymmetric interrupt lines and cc-NUMA machines is beyond the scope of this book, but they are the reason we prefer to use the term *multiprocessor (MP)* in place of the more restrictive term *symmetric multiprocessor (SMP)*.

So what does it take for an operating system to support MP machines? First, there needs to be a facility to boot each CPU. Second, there needs to be a way to assign tasks for execution. In Linux, each CPU normally watches the run queue on its own and executes the next task whenever one becomes available. However, when all CPUs are busy and a high-priority task becomes runnable, scheduling must be coordinated to ensure that all highest-priority tasks are running. For this purpose, there needs to be a facility to communicate information between CPUs. Both of these facilities are provided by the MP support interface we discuss in Section 8.3.

The third, and by far the most challenging, issue is how to prevent the CPUs from getting into each other's way. Specifically, the kernel needs to be careful to avoid race conditions when accessing or updating shared resources such as global variables or shared I/O devices. Otherwise, kernel internal data structures could become corrupted or devices could malfunction. Avoiding race conditions is difficult because of two conflicting goals: on the one hand, the kernel needs to be *MP-safe*, i.e., execution needs to be sufficiently serialized to ensure that no race conditions exist. On the other hand, if there is too much serialization, *MP-scalability* suffers. MP-scalability measures an operating system's ability to get more work done per time unit (increase throughput) as more CPUs are added to a machine. With perfectly linear scalability, a machine with n CPUs would achieve exactly n times the throughput of a machine with just a single CPU. But since even the most sophisticated kernels require some level of serialization, this ideal cannot be attained in practice. However, if serialization is minimized in the kernel, scalability can be improved and near-linear speedups are possible for broad classes of applications and for moderate numbers of CPUs. Still, the bottom line is that there are two conflicting forces: the more serialization, the easier it is to achieve MP-safety, but the worse MP-scalability becomes, and vice versa.

8.2 LINUX LOCKING PRINCIPLES

As alluded to previously, an easy way to build an MP-safe kernel is to serialize *all* execution with a single lock that is acquired on entry to the kernel and released before exiting from it. Since a lock can be acquired only once, this approach would ensure that at most one CPU can be inside the kernel at any given time. In other words, all execution would be serialized and there could be no race conditions. This solution works and was indeed used in early versions of Linux, but clearly it is not scalable. However, we should point out that it is not entirely useless either: multiple tasks still can execute in parallel while they are executing at the user level. Indeed, there are so-called *embarrassingly parallel applications* that spend almost all of their execution time at the user level. They can achieve near-linear scalability even with a kernel that completely serializes execution. However, even applications with just moderate I/O requirements would not scale well. I/O intensive applications might not scale at all. For example, a busy Internet server has to be able to handle thousands of

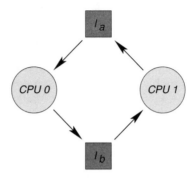

Figure 8.2. Resource-allocation graph illustrating a deadlock condition.

simultaneous network connections, and if each network packet had to be processed serially in the kernel, server throughput would be virtually the same, whether the machine had one CPU or a dozen.

To alleviate the MP-scaling problem, the Linux kernel uses multiple, more *fine-grained locks*. The idea is to have a lock for each major subsystem and data structure. With this, CPUs executing in different kernel subsystems or accessing different data structures can execute in parallel and overall throughput is increased. The question of how many locks are needed is a difficult one. On the one hand, the more fine-grained the locks are, the higher the potential parallelism and the better the scalability of the kernel. On the other hand, each lock creates additional overhead since the lock needs to be acquired before an operation can be performed and released afterward. Thus, a kernel that uses thousands of locks might scale superbly but its performance on a machine with just two or three CPUs would be poor. Linux attempts to strike a balance by using as many locks as needed but as few as it can get away with. In other words, before a new lock is introduced in Linux, it must be possible to show that it solves a real scalability problem and not just a theoretical issue that might show up when thousands of CPUs are used or when unrealistic workloads are imposed.

Another downside of using multiple fine-grained locks instead of a single heavyweight lock is the increased risk of *deadlock* (sometimes called *deadly embrace*). Without proper care, deadlocks can occur easily. For example, suppose that a CPU is holding a lock, l_a, and then attempts to acquire another lock, l_b. If that lock is presently held by a second CPU and that CPU attempts to acquire lock l_a, we have a deadlock condition: the first CPU cannot make progress because it is waiting for lock l_b to become available and the second CPU cannot release that lock until it has acquired lock l_a, which will never happen. Figure 8.2 illustrates this situation with a resource-allocation graph [64, 69]. In this graph, CPUs are represented as circles and locks as squares. An arrow from a lock to a CPU indicates that the lock has been acquired by that CPU. Conversely, an arrow from a CPU to a lock indicates that the CPU is waiting for the lock to become available. Resource-allocation graphs are useful because they make it very easy to visually detect deadlock conditions: whenever there is a cycle in the graph, a deadlock condition exists. In the figure, a cycle starts at *CPU 0*, goes through l_b, *CPU 1*, l_a, and back to *CPU 0*, so clearly the two CPUs are deadlocked.

While it is useful to have an easy way to detect a deadlock after the fact, it is much more important to know whether a given program could ever run into such a situation. Unfortunately, even with just a single lock, this problem is already *undecidable*, meaning that it is impossible to write a verification program that would answer this question. At first glance, this may sound unbelievable because, with just a single lock, it surely should be trivial to avoid deadlock, right? But when considering the problem more carefully, we see that guaranteeing the absence of deadlock would require proving that every possible execution path through the kernel acquires the lock at most once before releasing it again. And anyone with practical experience knows just how easy it is to sometimes forget to release a lock after acquiring it. Of course, more locks make the problem harder still, and even though Linux attempts to minimize the use of locks as much as possible, it contains well over a hundred different types of locks [40].

8.2.1 Locking rules

In the face of this complexity, how can there be any hope that Linux does not contain subtle deadlock conditions? The textbook answer is that such complex programs should define a *lock hierarchy* and then ensure that locks are always acquired in the order defined by the hierarchy. If this rule is followed, it is impossible to end up with a cycle in the resource-allocation graph and consequently it is impossible to create a deadlock. Unfortunately, the distributed and dynamic development model that Linux embodies would make it virtually impossible to ensure that every single developer would be aware of the latest locking hierarchy and that he or she would always follow it. Instead, Linux defines a few principles that are designed to reduce the need for locking hierarchies as much as possible. These rules can be summarized as follows:

1. Avoid locks whenever possible.

2. If a lock is unavoidable, use a single lock.

3. If multiple locks are unavoidable, define a (small) lock hierarchy.

The first rule may seem obvious, but when faced with a synchronization problem, it easy to overlook lock-free solutions and jump to the conclusion that a lock is needed. As we have seen in Chapter 3, *Processes, Tasks, and Threads*, Linux encourages lock-free solutions by providing many atomic operations: *xchg()* can atomically exchange the content of a register with the content of a memory location, then we have the interface to atomically increment or decrement counters, and, finally, we have the interface to atomically manipulate bits in a set. If these operations are not powerful enough to solve a particular problem, it is often possible to avoid locks by organizing the data such that each CPU gets its own private piece to work on. An interesting example of this is the task data structure: at any given time, there is at most one CPU that is executing on behalf of a task and that CPU can usually access the structure without needing any locking.

The second rule states that if a lock really is unavoidable, the next-best solution is to solve the problem while holding a single lock at a time. Ideally, the lock should never be held while a routine is called that is outside the domain to which the lock applies. For example, the IA-64 *kernel unwinder* (file arch/ia64/kernel/unwind.c) uses a lock but is careful never to call any other kernel routines while holding it. If a kernel routine is known not to acquire any locks of its own, it would be acceptable to call it, but this analysis needs to be done with great care. The reason is that some kernel routines acquire locks in an indirect fashion, such as when triggering a fault. A prime example is the *get_user()* routine from Chapter 5, *Kernel Entry and Exit*. Its implementation does not perform any explicit locking, but when it accesses user space, it may trigger a page fault, and resolving the fault may require additional locking.

Interfaces that employ some sort of callback interface are also notorious for creating deadlocks. For example, in the next section we describe *smp_call_function()*, which invokes a callback function on all CPUs while holding a lock. The lock being held is internal to the module implementing the routine, so just by looking at the interface definition, a programmer would not notice the locking constraint and could inadvertently specify a callback function that would create a deadlock condition.

When all else fails and a situation arises in which simultaneous acquisition of multiple locks is unavoidable, it is essential to define a lock hierarchy and encourage everybody to follow it. There are really two cases to consider here: individual locks and locks that are part of a data structure. For the former case there is no magic bullet and it necessary to explicitly spell out the order in which the locks are to be acquired. For example, the *Linux scheduler* (file kernel/sched.c) sometimes needs to simultaneously acquire the lock that guards the task list (*tasklist_lock*) and the lock that guards the queue of runnable tasks (*runqueue_lock*). For this pair, Linux requires that the *tasklist_lock* is always acquired before the *runqueue_lock*. For the cases in which it is necessary to acquire locks that are inside a data structure, Linux uses the general rule that such locks should be acquired in order of decreasing lock address. For example, when moving a directory in a filesystem, the *rename()* system call may have to acquire the locks of up to three different directory entry data structures, so it uses this rule to avoid deadlock. Clearly, locking hierarchies are cumbersome to use. The good news is that since the Linux kernel uses this technique only as a last resort, there are few of them. On the downside, the few hierarchies that do exist are not well documented and, often, reading the source code is the only way to find them.

8.2.2 The big kernel lock (BKL)

One lock that deserves special attention is the *big kernel lock (BKL)*. It once was the *only* lock in the kernel and was designed to emulate as much as possible the non-preemptive nature of a UP kernel. Because of this, the BKL has two special properties: first, it is *recursive* and, second, it can be held while the Linux scheduler is called. The former means that a task can acquire the BKL multiple times without creating a deadlock: the kernel automatically keeps track of how many times the task has acquired the lock and unlocks it only after a matching number of releases. The idea behind allowing the BKL to be held while the scheduler is called is to emulate UP behavior, where a task is assured that execution

lock_kernel();	/* acquire big kernel lock */
unlock_kernel();	/* release big kernel lock */
int **kernel_locked**();	/* test whether big kernel lock is taken */
/* scheduler support routines: */	
release_kernel_lock(task, cpu);	/* conditionally release big kernel lock */
reacquire_kernel_lock(task);	/* conditionally acquire big kernel lock */

Figure 8.3. Big kernel lock interface.

remains atomic until the task is put asleep and that execution is atomic again as soon as the task is woken up. These properties make the BKL convenient to use, but they also mean that the lock is often held for long periods of time. Because of this, MP-scalability is poor for code that is using the BKL, and, over the years, Linux has been enhanced to avoid it as much as possible. It is expected that eventually all code will be converted to fine-grained locking, and at that point the BKL can be removed. On the other hand, the BKL has such convenient properties that it may remain forever as a means to serialize execution of non-performance-critical parts of the kernel. In the v2.4 series of the Linux kernel, the BKL is already used mostly in this fashion, serializing non-performance-critical operations such as opening or closing a device.

Access to the BKL is abstracted through the *big kernel lock interface* (file include/-asm/smplock.h), illustrated in Figure 8.3. Each platform needs to provide a suitable implementation. Normal platform-independent code should only use the first three routines: *lock_kernel()*, *unlock_kernel()*, and *kernel_locked()*. As their name suggests, they are used to, respectively, acquire the BKL, release it, and test whether it is taken.

Since the BKL is recursive, a task can call *lock_kernel()* multiple times without creating a deadlock. The only condition is that, eventually, the task must call *unlock_kernel()* a matching number of times so that the BKL can be made available again for locking by other tasks.

The remaining two routines in the interface are intended for use by the Linux scheduler only. They are called *release_kernel_lock()* and *reacquire_kernel_lock()* and are used to temporarily relinquish the BKL while a task is blocked (sleeping). Specifically, *release-_kernel_lock()* checks whether the task pointed to by the *task* argument is holding the BKL and, if so, immediately makes the BKL available for locking by other tasks. On the other hand, *reacquire_kernel_lock()* checks whether the task pointed to by the *task* argument was holding the BKL before the task went to sleep and, if so, immediately reacquires the BKL before continuing execution. Apart from affecting the BKL, *release_kernel_lock()* also must ensure that both local and global interrupt delivery is enabled. The routine therefore takes a second argument, *cpu*, to identify the CPU that is currently executing. This argument is needed to determine whether global interrupts must be unmasked. Recall from Chapter 3, *Processes, Tasks, and Threads*, that global interrupt masking is supported for backward compatibility only and should not be used in new code.

IA-64 implementation

The fact that the BKL interface is implemented in the platform-specific portion of the kernel means it can be tuned for each architecture. However, since the BKL is no longer used for performance-critical operations, most platforms, including IA-64, use a generic implementation. The following description therefore applies not just to IA-64 but to most other architectures as well.

The generic implementation is built on top of a global spinlock and a nesting depth counter that Linux reserves for this purpose in the task structure. The nesting depth counter is called *lock_depth*, and when a task is created, *lock_depth* is initialized to -1. Each time *lock_kernel()* is called, the nesting depth is incremented, and each time *unlock_kernel()* is called, the nesting depth is decremented. The spinlock needs to be acquired only when the nesting depth changes from -1 to 0 and released only when it changes back from 0 to -1. Assuming the spinlock is called *l*, this could be implemented by macros along the lines of:

```
#define lock_kernel()   if (!++current->lock_depth) spin_lock(&l)
#define unlock_kernel() if (!current->lock_depth--) spin_unlock(&l)
```

Note that the nesting depth is incremented and decremented in a nonatomic fashion. This is safe because the task structure is effectively a CPU-private data structure. Even though the structure does not *belong* to any particular CPU, Linux ensures that at most one CPU is executing on behalf of the task, so no race condition is possible. Given that *l* is an ordinary spinlock, *kernel_locked()* can be implemented simply by a call to the *spin_is_locked()* routine from Chapter 3, *Processes, Tasks, and Threads*.

For the *release_kernel_lock()* and *reacquire_kernel_lock()* routines, the nesting depth indicates whether the task owns the BKL: a non-negative value indicates ownership. The *release_kernel_lock()* routine can therefore be realized by checking whether the nesting depth is non-negative and, if so, releasing spinlock *l*. As required by the interface, the routine also must reenable both local and global interrupt delivery. The former can be achieved by an unconditional call to *local_irq_enable()*. The latter requires more care: global interrupts should be enabled only if they were previously disabled by the current CPU. On IA-64, this is achieved with a call to the platform-specific routine *release_irqlock()*. The routine expects a single argument that identifies the current CPU, which is just what is passed in the *cpu* argument of *release_kernel_lock()*. Implementing *reacquire_kernel_lock()* is even easier: it just needs to check whether the nesting depth is non-negative and, if so, reacquire spinlock *l*. The routine does not affect interrupt masking in any fashion.

8.3   MULTIPROCESSOR SUPPORT INTERFACE

The interface needed to abstract the platform-specific aspects of MP machines is surprisingly simple. The reason is partly that many MP issues can be hidden behind *other* platform-specific interfaces. For example, in Chapter 4, *Virtual Memory*, we encountered *tlb_flush_all()*, a routine to flush the content of the translation lookaside buffer (TLB). This routine usually needs different implementations for UP and MP machines, but since the interface remains the same, the difference is not visible in the platform-independent part of Linux.

```
/* boot & shutdown support: */
extern int smp_num_cpus;                            /* number of active CPUs */
smp_boot_cpus();                                    /* boot secondary CPUs (APs) */
smp_commence();                                     /* release secondary CPUs (APs) */
smp_send_stop();                                    /* halt all other CPUs */

/* CPU numbering & identification: */
int smp_processor_id();                             /* get current CPU number */
int cpu_logical_map(i);                             /* map dense CPU number */
int cpu_number_map(n);                              /* map sparse CPU number */

/* scheduling support: */
#define PROC_CHANGE_PENALTY                         /* priority boost for CPU affinity */
smp_send_reschedule(cpu);                           /* force scheduling decision */

/* remote CPU invocation facility: */
int smp_call_function(func, arg, ignore, wait);    /* call function on all other CPUs */

/* memory-access ordering support: */
smp_rmb();                                          /* MP read memory barrier */
smp_wmb();                                          /* MP write memory barrier */
smp_mb();                                           /* MP full memory barrier */
```

Figure 8.4. Multiprocessor support interface.

8.3.1 Support facilities

Apart from synchronization primitives, Linux needs just a handful of facilities that enable the following tasks:

- Starting and stopping other CPUs.

- Identifying each CPU.

- Forcing a scheduling decision on another CPU.

- Invoking an arbitrary function on other CPUs.

- Enforcing memory-access order.

These facilities are provided by the *MP support interface* (file include/asm/smp.h), illustrated in Figure 8.4. The first part of the interface is used primarily during booting and when shutting down the machine. As described in Chapter 10, *Booting*, Linux assumes that a machine powers up with only one CPU active (the primary CPU, or bootstrap processor, BP). Linux uses this CPU to initialize most of the machine and then activates the *application processors (APs)* by calling the platform-specific routine *smp_boot_cpus()*. Apart from starting the APs, this routine also counts the total number of CPUs running in the system and stores the result in global variable *smp_num_cpus*. The value of this variable must not exceed the *maximum CPU count limit* (NR_CPUS in file include/linux/threads.h). Once the APs are started, they must wait for a signal from the BP before continuing execution. They wait by looping until function *smp_commence()* is called. At this point, all CPUs are fully operational and independently select and execute tasks from the Linux run queue. This continues until the machine is shut down. When that happens, the Linux kernel calls the *smp_send_stop()* routine, which halts execution on all CPUs other than the one that was used to call the routine.

The second part of the interface provides the means to uniquely identify the CPUs in a machine. Specifically, *smp_processor_id()* returns the unique ID of the currently executing CPU. This ID is a *sparse CPU number* and must be a valid bit number for a variable of type **long**. That is, on 32-bit platforms, it must be in the range of 0 to 31, and on 64-bit platforms, it must be in the range of 0 to 63. Apart from this constraint, the numbering can be arbitrary. When Linux needs to enumerate the CPUs in the system, it uses a *dense CPU numbering* scheme. Dense CPU numbers must be in the range of 0 to *smp_num_cpus* − 1 and there must be a one-to-one mapping between sparse and dense CPU numbers. To convert between the two, the interface provides routines *cpu_logical_map()* and *cpu_number_map()*. The former translates a dense CPU number to the corresponding sparse number, and the latter performs the reverse translation. Both routines are performance-critical, so they are commonly implemented with a simple arithmetic transformation or with an array lookup. To get a better sense of how these routines are used, let us look at the following example:

```
print_cpu_nums (void) {
    int i, self = smp_processor_id();
    for (i = 0; i < smp_num_cpus; ++i)
        printk("CPU%u: dense CPU # = %u%s\n", cpu_logical_map(i),
                i, (i == cpu_number_map(self)) ? " (self)" : "");
}
```

This function prints a listing that shows the mapping from dense CPU numbers to sparse CPU numbers. It also identifies the currently executing CPU by printing the additional string "self" for the corresponding entry. For example, if the third CPU on a four-way machine called this function, the resulting output might look as shown below:

```
CPU0: dense CPU # = 0
CPU3: dense CPU # = 1
CPU4: dense CPU # = 2 (self)
CPU5: dense CPU # = 3
```

In this output, there is a gap in the sparse numbering: CPUs 1 and 2 are missing. Depending on the platform, this could happen for a number of reasons. For example, the gap might be because the corresponding CPU sockets are empty or because the system administrator disabled the CPUs before booting the machine. We should point out that the implementation of *print_cpu_nums()* should not be taken too literally: it is meant to illustrate how *smp_processor_id()*, *cpu_logical_map()*, and *cpu_number_map()* relate to each other, and because of this, it contains extra conversion calls that would normally be avoided.

The third part of the interface assists the Linux scheduler. PROC_CHANGE_PENALTY is an integer constant that estimates the penalty incurred when a task is scheduled on a CPU different from the one it last ran on. The penalty is a negated nice value, so that 0 corresponds to no priority boost and 20 to a maximal priority boost. This value should take into account the cost of starting execution on a CPU with a cold cache and a cold TLB. No single value is correct for all cases, but generally, larger values increase the likelihood of a task continuing to be scheduled on the same CPU, a property called *CPU affinity*. On the other hand, if too large a value is chosen, it could happen that a high-priority task does not get scheduled for a while, even though some of the CPUs may be running lower-priority tasks. In other words, picking the right value for this constant is a tradeoff between ensuring that the highest-priority tasks run at all times and maximizing CPU affinity. Platform-dependent code also needs to provide a routine called *smp_send_reschedule()*. This routine takes a single argument, *cpu*, which is the sparse number of the CPU on which a scheduling decision should be forced. By the time this routine is called, the Linux scheduler already has taken care of marking the current task on the target CPU for rescheduling. It does this by setting task flag *need_resched* to **true**. This means that *smp_send_reschedule()* can accomplish its task by simply forcing any dummy interrupt on the target CPU: an interrupt handler will be invoked and, upon return from it, the kernel exit path will be executed. As we may recall from Chapter 5, *Kernel Entry and Exit*, the exit path checks the *need_resched* flag and if **true**, the exit path invokes the Linux scheduler. In other words, it is really the kernel exit path that initiates the scheduling decision. Triggering a dummy interrupt on the target CPU is one way of forcing a scheduling decision, but depending on the platform, there may be other ways to do that. Also, if a target CPU already has an interrupt pending, *smp_send_reschedule()* would not have to perform an operation at all. Despite its simplicity, this routine is important because it is performance critical.

The fourth part of the interface consists of just one routine: *smp_call_function()*. It invokes an arbitrary callback routine on all CPUs other than the one on which it is called. The routine takes four arguments, though the third one exists only for historic reasons and its value is ignored completely. The first argument, *func*, is a pointer to the function that should be invoked. The second argument, *arg*, is an arbitrary pointer that is passed as an argument to *func*. The last argument, *wait*, is a flag that selects the waiting behavior. A value of 0 indicates that *smp_call_function()* should return as soon as it has initiated execution of the callback function. A value of 1 indicates that it should wait until the CPUs have executed the callback function. The caller of *smp_call_function()* must ensure that the *arg* pointer remains valid while the CPUs are executing the callback function. This requires special care when the nonwaiting behavior (*wait* = 0) is used because, in that case, the callback function will continue to run even after the routine has returned.

The last portion of the MP support interface provides memory-access ordering routines similar to the ones we encountered in the memory-mapped I/O interface in Chapter 7, *Device I/O*. There are three such routines, called *smp_rmb()*, *smp_wmb()*, and *smp_mb()*, that, respectively, implement a read barrier, write barrier, or full barrier. The difference is that these ensure ordering on MP machines only. On UP machines, their only effect is to inform the compiler that it should assume that the barriers may change memory in an unpredictable fashion (the MP versions of the barriers do the same). This will prevent the compiler from moving memory accesses across barriers. Furthermore, it also forces the compiler to reread all variables from memory after a barrier. The MP-only barriers are sometimes useful because, on certain architectures, enforcing memory-access order slows down execution significantly; with these routines, it is easy to force the ordering needed for MP execution without unduly impacting UP performance. However, the routines should be used with great care because if it turns out that the memory ordering really *is* needed for UP machines as well, the MP-only barriers could cause subtle and elusive errors. As a general rule, it is safe to use the MP-only barriers when the goal is to enforce ordering only with respect to other CPUs and not, e.g., with respect to I/O devices. When in doubt, it is safer to use one of the regular access-ordering routines: *rmb()*, *wmb()*, or *mb()*.

8.3.2   IA-64 implementation

Let us now take a look at the IA-64 implementation of the MP support interface. Rather than describing the routines in sequential order, we start with the simple ones and then move on to the more challenging ones. Also, since *smp_boot_cpus()* and *smp_commence()* are covered in Chapter 10, *Booting*, there is no need to discuss them here.

As far as the CPU numbering is concerned, there is no good reason to distinguish between sparse and dense CPU numbers on IA-64. Instead, it is better to assign each CPU a dense number and to use that number as the sparse number as well. Consequently, *cpu_logical_map()* and *cpu_number_map()* are identity mappings that simply return the value passed as the argument of the respective function. The implementation of *smp_processor_id()* takes advantage of the fact that the Linux scheduler already stores the sparse CPU number in the *processor* member of the current task structure. Because of this, the routine can be implemented with a macro along the lines of:

```
#define smp_processor_id() (current->processor)
```

Incidentally, this implementation is used not just on IA-64, but on most Linux platforms.

The MP memory-ordering routines are similarly easy to implement: when a kernel that supports MP machines is compiled, these routines expand directly into the respective ordering routines of the memory-mapped I/O interface from Chapter 7, *Device I/O*. When compiling a UP kernel, the routines instead expand into an optimization barrier that instructs the compiler to assume that memory changes in an unpredictable fashion. In GNU C, such a barrier can be realized with a macro along the lines of:

```
#define barrier() asm volatile ("" ::: "memory")
```

This macro generates a dummy inline assembly code that emits no actual instruction (empty string), but the "memory" part of the statement tells the compiler that this dummy instruction may potentially write to *any* memory location. The net effect is that the compiler's optimizer is prevented from moving memory accesses across this barrier and is forced to reload all variables from memory after the barrier, which is exactly the goal of this construct.

Generating interprocessor interrupts (IPIs)

All other routines in the interface require some level of communication with other CPUs in the machine. Linux gives platform-specific code complete freedom on how this is achieved,

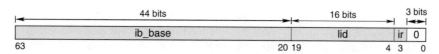

Figure 8.5. Address format for interprocessor-interrupt (IPI) messages.

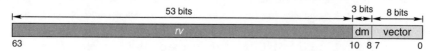

Figure 8.6. Data format for interprocessor-interrupt (IPI) messages.

but most commonly, it is realized with *interprocessor interrupts (IPIs)*. As we have seen in Chapter 7, *Device I/O*, IA-64 provides an IPI facility with the processor interrupt block. Since the entire interrupt system of IA-64 is transaction based, IPIs are really no different from ordinary interrupt messages. In Linux/ia64, the vector used for IPI purposes is called the *IPI vector number* (IA64_IPI_VECTOR in file include/asm-ia64/hw_irq.h). IPIs are high-priority events and because of this, it is advisable to choose a number for this vector that is large enough to put it into the highest-priority class. For this reason, Linux/ia64 uses number 254 (0xfe). Vector 255 is reserved for future use, so the IPI vector number is indeed the highest-priority interrupt in Linux/ia64.

Now, as explained in Chapter 7, *Device I/O*, before we can generate an IPI, we also need to know the local SAPIC ID of the destination CPU. Linux/ia64 provides a routine called *cpu_physical_id()* for this purpose: it takes a dense CPU number as the only argument and returns the corresponding local SAPIC ID. At this point we might wonder: why not use the local SAPIC ID as the sparse CPU number? The reason is simple. As explained earlier, sparse CPU numbers must be valid bit numbers (i.e., they must be in the range of 0 to 63), but since local SAPIC IDs are 16-bit wide, it is not possible to guarantee that they will will be smaller than 64. Of course, depending on how firmware assigns local SAPIC IDs, this could be the case, but since Linux/ia64 must run on *any* IA-64 machine, it would not be safe to make such firmware-specific assumptions. Fortunately, using *cpu_physical_id()* is not just a more general solution, it also helps to improve overall system performance because *cpu_logical_map()* and *cpu_number_map()* tend to be called more frequently than *cpu_physical_id()*. For example, the scheduler calls the first two routines each time it runs, whereas the kernel usually calls the last routine only when sending an IPI. In other words, it is better to make sparse and dense numbers identical so that converting between them is trivial. Also, *cpu_physical_id()* can be implemented efficiently with a simple forward-mapping table. For completeness, Linux/ia64 does provide a reverse mapping routine called *cpu_logical_id()*. It translates a local SAPIC ID to the corresponding dense CPU number. The routine is not meant to be used on any performance-critical paths and can therefore be implemented with a simple linear search through the forward-mapping table.

Given an interrupt vector number and a local SAPIC ID, the kernel can generate an IPI by writing a 64-bit word to the processor interrupt block (see Chapter 7, *Device I/O*). The local SAPIC ID of the target CPU is encoded as part of the address that the word is written to, and the vector number is encoded as part of the data word. Figure 8.5 shows the address format used for this purpose. The address is divided into three fields and must be an integer multiple of 8, so that the least significant three bits are always 0. The ib_base field encodes the top 44 bits of the base address of the processor interrupt block. This block must be aligned to a 2-Mbyte boundary, so the remaining bits of the base address are guaranteed to be 0. The second field, lid, holds the local SAPIC ID of the target CPU. The third field is ir, the *interrupt redirection* bit. Turning this bit on enables xtp-based re-steering of the IPI in the same fashion as for I/O SAPIC generated interrupts (see Chapter 7, *Device I/O*). Of course, when the operating system is generating an IPI, it normally wants to send the IPI to a particular CPU, so this bit is normally turned off. Figure 8.6 shows the data format. The top 53 bits are reserved for future use and must be 0. The remainder is divided into two fields: dm and vector. As the name suggests, vector encodes the IA-64 vector number of the interrupt that should be generated on the target CPU. The dm field encodes the *delivery mode*. For a normal interrupt to be generated, this field must be set to 0. Other values can be used to generate special transactions such as a nonmaskable interrupt (NMI) or machine-check-related interrupts (see Chapter 5, *Kernel Entry and Exit*). Given this, Linux/ia64 can generate an arbitrary IPI with the *ia64_send_ipi()* function shown below:

```
ia64_send_ipi (int cpu, int vector, int dm, int ir) {
    unsigned long addr, data, lid;
    lid = cpu_physical_id(cpu);
    data = (dm << 8) | vector;
    addr = ib_base | (lid << 4) | (ir << 3);
    writeq(data, addr);
}
```

In this code, we assume that global variable *ib_base* has been initialized to the uncached kernel address that corresponds to the physical base address of the processor interrupt block (as obtained by a call to *ioremap()*, for example). The function expects four arguments: *cpu*, the logical number of the target CPU; *vector*, the IA-64 vector number (normally IA64_IPI_VECTOR); *dm*, the delivery mode (normally 0); and *ir*, the re-steering enable bit (normally 0). It uses *cpu_physical_id()* to translate the CPU number to the corresponding local SAPIC ID and then encodes the various values to calculate the final address and the data word. In the last step, it calls *writeq()*. This routine writes the data word to the calculated address inside the processor interrupt block and thereby generates the interrupt.

IPI handling

To intercept interrupts generated for vector IA64_IPI_VECTOR, Linux/ia64 registers the *IPI interrupt handler* (*handle_IPI()* in file arch/ia64/kernel/smp.c). Whenever a CPU receives an IPI, control is transferred to this handler. To support multiple IPI operations, the IPI interrupt vector is combined with a 64-bit *IPI operation bitmask*, which is part of the CPU-specific data area (see Section 8.4). Up to 64 different operations can be supported in this fashion. When invoked, the handler simply walks through this bitmask and whenever it finds a bit set to 1, it executes the corresponding operation. If multiple bits are set, the handler will execute all corresponding operations one by one.

Note that there is only one bitmask per CPU and only one bit per operation. This implies that if the same operation is issued multiple times in quick succession and the target CPU is slow to respond to the first IPI, the operation may be executed only once. In this sense, IPIs behave like UNIX signals. For operations in which this would cause a problem, the caller of *ia64_send_ipi()* must properly serialize execution. A related issue is that multiple CPUs may attempt to simultaneously invoke different operations on a given target CPU. This could create a race condition that could cause the loss of one or more of the requests. To avoid this, Linux/ia64 manipulates the IPI operation bitmask with the bitset operations interface described in Chapter 3, *Processes, Tasks, and Threads*. Since the operations in this interface are guaranteed to execute atomically, there is no race condition and no risk of losing IPI requests.

Using IPIs to realize the MP support interface

Let us now look at how the IPI infrastructure can be used to implement the remaining routines in the MP support interface.

Both *smp_send_stop()* and *smp_call_function()* use this infrastructure, but *smp_send_reschedule()* does not. The last routine is both performance-critical and trivial enough to warrant a slightly different approach, which we describe in more detail toward the end of this section. On the other hand, *smp_send_stop()* and *smp_call_function()* are ideal candidates for the IPI infrastructure either because they are not performance-critical or because they perform relatively heavyweight operations that make the overhead of the IPI infrastructure insignificant. To support these operations, Linux/ia64 reserves two bits in the IPI operation bitmask. The manifest constants identifying these bits are called IPI_CPU_STOP and IPI_CALL_FUNC, respectively.

Routine *smp_send_stop()* can be implemented straightforwardly. For all other CPUs in the machine, the routine sets the IPI_CPU_STOP bit in the IPI operation mask of the target CPU and then calls *ia64_send_ipi()* to trigger an IPI on that CPU. After sending the IPIs, it resets *smp_num_cpus* to 1, since the calling CPU is now the only one left running. When an IPI arrives on a target CPU, will trigger the execution of the IPI handler. As explained earlier, the handler will then traverse the IPI operation bitmask and when it finds that the IPI_CPU_STOP bit is set, will call *stop_this_cpu()*. This function takes care of disabling interrupt delivery and entering an endless loop that calls *ia64_pal_halt()*. This PAL call effectively halts all CPU activity and may reduce power consumption of the stopped CPU (see Chapter 10, *Booting*). However, should a machine check occur, the CPU could become active again; this is why *ia64_pal_halt()* needs to be called repeatedly.

Implementing *smp_call_function()* is more challenging because the routine needs to communicate additional information from the calling CPU to the target CPUs. Specifically, the target CPUs must be informed of (a) the function to invoke, (b) the argument to pass to the function, and (c) the waiting behavior that is in effect. To support this, Linux/ia64 defines a globally shared variable, *call_data*, which is a pointer to a *call data structure* (struct call_data_struct in file arch/ia64/kernel/smp.c). This structure contains copies of the *func*, *arg*, and *wait* arguments to *smp_call_function()*, as well as two atomic counters: *started* and *finished*. Since *call_data* is a pointer that is shared across all CPUs, calls to *smp_call_function()* must be serialized. The function achieves this serialization by using a spinlock. Because this spinlock is hidden inside *smp_call_function()*, a caller must be careful not to accidentally create a deadlock condition. In particular, the callback function specified in the call to *smp_call_function()* must under no circumstances trigger another call to *smp_call_function()* as otherwise the routine would attempt to reacquire the lock when it is holding it already.

Once the *call_data* lock is acquired, the call data can be initialized with the arguments passed to *smp_call_function()* and the two counters can be cleared to 0. The calling CPU then sends an IPI_CALL_FUNC request to all other CPUs. When this request arrives on a target CPU, it copies the call arguments into local variables and then atomically increments the *started* counter. The handler then invokes the desired callback function with the specified argument. Once the callback returns, the handler checks which waiting behavior is in effect. If the caller is not waiting, the handler is done and returns directly. Otherwise, the handler needs to atomically increment the *finished* counter before returning. For the calling CPU, this means that once it has sent the IPIs, it can simply execute a tight loop and wait for the *started* counter to become equal to *smp_num_cpus* − 1. After reaching that value, the calling CPU knows that all target CPUs have finished copying the information from the call data structure. If nonwaiting behavior was selected, the routine can then release the *call_data* spinlock and return immediately. With waiting behavior, the calling CPU must wait until the *finished* counter also reaches *smp_num_cpus* − 1 before releasing the spinlock and returning.

The interesting part about the *smp_send_reschedule()* is that just triggering any interrupt on the target CPU will achieve the goal of forcing a scheduling decision. To support this, Linux/ia64 reserves a special *CPU reschedule vector number* (IA64_IPI_RESCHEDULE in file include/asm-ia64/hw_irq.h). This interrupt vector is used solely to force a scheduling decision. The IA-64 low-level interrupt handler explicitly checks for this vector and does nothing when it occurs. When the low-level interrupt handler has processed all pending interrupts, it will return and the normal kernel exit path will be executed, during which the scheduler will be invoked. With this approach, the overhead of invoking an ordinary interrupt handler such as *handle_IPI()* can be saved and CPU scheduling decisions can be forced in the most efficient way possible. This approach also makes it easy to implement *smp_send_reschedule()*: all this routine needs to do is call *ia64_send_ipi()* as usual, except for specifying interrupt vector IA64_IPI_RESCHEDULE instead of IA64_IPI_VECTOR.

8.4 CPU-SPECIFIC DATA AREA

Earlier we mentioned that it is often possible to avoid MP locking by giving each CPU its own piece of data to work with. The obvious way to declare such data would be to use an array with one element per CPU. For example, the kernel employs this approach to maintain the count of the number of interrupts that have occurred so far. If we assume that the maximum number of CPUs is given by macro NR_CPUS, we could declare a per-CPU array of counters as follows:

```
unsigned int icount[NR_CPUS];
```

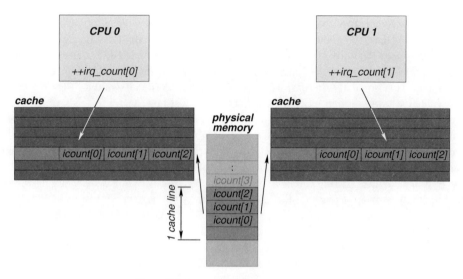

Figure 8.7. Example illustrating false sharing.

Since each CPU will only increment its own counter, no race conditions are possible and no locking is required.

8.4.1   False sharing

Although simple, the obvious way of declaring per-CPU data often works poorly in practice. To see why, let us assume that we have two CPUs that alternately increment their own counter. For example, CPU 0 may first increment *icount*[0], followed by CPU 1 incrementing *icount*[1], followed by CPU 0 incrementing *icount*[0] again, and so on. While this exact sequence may not occur frequently, it certainly is a possibility. The problem with this and similar sequences is that modern CPUs use private caches that are divided into fixed-size *cache lines*. These lines are usually at least 16 bytes long, but the trend is toward ever-increasing line sizes. For instance, Itanium uses a line size of 64 bytes in some of its caches. Because of this, it is likely that two neighboring counters will share the same cache line. For the *icount* example, we assume the configuration illustrated in Figure 8.7. The figure shows two CPUs, each with its own cache, and the shared physical memory. The cache line size illustrated is 16 bytes, so that four 32-bit counters fit into a single cache line. We also assume that *icount* is aligned such that the first counter falls into the second word of a cache line.

Now, before a CPU can increment its counter, it needs to acquire exclusive ownership of the cache line containing the counter. Otherwise, the other CPU could simultaneously update its counter in its own cache and create a situation where two CPUs cache the same memory area with different content. In other words, memory would no longer be *coherent*, which is not acceptable (see Chapter 4, *Virtual Memory*). But if exclusive ownership is needed, only one CPU may have the line in its cache at any given point in time. This implies that if the two CPUs alternately increment their own counters, the cache line containing these counters will have to move back and forth from one CPU cache to the other. This ping-pong effect is costly and occurs because two different counters share the same cache line. This is called *false sharing* because from the perspective of the CPUs, the cache line is shared, even though its content is not. To see just how costly false sharing can be, consider that writing to a cached memory location normally takes just one or two cycles. But if exclusive ownership of a line has to be obtained first, this can easily take several hundred cycles. Thus, the net effect of two counters sharing the same cache line is that each increment runs orders of magnitudes slower than it should.

Fortunately, false sharing can be avoided easily by alignment of the array elements such that they fall into separate cache lines. Linux supports this with a platform-specific *maximum cache line size constant* (SMP_CACHE_BYTES in file include/asm/cache.h). Aligning data according to this constant ensures that false sharing is avoided. The GNU C compiler supports this with an extension that specifies the desired alignment of a data object [16]. For example, the following declaration would avoid false sharing in the *icount* array:

```
typedef struct {
    unsigned int w __attribute__ ((__aligned__(SMP_CACHE_BYTES)));
} aligned_int;
aligned_int icount[NR_CPUS];
```

The __attribute__ declaration attached to member *w* forces it to be aligned according to the value of SMP_CACHE_BYTES and ensures that each element of *icount* will occupy its own cache line. Purely from a performance perspective, this is a good solution: each CPU can now acquire ownership of the cache line containing its own counter once, and from then on, subsequent writes will hit in the cache and execute at full speed. But the downside is that each element now consumes a full cache line. Only four bytes are actually used, so with a 64-byte line size, the remaining 60 bytes would be wasted. To minimize this waste, most platforms define a *CPU info structure* (struct cpuinfo in file include/asm/processor.h). This structure collects various per-CPU data objects. The cache line alignment then has to be enforced only once for the entire collection of objects instead of once for each object. This not only reduces the amount of wasted space but also increases cache effectiveness because most bytes in each line now contain useful data. For example, *icount* could be declared as shown below:

```
struct cpuinfo {
       ⋮
    unsigned int icount;
       ⋮
};
```

Linux/ia64 provides a routine called *cpu_data()* to obtain the CPU info pointer that corresponds to a given sparse CPU number. For convenience, it also provides a macro to obtain the CPU info pointer for the local CPU, i.e., the CPU that is performing the access:

```
#define local_cpu_data cpu_data(smp_processor_id())
```

As we see next, *local_cpu_data* not only saves typing, but also improves performance.

8.4.2   Virtual mapping of CPU-specific data area

Placing per-CPU data in the CPU info structure avoids false sharing and minimizes the amount of wasted memory, but still leaves another problem: the *cpu_data()* routine can be relatively expensive to execute. Even if we assume that this routine is implemented as a macro and simply indexes an array of CPU info structures, we still have to consider its cost: to access the ith element in an array, it is necessary to load its base address, multiply i by the size of the array element, and then add the result to the base address. For latency-sensitive execution paths, this is often more overhead than wanted. This is particularly true for IA-64, where integer multiplication is optimized more for high throughput than for low latency. Of course, some of the overhead could be avoided by forcing the CPU info data structure to a size that is an integer power of 2. This way, integer multiplication could be replaced with a shift instruction.

But Linux/ia64 goes beyond this and uses an additional trick that completely eliminates the overhead: it aligns the CPU info structure not just to the size of a cache line, but to the size of a page. That way, each CPU info structure occupies its own page, which can be remapped into virtual memory. In Chapter 4, *Virtual Memory*, we described the *per-CPU page*, which is used for this purpose. As explained there, the page is part of region 5, and its address is given by the *per-CPU page address constant* (PERCPU_ADDR in file include/-asm-ia64/system.h). There is just one little problem: region 5 uses a single page table that is shared across all CPUs. Thus, it seems like PERCPU_ADDR could be mapped to only one CPU info data structure at any given time, right? This is true, but Linux/ia64 avoids the problem by not using the page table at all; instead, it uses a translation register to pin the translation into the TLB. Since each CPU has its own TLB, they can map one and the same virtual address to different physical addresses without any difficulty. In other words, even though the Linux kernel officially supports only per-process (regions 0–4) and kernel-wide (regions 5–7) address spaces, the per-CPU page effectively creates a tiny address-space window that is CPU private. This is illustrated in Figure 8.8. The figure is not drawn to scale and, for simplicity, only three CPU info structures are shown. But as the arrows indicate, CPU 0 set up its translation register such that PERCPU_ADDR maps to *cpu_data(0)*, whereas CPU 1 set it up such that the same virtual address maps to *cpu_data(1)*. This arrangement lets us simplify the *local_cpu_data* macro to the version shown below:

```
#define local_cpu_data ((struct cpuinfo *) PERCPU_ADDR)
```

This means that accessing the local CPU info structure is extremely efficient: it is no longer necessary to read the current CPU ID with *smp_processor_id()* or to perform any array indexing.

The trick also has another welcome benefit: since a translation register is used, there is no risk that accessing the per-CPU page will ever generate a TLB miss fault. This means that it is perfectly safe to access it while executing in a bank 0 interruption handler (see Chapter 5, *Kernel Entry and Exit*). Indeed, Linux/ia64 takes advantage of this property. For

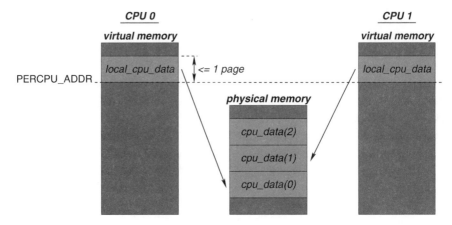

Figure 8.8. Using PERCPU_ADDR to access local CPU info structure.

example, in the kernel exit path it is necessary to clear the **invalid** partition of the register stack engine (RSE) before returning to the user level. This requires knowing how many physical stacked registers are implemented in the CPU. Since this number can change from one CPU model to another, it is best to store it in the CPU info structure and, thanks to the per-CPU page, the exit path can read it without risking a TLB miss fault.

8.5   TRACKING WALL-CLOCK TIME WITH HIGH RESOLUTION

Linux maintains the wall-clock time (real time) with the help of a periodic timer interrupt. The frequency of this timer is fixed and specified by the *clock tick frequency constant* (HZ in file include/asm/param.h). Like most UNIX-compatible systems, Linux represents wall-clock time internally as the number of seconds and microseconds elapsed since the beginning of January 1st, 1970 UTC (the UNIX *epoch*). Conceptually, maintaining time is simple: on each timer interrupt, Linux increments wall-clock time by the period of the clock tick (1/HZ).

8.5.1   MP challenges and options in maintaining wall-clock time

On an MP machine, each CPU uses its own periodic timer interrupt for scheduling, but it would not be desirable for each CPU to maintain its own wall clock. Otherwise, the per-CPU wall clock times could drift away from each other and, after running for a while, each CPU might have a completely different wall-clock time. To avoid such problems, Linux selects one CPU as the *time master*, and only this CPU maintains the wall-clock time. This time is then made available to the other CPUs through a shared *current time variable* (*xtime* in file kernel/timer.c).

Since the wall-clock time is incremented only once per timer interrupt, its resolution is quite limited. For example, Linux/ia64 normally uses a clock tick frequency of 1024 Hz

(HZ = 1024), which limits resolution to about 0.977 milliseconds. For modern machines, this is a long time: almost a million cycles for a CPU running at 1 GHz! For this reason, Linux attempts to improve the resolution of the wall-clock time by estimating how much time has elapsed since the last clock tick and adding this estimate as an offset to wall-clock time. On UP machines, this can be accomplished with the help of the cycle counters that most modern CPU architectures provide. On IA-64, this counter, called the interval time counter, can be read through the itc application register. Linux/ia64 already uses this register together with control register itm (interval timer match register) to implement the periodic timer interrupt (see Chapter 10, *Booting*), so estimating the elapsed time offset is indeed easy. For example, suppose the most recent clock tick occurred when the itc had a value of t_0. The time elapsed since the last tick is then given by $(\text{itc} - t_0)/F$, where F is the frequency (in hertz) at which the itc register is incremented.

Unfortunately, this scheme does not work on MP machines: there is no guarantee that the cycle counters in the CPUs are synchronized with each other. They may run at completely different frequencies, and even when the frequency is the same, there is no guarantee of no drift between them. There are multiple ways to solve this problem, but they all involve different tradeoffs in accuracy, complexity, and efficiency. Linux/ia64 supports one of two solutions, depending on what kind of machine it is running on. For machines that share a common clock for the cycle counters (no drift possible), Linux/ia64 synchronizes the counters at boot time and from then on uses the same interpolation algorithm used on UP machines. For machines that use different clocks for the cycle counters (drift possible), Linux/ia64 assumes that an external high-precision timer is shared by all CPUs. Time interpolation is then performed with the resolution provided by this timer. For example, a timer that follows the Multimedia Timer Specification would be suitable for this purpose [29].

8.5.2 Synchronizing the cycle counters in an MP machine

The problem of synchronizing cycle counters is interesting because it requires multiple parties (CPUs) to agree on something (time) that is continually changing. Since communication between the CPUs takes some time, this means that perfect synchronization is not possible. However, as we see below, it is often possible to get close to the ideal point. The algorithm that Linux/ia64 uses for synchronization has been designed with several factors in mind:

1. It must be possible to synchronize cycle counters in a pairwise fashion between an arbitrary CPU, called the *slave*, and the time master.

2. Synchronization should be achieved by modifying only the cycle counter on the slave CPU, not the cycle counter on the time master.

3. The synchronization must be done in a *closed loop* to ensure a bounded error.

4. Synchronization should be achieved quickly so that even machines with dozens of CPUs can boot without undue delay.

The first two points ensure that CPUs can be synchronized not just at boot time, but at any later time as well. This is useful, for instance, during recovery from temporary CPU

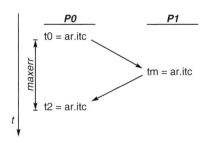

Figure 8.9. Cycle-counter synchronization.

failures: if such a failure occurs, the cycle counter may stop counting and fall behind. If the failure turns out to be nonfatal, the CPU can be brought back online again, but before that happens, the cycle counter would first have to be resynchronized. The third point is important because modern CPUs are not deterministic: at any time, an exceptional event such as a memory parity error might occur. Such an event could affect execution speed of the CPU just enough to throw off an open loop algorithm. With a closed loop algorithm, the event could still affect the accuracy of the synchronization, but at least the magnitude of the error would be known.

Based on these considerations, Linux/ia64 uses the synchronization algorithm illustrated in Figure 8.9. In the figure, we assume that P_0 is the slave CPU and P_1 is the time master. The algorithm starts with P_0 reading its cycle counter and storing the value in the t_0 variable. This value is then sent to P_1, and as soon as it arrives there, the CPU reads its own cycle counter and stores it in a variable, t_m. This value is sent back to P_0, and once it arrives there, P_0 reads its cycle counter for a second time and stores the result in t_2. To increase robustness against noise such as system bus traffic from other CPUs, this measurement step is repeated five times and only the values from the iteration for which $(t_2 - t_0)$ is minimal are retained.

Now, if the counters were perfectly synchronized, the value of t_m would definitely have to be somewhere between t_0 and t_2. Conversely, if t_m falls outside this range, the cycle counter on P_0 needs to be adjusted. The amount of the adjustment is given by the distance of t_m from the range. But what point in the range from t_0 to t_2 should the algorithm aim for? Without knowledge of the interconnect between P_0 and P_1, we cannot be sure. However, if the algorithm aims for the halfway point, it maximizes the chance that the adjustment will hit the target range. The halfway point would also be the theoretically correct point for machines with a symmetric interconnect between CPUs. Given this, the algorithm can calculate the distance between $(t_0 + t_2)/2$ and t_m and adjust the cycle counter on P_0 accordingly. For example, assuming the measured values were $t_0 = 5$, $t_2 = 7$, and $t_m = 15$, the distance is $(5 + 7)/2 - 15 = -9$ cycles. This implies that P_0 is running behind and that its counter should be adjusted forward by nine cycles.

Making the adjustment is not as simple as it may seem. It requires (1) reading the cycle counter register, (2) adding the correction value, and (3) writing back the result to the

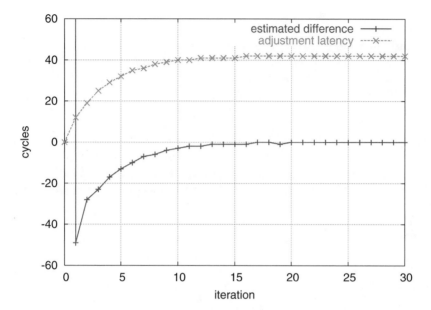

Figure 8.10. Dynamic behavior of cycle-counter synchronization algorithm.

register. Each step takes some time. For example, on Itanium, reading register itc nominally takes 38 cycles, writing it takes 35 cycles, and adding the correction value takes another cycle [30]. The algorithm therefore has to calculate a counter value that is far enough in the future to compensate for these delays. It does this by adding the sum of the delays to the desired target value. For Itanium, the adjustment delay would in theory be $38 + 35 + 1 = 74$ cycles. For example, to move the cycle counter value forward by 9 cycles, the adjustment step would have to add 83 to the value read from itc before writing it back. Unfortunately, many factors influence the adjustment latency. For example, it may be affected by the optimization level of the compiler, the CPU model, or by power-saving features that dynamically adjust execution speed.

The synchronization algorithm solves this problem by automatically estimating the latency as it is making adjustments. Initially, it assumes a latency of zero, and after each adjustment it refines the estimate by looking at the effect of the most recent adjustment. For example, if the most recent adjustment attempted to move the counter forward by nine cycles but ended up moving it forward by only five cycles, the algorithm can infer that the adjustment latency was four cycles too low. However, to make the algorithm more robust against noise, the adjustment latency is updated only by a fractional amount of the remaining difference (e.g., 1/16th).

The *complete synchronization algorithm* (*ia64_sync_itc()* in file arch/ia64/kernel/smp-boot.c) consists of multiple iterations of the measurement and adjustment phases. In practice, just a few iterations are sufficient to achieve near-perfect synchronization, but to be on the safe side, Linux/ia64 executes 64 iterations. The dynamic behavior for the first few iterations of the algorithm is illustrated in Figure 8.10.

The measurements shown there were obtained on an 800 MHz Itanium machine with two CPUs. The curve with the "+" markers represents the measured itc difference $(t_0 + t_2)/2 - t_m$ and the curve with the "×" markers shows the estimated adjustment latency. Looking at the former, we see that the initial difference between the cycle counters was so large (over 8800 cycles) that it is beyond the range of the figure. After the first iteration, the algorithm corrected most of this difference, but since the initial adjustment latency was assumed to be zero, the cycle counter is now running behind by 49 cycles. Looking at the curve with the "×" markers, we see that the algorithm then gradually refines the adjustment latency until it reaches 42 cycles in iteration 17. At that point, the difference between the cycle counters reached zero. The measured adjustment latency of 42 cycles is quite different from the theoretical value of 74 cycles. The discrepancy cannot readily be explained from the publicly available microarchitecture documentation [30]. One possibility is that the instruction reading the itc register is transferring the actual counter value at a late stage, when the instruction is almost finished executing. For example, the latency of reading the itc is specified as 38 cycles, but if the counter value was transferred only in cycle 32, the overall latency adjustment would indeed have to be 42 cycles. Fortunately, since the algorithm is self-tuning, it does not matter what is going on inside the CPU. As long as the adjustment converges, all error sources have been taken into account and the final calibration is correct.

The figure also shows that the curves are relatively smooth, meaning that there was virtually no noise during this measurement. Because of this, the algorithm could have been more aggressive in correcting the adjustment latency. But tuning this is clearly a tradeoff: the more aggressive it is, the less noise it can tolerate. Even with the relatively conservative tuning, the algorithm was able to achieve perfect synchronization after less than 20 iterations. Moreover, after just 4 iterations the difference is less than 20 cycles or 25 nanoseconds! However, it is important to keep in mind that a difference of 0 cycles implies perfect synchronization only if the interconnect truly is symmetric. For asymmetric interconnects, the error is bounded by the round-trip latency $(t_2 - t_0)$. This latency is not shown in the graph, but was measured to be about 558 cycles. The worst-case error therefore is ±279 cycles. But this would still be an error of less than ±0.35 microseconds! Compared to the resolution of 0.977 milliseconds that can be achieved with the periodic timer interrupt alone, this example shows that it clearly is worthwhile to use time interpolation. Also note that with a round-trip latency of 558 cycles, 5 round-trips per measurement, and 64 iterations, it takes less than 180,000 cycles or less than 225 microseconds to synchronize one CPU. Put differently, this algorithm is capable of synchronizing more than 4000 CPUs per second, so scalability is not really an issue.

The synchronization algorithm works extremely well in practice, but even with near-perfect synchronization, the kernel must guard against the possibility of ever returning a decreasing time value. To do this, it keeps track of the highest time value ever calculated by any CPU and always returns the maximum of this value and the interpolated time. The net effect is that sometimes a task may observe that time stands still for a tiny moment, but this just reflects the fact that time *resolution* is not the same as time *accuracy*. On an MP machine that uses cycle-counter synchronization, resolution is determined by the frequency at which the counter is incremented, but accuracy is determined by how well the different counters are synchronized.

8.6 SUMMARY

In this chapter, we discussed the MP-related aspects that are not covered elsewhere in this book. Most importantly, we described the locking principles that provide the foundation of MP-support in Linux. For a more detailed look at how these principles are applied in practice, see Rusty Russel's guide to kernel locking issues [58]. Though we should warn that it occasionally uses language that renders it unsuitable for the faint-of-heart.

This chapter also described the Big Kernel Lock that was originally the only lock in Linux. Since then, the kernel has evolved to a more fine-grained model. It now uses several dozens of different locks, some global and some part of a data structure. Describing each of them in detail would be beyond the scope of this book. Moreover, such a description would not be very useful because the locking details continue to change at a fairly rapid pace. There are, however, attempts to provide up-to-date, complete, and detailed lock descriptions. The document maintained by Rick Lindsley is probably closest to reaching this goal [40]. However, reading the source code is often the best way to answer specific locking questions.

In the remainder of the chapter we covered two other often overlooked but essential aspects of MP-support: how to provide efficient access to CPU-specific data and how to maintain time with high resolution. The former is important because the naive approach of using a simple array for CPU-private data can lead to false sharing, which can reduce performance by orders of magnitudes. For the latter, we have seen that maintaining high-resolution time in general requires extra hardware such as a shared multimedia timer. For the special case where all CPUs in a machine are driven off a common clock, we showed that a software-only solution is also possible.

Chapter 9

Understanding System Performance

Understanding the performance of a system comprising applications and an operating system kernel requires answering two fundamental questions: *how is the time spent* and *where is the time spent*? Answers to these two questions will provide insights on how applications and the operating system kernel behave under certain workloads, where the problems are, what they are, and possibly how to remove or minimize their impact.

The answer to the first question requires an understanding of how the hardware resources are used by the system. This is normally achieved by a technique called *cycle accounting*. Each cycle is either spent actually executing an instruction of the program or waiting for some resource to become available. The former is referred to as an *inherent execution cycle*, and the latter as a *CPU stall cycle*. Once every cycle has been accounted for, a complete breakdown showing the time spent waiting for memory (*memory access stalls*), waiting for execution units in the CPU (*issue limitation stalls*), or inherent program execution can be constructed. Another way of answering the first question is to capture the rate at which certain events occur during execution: the higher the rate, the more the corresponding hardware resource is used. This time-based sampling technique is called *event rate monitoring*. It collects the frequency at which events such as instruction completion or cache misses occur.

When we have answered the first question, we have characterized the workload, meaning that we know which hardware resource it relies on and which one it uses the most. For instance, a high rate of cache misses likely indicates that the workload is manipulating a large amount of data with little locality, such as sequentially reading a large file.

To answer the second question, we need to find the locations in the system where most of the time is spent. This leads to the identification of *bottlenecks*. One way to find those locations is to use a technique called *profiling*, which is also a time-based sampling technique. It records the value of the instruction pointer at regular intervals and is based on the statistical fact that the more often the same address shows up, the more likely it is that a lot of time is spent there. There can be several causes for performance bottlenecks, such as the CPU stalling on memory accesses for code or data or because the code is simply executed a lot. Once the bottlenecks are identified and the reasons for their presence are understood, we have a complete understanding of the performance of the system.

The techniques we described are just examples of how *performance monitoring* can be done. They are generic and have been used on many CPU architectures with success. They can also be used on IA-64, but as we see in this chapter, they become even more important for this architecture. So why is performance monitoring so important for IA-64?

The IA-64 architecture follows the EPIC paradigm (see Chapter 2, *IA-64 Architecture*). The key idea behind EPIC is that the compiler is the best place to extract parallelism from a program because the compiler has access to most of the underlying source code and is not as limited by resources as a CPU. For instance, the compiler can afford to take quite some time and memory to come up with the best possible code sequences for a given problem. This is acceptable because programs are compiled once and then run multiple times.

Although the compiler can come up with good optimizations, some of which are based on heuristics, it is sometimes difficult to *predict* how a program will behave because so much is driven by the workload. One way to handle this is to run the program and *measure* its behavior. This can be done with any of the techniques presented earlier. The collected information can then be analyzed by performance tools or can be fed back to the compiler, which will then be able to adjust its optimization strategy. This latter technique is referred to as *profile-based optimization (PBO)* and is important for IA-64 because much of the performance is, in fact, driven by the quality of the code generated by the compiler.

To illustrate the importance of PBO for IA-64, we show an example in which PBO is used to improve the effectiveness of predication. In the case of an **if**-statement as shown at the top of Figure 9.1, the length, in term of code size, of path A is much shorter than for path B. If the compiler relies only on static analysis, it may choose to mix both paths into a single instruction stream by using predicates which, when executed, will cause the instructions of one path or the other to be executed. Given the code size difference between the two paths, the cost of predicating off one or the other is dramatically different because predicated-off instructions are still executed by the CPU except that they have no effect (see Chapter 2, *IA-64 Architecture*). If path A is the dominant (more frequently executed) path, as shown in the figure with the thick line, then it can be quite expensive to execute all the instructions of path B for nothing. In this case, a branch to skip over the instructions of path B may be more efficient. On the other hand, if path B is more frequently executed, there is almost no penalty for executing path A for nothing. In that case, the compiler's choice to use predication would have been correct. To ensure that it always makes the right choice, the compiler needs dynamic information; in this case, the information is which path is executed more frequently. PBO provides just this kind of information, assuming the training workload is representative of the workloads the program is expected to encounter in real use. The same kind of feedback loop can be applied to other IA-64 features such as speculation.

The example shows how PBO can improve the quality of the code generated by the compiler and illustrates the importance of detailed monitoring capabilities for IA-64. PBO and other monitoring techniques are important to IA-64 compilers but also to developers who want to understand the behavior of their applications.

For Linux, some monitoring tools exist, such as the classic profiling tool `gprof`, which is available as part of the GNU toolchain. With `gprof` it is possible to collect simple profile information on user programs. It provides information on where the time is spent

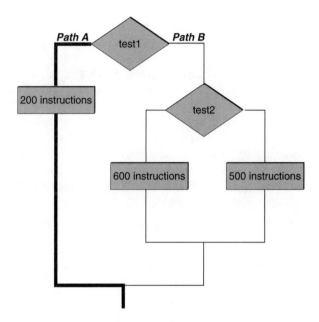

Figure 9.1. PBO and predication.

by using a time-based sampling of the instruction pointer. It can also record the call graph, which helps identify the critical execution paths. It requires programs to be recompiled with a special option to insert instrumentation code. This comes with a certain overhead in terms of execution speed and also implies that only programs for which the source code is available can be monitored. Because `gprof` is a user-level-only tool, it does not report how the time is spent in the kernel. When it comes to monitoring at the kernel level, Linux has a built-in profiling capability that generates a flat execution-time profile similar to `gprof`. It is compiled into the kernel by default and can be activated from the boot loader with the `profile` option.

Neither of these tools requires special hardware. Because of that, they are portable but also rather limited in the kind of information they provide. While they report *where* time is spent, they do not tell us *how* it is spent. We do not know whether the time spent is because of the inherent execution of the program or because of resource bottlenecks, such as cache misses, TLB misses, or branch mispredictions. Without detailed monitoring capabilities, we are left guessing.

The IA-64 architecture provides special hardware to help the programmer determine how applications perform. This support can logically be viewed as a single hardware component called the *performance monitoring unit (PMU)*. The PMU can be used as a facility to provide detailed low-level information to the monitoring techniques we outlined earlier. The interface of the PMU consists of a set of dedicated registers that can be programmed to count occurrences of certain microarchitecture events, such as the number of elapsed cycles, the number of instructions executed, or the number of cache misses in the level-one cache, for instance. The instruction set architecture defines only a set of generic monitoring features because most of the events of interest are intimately tied to the underlying microarchitecture of each CPU model. For instance, not all CPU models necessarily use a three-level cache hierarchy. It does not, therefore, make sense to specify level-three events in the architecture. Instead, the generic specification is refined by each CPU model.

The remainder of this chapter is organized as follows. In the first section, we give an overview of the architected PMU features. The second section uses Itanium as an example of how the architecture can be refined. The Itanium PMU defines several interesting capabilities such as support for hardware-level sampling. In the third section, we describe the design of the Linux/ia64 support for monitoring performance with the PMU.

9.1   IA-64 PERFORMANCE MONITORING UNIT OVERVIEW

In this section, we describe the main features of the generic PMU facility as specified by the IA-64 architecture. It is required that every CPU model implement these features.

9.1.1   PMU register file

The interface to the PMU consists of a set of specialized registers that can be programmed to capture occurrences of certain architectural events, such as the number of instructions executed or the number of cycles elapsed. The register file is composed of the *performance monitor data* registers (pmd), which collect the data, and the *performance monitor configuration* registers (pmc), which configure what is to be monitored. Three other registers control the overall behavior of the PMU. Figure 9.2 shows the entire set of registers used by the PMU. The registers represented with dashed lines are specified by the architecture, but whether they are implemented and their exact purpose is CPU model specific.

The architecture defines up to 256 pmc and 256 pmd registers, each of them 64 bits wide. A *monitor* is defined to be a combination of a pmc for the configuration and one or more pmd registers for collecting data. The architecture specifies only *counting monitors*, which are event counters. Counting monitors need only one pmd register. As we see in Section 9.2, CPU-model-specific monitors may use pmd registers for purposes other than counting. However, in this section, we focus on the architected counting monitors.

Each counting monitor can be programmed to count one event at a time. The architecture requires that at least four monitors, which use four pairs of registers, be supported. The minimal set consist of pmd4–pmd7 and pmc4–pmc7, such that pmc4 controls pmd4 and so on. The remainder of the pmd registers are CPU model specific, and they could be used to add more counting monitors or to collect other sorts of performance information. The four required pmd registers contain a counter that is incremented each time a specific event occurs. When a counter eventually overflows and wraps around to 0, this condition is detected and stored in the pmc0–pmc3 registers, the *overflow status registers*.

As shown in Figure 9.2, the PMU uses three other system registers: psr, dcr, and pmv. We have already encountered the first two registers in Chapter 2, *IA-64 Architecture*. The psr contains bits to start and stop monitoring, dcr controls whether monitoring can continue

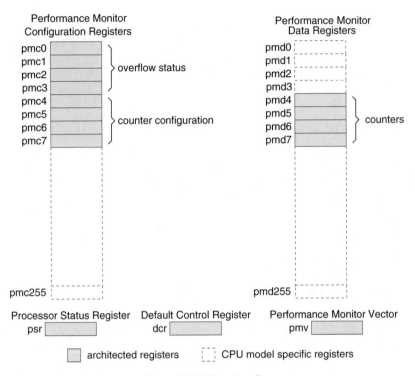

Figure 9.2. PMU register file.

during interruption handling, and pmv contains the IA-64 interrupt vector used by the PMU when an overflow must be signaled.

On Linux, it is possible to retrieve CPU-model-specific information about the PMU with the *ia64_pal_perf_mon_info( )* routine (see Chapter 10, *Booting*). Users can access this information with the *palinfo* kernel module. The module can be accessed through the /proc filesystem. For example, the PMU information for Itanium looks as follows:

```
$ cat /proc/pal/cpu0/perfmon_info
PMC/PMD pairs                   : 4
Counter width                   : 32 bits
Cycle event number              : 18
Retired event number            : 8
Implemented PMC                 : 0-13
Implemented PMD                 : 0-17
Cycles count capable            : 4-7
Retired bundles count capable : 4-5
```

This output illustrates that Itanium implements pmc0–pmc13 and pmd0–pmd17. The first line shows that four pmc/pmd pairs implement the counting monitors required by the IA-64

Figure 9.3. Format of pmd4–pmd7.

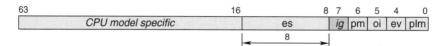

Figure 9.4. Format of pmc4–pmc7.

architecture. The remaining registers refine the measurement capabilities of the architecture and provide additional features, as we see in Section 9.2.

Format of the pmd registers

The format of a pmd register is shown in Figure 9.3. A pmd register is 64 bits wide, but depending on the CPU model, not all bits may be implemented. Bits 0 to $w - 1$ represent the counter; bits w to 63 are the sign extension of bit $w - 1$. A pmd register can be read from the user level but can only be written at the kernel level. The value returned on read depends on the configuration of the monitor, as we will see shortly. Writes to the sign extension part are ignored, and reads always return the value of bit $w - 1$. In other words, if we suppose that the counter is 32 bits wide and its value is 0x80000000, then a read of the pmd will return 0xffffffff80000000. To obtain the proper counter value, software must mask off the sign extension part.

When an overflow occurs, the counter wraps around to 0. For our example, this happens when the counter reaches the value of 0xffffffff + 1 (2^{32}). Under most circumstances, the overflow must be communicated to the monitoring software so that an adjustment can be made to ensure that the correct count is reported. It is possible to program the PMU to generate an interrupt whenever a pmd register overflows. When such an interrupt is received, there is a mechanism to determine which of the pmd registers overflowed. Specifically, for every pmd, there is a bit in pmc0–pmc3 that indicates the particular register that overflowed. It is important to note that more than one pmd can overflow at once.

Format of the pmc registers

There are two kinds of pmc registers; the first set (pmc4–pmc7) configures performance monitors and the second (pmc0–pmc3) holds the overflow status information. As opposed to pmd, the pmc registers are accessible only at the kernel level.

The format of pmc4–pmc7 is depicted in Figure 9.4. The description of each field in given in Table 9.1. The central element is the *event selector* (es), which indicates the event to monitor. This field can be up to 8 bits wide, so up to 256 distinct events can be supported.

Table 9.1. Description of the pmc fields.

Field	Description
plm	**privilege level mask**: each bit represents a privilege level
ev	**external visibility**: pin or transaction provided on interrupt
oi	**overflow interrupt**: generates an interrupt on counter overflow
pm	**privileged monitor**: specifies the type of the monitor
ig	*ignored*
es	**event selector**: the event to monitor

The architecture requires that the following two events be implemented by each PMU:

- Number of CPU clock cycles

- Number of instructions executed (retired)

However, they do not have preassigned es values. Instead, each CPU model defines its own values, which can be retrieved from PAL.

Apart from the event selector, several fields inside a pmc register can be used to constrain how counts are collected. The *privilege level mask* (plm) specifies the privilege level at which the monitor can count. Each of the four bits of this field represents a privilege level. Because it is a bit-field, more than one bit can be set, thereby allowing monitoring across several privilege levels. For instance, the Linux/ia64 kernel uses two privilege levels: the kernel level (0) and the user level (3). Setting plm to 0x9 makes is possible to monitor an event at both levels. Setting plm to 0 disables the monitor.

The oi bit controls whether an interrupt is generated when the counter overflows. If set, an overflow will generate an interrupt with the vector contained in pmv. The ev bit enables overflow notification outside the CPU, through a bus transaction or a pin. In most cases, this bit is cleared.

There are two types of monitors, which differ in how they can be enabled:

- *user monitor* (pm = 0): can be enabled or disabled from the user level.

- *privileged monitor* (pm = 1): can be enabled or disabled only at the kernel level.

Let us emphasize that the term *privileged monitor* denotes only the type of monitor and not where it can measure. Both types can count events at any privilege level. A better term for a privileged monitor would be a *system monitor*. Another distinction between the two types of monitor exists for reading the pmd registers directly from the user level. For a privileged monitor, the value returned will always be 0, whereas the actual value is returned for user monitors (unless the secure monitoring bit, psr.sp, is set in the processor status register).

But why is it important to have two types of monitors? Monitoring is usually applied to a single task or to an entire system. In each case, the accessibility and controllability requirements are different. For systemwide monitoring, unauthorized tasks must be prevented from randomly starting or stopping the monitoring. Furthermore, information should not

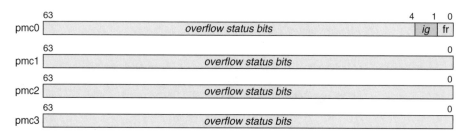

Figure 9.5. Format of pmc0–pmc3.

be leaked to unauthorized tasks. Finally, it must be possible to run systemwide monitoring in parallel with per-task monitoring. On the other hand, for a single task, it is desirable to control the monitors and read the pmd registers without the need to call the kernel. Hence, privileged monitors should be used for systemwide monitoring, because they provide the degree of security required and are controlled independently from user monitors, as we will see shortly. User monitors should be used for per-task monitoring because they provide user-level access to the monitors.

The format of registers pmc0–pmc3, the overflow status registers, is shown in Figure 9.5. The first four bits of pmc0 are special. Bits 1–3 are ignored, but bit 0 is called the *freeze bit* (fr). When this bit is set, the PMU is said to be *frozen*, i.e., it does not record anything new. When the bit is cleared, the PMU is *enabled*. This does not necessarily mean that counts are instantly collected. We see how this is controlled in the next sections. When a monitor with the oi bit set overflows, the PMU does the following:

- Sets the corresponding overflow bit

- Stops all monitoring by setting the freeze bit

- Sends an interrupt

In other words, when an overflow interrupt occurs, the PMU is frozen and all monitors stop, including those that did not overflow. An overflow on a monitor without the oi bit set will not freeze the PMU but will still set the corresponding overflow bit.

An overflow interrupt handler can determine which pmd registers overflowed by looking at the bits in pmc0–pmc3. To detect whether pmd_i overflowed, the handler must check bit i in pmc0. When more than 60 monitors are supported, it is necessary to inspect pmc1–pmc3. More than one bit can be set when several pmd registers overflow at the same time. The overflow bits are sticky, meaning that once set, they remain set until explicitly cleared by software. If the handler clears the freeze bit by writing zero to pmc0, the overflow status bits in this register are also cleared. The overflow status bits in pmc1–pmc3 must be cleared separately.

Table 9.2. Processor status register bits controlling monitors.

Name	Description
psr.up	user performance monitor enable
psr.pp	privileged performance monitor enable
psr.sp	secure performance monitors

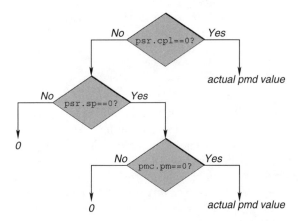

Figure 9.6. Effect of psr.sp on pmd read for user monitors.

The role of the processor status register

The processor status register psr contains three bits that control performance monitoring. The relevant bits are listed in Table 9.2, and a full description of psr can be found in Chapter 2, *IA-64 Architecture*. The psr.up bit enables or disables all user monitors, i.e., monitors for which pmc.pm is cleared. The psr.up bit is part of the user mask; therefore, it can be modified from the user level with the rum and sum instructions.

The role of the psr.pp bit is very similar to that of psr.up but applies only to privileged monitors. It has no effect on user monitors, and, conversely, psr.up has no effect on privileged monitors. The psr.pp bit is part of the system mask and therefore can only be accessed from privilege-level 0 with the ssm and rsm instructions (see Chapter 2, *IA-64 Architecture*). This bit can also be implicitly modified by the rfi instruction. The existence of these two bits provides independent control between user and privileged monitors.

The psr.sp bit can be used to secure access to the PMU from the user level and therefore applies to user monitors only. When this bit is set, it is not possible to start or stop monitoring with psr.up and reading a pmd will return 0. Figure 9.6 summarizes how the reading of a pmd register is affected by psr.sp.

Table 9.3 lists all the instructions used to control the PMU, along with their accessibility according to privilege level. None of the pmc registers are accessible at a level other than 0. Similarly, writes to the pmd registers are allowed only at privilege-level 0.

Table 9.3. Accessibility of instructions controlling the PMU.

Instruction	Accessibility
ssm/rsm	privilege-level 0
sum/rum	any level, no effect if psr.sp $= 1$
mov rX=pmc[i]	privilege-level 0
mov pmc[i]=rX	privilege-level 0
mov pmd[i]=rX	privilege-level 0
mov rX=pmd[i]	any level, read 0 if pmc.pm $= 1$ or psr.sp $= 1$

The role of dcr.pp

The default control register (see Chapter 2, *IA-64 Architecture*) contains the *privileged monitor default bit*, dcr.pp. This bit should not be confused with psr.pp.

This bit is used with privileged monitors and has no effect on user monitors. The value of dcr.pp is copied to psr.pp when an interruption occurs. This mechanism is, therefore, only relevant to monitoring happening at privilege-level 0. The goal is to provide a mechanism by which interruption handlers can be isolated from the rest of the execution happening at this level. The isolation works both ways: it is possible to monitor only what is happening during interruption processing, or it is possible to monitor what is happening at this level with the exclusion of interruption processing. This mechanism is mostly interesting for systemwide monitoring, so it applies only to privileged monitors.

9.1.2 Controlling monitoring

A monitoring session consists of several steps that must be followed to collect valid measurements. Those steps can be summarized as follows:

1. Program the monitors (pmc and pmd registers).

2. Enable the monitors.

3. Run the code to be monitored.

4. Disable the monitors.

5. Collect results.

Before the monitors can be programmed, it is necessary to ensure that monitoring is inactive. There are two methods to do this. The first method is to freeze the PMU by setting the freeze bit; the second is to clear psr.up and psr.pp.

Once the monitors are programmed, monitoring can be activated. The PMU must be unfrozen, and the relevant psr bits must be set. A monitor is said to be *enabled* when the conditions depicted in Figure 9.7 are met.

The various state transitions of a monitoring sessions are presented in Figure 9.8. Three states are possible, based on the value of the psr bits and the freeze bit. While in the active

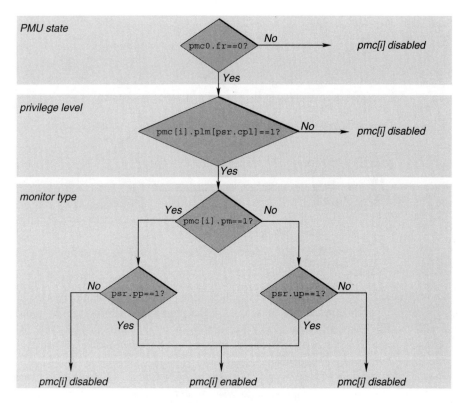

Figure 9.7. How a monitor is enabled.

state, the PMU can suddenly freeze when an overflow occurs and causes the freeze bit to be set. At that point, the PMU is frozen but the psr bits are still set. When the overflow interrupt handler eventually clears the freeze bit, the PMU goes back to the active state. When the PMU is not frozen, toggling the psr.up and the psr.pp bits switches the PMU between the enabled and active states.

9.1.3 Dealing with counter overflows

In our description of the pmd registers, we indicated that even though those registers are all 64 bits wide, the counter field can be smaller. The architecture does not specify a minimum width but instead provides a recovery mechanism in case of overflow.

An overflow happens when the counter rolls back to zero. We might think this does not happen easily, but if we consider a CPU running at 1 GHz, a 32-bit counter measuring the number of elapsed cycles would overflow in just 4.3 seconds! To put things in perspective, at the same frequency, it would take a little over five million hours (about 584 years) to overflow a 64-bit counter, so this limit is reasonably safe.

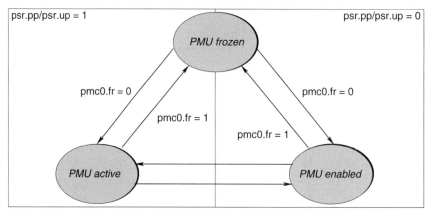

Figure 9.8. Operating states of the PMU.

Another factor worth mentioning is that some events happen more than once a cycle. If the PMU is programmed to capture those events, the time to an overflow can be reduced even more. As an example, Itanium can execute up to two bundles in one cycle, so if we assume perfect scheduling of instructions, an event such as the number of instructions executed would increase by six in each cycle.

The overflow mechanism is designed to notify the software when a counter wraps around. Using this mechanism, an operating system can maintain a 64-bit *software* counter for every *hardware* counter. On overflow, the software counter is incremented by 2^w where w is the width of the hardware counter. We describe this technique in Section 9.3.

Relying on overflows and software counters to collect measurements comes with its own set of problems and dangers. Some latency is always involved between the moment the overflow occurs and the time the interrupt handler is invoked. Such delays may lead to race conditions that could affect the accuracy of the measurements. This is the case when an application tries to read the value of the 64-bit software counter with a system call and an overflow interrupt is in-flight, i.e., pending but not yet delivered. In this case, it is possible that the application will retrieve an invalid count with a potential error of 2^w. Note that it is not even necessary to have monitoring active to get to this situation: it can happen even after the psr bits have been cleared. To prevent this, software must check the overflow status bit corresponding to the pmd register being read before returning its value.

Because the PMU is frozen when an overflow occurs, it is not possible to record events while running in the overflow interrupt handler until the freeze bit is cleared. This ensures that the correct counts are observed and that no nested overflows can happen. Such a behavior is reasonable because the handler is just here to alleviate the small width of the counters and so it is overhead that should not normally be included in the counts. The execution of the overflow handler is one of the *monitoring blind spots*.

So far we have described overflow interrupts as being an inevitable *problem* that requires special attention in the kernel. But sometimes overflows can be turned into an advantage when it comes to sampling, in particular, event-based sampling. With this technique, the sampling period is determined by a number of occurrences of an event, not by time. Hence, it is useful to be able to program a counter such that it will overflow after exactly n occurrences have been observed, where n is the sampling period. We describe how this is implemented for Linux/ia64 in Section 9.3.

9.2   EXTENDING THE PMU: THE ITANIUM EXAMPLE

The Itanium PMU provides the architected features outlined in the previous section and adds many other features that we describe here. Other CPU models may implement the same extensions, replace them, or build on them. We describe the Itanium PMU because it shows how the architecture can be refined and also because the additional features provide some unique monitoring capabilities.

9.2.1   Itanium PMU additional capabilities

There are two categories of enhancements. The first category adds more configuration capabilities to existing monitors with new ways of fine-tuning what is to be monitored. The second category adds new features that help pinpoint the performance characteristics of programs by providing hardware support for sampling cache misses, TLB misses, and branches. For this purpose, Itanium adds 6 pmc and 14 pmd registers. The list of major additional features can be summarized as follows:

- **Opcode matching**: Monitoring can be constrained to certain instructions, based on their encoding or based on the execution unit they use.

- **Address range checking**: The PMU can be programmed to record events only when they occur within a certain range of data or code addresses.

- **Event thresholding**: With a threshold, an event is recorded only when it occurs more than a certain number of times per cycle.

- **IA-32 execution monitoring**: The PMU can monitor execution of IA-32 programs. Most of the monitoring features are available in this mode.

- **Event address registers (EAR)**: The PMU can record cache or TLB misses caused by data accesses or instruction fetches. Each sample collects the address where the miss happened, along with other information such as the data address, the latency of the miss, or the TLB level in which the miss was handled.

- **Branch trace buffer (BTB)**: The PMU can record a trace of the branch instructions executed. It is possible to configure what kind of branches are captured: taken, not taken, predicted correctly, predicted incorrectly. Up to four branches can be recorded in the buffer, and for each the source and target addresses are provided.

In the remainder of this section, we describe each of these features in more detail. We focus mostly on the EAR and BTB since they are the most powerful enhancements of Itanium.

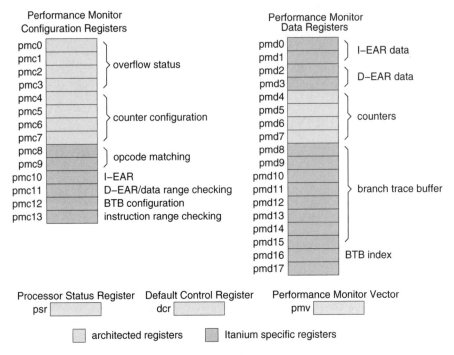

Figure 9.9. Itanium PMU register file.

9.2.2   Itanium PMU register file

Itanium implements the pmc and pmd registers shown in Figure 9.9. The counter width w is limited to 32 bits.

Format of the pmd and pmc registers

Figure 9.10 shows the format of the pmc and pmd for counting monitors. Compared with the architected format, there are three additional fields in the configuration registers: ism (instruction set mask), thr (threshold), and umask (unit mask). When the threshold is not 0, the corresponding counter will be incremented only when the number of occurrences of an event exceeds the number in this field. For instance, by setting the threshold to 5, the monitor captures the event only when it occurs six or more times per cycle. The width of this field is not the same for all of the four pmc registers. For pmc4–pmc5, the width is three bits, whereas it is only two bits for pmc6–pmc7. This means that the latter can only use thresholds up to three, whereas the former can go up to seven. The 2-bit ism field indicates which instruction set is to be monitored. Bit 24 and bit 25 represent the IA-64 and IA-32 instruction set, respectively. If both bits are set, the PMU monitors both instruction sets simultaneously. The umask field denotes small variations of an event. For

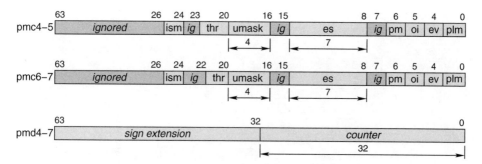

Figure 9.10. Format of a monitor pair on Itanium.

instance, the Itanium-specific event INST_FAILED_CHKS_RETIRED counts the number of failed chk.s instructions executed. It has three variants, which are named by appending one of the following suffixes to the main event name: .INTEGER, .FP, and .ALL. The first two suffixes make it possible to separate instructions that check integer registers from those that check floating-point registers, whereas the third ignores the distinction. Itanium encodes these variations in the umask rather than using a different event code in the es field.

The architecture specifies that the event select field (es) is up to 8 bits wide with a minimum width of 1 bit. Itanium uses seven bits, which means that it can support a total of 128 distinct events. However with the 4-bit umask, a maximum of 2048 events ($2048 = 128 \cdot 2^4$) is possible.

9.2.3   Itanium PMU events

The architecture requires only two events, but Itanium goes well beyond that and defines approximately 230 different events. Of course, since there are only four counters, only 4 events out of 230 can be measured at any given time. Not all events support the Itanium-specific enhancements we presented earlier. For example, some events cannot be used in conjunction with address range checking or opcode matching. All Itanium events names are listed in Appendix D.

Cycle accounting with the Itanium PMU

During the execution of a program, the consumed CPU cycles can be separated in two categories:

- **Inherent execution cycles**: The cycles used to do the real work of the program.

- **Stall cycles**: The cycles lost waiting for a hardware resource to become available. For instance, a program may have to wait several cycles for data to come from a cache or main memory. Stalls also happen when too many instructions need the same execution unit or when a branch is incorrectly predicted, i.e., mispredicted.

Table 9.4. Itanium cycle accounting categories and formulas.

Category	Event formula
Data access	DATA_ACCESS_CYCLES
Dependencies	DEPENDENCY_SCOREBOARD_CYCLE
RSE activities	MEMORY_CYCLE – DATA_ACCESS_CYCLES
Issue limit	DEPENDENCY_ALL_CYCLE – DEPENDENCY_SCOREBOARD_CYCLE
Instruction access	INST_ACCESS_CYCLE
Branch re-steers	PIPELINE_BACKEND_FLUSH_CYCLE
Taken branches	PIPELINE_ALL_FLUSH_CYCLE – PIPELINE_BACKEND_FLUSH_CYCLE
Inherent execution	UNSTALLED_BACKEND_CYCLE – INST_ACCESS_CYCLE

The second category is more useful for identifying performance problems and possible solutions. For instance, if we know that a lot of the stalls are due to data accesses, prefetching
the data or modifying the data layout might improve performance. Similarly, using predication might help remove some branch stall cycles.

On Itanium, every cycle can be accounted as one of four events: DEPENDENCY_ALL-
_CYCLE, MEMORY_CYCLE, PIPELINE_ALL_FLUSH, or UNSTALLED_BACKEND_CYCLE.
The last event represents inherent execution cycles, and the three others account for different types of stalls. The sum of these four events must add up to CPU_CYCLES, the number
of elapsed CPU cycles. It is possible to generate a more detailed cycle breakdown by using
combinations of events. Specifically, the stalls can be subdivided into seven categories. If
we add inherent execution cycles, this gives a total of eight categories. Four stall categories
can be measured directly, but the other four categories must be obtained indirectly, by combining events as shown in Table 9.4. The table shows that a complete breakdown requires
collecting nine events (eight events plus CPU_CYCLES). Given that only four events can
be measured at a time, a minimum of three runs is required. In practice, an accurate breakdown requires several such runs to average out fluctuations. In particular, it is often a good
idea to measure CPU_CYCLES in each run to get an estimate of the fluctuations. We give
an example of how to collect a simple breakdown in Section 9.3.3.

9.2.4   Hardware support for event sampling

The cycle accounting support we described in the previous section provides some insights
as to *how* the CPU spends its time, but not *where* it is spent. The *where* can be determined
with traditional time-based sampling (profiling), which periodically samples the instruction
pointer (IP) of the CPU. Each sample is recorded into a sampling buffer. The time between
samples can vary and, in fact, is better if it is random to make sure that sampling is not
in lockstep with the execution. The collected samples can then be analyzed. For example,
hot spots can be detected with a histogram of the recorded addresses. The main assumption
is that the more often a certain address occurs, the more time was spent there, suggesting
the possible presence of a bottleneck. Of course, this technique works reliably only if the
recorded IP is accurate. Considering the instruction recorded by the IP and mapping it

back to the source code, may make it possible to figure out the source of the problem. For instance, if the instruction is a load from memory, the problem could be a cache miss.

Limitations of traditional sampling techniques

A first and obvious problem with traditional sampling is that it provides information about *instructions* only. It does not help answer questions such as whether a particular *data structure* might be causing an excessive number of cache or TLB misses. For example, if a profile indicates that a particular load instruction is slow to execute, it would not be possible to say whether it was slow because (a) the instruction was not in the cache, (b) the data was not in the cache, or (c) the necessary translation was missing in the TLB.

A more insidious problem is that with modern architectures, traditional IP-based sampling techniques tend to be less and less accurate because of features such as parallel instruction issue, deep pipelining, and nonblocking caches [4]. Figure 9.11 (a) illustrates how this might cause problems. On Itanium, the load of register r32 at address 0x1000 might cause a data cache miss. Itanium can tolerate several outstanding misses, so this might not stall execution immediately. Instead, it might continue up to the point at which the code is trying to use r32 for the addition in the bundle at address 0x1040. At that point, Itanium would stall until the data arrives from the cache. With time-based sampling, the more time spent at an address, the more likely the timer interrupt will occur there. This means that the interrupt is likely to hit in the bundle where the addition is. On IA-64, interrupts can only occur at bundle boundaries, so the actual IP value recorded would be 0x1050. Even if we account for this one-bundle skew, the problem is that the bundle at 0x1040 has no direct relationship to the load that is the actual source of the problem.

Now, given the Itanium PMU, we might think this problem could be fixed by the use of event-based sampling instead of time-based sampling. For example, we could use the L2_MISSES event to sample the IP after a certain number of cache misses have occurred. Indeed, with a sampling period of one, we could record every single miss as it occurs. To achieve this, an counting monitor would have to be programmed such that it overflows after just one event. That is, the counter would have to be set to $2^w - 1$, where w is the width of the counter. Unfortunately, this does not really help. When the load at 0x1000 is executed, it takes the CPU some time to realize that there is a cache miss and for the event to be qualified as an L2 cache miss. During this time, the CPU will continue executing other instructions. By the time the PMU finally increments the counter, detects the overflow, and generates the interrupt, the IP can be several bundles beyond the instruction that triggered the event. The recorded IP will be the address of the bundle that was about to be executed at the time the interrupt was generated. In the example illustrated in Figure 9.11 (b), the IP is at address 0x10a0, which is 10 bundles away from the load. So again, the sample is skewed and of limited value. This is not just a theoretical problem. On Itanium, the maximum distance by which the IP can be off is 16 bundles, or 48 instructions!

The two examples show that neither time- nor event-based sampling can identify the source of the problem. In the case of time-based sampling, we tend to find the effect rather than the cause of the problem: the addition stalls because the load missed. Event-based sampling fails because by the time the interrupt captures the IP, it is already too late.

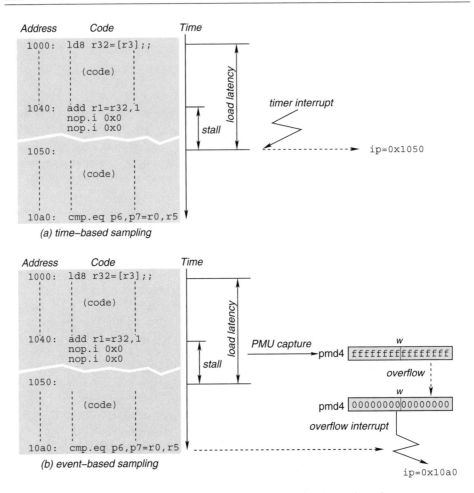

Figure 9.11. Inaccuracy of interrupt driven sampling of the instruction pointer.

What does Itanium provide?

Itanium addresses all of these problems with *event address registers (EAR)*. As their name suggests, they record where certain events occur. Specifically, the PMU can record where cache and TLB misses occur. For each miss, the PMU records additional information such as the latency of a cache miss or the level of the TLB in which a miss is resolved. This kind of recording is supported for both instruction (*I-EAR*) and data (*D-EAR*) addresses. For the example in Figure 9.11, if the PMU was programmed for D-EAR sampling, it would record the address of the load instruction (0x1000), the data address being accessed (the value of register r3), and the load latency. In addition, the BTB can also be used for sampling purposes. For example, it can be used to sample every 1000th mispredicted branch.

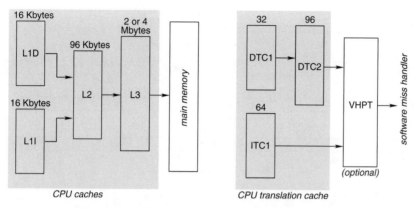

Figure 9.12. Itanium cache and TLB hierarchies.

9.2.5 Event address registers (EAR)

The EAR capture events related to the memory system. Before we can describe them, it is useful to briefly review the Itanium memory system. The left side of Figure 9.12 depicts the three-level cache hierarchy of this CPU model. It has separate level-one data (L1D) and instruction (L1I) caches, and unified level-two (L2) and level-three (L3) caches. A load takes 2 cycles from L1D, 6 cycles from L2, and 21 cycles from L3.

The TLB cache structure is shown on the right of Figure 9.12. The data TLB is composed of two levels of fully associative caches with 32 and 96 entries, respectively. If both levels miss, then it may be possible to resolve the miss with the VHPT walker. The instruction side has only one level before going to the VHPT. If there is a miss in the VHPT or if the VHPT is disabled, the CPU raises a TLB miss fault, which is then handled by software.

Data event address registers (D-EAR)

The D-EAR capture events related to loads, stores, semaphore instructions, and RSE loads and stores. The set of registers used by the D-EAR is shown in Figure 9.13. One register, pmc11, configures the D-EAR and three data registers (pmd2, pmd3, and pmd17) are used as buffers. The D-EAR is an example of a monitor using more than two registers. The format of pmc11 is similar to the configuration register of a counting monitor (pmc4–pmc7). Many of the fields have indeed the same meaning, such as plm, ism, and pm. Similarly, the activation of a D-EAR monitor follows the rules we outlined earlier.

The tlb field indicates whether the D-EAR capture TLB (tlb = 1) or cache (tlb = 0) misses. The pt (pass tag) field enables data address range checking (pt = 0) and has no direct effect on the D-EAR themselves.

When a TLB miss or a cache miss occurs, it is useful to know the memory address and the IP of the instruction that caused it. This information is recorded in pmd2 and pmd17, respectively. Because instruction bundles are 16 bytes long, the low 4 bits are always 0.

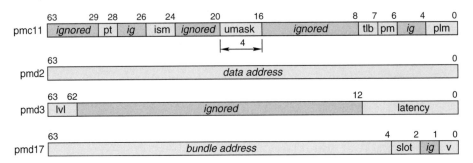

Figure 9.13. Itanium D-EAR.

Table 9.5. Description of umask values for pmc11.

	Cache mode	TLB mode
umask	Miss latency	TLB level
0x0	$\geq$ 4 cycles	reserved
0x1	$\geq$ 8 cycles	hit in L2 TLB
0x2	$\geq$ 16 cycles	hit in VHPT
0x3	$\geq$ 32 cycles	handled by software
0x4	$\geq$ 64 cycles	ignored
0x5	$\geq$ 128 cycles	ignored
0x6	$\geq$ 256 cycles	ignored
0x7	$\geq$ 512 cycles	ignored
0x8	$\geq$ 1024 cycles	ignored
0x9	$\geq$ 2048 cycles	ignored
0xa	$\geq$ 4096 cycles	ignored
0xb–0xf	nothing captured	ignored

Hence, pmd17 uses bit 0 (v) to indicate whether a qualified event was captured in the D-EAR. The latency of a cache miss is reported in the latency field, and the level at which the TLB miss was handled is reported in the lvl field.

The *umask* field in pmc11 is a filter on the kinds of misses to capture. Table 9.5 lists all possible values for both modes. In cache mode, the filter is based on the latency to resolve the miss, expressed in CPU cycles. For instance, if umask is set to 0x4, the D-EAR will capture all misses taking at least 64 cycles. In TLB mode, the umask designates the TLB level at which the miss was resolved. For instance, if the umask equals 0x2, the D-EAR will capture a miss that is resolved in the VHPT, i.e., missed in the level-two TLB.

Figure 9.14 illustrates how the information captured by the D-EAR relate to the instruction that triggered the event. We assume that the D-EAR are configured to capture cache misses that take more than four cycles to resolve (umask = 0). The right side of the figure shows the code of function *f()*. We assume that the load instruction at address

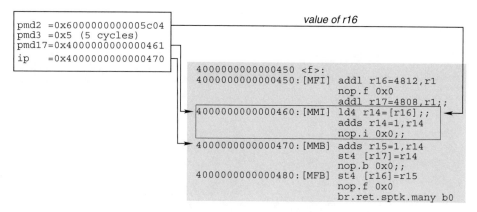

Figure 9.14. Example of a D-EAR sample.

0x4000000000000460 caused a data cache miss that is captured by the D-EAR. On the left side, we show the content of the D-EAR once the miss is resolved. The sample is valid because bit 0 of pmd17 is set. If we mask off the low four bits of pmd17, we obtain the address of the instruction bundle that caused the miss. The data address that the load was accessing is in pmd2. It reflects the value of r16 at the time of the load. Finally, the D-EAR show the latency of the miss at five cycles, as indicated by pmd3. This example is similar to the one we used in Figure 9.11 and clearly shows how the D-EAR avoid the problems encountered with traditional IP sampling. Here, we still use an interrupt; however, by the time it is generated, the D-EAR have already captured the relevant information.

It is important to realize that none of the pmd registers used by the D-EAR behave like counters, so they do not generate overflow interrupts. In fact, the D-EAR constantly record any qualified events, and the pmd registers act like a ring buffer of size 1. To make it possible to detect when a qualified event is captured, we need to program a monitor to count DATA_EAR_EVENT. The counter will be incremented by 1 each time a qualified miss is captured.

Instruction event address registers (I-EAR)

The I-EAR follow the same principles as the D-EAR but they capture cache and TLB misses triggered by instruction fetches. The I-EAR are shown in Figure 9.15. The configuration is held in pmc10, which is similar to pmc11. The pmd1 register contains the latency of a cache miss, and pmd0 holds the address of the instruction cache line that triggered the miss. On Itanium, an L1 cache line is 32 bytes long (2 bundles). This means that in cases in which execution jumps directly in the middle of a cache line, pmd0 does not give the address of the bundle that was about to be executed. Similarly, the TLB uses a page as the basic unit for a miss. Hence, pmd0 must be rounded down to the closest page boundary to get the correct TLB miss address. Because the IA-64 TLB supports multiple page sizes, the analysis of the sampling trace must use the proper page size in the rounding calculations.

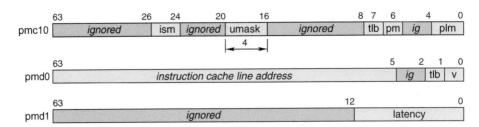

Figure 9.15. Itanium I-EAR.

Table 9.6. Description of umask values for pmc10.

umask	Cache mode Miss latency	TLB mode TLB level
0x0	≥ 4 cycles	ignored
0x1	≥ 8 cycles	ignored
0x2	≥ 16 cycles	hit in VHPT
0x3	≥ 32 cycles	handled by software
0x4	≥ 64 cycles	ignored
0x5	≥ 128 cycles	ignored
0x6	≥ 256 cycles	ignored
0x7	≥ 512 cycles	ignored
0x8	≥ 1024 cycles	ignored
0x9	≥ 2048 cycles	ignored
0xa	≥ 4096 cycles	ignored
0xb–0xf	nothing captured	ignored

Because of the minimum cache line size of 32 bytes, the first five bits ($2^5 = 32$) of pmd0 can store other information. Bit 0 holds a valid bit, and bit 1 indicates which level of TLB resolved the miss when the I-EAR are programmed to capture TLB misses.

The possible values of the umask field for pmc10 are shown in Table 9.6. This table is similar to Table 9.5, except that in TLB mode, only two choices are available because the I-TLB only has two levels.

The pmd0–pmd1 registers are managed as a ring buffer of size 1. To count the number of qualified events captured by I-EAR, it is necessary to program a monitor to count INSTRUCTION_EAR_EVENT. The counter will be incremented by 1 each time a qualified miss is captured.

9.2.6 Branch trace buffer (BTB)

Another type of information that can be useful for performance analysis is a taken branch trace. With such a trace, the execution path can be reconstructed. Once the path is known, it can be optimized to minimize instruction cache misses, for instance. This information can

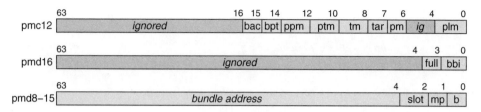

Figure 9.16. Itanium BTB registers.

also be used to place prefetch instructions in such a way that by the time execution reaches a certain point in the path, the data is already present in the cache. For this purpose, the Itanium PMU provides the *branch trace buffer (BTB)*.

The BTB records the outcome of certain branches. The kind of branches to record can be constrained with pmc12, the BTB configuration register. The collected information is stored in eight pmd registers. For each qualified branch, the address of the branch instruction and its target are recorded in pairs. This means that up to four pairs can be kept in registers. The buffer consists of pmd8–pmd15 and is managed like a ring buffer. After the last pair in pmd14–pmd15 is written, the first pair in pmd8–pmd9 gets overwritten. Register pmd16 serves as an index register. It also incorporates a mechanism to keep track of wrap-around conditions, which we describe shortly.

The format of pmc12 is shown in Figure 9.16. The plm and pm fields have the same meaning as for counting monitors. Note that there is no ism field. The reason is that the BTB works only for the IA-64 instruction set. The purpose of the other fields is as follows:

- tm: This 2-bit *taken mask* field indicates whether to record taken, not taken, or all branches.

- ptm: This 2-bit *predicted target address mask* field indicates whether to record branches for which the target address has been predicted correctly or incorrectly (mispredicted).

- ppm: This 2-bit *path prediction mask* field indicates whether to record branches regardless of the path prediction outcome (taken or not taken), only when the prediction was correct, or only when the prediction was incorrect.

The remaining fields pertain to the branch architecture of Itanium. Explaining this architecture is beyond the scope of this book. Here, we simply give the minimal information to describe the fields of pmc12. The *target address registers (TAR)* and *target address cache (TAC)* are two elements of the branch architecture involved with branch predictions. If they failed to predict the target of a branch, the CPU uses the static hints encoded in the branch instructions, such as .sptk or .dpnt. In this case, the target address is calculated by the *branch address calculator (BAC)*. The tar, bpt, and bac fields can be used to further qualify branches according to whether they were predicted with TAR, TAC, or BAC, respectively.

Table 9.7. Configuration of pmc12 to capture all mispredicted branches.

Field	Value	Description
tm	0x3	capture taken and not taken branches
ptm	0x1	capture branches with mispredicted target address
ppm	0x1	capture branches with mispredicted path
bpt	0x1	capture branches predicted by TAC
tar	0x1	capture branches predicted by TAR
bac	0x1	capture branches which used the BAC

As an example of how to use pmc12, we show in Table 9.7 how to configure the various fields to capture all mispredicted branches.

Registers pmd8–pmd15 all have the same format, which is illustrated in Figure 9.16. Each register may contain information about a branch instruction or a branch target. The b bit distinguishes the two possibilities. If b is set, the register contains information about the branch instruction; otherwise, about the branch target. The meaning of the mp field depends on the type of entry. For a branch instruction, the field indicates how the branch was predicted: if it is set, the branch was mispredicted. For a branch target, the mp field indicates whether the record is correct. The remainder of the register contains the address of the branch instruction or the branch target, expressed as a 60-bit bundle address.

The BTB will not always record both the branch instruction and branch target. Possible reasons for this include situations in which the branch traps or faults and hence does not reach the intended target. Also, when the target of the branch is a bundle that contains another qualifying branch, the BTB may record the two branches as two separate pairs or it may combine the two. In the former case, the second branch instruction appears as both the branch target of the first pair and source address in the second. In the latter case, the target address comes from the second branch instruction.

Register pmd16 serves as the *branch buffer index*. Its format is shown in Figure 9.16. The bbi field is the index of the next register to be written expressed as a value in the range of 0 to 7. When bbi = 0, it means that pmd8 is to be written next. When bbi = 7 and an entry is recorded, bbi wraps around to 0. The PMU indicates the wrap-around condition by setting the full bit. The bit will stay set until cleared by software. Because the branch buffer is often used to trace the history of branches, the sequencing information which shows that a branch was executed after another must always be preserved. The full bit is designed just for this reason; when it is set, the bbi field not only points to the next entry to be written, but it also becomes a pointer to the oldest entry in the buffer.

The best way to visualize this is to look at the examples shown in Figure 9.17. The left side of the figure shows a situation in which the buffer has not yet overflowed, so full is cleared. The oldest entry is in pmd8, the newest recorded entry is in pmd14, and the next entry will go in pmd15. The right side shows a situation in which the buffer has overflowed, possibly multiple times, so full is set. The bbi field points to the next entry to be written; this entry is also the oldest entry in the buffer. In this configuration, the sequential branch history is pmd11–pmd15 followed by pmd8–pmd10.

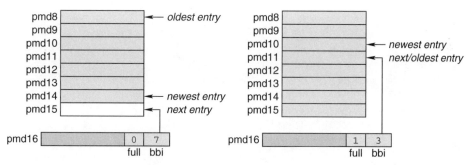

Figure 9.17. Interpreting the value of pmd16.

No overflow interrupt is generated when the buffer wraps around. To count the number of branches captured, a monitor must be programmed to count the BRANCH_EVENT. The counter will be incremented by 1 for each pair of registers written.

To make the description of the BTB more concrete, let us examine an example. Suppose we want to capture a trace of the taken branches on a simple program that iterates forever, incrementing a counter each time. If the counter is an odd number, the program also calls *func1()*. The simplified C code is as follows:

```
long func1 (void) { return 0; }

void do_it (void) {
    long p = 0;
    for (;;) {
        if (p & 0x1) func1();
        p++;
    }
}
```

The relevant portion of the assembly code generated for this program is shown at the top of Figure 9.18. We configure the BTB to record taken branches, independently of whether they were predicted correctly. We do this by setting pmc12 such that all fields have a value of 1. The privilege level is set to the user level to make sure we only capture user-level execution. We program a counting monitor (pmc4, pmd4) to count the BRANCH_EVENT and set the counter such that it will overflow once the BTB is full, i.e., $pmd4 = 2^{32} - 4$. This ensures that we do not lose any branches. Note that this setting imposes quite some overhead because every four branches, pmd4 will overflow. However, this does not affect the accuracy of the trace because it does not change which branches are taken.

The bottom of the figure shows a sample with the branches sorted by order of execution. For this sample, the full bit must have been set because the pmd8–pmd9 pair does not contain the first branch recorded. Instead, the pmd10–pmd11 pair contains the first branch. The pair recorded the source and destination of the last branch in the code. The second pair shows that *p* must have been even since the next recorded branch caused the CPU to loop

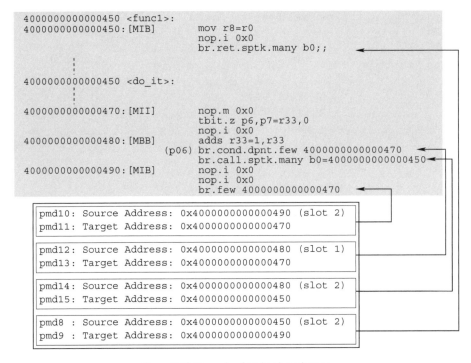

```
4000000000000450 <func1>:
4000000000000450:[MIB]          mov r8=r0
                                nop.i 0x0
                                br.ret.sptk.many b0;;

4000000000000450 <do_it>:

4000000000000470:[MII]          nop.m 0x0
                                tbit.z p6,p7=r33,0
                                nop.i 0x0
4000000000000480:[MBB]          adds r33=1,r33
                         (p06)  br.cond.dpnt.few 4000000000000470
                                br.call.sptk.many b0=4000000000000450
4000000000000490:[MIB]          nop.i 0x0
                                nop.i 0x0
                                br.few 4000000000000470
```

```
pmd10:  Source Address:  0x4000000000000490 (slot 2)
pmd11:  Target Address:  0x4000000000000470

pmd12:  Source Address:  0x4000000000000480 (slot 1)
pmd13:  Target Address:  0x4000000000000470

pmd14:  Source Address:  0x4000000000000480 (slot 2)
pmd15:  Target Address:  0x4000000000000450

pmd8 :  Source Address:  0x4000000000000450 (slot 2)
pmd9 :  Target Address:  0x4000000000000490
```

Figure 9.18. Example of a taken branch trace.

again. The third pair recorded a call to *func1()*. It is followed by the return branch (br.ret) from *func1()* as recorded in the fourth pair.

9.2.7 Miscellaneous features

The Itanium PMU provides two additional features. The *address range check* feature provides a mechanism to constrain the range of data or code addresses to which monitoring applies. The *opcode match registers* constrain monitoring to specific instruction patterns. These two features can usually be combined with all the other PMU features of Itanium.

Address range checking

Address range checking uses two control registers, one for code (pmc13) and one for data (pmc11). We already encountered pmc11 when talking about the D-EAR (see Figure 9.13). The pt field of pmc11 enables (pt = 0) or disables (pt = 1) data address range checking. For code range checking, bit 0 of pmc13 serves the equivalent purpose. That is, when the bit is cleared, range checking is enabled.

The address ranges to be monitored are stored in debug registers ibr and dbr. Normally, debug registers hold hardware breakpoints. The dual use of these registers implies that it

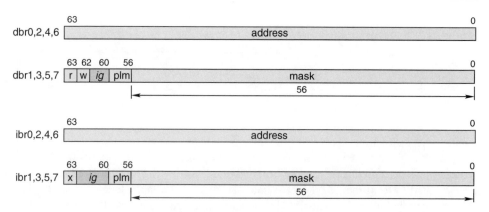

Figure 9.19. Format of the debug registers.

is not possible to use address range checking when the debug registers are used for break-points, and vice versa. In practice, this limitation is not an issue because debugging and performance monitoring are rarely done at the same time.

The IA-64 debug registers have the format shown in Figure 9.19 and are paired just like the pmc and pmd registers. Each even-numbered debug register holds an address field. Each odd-numbered register contains a mask field and a set of 1-bit fields: r and w for data debug registers; x for instruction debug registers. The 1-bit fields determine whether or not a breakpoint is enabled on reads, writes, or execution, respectively. Those three bits must be cleared for the PMU to consider the debug registers as holding a valid instruction or data range. The range is expressed by the mask field that indicates which address bits are compared between the address field and the instruction pointer. For instance, setting all bits in the mask to a value of 1 means that the instruction pointer must match exactly the value in the address field.

Because of the alignment and size restrictions of this mechanism, it may be necessary to use more than one debug register to cover a function or data structure. And even then, the covered area may include chunks of code or data in front of or after the range that could perturb the measurements, especially if those extra chunks are heavily used.

When the mask is programmed to cover just one bundle, range checking behaves like a checkpoint. This behavior can be useful for counting the number of times a particular func-tion is called. To realize such a counter, software must write the address of the function's entry point to the address field and program a monitor to count the number of instructions executed (with the IA64_INST_RETIRED event). The number of calls to the function is ob-tained by dividing the resulting count by 3 since there are three instructions in a bundle.

Opcode matching

Itanium provides two opcode matching registers, pmc8 and pmc9. Their format is shown in Figure 9.20. Any particular opcode can be encoded in either of those two registers. In a

Figure 9.20. Format of pmc8 and pmc9.

bundle, each instruction is encoded in 41 bits, but here only 27 bits are used. The 27 bits are composed of bits 27–40, which include the major opcode in 37–40, and bits 0–12, which typically encode a predicate and one of the operands of the instruction. Both chunks are concatenated to form the 27-bit match field. There is also a mask field that can be used to ignore certain bits in the match field. An instruction matches if bits 40–27 and 12–0 are identical to the corresponding bits in the match field or if the corresponding bits in the mask field are set.

Both pmc registers also include fields to restrict opcode matching according to the execution unit of an instruction slot. Setting one or more bits in the m, i, f, and b fields makes it possible to specify exactly which instructions and units are to be monitored. For instance, the adds instruction can execute on the M and I units and uses the same encoding for both cases. By setting the m and i fields appropriately, software can therefore choose to monitor all adds instructions, only those executed by the M-unit, or only those executed by the I-unit.

Once an opcode matching register is programmed for a particular instruction pattern, the number of qualified instructions executed can be counted with the IA64_TAGGED_INST-_RETIRED event. If pmc8 contains the instruction pattern, the event suffix .PMC8 must be used; otherwise, the event suffix .PMC9 must be used.

As an example, the opcode matching registers can be used to count the number of system calls executed by a program. In the case of Linux/ia64, system calls are triggered by a break with an operand of 0x100000 (see Chapter 5, *Kernel Entry and Exit*). If the opcode of break is programmed into pmc8, programming a monitor to count the number of matching occurrences with the IA64_TAGGED_INST_RETIRED.PMC8 event at the user level only will yield the number of system calls.

9.3 KERNEL SUPPORT FOR PERFORMANCE MONITORING

The Linux/ia64 kernel can be compiled to include support for the IA-64 PMU. This support is called *perfmon* and is the topic of this section. The principal goal of perfmon is to provide Linux/ia64 with the support needed to allow advanced performance analysis with the PMU.

Perfmon supports all architected PMU features and also the model-specific refinements such as the ones we described for Itanium. The user-level interface of perfmon consists of a single system call, *perfmonctl( )*, which supports a set of requests to configure, measure, and collect performance monitoring information. Event-based sampling is also supported. The interface provides 64-bit counters that are independent of the width of the hardware counters implemented by the underlying PMU.

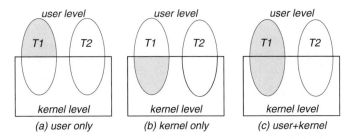

Figure 9.21. Per-task monitoring configurations.

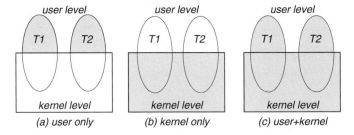

Figure 9.22. Systemwide monitoring configurations.

The sequence of actions from configuring the PMU, activating the monitoring, to collecting the results constitutes a *monitoring session*. Perfmon supports two types of sessions:

- **per-task**: monitoring is applied to only one task or a designated group of tasks

- **systemwide**: monitoring is applied to the entire system across all tasks

For per-task sessions, programs can be modified to use the perfmon interface to become *self-monitoring*, or an external program can be used to monitor unmodified binaries.

Within a session, each PMU monitor can be configured to measure at user level, kernel level, or both levels. For a per-task session, this leads to the three possible configurations shown in Figure 9.21. To keep our discussion simple, we limit our description of per-task sessions to configurations where only one task is monitored. For a systemwide session, there are also three possibilities, as shown in Figure 9.22. At any time there can be several distinct per-task sessions. Furthermore, perfmon does not preclude running per-task sessions and systemwide sessions in parallel.

In the remainder of this section we explore the perfmon interface and its implementation. We conclude by describing how perfmon can be used with pfmon, a simple tool for collecting performance information on unmodified binaries.

Table 9.8. List of requests for *perfmonctl()*.

Request	Description
PFM_CONTEXT_CREATE	create a new perfmon context
PFM_DESTROY_CONTEXT	destroy an existing context
PFM_ENABLE	set PMU in stable state and unfreeze
PFM_DISABLE	stop monitoring and freeze PMU
PFM_START	start monitoring
PFM_STOP	stop monitoring
PFM_READ_PMDS	read 64-bit virtual pmd registers
PFM_WRITE_PMDS	write pmd registers
PFM_WRITE_PMCS	write pmc registers
PFM_RESTART	restart monitoring after notification
PFM_PROTECT_CONTEXT	make context accessible only to owner
PFM_UNPROTECT_CONTEXT	make context accessible to everyone
CPU-model-specific extensions	
PFM_WRITE_IBRS	write instruction debug registers
PFM_WRITE_DBRS	write data debug registers

9.3.1 The perfmon interface

The *perfmon interface* (file include/asm/perfmon.h) is designed to be as close as possible to the hardware interface, i.e., the PMU interface. It mostly provides a mechanism to read and write PMU registers. The number of software abstractions layered on top of the PMU is kept to a bare minimum. This ensures that perfmon is portable across CPU models and that it can evolve as new features are added.

Perfmon provides a single system call, which has the following prototype:

```
int perfmonctl(pid, req, arg_ptr, narg);
```

The *req* argument indicates the request to execute and applies to the task designated by *pid*. Some requests take arguments that are pointed to by *arg_ptr*. The number of arguments is indicated by *narg*.

Table 9.8 lists the supported requests. Applications can use the first two requests to create or destroy a *perfmon context*. We discuss this notion in the next section. Once a context is created, the application must enable the PMU with PFM_ENABLE. The pmd and pmc registers can then be programmed with PFM_WRITE_PMDS and PFM_WRITE_PMCS, respectively. Self-monitoring applications can start and stop monitoring directly by toggling the psr.up bit. Other applications must use PFM_START and PFM_STOP instead. After monitoring is started, the PMU collects data as qualified events occur. Once the necessary data has been collected, the application can stop monitoring and retrieve the results by reading the pmd registers with PFM_READ_PMDS. The system call supports three other requests: PFM_RESTART, PFM_PROTECT_CONTEXT, and PFM_UNPROTECT_CONTEXT. The first is needed during overflow processing and the last two modify access control on the context. We describe them in more detail later on.

Table 9.9. Format of PFM_CREATE_CONTEXT argument.

Name	Description
ctx_smpl_entries	number of entries in the sampling buffer
ctx_smpl_regs	the pmd registers to record in each sample
ctx_smpl_vaddr	address of sampling buffer
ctx_notify_pid	task to notify on overflow
ctx_flags	set of flags

The system call may also support CPU-model-specific requests. At the bottom of Table 9.8, two such requests are shown. PFM_WRITE_DBRS and PFM_WRITE_IBRS program the data and instruction debug registers, respectively. As we have seen, this is needed to take advantage of the address range checking feature implemented, e.g., by Itanium.

The perfmon context

A *perfmon context* encapsulates the state of a monitoring session. The state includes the 64-bit software counters and the storage area used to save the PMU registers during a context switch for per-task sessions. At any time, a context is attached to only one task. For a per-task session, the context is attached to the task being monitored; for a systemwide session, it is attached to the task controlling the session. The controlling task can also be the one being monitored in the case of a self-monitoring task. For externally monitored tasks, the context is dynamically attached to an unmodified program when it gets created. To support this, the context can be cloned during a *clone2()* system call and inherited across a call to *execve()*. This mechanism allows monitoring of complex chains of tasks.

A context remains attached to a task until it is explicitly removed with PFM_DESTROY-_CONTEXT or until the task terminates. In the latter case, the perfmon context remains valid until the task is collected by a call to *wait4()*. This allows the task controlling the session to retrieve the results before the monitored task vanishes completely. For a systemwide monitoring session, results are collected when monitoring is stopped. The context is destroyed either explicitly or when the controlling task terminates.

The characteristics of the session are specified in the argument to PFM_CREATE_CON-TEXT. The format of this argument is shown in Table 9.9. The first three elements are used to configure a sampling session. We describe them shortly. The session type is indicated by a flag in *ctx_flags*. If PFM_FL_SYSTEM_WIDE is set, the context is created for a systemwide session. Otherwise, the context is created for a per-task session. When *ctx_notify_pid* is set to a non-zero value, it identifies the task that will receive the overflow notifications.

Configuring PMU registers

The perfmon interface provides write access to the pmc registers with PFM_WRITE_PMCS. Similarly, pmd registers can be written with PFM_WRITE_PMDS. For all CPU models, the interface is uniform and exports counting monitors with a counter width of 64 bits. On CPU models for which the PMU does not provide 64-bit counters, perfmon virtualizes

Table 9.10. Format of PFM_WRITE_PMCS and PFM_WRITE_PMDS argument.

Name	Applies to	Description
reg_num	pmd, pmc	register number
reg_value	pmd, pmc	64-bit value for the register
reg_short_reset	pmd	64-bit short overflow reset value
reg_long_reset	pmd	64-bit long overflow reset value
reg_flags	pmc	set of flags

them by using software counters. Just as hardware counters can be configured to interrupt on overflow, their corresponding software counters can be configured to send a signal on overflow, i.e., when they wrap around from $2^{64} - 1$ to 0. Not all pmd registers are counters, so this virtualization applies only to the subset of the pmd registers used as counters.

To allow a systemwide session to coexist with per-task sessions and guarantee that both can be started and stopped independently, perfmon forces all per-task sessions to employ user monitors and forces systemwide sessions to employ privileged monitors.

The PFM_WRITE_PMCS and PFM_WRITE_PMDS requests both take an argument with the format shown in Table 9.10. The number of the register to program is specified in *reg_num*, and its 64-bit value is stored in *reg_value*. For pmc registers controlling a counter, if *reg_flags* is set to PFM_REGFL_OVFL_NOTIFY, overflows will be propagated to the application with a SIGPROF signal. For pmd registers, the *reg_short_reset* and *reg_long_reset* specify two distinct reset values that are mostly used during sampling. We describe them in more detail later on.

Typically, it is necessary to program several pmc and pmd registers to configure a session. For this reason, both requests accept an array of arguments. Each entry in the array will program one register. This approach makes it possible to program an arbitrary number of pmc or pmd registers with the overhead of just a single system call.

Dealing with overflows

An overflow happens when a 64-bit counter wraps around to 0. In this case, perfmon can generate an overflow notification. This option is controlled by the PFM_REGFL_OVFL-_NOTIFY flag used when a pmc register is written. The notification uses the SIGPROF signal and is sent to the task with the process ID that was passed in *ctx_notify_pid* when the context was created. Supposing that this task has registered a SIGPROF signal handler, it will receive the notification along with information about the overflows. More than one overflow can be reported per notification. The information is provided in the siginfo structure passed to the signal handler (see Chapter 5, *Kernel Entry and Exit*). This structure contains a bitmask, called *si_pfm_ovfl*, where each bit represents a pmd register. The registers that overflowed have their corresponding bit set.

In the case of a per-task session, there are two possibilities for what may happen to the monitored task while the signal is handled: the task may keep running with monitoring turned off, or it may be blocked. The former allows the caches and TLB to remain somewhat warm but incurs some blind spots. The latter avoids the blind spots but perturbs the caches more. Because there is no perfect solution, perfmon leaves the decision to each application. By default, the task is not blocked. An application can request blocking mode by specifying the PFM_FL_OVFL_BLOCK flag when creating the context. In either case, an overflow signal handler must restart monitoring explicitly with PFM_RESTART. In nonblocking mode, the request will reenable monitoring by unfreezing the PMU. In blocking mode, the monitored task is woken up and once it resumes execution, the task also reenables monitoring by unfreezing the PMU. To avoid deadlock, self-monitoring tasks and systemwide sessions must use nonblocking mode.

After an overflow, only the counters that overflowed are reset. Perfmon uses the reset values that were passed in *reg_short_reset* and *reg_long_reset* when the context was created. Depending on the type of overflow, it uses the former or the latter. We explain the difference between the two values in the next section.

Support for sampling

Perfmon provides direct support for event-based sampling. Time-based sampling of the instruction pointer as we described it in Section 9.2.4 is also possible but does not necessitate any PMU support and is therefore outside the scope of perfmon.

In order to make event-based sampling work, it is necessary to have all of the following:

- At least one counter to generate the sampling period

- The PMU programmed to count occurrences of some events

- A list of the pmd registers to record in each sample

- A sampling buffer to record each sample

- A mechanism to indicate that the sampling buffer is full

- A mechanism to indicate that the sampling buffer has been processed

The sampling period defines the distance between two samples as an event count. Perfmon realizes this period with the overflow mechanism of the PMU. To request a sampling period of n events, perfmon sets the counter to $2^{64} - n$. The resulting overflow interrupt marks the end of the sampling period and triggers the recording of a sample. After the sample is processed, perfmon programs the next period by loading the counter with a new value.

For each overflow, perfmon records a set of pmd registers in the sampling buffer. The list of registers can vary from one session to another and is specified by the *ctx_smpl_regs* bitmask in the argument that is passed when the context is created.

For performance reasons, the sampling buffer is maintained by perfmon. It acts like a first-level sampling cache and avoids involving the application for each overflow—an involvement that would be quite expensive. The buffer length is specified by the application as a number of entries (*ctx_smpl_entries*) when the context is created. To avoid copying possibly large amounts of data from the kernel to the application, perfmon automatically maps the buffer read-only into the user address space of the task that creates the context. Perfmon

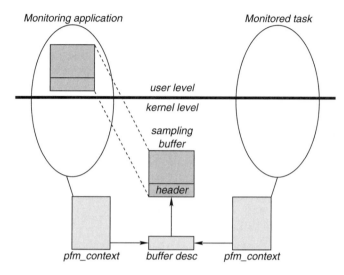

Figure 9.23. Sampling buffer configuration for monitoring an unmodified binary.

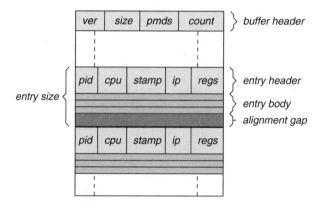

Figure 9.24. Format of the sampling buffer.

returns the address at which the buffer is mapped through *ctx_smpl_vaddr* in the argument
that is passed when the context is created. The mapping is illustrated in Figure 9.23 for
a per-task session monitoring an unmodified binary. With this mapping, samples can be
directly accessed by the monitoring application.

The sampling buffer consists of two parts: a fixed-size header and a variable-sized body.
The header shown in Figure 9.24 contains information about the format of the samples. For
instance, *pmds* is a bit vector indicating which pmd registers are recorded in each sample.
The size in bytes of each sample is also provided and can be used to access the buffer. Even

though the samples are all identical, they are always aligned on cache line boundaries for performance reasons; therefore, the distance between two samples can be more than the sum of the sizes of each of its elements. The header also provides the number of recorded samples in *count*. This information is necessary because there may be situations where monitoring stops before the buffer becomes full.

Each sample also consists of two parts: a fixed-size header and a variable-sized body. The entry header describes the sample and is shown in Figure 9.24. The ID of the task and the CPU that were executing when the overflow occurred are recorded in *pid* and *cpu*, respectively. A bit vector indicating which counters overflowed for this sample is recorded in *regs*. The instruction pointer is recorded in *ip*. The header is immediately followed by the entry body, a set of 64-bit words. Each word records the value of a pmd register at the time of the overflow. Remember that the PMU is always frozen on overflow, so the values in the pmd are the latest values captured while the task was still running. When recording the pmd of a counting monitor, perfmon uses the 64-bit software counter value.

During sampling, overflows are handled in the kernel. No notification is sent to the application until the buffer becomes full. At that point, no more samples can be recorded and the buffer must somehow be drained. This always happens as a consequence of a counter overflow; therefore, perfmon uses the same signal-based notification mechanism as used for a regular counter overflow. When the application receives the signal, it processes the buffer and eventually uses the PFM_RESTART request to resume monitoring. This request will mark the buffer as empty and monitoring will resume.

This sampling mechanism can also be used for simple event-based sampling of the instruction pointer. In this case, an empty bit vector is specified for *ctx_smpl_regs* when the context is created.

As we saw in Section 9.2, Itanium provides hardware support for sampling with the EAR and BTB monitors. Perfmon supports these features in a generic fashion. The relevant configuration registers, namely, pmc10–pmc12, can be programmed with PFM_WRITE-_PMCS. The EAR and BTB data buffers can be recorded in the sampling buffer by setting the corresponding bits in the *ctx_smpl_regs* bitmask. For instance, a sampling session using the D-EAR must record pmd2, pmd3, and pmd17 in each sample. The sampling period is loaded into a 64-bit counter, and the corresponding pmc is programmed to count the DATA_EAR_EVENT. The reset values can be adjusted to take into account the size of the hardware buffers. For instance, to record all branches, the sampling period must be set to 4.

Even with a kernel-level buffer, sampling incurs some overhead because interrupting the monitored task, running an interrupt handler, and returning to the task takes time and will necessarily modify the content of the caches and the TLB, thus introducing noise that can make the measurements inaccurate. This is illustrated in Figure 9.25. The black bars represent events recorded by the EAR. In this example, we illustrate a case with a highly regular pattern of events to emphasize the disruption. The overhead incurred by the overflow interrupt is labeled the *direct overhead*. After the overflow is processed, the task resumes execution but is now affected by another kind of overhead, called *indirect over-head*. Indirect overhead is more subtle and more difficult to measure because it is caused by disturbances to the caches and TLB generated during the execution of the overflow handler. This overhead may impact the behavior of the program and is shown as an irregular pattern

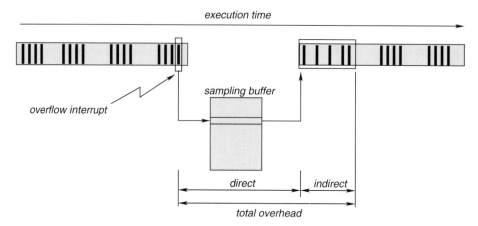

Figure 9.25. Overhead generated by sampling.

of events in the rectangle after the resumption point. Those events are in the *shadow* of the overflow and are not representative of the program. Therefore, they should not be recorded. The only way to avoid them is by carefully choosing the sampling period. The choice is always difficult because the period must not be too large; otherwise, we may not collect enough events to have a high probability that the sample collection is representative. But it cannot be too small either; otherwise, the overhead increases and the risk of capturing *contaminated* samples is higher.

Perfmon provides two distinct sampling periods: *reg_short_reset* and *reg_long_reset*. Both values are used to reset a counter after an overflow. The former is used to reset the counter when the overflow is entirely processed in the kernel, and the latter is used when user-level notification is necessary, i.e., the sampling buffer is full. This distinction accounts for the fact that user-level notification necessarily incurs a larger overhead since the large amount of data in the sampling buffer needs to be processed, causing more disruption in the caches and TLB. Generally, it is expected that applications will always set up the two periods such that *reg_long_reset* ≥ *reg_short_reset*. If both periods are equal, this is equivalent to having only one sampling period. The sampling periods try to hide the overhead but do not attempt to minimize it. The nonblocking mode provided by perfmon can help minimize some of the overhead by keeping the program running while the user-level notification is being processed. Of course, this is effective only on MP machines when the monitored task runs on a different CPU than the monitoring task.

The sampling mechanism just described works for both systemwide and per-task sessions, including self-monitoring sessions.

Security considerations

Three main security guarantees are provided by perfmon. First, perfmon ensures that a context can only be accessed by authorized tasks. For instance, it is not possible to operate on a context owned by a different user unless the task has root privileges. The task creating a context is called the *owner* of the context. If it is necessary to restrict access to only this task, applications can use the PFM_PROTECT_CONTEXT request. Alternatively, the PFM_UNPROTECT_CONTEXT request can be used to lift this restriction.

The second aspect of security covers the activation and deactivation of user monitors with the psr.up bit. As indicated earlier, users monitors are used for all per-task sessions. Perfmon ensures that only the owner of a context can use psr.up to start and stop user monitors. It achieves this by turning on the psr.sp bit (secure monitoring) for all monitored tasks that are not owners of their attached context. This ensures that self-monitoring tasks can start and stop their monitoring by using psr.up and that unmodified binaries which are externally monitored cannot. Systemwide sessions use privileged monitors and are not subject to this problem.

The third aspect of security deals with leaking measurement information to unauthorized tasks. This problem affects only per-task sessions because the pmd registers of user monitors can be read at the user level. The use of the secure monitoring bit (psr.sp) guarantees that no unauthorized task can read the actual value of a hardware register.

For CPU models, such as Itanium, that support PMU address range checking through the debug registers, both PFM_WRITE_DBRS and PFM_WRITE_IBRS ensure that no malicious breakpoints can be set by always clearing the r, w, and x bits of all odd-numbered debug registers (see Figure 9.19).

9.3.2 Implementation aspects

Let us now look at some aspects of the *perfmon implementation* (file arch/ia64/kernel/-perfmon.c). Specifically, we describe the effect of dcr.pp on Linux/ia64, how counting monitors are virtualized to 64 bits, and how event-based sampling is implemented. We round out the discussion with a description of how context switching works for per-task sessions.

Systemwide sessions and dcr.pp

As alluded to earlier, perfmon mandates that all systemwide sessions use privileged monitors to isolate them from concurrent per-task sessions.

Normally, the Linux/ia64 kernel is entered through some sort of interruption. As we saw in Chapter 5, *Kernel Entry and Exit*, system calls use the break instruction for this purpose. Since break is indistinguishable from any other interruption, it is not possible to isolate interruption handler execution from system call execution. Hence, perfmon cannot take advantage of dcr.pp and always sets it to 1. If, instead, system calls were initiated with an epc instruction, it would be possible to clear this bit when it is desirable to exclude interruption handling from other kernel-level execution.

Virtualizing the counters

Not all PMUs implement full 64-bit counters. For instance, the Itanium PMU only implements 32-bit counters. To maintain a uniform interface, perfmon emulates 64-bit counters by using software counters when necessary. To update the software counters, perfmon relies

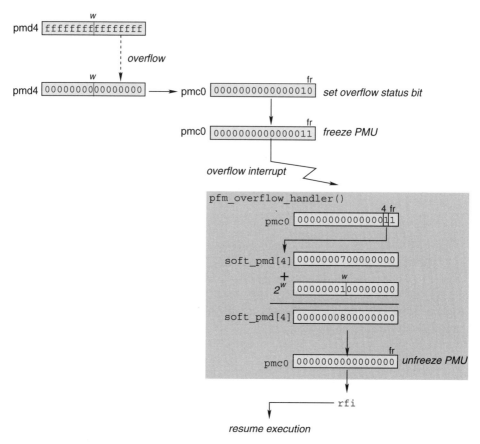

Figure 9.26. Virtualization of counters by the perfmon interrupt handler.

on the overflow interrupt of the hardware counters. For this reason, perfmon always forces the oi bit to be set for all counting monitors. The overflow is processed by the *perfmon over-flow interrupt handler (pfm_overflow_handler()* in file arch/ia64/kernel/perfmon.c). Once the monitor that overflowed is determined from the overflow status bits in pmc0–pmc3, the corresponding software counter is incremented by 2^w, where w is the width of the *hardware* counter. This mechanism is illustrated in Figure 9.26 in which we show what happens when pmd4 overflows. Once the handler has updated the software counter, the PMU is unfrozen and execution resumes.

When the 64-bit software counter overflows, a signal is sent to the task indicated by *ctx_notify_pid* if the PFM_REG_FL_OVFL_NOTIFY flag was set for the monitor. In a sense, this flag is equivalent to the oi bit of a monitor. The overflow condition is detected when 2^w is added to the software counter. If the value of the software counter is smaller than before the addition (of a positive value), the counter overflowed.

Any PFM_READ_PMDS request on a pmd used as a counter returns the sum of the software counter and the current hardware counter according to the following formula:

$$pmd\_64bit_i = soft\_pmd_i + (pmd_i \wedge (2^w - 1))$$

where pmd_i represents the hardware register. The last element of this formula masks off the sign extension of the counter. Similarly, PFM_WRITE_PMDS splits the 64-bit value between the software pmd and the hardware counter: bits 0 to $w - 1$ go directly to the hardware counter, and bits w to 63 go to the software counter.

For a context in blocking mode, perfmon uses a semaphore to ensure that the corresponding task does not return to the user level while a notification is in progress. Specifically, perfmon intercepts the task while executing the kernel's exit path and calls *down-_interruptible()* to block execution. When the monitoring task is done processing the notification, it calls PFM_RESTART. In response, perfmon wakes up the blocked task by signaling the semaphore with *up()*. Once the task resumes execution, it resets the overflowed counters to the value in *reg_long_reset*, unfreezes the PMU, and returns to the user level.

How sampling works

A sample is recorded only when a 64-bit software counter overflows. The necessary code is therefore executed after counter overflows have been processed. When a counter overflows and a sampling buffer is attached to the context, a new entry is allocated in that buffer, an entry header is generated, and the pmd registers specified in *ctx_smpl_regs* are recorded. When the entry is not the last one of the buffer, the counter is reloaded with the short reset value (*reg_short_reset*), the PMU is unfrozen, and execution resumes. Otherwise, a SIGPROF signal is sent to the task identified by *ctx_notify_pid*. This task will then determine the counter that overflowed by using the *si_pfm_ovfl* bitmask in the siginfo structure. When the task recognizes that the counter was controlling the sampling period, it will process the sampling buffer. During this processing, there is no risk of getting overflows or of the sampling buffer being modified by the kernel, even when the context is in nonblocking mode. The reason is that the PMU remains frozen until PFM_RESTART is invoked. After processing the buffer, the task invokes PFM_RESTART. In response, perfmon starts a new sampling period by reloading the overflowed counter with the long reset value (*reg_long-_reset*), marking the buffer as empty, unfreezing the PMU, and resuming execution.

This mechanism is illustrated in Figure 9.27 for a session sampling using the D-EAR. The figure assumes monitor pmc4/pmd4 is programmed to count the DATA_EAR_EVENT. The sampling period is assumed to be 2000. To realize this, the counter and the short reset value (*reg_short_reset*) need to be set to 0xfffffffffffff830 ($2^{64} - 2000$). The figure shows what happens when the 2000th event is detected. The top-left corner of the figure shows the current values of the software counter and the hardware counter just before the event is detected. When the overflow occurs, the value of pmd4 wraps around to 0, the overflow status bit is set, the PMU is frozen, and execution is transferred to the perfmon overflow handler. The software counter is updated as described in the previous section. If the 64-bit counter overflowed and there is a sampling buffer, a new entry is allocated and pmd2, pmd3, and pmd17 are recorded. Next, the 64-bit counter is reset to the short reset

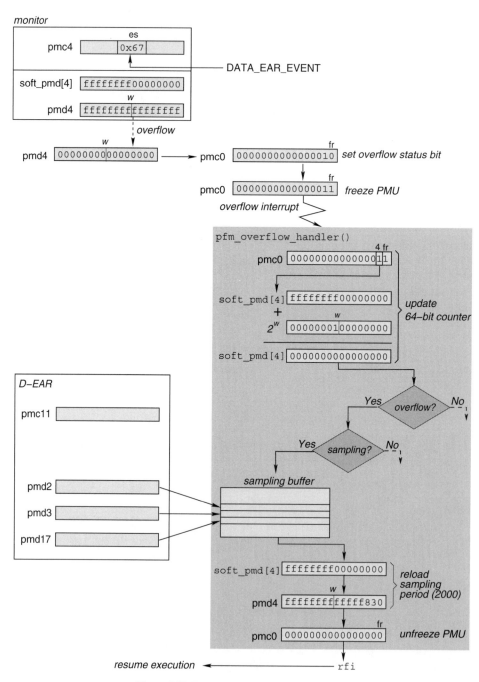

Figure 9.27. Example of sampling with perfmon.

value. As explained earlier, the 64-bit value is split between the software counter and the hardware counter. Finally, the PMU is unfrozen and execution resumes. When the 64-bit counter does not overflow, nothing is recorded in the sampling buffer, the PMU is simply unfrozen, and execution resumes.

Context switching

It is only necessary to save and restore the PMU state for per-task sessions. By nature a systemwide session relies on the fact that the state is shared among all the tasks running on the system and the most efficient way of sharing state is to leave it in the PMU. The PMU context-switch code is attached to the normal context-switch routines in *ia64_save_extra()* and *ia64_load_extra()* (see Chapter 3, *Processes, Tasks, and Threads*). It is implemented by three functions: *pfm_save_regs()*, *pfm_load_regs()*, and *pfm_lazy_save_regs()* (file arch/-ia64/kernel/perfmon.c).

Before discussing how the context switch works, we need to identify the PMU state that must be preserved in the perfmon context. As described at the beginning of this chapter, the PMU state consists of the pmc and pmd register files, the dcr.pp bit, and three psr bits. There is no need to preserve dcr.pp because it is a systemwide setting. On the other hand, the psr bits must be preserved in the perfmon context even though they are already preserved in pt-regs during normal kernel entry and exit. We explain the reason for this shortly. Similarly, the content of the pmc and pmd registers also must be preserved in the perfmon context because more than one per-task session can be competing for the PMU. Also, on MP machines the task may get rescheduled on another CPU, and in this case, the PMU state has to follow to that CPU. The number of implemented pmc and pmd registers can vary from one CPU model to another. To handle this, the context-switch code uses the PAL information returned by *ia64_pal_perf_mon_info()* to determine exactly which registers need to be saved and restored during a context switch (see Chapter 10, *Booting*).

There are three important aspects to the PMU context-switch code. The first aspect is efficiency. The overhead of saving and restoring the pmd and pmc registers must be minimized especially because accessing those registers is often slow. Perfmon combines three levels of lazy techniques to achieve this goal:

1. Perfmon avoids penalizing the many tasks that do not use the PMU by defining a thread flag called THREAD_PFM_FLAG. Only when this flag is set does the general context-switch code invoke the PMU save and load routines.

2. For tasks using the PMU, perfmon avoids saving and restoring registers by managing them in a lazy fashion. On context switch out, the state is left in the hardware registers in hopes that no other task will use the PMU. If no conflict arises, the task reacquires its own state at no cost. When there is a conflict, perfmon saves the old state before establishing the new state. For this purpose, perfmon maintains a variable, called *pmu_owner*, which indicates the task owning the PMU. For MP machines, there is one such variable per CPU. If a task is rescheduled from one CPU to another, perfmon must first fetch the state from the previous CPU. Perfmon does this by sending an interprocessor interrupt (IPI) to force the state to be saved on the old CPU. This

incurs some overhead, which is, however, mitigated by the fact that the scheduler tries to keep tasks on the same CPU to maintain good cache locality (CPU affinity).

3. When it is absolutely necessary to save the state, perfmon minimizes the cost by saving only the minimal set of registers. A first approach is to save only the pmd and pmc registers that are used by the task. This can easily be tracked because writing to a PMU register requires a *perfmonctl()* call. The approach can further be refined by differentiation of the pmc and pmd registers. The pmc1–pmc3 registers are directly modified by hardware; therefore, they must always be saved. The pmc0 register is always treated separately because of its side effect (freezing of the PMU). All other pmc registers remain constant throughout a session unless explicitly modified by the application. Perfmon keeps copies of the values installed and never saves these registers. In contrast, the pmd registers are directly modified by hardware; hence, they are always saved. When a saved PMU state is restored, all pmc registers must be restored to ensure that the task does not pick up a stale configuration from another task. Unused pmc registers are automatically initialized to a safe value. For instance, a pmc controlling a counter has its plm field cleared. Theoretically, perfmon could restore only the pmd registers that are used. However, to avoid leaking information between tasks, perfmon clears all the unused registers to 0.

The second aspect of context switching deals with stopping the monitoring when a task is switched out. Perfmon clears the psr.up bit after saving psr in the perfmon context. This has the effect of stopping the monitoring and ensures that the psr is not transferred to the next task with this bit set. Because the PMU is never frozen during the context switch and a lazy approach is used for saving the state, the kernel must enforce secure monitoring by setting psr.sp for all tasks except those that own their perfmon context. Otherwise, a task not using the PMU could modify the PMU state of another task by setting the psr.up bit.

The third and final aspect deals with correctness in the presence of an in-flight overflow interrupt. Linux/ia64 does not mask interrupts during context switches. Hence, it is possible to receive an overflow interrupt as a task is being switched out. In fact, any instruction up until the effect of clearing the psr.up bit takes hold could cause this overflow. While such a situation is unlikely, perfmon must handle it correctly and must guarantee that the effect of the interrupt is not lost, i.e., the software counters that overflowed are updated.

Perfmon must avoid the race condition between the overflow interrupt handler *pfm-_overflow_handler()* and the *pfm_lazy_save_regs()* function, which saves the pmd registers in memory. If the race is not handled correctly, the software counters may be updated incorrectly and stale pmd values may be saved in memory.

Masking interrupts while the pmd registers are saved would not eliminate the problem but simply postpone it. It would also increase interrupt response latency because reading the PMU registers can be quite slow. Similarly, it is not possible to cancel an overflow interrupt, once triggered. Since perfmon can neither ignore nor stop such interrupts, it must change the way it handles them. For this purpose, perfmon simply interprets overflow interrupts as *hints* that the overflow status bits (pmc0–pmc3) should be inspected. They contain the key information of which counters overflowed. As long as they are preserved, interrupts occurring at inopportune times can simply be dropped, i.e., treated as spurious. Thus,

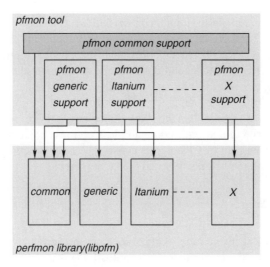

Figure 9.28. Architecture of pfmon.

the context-switch code uses a flag that is toggled in an atomic fashion. When the flag is cleared, the interrupt handler treats overflow interrupts as spurious and does not update the counters. The context-switch code takes advantage of this flag by clearing it after turning off monitoring but before saving the pmc and pmd registers. The flag remains cleared until a new task restores its PMU state. During this window of time, overflow interrupts will be treated as spurious. To make sure the effect of spurious interrupts is not lost, the saved overflow status bits are inspected after the pmc and pmd registers are restored. If some bits are set, the overflows are processed at that time. Once the saved overflow status bits have been processed, the flag is set and overflow interrupts will again be handled in the normal fashion. Perfmon uses *pmu_owner* as the flag because it is updated as required during the context switch and is also managed in an atomic fashion.

9.3.3   Using the perfmon interface: The pfmon example

In this section, we illustrate how perfmon can be used to collect performance information of unmodified binaries. We use pfmon for this purpose [14]. This is a versatile tool that can run on any Linux/ia64 system for which perfmon support has been enabled. It can monitor individual binaries with per-task sessions or the entire machine with a systemwide session. Both event counts and samples can be collected.

Because the PMU is CPU model specific, pfmon uses the modular architecture shown in Figure 9.28. The tool itself is built on a library of utility routines called *libpfm*. This library is also modular, and its interface consists of a set of common and CPU-model-specific routines. For instance, Itanium-specific features such as address range checking are handled by the Itanium module. Every module also contains a table of events supported by that CPU model. On top of this library, `pfmon` builds its own set of modules specialized for a particular CPU. For instance, all the EAR and BTB support is in the Itanium-specific module. At both levels, each CPU-specific module is independent of the others. The library is able to autodetect the host CPU and activates the appropriate module. When the host CPU is unknown, `pfmon` can still be used and will default to generic support, which implements the minimal architected support for the two events "CPU cycles" and "number of instructions executed." In this section we show examples of `pfmon` running on Itanium.

The tool can be configured with command-line options. For instance, the following command counts the number of CPU cycles consumed and instructions executed (retired) by the `date` command, both at the user and the kernel level:

```
$ pfmon -u -k -e cpu_cycles,ia64_inst_retired /usr/bin/date
293523 CPU_CYCLES
231009 IA64_INST_RETIRED
```

The `-u` and `-k` options activate monitoring at the user and kernel levels, respectively. The `-e` option specifies the list of events to be monitored. This example shows that no modifications are required on the `date` command. Pfmon creates a perfmon context, then it forks a child task that inherits the context. After the *fork()* but before the *execve()*, the PMU is enabled, programmed, and protected to avoid random attempts to modify the context by the `date` command. Finally, the `date` command is launched. Next, `pfmon` waits for the command to terminate, at which point it receives the SIGCHILD signal. Pfmon then uses PFM_READ_PMDS on the child task to extract the counter values before invoking *wait4()* to clean up the child task.

Cycle accounting with `pfmon`

In the introduction to this chapter we mentioned that cycle accounting is a useful tool to determine how the execution time is spent. Later, in Section 9.2.3 we presented what Itanium provides to support this technique. On this CPU, cycles can be classified into eight categories, and nine events are required to get a complete breakdown. Given that Itanium only has four counters and that we need to collect nine measurements at a minimum, we need three runs to collect the information. We can easily use `pfmon` to collect the counts by invoking it three times. As an example, we use a simple empty loop (nop) program with a core loop as follows:

```
loop:       [MIB]      nop.m 0x0
                       nop.i 0x0
                       br.cloop.dptk.few loop
```

Itanium can execute this loop in a single cycle. If we suppose that the program is called `noploop` and that the number of iterations through the loop is 10^9, then one of the runs is invoked as follows:

```
$ pfmon -u -e cpu_cycles,memory_cycle,data_access_cycle noploop
1000423602 CPU_CYCLES
5154       MEMORY_CYCLE
5141       DATA_ACCESS_CYCLE
```

Once all three runs are completed it is possible to calculate the breakdown. Using only three runs to draw conclusions about a program is usually not recommended because there can be fluctuations between runs, but we use it to illustrate how pfmon could be used to construct the breakdown. For noploop, it might look as follows:

```
                               cycles        % of cycles
   ----------------------------------------------------------
   1. dependency cycles         1544            0.00%
   2. issue limit cycles        4402            0.00%
   3. data access cycles        5141            0.00%
   4. instruction access cycles 422267          0.04%
   5. RSE memory cycles         13              0.00%
   6. inherent execution cycles 1000001803      99.93%
   7. branch resteer cycles     20195           0.00%
   8. taken branch cycles       6890            0.00%
   ----------------------------------------------------------
   Total                        1000462255      99.97%
```

This output confirms that, indeed, virtually all cycles were actually spent in the loop (inherent execution) and that no major stalls were incurred. Furthermore, we can also use it to verify that the loop was executed in one cycle by dividing the number of cycles by the number of iterations: $1000462255/10^9 \approx 1$.

9.4 SUMMARY

In this chapter, we described the general performance monitoring framework of the IA-64 architecture and the additional features provided by Itanium. We explained how the PMU support for Linux/ia64, perfmon, is designed, and we discussed the most important aspects of its implementation. We concluded by showing examples of how it can be used with pfmon, a sample tool for monitoring unmodified programs.

Chapter 10

Booting

Booting a machine has always been an obscure and complex procedure. There are good reasons for this. The bootstrap procedure brings a machine to life and, by definition, involves almost every single component of the machine: the CPUs, the bus bridges and I/O chipsets, the I/O devices themselves, the physical memory, and, of course, the operating system. Within the operating system kernel, much of the same picture emerges: almost every single subsystem is affected by the bootstrap procedure. Understanding this procedure therefore requires familiarity with all of these components and subsystems. This is the reason the boot procedure is described here, near the end of this book: it allows us to draw from the material covered in the earlier chapters. As we will see, against this background the bootstrap procedure is not nearly as daunting as it may seem at first.

Figure 10.1 provides a high-level view of how the various components of a machine interact during the bootstrap procedure. At the lowest level is the hardware. From its point of view, the bootstrap procedure starts when the machine is powered up and a reset line is asserted. Once the machine comes out of the hardware reset, the bootstrap procedure moves into the first level of software, which is firmware. Firmware is stored in nonvolatile memory such as ROM and is therefore available immediately after a hardware reset. Once execution starts there, the firmware detects, configures, and tests the hardware that is present in the machine. On an MP machine, firmware also is responsible for electing a bootstrap processor (BP), which will take care of executing most of the bootstrap procedure. The remaining CPUs are called application processors (APs), and they typically remain inactive until the operating system wakes them up near the end of the bootstrap procedure. Once the

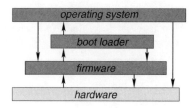

Figure 10.1. Boot components and control flow.

hardware is tested and the BP elected, the firmware searches for devices that are bootable. Typically, firmware can boot from hard disks, floppy disks, DVD-ROMs, or even from remote machines (by means of a network interface). From the list of bootable devices, the firmware picks one and uses it to load and start a bootloader. The bootloader represents the second level of software. It is responsible for locating, loading, and starting the kernel of the operating system. The bootloader is needed only until control is handed over to the kernel. Afterward, its memory can be freed up and used for other purposes. As soon as the operating system has control, it starts its own bootstrap procedure. This normally consists of initializing all its subsystems, such as the interrupt system, the virtual memory system, the device drivers, and so on. The kernel initialization comes to its end when the kernel creates the first user-level task. From a user perspective, many initialization steps still need to be performed at that point. For example, it might be necessary to start a windowing system. On Linux, this procedure is driven by the `/sbin/init` command. However, a detailed description of the user-level bootstrap procedure is beyond the scope of this book.

The remainder of this chapter is organized as follows: the first section explores the operation of the firmware in more detail. As usual in this book, we use IA-64 as an example. Although other platforms use sometimes drastically different firmware, the problems and principles described in this section tend to be the same on every platform. Another good reason for basing this discussion on the IA-64 firmware is that it has a clean design and well-defined interfaces. In the second section, we describe how the Linux/ia64 bootloader uses the firmware to load and start the Linux kernel. The third section then introduces and explains the bootstrap procedure of the Linux kernel. Not surprisingly, several steps in this procedure are platform specific. We describe those in terms of their IA-64 implementations.

10.1 IA-64 FIRMWARE OVERVIEW

Figure 10.2 presents a graphical overview of the IA-64 firmware and illustrates how it interacts with the underlying hardware and the higher-level software such as the bootloader and the operating system kernel. The figure shows that IA-64 firmware breaks down into four separate components: PAL, SAL, EFI, and ACPI. Each component serves a particular purpose:

- **PAL (Processor Abstraction Layer):** Provides a uniform way for obtaining CPU-model-specific information and for performing CPU-model-specific operations. For example, PAL can provide the number of physical address bits implemented by a CPU.

- **SAL (System Abstraction Layer):** Provides a uniform way for obtaining machine-specific information and performing machine-specific operations. For example, SAL provides the means to wake up application processors (APs).

- **EFI (Extensible Firmware Interface):** Provides an initial operating environment that can be used to boot an operating system.

- **ACPI (Advanced Control and Power Interface):** Provides a generic way of describing and controlling machine-specific hardware.

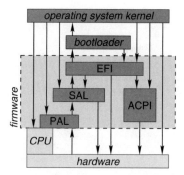

Figure 10.2. Overview of the IA-64 firmware components and their interactions.

The first two firmware components, PAL and SAL, are IA-64 specific. Indeed, PAL is specified by the architecture manual itself [26]. Figure 10.2 represents the tight coupling between the CPU and PAL by the fact that the latter sits right on top of the former. The need for an IA-64 boot manager originally motivated the design of EFI. However, EFI is not limited to IA-64 and is indeed available for other platforms, including IA-32. The same is true for ACPI: it is architecture neutral and is used on a number of platforms, including IA-64 and IA-32.

In Figure 10.2, upward arrows indicate the flow of control during the bootstrap procedure. If we follow these arrows, we see that the procedure starts with the hardware, then works its way up through PAL, SAL, and then EFI. At that point, a user can select an operating system to boot. Once the user has made a choice, the appropriate bootloader is invoked. The bootloader then takes care of loading and starting the operating system kernel. ACPI is not directly involved in the bootstrap procedure. However, it is initialized early on, and various components, including EFI and the operating system kernel, occasionally rely on the services it provides.

Downward arrows show how the different components depend on each other. Note how the kernel depends on every single firmware component. What this means is that the firmware is not limited to strict layering, where only neighboring layers can interact with each other. Instead, the kernel can access all firmware layers directly, without necessarily having to first go through the highest level of firmware. For example, Linux/ia64 includes a user-level interface that provides convenient access to the information provided by PAL.

10.1.1   Processor Abstraction Layer (PAL)

The *processor abstraction layer (PAL)* is the firmware layer responsible for abstracting differences between IA-64 *CPU models*. Though implemented as firmware, PAL is an integral part of the IA-64 architecture and is as rigorously specified as the instruction set architecture itself. PAL is specific to the particular CPU that it represents and, as such, has no knowledge of the machine surrounding it. During power-up, PAL performs low-level

Table 10.1. PAL procedure groups.

Index	Group
0	*reserved*
1 – 255	architected, **static** convention
256 – 511	architected, **stacked** convention
512 – 767	CPU model specific, **static** convention
768 – 1023	CPU model specific, **stacked** convention
1024 – n	*reserved*

testing and initialization of the CPU. Once powered up, PAL provides several procedures that can be used to extract CPU-model-specific information, such as the number, types, and sizes of the caches that are present. Other procedures can be used to perform CPU-model-specific operations, such as invalidating the CPU caches. Finally, PAL responds to asynchronous events triggered by the hardware. For example, if error detection logic in a cache determines that a data bit was corrupted, the hardware would report this problem to PAL, which may then either attempt to fix the problem or report it to higher-level software, such as SAL.

PAL procedures

The IA-64 architecture defines about 40 separate PAL procedures [26]. These procedures can be invoked through a single PAL entry point called PAL_PROC. The address of this entry point can be obtained from SAL (see Section 10.1.2). An index passed to the entry point selects which procedure is to be executed. PAL procedures are therefore invoked through a dispatch table that is similar to the system call table used by Linux. Besides identifying the procedure, the index also identifies the group the procedure belongs to. As shown in Table 10.1, there are four such groups. The four groups are divided according to whether a procedure is architected or CPU model specific and whether a procedure uses the **static** or **stacked** argument-passing convention. We describe the argument-passing conventions in more detail later on. Architected calls are specified in the IA-64 architecture manual and, as such, must be supported on any CPU model. On the other hand, the presence and semantics of particular CPU-model-specific procedures may be different from one CPU model to another. Operating systems generally rely on architected calls only. Consequently, the remainder of this section focuses on the architected calls.

PAL calling conventions

PAL must be able to operate in an extremely limited environment. For example, right after a machine is powered up, no tested memory may be available, so almost all PAL procedures avoid passing arguments through memory and use registers instead. The flip side of this coin is that an operating system must be careful to establish the environment expected by PAL before calling a PAL procedure. Specifically, PAL procedures must always be invoked at privilege-level zero (most privileged). For Linux, this means that only the kernel

Table 10.2. Processor status register (psr) settings required for PAL procedures.

psr *bit*	*Value*	*Description*
be	0	little-endian byte order
i	0	interrupts disabled
dfl	0	disable floating-point low partition
db	0	disable debug breakpoint fault
lp	0	disable lower privilege transfer trap
tb	0	disable taken branch trap
cpl	0	privilege-level 0
is	0	IA-64 instruction set
id	0	disable instruction breakpoint fault
da	0	disable data access and dirty-bit fault
dd	0	disable data breakpoint fault
ss	0	disable single step trap
ia	0	disable ignoring of instruction access-bit fault
bn	1	register bank 1

can invoke PAL procedures. In addition, most procedures must be invoked while the CPU is executing in physical address space. However, some procedures can also be invoked in virtual address space, which is more convenient for the Linux kernel. But even those procedures cannot tolerate ITLB misses. To guarantee this, the entire PAL code must be pinned into the TLB with an instruction translation register (itr). PAL also places restrictions on the settings of many of the bits in the processor status register (psr). These requirements are summarized in Table 10.2. As shown there, for example, psr.be must be cleared on entry to PAL, meaning that memory accesses use little-endian byte order. Similarly, interrupts must be disabled, as indicated by the requirement that psr.i must be 0.

PAL procedures always expect four arguments, which are passed in registers. If a procedure takes fewer than four inputs, the remaining argument registers must be cleared to 0. Which registers are used for this purpose depends on the convention. The **stacked** convention uses stacked registers r32–r35 and follows the rules specified by the IA-64 software conventions [28]. The **static** convention uses static general registers r28–r31. This convention is used by procedures that may be called when the register stack engine (RSE) is not operational (e.g., because no memory is available for the register backing store). Independently of the argument-passing convention, the first argument (r28 or r32) always identifies the index of the procedure to call. Results are always returned in registers r8–r11, just as for ordinary function calls.

Example: The PAL_FREQ_RATIOS procedure

To get a better idea of how PAL procedures work, let us take a look at one specific example. The PAL_FREQ_RATIOS procedure can be used to obtain information about how various clocks relate to each other. As we see later in this chapter, this will prove helpful in setting up the periodic timer interrupt needed by the Linux kernel.

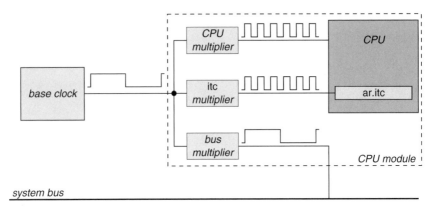

Figure 10.3. Frequency ratios returned by PAL_FREQ_RATIO.

The PAL_FREQ_RATIOS procedure assumes that on any given machine, there is a base clock that can be generated either by the CPU or by the machine itself (e.g., by the motherboard). Other clocks in the machine are then assumed to be derived from the base clock. This happens by means of clock multipliers, which may multiply the base clock frequency to a higher frequency or divide it down to a lower frequency. Figure 10.3 illustrates the case where the machine generates the base clock. This clock is then used to derive the bus clock, the CPU clock, and the clock that drives the interval time counter register ar.itc. Accordingly, there are three separate multipliers. In the figure, we assumed that the CPU and itc clock frequencies are obtained by multiplying the base clock by a factor of 11/2. For example, if the base clock was 133.3 MHz, the calculation would yield a clock frequency of 733 MHz. Note that the CPU and the itc have their own multipliers, so there is no guarantee that the itc will always run at core clock frequency of the CPU. For the bus clock, we assumed that a multiplier of 1 is used, so the bus clock frequency is the same as the frequency of the base clock.

Now, PAL_FREQ_RATIOS can be used to obtain the frequency ratios of the three multipliers shown in Figure 10.3. The interface for this procedure is described in Table 10.3. As shown there, this procedure has index 14 and is therefore an architected call using the **static** convention. Furthermore, the procedure can be called while the CPU is executing either in physical or virtual address space. Apart from the procedure index passed in register r28, there are no inputs to the procedure, so r29–r31 must be cleared to 0. On return, r8 contains a status indicator. Zero indicates successful completion, negative values indicate failure, and the exact value returned specifies the reason for the failure. Result registers r9–r11 each return the frequency ratio of one of the multipliers. The ratios are specified as rational numbers with the numerator in the top 32 bits and the denominator in the low 32 bits of the register. In our example, r9 (CPU ratio) and r11 (itc ratio) would both return a value of 0xb00000002, and r10 (bus ratio) would return a value of 0x100000001. These correspond to ratios of 11/2 and 1/1, respectively.

Table 10.3. Interface of PAL_FREQ_RATIOS procedure.

Name: PAL_FREQ_RATIOS	Index: 14
Convention: static	Space: physical or virtual
Arguments:	
r28	PAL_FREQ_RATIOS (14)
r29	0
r30	0
r31	0
Returns:	
r8	Return status (success or error indication).
r9	CPU clock frequency ratio.
r10	Bus frequency ratio.
r11	Interval time counter (itc) ratio.

Kernel interface to PAL

The Linux/ia64 kernel needs to call PAL procedures on several occasions, for example, to obtain CPU-model-specific information such as the number of physical address bits implemented. To make this convenient, the kernel implements a *PAL interface* (file include/asm-ia64/pal.h). This interface provides access to all architected PAL procedures and is shown in Figure 10.4. From the caller's point of view, these routines operate like normal function calls. For example, the frequency ratios returned by PAL_FREQ_RATIOS could be obtained with a call of the form:

```
unsigned long cpu, bus, itc;
long status = ia64_pal_freq_ratios(&cpu, &bus, &itc);
```

Each routine is implemented as an invocation of a small stub that takes care of establishing the environment needed by PAL. For procedures using the **static** convention, the stub also takes care of copying the incoming arguments from the stacked registers to the corresponding static registers. Since there are two argument-passing conventions and some procedures must be called in physical address space while others may be called in virtual address space, four stubs are needed: *ia64_pal_call_static()* and *ia64_pal_call_stacked()* handle the **static** and **stacked** conventions for procedures that may be called in virtual address space; *ia64_pal_call_phys_static()* and *ia64_pal_call_phys_stacked()* handle the two conventions for procedures that must be called in physical address space.

Recall that PAL code must not trigger any ITLB misses. When the kernel initializes the firmware interfaces, it uses an instruction translation register (itr) to ensure this. PAL code is position independent, so it can be mapped anywhere in virtual address space. For the Linux kernel, it is easiest to map PAL code through the identity mapping provided by region 7. The mapping is further simplified by the fact that the IA-64 architecture guarantees that at most one translation register is needed to map the entire PAL code. This is ensured by aligning PAL code on a page-size boundary that is large enough to cover the entire PAL code. For instance, if the PAL code was 31 Kbytes in size, it would have to be aligned on at

long **ia64_pal_bus_get_features**(*avlp, statp, ctrlp*);	/* get configurable bus features */
long **ia64_pal_bus_set_features**(*select*);	/* set configurable bus features */
long **ia64_pal_cache_config_info**(*lvl, type, confp*);	/* get detailed cache info */
long **ia64_pal_cache_flush**(*type, inv, progp, vecp*);	/* flush caches */
long **ia64_pal_cache_init**(*lvl, type, restr*);	/* initialize CPU caches */
long **ia64_pal_cache_line_init**(*paddr, val*);	/* initialize cache line */
long **ia64_pal_cache_prot_info**(*lvl, type, protp*);	/* get cache protection info */
long **ia64_pal_cache_read**(*line, paddr*);	/* read a cache line */
long **ia64_pal_cache_summary**(*lvlp, uniqp*);	/* get cache hierarchy */
long **ia64_pal_cache_write**(*line, paddr, val*);	/* write a cache line */
long **ia64_pal_copy_info**(*t, ncpu, nio, szp, alignp*);	/* get info for PAL copy */
long **ia64_pal_copy_pal**(*t, asz, cpu, off*	/* copy PAL from ROM to memory */
long **ia64_pal_debug_info**(*instrp, datap*);	/* get debug regs info */
long **ia64_pal_fixed_addr**(*addrp*);	/* get address of CPU */
long **ia64_pal_freq_ratios**(*cpup, busp, itcp*);	/* get freq multipliers ratios */
long **ia64_pal_get_ptce**(*ptcep*);	/* set TC purge info */
long **ia64_pal_halt_info**(*infop*);	/* get power management info */
long **ia64_pal_halt_light**();	/* enter the LIGHT HALT state */
long **ia64_pal_halt**(*state*);	/* enter the HALT power state */
long **ia64_pal_mc_clear_log**(*vecp*);	/* clear CPU error log */
long **ia64_pal_mc_drain**();	/* complete all transactions */
long **ia64_pal_mc_dynamic_state**(*offs, szp, pdsp*);	/* return MC dynamic state */
long **ia64_pal_mc_error_info**(*idx, type, szp, infop*);	/* return MC info */
long **ia64_pal_mc_expected**(*expect, prevp*);	/* inform PAL MC is expected */
long **ia64_pal_mc_register_mem**(*paddr*);	/* register save state area */
long **ia64_pal_mc_resume**(*cmci, save*);	/* restore minimal state */
long **ia64_pal_mem_attrib**(*attribp*);	/* get supported mem attr. */
long **ia64_pal_mem_for_test**(*neededp, alignp*);	/* get mem req. for CPU test */
long **ia64_pal_perf_mon_info**(*bufp, infop*);	/* get PMU config */
long **ia64_pal_platform_addr**(*type, padr*);	/* set phys addr for I/O space */
long **ia64_pal_pmi_entrypoint**(*addr*);	/* set SAL PMI entrypoint */
long **ia64_pal_prefetch_visibility**()	/* remove page cacheability */
long **ia64_pal_proc_get_features**(*avlp, statp, ctrp*);	/* get CPU features */
long **ia64_pal_proc_set_features**(*select*);	/* set CPU features */
long **ia64_pal_register_info**(*req, inf1p, inf2p*);	/* get info on appl. & control registers */
long **ia64_pal_rse_info**(*stackedp, hintsp*);	/* get RSE info */
long **ia64_pal_test_proc**(*addr, sz, attr, statep*);	/* perform 2nd phase self-test */
long **ia64_pal_tr_read**(*n, type, bufp, vp*);	/* read translation register */
long **ia64_pal_version**(*minp, curp*);	/* get PAL version */
long **ia64_pal_vm_info**(*lvl, type, infop, tcp*);	/* get VM info */
long **ia64_pal_vm_page_size**(*trp, vwp*);	/* get page size info */
long **ia64_pal_vm_summary**(*inf1p, inf2p*);	/* get VM info */

Figure 10.4. PAL interface provided by Linux/ia64.

least a 64-Kbyte boundary because that is the smallest page size that is both big enough and supported by IA-64. The address range occupied by the PAL code can be obtained from the EFI memory map (see Section 10.1.4).

User-level interface to PAL

For convenience, the Linux/ia64 kernel also provides an optional user-level interface to access the information provided by PAL. It is accessible through a virtual directory tree that is normally mounted at /proc/pal. In this tree, there is one subdirectory per CPU (e.g., cpu0 for the first CPU), which contains several separate files. For example, the file vm_info provides information related to the virtual memory support implemented by the CPU. There is also a file called frequency_info, which contains information about the clock frequency. At the user level, this information can be inspected with a command of the form:

```
$ cat /proc/pal/cpu0/frequency_info
Output clock          : not implemented
Processor/Clock ratio : 11/2
Bus/Clock ratio       : 1/1
ITC/Clock ratio       : 11/2
```

The first line shows the output clock frequency, which is obtained from the PAL procedure called PAL_FREQ_BASE. This procedure returns the base clock frequency of the machine. However, since we assumed in our example that the machine, not the CPU, is generating this clock, it is reported as "not implemented." The remaining lines show the values returned by PAL_FREQ_RATIOS: a clock multiplier value of 1 for the bus clock and a value of 11/2 for the CPU and the itc clocks.

10.1.2 System Abstraction Layer (SAL)

The *system abstraction layer (SAL)* is the firmware layer responsible for abstracting differences between IA-64 *machines* [31]. While not part of the actual CPU architecture, it is an integral part of the IA-64 platform architecture called *DIG64* [13].

SAL provides machine-related information through two mechanisms: a table called the *SAL system table* and a set of procedures called the *SAL procedures*. Beyond providing basic information, the procedures can also be used to control certain aspects of the machine. For example, SAL provides a procedure to invalidate *all* caches in a machine, including CPU-external caches, which cannot be invalidated with PAL. SAL defines an elaborate *machine check architecture (MCA)* that is designed to make machines more resilient against partial or temporary hardware failures. This architecture is beyond the scope of this book and we do not discuss it in more detail.

On a few occasions, SAL must be able to perform an *upcall* into the operating system. For instance, after an application processor (AP) is woken up, SAL uses an upcall to hand over control of the CPU to the operating system. To support this, SAL defines a handful of *SAL OS entrypoints*. The operating system can register callback functions for these entrypoints. Once registered, SAL will invoke them whenever the corresponding event occurs.

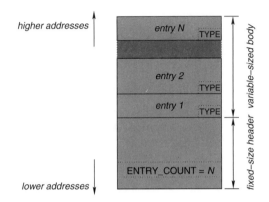

Figure 10.5. The SAL system table.

Table 10.4. SAL system table descriptor types.

TYPE	Size	Description
0	48 bytes	entrypoint descriptor
1	32 bytes	memory descriptor (obsolete)
2	16 bytes	platform features descriptor
3	32 bytes	translation register descriptor
4	16 bytes	purge translation cache coherence descriptor
5	16 bytes	AP wakeup descriptor

SAL system table

The SAL system table occupies a contiguous range of memory. Its starting address can be obtained from EFI (see Section 10.1.4). The table is divided into two sections: a fixed-size header and a variable-sized body. The format of this table is illustrated in Figure 10.5. The header contains miscellaneous bits such as a SAL version number, a checksum, and the total size of the table (in bytes). Most importantly, the member ENTRY_COUNT specifies the number of entries that are contained in the variable-sized portion of the table.

Each entry in the system table contains a *SAL descriptor* and starts with a 1-byte TYPE member. The TYPE of a descriptor determines both its format and its size. Table 10.4 lists each supported type as well as the size and the purpose of the corresponding descriptor. For example, a TYPE of 0 would indicate an entrypoint descriptor, which has a size of 48 bytes. Note that the memory descriptor is obsolete; it has been replaced by the more versatile EFI memory map (see Section 10.1.4).

The entrypoint, platform features, and AP wakeup descriptors are the most interesting descriptors. Let us start with the *entrypoint descriptor*. Its format is shown in Table 10.5. The descriptor contains the physical addresses of the entry point to the PAL and SAL

Table 10.5. SAL entrypoint descriptor.

Size	Description
1 byte	TYPE = 0
7 bytes	*reserved*
8 bytes	Physical address of PAL entry point (PAL_PROC).
8 bytes	Physical address of SAL entry point (SAL_PROC).
8 bytes	Physical address of global pointer (GP) for SAL.
16 bytes	*reserved*

Table 10.6. SAL platform features descriptor.

Size	Description
1 byte	TYPE = 2
1 byte	Platform feature list:
	bit 0: Set if bus lock is fully supported.
	bit 1: Set if re-steering of I/O SAPIC interrupts is supported.
	bit 2: Set if re-steering IPIs is supported.
	bit 3: Set if clocks for ar.itc may drift.
14 bytes	*reserved*

procedures (PAL_PROC and SAL_PROC, respectively). A third value specifies the global pointer value (GP) that needs to be loaded into register gp before the SAL entry point is called. No such value is needed for the PAL entry point because PAL does not use a short data segment (see Chapter 2, *IA-64 Architecture*).

The *platform features descriptor* contains several bits indicating the presence or absence of certain machine features. Its format is shown in Table 10.6. In the second byte, bits 1 and 3 are of interest to the Linux kernel: if bit 1 is turned on, the kernel can take advantage of the interrupt re-steering mechanism described in Chapter 7, *Device I/O*. As discussed there, this mechanism is useful for automatically distributing the interrupt load across multiple CPUs. If bit 3 is turned on, the interval time counters (ar.itc) of the CPUs in an MP machine are driven by separate clocks. In other words, the counters do not operate in lockstep and may drift away from each other, even if nominally they operate at the same frequency. This implies that the kernel cannot readily use the interval time counters to calculate high-resolution timestamps (see Chapter 8, *Symmetric Multiprocessing*).

After an MP machine is powered up, only the bootstrap processor (BP) is active. To enable the remaining CPUs, we need a mechanism to wake up the application processors (APs). SAL provides this mechanism: to wake up a specific AP, an operating system must send a special interprocessor interrupt (IPI) to that CPU. The IA-64 interrupt vector number that must be used for this purpose is specified in the *AP wakeup descriptor*. The format of this descriptor is shown in Table 10.7. As shown in the table, the last value in this descriptor specifies the IA-64 interrupt vector that will wake up an AP.

Table 10.7. SAL AP wakeup descriptor.

Size	Description
1 byte	TYPE = 5
1 byte	Wakeup mechanism
6 bytes	*reserved*
8 bytes	IA-64 interrupt vector (in range `0x10–0xff`)

Table 10.8. Processor status registers (psr) settings required for SAL procedures.

psr *bit*	Value	Description
be	0	little-endian byte order
cpl	0	privilege-level 0
is	0	IA-64 instruction set
da	0	disable data access and dirty-bit fault
dd	0	disable data breakpoint fault
ss	0	disable single step trap
ia	0	disable ignoring of instruction access-bit fault
bn	1	register bank 1

SAL procedures

SAL provides a set of procedures that are invoked through a single entry point. In the case of SAL, this entry point is called SAL_PROC. As described earlier, its address is contained in the entry point descriptor of the SAL system table. SAL procedures are divided into two groups: the *SAL architected procedures* and the *SAL OEM procedures*. The former are defined by the SAL specification and must be supported by all machines. The latter are specific to an OEM (original equipment manufacturer) and their presence and semantics can vary from one machine to another. Furthermore, they have been deprecated and replaced with the more flexible *extensible SAL interface (ESI)* [21]. The SAL architected procedures are position independent and can be called in physical or virtual address space. In virtual space, they can tolerate both instruction and data TLB misses, so there is no need to pin translations into the TLB as is the case for PAL code.

SAL procedures pass arguments in stacked registers r33–r39. The first stacked register, r32, is used to pass the index of the SAL procedure to invoke. If a procedure expects fewer than seven inputs, the remaining registers must be cleared to 0. As usual, result values are returned in registers r8–r11. Before making a call, the global pointer register gp must be loaded with the GP value in the SAL entrypoint descriptor. If the call is performed in virtual address space, this value must first be mapped to a corresponding virtual address.

The processor status register (psr) must have specific values in certain bits. These restrictions are shown in Table 10.8. For example, the table shows that SAL procedures must be called while the CPU is executing the IA-64 instruction set (psr.is must be 0) and with little-endian byte order (psr.be must be 0). Note that SAL procedures theoretically could be

long **ia64_sal_cache_flush**(*cache_type*);	/* flush CPU & machine caches */
long **ia64_sal_cache_init**();	/* init CPU & machine caches */
long **ia64_sal_clear_state_info**(*info_type*);	/* clear machine state log info */
long **ia64_sal_freq_base**(*which, ticksp, drift*);	/* extract base clock frequency */
long **ia64_sal_get_state_info_size**(*type*);	/* get CPU state log info size */
long **ia64_sal_get_state_info**(*type, infop*);	/* get CPU state log info */
long **ia64_sal_mc_rendez**();	/* go into spinloop in SAL */
long **ia64_sal_mc_set_params**(*type, im, val, tm, rz*);	/* set MC/rendezvous params */
long **ia64_sal_pci_config_read**(*addr, size, valp*);	/* read from PCI config space */
long **ia64_sal_pci_config_write**(*addr, size, val*);	/* write to PCI config space */
long **ia64_sal_register_physical_addr**(*pent, paddr*);	/* register physical addr */
long **ia64_sal_set_vectors**(*vec, ip, gp, sz, ip2, gp2, sz2*);	/* set SAL OS entrypoints */
long **ia64_sal_update_pal**(*parm, buf, sz, errp, szp*);	/* update PAL in NVRAM */

Figure 10.6. SAL interface provided by Linux/ia64.

called with interrupts enabled because psr.i is not required to be 0. However, SAL handles neither interrupt nor CPU concurrency (see Chapter 3, *Processes, Tasks, and Threads*). To protect against the former, it is necessary to mask interrupts before calling SAL. For the latter, MP machines need to serialize all calls, e.g., with a global spinlock.

Kernel interface to SAL

The Linux/ia64 kernel needs to call SAL architected procedures on several occasions. Since these procedures expect the input arguments in the stacked registers and since they can be called in virtual address space, there is no need for a stub routine. Instead, the procedures can be called directly through a function pointer. However, since SAL procedures always expect eight arguments, it would be inconvenient to do that. Instead, the kernel implements a *SAL interface* (file include/asm-ia64/sal.h). This interface provides access to all architected SAL procedures, as illustrated in Figure 10.6. In this interface, each routine maps to the SAL procedure with the corresponding name. For example, routine *ia64_sal_cache_flush()* maps to SAL procedure SAL_CACHE_FLUSH. As described previously, all calls to SAL need to be serialized. To ensure this, the routines automatically mask interrupt delivery and, on MP machines, acquire a spinlock before calling into SAL.

Example SAL procedures

For this book, it is not necessary to be familiar with every SAL procedure. However, it is useful to present some of them. For example, in our earlier clock frequency example, we saw that PAL is not always able to provide the frequency of the base clock of a machine. SAL fills this hole with the *ia64_sal_freq_base()* routine. The platform base frequency can be obtained by a call to this routine with the *which* argument set to 0. The other arguments, *ticksp* and *driftp*, must both be pointers to 64-bit words. The former returns the clock frequency (in hertz), and the latter returns the maximum rate at which this clock drifts over time (in parts per million, relative to the returned frequency).

Two routines, *ia64_sal_pci_config_read( )* and *ia64_sal_pci_config_write( )*, help us manage PCI buses. They read and write PCI configuration space, respectively. This is handy because they provide consistent interfaces that are independent of the actual mechanism a machine uses to access this space. Both routines use the first two arguments, *addr* and *size*, to pass a PCI device address and the number of bytes to transfer. The PCI device address consists of an integer value that encodes the PCI bus, slot, and function number of the device whose configuration space should be accessed. For writing to configuration space, the third argument, *val*, specifies the value to write. For reading configuration space, the third argument, *valp*, specifies the address at which the value read should be returned.

Earlier, we said that SAL sometimes needs to perform an upcall by invoking a SAL OS entrypoint. Before SAL can do so, an operating system must register a handler for the respective entrypoint. This can be accomplished with the *ia64_sal_set_vectors( )* routine.

At first sight, this looks like a complicated routine because it takes seven arguments. However, the routine is actually quite easy to use: the first argument, *vec*, selects which entrypoint the handler is for. The next three arguments specify the handler itself: *ip* is the physical address at which the handler starts, *gp* is the physical address of the GP value that SAL needs to install before calling the handler, and *sz* is the size of the handler. If *sz* is non-zero, SAL uses it to ensure that, at the time of an upcall, the handler is still intact. SAL does this in two steps: at the time the handler is registered, it calculates and saves a checksum of the address range from *ip* to $ip + sz - 1$. The second step takes place when an upcall must be performed. At that point, SAL recalculates the checksum and compares it with the saved checksum. If they match, SAL assumes that the handler is intact and performs the upcall. Otherwise, SAL considers the handler corrupted and skips the upcall. The remaining arguments, *ip2*, *gp2*, and *sz2* can be used to specify a second handler, which is needed only for certain entrypoints.

When an AP is woken up, SAL invokes the OS_RENDEZ entrypoint. An operating system can register a handler for this entrypoint with *ia64_sal_set_vectors( )*, passing 2 in the *vec* argument. The entrypoint requires only a single handler, so the last three arguments remain unused (must be zero). Once a handler is registered, an operating system can wake up an AP by sending it an IPI with the interrupt vector number specified in the SAL AP wakeup descriptor. Eventually, this interrupt will arrive at the AP. Once that happens, SAL will use the AP to perform an upcall so that execution will start at the registered handler. From then on, the operating system is in control of the AP.

10.1.3   Advanced configuration and power interface (ACPI)

The *advanced configuration and power interface (ACPI)* is a firmware component that describes machine-specific hardware features in a generic fashion [1]. Not only does ACPI *describe* these features, but it also provides a portable means to *control* them. Its original aim was primarily to control power consumption, but because it is generic, it has much wider applicability. ACPI is a complex standard that comes with its own programming language and even its own filesystem-like namespace.

ACPI consists of a hardware and a software component. The hardware component defines a control register interface that all ACPI-compliant devices must implement. This

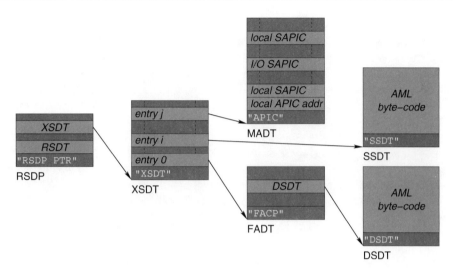

Figure 10.7. The tree of ACPI tables.

interface provides a generic way of controlling the power consumption of a device. For example, it can put a device into a sleep mode, turn it off completely, or turn it back on again. Devices that support this interface fall into the category of *ACPI fixed hardware*. Legacy devices that do not support this interface fall into the category of *ACPI generic hardware*.

ACPI tables

The software component of ACPI consists of a tree of tables that contain static configuration information and executable bytecode called AML. For now, let us focus on the static portions of these tables. An example of the tree of ACPI tables as it might exist on a typical IA-64 machine is illustrated in Figure 10.7. The strings in double quotes indicate that each ACPI table starts with a signature string that uniquely identifies the content of the table. The root of the tree is formed by the *root system description pointer (RSDP)* table whose physical address can be obtained from EFI (see Section 10.1.4). This table principally contains two pointers: one to the *root system description table (RSDT)* and the other to the *extended system description table (XSDT)*. The former is used for ACPI v1.0, and the latter is used for ACPI v2.0. IA-64 machines must use XSDT because ACPI v2.0 is the first version of ACPI that can support 64-bit platforms.

The XSDT is a variable-length table that primarily contains a list of pointers to other tables. ACPI v2.0 defines more than a dozen such tables, and OEMs can define their own machine-specific tables. For our purposes, it is sufficient to take a closer look at three of them: the FADT, MADT, and SSDT.

The *fixed ACPI description table (FADT)* contains information about the ACPI fixed hardware, such as the addresses at which their ACPI registers can be accessed. The FADT also contains a pointer to the DSDT, which we describe later.

The *multiple APIC description table (MADT)* is vital to an IA-64 operating system because it describes all local SAPICs and I/O SAPICs that are present in a machine at boot time. Since there is exactly one local SAPIC per CPU, this table implicitly also enumerates all the CPUs that are present in the machine. The MADT is generic in the sense that it can describe many different types of interrupt controllers, including IA-32 style APIC controllers. However, on IA-64, the table only contains entries for SAPIC style controllers.

The MADT consists of a fixed header and a variable portion with one entry per SAPIC. Among other things, the header contains the local APIC address, which, on IA-64, specifies the base address of the processor interrupt block (see Chapter 7, *Device I/O*). This block is used to generate IPIs and since there is only one such entry, it applies to all CPUs in the machine. In the variable portion, each MADT entry that describes an I/O SAPIC provides the physical address at which the controller is located and its *global interrupt base*, which is the global interrupt line number of the first interrupt pin (see Chapter 7, *Device I/O*). MADT entries describing local SAPICs primarily contain the local ID of the corresponding CPU and a flag that indicates whether the CPU is enabled.

The SSDT contains dynamic information about the hardware features of a machine. It is closely related to the DSDT; we describe both of them in the next section.

ACPI source language (ASL) and ACPI machine language (AML)

ACPI uses its own declarative language to describe hardware features and to provide methods to control the hardware. This language is called *ACPI source language (ASL)*. ASL is a complete programming language and comes with its own type system, control structures such as **while**-loops and **if**-statements, and a runtime system that provides I/O and dynamic memory allocation facilities.

The ASL type system is fairly extensive and includes basic types such as integers of different sizes, character strings, and bit-fields. Structured data can be defined with *packages*. A package consists of an integer count and a list of elements. The count specifies the length of the list. Each element in the list can be an ACPI object of arbitrary type and may even consist of a package itself. ACPI packages can be thought of as being similar to C arrays, except that each element in the array may have its own type.

ASL is object oriented in the sense that each code fragment has a unique name in a global, hierarchical namespace. The top level (root) of this namespace is identified by a single backslash character ("\") and is subdivided into the five subspaces described in Table 10.9. The absolute path of an object in the ACPI namespace can be obtained by concatenation the names of its ancestors, using a dot (".") as a separator. For example, if object _IDE0 is a child of object _PCI0 and this in turn is a child of _SB, the corresponding absolute path would be _SB._PCI0._IDE0. This path might represent the first IDE disk controller on the first PCI bus of the machine.

Once a machine is fully described in ASL, a compiler translates the description into *ACPI machine language (AML)*. This is a compact and platform-independent bytecode. AML is packaged into *definition blocks* that can be stored in ACPI tables. The first definition block is always stored in the *differentiated system description table (DSDT)*. As shown in Figure 10.7, this table can be located through the FADT. The figure also shows that the

Table 10.9. Top-level organization of the ACPI namespace.

Name	Contains objects for
_GPE	ACPI events
_PR	processors (deprecated in ACPI v2.0)
_SB	system bus (devices and secondary buses)
_SI	system indicators (LEDs, small LCD panels, etc.)
_TZ	thermal zones

XSDT can refer to one or more *secondary system description tables (SSDTs)*. These tables contain additional definition blocks that extend the DSDT. The motivation for this split is that normally the DSDT is a static table (e.g., residing in ROM) and the SSDTs are dynamic tables, which are created by firmware at boot time. AML code may dynamically load or unload other definition blocks. The only exception is that the DSDT cannot be unloaded.

When a definition block is loaded, the AML objects defined in it will be installed in the ACPI namespace. An operating system can then use an *AML interpreter* to execute (evaluate) the AML objects. ACPI classifies objects into one of three categories, based on the effect they have when they are evaluated. The categories are *device identification*, *device configuration*, and *device removal/insertion*. For example, an object with name _ADR is defined to be an identification object that, when evaluated, yields the address of the device its parent represents. With our IDE disk controller example, the object with path _SB._PCI0._IDE0._ADR would evaluate to the address of the controller. Configuration objects also can return information about a device, but in addition, they can modify the device configuration. An example of such an object is _PRT, which is defined to be an object that corresponds to a PCI interrupt routing table. We describe this table in more detail below. As a final example, the _DIS method belongs to the device removal/insertion category because it is defined to be an object that, when evaluated, disables (deactivates) a device.

Example: The PCI routing table (_PRT)

To get a better sense of how AML describes hardware, let us consider a specific example. For this purpose, we look at the _PRT object. Recall that in Chapter 7, *Device I/O*, we found that programming the I/O SAPIC requires knowing how the interrupt pins of each PCI slot are wired to the I/O SAPIC pins. In ACPI, this information is called the *PCI routing table (PRT)* and is provided by the _PRT object. This type of object is defined to evaluate to a package that contains a list of packages. Each of the subpackages describes the wiring of one PCI interrupt pin. The entire list of subpackages describes the wiring of all interrupt pins of the PCI slots on a particular bus. For example, Figure 10.8 shows the AML code that object _SB._PCI3._PRT might evaluate to. In this case, the object evaluated to a package with two subpackages. The first subpackage indicates that on device 0 the INTA pin is wired to global interrupt line 11. The second subpackage indicates that the INTB pin of the same device is wired to global interrupt line 10.

```
Name _PRT (\_SB._PCI3._PRT)
    Package
        0x02            --> number of elements (2 subpackages)
        Package
            0x04        --> number of elements (4 numbers)
            0x0000ffff  --> device 0, any function (0xffff)
            0x00        --> pin INTA
            0x00        --> not used
            0x0b        --> global interrupt line 11
        Package
            0x04        --> number of elements (4 numbers)
            0x0000ffff  --> device 0, any function (0xffff)
            0x01        --> pin INTB
            0x00        --> not used
            0x0a        --> global interrupt line 10
```

Figure 10.8. Example of values returned by PCI routing table object (_PRT).

Since there is one _PRT object for each PCI bus, obtaining the complete PCI interrupt routing table requires scanning the entire ACPI system bus namespace (_SB) and evaluating all _PRT objects found along the way.

Kernel interface to ACPI

For IA-64 machines, some critically important information is stored in AML code. For example, without the information from the PCI routing table, an IA-64 machine cannot program the I/O SAPICs and would therefore not be able to boot. For this reason, the Linux kernel comes with an ACPI subsystem that includes a full AML interpreter. A complete description of the ACPI subsystem is beyond the scope of this book. As far as the PCI routing table is concerned, it can be obtained by a single call to a routine called *acpi_cf_get_pci_vectors()*. This routine takes care of scanning the _SB namespace for _PRT objects, evaluating them, and collecting the results.

10.1.4   Extensible firmware interface (EFI)

IA-64 machines use the *extensible firmware interface (EFI)* to provide an initial operating environment that lets users configure, select, and boot an operating system. EFI represents the first point at which a user can interact with an IA-64 machine. For this purpose, EFI provides a *boot manager*, which is a simple, menu-oriented interface. The boot manager also can be used to manage *EFI environment variables*. They are similar to UNIX environment variables in that they consist of name/value pairs. However, they are different because they are not limited to ASCII strings. Instead, they can contain arbitrary binary data. Furthermore, EFI environment variables are nonvolatile, meaning that they will not be lost when a machine is rebooted or powered down. Among other things, EFI environment variables often are used to configure exactly how an operating system is booted (e.g., whether it is booted into single- or multiuser mode).

However, EFI is much more than a boot manager. It is a complete programming environment. This environment can be used to implement helper applications, such as a *bootloader*, which loads and starts an operating system. EFI even comes with an optional command-line shell, called `nshell`. Advanced users can use this shell to boot an operating system from a command line, or to run utilities such as hardware configuration or testing tools. Such helper applications are called *EFI applications* and are stored in files that are called *EFI binaries*. To store all these files, EFI requires a nonvolatile storage area called the *EFI system partition*. This partition uses the EFI filesystem format, which is a slightly modified version of the FAT (MS-DOS) filesystem.

Apart from applications, there are also *EFI drivers*. The primary difference is that drivers do not just run and then exit (or hand off control to an operating system). Instead, they are *loaded* for the purpose of extending the functionality of EFI in some fashion. For example, an EFI driver could be used to enable booting from a new hardware device or to enable booting from a new filesystem format.

Boot and runtime services

After a machine is powered up, EFI is in full control of all hardware resources. This remains true until an operating system is ready to take over. When that happens, EFI relinquishes control and, from then on, the operating system manages the hardware resources. The state where EFI is in full control is called the ***boot*** *mode*, and the state where the operating system is in full control is called the ***runtime*** *mode*. Most EFI-related work gets done in **boot** mode. To support this, EFI provides a set of *boot services* that can access the full spectrum of EFI's programming environment. For example, there are services (routines) to allocate and free memory, to load EFI drivers, and to gain access to support interfaces, such as an interface to open and read files on an EFI filesystem.

In **runtime** mode, EFI still provides some services to the operating system, but these *runtime services* are much more limited. Their primary purpose is to abstract differences in how minor parts of a machine are implemented. For example, one runtime service lets the operating system read a machine's wall-clock time. Others can be used to access and manage the EFI environment variables.

As we see later, EFI defines a sequence of steps that must be followed to ensure an orderly transition from **boot** to **runtime** mode. The routine that actually effects this switch is a boot service called *ExitBootServices()*. Once in **runtime** mode, there is no way of switching back to **boot** mode, short of rebooting the machine.

Programming environment

EFI defines a programming environment for EFI applications and drivers. The goal of this environment is to be both architecture neutral and operating system neutral. It consists of a collection of interfaces that are defined in the ANSI C language. Nominally, these interfaces assume the *P64* data model, where **int** and **long** are both 32 bits wide and only pointers are 64 bits wide. We say "nominally" here because it turns out that none of the EFI interfaces use these types directly. Instead, the interfaces are all defined with EFI-specific type names. For example, EFI type **UINT64** is an unsigned integer that is 64 bits wide. Similarly, EFI type **UINTN** is an unsigned integer of natural width, which is 32 bits on a 32-bit platform and 64 bits on a 64-bit platform. In effect, EFI defines its own data model. EFI represents all strings with 2-byte characters in UTF-16 encoding, as defined by Unicode [74]. Other than that, when EFI is running on an IA-64 machine, it uses the normal IA-64 software conventions with little-endian byte order [28].

In **boot** mode, EFI always executes in physical address space and manages physical memory at a granularity of 4-Kbyte page frames (the smallest page size supported by IA-64). In **runtime** mode, EFI can be switched into virtual address space. This is achieved with a runtime service called *SetVirtualAddressMap()*. Later, we will see an example of how this is used by Linux/ia64.

EFI applications and drivers written in ANSI C are compiled and linked into *EFI binaries*. These binaries normally have a file extension of .efi and are in the Microsoft *portable executable (PE32+)* format [46], which is an extension of the *common object file format (COFF)*. PE32+ binaries are quite different from the ELF binaries that Linux/ia64 normally uses. However, a software package called GNU-EFI hides these differences and enables the development of EFI binaries under Linux/ia64 [15]. With this package, EFI applications can be written much like ordinary C programs, except that the main program is *efi_main()* instead of *main()*. The prototype of *efi_main()* is shown below:

```
EFI_STATUS efi_main(EFI_HANDLE image, EFI_SYSTEM_TABLE *systab);
```

The first argument passed to this routine, *image*, provides access to various information about the application itself, including its filename and the command line that was used to invoke it. The second argument, *systab*, is a pointer to the EFI system table. As we will see, this table provides access to both boot and runtime services.

Globally unique identifier (GUID)

A central concept in EFI is the *globally unique identifier (GUID)*, as defined by the Wired for Management (WfM) specification [24]. EFI uses GUIDs to identify firmware tables, programming interfaces, disk partitions, and anything else that needs a unique identifier.

GUIDs are sometimes called *universal unique identifiers (UUIDs)* and can be thought of as 128-bit keys that consist of a timestamp and a location ID [34, 51]. Any machine can create a GUID at any time by following an algorithm defined in the WfM specification. The basic idea is to generate a GUID by using the time of creation as the timestamp and the Ethernet address of the machine as the location ID. If done properly, this scheme guarantees that the resulting GUID is unique in time and space even though it is generated locally, without help from a centralized registration authority.

Strings of hexadecimal numbers are used to represent GUIDs in human-readable form. WfM recommends the use of big-endian byte order for this purpose. Unfortunately, EFI uses neither big-endian nor little-endian byte order, but instead a mixture of the two. For example, EFI represents the GUID called FPSWA_PROTOCOL in the following form:

```
FPSWA_PROTOCOL = c41b6531-97b9-11d3-9a290090273fc14d
```

The first component (c41b6531) is a 32-bit number in little-endian byte order, the second and third components (97b9 and 11d3) are 16-bit numbers in little-endian byte order, and the fourth component is a 64-bit number in *big-endian* byte order.

EFI interfaces

The EFI abstraction that provides extensibility is the *EFI interface*. Each interface is defined by a C structure that primarily contains a set of function pointers. Associated with each interface is a GUID that can be used to obtain an implementation of the interface.

Let us look at an EFI driver called FPSWA to see how EFI interfaces are used in practice. First, some background on FPSWA. IA-64 does not mandate that the floating-point architecture be fully implemented in hardware. Instead, a CPU may generate a fault or a trap for certain floating-point operations and rely on software to provide the architected behavior. For example, Itanium does not fully support IEEE denormals and requires software assistance to handle them (denormals can be thought of as floating-point numbers that are so tiny that they are almost zero). It may seem that the necessary software would be ideally suited for implementation in PAL. However, size, complexity, and performance issues make this impractical. Instead, Itanium machines ship with an EFI driver called *floating-point software assist (FPSWA)* that provides the necessary emulation software in the form of an EFI interface. The C structure defining this interface is shown below:

```
struct fpswa_interface {
    unsigned int revision; /* version code */
    unsigned int reserved; /* reserved for future use */
    long (*fpswa)();       /* pointer to the FPSWA handler */
};
```

This is a simple interface: apart from a version code, it contains just a single function pointer. For space reasons, the arguments to this function have been omitted, but the idea is that whenever an Itanium CPU triggers a floating-point fault or trap, the routine identified by function pointer *fpswa* can be called to obtain the correct result.

The FPSWA driver is normally implemented in a file called fpswa.efi and stored in non-volatile memory (e.g., ROM) or on the EFI system partition. EFI boot services can be used to load the driver into memory. Once loaded, the GUID defined for FPSWA (FPSWA_PROTOCOL) can be used to obtain a pointer to the FPSWA interface (struct fpswa_interface). With this pointer, an operating system would have everything it needs to call the FPSWA handler. In other words, the combination of the FPSWA interface, its GUID, and the fpswa.efi file extends the functionality of EFI with a software floating-point emulator.

Apart from the interfaces provided by EFI drivers, the EFI programming environment offers many built-in interfaces. For example, there are interfaces for console I/O, disk I/O, network I/O, and for accessing files on an EFI filesystem. Interestingly, even the boot and runtime services are EFI interfaces. However, since the boot services are needed to find an interface by GUID, there must be an alternate mechanism to locate them. As we see next, the EFI system table serves this purpose.

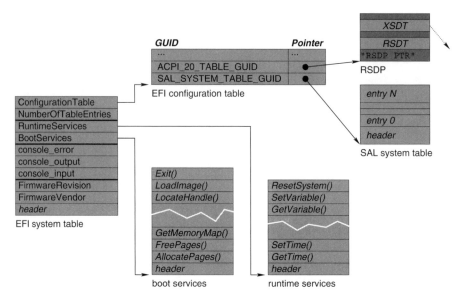

Figure 10.9. The EFI system table.

EFI system table

The EFI system table is key to gaining access to the EFI boot and runtime services as well as to all other firmware tables, including the SAL system table and the ACPI tables. As shown in Figure 10.9, the EFI system table consists of four sections. The first section is a header that identifies the table. Next is a section with three descriptors that are used for console I/O. They serve a similar purpose as the *stdin*, *stdout*, and *stderr* file descriptors defined by the standard C library. The third section contains pointers to the interfaces for the boot and runtime services. The last section consists of a count and a pointer to an array of configuration tables. The count specifies the length of this array. Each entry in the array contains a GUID and a pointer. The GUID uniquely identifies what kind of table the pointer refers to. The length and content of the configuration table array can vary from one machine to another. However, as indicated in Figure 10.9, IA-64 machines must have entries for the SAL system table and the ACPI Root System Description Table (RSDP).

EFI memory management

The EFI boot services provide several routines to allocate and free memory. The primary allocation routine is *AllocatePages()*. It allocates an integral number of 4-Kbyte pages. Normally, the routine allocates memory wherever it is available. However, it is also possible to specify arguments that will force it to allocate memory from a specific address range. In this case, the call fails if the memory in the specified address range is already in use. The *AllocatePages()* routine needs to be told what the allocated memory is used for. For

Table 10.10. EFI memory types.

Memory type	Description
EfiACPIMemoryNVS	reserved for firmware
EfiACPIReclaimMemory	ACPI tables
EfiBootServicesCode	boot service driver code
EfiBootServicesData	boot service driver data
EfiConventionalMemory	free memory
EfiFirmwareReserved	reserved for firmware
EfiLoaderCode	application code
EfiLoaderData	application data
EfiMemoryMappedIOPortSpace	legacy port I/O
EfiMemoryMappedIO	memory-mapped I/O
EfiPalCode	PAL code
EfiReservedMemoryType	not used
EfiRuntimeServicesCode	runtime service driver code
EfiRuntimeServicesData	runtime service driver data
EfiUnuseableMemory	faulty memory

this purpose, EFI uses the memory types listed in Table 10.10. Typically, memory type EfiBootServicesData is used to allocate memory that is needed only while EFI is operating in **boot** mode. In contrast, memory that needs to be retained across the switch to **runtime** mode should be allocated with a memory type of EfiLoaderData or EfiLoaderCode. The other types serve special purposes and should not be used for memory allocation.

A description of current memory usage can be obtained with the EFI boot service *GetMemoryMap()*. It takes a memory buffer as an input argument and uses it to return the current *EFI memory map*. Each entry in this map describes one contiguous range of physical memory by providing its type, starting address, size (in 4-Kbyte pages), and attributes. The attributes consist of a collection of flags that provide usage information in addition to the memory type. For example, if attribute EFI_MEMORY_UC is set, the memory can be accessed via uncached space. Attribute EFI_MEMORY_WB indicates that the memory can be accessed through normal, cached space (WB stands for *writeback*). Another important attribute is EFI_MEMORY_RUNTIME. It is used for switching EFI to virtual address space. We will describe this in more detail later on. Apart from the actual map, *GetMemoryMap()* also returns a cookie, which is an opaque integer that encodes the version of the returned memory map. Any time the memory map changes, e.g., because of a call to *AllocatePages()*, the version of the memory map changes and *GetMemoryMap()* will return a different cookie. This cookie is of no direct use to the caller. However, as we will see later, EFI uses it to ensure that **runtime** mode is entered only after the latest memory map has been obtained.

Figure 10.10 illustrates a typical memory map as it might exist while an EFI application is running. For space reasons, the figure uses UC, WB, and RT instead of EFI_MEMORY_UC, EFI_MEMORY_WB, and EFI_MEMORY_RUNTIME, respectively. The map shows that the bulk of the memory consists of 257921 pages of type ConventionalMemory. According to

Memory type	Physical address range	Pages	Attributes
BootServicesData	0x00000000000–0x00000000fff	1	UC|WB
ConventionalMemory	0x00000001000–0x00000088fff	136	UC|WB
BootServicesData	0x00000089000–0x0000009ffff	23	UC|WB
RuntimeServicesCode	0x000000c0000–0x000000fffff	64	UC|WB|RT
ConventionalMemory	0x00000100000–0x0003f080fff	257921	UC|WB
LoaderData	0x0003f081000–0x0003f086fff	6	UC|WB
LoaderCode	0x0003f087000–0x0003f0a8fff	33	UC|WB
LoaderData	0x0003f0a9000–0x0003f0cbfff	35	UC|WB
BootServicesData	0x0003f0cc000–0x0003f0ccfff	1	UC|WB
ConventionalMemory	0x0003f0cd000–0x0003f0d0fff	4	UC|WB
BootServicesData	0x0003f0d1000–0x0003f0d2fff	2	UC|WB
ConventionalMemory	0x0003f0d3000–0x0003f0d5fff	3	UC|WB
BootServicesData	0x0003f0d6000–0x0003f0e7fff	18	UC|WB
RuntimeServicesData	0x0003f0e8000–0x0003f0e9fff	2	UC|WB|RT
BootServicesData	0x0003f0ea000–0x0003f0ebfff	2	UC|WB
RuntimeServicesData	0x0003f0ec000–0x0003f156fff	107	UC|WB|RT
BootServicesData	0x0003f157000–0x0003f1b8fff	98	UC|WB
RuntimeServicesData	0x0003f1b9000–0x0003f1b9fff	1	UC|WB|RT
BootServicesData	0x0003f1ba000–0x0003f1cdfff	20	UC|WB
RuntimeServicesData	0x0003f1ce000–0x0003f206fff	57	UC|WB|RT
BootServicesData	0x0003f207000–0x0003f24efff	72	UC|WB
RuntimeServicesData	0x0003f24f000–0x0003f24ffff	1	UC|WB|RT
RuntimeServicesCode	0x0003f250000–0x0003f423fff	468	UC|WB|RT
BootServicesData	0x0003f424000–0x0003f425fff	2	UC|WB
ACPIReclaimMemory	0x0003f426000–0x0003f42dfff	8	UC|WB
BootServicesData	0x0003f42e000–0x0003f42efff	1	UC|WB
RuntimeServicesCode	0x0003f42f000–0x0003ff3ffff	2833	UC|WB|RT
PalCode	0x0003ff40000–0x0003ff7afff	59	UC|WB|RT
BootServicesData	0x0003ff7b000–0x0003ff7cfff	2	UC|WB
RuntimeServicesData	0x0003ff7d000–0x0003ff7dfff	1	UC|WB|RT
BootServicesData	0x0003ff7e000–0x0003ff7ffff	2	UC|WB
RuntimeServicesData	0x0003ff80000–0x0003fffffff	128	UC|WB|RT
RuntimeServicesData	0x000ffc00000–0x000ffffffff	1024	UC|RT
MemoryIOPortSpace	0xffffc000000–0xfffffffffff	16384	UC|RT

Figure 10.10. Example of a typical EFI memory map.

Table 10.10, this is free memory. Most remaining entries are either of type BootServices-Data or RuntimeServicesData. The only difference between the two is that the latter will still be in use after EFI is switched to **runtime** mode. Near the end of the map, we see an entry of type PalCode. This entry marks the address range occupied by PAL code. As described in Section 10.1.1, this address range is needed to support PAL calls in virtual space. Also note that the last entry is of type MemoryIOPortSpace. This entry describes the address range of the legacy I/O space (see Chapter 7, *Device I/O*) used for accessing

```
/* time services: */
efi_status_t get_time(tm, tc);                  /* get time and date from wall clock */
efi_status_t set_time(tm);                      /* set time/date of wall clock */
efi_status_t get_wakeup_time(ena, pend, tm);    /* return wakeup alarm clock settings */
efi_status_t set_wakeup_time(ena, tm);          /* set wakeup alarm clock time */

/* environment variable services: */
efi_status_t get_variable(nm, vndr, attr, sz, val);   /* get environment variable */
efi_status_t get_next_variable(sz, nm, vndr);         /* get next environment variable */
efi_status_t set_variable(nm, vndr, attr, sz, val);   /* set environment variable */

/* miscellaneous services: */
efi_status_t get_next_high_mono_count(val);     /* return high bits of monotonic counter */
efi_status_t reset_system(type, status, sz, data);  /* reboot the machine */
```

Figure 10.11. EFI runtime services interface provided by Linux/ia64.

I/O devices. Since it does not represent real memory, we could more accurately say that *GetMemoryMap()* returns an *address* map, rather than a memory map. However, for consistency with the EFI specification, we continue to call it a memory map.

Switching EFI to runtime mode

As alluded to earlier, the boot service routine *ExitBootServices()* can be used to switch EFI into **runtime** mode. This is normally done by a bootloader shortly before control is handed over to an operating system. A successful return from this routine implies that the EFI boot services are no longer available and that EFI no longer controls the machine's hardware (particularly memory). The routine takes two arguments: the first one must be the image handle that was passed as the first argument to *efi_main()*, and the second must be a cookie returned by *GetMemoryMap()*. EFI checks this cookie to ensure that it corresponds to the latest version of its memory map. If it does not, the call to *ExitBootServices()* fails. In other words, EFI forces the caller to obtain the latest version of the memory map before allowing the switch into **runtime** mode. This is a simple precaution to protect against accidental use of a stale memory map. Once EFI is in **runtime** mode, memory map entries of type BootServicesCode and BootServicesData can be treated as free memory.

Kernel interface to EFI

The Linux/ia64 kernel provides access to the EFI runtime services through the *EFI interface* (file include/asm-ia64/efi.h). This interface is summarized in Figure 10.11. There are three primary types of services: time related, environment variable related, and miscellaneous. Among the time-related services are routines to get and set the wall-clock time. The Linux kernel uses *get_time()* to initialize the date and the time of day when it boots. Two other routines provide the capability to set and get the wakeup time. On machines that implement these features, they can be used to power up the machine automatically at a specified time. The environment-variable-related services make it possible to get and set the content of an EFI environment variable. Furthermore, the *get_next_variable()* routine provides the capability to read existing EFI environment variables one at a time. Among the miscellaneous services, *reset_system()* provides the capability to reboot a machine. The *get_next_high_mono_count()* routine provides the capability to get the next high 32 bits of a monotonic counter. This is a foundation for implementing a 64-bit counter that is guaranteed to return increasingly large values, despite the fact that the machine may be rebooted or powered down between subsequent calls.

The interface shown in Figure 10.11 is actually implemented with a set of function pointers that are contained in a global variable called *efi*. For instance, with this variable the *reset_system()* routine could be invoked as follows:

```
(*efi.reset_system) (args...);
```

The reason for this implementation approach is that the EFI runtime services must initially be called in physical address space. To this end, the kernel implements separate stubs for each of the runtime service routines. These stubs convert pointer arguments to their physical equivalents and switch to physical address space before calling the real EFI routine. Once an EFI routine returns, the stubs switch back to virtual address space. The function pointers in *efi* are initialized to point to these stubs. This makes it possible to call EFI runtime services as soon as the kernel is started.

Once the kernel has initialized its virtual memory system, it can tell EFI to switch to virtual address space. This will let the kernel call EFI runtime services directly, without having to go through the conversion stubs. In other words, with EFI in virtual address space, the kernel can replace the function pointers in *efi* with values that map directly to the EFI runtime service entry points. The bottom line is that EFI runtime services can be invoked through the function pointers in the *efi* variable at *any* time, without having to worry about which address space EFI is operating in. If it is still in physical space, the function pointers lead to stubs that perform the necessary conversions. On the other hand, if EFI is in virtual space, the function pointers will lead directly to the corresponding EFI routines.

So, how can the kernel switch EFI into virtual address space? The answer comes in the form of EFI runtime service *SetVirtualAddressMap()*. This routine is not exported by the kernel interface shown in Figure 10.11 because it needs to be called only once. To operate in virtual mode, EFI needs to have certain memory regions mapped into virtual space. These memory regions are marked in the EFI memory map with attribute EFI_MEMORY_RUNTIME (RT in Table 10.10). In other words, before the kernel can call *SetVirtualAddressMap()*, it needs to obtain the latest EFI memory map and update each map entry marked with EFI_MEMORY_RUNTIME by taking the physical starting address and translating it to the corresponding virtual address. The memory map is normally obtained by a bootloader just before it calls *ExitBootServices()* and the memory map is then passed to the kernel.

If we consider the map shown in Figure 10.10, the fourth entry has the RT attribute set and would have to be updated. Its physical address is 0xc0000, and since it can be mapped cacheable (WB is set), the equivalent virtual address would be 0xe0000000000c0000. The last entry with physical address 0xffffc000000 would also have to be updated. However, since it must be mapped uncached (only UC is set), the kernel must instead map

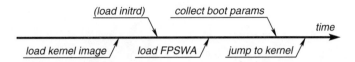

Figure 10.12. Time line of the bootloader.

it through region 6, the uncached identity-mapped region. In other words, the equivalent virtual address would be 0xc0000ffffc000000.

Once the memory map entries have been updated in this fashion, the kernel can call *SetVirtualAddressMap( )*, passing the updated map as an argument. EFI will then relocate its code and data according to this updated map. Should something go wrong, EFI remains in physical address space and the call returns with a failure status. When this happens, the kernel skips the update of the function pointers in *efi*. The effect of this would be that the EFI runtime services would continue to be called through the stubs. This would be slower than if the switch had succeeded, but at least the EFI runtime services would continue to be available.

10.2   THE BOOTLOADER

We now know enough about the IA-64 firmware to move up one level in the hierarchy of software layers shown in Figure 10.2 on page 411. Specifically, we can now take a look at the bootloader. On IA-64, this is an EFI application that loads a kernel image from boot media into memory and transfers control to it. In between, the bootloader has to collect other information that the kernel needs for proper operation. For example, if the user specified kernel command-line options, the bootloader needs to collect them and pass them on to the kernel. A complete bootloader offers many additional features, such as the ability to load compressed kernel images (for faster load times and to save disk space), the ability to boot not just from local disks, but also through the network, and so on. However, the description of such additional features is beyond the scope of this book. Instead, we focus on the minimal functionality that needs to be supported by all Linux/ia64 bootloaders. For this purpose, we use the timeline in Figure 10.12 as a guide.

The bootloader is invoked by EFI, either through the EFI boot manager or from the command-line interface provided by the EFI shell (nshell). In either case, once the bootloader is running, it starts by loading the kernel image into memory. In an optional second step, the bootloader loads an *initial RAM disk* into memory. Such a RAM disk typically contains kernel modules that may be needed by the kernel early on in the bootstrap procedure. In a third step, the bootloader ensures that the latest version of the FPSWA driver is loaded. In the second-last step, the bootloader collects boot parameters such as the command-line options and the EFI memory map. Once that is taken care of, the bootloader hands over control to the kernel by jumping to its entry point.

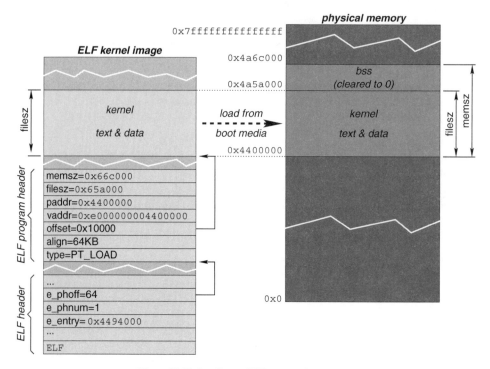

Figure 10.13. Loading an ELF segment in memory.

10.2.1   Loading the kernel image

The filename of the kernel image to be loaded is normally specified with a command-line option at the time the bootloader is invoked. The bootloader can open and read this file with the EFI boot services. For Linux/ia64, the file containing the kernel image is in the ELF format [60, 71]. The kernel image is a self-contained file in the sense that it has no dependencies on other ELF files, such as shared libraries.

As described in Chapter 4, *Virtual Memory*, the kernel normally executes in region 7. A typical starting point for the kernel image might be address 0xe000000004400000. However, since the bootloader is an EFI application, it runs in physical address space and must load the kernel image into physical memory. Indeed, as we see later, the bootloader even *invokes* the kernel while executing in the physical address space. This is not a problem because the kernel's entry code is designed to be position independent and takes care of switching over to virtual address space before invoking any kernel code that is not position independent.

EFI has no support for loading ELF binaries, so the bootloader must load them on its own. Fortunately, this is fairly straightforward: as illustrated in Figure 10.13, an ELF executable image starts with a fixed-size *ELF header*. Among other things, this header contains the file offset e_phoff at which the *ELF program headers* start. The number of such headers is given by e_phnum. Each ELF program header describes a contiguous segment of memory. Program headers start with a type field that indicates the kind of segment they describe. Only segments of type PT_LOAD need to be loaded. Other fields in the program header indicate where and how the segment should be loaded. Specifically, paddr specifies the physical address at which it should be loaded, memsz specifies its size, and offset specifies the file offset at which the content of the segment is stored. If the segment ends with a block of memory that contains all zeroes, that block is not actually stored in the file. The number of bytes that are actually stored in the image is given by the filesz field. With this information, the bootloader can load each segment of type PT_LOAD by allocating memsz bytes of memory at address paddr, copying filesz bytes from the file to memory, and then clearing the remaining (memsz − filesz) bytes in the segment.

The EFI routine *AllocatePages()* can be used to allocate memory at a specific physical address range. Such an allocation succeeds as long as the requested memory range is not already in use. If the call were to fail, the bootloader would be unable to load the kernel, because the ELF image is not relocatable (apart from the kernel's entry code). For this reason, the Linux/ia64 kernel needs to be linked for an address range that corresponds to physical memory that is likely to be available. EFI does not guarantee that *any* fixed address range is available for such purposes, but in practice, the first several megabytes above 64 Mbytes tend to be free. The call to *AllocatePages()* also needs to specify the EFI memory type. Since the allocated memory must persist across the later call to *ExitBootServices()*, types EfiLoaderCode and EfiLoaderData are the only possible choices (see Table 10.10). It does not matter which of the two is used. However, since the loaded image is data as far as the bootloader is concerned, it makes sense to use EfiLoaderData. The bootloader uses this memory type not just for the kernel image, but for all allocations that need to persist across the call to *ExitBootServices()*.

Figure 10.13 shows that ELF program headers also contain a field called vaddr which specifies the virtual address of the segment. The bootloader completely ignores this field and simply trusts that loading the segments at the specified physical addresses will do the right thing. However, since we know from Chapter 4, *Virtual Memory*, that region 7 is identity mapped, it is clear that the virtual load address 0xe000000004400000 shown in the figure does indeed correspond to the physical load address of 0x4400000.

A final piece of information that the bootloader can extract from the ELF image is the entry point at which the kernel needs to be started. This is specified in field e_entry of the ELF header. As shown in the figure, this is also a physical address. The bootloader will need this address later on to start the kernel.

10.2.2 Loading the initial RAM disk

The purpose of the initial RAM disk is to enable booting Linux in situations where it needs to load a kernel module before it can mount the root filesystem. Normally, kernel modules are loaded from the filesystem, but without the root filesystem, there is a cyclic dependency: the root filesystem cannot be mounted without the module, but the module cannot be loaded without the root filesystem. The initial RAM disk breaks this cycle by providing a temporary root filesystem in memory. The sole purpose of this temporary filesystem is to collect all the modules that might be needed to mount the real root filesystem. The initial RAM disk is popular with Linux distributors because it lets them ship small kernels that can boot on any machine, provided the necessary drivers are available as kernel modules in an initial RAM disk.

From the perspective of the bootloader, the initial RAM disk is simply a file whose content needs to be loaded somewhere in memory. The bootloader can use the EFI boot services to determine the size of the file, allocate the necessary memory with *AllocatePages()*, and read the file content into this memory. The only caveat is that *AllocatePages()* returns memory that is aligned to a 4-Kbyte boundary. If the Linux/ia64 kernel uses a larger page size, this does not guarantee alignment on a page-size boundary. Thus, when the kernel is done with the initial RAM disk and is ready to free up the memory for other purposes, it needs to be careful to avoid accidentally freeing too much memory.

10.2.3   Loading the FPSWA

The FPSWA driver may be stored with other firmware in nonvolatile memory, such as Flash ROM. If so, EFI will load it automatically. However, to enable updating FPSWA without forcing an update of the entire firmware, the bootloader must also check whether a file of name fpswa.efi exists in the EFI filesystem. If the file exists, the bootloader must load it with the boot services that exist for loading EFI drivers. Once the latest version of FPSWA is loaded, the bootloader can use the GUID of FPSWA to obtain a pointer to its interface.

10.2.4   Collecting the boot parameters

Before the bootloader can start the kernel, it needs to collect various pieces of information and place them in the *boot param structure* (struct ia64_boot_param in file include/asm-ia64/system.h). Later on, a pointer to this structure is passed to the kernel. The boot param structure therefore serves as the central hub that makes it possible to pass information from the bootloader to the kernel. As we will see, the boot param structure could comfortably fit in a few dozen bytes of memory. However, to enable backward-compatible extensions, the bootloader dedicates 2 Kbytes to the boot param structure. The unused portion of this memory is cleared to 0. This way, an old bootloader can be used to load a kernel that expects a bigger boot param structure, provided the kernel can gracefully handle the situation where the missing portion of the structure contains zeroes.

The bootloader needs to collect five primary pieces of information:

1. The pointer to the EFI system table.

2. The pointer to the FPSWA interface.

3. The address and size of the initial RAM disk (if one was loaded).

4. The pointer to the string containing the kernel boot command-line options.

5. The EFI memory map.

The first four are easy to handle. EFI passes a pointer to the EFI system table as the second argument to the *efi_main()* routine. The bootloader simply takes this argument and copies it to the boot param structure. Similarly, the bootloader already has the addresses of the FPSWA interface and the initial RAM disk, since it loaded them previously. If the FPSWA interface could not be loaded, the corresponding pointer in the boot param structure is set to 0. If no initial RAM disk was loaded, the corresponding address and the size members in the boot param structure are set to 0. The boot command-line options can be extracted from the command-line string that was used to invoke the bootloader. This string can be obtained from the first argument (*image*) that EFI passes to the *efi_main()* routine.

Collecting the EFI memory map is a bit trickier. Ideally, the bootloader would obtain the memory map with the following three steps. First, it would call the EFI routine *GetMemoryMap()* just to obtain the size of the memory map. Second, it would allocate the necessary memory from EFI, and, third, it would call *GetMemoryMap()* again to obtain the actual memory map. Unfortunately, this procedure may not work because the second step allocates memory. If the newly allocated memory needs a new entry in the memory map, this would increase the size of map. Of course, the updated memory map would then no longer fit into the allocated memory anymore and the third step would fail. The bootloader solves this problem simply by always allocating sightly more memory than strictly needed and by repeating the three steps until the last one completes successfully. Normally, just one or two iterations are sufficient.

Once the bootloader has filled in the boot param structure, it is almost ready to start the kernel. The last thing it needs to do is switch EFI from **boot** mode to **runtime** mode because neither the kernel nor the bootloader will need the boot services anymore. This also ensures that the kernel has full ownership of all hardware resources in the machine, including memory. The switch must be done by a call to *ExitBootServices()*. For this to work, the bootloader must pass the memory map cookie that was returned by the last call to *GetMemoryMap()*. Since the bootloader is careful not to allocate any memory once the memory map has been obtained, EFI will find the cookie to be valid and the switch to **runtime** mode will succeed.

10.2.5 Starting the kernel

In the last step, the bootloader starts the kernel by jumping to the entry point specified in the kernel image. The bootloader assumes that the entry point has the following interface:

```
void _start(struct ia64_boot_param *bp);
```

Argument *bp* is the physical address of the boot param structure. To avoid relying on the register stack engine (RSE), the kernel chooses to use the PAL **static** convention for this routine. That is, *bp* is passed in register r28 instead of the first stacked register (r32). The bootloader assumes that, once called, the entry point never returns. Note that the bootloader does not know the name of the kernel entry point. It simply jumps to whatever physical address is listed as the entry point in the ELF header. That said, the entry point in the Linux/ia64 kernel is indeed called *_start()*.

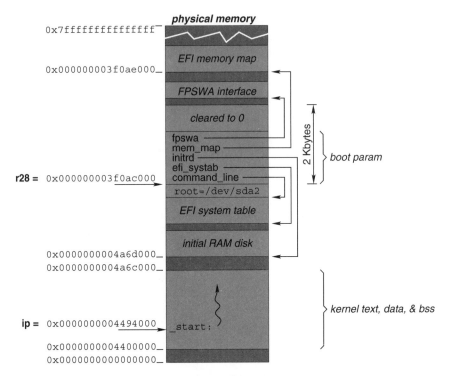

Figure 10.14. Example illustrating the kernel handoff state.

Summary of kernel handoff state

Figure 10.14 illustrates the memory layout as it might exist at the time the kernel's entry point is called. In this example, the kernel was loaded at address 0x4400000 (68 Mbytes) and the entry point in the kernel image points to the physical address of label _start (0x4494000). The figure also shows that register r28 points to the boot param structure, which happens to reside at address 0x3f0ac000.

Note that the kernel handoff state has been designed to keep the bootloader as independent of the kernel as possible. There are, however, a few dependencies. First, the bootloader operates entirely in physical space. This implies that the kernel's ELF image must specify valid physical load addresses, even though it is linked for execution in region 7. Similarly, the entry point in the ELF header of the image must be a physical address. Second, the bootloader and the kernel must agree on the layout of the boot param structure. Third, all memory allocated by the bootloader on behalf of the kernel must be allocated as EfiLoader-Data. Finally, the kernel must provide an entry point that expects to be called in the physical address space and with the physical address of the boot param structure in register r28. This minimal set of dependencies increases the likelihood that a single bootloader is capable of booting *any* Linux/ia64 kernel, no matter how old or how new it is.

10.3   KERNEL INITIALIZATION

Now that we understand how the IA-64 firmware works and how the EFI bootloader manages to load and start the Linux/ia64 kernel, it is time to explore the bootstrap procedure that Linux uses to bring itself into an operational state. This bootstrap procedure is driven by the platform-independent part of the kernel. In the first part of this section, we describe the general steps that take place during this procedure and how they rely on the *bootstrap interface* to take care of the platform-specific initializations. In the second half of the section, we describe how the bootstrap interface is realized on IA-64.

10.3.1   The bootstrap interface

After the bootloader hands off control to the Linux kernel, execution starts in a platform-specific startup routine. This routine should perform the minimum amount of initialization required before control can be turned over to the platform-independent *start-kernel routine* (*start_kernel()* in file init/main.c). As we will see shortly, the latter then takes care of booting the entire machine and initiating the user-level boot procedure. The prototype of the start-kernel routine is shown below:

```
void start_kernel(void);
```

The routine takes no arguments and returns no result. Indeed, the routine never even returns! Given this trivial interface, would it not be possible for the bootloader to directly call this routine? The answer is no because the routine must be invoked in a particular execution environment. Specifically, the routine expects to be executing in the context of the *initial task* (not to be confused with the user-level `init` command). This implies that the *current* pointer must be valid (see Chapter 3, *Processes, Tasks, and Threads*) and that the CPU must be using the stack memory provided by this task. Furthermore, interrupts must be disabled and all platform-specific requirements for executing kernel code must be met.

Fortunately, switching to the initial task is much easier than it may sound. The reason is that the necessary task structure is created at compile time in statically initialized memory. This task structure contains a process ID (task ID) of 0, which is a special ID that is invisible at the user level. A pointer to this task structure can be found in the first element of a global array called *init_tasks*. In other words, before calling the start-kernel routine, platform-specific code must load init_tasks[0] into the *current* pointer, switch the stack over to the memory area of this task, disable interrupts, and perform any other platform-specific initializations that might be necessary.

Once the start-kernel routine has control, it initializes each subsystem in the kernel, step by step. Not surprisingly, some of these steps are platform specific, and to abstract such differences, the Linux kernel employs the bootstrap interface shown in Figure 10.15. The interface consists of ten routines. All but *setup_arch()* take no arguments and return no result value. Even *setup_arch()* takes just a single argument. The fact that these routines have such trivial interfaces indicates that they cannot be understood in isolation. Instead, they must be viewed in the context in which they are used.

For this purpose, Figure 10.16 illustrates a slightly simplified version of the Linux bootstrap procedure as it might unfold on a hypothetical machine with two CPUs (CPU0 and

setup_arch(*cmdline_ptr*);	/* *perform basic platform-specific initialization* */
trap_init();	/* *initialize trap and fault handlers* */
init_IRQ();	/* *initialize interrupt system* */
time_init();	/* *initialize wall-clock time and periodic timer interrupt* */
mem_init();	/* *initialize physical page frame list* */
smp_boot_cpus();	/* *wake up application processors (APs)* */
smp_commence();	/* *release APs for general execution* */
pcibios_init();	/* *scan and register PCI buses and installed devices* */
free_initmem();	/* *free memory occupied by initialization code and data* */
cpu_idle();	/* *idle loop* */

Figure 10.15. The bootstrap interface.

CPU1). The darker-shaded boxes represent steps that are platform-independent, and the lighter-shaded boxes represent calls to the routines defined by the bootstrap interface.

Starting at the top, we see that *setup_arch()* is called right at the beginning. It takes one argument: *cmdline_ptr*. The start-kernel routine expects *setup_arch()* to initialize *cmdline_ptr* such that it points to the string representing the boot command-line options passed by the bootloader. If there are no such options, a pointer to an empty string should be returned. Apart from returning the boot command-line options, the routine should also perform as many platform-specific initializations as are possible at this early stage. In particular, the routine must locate available physical memory and register it with the kernel's *bootmem allocator* (file include/linux/bootmem.h). This is a simple and platform-independent memory allocator that can be used to allocate physically contiguous memory before the normal kernel allocators (such as the page allocator) are ready for use.

In the second step, the boot command-line options returned by *setup_arch()* are parsed into an internal format that is easy to handle. This internal format is basically an array of strings, much like the *argv* argument vector passed to C programs. Later steps in the bootstrap procedure can then use these arguments to adjust their behavior. For example, there is a boot command-line option to select the disk partition that contains the root filesystem, another option selects whether the machine should be booted into single-user mode, and so on. The important point here is that the command-line options are processed *after* *setup_arch()* has returned.

In the third and fourth steps, the platform-specific routines *trap_init()* and *init_IRQ()* are called. The former initializes the machine such that traps and faults can be handled. The latter is related in that it initializes the interrupt handling system of the machine, though without actually enabling interrupts.

In the fifth step, the kernel initializes enough of the scheduler that new tasks can be created. However, this does *not* mean that the initial task may block after this step. It is still too early for that. Blocking is possible only after the initial task has completed its initialization steps and turned itself into an idle task (more on this later).

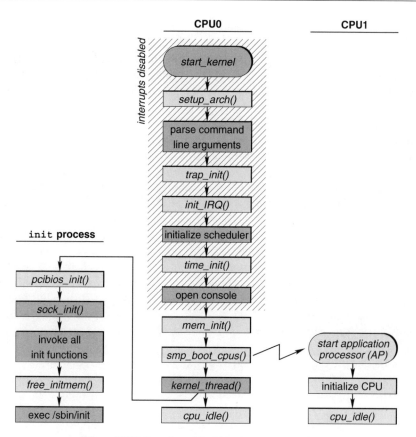

Figure 10.16. Overview of the Linux bootstrap procedure.

The sixth step is again platform specific and consists of a call to *time_init()*. This routine is responsible for initializing the wall-clock time and setting up the periodic timer interrupt needed by the Linux scheduler.

In step seven, the Linux kernel selects and opens its console device. Typically, a VGA graphics card or a serial-line interface is used for this purpose. Messages printed with *printk()* are output through the console device. Note that *printk()* can be called even before the console device is open. In such cases, the printed messages are stored in a ring buffer in memory. Once the console device is opened, all buffered messages are printed. However, the ring buffer has a fixed size so it is possible to overrun it and lose early boot messages. To avoid this, early bootstrap steps should be terse and produce output messages only when there is a good reason (such as to warn the user of potential problems).

In the eighth step, the platform-specific routine *mem_init()* is called. The primary purpose of this routine is to terminate the bootmem allocator and to count the number of physical page frames available in the machine. Immediately after this routine returns, the kernel will finish initializing the page allocator and for this reason the bootmem allocator is no longer needed.

On an MP machine, the ninth step calls the platform-specific *smp_boot_cpus()* routine to wake up all application processors (APs). Apart from waking them up, the routine also needs to count them and store the total number of CPUs in a global variable called *smp_num_cpus* (see Chapter 8, *Symmetric Multiprocessing*). Most platforms wake up APs with interprocessor interrupts (IPIs, see Chapter 7, *Device I/O*). In Figure 10.16, the wakeup is represented by the lightning bolt (jagged arrow) that brings life to CPU1. Before waking up an AP, the initial task clones itself by a call to *clone2()* with the CLONE_VM and the CLONE_PID flags set (see Chapter 3, *Processes, Tasks, and Threads*). The CLONE_PID flag ensures that the cloned task will also have a process ID of 0, so it, too, will be invisible at the user level. Once the task is cloned, a pointer to the new task structure is stored in the first unused element of the *init_tasks* array. The AP picks up the pointer from there and uses the cloned task to provide its own execution environment. Once running, the AP initializes its own CPU state and then waits until the BP invokes the *smp_commence()* routine. For space reasons, the call to *smp_commence()* has been omitted from the figure, but it happens right after all APs have been woken up. Once released, the AP turns its clone of the initial task into an idle task by calling the platform-specific *cpu_idle()* routine. This routine must lower the task scheduling priority to the lowest possible value and then enter an endless loop that performs little else beyond repeatedly calling *schedule()* to check whether another task is available for execution.

Back on the BP, the second-last step calls *kernel_thread()* (see Chapter 3, *Processes, Tasks, and Threads*) to create a separate task that will initialize the remainder of the machine. The newly created task is guaranteed to have a process ID of 1. For reasons that will become clear shortly, we call this new task the init process. As soon as *kernel_thread()* returns, the initial task turns itself into the idle task of the BP by calling *cpu_idle()*.

Eventually, one of the idle CPUs (CPU0 or CPU1, in our hypothetical machine) will start executing the init process. In its first step, this process initializes all system buses. For PCI machines, this requires calling *pci_init()*, a routine that takes care of initializing most of the PCI subsystem. It relies on the platform-specific *pcibios_init()* routine to scan the available PCI buses for installed devices and to register them with the kernel. Note that since the kernel now has one idle task per CPU, this step as well as all subsequent steps may block execution. In other words, all facilities of the Linux scheduler, including timeouts, are available at this point. The init process initializes the networking subsystem in the second step with a call to *sock_init()*. In the third step, it calls all *init functions*. These functions are routines that have been registered with the *initcall macro* (__initcall in file include/linux/init.h); they take no arguments. Furthermore, the order in which these functions are invoked is mostly undefined, so they need to be independent of each other. The init functions represent the bulk of the platform-independent initializations. It is here that all the device drivers, filesystems, network protocols, and so on, get initialized.

In the second-last step, the init process calls the platform-specific *free_initmem()* routine. The primary purpose of this routine is to free all the memory that is no longer needed now that the bootstrap procedure is almost complete. This covers both memory used for bootstrap data as well as for bootstrap functions. Bootstrap data is normally declared with the *initdata macro* (__initdata in file include/linux/init.h). Similarly, bootstrap functions are normally declared with the *init macro* (__init in file include/linux/init.h).

Last but not least, the `init` process invokes the `init` command with a call to *execve()*. Normally, this command is located in /sbin/init, but if it cannot be found, the kernel also attempts some alternate locations, such as /etc/init or /bin/init. As a last resort, it will even try to start a shell by invoking /bin/sh. If none of these files can be found, the kernel will panic and stop execution. On the other hand, the first file found in this fashion will cause the CPU to start executing at the user level. With the first user-level process created, the kernel bootstrap procedure is complete. Of course, before the machine is usable for an ordinary user, the `init` command will have to execute many other initialization steps, such as starting the X11 windowing system. However, the details of this user-level bootstrap procedure are beyond the scope of this book.

Discussion

The description of the bootstrap procedure showed that each individual step tends to be simple, if not downright trivial. However, the overall procedure is still quite complex because so many separate steps are involved and because the order in which they are executed has to be orchestrated carefully. When adding to or changing the bootstrap procedure, it is worthwhile to keep the following points in mind:

- Interrupts are disabled initially and must remain disabled until the kernel enables them. In Figure 10.16, this period is represented by the diagonally shaded area.

- The bootmem allocator is available after *setup_arch()* until *mem_init()* is called. The page allocator is available right after that.

- None of the steps executed in the initial task may block execution. In contrast, the steps executed in the `init` process may block.

These are of course not the only constraints on initialization order. Indeed, each platform usually brings its own set of constraints. The bottom line is that any change to the bootstrap procedure is risky and error prone. On the positive side, platform-specific code can assume that the bootstrap procedure will remain fairly stable, even as the rest of the Linux kernel evolves over time.

10.3.2   IA-64 implementation

In Section 10.2.5, we described that the IA-64 bootloader will start the kernel by calling *_start()*. At the time this routine is invoked, the CPU is still executing in physical address space and uses the memory stack and the register backing store area set up by EFI. Before doing anything else, the routine needs to switch the CPU to virtual address space. This is achieved with the following steps:

1. Write control register iva with the address of the Linux/ia64 *interruption vector table* (*ia64_ivt* in file arch/ia64/kernel/ivt.S).

2. Set up a translation register to pin the interruption vector table (IVT) into the TLB.

3. Set region registers rr6 and rr7 to the *kernel region ID* (IA64_REGION_ID_KERNEL in file include/asm-ia64/mmu_context.h).

4. Turn on virtual address translation by setting psr.it, psr.dt, and psr.rt. Since psr.it is not part of the system mask, this requires executing a dummy rfi instruction (see Chapter 2, *IA-64 Architecture*).

These steps ensure that the CPU can execute in the IVT without triggering TLB miss faults and that all TLB misses due to accesses to the identity-mapped regions can be handled by the alternate DTLB/ITLB miss handlers (see Chapter 4, *Virtual Memory*).

Once virtual addressing is enabled, the _start() routine can switch the CPU over to the initial task. The routine does this by reading the address of the task from the first element of the *init_tasks* array and switching the memory stack and the register backing store to the memory area of this task. On the memory stack, a dummy pt-regs structure needs to be allocated. As explained in Chapter 3, *Processes, Tasks, and Threads*, the presence of this dummy structure makes the kernel stack layout more uniform and facilitates certain optimizations. The routine then establishes the *current* pointer by writing the address of the initial task to register r13 (tp). With this setup in place, the routine can start the Linux kernel bootstrap procedure by calling *start_kernel()*.

As we explained earlier, the bootstrap procedure will then call the various routines in the bootstrap interface (Figure 10.15) to perform platform-specific initializations. For IA-64, most of these routines are straightforward and do not require further discussion. The exceptions are *setup_arch()*, *time_init()*, and *pcibios_init()*, which we discuss next. A description of how *smp_boot_cpus()* and *smp_commence()* are used to wake up the APs follows a little later.

General initializations

The *setup_arch()* routine represents the bulk of the IA-64–specific work and takes care of initializing the kernel unwinder (Chapter 6, *Stack Unwinding*), initializing the firmware interfaces, and collecting various information from PAL and the EFI, SAL, and ACPI tables. In particular, the routine locates all available physical memory by scanning the EFI memory map passed by the bootloader. During this scan, memory types EfiLoaderCode, EfiLoader-Data, EfiBootServicesCode, EfiBootServicesData, and EfiConventionalMemory are treated as memory available to the kernel. However, since the kernel image, the boot parameters, and the initial RAM disk all reside in memory marked as EfiLoaderData, the routine must be careful not to treat those areas as free memory. The *setup_arch()* routine also uses the EFI memory map to locate the legacy I/O space (see Chapter 7, *Device I/O*). This area is represented by the first entry of type EfiMemoryMappedIOPortSpace.

The *time_init()* routine uses EFI runtime routine *get_time()* to initialize the Linux wall-clock time variable *xtime* (see Chapter 8, *Symmetric Multiprocessing*). For the periodic timer interrupt, the DIG64 standard requires that the CPU internal interval timer counter be used for this purpose [13]. Conceptually, this is straightforward: once the vector number desired for the timer interrupt is written to itv (see Chapter 7, *Device I/O*), a timer interrupt can be triggered in x cycles simply by writing the value itc $+ x$ to the interval timer match register (itm). As described in Chapter 8, *Symmetric Multiprocessing*, the clock tick frequency is defined by the HZ macro. This means that the value of x needs to be chosen such that it corresponds to a period of $1/HZ$ (0.977 milliseconds, with a HZ value of 1024). If the itc counts at a frequency of f_{itc}, the value of x should be equal to f_{itc}/HZ. But how can the routine determine the correct value of f_{itc}? The answer can be found in PAL and SAL. Specifically, *ia64_sal_freq_base()* can be called to obtain the base clock frequency f_b, and *ia64_pal_freq_ratios()* can be used to obtain the ratio r between the itc frequency and the base clock frequency. The value of x would therefore be given by $x = f_b \cdot r/HZ$. For example, an Itanium machine might use a base block frequency of $f_b = 133.3$ MHz and multiply it by a factor of $r = 5.5$ to obtain an itc frequency of approximately 733 MHz. With a clock timer frequency of 1024 Hz, this would yield a value of x that is equal to $133.3 \cdot 10^6 \cdot 5.5/1024$, or approximately 716,000 itc cycles. Once the value of x is known, the routine can use it to program the itm register so that it will generate the first timer interrupt. The *timer interrupt handler* (*timer_interrupt()* in file arch/ia64/kernel/time.c) can then use x again to program the next interrupt. By doing this repeatedly, the handler effectively generates the periodic and regular stream of clock ticks that Linux requires.

The *pcibios_init()* routine primarily scans all PCI buses. Most of this scanning logic is platform independent and implemented in the *PCI bus scanner* (*pci_scan_bus()* in file drivers/pci/pci.c). The PCI bus scanner checks each PCI slot of a bus. For each slot that is found to have a device installed, the scanner will create a PCI device structure (see Chapter 7, *Device I/O*) and fill it with essential information about the device such as the device class, the address ranges that the device occupies in I/O and memory space, and so on. Each device structure is inserted into the global *PCI device list* (*pci_devices* in file include/linux/pci.h). The only information the PCI bus scanner needs from platform-specific code is (a) the bus number at which to start the scan and (b) a set of routines (function pointers) that provide access to the PCI configuration space. For the latter, SAL routines *ia64_sal_pci_config_read()* and *ia64_sal_pci_config_write()* can be used. On IA-64 machines, there is no easy way to enumerate the bus numbers that correspond to primary PCI buses. Instead, *pcibios_init()* can simply invoke the PCI bus scanner once for each of the 256 possible PCI bus numbers. This works fine because the PCI bus scanner will automatically skip any bus numbers that turn out to be secondary buses. In a second phase, *pcibios_init()* traverses the PCI device list and uses the ACPI PCI routing table (PRT) to map the four interrupt pins (INTA to INTD) of each device to the machine-specific global interrupt line numbers (see Chapter 7, *Device I/O*).

Waking up the application processors (APs)

The initialization of the APs occurs in two phases: first, the kernel calls *smp_boot_cpus()* to wake them all up. Second, the APs wait for the BP to call *smp_commence()*. This two-phase protocol simplifies the wakeup procedure because it guarantees that between the call to *smp_boot_cpus()* and the call to *smp_commence()* at most one AP is executing at any given time (all other APs are either still sleeping or waiting for the *smp_commence()*

signal). On IA-64, the *smp_commence()* signaling is implemented with a shared variable called *smp_commenced*. Its value is initially 0. The *smp_commence()* routine will set the variable to 1, meaning that the APs can wait for the signal simply by executing a tight loop (spinloop) that checks whether the variable has a non-zero value.

The more interesting question is how *smp_boot_cpus()* is able to wake up the APs. In a first step, the goal is to trigger the APs to execute the *AP bootstrap routine* (*start_ap()* in file arch/ia64/kernel/head.S). On an MP machine, *setup_arch()* already takes care of calling *ia64_sal_set_vectors()* to establish this routine as the OS_RENDEZ entrypoint. With this handler in place, all that is left to do is to send an interrupt to each AP to trigger the wakeup. The IA-64 interrupt vector that needs to be used for this purpose is selected by SAL and can be obtained from the SAL AP wakeup descriptor (see Section 10.1.2). The list of the APs in the machine can be obtained from ACPI by scanning the Multiple APIC Description Table (MADT). For each entry in this table, *smp_boot_cpus()* checks a flag to see if the corresponding CPU is enabled and, if so, extracts from it the AP's local ID. With the wakeup vector and the local ID, the BP has all the information needed to send an interprocessor interrupt (IPI) to the AP. SAL will intercept this interrupt on the AP and will then perform an upcall to the OS_RENDEZ entrypoint. For Linux/ia64, this will invoke the AP bootstrap routine *start_ap()*.

Just like the BP, the AP will start execution in physical address space and with a temporary memory stack and register backing store provided by firmware. Accordingly, the AP bootstrap routine needs to switch execution into virtual address space and then get its clone of the initial task from the *init_tasks* array. The *smp_boot_cpus()* routine informs the AP bootstrap routine of which entry to use by setting global variable *cpu_now_booting* to the desired value. Incidentally, this number later on serves as the logical CPU number of the AP (see Chapter 8, *Symmetric Multiprocessing*). Once the AP obtains the address of its clone of the initial task, it switches the stacks over to this task (in the same fashion as the BP did) and then invokes the *start AP routine* (*start_secondary()* in file arch/ia64/kernel/smpboot.c). There, the AP finishes initializing its own machine state, sets up its own timer interrupt, and then waits for the *smp_commence()* signal from the BP. As soon as that arrives, the AP calls *cpu_idle()*. At that point, the AP has reached its operational state and is ready to execute tasks as soon as they become available.

10.4 SUMMARY

In this chapter we described one of the more obscure aspects of modern computers: the bootstrap procedure. We have seen that an IA-64 machine is booted with the help of several firmware components and that these firmware components provide useful services even after a machine is up and running. In the second section, we described the basic steps that a bootloader needs to go through to load and start the Linux/ia64 kernel. Near the end, we described the handoff state that exists at the time the kernel is invoked. In the last section, we focused on Linux kernel initialization. As described there, platform-independent code is responsible for driving the kernel bootstrap procedure, but while doing so, it relies heavily on platform-specific code, which it invokes through the Linux kernel bootstrap interface.

Chapter 11

IA-32 Compatibility

Although the IA-64 architecture differs radically from previous mainstream CPU architectures, its designers recognized the importance of providing smooth transition paths that enable the gradual adoption of IA-64. For this purpose, IA-64 has been designed to enable compatibility with both the Intel IA-32 architecture and the Hewlett-Packard PA-RISC architecture [25, 35]. From a Linux perspective, backward compatibility with IA-32 is more important because IA-32 Linux has been so popular that it has more applications available. So, while nothing in principle would stop Linux/ia64 from supporting PA-RISC Linux binaries, this chapter focuses on IA-32 Linux compatibility support.

The goal of this compatibility support is to enable users to transparently run existing IA-32 Linux applications side by side with native IA-64 applications. It is important to recognize that the goal here is *not* to provide backward compatibility with foreign operating systems, such as Windows. This is for a good reason: cross-architecture emulation is really a problem quite different from cross-operating system emulation. Since they are so distinct, the two problems often require very different solutions and it makes little sense to mix them together. Furthermore, if cross-architecture emulation is done well, it should be possible to run cross-operating system emulators that exist for the emulated architecture. For example, Linux/ia64 can run the WINE emulator, which is an IA-32 Linux application that emulates the Windows operating system [63].

The focus on IA-32 application compatibility also implies that it is not a goal to enable running IA-32 device drivers or kernel modules inside the Linux/ia64 kernel. This is for two reasons: first of all, it would be difficult to implement a driver emulation framework that works well and efficiently, and without impacting the stability of the Linux/ia64 kernel. Second, and more importantly, since Linux is an Open Source operating system, there is little need for such a feature. It is generally much easier to recompile an existing Linux driver and make it work as a native IA-64 driver than to use a potentially fragile IA-32 driver emulation framework. This is particularly true because Linux already supports many different platforms, including several 64-bit platforms. In other words, supporting the IA-64 platform generally requires either no or very little additional driver development work. Binary-only kernel modules could potentially benefit from an IA-32 driver emulation framework, but since Linux does not even guarantee binary compatibility across different versions of the IA-32 Linux kernel, there is little point in trying to provide binary compatibility across architectures.

So what are the challenges of transparently running IA-32 Linux applications? An obvious issue is that the emulated applications use a different instruction set, so there needs to be some kind of a translator that maps the IA-32 instructions into a sequence of corresponding IA-64 instructions. As we see in the next section, the IA-64 architecture solves this problem for Linux. From the operating system perspective, the major issue is the difference in the data model: Linux/ia64 uses the LP64 model, but IA-32 Linux is a traditional 32-bit platform and therefore uses the ILP32 model (C types **int**, **long**, and pointers are all 32 bits in size). What this means is that any data structure that contains values of type **long** or any pointers will have a different size and layout on the two platforms. Another implication is that since pointers are 32 bits wide, IA-32 Linux applications can address only the first 4 Gbytes of address space. Apart from the data model issue, there are dozens of other differences that need to be taken care of. For example, IA-32 uses a page size of 4 Kbytes, whereas Linux/ia64 may use a page size of 4, 8, 16, or 64 Kbytes. Similarly, the clock tick rate of IA-32 is fixed to 100 Hz, whereas IA-64 can be configured for any rate and normally uses 1024 Hz. Then there are filename issues: the content of a given file may have to differ depending on whether it is used by an IA-32 or an IA-64 application. The canonical example here is shared libraries. For example, both IA-32 and IA-64 applications might expect that the C library is installed in /lib/libc.so.6. Fortunately, most of these issues are easy to handle and require no special discussion in this chapter. The remaining, more challenging, and more interesting issues are discussed in Section 11.2.

In the remainder of this chapter, we occasionally use the term "*bug-for-bug compatible.*" This is an important aspect of almost any emulator. What it means is that a successful emulator often must adhere not just to the officially defined aspects of the emulated system, but also to various implementation-dependent aspects. For example, in theory, an IA-32 application should work correctly no matter what the starting address of the stack is. However, some IA-32 applications may erroneously or mistakenly depend on the specific value used by IA-32 Linux. Bug-for-bug compatibility therefore would mandate that the emulator place the stack at the same address as a real IA-32 Linux kernel, just to ensure that such applications could also run correctly.

11.1 ARCHITECTURAL SUPPORT FOR IA-32

IA-64 defines all the architectural support needed for running IA-32 applications. This support is implemented in the *Intel value engine (IVE)*, illustrated in Figure 11.1. As shown there, the IVE can be thought of as being a translator that takes IA-32 instructions as input and generates corresponding IA-64 instructions as output. The translated instructions are then fed to the IA-64 engine that is also used for executing native applications. The interface to the IVE has been designed carefully so it can be implemented purely in hardware, purely in software, or as a combination of the two. The expectation is that IVE will initially be implemented mostly in hardware. Later, as IA-32 performance becomes less a priority or as software emulation becomes faster, more and more of the IVE will be implemented in software. Itanium certainly set the starting point for this process: since it is the first implementation of IA-64, it implements IVE almost entirely in hardware and

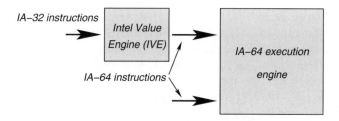

Figure 11.1. The Intel value engine (IVE).

can execute virtually all user-level IA-32 instructions. The only time the Itanium IVE requires assistance from software is for difficult corner cases of certain instructions or for any security-sensitive instruction.

11.1.1   IA-32 user-level machine state

The IA-32 architecture has a long history, and its roots can be traced back to one of the first popular 8-bit CPUs, the Intel 8080. Because of this history, the architecture comes with many architectural features that are no longer needed by modern operating systems such as Linux. Since we are primarily interested in Linux, we focus on the subset of the architecture that it uses. This subset is generally known as the *32-bit protected mode*. In this mode, IA-32 provides eight 32-bit general-purpose registers called EAX, EBX, ECX, EDX, ESP, EBP, ESI, and EDI. Register ESP serves as a hardware-supported memory stack that grows toward lower addresses, and EBP serves as the frame pointer (see Chapter 6, *Stack Unwinding*). Registers ESI and EDI are primarily intended as memory base registers and are implicitly used by several string-related instructions.

To support floating-point operations, IA-32 provides a traditional set of eight 80-bit floating-point registers called FP0–FP7. Unlike normal register files, these are accessed indirectly and managed as a cache of a floating-point operand stack that resides in memory. Starting with later models of the Pentium implementation, these registers can also be used as eight 64-bit multimedia registers. In this capacity, they are known as MM0–MM7 and are directly accessible by the Pentium MMX instructions. These instructions are similar to the IA-64 multimedia operations in the sense that they treat each register as a (small) vector of integer values. Note that since the MMX and the traditional floating-point registers occupy the same physical registers, only one set of registers can be active at any given time. Yet another register file was introduced starting with the Pentium III implementation. At that time, eight 128-bit floating-point registers were added. These registers are called XMM0– XMM7 and are generally referred to as the *streaming SIMD extension (SSE)* registers. SSE is basically a generalization of the MMX extension since it can treat each register not just as a vector of integer values but also as a pair of floating-point values.

The memory addressing scheme of IA-32 is quite unique: it supports not just normal paging but also segmentation. Segmentation was originally conceived for the 8086 implementation as a means to work around the 16-bit address-space limit that was present in the

8080 CPU. But when the architecture was extended to 32 bits, segmentation was kept for backward compatibility and to provide an additional level of indirection and protection. To support this, the IA-32 architecture defines six 16-bit wide *segment selector* registers called CS, DS, ES, SS, FS, and GS. Each of them identifies the segment that is used for the particular type of memory access that they represent. For instance, CS (code segment) is used for instruction fetches, DS (data segment) for normal data accesses, and SS (stack segment) for accesses to the memory stack. In other words, the type of memory access normally implicitly determines which segment selector is used during the access. However, in some cases it is necessary to have explicit control over which segment selector is used for a data access. IA-32 supports this control with an instruction modifier called *segment-override prefix*. This prefix modifies the behavior of the next instruction such that memory accesses that would normally use the implied selector use the specified segment selector instead. In addition to the six normal segment selectors, there are two special segment selectors called TSS and LDT. We discuss them in more detail later on.

11.1.2   Mapping the IA-32 user-level machine state to IA-64

Given that IVE translates IA-32 instructions to their IA-64 equivalent, it must also define a way to represent the user-level IA-32 machine state with IA-64 registers. Figure 11.2 illustrates how this is accomplished. As shown there, the general-purpose registers EAX–EDI are mapped to the low 32 bits of IA-64 registers r8–r15. When reading these registers, IVE ignores the top 32 bits, but when writing them, it sets the top 32 bits to the sign extension of bit 31. For example, if an IA-32 instruction were to write 2^{31} to register EAX, IVE would place the value 0xffffffff80000000 in register r8.

The traditional floating-point registers FP0–FP7 and their MMX-aliases MM0–MM7 are mapped to f8–f15. When these are used as floating-point registers, the IA-32 register values are maintained in the 82-bit floating-point register format that IA-64 normally uses. On the other hand, when they are used as MMX registers, the 64-bit mantissa of each register stores the 64-bit value of each MMX register and the 17-bit exponent and sign fields are set to all ones. SSE registers are 128 bits wide and therefore too big to fit into any individual IA-64 register. Instead, IVE uses a pair of IA-64 floating-point registers for each SSE register. Specifically, XMM0–XMM7 are mapped to registers f16–f31. The 64-bit mantissa of each IA-64 register is used to store half of an SSE register. The sign bit is set to 0 and the exponent field is set to 0x1003e. This exponent corresponds to a factor of 2^{63}, meaning that the floating-point value of the entire register is equal to the integer value stored in the mantissa bits.

The segment selector registers are only 16 bits wide. This makes it possible to pack four of them into a single 64-bit register and, as shown in Figure 11.2, IVE uses IA-64 registers r16 and r17 for this purpose. For example, CS is stored in the low 16 bits of register r17. Right below the segment selectors, we see that register r24 is used to hold ESD. This is the segment *descriptor* register for ES. If we look at the entire figure, we see that there is one such descriptor register for each segment selector. These registers do not correspond to directly visible IA-32 machine state but instead serve as a cache for in-memory data structures. We return to this topic in the next section.

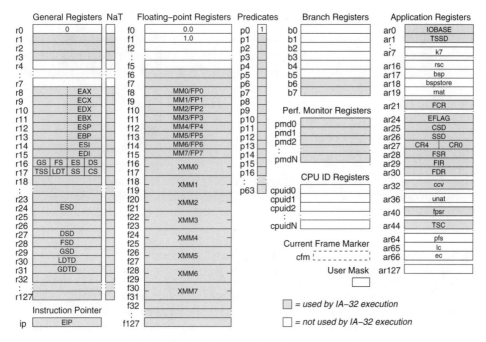

Figure 11.2. Mapping of IA-32 user-level machine state to IA-64 registers.

Apart from the main user-level machine state, IA-32 defines several control and system registers. For example, the IA-32 instruction pointer is called EIP, and IVE maps it directly to the IA-64 instruction pointer ip. However, since IA-32 instruction are not 16-byte aligned, IVE may store arbitrary values in the least significant four bits of this register. Most other special registers are mapped to IA-64 application registers. For example, k0 is used as the IOBASE register. This register plays a role when an IA-32 application accesses I/O port space (see Section 11.2.7).

To perform its job, IVE sometimes needs to use an IA-64 register as a scratch register, and the architecture reserves several registers for this purpose. In Figure 11.2, all registers that can be modified by IVE are shown as shaded boxes. Looking at the figure, we can see that, for example, IVE can modify all predicate registers (except for p0, which is read-only), all stacked registers, and all floating-point registers in the high partition. On the other hand, the architecture also mandates that IVE must preserve the content of certain registers. In the figure, these registers are shown as white boxes. As the figure illustrates, r4–r7 are among the few registers in this class. Since there are so few preserved registers, switching to IA-32 execution requires saving almost the entire IA-64 machine state, which makes this a relatively slow operation.

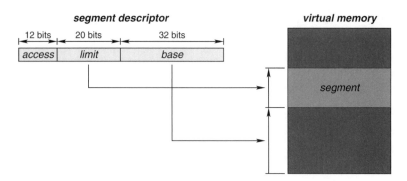

Figure 11.3. Format of IA-32 segment descriptor and associated segment.

11.1.3   IA-32 segmentation and memory addressing

Before we continue, let us take a closer look at how IA-32 segmentation works and how the IVE translates segmented addresses to IA-64 virtual addresses. Fundamentally, a segment consists of a contiguous region of virtual memory and a set of access attributes that define the exact properties of the segment. For example, the access attributes determine whether the segment is writable or executable. At any given time, thousands of segments may exist and each segment can be installed either globally, so that it is visible to all processes, or locally, so that it is visible to only one process.

To keep track of the potentially large number of segments, IA-32 defines two tables: the *global descriptor table (GDT)* and the *local descriptor table (LDT)*. Both can contain up to 8,192 *segment descriptors*. Each descriptor is 64 bits in size and defines one segment.

As illustrated in Figure 11.3, a descriptor contains three primary fields: the *base*, *limit*, and *access* fields. The *access* field specifies the segment's attributes and contains several flags that control miscellaneous aspects. The starting address of the segment is given by *base*, which is a 32-bit virtual address. The *limit* field determines the size of the segment by specifying the largest valid offset within the segment. Since this field is only 20 bits wide, a flag in the *access* field controls whether it is interpreted as a byte count (for segments of up to 1 Mbyte in size) or as a 4-Kbyte page count (for segments up to 4 Gbytes in size).

In addition to normal segments, the *access* field also provides encodings that represent special *system segments*. While these system segments also define contiguous regions of virtual memory, they additionally have various side effects. For example, segments of type *task state segment (TSS)* can be used for context switching and even contain a bitmap that controls which I/O ports a task can access! Another example is the LDT: the location and size of this table is specified by special system segment descriptors that reside in the GDT. Given these capabilities, it is clear that the descriptor tables are security sensitive and must be protected from direct access by user-level software. For this reason, operating systems generally maintain the GDT and LDT in protected kernel memory.

So what is the relationship between segment *selectors* and *descriptors*? The former basically serve as an index into a descriptor table, so each selector corresponds to a segment

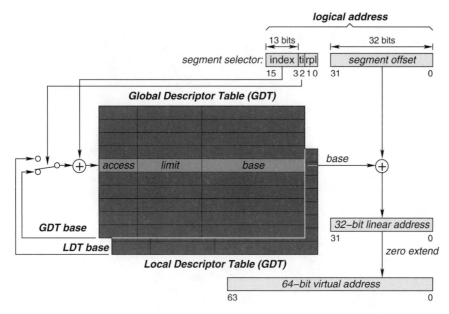

Figure 11.4. Translating IA-32 segmented addresses to IA-64 virtual addresses.

descriptor that may be either in the GDT or the LDT. To see how this works, let us look at the exact procedure for translating a segmented address to a linear virtual address, as illustrated in Figure 11.4.

As shown at the top right, IA-32 starts with a *logical address* that consists of a segment selector and an offset. The segment selector is a 16-bit value that can be broken up into three subfields: rpl, ti, and index. The first field, rpl (*requested privilege level*), is related to segment protection and we will ignore it for now. The second field, ti, is a 1-bit *table indicator* that controls whether the descriptor resides in the GDT or the LDT. The third field, index, is the index of the descriptor within the selected table. Since each descriptor is eight bytes in size, the address of the descriptor can be calculated as $8 \cdot \text{index} + tbase$, where *tbase* is the base address of the descriptor table (GDT if ti is zero, LDT otherwise).

Once its address is determined, the descriptor can be read from memory and the segment offset compared with the value in the descriptor's *limit* field. If the offset is greater, the memory access is beyond the boundaries of the segment and a fault is raised. Otherwise, the segment offset is valid and can be added to the descriptor's *base* address to form a *32-bit linear address*. At this point, a real IA-32 CPU would have finished translating the segmented address, but since IA-64 is a 64-bit platform, IVE needs one more step to zero-extend the 32-bit linear address to a 64-bit virtual address.

When the resulting 64-bit address is accessed, the normal IA-64 TLB and page-table mechanisms are used to obtain the final physical address and access rights. Note that with the top 32 bits of the virtual address always cleared to 0, IVE can access only the first

4 Gbytes of region 0 (see Chapter 4, *Virtual Memory*). Also, the zero-extension is in contrast to the sign-extension IVE uses when placing a 32-bit value in an IA-64 register. This implies that IA-64 software must clear the top 32 bits of a register written by IVE before using its content as an address.

Now, what is the segment selector's rpl field good for? It specifies the highest privilege level with which a memory access is issued. This feature can be used to artificially lower the privilege level when a particular segment is accessed. For example, when the Linux kernel accesses memory on behalf of the user level, it could place the lowest priority-level (3) in this field and then the segment's memory could be accessed only if the user level was already entitled to access it. However, since user level runs at the lowest priority already, IA-32 applications cannot lower priority even further and the rpl field is not useful to applications.

From a performance perspective, segmented address translation would run slowly if every memory access required that a descriptor be read from memory. To avoid this problem, real IA-32 CPUs cache descriptors in a hidden portion of the segment selector registers. For example, whenever a new selector is loaded into DS, the CPU loads the corresponding descriptor into the hidden portion of DS. With this approach, descriptor tables need to be accessed only once per update to a segment selector, instead of once per memory access. As illustrated in Figure 11.3, IVE emulates the hidden portion of the segment selector registers with separate descriptor registers. It uses r24 (ESD) to hold the descriptor for ES, r27 (DSD) to hold the descriptor for DS, and so on. Note that some of these registers are mapped to the application register file. For instance, TSSD is mapped to ar.k1 and CSD is mapped to ar25. We should also mention that these registers use the so-called *de-scrambled segment descriptor format*. This format is simply a rearrangement of the normal memory format of segment descriptors, intended to simplify and accelerate segment limit checking in IVE.

11.1.4   Transferring control between IA-32 and IA-64

Now that we understand how IVE maps the IA-32 machine state to IA-64 registers and how it addresses memory, let us look at how to turn it on, i.e., how to turn on IA-32 instruction execution. There are two primary ways of doing this: first, as described in Chapter 2, *IA-64 Architecture*, the processor status register contains a bit called is (instruction set) which, when set to 1, turns on IVE. Since this bit is in the upper half of psr, the only direct way of changing it is by execution of an rfi instruction (return from interruption). The second way of turning on IVE is to execute the special br.ia instruction. This is an unconditional branch instruction that will turn on the psr.is bit before execution starts at the target address. Since IA-32 is limited to the first 4 Gbytes of region 0, the branch target must lie below this boundary. The br.ia instruction is unprivileged and can therefore be used by IA-64 applications. Applications that contain both IA-32 and IA-64 code are called *mixed-mode* applications. Not all operating systems support them, and for this reason, this instruction can be disabled by turning on psr.di (disable instruction set transition). If this bit is set and the br.ia instruction is executed, the CPU raises a DISABLED INSTRUCTION SET TRANSITION fault.

There are also two ways for turning IVE off. Most commonly, this happens because of interruptions. Indeed, *any* interruption will automatically turn off IVE because the CPU clears the psr.is bit before it starts executing in the interruption vector table (see Chapter 2, *IA-64 Architecture*). IVE also implements a special IA-32 jump instruction called JMPE. It has the reverse effect of br.ia in that it clears the psr.is bit before execution begins at the target address. Since the jump target will be interpreted as a bundle of IA-64 instructions, it must be 16-byte aligned. Furthermore, because IA-32 can address only the first 4 Gbytes of region 0, the target must lie below this boundary. Of course, the JMPE instruction is not implemented on any real IA-32 CPU, and legacy applications will therefore never execute it. However, for mixed-mode applications, the instruction could be useful. For example, if IA-64 firmware needed to execute IA-32 BIOS code that may be present on a peripheral card such as a network interface controller, it could use the br.ia instruction to turn on IVE before executing the BIOS code and afterward it could use JMPE to return control to IA-64 code. Like br.ia, the execution of JMPE can be disabled by turning on the psr.di bit.

We need to emphasize that switching instruction sets does *not* automatically switch the machine state. For example, before IVE is turned on, the old IA-64 machine state must be saved and the new IA-32 machine state loaded according to the register mapping conventions described in Section 11.1.2. Only once the IA-32 state has been loaded can IVE be turned on. This is true even for the segment descriptor registers: despite not being part of the user-visible machine state, they must be initialized with the descriptors identified by the corresponding segment selector registers. For example, if CS were initialized to 0x23 (*index* = 4, *ti* = 0, *rpl* = 3), CSD would have to be initialized with the de-scrambled version of the descriptor in *GDT*[4].

11.2   LINUX SUPPORT FOR IA-32 APPLICATIONS

In the introduction to this chapter we explained that the goal of Linux/ia64 is to facilitate the transparent execution of existing IA-32 Linux applications. This goal is realized with the help of an optional *IA-32 Linux emulator*. When enabled, it will detect attempts to invoke IA-32 applications and transparently set up an execution environment that, with the help of IVE, will make it appear as if the application were running on a Pentium III Linux machine.

As illustrated in Figure 11.5, the IA-32 Linux emulator is part of the kernel. Just like the rest of the kernel, this emulator consists entirely of IA-64 code. That is, the Linux/ia64 kernel itself never executes any IA-32 instructions. IA-32 applications interact with the emulator through system calls, faults, and signals. The IVE takes care of executing virtually all user-level IA-32 instructions, so all the emulator needs to do is provide an execution environment that looks like the one provided by a real IA-32 Linux kernel. The emulator achieves this not by directly emulating the behavior of an IA-32 Linux kernel, but instead by translating the IA-32 environment into an equivalent IA-64 environment. This translation approach makes it possible to implement the emulator as a thin layer that is built on top of the regular Linux/ia64 kernel. For example, the emulator implements IA-32 system calls by forwarding them to the corresponding IA-64 system call handlers, making just the

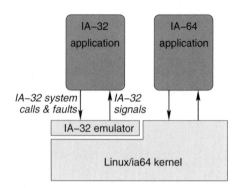

Figure 11.5. Role of the IA-32 Linux emulator inside Linux/ia64.

minimal adjustments needed to take care of the differences between IA-32 and IA-64 calling conventions and interfaces. Similarly, signal handling is managed almost entirely in the
Linux/ia64 kernel. The emulator is involved only in the last step, when an IA-32 signal
handler actually needs to be invoked.

Earlier we alluded to the fact that the IA-64 architecture can support mixed-mode applications. Such applications, however, are not supported by Linux/ia64. To enforce this ban,
Linux/ia64 sets the di bit in the processor status register and thereby inhibits the execution
of the br.ia and JMPE instructions. This is done for two reasons. First, there is a potential
for mixed-mode applications to create security holes. For example, an IA-32 application
might use JMPE to turn off IVE and use that as a way to bypass segment-based access
restrictions the emulator might rely on. Whether or not this would create an exploitable
security hole is a good question, and answering it would require careful review of all IA-32
instructions. To be on the safe side, it is better to disable the execution of JMPE and br.ia. A
second reason is that, over time, the importance of IA-32 compatibility will decrease and,
eventually, both IA-64 hardware and software are expected to drop this support entirely.
But if programmers started to write new mixed-mode applications, it might never be possible to reach this point. To put this another way, disabling mixed-mode support is intended
to encourage programmers to come up with pure IA-64 solutions that do not rely on the
existence of IVE.

In the remainder of this section, we discuss some of the more interesting challenges
that the emulator has to solve. Specifically, we describe how the emulator maps IA-32
tasks and processes to their IA-64 equivalents, how IA-32 applications get invoked, and
how system calls are emulated. We round out the discussion with brief descriptions of how
signal delivery is implemented and what facilities exist to let privileged IA-32 applications
access I/O ports directly, without involvement from the kernel.

11.2.1   Kernel representation of an IA-32 task

Given how IVE maps the IA-32 machine state to IA-64 registers, it should not come as
a surprise that IA-32 tasks can directly use the IA-64 task-related structures. Specifically,
the pt-regs, task, and thread structures normally used for IA-64 tasks can also be used
for IA-32 tasks. There is virtually no difference, except that the emulator reserves some
additional space in the thread structure so it can preserve those registers that are used only
while the IA-32 instruction set is executing. This set of registers consists of EFLAG, FSR,
FCR, FIR, FDR, and TSSD. A special case is registers IOBASE and TSSD, which map to
IA-64 kernel registers ar.k0 and ar.k1. They are special because, as far as IA-64 tasks are
concerned, they are constant. The normal IA-64 context-switch routines therefore do not
save or restore these registers. To avoid interfering with IA-64 tasks, the emulator therefore
must save these registers before installing its own values. Similarly, when switching away
from an IA-32 task, the emulator has to restore the original values again. As with the other
IA-32–specific registers, the emulator reserves extra space in the thread structure for the
purpose of preserving these registers.

   To avoid slowing down normal IA-64 context switching, the emulator saves and restores the extra words in the thread structure in separate *IA-32 context-switch routines*
(*ia32_load_state()* and *ia32_save_state()* in file arch/ia64/ia32/ia32_support.c). The emulator hooks these routines into the normal context-switch routine by treating the IA-32–
specific state as *extra state* (see Chapter 3, *Processes, Tasks, and Threads*). This implies
that the IA-32–specific state is switched in a lazy fashion, i.e., it is loaded only for a switch
to an IA-32 task and saved only for a switch away from an IA-32 task. Finding out whether a
given task is an IA-32 task is easy: it simply requires checking whether the is bit is set in the
psr value saved in the pt-regs structure. Since this is a fairly common test, Linux/ia64 provides a convenience routine called *IS_IA32_PROCESS()* for this purpose. This routine takes
a single argument, which must be a pointer to a pt-regs structure, and returns a non-zero
value if the corresponding task is running under IVE. Apart from being more legible, this
approach has the advantage that when a kernel is being built with IA-32 support disabled,
the routine evaluates to a constant value of 0. If the routine is implemented as a macro, a
compiler can detect this and automatically optimize away all IA-32–specific code.

11.2.2   Address space of an emulated IA-32 task

The layout of the IA-64 address space for an emulated IA-32 task is illustrated in Figure 11.6. The left part of the figure shows that the emulated task occupies the first 4 Gbytes
of the 64-bit address space. This means that it lies entirely inside the user address space
and, in fact, occupies just a tiny portion of region 0. The first 4 Gbytes of a task are guaranteed to be mappable by the Linux page tables because even with the smallest page size
of 4 Kbytes, a three-level page table can map a total of 39 bits, or 36 bits per region.

   The right part of Figure 11.6 is a zoomed view of the first 4 Gbytes of the address space.
This space is divided into two segments: a 3-Gbyte *user segment* and a 1-Gbyte *emulator
segment*. The user segment is accessible to IA-32 applications; it extends from address 0
up to 0xbfffffff. The emulator segment occupies the space above that. On a real IA-32
machine, this space would be occupied by the Linux kernel.

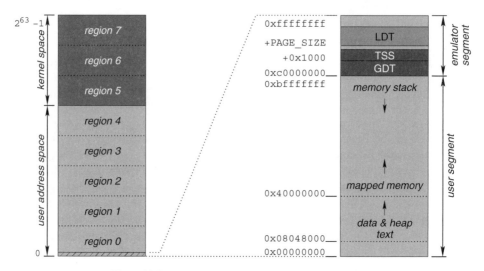

Figure 11.6. Virtual address space of an emulated IA-32 task.

User segment

IA-32 applications have full control over the user segment and can use the available address space almost any way they want. The only exceptions are that the starting address of the memory stack and the map base are fixed by the emulator. The stack starts at address 0xc0000000 and grows toward lower addresses. The map base is equal to 0x40000000 and defines the address at which the kernel starts searching for available virtual memory when mapping an object such as a file or a System V shared memory segment [9]. If we compare these addresses to those used by a real IA-32 Linux kernel, we would find that they are the same. While this is not strictly necessary (most applications do not depend on them), using the same values increases the likelihood of being bug-for-bug compatible with a real IA-32 Linux machine.

The figure also shows that IA-32 applications are normally linked such that the text, data, and heap segments are loaded at a starting address of 0x8048000, i.e., just above 128 Mbytes. Memory below that address normally remains unmapped to guarantee that dereferencing NULL pointers to data objects of up to 128 Mbytes in size will result in a segmentation violation signal (SIGSEGV). The offset of 0x48000 was intended to provide initial stack space so that small programs could be mapped with just two page-table pages (a global directory and a PTE directory, see Chapter 4, *Virtual Memory*). However, Linux does not use this space and instead places the memory stack at the upper end of the user segment. Let us emphasize that the load address of IA-32 applications is *not* in any way limited by the emulator: it simply loads the application at the address indicated by the ELF executable header, and, by convention, IA-32 Linux applications use address 0x8048000 for this purpose.

To summarize, the text-, data-, and heap-segments of an IA-32 application occupy the first 1 Gbyte of the user segment, and the remaining 2 Gbytes hold the mapped memory area (which includes all shared libraries) and the memory stack.

Emulator segment

The emulator segment occupies the address range that, on a real IA-32 machine, would be occupied by the Linux kernel. But since the emulator is part of the IA-64 kernel in region 7, this address range remains mostly empty. The exception is that three tables need to be accessible by the IVE but not from the IA-32 user level and, as we will see below, the emulator segment can provide just that.

As shown in the right part of Figure 11.6, the three tables are the GDT, TSS, and LDT.

The GDT is managed by the kernel and contains the global segment descriptors that apply regardless of the IA-32 process that is currently running. In contrast, the LDT contains segment descriptors that are process-private. This table starts out empty (no segments) but applications can use it to define their own segments.

The TSS is a memory area big enough to hold the machine state of an IA-32 CPU and can be used by IA-32 CPUs to support hardware thread context switching. The TSS can be thought of as the IA-32 hardware equivalent of the Linux thread structure (see Chapter 3, *Processes, Tasks, and Threads*). Indeed, early versions of the IA-32 Linux kernel defined the thread structure such that first 236 bytes corresponded exactly to the TSS. These 236 bytes provided enough space for the actual IA-32 machine state (104 bytes) and an I/O bitmap (132 bytes). The I/O bitmap controls user-level access to the first 1024 I/O ports (see Chapter 7, *Device I/O*). Later versions of IA-32 Linux abandoned the use of the TSS because it turned out that hardware context switching is both slower and less flexible than a software-only solution. Similarly, in the IA-32 Linux emulator, the TSS serves no direct purpose: since the IA-32 machine state is mapped to IA-64 registers, the first 104 bytes of the TSS remain completely unused. The I/O bitmap in the TSS also remains unused, though the emulator could conceivably take advantage of it if there was ever a need. The bottom line is that the IA-32 Linux emulator maintains the TSS simply as a 236-byte memory area that contains all zeroes.

Let us now take a closer look at how the GDT is set up by the emulator. This table is illustrated in Figure 11.7. If we start at the bottom, we see that the first four entries are unused and contain NULL descriptors. These define empty segments, such that any access to them will raise a segmentation fault. Even though the emulator does not use them, the figure shows the labels KERNEL_CS and KERNEL_DS next to the descriptors for entries two and three, respectively. This indicates that a real IA-32 Linux kernel would use them for mapping the kernel's code and data segments. But since the emulator consists of IA-64 code, there is no need to define these segments. The next two descriptors are the most important ones because they define the address range that is accessible to IA-32 applications. Specifically, the descriptor labeled USER_CS (entry four) maps the code segment, and the one labeled USER_DS (entry five) maps the data segment. The figure shows that both span the address range from 0 to 0xbfffffff. Thus, they encompass the entire user segment, just as we might expect. The remaining entries in the GDT define one TSS and one LDT

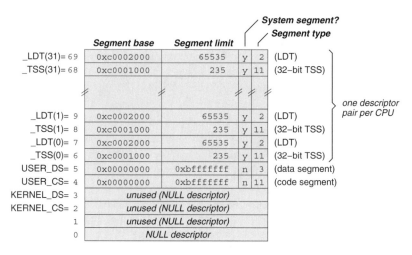

Figure 11.7. Content of global descriptor table (GDT).

descriptor for each of up to 32 CPUs. Since the descriptors refer to tables that reside in IA-64 virtual memory, the same descriptors can be used for all 32 entries: the TSS starts at address 0xc0001000 and is 236 bytes long, and the LDT is 64 Kbytes long and starts at address 0xc0000000 + max(PAGE_SIZE, 0x2000).

In the figure, we assumed an IA-64 page size of 8 Kbytes, so the LDT would start at address 0xc0002000. Given that the LDT/TSS descriptors are identical for each CPU, would it not be possible to share a single pair of descriptors for all CPUs? The answer is "probably yes," but it would mean that the segment selectors for the TSS and the LDT would be different from those of a real IA-32 Linux machine. It is unlikely that any applications depend on these values, but the principle of being bug-for-bug compatible suggests that the same values should be used.

With the content of the GDT explained, let us turn our attention to the LDT. The LDT also contains segment descriptors, just like the GDT, but its content is private to each process (address space). Neither the emulator nor a real IA-32 Linux kernel uses this table on its own. Instead, it is available for use by applications. For security, user-level code must not be allowed to directly write to this table. For that reason, the LDT is placed in the emulator segment. While applications cannot directly access the LDT, they can do so indirectly with the IA-32–specific *modify_ldt()* system call. This system call rejects any attempt to install problematic descriptors such as system descriptors and is therefore safe for use even by unprivileged applications.

But why would an application ever want to define its own segments? The short answer is that segments provide a somewhat clunky way to work around the fact that IA-32 has so few general-purpose registers. For example, the Linux pthread library could benefit from a dedicated register that points to the thread control block. Since this is a frequently accessed data structure, a dedicated register would improve performance by providing direct, register-relative addressing for the data in the thread control block. But since there are too few IA-32 registers to begin with, this is not a feasible option. The solution adopted by the pthread library is based on the recognition that a segment effectively provides a 32-bit base address register. Thus, the library uses the LDT to define one segment for each thread control block. When a thread is scheduled for execution, the segment selector for its thread control block is loaded into register GS and from then on, variables in the thread control block can be accessed through GS-relative memory addresses. In effect, the hidden GSD register serves as a dedicated pointer to the thread control block. Of course, this means that code outside the pthread library may not use GS, but since most IA-32 Linux applications do not use segmentation on their own, this limitation is not serious.

One remaining question is why the GDT, LDT, and TSS have to be stored in the emulator segment. There are really two issues here: accessibility and protection. The IVE may need to access these tables in the course of normal IA-32 user-level instruction execution. For example, whenever a new value is written to one of the segment selector registers, the IVE needs to access the GDT or LDT to update the corresponding descriptor register. But since the IVE is limited to 32-bit addressing, this means that the tables must be stored below the 4-Gbyte boundary. Since the tables contain security-sensitive information (such as privilege levels), they must be protected from direct access by user-level code. For Linux, it would be most natural to use page protection for this purpose: the pages in the emulator segment would be mapped such that only the kernel can access them. This is indeed what a real IA-32 Linux kernel does. Unfortunately, this approach does not work with IVE. The reason is that when the IVE needs to access the tables, it accesses them in the virtual, not physical, address space and with whatever privilege level happens to be in effect at the time. For example, if a user-level instruction writes a new value to a segment selector register, IVE would access the GDT or LDT with user-level privilege only. In other words, at the page level, there is no way to distinguish a direct user-level access from an IVE access, and this renders page protection useless. Fortunately, when IVE accesses the tables, it does so directly with a linear 32-bit address, bypassing all segment-related translations and checks. Thus, by limiting the user segment to the address range from 0 to 0xbfffffff, the user level is prevented from accessing the tables but IVE is not, which is just what is needed.

11.2.3   Dealing with absolute filesystem paths

There are a few occasions where IA-32 applications use absolute paths to open IA-32–specific files. If there is an IA-64–specific version of the same file, this creates a name collision that must be resolved. Most applications provide a means to specify alternative locations for such files. For instance, the directories listed in environment variable LD-_LIBRARY_PATH are usually searched when the runtime loader is trying to locate a shared library. Unfortunately, for security-sensitive applications, environment variables are not an acceptable solution because they would create security holes. Just imagine what would happen if an ordinary user could create his or her own version of /etc/passwd and trick the system into using it. Before long the user would have all root privileges!

For this reason, security-sensitive software such as the *pluggable authentication modules (PAM)* use configuration files that specify the absolute paths of the shared libraries

Table 11.1. Examples showing the effect of the emulator prefix.

Original path	Final IA-64 path	Final IA-32 path
/lib/libc.so.6	/lib/libc.so.6	/emul/ia32-linux/lib/libc.so.6
./libc.so.6	./libc.so.6	./libc.so.6
/etc/passwd	/etc/passwd	/etc/passwd
/lib/	/lib/	/lib/

they rely upon [48]. For example, configuration file /etc/pam.d/system-auth might specify library /lib/security/pam_unix.so as the module implementing the authentication policy for the normal UNIX password mechanism. Now, this file may contain either the IA-64 version or the IA-32 version of the shared library, but not both at the same time. This means that only one kind of application could use PAM, but not the other. Of course, this is not acceptable. To handle such situations, the kernel supports an *emulator prefix* (*__emul_prefix()* in file include/asm/namei.h). This routine returns a prefix that should be used when an absolute path of an emulated application is translated. On IA-64, this routine returns the string "emul/ia32-linux" for IA-32 applications and an empty string for native applications. The effect is that for IA-32 applications, absolute paths are first searched in /emul/ia32-linux and only if the file does not exist there, is an attempt made to open the original path. As a special case, absolute paths that resolve to a directory never use the emulator prefix. The emulator prefix effectively creates an overlay in the filesystem namespace such that nondirectory files in /emul/ia32-linux substitute the files of the same name in the normal filesystem tree. Given this, we can fix the PAM problem simply by installing the IA-32 version of the shared library in /emul/ia32-linux/lib/security/pam_unix.so.

To get a better sense of how the emulator prefix works in practice, let us look at the examples listed in Table 11.1. They assume that only one file actually exists in the filesystem, namely /emul/ia32-linux/lib/libc.so.6. The first line shows that for an IA-64 application, the path /lib/libc.so.6 would be used directly, without any prefix. In contrast, an IA-32 application would pick up the file from the overlay tree. The second line shows that relative paths are unaffected by the emulator prefix. The third line shows that paths that do not exist in the overlay tree are also unaffected by the emulator prefix. The last line shows that directory paths are *also* not affected by the emulator prefix, even if they exist in the overlay tree.

We should point out that the emulator prefix creates small inconsistencies that could be observed by applications. For example, if we assume that ls.ia32 is an IA-32 version of the ls command, we might observe the following behavior:

```
$ ls.ia32 -l /lib | fgrep libc.so.6
$ ls.ia32 -l /lib/libc.so.6
-rwxr-xr-x 2 root root 1179756 Mar 13 2001 /lib/libc.so.6
```

In this example, the empty output from the first command seems to suggest that file /lib/libc.so.6 does not exist. Yet the second command shows that the file is there. This apparent paradox can be observed when a file exists in the overlay tree, but not in the original tree. Of course, there are ways to fix this particular problem, but if we step back for a minute, we can see that no matter how the overlay tree is implemented, there is *always* a chance of an application detecting a discrepancy. For example, an IA-32 application could calculate a checksum of the content of a given file and then pass the absolute filename and the checksum to an IA-64 application. If the native application were to recalculate the checksum, it could readily discover any change in the file content, no matter what the overlay scheme. The only way to prevent discrepancies completely is to disallow any sharing between the original and the emulated filesystems and that would, of course, be equivalent to throwing out the baby with the bathwater.

Despite the potential problems, the emulator prefix approach works well in practice, largely because few applications use hardcoded, absolute paths. Because of this, only a minimal number of files need to be stored in the overlay tree, and the smaller the number of files in the overlay tree, the smaller the chance that an application would accidentally encounter a discrepancy. This is not to say that the emulator prefix is the only practical solution. Other possible solutions go by colorful names such as *fat binaries, namespaces, dynamic symlinks,* and so on. But as explained earlier, any solution that allows sharing of portions of the namespace runs the risk of applications discovering discrepancies. In addition, the emulator prefix solution does have the nice aspect of isolating all emulator-related changes to a single subtree in the filesystem. In other words, none of the files or directories used by native applications have to be modified in any shape or form.

On a final note, we should point out that shared libraries are normally specified with relative, not absolute, paths. For example, an executable image such as /bin/ls might depend on the shared library with relative path libc.so.6. It is the responsibility of the runtime loader to locate the correct file for this relative path. The Linux loader achieves this with the help of the configuration file /etc/ld.so.conf, which lists directories that contain shared libraries. Fortunately, when searching these directories, the Linux loader (and all associated tools such as `ldconfig`) qualifies the search by platform type. That is, for IA-32 applications, it will only consider IA-32 shared libraries, and for IA-64 applications, it will only consider IA-64 shared libraries. This makes it possible to list any directory with shared libraries in /etc/ld.so.conf, independently of whether it contains IA-64 or IA-32 shared libraries. This also means that for normal shared library dependencies with relative paths, the emulator prefix mechanism is not used.

11.2.4   Starting an IA-32 executable

Users normally invoke IA-32 applications from an IA-64 command-line shell such as `bash`. When this happens, the shell locates the executable image for the application, forks a new IA-64 task, and then transfers control to the executable image with the *execve()* system call. This system call is responsible for detecting that the executable image is an IA-32 application and for transforming the IA-64 task into an emulated IA-32 task. Fortunately, the Linux kernel provides a generic facility for handling nonnative executable formats. For this purpose, it maintains a list of *binary formats* (struct linux_binfmt in file include/linux/binfmts.h). When *execve()* is invoked, the kernel traverses this list and asks each binary format to attempt to load the executable image. The first binary format that succeeds in loading the image wins and gains control of the task.

The emulator takes advantage of this facility by registering its own *IA-32 binary format* (file arch/ia64/ia32/binfmt_elf32.c). When asked to load an executable image, this binary format checks whether the image is an ELF-32 file for the IA-32 architecture. If not, it returns a failure indication; otherwise, it goes ahead and starts the executable image with the following steps:

- Map the executable image into the emulated address space.

- Set up the IA-64 task state for IA-32 execution.

- Return from *execve()* system call.

Note that as the kernel returns from *execve()*, it will eventually return to the user level with an rfi instruction. Since the second step will have turned on the psr.is in the pt-regs structure, this will have the effect of launching the IVE and initiating IA-32 instruction execution. If we look at the overall procedure, we see that starting an IA-32 executable is fundamentally very similar to starting a native IA-64 executable. Indeed, the two cases are almost identical, except for the following three differences:

1. Addresses are only 32 bits wide and are therefore limited to addressing the first 4 Gbytes of the address space.

2. Regardless of the actual IA-64 page size, the virtual memory system must appear to allow mapping files at arbitrary 4-Kbyte boundaries.

3. IA-64 task state must be initialize as required by the IVE.

The emulator takes care of the first difference by lowering both the *task size limit* and the map base. Recall from Chapter 4, *Virtual Memory*, that the task size limit determines the largest virtual address that is accessible at the user level. Throughout the Linux kernel, this limit is represented by macro TASK_SIZE and treated like a constant. However, in the case of Linux/ia64, this macro actually evaluates to the value of the *task_size* member in the thread structure. This means that each task could potentially have its own task size limit. For IA-64 tasks, a value of 0xa000000000000000 is used, but when starting an IA-32 task, the emulator lowers this to 0xc0000000. Related to the task limit is the map base: as explained earlier, it is the address at which the kernel starts to search for available virtual memory when mapping an object. For IA-64 tasks, the map base is normally 0x2000000000000000, but the emulator lowers this address to 0x40000000 for IA-32 tasks.

The second difference is a bigger challenge: IA-32 use a fixed page size of 4 Kbytes whereas the page size in Linux/ia64 is configurable and generally bigger than 4 Kbytes. A page size of more than 4 Kbytes creates a problem because the kernel has a built-in assumption that all virtual mappings must be page aligned. For IA-64 executables, this is not an issue because they are always aligned according to the largest possible page size (64 Kbytes). However, IA-32 executables are aligned only to 4 Kbytes and this prevents the emulator from using the normal mapping routines. To solve this problem, the emulator redirects all mapping requests to a special routine called *ia32_do_mmap()*. To the degree possible, this routine emulates the mapping behavior of a machine with a 4-Kbyte page size, independently of the actual IA-64 page size. We describe the inner workings and limitations of this routine in more detail in Section 11.2.5. For now, we can think of it as being identical to *mmap()*, except that it allows mappings at arbitrary 4-Kbyte boundaries.

Handling the third difference is not particularly difficult but still requires some care, largely because the task state does not consist of the IA-32 registers alone. As is typical for CISC architectures, IA-32 has several instructions that implicitly access privileged data structures, such as the GDT, LDT, and TSS. Consequently, those data structures also must be initialized. But let us begin with the IA-32 registers. Initializing those primarily consists of clearing the general-purpose registers and setting up the segmentation-related registers, stack pointer (ESP), and instruction pointer (EIP). Given the register mapping used by IVE, this is straightforward. For example, register EAX is mapped to IA-64 register r8, so clearing it simply entails writing 0 to the corresponding member in the pt-regs structure. Similarly, various IA-32 status and control registers such as EFLAG, FCR, and FSR need to be initialized. As far as the privileged data structures are concerned, GDT and TSS can be handled in the same fashion because their content is constant and identical for each IA-32 task. Indeed, the emulator can create these tables at boot time, so that when the time comes to initialize an IA-32 task, it can simply map them into virtual space by creating a suitable vm-area structure (see Chapter 4, *Virtual Memory*). The LDT needs to be handled slightly differently because it is process-private. The emulator also creates a vm-area for the LDT, but instead of mapping it to an existing table, it maps it to anonymous memory. Such memory is process-private and initially contains all zeros. Since a segment descriptor full of zeros corresponds to a NULL descriptor, this is exactly what is needed for the LDT and no further initialization is necessary.

Example of starting an IA-32 task

Let us take a look at a specific example: Figure 11.8 illustrates the initial state of an emulated task that is just about to start executing the IA-32 version of the ls command. In the figure, we assumed that the task was invoked with the command line ls -l and, somewhat unrealistically, with just one environment variable (HOME=/).

The upper-left corner shows the major portions of the emulated IA-32 register state: all general-purpose registers have been cleared to 0, the instruction pointer EIP has been set to the entry point of the runtime loader (0x40001dd0), and the stack pointer ESP has been set to the address just below the argument area (0xbffffa50). Note that segment selector CS has been set to 0x23.

If we consider the segment selector format shown at the top of Figure 11.4 on page 455, we see that this breaks down to a requested priority-level of three (user level) and a GDT index of four. According to the GDT shown in Figure 11.7, this corresponds to the segment descriptor for the user code segment. Similarly, segment selectors SS, DS, and ES have been initialized to 0x2b, which also breaks down to a requested priority-level of three but to a GDT index of five. Again, by looking at the content of the GDT, we can see that this corresponds to the user data segment. The remaining two selectors FS and GS are initialized to 0 so that any attempt to use them will result in a fault.

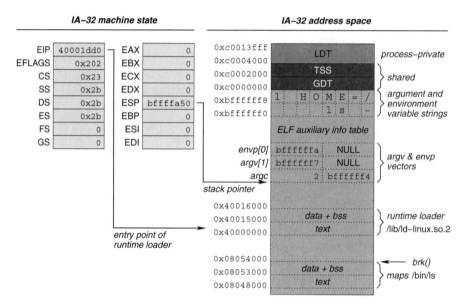

Figure 11.8. Initial state of an IA-32 task executing ls -l.

Since the emulator initializes the segment registers while executing the IA-64 instruction set, it must emulate all side effects that would normally take place when IA-32 instructions would write to these registers. In particular, this means that the corresponding segment descriptor registers must be loaded with the descriptor values from the GDT. For example, the descriptor register for ES is ESD and is mapped to IA-64 register r24. After initializing ES with 0x2b, the emulator therefore also must de-scramble the content of *GDT*[5] and place it in the pt-regs member for r24. However, for space reasons the segment descriptor registers have been omitted from Figure 11.8.

The right half of Figure 11.8 illustrates the address-space layout at the time IA-32 execution starts at the user level. We can see that near the bottom of the address space, the IA-32 executable image of /bin/ls has been mapped. This is achieved with the equivalent of two *mmap()* system calls: one to map the program text with read and execute permission and a second one to map the program's data and bss with read and write permission. The IA-32 runtime loader is called /lib/ld-linux.so.2, and since it is position independent, it can be mapped anywhere in the address space. But since it is the first position-independent mapping, it generally ends up right at the map base, which is 0x40000000 for IA-32 tasks. The last portion of user-accessible address space is occupied by the stack. As shown in the figure, the initial (top) portion of the stack holds the argument and environment variable strings, the ELF auxiliary info table, and the *argv* and *envp* argument vectors. This layout closely corresponds to the one used for native IA-64 tasks (see Chapter 1, *Introduction*); the primary difference is that the *argv* and *envp* vectors contain pointers that are only four bytes in size. Lastly, the emulator segment above 0xc0000000 maps

On entry   *On return*

EAX (r8)	syscall number
EBX (r11)	syscall arg 0
ECX (r9)	syscall arg 1
EDX (r10)	syscall arg 2
ESI (r14)	syscall arg 3
EDI (r15)	syscall arg 4
EBP (r13)	syscall arg 5

| EAX (r8) | syscall status |

Figure 11.9. IA-32 system call register usage convention.

the GDT, TSS, and LDT. It is important to keep in mind that even though segmentation prevents this area from being accessed by IA-32 user-level tasks, from the perspective of the Linux/ia64 kernel, it is normal user-space memory.

11.2.5   System call emulation

The system call conventions used by IA-32 tasks are, of course, different from those used by native IA-64 tasks. The emulator therefore has to intercept such calls and emulate them with the facilities provided by the Linux/ia64 kernel. The goal is for the emulated system calls to behave exactly like they would on a real IA-32 Linux machine, even though IA-64 is a 64-bit platform with a different instruction set. Depending on the system call, such perfect emulation may be entirely trivial, may require some work, or may be almost impossible to achieve. For example, emulating *getpid()* is rather trivial, emulating *execve()* requires some extra work, and emulating *mmap()* perfectly and efficiently is impossible when the page size is greater than 4 Kbytes.

IA-32 Linux applications invoke system calls with an INT 0x80 instruction. This triggers a software interrupt similar to the break instruction used for IA-64 system calls. Up to six arguments can be passed in general-purpose registers. The registers used for this purpose are, in order, registers EBX, ECX, EDX, ESI, EDI, and EBP. General-purpose register EAX is used to pass the system call number and, on return from the system call handler, it contains the system call status. The encoding of this status value is the same as the one used by the Linux system call handlers, i.e., small negative values indicate failure and all other values indicate success. On success, the status contains the result value that should be returned to the caller; on failure, it contains the negated error code that should be stored in the *errno* variable. This system call register usage convention is illustrated in Figure 11.9. The register names in parentheses are the IA-64 registers that the IVE uses to host the corresponding IA-32 registers. If we look at these, we see that an IA-32 system call involves only registers that the IA-64 software conventions consider **scratch** registers. As we see next, this is convenient because it means that these registers are part of the pt-regs structure created on entry to the kernel.

Now, what happens when the IVE encounters an INT 0x80 instruction? The answer is that it raises an IA-32 INTERRUPT TRAP, which initiates IA-64 interruption handling just as any other IA-64 interruption does. In particular, the trap will switch execution back to the IA-64 instruction set and, for this particular fault, the IA-64 CPU will place the instruction's trap number (i.e., 0x80) in bits 16–23 of the isr control register. The CPU then dispatches execution to interruption vector 47 (IA-32 interrupt vector).

Once execution reaches that point in the interruption vector table (IVT), Linux/ia64 executes the normal kernel entry path (see Chapter 5, *Kernel Entry and Exit*) and checks whether the trap number in isr is equal to 0x80. If not, the application executed an unsupported INT instruction, and the kernel responds by sending a SIGTRAP signal. If the trap number is equal to 0x80, the kernel invokes the emulator by looking up and calling the appropriate handler. For this purpose, the kernel maintains an *IA-32 system call table* (*ia32-_syscall_table* in file arch/ia64/ia32/ia32_entry.S). In this table, the entry with index *n* points to the handler for the IA-32 system call with number *n*. For example, system call number 13 is the IA-32 version of *time()*. Accordingly, the IA-32 system call table entry with index 13 points to function *sys32_time()*, which is the emulator's handler for the system call.

Before the handler can be called, the arguments must be set up according to the IA-64 software conventions. Specifically, the system call arguments need to be loaded into output registers out0–out5. As mentioned earlier, at the time of the software interrupt, the IA-32 system call arguments reside in **scratch** registers, which the kernel entry path copies to the pt-regs structure. The kernel can therefore retrieve the arguments by loading the content of the corresponding pt-regs members. For example, the first argument is passed in EBX, so the kernel can retrieve it by loading the pt-regs member for register r11. While loading the arguments, the kernel zero-extends them from 32 to 64 bits. Zero-extension is useful because it ensures that pointers passed as system call arguments remain valid when interpreted as 64-bit pointers. With sign-extension, this would not be true because any pointer above 2 Gbytes would end up with the top 32 bits set to 1. For example, 0xbfffc000 would become 0xffffffffbfffc000, which is not a valid user-space address.

Once the arguments are loaded, the kernel can invoke the system call handler. Since the handler uses the normal IA-64 software conventions, it will pick up the system call from the stacked registers and, before returning, will place the system call status in register r8. Upon returning from the handler, the kernel stores the system call status in the pt-regs member for r8. Since IVE maps EAX to r8, this has the desired effect of returning the system call status through EAX. In the last step, the normal kernel exit path returns control to the user level and IVE resumes executing IA-32 instructions.

Trivial system calls

It turns out that many IA-32 system calls can be emulated directly with the system call handlers normally used for IA-64. For instance, *open()* can be emulated simply by specifying the normal *sys_open()* handler in the corresponding entry of the IA-32 system call table. Since such system calls require no extra IA-32–specific work, we consider them *trivial system calls*. This group is surprisingly large and, beyond *open()*, includes other important system calls such as *read()*, *write()*, and *close()*.

To get a better sense of what system calls can be handled in this trivial fashion, let us look at the example shown in Figure 11.10. It illustrates an IA-32 system call invoked with:

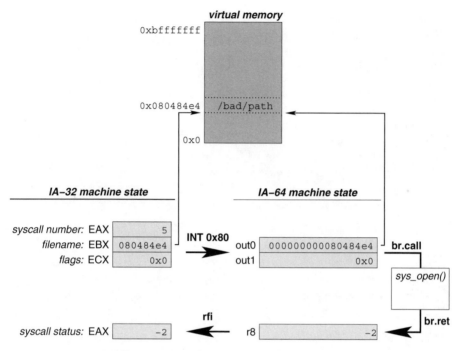

Figure 11.10. Example: Execution of IA-32 *open()* system call.

```
int ret = open("/bad/path", O_RDONLY);
```

In this example, we assume that file /bad/path does not exist and that the address of string /bad/path is equal to 0x080484e4. On IA-32, *open()* is system call number 5 and O_RDONLY is equal to 0. Thus, as illustrated in the left part of the figure, EAX is set to 5, the first system call argument (EBX) is set to the address of the string, and the second system call argument (ECX) is set to 0 (O_RDONLY). Then the INT 0x80 instruction is executed to transfer control to the kernel. As explained earlier, the kernel retrieves the system call arguments, zero-extends them to 64 bits and then places them into the output registers. In the figure, only out0 and out1 are shown, but in reality, the kernel always retrieves all six argument registers, even though not all arguments are needed by every system call handler.

The system call number is used as an index into the IA-32 system call table. In our case, the table entry with index five contains a pointer to function *sys_open()*, so the kernel ends up calling this routine. Now, since *sys_open()* is the normal handler for the IA-64 *open()* system call, it will interpret the two arguments according to the IA-64 conventions. But thanks to zero-extension, this is not a problem: the zero-extended filename pointer still points to /bad/path, and the *flags* argument is a 32-bit value even for IA-64, so the values in the upper 32 bits of out1 do not matter. When *sys_open()* returns, register r8 contains the return value as usual. In our example, we assumed that the file does not exist, so a value of -2 would be returned ($-$ENOENT). Fortunately, IA-64 uses the same error codes as IA-32 Linux, so this value can be stored directly in the pt-regs member that corresponds to EAX. In the final step, execution returns to the user level with the rfi instruction.

This discussion illustrates that trivial system calls must meet the following conditions:

1. The zero-extended value of each system call argument must have the same meaning as the original 32-bit argument. The *flags* argument of *open()* meets this requirement because both IA-32 and IA-64 treat it as an unsigned 32-bit integer and because they use the same values for O_RDONLY, O_WRONLY, and so on. A contrasting example is the *offset* argument of *lseek()*. This argument is a 32-bit signed number, so zero-extending it would change its meaning. For instance, a value of -1 (small negative number) would be zero-extended to 0xffffffff (large positive number), and because of this, *lseek()* cannot be treated as a trivial system call.

2. For arguments passed in memory, the data layout of the underlying type must be identical for IA-32 and IA-64. This is always the case for character strings such as the filename argument passed to *open()* but is rarely true for any moderately complex data structures. In particular, because of the different data model (ILP32 vs. LP64), structures containing pointers are never compatible with the IA-64 layout and system calls that pass pointers to such structures do not qualify as trivial system calls.

3. The return value from the system call handler must have the same meaning as the return value expected by the caller. This must be true even though the returned value will be truncated down to 32 bits when it is returned to the IA-32 caller. For the *open()* system call, this condition is met. On success, a small positive number, which is a file descriptor number, is returned; on failure, a small negative number, which is an error code number, is returned.

Despite these rather stringent conditions, more than half of the roughly 189 system calls supported by the IA-32 Linux emulator fall into the group of trivial system calls.

Nontrivial system calls

For nontrivial system calls, the emulator defines IA-32–specific system call handlers whose names generally start with a prefix of "*sys32_*". For example, the IA-32 version of *lseek()* is implemented by handler *sys32_lseek()*. Implementing these handlers is usually straightforward and consists of three steps: first, the incoming arguments need to be converted to 64-bit equivalents; second, the actual operation is performed; and, third, the 64-bit results need to be converted back to 32-bit results. Of course, if there are no incoming arguments or no results, the corresponding conversion step can be skipped.

For a concrete example, let us take a look at how the *gettimeofday()* system call might be implemented. Recall that this system call takes two pointer arguments: the first one is a pointer to a timeval structure and the second is a pointer to a time-zone structure. The timeval structure contains two members, *tv_sec* and *tv_usec*, that hold the seconds and microseconds elapsed since the UNIX epoch. The *tv_sec* member is 64 bits in size on IA-64, but only 32 bits on IA-32. In other words, the timeval argument requires conversion. On the other hand, the time-zone structure contains two **int**-typed variables. This type is 32 bits wide on both platforms, so no conversion is needed. A possible solution is illustrated below:

```
struct timeval32 {
    int tv_sec, tv_usec;
};

long
sys32_gettimeofday (struct timeval32 *tv, struct timezone *tz) {
    if (tv) {
        struct timeval tv64;
        do_gettimeofday(&tv64);
        if (put_user(tv->tv_sec, tv64.tv_sec)
            || put_user(tv->tv_usec, tv64.tv_usec))
            return -EFAULT;
    }
    if (tz && copy_to_user(tz, &sys_tz, sizeof(sys_tz)))
        return -EFAULT;
    return 0;
}
```

This routine shows that if the *tv* argument is not NULL, the kernel internal routine *do_get-timeofday()* is called to read the current time into a 64-bit timeval structure. The result is then converted to a 32-bit timeval structure through two calls to *put_user()*. Note here that copying the *tv_sec* member will automatically truncate it to 32 bits. This, of course, could cause problems if *tv_sec* happens to be greater than 0x7fffffff. Fortunately, this will happen only in the year 2038. We can assume that by then, IA-32 emulation will either not be important anymore or some other solution that does not suffer from the overflow problem will have been found (e.g., *tv_sec* could be widened to 64 bits even on IA-32). In any case, the point is that the overflow problem is inherent in the IA-32 interface and not a limitation of the emulator per se.

The *gettimeofday()* example illustrates that there is generally nothing fundamentally difficult about realizing an IA-32 system call handler, but we need to recognize that even though each handler is often quite simple, dozens of system calls need such handlers. More-over, some of the system calls have very complicated interfaces, involving literally dozens of different data types. The worst, but by no means the only, offender is *ioctl()*: since each device driver can extend this system call with its own data structures, accurate emulation requires lots and lots of simple argument conversions. Fortunately, most *ioctl()* calls are ob-scure enough that they do not have to be supported by the emulator, but given the number of nontrivial system calls and the amount of argument conversion that some of them require, it should be clear that complete and reasonably accurate system call emulation constitutes the bulk of the work that the emulator needs to perform.

One system call that is notable not for its complexity, but for its simplicity is *execve()*. We can emulate it easily by converting the argument and environment vectors to 64-bit ver-sions and using them to call the normal IA-64 *sys_execve()* handler. Beyond being simple, this solution is elegant because it lets an IA-32 task invoke *execve()* on an IA-64 executable. Thus, IA-32 and IA-64 applications can invoke each other without any difficulty.

Emulating *mmap()*

There are a few system calls whose operation depends on the granularity of the page size. For example, the *mmap()* system call is limited to mapping objects on page boundaries. Other examples include *mprotect()* and *munmap()*, but these can be handled with the same techniques that are used for *mmap()*, so we do not discuss them separately.

Emulating *mmap()* is easy *if* the page size of the host platform is no bigger than the page size of the emulated platform. For IA-64, this may or may not be the case: the smallest supported page size is 4 Kbytes and matches the IA-32 page size. However, for best performance, most Linux/ia64 machines are configured for a larger page size of 8 Kbytes or 16 Kbytes. As we see later, this creates some challenges.

Before getting into this discussion, let us remind ourselves how this system call works. Its prototype is shown below:

```
void *mmap(void *start, unsigned long length, int prot,
           int flags, int fd, long long offset);
```

The basic idea behind this system call is simple: it maps an arbitrary area of a file into virtual address space. The file to be mapped is identified by file descriptor *fd*. Arguments *offset* and *length* determine which portion of the file gets mapped: *offset* is the byte offset at which the area starts, and *length* specifies the number of bytes to be mapped. The virtual address at which the area gets mapped is determined by argument *start*. Argument *prot* determines the access rights for the mapped virtual memory (PROT_NONE, PROT_READ, PROT_WRITE, PROT_EXEC, or any combination of the last three). Finally, argument *flags* contains various flags that determine the exact semantics of the mapping. Linux supports almost a dozen different flags, but the ones that are relevant here are MAP_SHARED, MAP_PRIVATE, MAP_FIXED, and MAP_ANONYMOUS. The first two are mutually exclusive, so there are really just three independent binary flags:

- If MAP_PRIVATE is set, modifications to the mapped area are private to the process. If MAP_SHARED is set instead, modifications update the content of the mapped file. Other processes mapping the file in this fashion will also see the modified content.

- If MAP_FIXED is set, the area must be mapped *exactly* at the address specified by *start*. In this case, existing mappings in the range from *start* to *start* + *length* − 1 are unmapped before the new mapping is established (as if *munmap()* had been called). If MAP_FIXED is not set, the kernel is free to map the area at any address. In this case, the kernel chooses the final mapping address by searching the address space for an unused region of virtual memory that is large enough to hold the mapped area. If *start* is not NULL, this search begins at the specified address; otherwise, it begins at the map base (0x40000000 for IA-32). In both cases, the kernel searches only toward higher addresses. If no free region can be found, *mmap()* fails with ENOMEM.

- The MAP_ANONYMOUS flag can be set to create an area of anonymous memory. That is, the memory area being mapped is initially cleared to 0 and not associated with any file. Since no file is mapped, the *fd* argument is ignored. Similarly, the *offset*

Table 11.2. Translation rules for IA-32 protection bits.

Requested IA-32 protection bit	Corresponding IA-64 protection bits
PROT_NONE	PROT_NONE
PROT_READ	PROT_READ|PROT_EXEC
PROT_WRITE	PROT_READ|PROT_EXEC|PROT_WRITE
PROT_EXEC	PROT_READ|PROT_EXEC

argument serves no purposes and is usually set to 0. If MAP_ANONYMOUS is not set, the system call has the normal behavior of mapping a file.

Regardless of the settings of the *flags* argument, the system call always returns the address at which the object was mapped or -1 in the case of an error.

Considering this description, it might seem that if the IA-64 page size matches the IA-32 page size of 4 Kbytes, *mmap()* can be treated as a trivial system call. This is almost true, but a problem arises because of subtle differences in the handling of the page access rights specified in the *prot* argument. For IA-32, a page is either not accessible at all, readable, or writable. If the page is writable, it is also readable, and if it is readable, it is also executable. Since IA-64 supports a finer-grained protection model, effectively with separate bits for read, write, and execute rights, care needs to be taken to provide the page protection semantics that IA-32 applications expect. For example, when an IA-32 application maps a file, it might request only read permission, knowing full well that execution permission will be granted implicitly.

Table 11.2 illustrates how the individual IA-32 protection settings have to be mapped to IA-64 settings to provide the desired semantics. If multiple IA-32 bits are set in the *prot* argument, the union of the listed IA-64 protection bits must be used. To ensure that this mapping is applied consistently, the emulator defines an *IA-32 protection mapping routine* (*get_prot32()* in file arch/ia64/ia32/sys_ia32.c). It takes an integer argument that specifies a set of IA-32 protection bits and returns an integer with the corresponding IA-64 protection bits. With this routine, it is easy to translate the IA-32 *prot* argument to the corresponding IA-64 argument. Provided the IA-64 page size is 4 Kbytes, it is then possible to call the normal IA-64 system call handler of *mmap()*.

Now, if the IA-64 page size is larger than 4 Kbytes, translating the *prot* argument is not nearly enough. The problem is that the normal system call handler for *mmap()* executes successfully only if the arguments meet several constraints. Specifically, if MAP_FIXED has been specified, the starting address *start* must be page aligned. In the absence of this flag, the *start* argument serves only as a hint, so there is no alignment constraint. Implicitly, the ending address of the mapped area also must fall on a page boundary. If *start* + *len* is not page aligned, the kernel will automatically extend the size of the mapped area to force proper alignment. The *offset* argument always must be page aligned, regardless of the flag settings. This is strange since the argument is otherwise ignored for anonymous mappings (MAP_ANONYMOUS is set). Applications usually adhere to this constraint by passing 0.

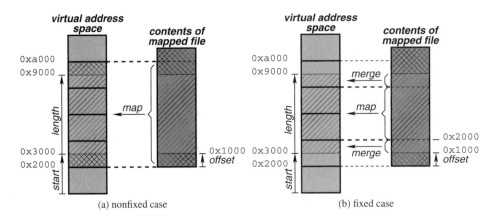

Figure 11.11. Emulating *mmap()*: fixed versus nonfixed mapping.

If we analyze the scenarios created by the different flag settings and mapping constraints, we find that there are two distinct issues: the first one is *mapping granularity*, and
the second one is *mapping congruence*. The former is easy to grasp: when Linux/ia64 employs a page size larger than 4 Kbytes, it is obviously possible for the starting and ending
addresses of a memory area to be 4-Kbyte aligned, but not page aligned. Thus, the IA-64
version of the *mmap()* handler might reject a mapping request as misaligned, even though
the mapped area is 4-Kbyte aligned. The second problem is more subtle, but equally important: the fact that both the starting address of the memory area and the file offset must be
page aligned implies that the memory content and the file content must be *congruent* with
each other. The easiest way to think of this constraint is that the beginning of the file must
always line up with a page boundary. Unfortunately, just as for the granularity problem, a
mapping that is congruent with 4-Kbyte pages is not necessarily congruent for any larger
page size, which creates another reason why the IA-64 version of the *mmap()* handler might
fail.

Let us focus on the mapping granularity problem first. It turns out that this problem
needs to be solved differently, depending on whether the mapping needs to be at a fixed
address (MAP_FIXED has been specified). The nonfixed case is easier to handle so we will
discuss it first.

The left half of Figure 11.11 illustrates the nonfixed case. It assumes that *mmap()* is
called to request the mapping of six 4-Kbyte pages worth of data (24 Kbytes) from a file
starting at file offset 0x1000. Furthermore, it assumes that the kernel picked a starting address 0x3000 for the mapping. The ending address would then be 0x9000, which means
that both the starting and the ending addresses are 4-Kbyte aligned but not aligned for any
larger page size, such as the 8-Kbyte page size assumed in the figure. Note that the congruence requirement prevents the emulator from fixing the problem by choosing a starting
address that is page aligned: if it were to do that, the beginning of the file would no longer
be page aligned and it merely would have turned the granularity problem into a congruence

problem. Given that the emulator has to live with the memory area not being page aligned, what can it do? The solution is to simply map a little too much of the file so that the starting address and the ending address of the expanded area fall on a page boundary. In the figure, the file content that was requested to be mapped is shown with diagonal shading and the rest of the file with cross shading. As illustrated there, the emulated *mmap()* ends up mapping the entire address range from 0x2000 to 0xa000, meaning that 4 Kbytes of extra file data get mapped on either end of the file area. This extended mapping approach is safe in the sense that every byte that was requested to be mapped ends up getting mapped. This is not to say that the emulation is perfect: there clearly are cases where an application could observe the difference. For example, an application might use such a mapping to protect against accesses to the first 4 Kbytes of file data. With the emulation, this protection would be lost. Fortunately, most applications do not rely on this.

The more difficult case is illustrated in the right half of Figure 11.11. When the MAP_FIXED flag has been specified, the emulator cannot simply expand the area being mapped. The reason is that the additional virtual memory area that would be covered by the expanded mapping might be needed for other existing or future mappings. Thus, instead of expanding the mapping, the emulator *shrinks* it such that both the starting and ending addresses fall on a page boundary.

Of course, that leaves the question of what to do with the file content that corresponds to the partial pages that do not get mapped. The emulator handles these by creating new anonymous pages that are initialized with the merged content of the remaining file area and the previous content of the page. This merging is achieved by the *subpage mapping routine* (*mmap_subpage()* in file arch/ia64/ia32/sys_ia32.c). In our example, this routine would map the file content from offset 0x1000 to 0x2000 by making a copy of the page at address 0x2000 and copying the file content to the second half of the copied page. Once the content has been merged in this fashion, the copied page is installed at address 0x2000 and substitutes whatever page was mapped there previously.

This approach ensures that the *content* of the entire mapped area is correct, but of course it does not guarantee that the *sharing properties* are preserved. For example, if the file content was mapped with the MAP_SHARED flag set, once the beginning and ending 4 Kbytes of the file content have been copied to anonymous pages, modifications to the copied areas would no longer be reflected in the file content. Of course, the sharing property of the previously existing portion of the copied page may also be broken. Clearly, this creates differences that could easily be visible to applications. Yet it is the best the emulator can do short of resorting to unreasonably expensive emulation methods such as trapping and simulating each memory access to such subpages. Fortunately, it turns out that even though there clearly is a potential for serious problems, in practice the solution works extremely well. This is largely because Linux applications are encouraged to avoid using the MAP_FIXED flag as much as possible. Indeed, the runtime loader is one of the few applications that makes frequent use of this flag, and it never uses the MAP_SHARED flag, so there is no real problem here. Still, the emulator attempts to detect whenever MAP_FIXED and MAP_SHARED are used together and in combination with misaligned addresses. If it detects such a case, it prints a warning message on the system console. The appearance of such a warning message indicates the definite potential for an emulated application not

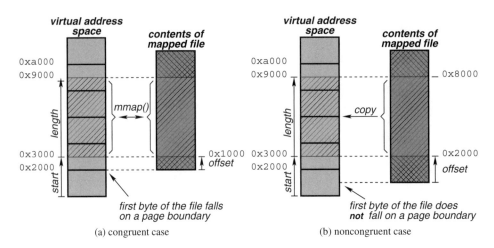

Figure 11.12. Emulating *mmap()*: congruent versus noncongruent mapping.

working properly and may be a sign that a Linux/ia64 kernel with a 4-Kbyte page size should be used instead.

Figure 11.12 illustrates the mapping congruence problem and its solution. The left half of the figure shows that as long as the first byte of the mapped file falls on a page boundary, there is no problem and whatever area needs to be mapped can be mapped directly with the IA-64 version of the *mmap()* handler. Note that if the MAP_ANONYMOUS flag is set, no file is involved and the congruence problem cannot occur. On the other hand, the right half of the figure illustrates a case where the first byte of a mapped file does not fall on a page boundary. In this particular case, we assume that the file area from offset 0x2000 to 0x8000 should be mapped at virtual address 0x3000. Since the first byte of the file falls on 0x1000, i.e., the middle of an 8-Kbyte page, the mapping is incongruent and it is impossible to use the IA-64 version of the *mmap()* handler. To fix this, the emulator allocates anonymous memory for the entire mapped address range and explicitly copies the file content to this memory. As with the subpage mapping in the MAP_FIXED case, this preserves the *content*, but not the *sharing properties* of the mapping. Fortunately, for non-fixed mappings, the emulator can always pick a mapping address that ensures congruence. And, as we explained earlier, applications seldom use MAP_FIXED in combination with MAP_SHARED, so this situation occurs rarely in practice.

In summary, the emulator handles *mmap()* on Linux/ia64 machines with a page size larger than 4 Kbytes by *expanding* nonfixed mappings. Fixed mappings are handled by being *shrunk* if necessary. In such cases, the emulator maps the leftover subpages by merging their content with the old page content. For congruent mappings, normal *mmap()* semantics are used for the possibly expanded or shrunk areas, whereas for incongruent mappings, the file content is copied to anonymous memory and the sharing properties are lost. In practice, this means that the IA-32 version of *mmap()* can be emulated almost perfectly except for the cases in which both the MAP_FIXED and MAP_SHARED flags are set and the start address or the file offset is not page aligned.

11.2.6   Signal delivery

Just as the emulator needs to take care of translating IA-32 state to IA-64 state during a system call, it must perform the reverse translation when delivering a signal. Delivery is surprisingly simple: outside the emulator, the kernel treats signal delivery to IA-32 tasks exactly the same as for IA-64 tasks. The user level, of course, employs the normal IA-32 signal handling conventions, so the emulator is responsible for translating between the two domains. This translation layer is implemented in the *IA-32 signal emulator* (file arch/ia64/ia32/ia32_signal.c). This portion of the emulator greatly benefits from the fact that most signal-related data structures are either the same or at least very similar in their IA-32 and IA-64 incarnations. For instance, all signal numbers are the same, signal sets have identical layout, and the siginfo structure has the same members. The only data structure that is significantly different is the sigcontext structure. Indeed, since the IA-32 machine state is so different from the IA-64 machine state, the two versions have almost nothing in common. But even so, translating the user-level machine state to an IA-32 sigcontext structure and back is straightforward. For example, in the IA-32 sigcontext, member *eax* stores the user-level value of register EAX. Since the IVE maps this register to IA-64 register r8, copying the user-level value of EAX to the sigcontext structure simply requires copying the least significant 32 bits from the r8 member of the pt-regs structure. The analog applies for the other members.

One slightly tricky problem arises from the fact that the IA-32 version of the sigaction structure contains the member *sa_restorer*, which is absent in the IA-64 version. As described in Chapter 5, *Kernel Entry and Exit*, this member can be used to simplify and accelerate signal delivery. This works as follows: when an application registers a signal handler by calling the *sigaction()* system call stub, the C library intercepts the call and sets the *sa_restorer* member in the sigaction structure to the address of a small routine whose sole purpose is to invoke system call *sigreturn()*. The C library also sets the SA_RESTORER flag in sigaction, and then forwards the call to the real *sigaction()* system call. When the time comes to deliver a signal, the kernel checks the SA_RESTORER flag and, if it is set, the kernel creates a signal frame such that when the signal handler returns, the routine at address *sa_restorer* is invoked. Once execution reaches that point, the CPU will immediately execute the *sigreturn()* system call and thereby complete the delivery of the signal. This approach allows IA-32 Linux to avoid dynamic code generation during signal delivery. And since dynamic code generation tends to be slow on modern CPUs, using *sa_restorer* is not just simpler, but also faster.

Given how this member is used, it is clear that the IA-32 signal emulator must be able to keep track of the *sa_restorer* value that has been established for each signal. That way, when the time comes and a signal needs to be delivered, the emulator can recover the appropriate value for *sa_restorer*. To support this, Linux provides a table of sigaction structures in the task structure, but since this table contains the IA-64 version of sigaction, there is no obvious place to store the IA-32 *sa_restorer* field. Fortunately, a little trick

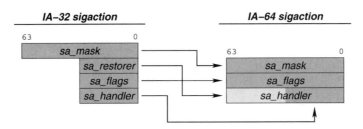

Figure 11.13. Mapping IA-32 sigaction to IA-64 version.

solves this problem: since the IA-32 sigaction members *sa_handler* and *sa_restorer* are only 32 bits wide, the emulator can simply pack them together and store them in the 64-bit-wide *sa_handler* member of the IA-64 version of this structure. This is illustrated in Figure 11.13.

As shown there, the IA-32 version of *sa_handler* is stored in the low-order 32 bits of the IA-64 *sa_handler*, and the high-order bits hold the IA-32 *sa_restorer* member. For this to really work, care needs to be taken when a special signal handler is established for an IA-32 signal. If it is set to one of SIG_DFL, SIG_IGN, or SIG_ERR, the 64-bit sign-extended version of these values must be stored in the IA-64 version of *sa_handler*. The reason is that the platform-independent signal handling code is unaware of the packing used by the emulator and if this code wanted to find out, e.g., whether a signal uses the default disposition, it would simply compare the IA-64 *sa_handler* with SIG_DFL. Storing the sign-extended version of the special values ensures that such comparisons will continue to work. To ensure that the IA-32 to IA-64 transformation is applied consistently, the emulator defines and uses a simple routine called the *IA-32 sigaction handler setter* (*sigact_set_handler()* in file arch/ia64/ia32/ia32_signal.c). This routine takes three arguments: a pointer to an IA-64 sigaction structure and two 32-bit values corresponding to the IA-32 *sa_handler* and *sa_restorer* members. Given these arguments, it encodes the IA-32 values in the sigaction structure, taking care of sign-extending any special signal handler values if necessary.

11.2.7 Accessing I/O port space

The IA-32 architecture provides special IN and OUT instructions for accessing the legacy I/O space (see Chapter 7, *Device I/O*, for a description of this space). When IVE encounters such an instruction, it uses the IOBASE register (ar.k0) to translate the instruction to a corresponding memory access. IN is translated to a memory read, OUT to a memory write, and the port number *p* specified in the instruction is translated to a virtual memory address according to the following formula:

    IOBASE + ((p & 0xfff) | ((p >> 2) << 12)).

With this translation, each 4-Kbyte–aligned memory area corresponds to four I/O ports. Recall from Chapter 7, *Device I/O*, that this is exactly the same encoding as that used for the memory-mapped IA-64 legacy I/O space. This means that the emulator can grant a suitably privileged IA-32 task direct access to the legacy I/O space by mapping the physical address range of this space into the task's virtual address space and placing the starting address of the mapped region in IOBASE. This is indeed the approach that the emulator uses for implementing the IA-32 version of the *iopl()* (I/O privilege level) and *ioperm()* (I/O permission) system calls. Applications with root privileges or the raw I/O capability (CAP_SYS_RAWIO) can call *iopl()* to gain access to the entire I/O port space or *ioperm()* to gain access to a specific range of ports. However, for simplicity, the emulator ignores the port range specified by *ioperm()* and, just like *iopl()*, simply enables or disables access to the entire space. This simplified implementation is slightly less secure than a proper implementation would be, but it is hardly an issue in practice because few applications use this system call and because privileged tasks have many other ways to disrupt the proper operation of a machine.

One question that we still need to answer is what virtual address the emulator should use to map the I/O port space. This choice is not critical, and the only real constraint is that the address must be aligned to a 64-Mbyte boundary. Of course, it is also desirable for the virtual address to be above 4 Gbytes, so that there is no risk of an IA-32 task accessing this region accidentally. For this reason, the emulator maps the I/O port space at the beginning of the second region, i.e., at address 0x2000000000000000. Note that since IVE accesses legacy I/O space through virtual space, the normal page protection mechanism could be used to grant or deny access to specific ports. The granularity for this would be 4 ports per 4-Kbyte page, 8 ports with 8-Kbyte pages, and so on. Moreover, the I/O bitmap in the TSS could be used to control access to the first 1024 ports on a port-by-port basis. However, as described previously, *ioperm()* does not take advantage of either facility and simply grants or denies access to the entire legacy I/O space.

11.3 SUMMARY

In this chapter we described how Linux/ia64 provides backward compatibility with IA-32 Linux application. The necessary support is realized as two components: the IVE, which is an IA-32 instruction set emulator defined by the IA-64 architecture and the IA-32 Linux emulator. The two combine to provide IA-32 Linux applications the illusion of running on a traditional Pentium III Linux machine. A key aspect is that this support is well isolated and entirely optional. At some point, backward compatibility will not be important anymore, and at that time, the extra complexity created by it can be shed both from the kernel and the architecture itself. In other words, the IA-32 support has been designed carefully to enable a smooth transition to IA-64 while keeping open the possibility of building simplified, legacy-free CPUs and operating systems.

Appendix A

IA-64 CPU MODELS

	Itanium	*McKinley (code name)*
Physical stacked registers:	96	96
Region ID width:	18 bits	24 bits
Physical address:	44 bits	50 bits
Virtual address:	54 bits	64 bits
Pipeline depth:	10 stages	8 stages
Issue width:	2 bundles/cycle	2 bundles/cycle
integer units:	4	6
memory units:	2	4 (2 load, 2 store)
System bus bandwidth:	2.1 Gbyte/s	6.4 Gbyte/s
L1 cache size	2 × 16 Kbytes	2 × 16 Kbytes
type:	split	split
associativity:	4-way	4-way
line size:	32 bytes	64 bytes
load latency:	2 cycles	1 cycle
L2 cache size	96 Kbytes	256 Kbytes
type:	unified	unified
associativity:	6-way	8-way
line size:	64 bytes	128 bytes
load latency:	6 cycles	5 cycles
L3 cache size	2 or 4 Mbytes	3 Mbytes
type:	unified, off-chip	unified, on-chip
associativity:	4-way	12-way
line size:	64 bytes	128 bytes
load latency:	21 cycles	12 cycles
L1 TLB entries	32 data, 64 instruction	2 × 32
type:	split	split
associativity:	full	full
L2 TLB entries	96 data	2 × 128
type:	data only	split
associativity:	full	full

Appendix B

KERNEL REGISTER USAGE

GENERAL REGISTERS

Register	Alias	Description
r1	gp	global pointer: points to current short data segment
r12	sp	stack pointer: current kernel stack pointer
r13	tp	thread pointer: *current* task pointer

KERNEL REGISTERS

Register	Description
ar.k0	IA-64: physical legacy I/O base; IA-32: virtual legacy I/O base
ar.k1	IA-64: *unused*; IA-32: task state segment descriptor (TSSD)
ar.k2	*unused*
ar.k3	*unused*
ar.k4	pointer to kernel page mapped by translation register dtr2
ar.k5	pointer to task structure that owns floating-point high partition
ar.k6	physical address of task structure of currently executing task
ar.k7	physical address of global directory (page table) of current process

TRANSLATION REGISTERS

Register	Description
itr0	maps kernel code
itr1	maps PALcode
dtr0	maps kernel data
dtr1	maps per-CPU page
dtr2	maps current kernel stack (unless already mapped by dtr0)

Appendix C

IA-64 INSTRUCTIONS

This appendix provides a complete listing of all IA-64 instructions. The instructions are grouped into eight tables according to their primary function. Each line in the table provides a synopsis of the instruction format, the type of units on which the instruction can execute (M, I, B, F, or X), and a brief description. The tables list only the major opcodes of the instructions; suffixes are omitted. For example, the integer compare instruction uses different suffixes to indicate the exact kind of comparison to perform. Comparison for equality uses a suffix of .eq, and comparison for inequality uses a suffix of .neq, but in the table below, these forms are represented by the single entry for cmp. Furthermore, curly braces are used to compact minor variations of the same instruction. For example, czx{1,2} represents the two instructions czx1 and czx2 because they perform the same basic operation (compute zero index) except that the former interprets the contents in the operand register as a sequence of eight bytes and the latter as a sequence of four 16-bit words.

For operands, r represents a general (integer) register, p a predicate register, b a branch register, ar an application register, cr a control register, and f a floating-point register. Branch targets are represented by L, and immediate (constant) values by n. If the same type of operand can occur multiple times, each occurrence is numbered with a subscript (e.g., r_1 and r_2 for the first two general registers). Certain operands can accept multiple types; for those, the tables list the acceptable types separated by vertical bars. For example, $r|n$ is an operand that can be either a general register or an immediate value.

C.1 INTEGER INSTRUCTIONS

Table C.1: Integer instructions.

Instruction Synopsis		Unit	Description
(p_q) add	$r_1 = r_2|n, r_3$	MI	integer add
(p_q) addp4	$r_1 = r_2|n, r_3$	MI	add 32-bit pointer
(p_q) and	$r_1 = r_2|n, r_3$	MI	logical AND
(p_q) andcm	$r_1 = r_2|n, r_3$	MI	logical AND with complement
(p_q) cmp	$p_1, p_2 = r_1|n, r_2$	MI	integer compare
(p_q) cmp4	$p_1, p_2 = r_1|n, r_2$	MI	32-bit integer compare
(p_q) dep	$r_1 = r_2|n, r_3, n_b, n_l$	I	deposit bit field

...continued on next page

Table C.1: Integer instructions *(continued)*.

Instruction Synopsis		Unit	Description
(p_q) dep.z	$r_1 = r_2 \| n, n_b, n_l$	I	deposit zero bit field
(p_q) extr	$r_1 = r_2, n_b, n_l$	I	extract bit field
(p_q) fand	$f_1 = f_2, f_3$	F	fp logical AND
(p_q) fandcm	$f_1 = f_2, f_3$	F	fp logical AND with complement
(p_q) fmix	$f_1 = f_2, f_3$	F	fp mix
(p_q) for	$f_1 = f_2, f_3$	F	fp logical OR
(p_q) fswap	$f_1 = f_2, f_3$	F	fp swap
(p_q) getf	$r = f$	M	get fp register contents
(p_q) mov	$r = ar$	MI	move from application register
(p_q) mov	$ar = r \| n$	MI	move to application register
(p_q) mov	$r = b$	I	move from branch register
(p_q) mov	$r_1 = ireg[r_2]$	M	move from indirect register
(p_q) mov	$ireg[r_1] = r_2$	M	move to indirect register
(p_q) mov	$r = ip$	I	read instruction pointer
(p_q) mov	$r = pr$	I	read predicate registers
(p_q) mov	$pr = r, n$	I	write predicate registers
(p_q) mov	$pr.rot = n$	I	write rotating predicate registers
(p_q) mov	$r = psr.um$	M	read user mask
(p_q) mov	$psr.um = r$	M	write user mask
(p_q) movl	$r = n$	X	load 64-bit constant
(p_q) nop	n	MIBFX	no operation
(p_q) or	$r_1 = r_2 \| n, r_3$	MI	logical OR
(p_q) popcnt	$r_1 = r_2$	I	population count
(p_q) setf	$f = r$	M	set fp register contents
(p_q) shladd	$r_1 = r_2, n, r_3$	MI	shift left and add
(p_q) shladdp4	$r_1 = r_2, n, r_3$	MI	shift left and add 32-bit pointer
(p_q) shr	$r_1 = r_2, r_3 \| n$	I	shift right
(p_q) shrp	$r_1 = r_2, r_3, n$	I	shift right pair
(p_q) sub	$r_1 = r_2 \| n, r_3$	MI	integer subtract
(p_q) sxt{1,2,4}	$r_1 = r_2$	I	sign-extend
(p_q) tbit	$p_1, p_2 = r, n$	I	test bit
(p_q) tnat	$p_1, p_2 = r$	I	test NaT bit
(p_q) xma	$f_1 = f_2, f_3, f_4$	F	integer multiply-and-add
(p_q) xor	$r_1 = r_2 \| n, r_3$	MI	logical exclusive-OR
(p_q) zxt{1,2,4}	$r_1 = r_2$	I	zero-extend

C.2 MEMORY INSTRUCTIONS

Table C.2: Memory instructions.

Instruction Synopsis		Unit	Description
(p_q) ld{1,2,4,8}	$r_1 = [r_2]$	M	load
(p_q) ld{1,2,4,8}	$r_1 = [r_2], r_3\|n$	M	load with post-increment
(p_q) ldf{s,d,e,8}	$f = [r]$	M	fp load
(p_q) ldf{s,d,e,8}	$f = [r_1], r_2\|n$	M	fp load with post-increment
(p_q) ldfp{s,d,8}	$f_1, f_2 = [r]$	M	parallel fp load
(p_q) ldfp{s,d,8}	$f_1, f_2 = [r], n$	M	parallel fp load with post-increment
(p_q) st{1,2,4,8}	$[r_1] = r_2$	M	store
(p_q) st{1,2,4,8}	$[r_1] = r_2, n$	M	store with post-increment
(p_q) stf{s,d,e,8}	$[r] = f$	M	fp store
(p_q) stf{s,d,e,8}	$[r] = f, n$	M	fp store with post-increment

C.3 SEMAPHORE INSTRUCTIONS

Table C.3: Semaphore instructions.

Instruction Synopsis		Unit	Description
(p_q) cmpxchg{1,2,4,8}	$r_1 = [r_2], r_3$, ar.ccv	M	atomic compare-and-exchange
(p_q) fetchadd{4,8}	$r_1 = [r_2], n$	M	atomic fetch-and-add
(p_q) xchg{1,2,4,8}	$r_1 = [r_2], r_3$	M	exchange

C.4 BRANCH INSTRUCTIONS

Table C.4: Branch instructions.

Instruction Synopsis		Unit	Description
(p_q) br.call	$b_1 = L\|b_2$	B	call subroutine
br.{ctop|cexit}	L	B	modulo-scheduled counted loop branch
br.cloop	L	B	counted loop branch
(p_q) br.cond	$L\|b$	B	conditional branch
br.ia	b	B	branch to IA-32 code
(p_q) br.ret	b	B	return from subroutine
(p_q) br.{wtop|wexit}	L	B	modulo-scheduled **while**-loop branch
(p_q) brl.call	$b = L$	X	long call subroutine
(p_q) brl.cond	L	X	conditional long branch

...continued on next page

Table C.4: Branch instructions *(continued)*.

Instruction Synopsis		Unit	Description
brp	$L_1\|b, L_2$	B	predict branch
(p_q) chk	$r\|f, L$	MI	speculation check
(p_q) fchkf	L	F	fp check flags
(p_q) mov	$b = r, L$	I	move to branch register

C.5   CONTROL INSTRUCTIONS

Table C.5: Control instructions.

Instruction Synopsis		Unit	Description
alloc	$r=\text{ar.pfs},n_i,n_l,n_o,n_r$	M	resize stack frame
(p_q) break	n	MIBFX	break (stop) execution
clrrrb		B	clear rotating register base
cover		B	cover stack frame
(p_q) fc	r	M	flush cache line
flushrs		M	flush register stack
(p_q) fwb		M	flush write buffers
(p_q) invala		M	invalidate ALAT
(p_q) lfetch	$[r_1]$	M	prefetch cache line
(p_q) lfetch	$[r_1], r_2\|n$	M	prefetch cache line with post-increment
loadrs		M	load register stack
(p_q) mf		M	memory fence
(p_q) rum	n	M	reset user mask
(p_q) srlz		M	serialize
(p_q) sum	n	M	set user mask
(p_q) sync.i		M	memory synchronization

C.6   MULTIMEDIA INSTRUCTIONS

Table C.6: Multimedia instructions.

Instruction Synopsis		Unit	Description
(p_q) czx{1,2}	$r_1 = r_2$	I	compute zero index
(p_q) mix{1,2,4}	$r_1 = r_2, r_3$	I	mix
(p_q) mux{1,2}	$r_1 = r_2, n$	I	permute register
(p_q) pack{2,4}	$r_1 = r_2, r_3$	I	pack register
(p_q) padd{1,2,4}	$r_1 = r_2, r_3$	MI	parallel add

...continued on next page

Table C.6: Multimedia instructions *(continued)*.

Instruction Synopsis		Unit	Description
(p_q) pavg{1,2}	$r_1 = r_2, r_3$	MI	parallel average
(p_q) pavgsub{1,2}	$r_1 = r_2, r_3$	MI	parallel average subtract
(p_q) pcmp{1,2,4}	$r_1 = r_2, r_3$	MI	parallel compare
(p_q) pmax{1,2}	$r_1 = r_2, r_3$	I	parallel maximum
(p_q) pmin{1,2}	$r_1 = r_2, r_3$	I	parallel minimum
(p_q) pmpy2	$r_1 = r_2, r_3$	I	parallel multiply
(p_q) pmpyshr2	$r_1 = r_2, r_3, n$	I	parallel multiply and shift right
(p_q) psad1	$r_1 = r_2, r_3$	I	parallel sum of absolute difference
(p_q) pshl{2,4}	$r_1 = r_2, r_3 \vert n$	I	parallel shift left
(p_q) pshladd2	$r_1 = r_2, n, r_3$	MI	parallel shift left and add
(p_q) pshr{2,4}	$r_1 = r_2, r_3 \vert n$	I	parallel shift right
(p_q) pshradd2	$r_1 = r_2, n, r_3$	MI	parallel shift right and add
(p_q) psub{1,2,4}	$r_1 = r_2, r_3$	MI	parallel subtract
(p_q) unpack{1,2,4}	$r_1 = r_2, r_3$	I	unpack register

C.7 FLOATING-POINT INSTRUCTIONS

Table C.7: Floating-point instructions.

Instruction Synopsis		Unit	Description
(p_q) famax	$f_1 = f_2, f_3$	F	fp absolute maximum
(p_q) famin	$f_1 = f_2, f_3$	F	fp absolute minimum
(p_q) fclass	$p_1, p_2 = f, n$	F	fp class
(p_q) fclrf		F	clear fp flags
(p_q) fcmp	$p_1, p_2 = f_1, f_2$	F	fp compare
(p_q) fcvt	$f_1 = f_2$	F	fp/integer conversion
(p_q) fma	$f_1 = f_2, f_3, f_4$	F	fp multiply-and-add
(p_q) fmax	$f_1 = f_2, f_3$	F	fp maximum
(p_q) fmerge	$f_1 = f_2, f_3$	F	fp merge
(p_q) fmin	$f_1 = f_2, f_3$	F	fp minimum
(p_q) fms	$f_1 = f_2, f_3, f_4$	F	fp multiply-and-subtract
(p_q) fnma	$f_1 = f_2, f_3, f_4$	F	fp negative multiply-and-add
(p_q) fpack	$f_1 = f_2, f_3$	F	fp pack register
(p_q) fpamax	$f_1 = f_2, f_3$	F	fp parallel absolute maximum
(p_q) fpamin	$f_1 = f_2, f_3$	F	fp parallel absolute minimum
(p_q) fpcmp	$f_1 = f_2, f_3$	F	fp parallel compare
(p_q) fpcvt	$f_1 = f_2$	F	parallel fp/integer conversion
(p_q) fpma	$f_1 = f_2, f_3, f_4$	F	fp parallel multiply-and-add
(p_q) fpmax	$f_1 = f_2, f_3$	F	fp parallel maximum
(p_q) fpmerge	$f_1 = f_2, f_3$	F	fp parallel merge
(p_q) fpmin	$f_1 = f_2, f_3$	F	fp parallel minimum

...continued on next page

Table C.7: Floating-point instructions *(continued)*.

Instruction Synopsis		Unit	Description
(p_q) fpms	$f_1 = f_2, f_3, f_4$	F	fp parallel multiply-and-subtract
(p_q) fpnma	$f_1 = f_2, f_3, f_4$	F	fp parallel negative multiply-and-add
(p_q) fprcpa	$f_1, p = f_2, f_3$	F	fp parallel reciprocal approx.
(p_q) fprsqrta	$f_1, p = f_2$	F	fp parallel reciprocal square root approx.
(p_q) frcpa	$f_1, p = f_2, f_3$	F	fp reciprocal approx.
(p_q) frsqrta	$f_1, p = f_2$	F	fp reciprocal square root approx.
(p_q) fselect	$f_1 = f_2, f_3, f_4$	F	fp select
(p_q) fsetc	n_1, n_2	F	fp set controls
(p_q) fsxt	$f_1 = f_2, f_3$	F	fp sign-extend

C.8   PRIVILEGED INSTRUCTIONS

Table C.8: Privileged instructions.

Instruction Synopsis		Unit	Description
bsw		B	switch register bank
epc		B	enter privileged code
(p_q) itc	r	M	insert translation cache
(p_q) itr.d	$dtr[r] = r_2$	M	insert data translation register
(p_q) itr.i	$itr[r] = r_2$	M	insert instruction translation register
(p_q) mov	$cr = r$	M	move to control register
(p_q) mov	$r = cr$	M	move from control register
(p_q) mov	$r = psr$	M	move from processor status register
(p_q) mov	$psr.l = r$	M	move to low processor status register
(p_q) probe	$r_1 = r_2, r_3\|n$	M	probe access
(p_q) probe.{r,w,rw}.fault	r, n	M	probe access, faulting version
(p_q) ptc	r_1, r_2	M	purge translation cache
(p_q) ptc.e	r	M	purge translation cache entry
(p_q) ptr	r_1, r_2	M	purge translation register
rfi		B	return from interruption
(p_q) rsm	n	M	reset system mask
(p_q) ssm	n	M	set system mask
(p_q) tak	$r_1 = r_2$	M	translation access key
(p_q) thash	$r_1 = r_2$	M	translation hashed entry address
(p_q) tpa	$r_1 = r_2$	M	translate to physical address
(p_q) ttag	$r_1 = r_2$	M	translation hashed entry tag

ITANIUM PMU EVENTS

Table D.1: Itanium PMU event list.

ALAT Events	
ALAT_INST_CHKA_LDC.ALL	ALAT_INST_FAILED_CHKA_LDC.INTEGER
ALAT_INST_CHKA_LDC.FP	ALAT_REPLACEMENT.ALL
ALAT_INST_CHKA_LDC.INTEGER	ALAT_REPLACEMENT.FP
ALAT_INST_FAILED_CHKA_LDC.ALL	ALAT_REPLACEMENT.INTEGER
ALAT_INST_FAILED_CHKA_LDC.FP	
Miscellaneous Execution Events	
ALL_STOPS_DISPERSED	EXPL_STOPS_DISPERSED
CPU_CPL_CHANGES	INST_ACCESS_CYCLE
CPU_CYCLES	INST_DISPERSED
DATA_ACCESS_CYCLE	MEMORY_CYCLE
DEPENDENCY_ALL_CYCLE	UNSTALLED_BACKEND_CYCLE
DEPENDENCY_SCOREBOARD_CYCLE	
Instructions Retirement Events	
DATA_REFERENCES_RETIRED	LOADS_RETIRED
FP_OPS_RETIRED_HI	MISALIGNED_LOADS_RETIRED
FP_OPS_RETIRED_LO	MISALIGNED_STORES_RETIRED
IA32_INST_RETIRED	NOPS_RETIRED
IA64_INST_RETIRED	PREDICATE_SQUASHED_RETIRED
IA64_TAGGED_INST_RETIRED.ALL	RSE_LOADS_RETIRED
IA64_TAGGED_INST_RETIRED.PMC8	RSE_REFERENCES_RETIRED
IA64_TAGGED_INST_RETIRED.PMC9	STORES_RETIRED
INST_FAILED_CHKS_RETIRED.ALL	UC_LOADS_RETIRED
INST_FAILED_CHKS_RETIRED.FP	UC_STORE_RETIRED
INST_FAILED_CHKS_RETIRED.INTEGER	
TLB Events	
DTC_MISSES	ITLB_INSERTS_HPW
DTLB_INSERTS_HPW	ITLB_MISSES_FETCH
DTLB_MISSES	
Cache Events	
ISB_LINES_IN	L3_MISSES
L1D_READS_RETIRED	L3_READS.ALL_READS.ALL

... continued on next page

Table D.1: Itanium PMU event list *(continued)*.

L1D_READ_FORCED_MISSES_RETIRED	L3_READS.ALL_READS.HIT
L1D_READ_MISSES_RETIRED	L3_READS.ALL_READS.MISS
L1I_DEMAND_READS	L3_READS.DATA_READS.ALL
L1I_FILLS	L3_READS.DATA_READS.HIT
L1I_PREFETCH_READS	L3_READS.DATA_READS.MISS
L2_DATA_REFERENCES.ALL	L3_READS.INST_READS.ALL
L2_DATA_REFERENCES.READS	L3_READS.INST_READS.HIT
L2_DATA_REFERENCES.WRITES	L3_READS.INST_READS.MISS
L2_FLUSHES	L3_REFERENCES
L2_FLUSH_DETAILS.ADDR_CONFLICT	L3_WRITES.ALL_WRITES.ALL
L2_FLUSH_DETAILS.BUS_REJECT	L3_WRITES.ALL_WRITES.HIT
L2_FLUSH_DETAILS.FULL_FLUSH	L3_WRITES.ALL_WRITES.MISS
L2_FLUSH_DETAILS.ST_BUFFER_FLUSH	L3_WRITES.DATA_WRITES.ALL
L2_INST_DEMAND_READS	L3_WRITES.DATA_WRITES.HIT
L2_INST_PREFETCH_READS	L3_WRITES.DATA_WRITES.MISS
L2_MISSES	L3_WRITES.L2_WRITEBACK.ALL
L2_REFERENCES	L3_WRITES.L2_WRITEBACK.HIT
L3_LINE_REPLACED	L3_WRITES.L2_WRITEBACK.MISS
Pipeline Events	
PIPELINE_ALL_FLUSH_CYCLE	PIPELINE_FLUSH.IEU_FLUSH
PIPELINE_BACKEND_FLUSH_CYCLE	PIPELINE_FLUSH.L1D_WAYMP_FLUSH
PIPELINE_FLUSH.DTC_FLUSH	PIPELINE_FLUSH.OTHER_FLUSH
Floating-point Events	
FP_FLUSH_TO_ZERO	FP_SIR_FLUSH
Bus Events	
BUS_ALL.ANY	BUS_RD_DATA.ANY
BUS_ALL.IO	BUS_RD_DATA.IO
BUS_ALL.SELF	BUS_RD_DATA.SELF
BUS_BRQ_LIVE_REQ_HI	BUS_RD_HIT
BUS_BRQ_LIVE__REQ_LO	BUS_RD_HITM
BUS_BRQ_READ_REQ_INSERTED	BUS_RD_INVAL.ANY
BUS_BURST.ANY	BUS_RD_INVAL.IO
BUS_BURST.IO	BUS_RD_INVAL.SELF
BUS_BURST.SELF	BUS_RD_INVAL_BST.ANY
BUS_HITM	BUS_RD_INVAL_BST.IO
BUS_IO.ANY	BUS_RD_INVAL_BST.SELF
BUS_IO.SELF	BUS_RD_INVAL_BST_HITM
BUS_IOQ_LIVE_REQ_HI	BUS_RD_INVAL_HITM
BUS_IOQ_LIVE_REQ_LO	BUS_RD_IO.ANY
BUS_LOCK.ANY	BUS_RD_IO.SELF
BUS_LOCK_CYCLES.ANY	BUS_RD_PRTL
BUS_MEMORY.ANY	BUS_SNOOPS.ANY
BUS_MEMORY.IO	BUS_SNOOPS_HITM.ANY
BUS_MEMORY.SELF	BUS_SNOOPS_REQ
BUS_PARTIAL.ANY	BUS_SNOOPS_STALL_CYCLES.ANY

. . . continued on next page

Table D.1: Itanium PMU event list *(continued)*.

BUS_PARTIAL.IO	BUS_SNOOPS_STALL_CYCLES.SELF
BUS_PARTIAL.SELF	BUS_WR_WB.ANY
BUS_RD_ALL.ANY	BUS_WR_WB.IO
BUS_RD_ALL.IO	BUS_WR_WB.SELF
BUS_RD_ALL.SELF	

Table D.2: Itanium PMU branch event list.

Multiway Branch Events
BRANCH_MULTIWAY.ALL_PATHS.ALL_PREDICTIONS
BRANCH_MULTIWAY.ALL_PATHS.ALL_PREDICTIONS
BRANCH_MULTIWAY.ALL_PATHS.CORRECT_PREDICTIONS
BRANCH_MULTIWAY.ALL_PATHS.WRONG_PATH
BRANCH_MULTIWAY.ALL_PATHS.WRONG_TARGET
BRANCH_MULTIWAY.NOT_TAKEN.ALL_PREDICTIONS
BRANCH_MULTIWAY.NOT_TAKEN.CORRECT_PREDICTIONS
BRANCH_MULTIWAY.NOT_TAKEN.WRONG_PATH
BRANCH_MULTIWAY.NOT_TAKEN.WRONG_TARGET
BRANCH_MULTIWAY.TAKEN.ALL_PREDICTIONS
BRANCH_MULTIWAY.TAKEN.CORRECT_PREDICTIONS
BRANCH_MULTIWAY.TAKEN.WRONG_PATH
BRANCH_MULTIWAY.TAKEN.WRONG_TARGET
Branch Outcome Events
BRANCH_PATH.1ST_STAGE.NT_OUTCOMES_CORRECTLY_PREDICTED
BRANCH_PATH.1ST_STAGE.NT_OUTCOMES_INCORRECTLY_PREDICTED
BRANCH_PATH.1ST_STAGE.TK_OUTCOMES_CORRECTLY_PREDICTED
BRANCH_PATH.1ST_STAGE.TK_OUTCOMES_INCORRECTLY_PREDICTED
BRANCH_PATH.2ND_STAGE.NT_OUTCOMES_CORRECTLY_PREDICTED
BRANCH_PATH.2ND_STAGE.NT_OUTCOMES_INCORRECTLY_PREDICTED
BRANCH_PATH.2ND_STAGE.TK_OUTCOMES_CORRECTLY_PREDICTED
BRANCH_PATH.2ND_STAGE.TK_OUTCOMES_INCORRECTLY_PREDICTED
BRANCH_PATH.3ND_STAGE.NT_OUTCOMES_CORRECTLY_PREDICTED
BRANCH_PATH.3ND_STAGE.NT_OUTCOMES_INCORRECTLY_PREDICTED
BRANCH_PATH.3ND_STAGE.TK_OUTCOMES_CORRECTLY_PREDICTED
BRANCH_PATH.3ND_STAGE.TK_OUTCOMES_INCORRECTLY_PREDICTED
BRANCH_PATH.ALL.NT_OUTCOMES_CORRECTLY_PREDICTED
BRANCH_PATH.ALL.NT_OUTCOMES_INCORRECTLY_PREDICTED
BRANCH_PATH.ALL.TK_OUTCOMES_CORRECTLY_PREDICTED
BRANCH_PATH.ALL.TK_OUTCOMES_INCORRECTLY_PREDICTED
Branch Predicator Events
BRANCH_PREDICATOR.1ST_STAGE.ALL_PREDICTIONS
BRANCH_PREDICATOR.1ST_STAGE.CORRECT_PREDICTIONS
BRANCH_PREDICATOR.1ST_STAGE.WRONG_PATH

. . . continued on next page

Table D.2: Itanium PMU branch event list *(continued)*.

BRANCH_PREDICATOR.1ST_STAGE.WRONG_TARGET	
BRANCH_PREDICATOR.2ND_STAGE.ALL_PREDICTIONS	
BRANCH_PREDICATOR.2ND_STAGE.CORRECT_PREDICTIONS	
BRANCH_PREDICATOR.2ND_STAGE.WRONG_PATH	
BRANCH_PREDICATOR.2ND_STAGE.WRONG_TARGET	
BRANCH_PREDICATOR.3RD_STAGE.ALL_PREDICTIONS	
BRANCH_PREDICATOR.3RD_STAGE.CORRECT_PREDICTIONS	
BRANCH_PREDICATOR.3RD_STAGE.WRONG_PATH	
BRANCH_PREDICATOR.3RD_STAGE.WRONG_TARGET	
BRANCH_PREDICATOR.ALL.ALL_PREDICTIONS	
BRANCH_PREDICATOR.ALL.CORRECT_PREDICTIONS	
BRANCH_PREDICATOR.ALL.WRONG_PATH	
BRANCH_PREDICATOR.ALL.WRONG_TARGET	
Taken Branch Events	
BRANCH_TAKEN_SLOT.NT	BRANCH_TAKEN_SLOT1
BRANCH_TAKEN_SLOT0	BRANCH_TAKEN_SLOT2

Appendix E

GLOSSARY

ABI: Application Binary Interface. ABIs are intended to ensure application compatibility across different operating systems at the binary level. This is in contrast to APIs, which attempt to ensure application compatibility at the source-code level.

ACPI: Advanced Configuration and Power Interface. See Chapter 10, *Booting*.

ALU: Arithmetic Logic Unit. An execution unit in a CPU that can perform arithmetic and logical calculations.

AP: Application Processor. In an MP machine, all processors other than the bootstrap processor.

BP: Bootstrap Processor. In an MP machine, the bootstrap processor is the CPU that starts executing first and is responsible for waking up all the other processors.

BSP: Bootstrap Processor. *See also* **BP**.

BSS segment: Block Started by Symbol segment. A segment in the address space of a process that is initialized to 0 on program startup. Sometimes "BSS" is interpreted to mean "block structured storage/segment" or "blank static storage," but according to Dennis Ritchie, BSS derived from the FAP assembler for the IBM 709x series of machines. FAP defined a **BSS** directive that reserved a given number of words in memory and used the starting address of the reserved memory as the value of the associated label (symbol). A corresponding directive called **BES** (block ended by symbol) worked the same way except that the value of the symbol was set to the first word beyond the end of the reserved memory area.

cc-NUMA: cache-coherent Nonuniform Memory Access. A type of NUMA machine that keeps all caches coherent. *See also* **NUMA**.

CISC: Complex Instruction Set Computing. See Chapter 1, *Introduction*.

CPP: C preprocessor. A compiler stage that processes C source code before compilation. In particular, it provides the facilities needed for conditional compilation and expands include files as well as macros.

CPU: Central Processing Unit. Also known as microprocessor. It refers to the part of a computer system that executes a single stream of instructions. These instructions operate on the CPU's registers (its *machine state* or *CPU state*) and memory.

DMA: Direct Memory Access. The ability of I/O devices (peripheral devices) to directly read and/or write a machine's system memory. DMA is generally more efficient than Programmed I/O. *See also* **PIO**.

ECC: Error Correcting Code. Memory, caches, and system buses often use ECCs to improve reliability. A typical ECC uses 36 bits to encode 32 bits of data and can detect all 1- and 2-bit errors and correct all 1-bit errors.

EFI: Extensible Firmware Interface. See Chapter 10, *Booting*.

ELF: Executable and Linking Format. See Chapter 1, *Introduction*.

EPIC: Explicitly Parallel Instruction set Computing. See Chapter 1, *Introduction*.

Floating-point high partition: Registers f32–f127 form the high partition of the floating-point register file. *See also* **Floating-point low partition**.

Floating-point low partition: Registers f0–f31 form the low partition of the floating-point register file. *See also* **Floating-point high partition**.

Gbyte: Gigabyte. Equals 2^{30} bytes.

IA-32: Intel Architecture, 32-bit. This name refers to the instruction set architecture implemented by Pentium III.

IA-64: Intel Architecture, 64-bit. This name refers to the instruction set architecture implemented by the Itanium family of chips. The architecture is sometimes called *Itanium processor family (IPF)*.

IA-64 vector: An 8-bit (0..255) number that indicates the type of external device interrupt that is to be raised on a CPU. Depending on the machine, the IA-64 vectors can be shared across all CPUs or they can be specific to certain groups of CPUs (e.g., individual CPUs or the CPUs in a node of a NUMA system).

ILP32: Integer, Long-integer, and Pointer 32-bits. A data model that specifies that the C types **int**, **long**, and all pointers have a size of 32 bits. *See also* **LP64** *and* **P64**.

Inner function: A function that is not a **leaf function**.

I/O MMU: I/O Memory Management Unit. *See also* **I/O TLB**.

I/O subsystem: Input/Output (I/O) subsystem. Defines the low-level interfaces to access peripherals such as disks, network interface cards, or graphics cards.

I/O TLB: I/O Translation Lookaside Buffer. A hardware structure that some machines implement in support of DMA. See Chapter 7, *Device I/O*.

IP: Instruction Pointer. A 64-bit register that addresses the instruction bundle to be executed next. Its contents can be read through register ip. Since instruction bundles are 16-byte aligned, the least significant four bits are 0 when IA-64 instructions are executed. When IA-32 instructions are executed, the IP may contain an arbitrary byte address.

IPF: Itanium Processor Family. *See also* **IA-64**.

Irq number: An abstraction for managing interrupts. Each interrupt source maps to one and only one irq number in the range of 0 to NR_IRQS − 1. Multiple interrupt sources can share the same irq number.

IVE: Intel Value Engine. A mechanism responsible for executing IA-32 instructions. Depending on the IA-64 CPU model, the IVE can be implemented entirely as hardware, as a combination of hardware and software, or entirely as software.

Kbyte: Kilobyte. Equals 2^{10} bytes.

Leaf function: A function that never calls any other function. In other words, when all possible calling trees are considered, the functions that always appear as the leaves of the tree are leaf functions. *See also* **Root function**.

LP64: Long-integer and Pointer 64-bits. A data model that specifies that the C type **long** and all pointers have a size of 64 bits. Type **int** is implicitly assumed to have a size of 32 bits. *See also* **ILP32** *and* **P64**.

Mbyte: Megabyte. Equals 2^{20} bytes.

MP: Multiprocessor. A machine architecture that uses multiple CPUs. *See also* **SMP** *and* **NUMA**.

NaT token: A set NaT (Not a Thing) bit in the case of a general register. A special NaTVal (Not a Thing value) in the case of a floating-point register.

Naturally aligned: The case in which the address of an object is an integer multiple of the byte size of the object. For example, the address `0x1004` is naturally aligned for an object that is four bytes in size.

Nonleaf function: *See also* **Inner function**.

NUMA: Non-Uniform Memory Access. A type of machine where different portions of the system memory may have different access latencies. In addition, different CPUs will generally observe different access latencies for any given portion of memory. *See also* **cc-NUMA**.

OEM: Original Equipment Manufacturer. A manufacturer of computer equipment.

Opaque type: A platform-specific data type whose exact definition is of no concern to the part of Linux that is platform independent. Linux never directly manipulates values with an opaque type and instead uses platform-specific routines to do that.

P64: Pointer 64-bits. A data model that specifies that all pointers have a size of 64 bits. The C types **int** and **long** are implicitly assumed to have a size of 64 bits. *See also* **ILP32** *and* **LP64**.

PAL: Processor Abstraction Layer. See Chapter 10, *Booting*.

Pbyte: Petabyte. Equals 2^{50} bytes.

PIO: Programmed I/O. The opposite of **DMA**. With PIO, the CPU itself is responsible for moving data between system memory and an I/O (peripheral) device.

Polymorphic: Of multiple forms. The characteristic of a routine that can accept multiple types for certain arguments. The C language does not support polymorphism, but the C preprocessor does. Examples are the well-known *min( )* and *max( )* macros, since they can operate on any numeric type (including floating-point types).

Procedure: For unwinding purposes, a procedure is defined to be a contiguous sequence of instructions. Each procedure has (at most) one entry in the IA-64 unwind table.

RBS: Register Backing Store. The memory that holds the part of the register stack that does not fit in the CPU's physical stacked registers. The top of the register backing store is given by application register bspstore. It grows toward higher addresses.

Register stack: A virtually infinite large stack of registers. A call to a nested function allocates new registers on this stack, and a return from a nested function restores the previously active registers. The top portion of the register stack stores the physical stacked registers. The remainder of the register stack is stored in the **RBS**. The CPU automatically takes care of moving the virtual registers from the physical stacked registers to the **RBS**, and vice versa.

RISC: Reduced Instruction Set Computing. See Chapter 1, *Introduction*.

Root function: A kernel function that never gets called by another kernel function. In other words, when all possible kernel calling trees are considered, the functions that always appear at the root of the tree are the kernel's root functions. These functions are sometimes also called kernel system call handlers, interrupt handlers, trap handlers, or fault handlers.

SAL: System Abstraction Layer. See Chapter 10, *Booting*.

SMP: Symmetric Multiprocessor. A machine architecture that uses multiple CPUs in a shared physical address space. These machines are symmetric in the sense that each CPU has equal access to all the resources of the machine (memory, I/O devices, etc.). SMP machines are generally cache-coherent. *See also* **MP** *and* **NUMA**.

Stacked registers: General registers r32–r127. These registers form the current frame of the register stack. *See also* **Static registers** *and* **Register stack**.

Static registers: General registers r0–r32. *See also* **Stacked registers**.

Tbyte: Terabyte. Equals 2^{40} bytes.

UP: Uniprocessor. A machine architecture that uses only one CPU. *See also* **MP**.

UTC: Universal Time, Coordinated. Equivalent to mean solar time at the prime meridian ($0°$ longitude), formerly expressed in GMT (Greenwich Mean Time) [70].

VLIW: Very Long Instruction Word. See Chapter 1, *Introduction*.

BIBLIOGRAPHY

[1] ACPI Special Interest Group. *Advanced Configuration and Power Interface Specification, Revision 2.0*, July 2000.
http://www.acpi.info/spec.htm.

[2] Sarita V. Adve and Kourosh Gharachorloo. Shared memory consistency models: A tutorial. *IEEE Computer*, 29(12):66–76, December 1996.
http://www.computer.org/computer/co1996/rz066abs.htm.

[3] C. Amza, A. L. Cox, S. Dwarkadas, P. Keleher, H. Lu, R. Rajamony, W. Yu, and W. Zwaenepoel. TreadMarks: Shared memory computing on Networks of Workstations. *IEEE Computer*, 29(2):18–28, February 1996.

[4] Jennifer M. Andersen, Lance M. Berc, Jeffrey Dean, Sanjay Ghemawat, Monika R. Henzinger, Shun-tak A. Leung, Richard L. Sites, Mark T. Vandevoorde, Carl A. Waldspurger, and William E. Weihl. Continuous profiling: Where have all the cycles gone? *ACM Transactions on Computer Systems*, 15(4):357–390, 1997.
http://www.tru64unix.compaq.com/dcpi/.

[5] Don Anderson, John Swindle, and Tom Shanley. *ISA System Architecture*. Addison-Wesley, April 1995.

[6] Gregory R. Andrews. *Concurrent Programming: Principles and Practice*. Benjamin/Cummings, 1991.

[7] ANSI. ANSI C. American National Standard X3.159-1989, 1989.

[8] K. Arnold and J. Gosling. *The Java Programming Language*. Addison-Wesley, 1996.

[9] Maurice J. Bach. *The Design of the UNIX Operating System*. Prentice Hall, 1986.

[10] John Bayko. Great microprocessors of the past and present (v12.1.2), June 2001.
http://www3.sk.sympatico.ca/jbayko/.

[11] Lubomir Bic and Alan C. Shaw. *The Logical Design of Operating Systems*. Prentice Hall, 2nd edition, 1988.

[12] Jeff Bonwick. The slab allocator: An object-caching kernel. In *USENIX Summer 1994 Technical Conference*, pages 87–98, Boston, MA, June 1994.
http://www.usenix.org/publications/library/proceedings/bos94/bonwick.html.

[13] DiG Forum. *Developer's Interface Guide for IA-64 Servers (DIG64) Version 1.1*, June 2001.
http://dig64.org/.

[14] Stéphane Eranian. The pfmon performance monitoring tool for Linux/ia64, June 2001.
ftp://ftp.hpl.hp.com/pub/linux-ia64/.

[15] Stéphane Eranian and David Mosberger. The GNU-EFI package for Linux/ia64, 2001.
ftp://ftp.hpl.hp.com/pub/linux-ia64/.

[16] Free Software Foundation. *Using and Porting the GNU Compiler Collection (GCC)*, 2001.
http://gcc.gnu.org/onlinedocs/gcc-3.0.1/gcc.html.

[17] Bill O. Gallmeister. *POSIX.4: Programming for the Real World*. O'Reilly & Associates, January 1995.

[18] Jon Hall and David Rusling. An interview with DEC. *Linux Journal*, May 1997.
http://www.linuxjournal.com/article.php?sid=2105.

[19] John L. Hennessey and David A. Patterson. *Computer Architecture: A Quantitative Approach*. Morgan Kaufman, 1990.

[20] Maurice Herlihy. A methodology for implementing highly concurrent data objects. *ACM Transactions on Programming Languages and Systems*, 15(5):745–770, November 1993.

[21] Hewlett-Packard. *Extensible SAL Specification Version 1.0*, October 2001.
http://devresource.hp.com/devresource/Docs/TechPapers/IA64/esi.pdf.

[22] IEEE. IEEE standard for binary floating-point arithmetic. *SIGPLAN Notices*, 22(2):9–25, 1985. Reprint of IEEE 754 standard.

[23] Intel Corp. *Intel386 Binary Compatibility Specification (iBCS)*. McGraw-Hill, 1995.

[24] Intel Corp. *Wired for Management Baseline*, December 1998.
http://developer.intel.com/ial/WfM/wfmspecs.htm.

[25] Intel Corp. *Intel Architecture Software Developer's Manual*, 1999. Document #243190.
http://developer.intel.com/design/PentiumIII/manuals/.

[26] Intel Corp. *The IA-64 Architecture Software Developer's Manual*, July 2000. Document #245317-002.
http://developer.intel.com/design/itanium/.

[27] Intel Corp. *IA-64 Assembly Language Reference Guide*, January 2000. Document #248801-002.

[28] Intel Corp. *IA-64 Software Conventions & Runtime Architecture Guide*, January 2000. Document #245358-001.

[29] Intel Corp. *IA-PC Multimedia Timers*, draft edition, June 2000.
http://developer.intel.com/ial/home/sp/pcmmspec.htm.

[30] Intel Corp. *Itanium Processor Microarchitecture Reference*, August 2000. Document #245473-002.
http://developer.intel.com/design/itanium/.

[31] Intel Corp. *System Abstraction Layer (SAL) Specification*, July 2000. Document #245359-002.
http://developer.intel.com/design/itanium/firmware.htm.

[32] Intel Corp. *UNIX System V Application Binary Interface: IA-64 specific supplement*, September 2000. Document #245370-002.
http://developer.intel.com/design/itanium/.

[33] Intel Corp. *Intel 460GX Chipset System Software Developer's Manual*, June 2001. Document #248704-001.
http://developer.intel.com/design/itanium/.

[34] International Organization for Standardization. Open Systems Interconnection: Remote Procedure Call (RPC). ISO/IEC 11578, 1996.

[35] Gerry Kane. *PA-RISC Architecture*. Hewlett-Packard Professional Books, 1995.

[36] Brian W. Kernighan and Dennis M. Ritchie. *The C Programming Language*. Prentice Hall, 1978.

[37] Donald E. Knuth. *The Art of Computer Programming*, volume 1. Addison-Wesley, 2nd edition, 1973.

[38] Chris Lawrence. Linux/m68k frequently asked questions, 1999.
http://www.linux-m68k.org/faq/faq.html.

[39] Samuel J. Leffler, Marshall K. McKusick, Michael J. Karels, and John S. Quarterman. *The Design and Implementation of the 4.3BSD UNIX Operating System*. Addison-Wesley, 1988.

[40] Rick Lindsley. Global spinlock list and usage, June 2001.
http://lse.sourceforge.net/lockhier/global-spin-lock.

[41] Scott Lurndal, Keith Owens, et al. KDB v1.2: Built-in kernel debugger for Linux, 2001.
http://oss.sgi.com/projects/kdb/.

[42] Udi Manber. *Introduction to Algorithms*. Addison-Wesley, 1989.

[43] Peter Markstein. *IA-64 and Elementary Functions: Speed and Precision*. Hewlett-Packard Professional Books, 2000.

[44] Henry Massalin and Calton Pu. A lock-free multiprocessor OS kernel. Technical Report CUCS-005-91, Columbia University, New York, NY, June 1991.
http://www.cs.columbia.edu/~library/1991.html.

[45] Maged M. Michael and Michael L. Scott. Simple, fast, and practical non-blocking and blocking concurrent queue algorithms. In *Proc. of the Fifteenth ACM Symposium on Principles of Distributed Computing*, pages 267–275, May 1996.
http://www.cs.rochester.edu/u/michael/PODC96.html.

[46] Microsoft Corp. *Microsoft Portable Executable and Common Object File Format Specification, Revision 6.0*, February 1999.
http://www.microsoft.com/hwdev/hardware/PECOFF.htm.

[47] Jeffrey C. Mogul, Joel F. Bartlett, Robert N. Mayo, and Amitabh Srivastava. Performance implications of multiple pointer sizes. In *USENIX Winter 1995 Technical Conference*, pages 187–200, New Orleans, LA, January 1995.
http://www.usenix.org/publications/library/proceedings/neworl/mogul.html.

[48] Andrew G. Morgan. *The Linux-PAM System Administrators' Guide*, 2001.
http://www.kernel.org/pub/linux/libs/pam/Linux-PAM-html/pam.html.

[49] Michael Morrell, David Mosberger, and Stéphane Eranian. The Ski simulator, 2001.
http://software.hp.com/ia64linux/.

[50] Bradford Nichols, Dick Buttlar, and Jacqueline P. Farrell. *Pthreads Programming: A POSIX Standard for Better Multiprocessing*. O'Reilly & Associates, September 1996.

[51] The Open Group. *DCE 1.1: Remote Procedure Call*, 1997. Document C706.
http://www.opengroup.org/onlinepubs/9629399/toc.htm.

[52] The Open Group. *Single UNIX Specification V2 (UNIX 98)*, volume 1–6. Open Group Books, February 1997.
http://www.opengroup.org/online-pubs?DOC=007908799&FORM=HTML.

[53] PCI Special Interest Group. *PCI Local Bus Specification Revision 2.2*, December 1998.
http://www.pcisig.com/.

[54] R. Pike, D. Presotto, S. Dorward, B. Flandrena, K. Thompson, H. Trickey, and P. Winterbottom. Plan 9 from Bell Labs. *Computing Systems*, 8(3):221–254, Summer 1995.
http://plan9.bell-labs.com/sys/doc/9.html.

[55] POSIX working group. *Portable Operating System Interface (POSIX) — Part 1: System Application Program Interface (API), Amendment 2: Threads Extension (C Language)*, 1995. IEEE/ANSI Std 1003.1c-1995.

[56] Charles Price. *MIPS IV Instruction Set*. MIPS Technologies, Inc., 1995.

[57] Eric S. Raymond. The jargon file, version 4.3.1, June 2001.
http://www.tuxedo.org/˜esr/jargon/.

[58] Paul Rusty Russell. *Unreliable Guide to Locking*, 2000.
http://netfilter.samba.org/unreliable-guides/kernel-locking/kernel-locking.docbook/lklockingguide.html.

[59] Julio Sanchez and Maria P. Canton. *IBM Microcomputers: A Programmer's Handbook*. McGraw-Hill, 1990.

[60] The Santa Cruz Operation. System V Application Binary Interface (ABI), Edition 4.1, March 1997.
http://www.caldera.com/developers/devspecs/gabi41.pdf.

[61] Michael S. Schlansker and Bob R. Rau. EPIC: Explicitly parallel instruction computing. *IEEE Computer*, 33(2):37–45, February 2000.

[62] Robert Sedgewick. *Algorithms*. Addison-Wesley, 2nd edition, 1988.

[63] John Sheets, Ove Kåven, et al. WINE user guide, 2001.
http://www.winehq.com/Docs/wine-user/.

[64] Abraham Silberschatz, James L. Peterson, and Peter B. Galvin. *Operating System Concepts*. Addison-Wesley, 3rd edition, 1991.

[65] Richard L. Sites, editor. *Alpha Architecture Reference Manual*. Digital Press, 1992. Order number EY-L520E-DP.

[66] Bjarne Stroustrup. *The C++ Programming Language*. Addison-Wesley, 3rd edition, 1997.

[67] Andrew S. Tanenbaum. *Operating Systems: Design and Implementation*. Prentice Hall, 1987.

[68] Andrew S. Tanenbaum. *Distributed Operating Systems*. Prentice Hall, 1992.

[69] Andrew S. Tanenbaum. *Modern Operating Systems*. Prentice Hall, 1992.

[70] Tech. Subcommittee on Performance and Signal Processing. *Telecom Glossary 2000*, 2000. American National Standard T1.523-2001.
http://www.its.bldrdoc.gov/projects/telecomglossary2000/.

[71] Tool Interface Standard (TIS). *Executable and Linking Format (ELF) Specification*, May 1995.

[72] Linus Torvalds. Linux history, July 1992.
http://www.li.org/linuxhistory.php.

[73] Linus Torvalds. Linux: a Portable Operating System. Master of Science Thesis, University of Helsinki, Finland, 1997.

[74] The Unicode Consortium. *The Unicode Standard Version 3.0*. Addison-Wesley, 2000. http://www.unicode.org/.

[75] David L. Weaver and Tom Germond, editors. *The SPARC Architecture Manual, Version 9*. Prentice Hall, 1993.

[76] Rumi Zahir, Jonathan Ross, Dale Morris, and Drew Hess. OS and compiler considerations in the design of the IA-64 architecture. In *Proceedings of the 9th International Conference on Architectural Support for Programming Languages and Operating Systems*, pages 212–219, Cambridge, MA, November 2000. ACM.

INDEX

fulfill your
needs

invent

Want to know about new products, services and solutions from Hewlett-Packard Company — as soon as they're invented?

Need information about new HP services to help you implement new or existing products?

Looking for HP's newest solution to a specific challenge in your business?

HP Computer News features the latest from HP!

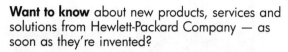

4 easy ways to subscribe, and it's FREE:

* **fax** complete and fax the form below to (651) 430-3388, or

* **online** sign up online at www.hp.com/go/compnews, or

* **email** complete the information below and send to hporders@earthlink.net, or

* **mail** complete and mail the form below to:

Twin Cities Fulfillment Center
Hewlett-Packard Company
P.O. Box 408
Stillwater, MN 55082

reply now to receive the first year FREE!

name	title
company	dept./mail stop
address	
city	state zip
email signature	date

please indicate your industry below:

☐ accounting	☐ healthcare/medical	☐ online services	☐ telecommunications
☐ education	☐ legal	☐ real estate	☐ transport and travel
☐ financial services	☐ manufacturing	☐ retail/wholesale distrib	☐ utilities
☐ government	☐ publishing/printing	☐ technical	☐ other: _____

integrated
hp education training
it just works

invent

HP's world-class education and training offers hands on education solutions including:

- Linux
- HP-UX System and Network Administration
- Advanced HP-UX System Administration
- IT Service Management using advanced Internet technologies
- Microsoft Windows NT/2000
- Internet/Intranet
- MPE/iX
- Database Administration
- Software Development

HP's new IT Professional Certification program provides rigorous technical qualification for specific IT job roles including HP-UX System Administration, Network Management, Unix/NT Servers and Applications Management, and IT Service Management.

become hp certified

http://education.hp.com

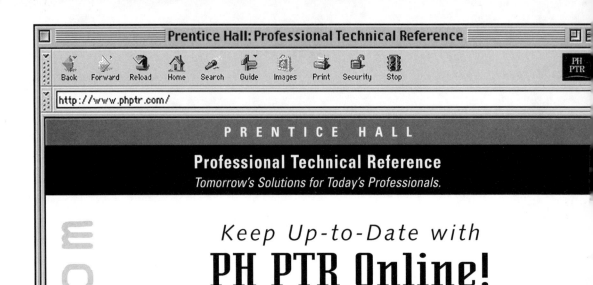